# Hello Kitty Dictionary

Collins

HarperCollins Publishers
Westerhill Road
Bishopbriggs
Glasgow
G64 2QT

First Edition 2012
This edition published 2014 for Index Books.
ISBN 978-0-00-745719-9 – HC edition
ISBN 978-0-00-748763-9 – X edition

Reprint 10 9 8 7 6 5 4 3 2

© HarperCollins Publishers 2012

© 1976, 2012 Sanrio Co., Ltd

Collins® is a registered trademark of HarperCollins Publishers Limited

www.collinslanguage.com

A catalogue record for this book is available from the British Library

Printed and bound at Leo Paper Products Ltd

**Acknowledgements**
We would like to thank those authors and publishers who kindly gave permission for copyright material to be used in the Collins Corpus. We would also like to thank Times Newspapers Ltd for providing valuable data.

All rights reserved. No part of this book may be reproduced, stored in a retrieval system, or transmitted in any form or by any means, electronic, mechanical, photocopying, recording or otherwise, without the prior permission in writing of the Publisher. This book is sold subject to the conditions that it shall not, by way of trade or otherwise, be lent, re-sold, hired out or otherwise circulated without the Publisher's prior consent in any form of binding or cover other than that in which it is published and without a similar condition including this condition being imposed on the subsequent purchaser.

Entered words that we have reason to believe constitute trademarks have been designated as such. However, neither the presence nor absence of such designation should be regarded as affecting the legal status of any trademark.

HarperCollins does not warrant that www.collinsdictionary.com, www.collinslanguage.com or any other website mentioned in this title will be provided uninterrupted, that any website will be error free, that defects will be corrected, or that the website or the server that makes it available are free of viruses or bugs. For full terms and conditions please refer to the site terms provided on the website.

**Page design**
Sally Griffin

**Page make-up**
Q2AMedia Services Pvt. Ltd.

**Typesetting**
Davidson Publishing Solutions, Glasgow

**Editorial consultants**
Andrew Holmes
Elspeth Summers

**For the publisher**
Gerry Breslin
Lucy Cooper
Julianna Dunn
Kerry Ferguson
Elaine Higgleton
Catherine Lutman
Ruth O'Donovan

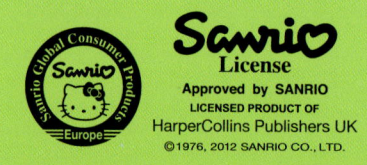

Sanrio License
Approved by SANRIO
LICENSED PRODUCT OF
HarperCollins Publishers UK
© 1976, 2012 SANRIO CO., LTD.

# How To Use The Dictionary

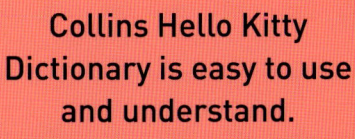

Collins Hello Kitty Dictionary is easy to use and understand. Below is a list of all its features and how to recognize them.

★ **Main entry words are printed in large bold pink type:**

   **bookmark**

★ **Some words can be spelt in more than one way. These spellings are shown in large bold pink type:**

   **connection** or **connexion**

   **criticize**, criticizes, criticizing, criticized (also **criticise**)

★ **A pronunciation shows how to say the word. It comes after the entry word or variant and is in italics inside square brackets. The part in bold is the one with most force on it when the word is said:**

   **cashew** [*kash-oo*] NOUN

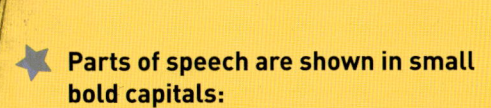

★ **Parts of speech are shown in small bold capitals:**

   **absorb** VERB

★ **When a word can be used with more than one part of speech, the change of part of speech is shown after a pink flower:**

   **glitter** VERB ❶ If something glitters, it shines in a sparkling way ✿ NOUN ❷ Glitter is sparkling light

★ **Parts of speech may be combined for some words:**

   **about** PREPOSITION OR ADVERB

★ **Cross-references are shown in bold type. These are places where you are told to look at another entry:**

   **been** the past participle of **be**

★ **Forms of verbs, nouns, and adjectives that can be tricky to spell are shown in pink type after the entry word:**

> **achieve**, achieves, achieving, achieved
> **angry**, angrier, angriest

★ **If a word has more than one meaning they are separated by numbers:**

> **handsome** ADJECTIVE ❶ very attractive in appearance ❷ large and generous

★ **Some meanings contain advice on when the word is used. This is shown in small capitals after the part of speech or sense number:**

> **boiling** ADJECTIVE INFORMAL very hot
> **conduct** ... ❷ FORMAL The way you conduct yourself is the way you behave

★ **Sometimes the entry word is used as a plural, this is shown by the words IN PLURAL in small capitals:**

> **affair** ... ❸ IN PLURAL Your affairs are your private and personal life

★ **Related words are shown in bold pink type at the end of the entry:**

> **aggressive** ADJECTIVE full of hostility and violence
> **aggressively** ADVERB

★ **Feature boxes provide extra help on spelling and punctuation, where words come from, how English works, and which words you shouldn't mix up:**

### don't mix up

## Hello Kitty...

never mixes up **bare** (not having any clothes on) and **bear** (the wild animal with thick fur).

# a – abstract

**a** or **an** ADJECTIVE The indefinite article 'a', or 'an' if the next sound is a vowel, is used when you are talking about one of something

**abandon** VERB ❶ If you abandon someone or something, you leave them or give them up for good ❋ NOUN ❷ If you do something with abandon, you do it in an uncontrolled way **abandoned** ADJECTIVE

**abbreviation** NOUN a short form of a word or phrase. An example is 'W', which is short for 'West'

**abdomen** NOUN the front part of your body below your chest, containing your stomach and intestines **abdominal** ADJECTIVE

**ability**, abilities NOUN the intelligence or skill needed to do something

**able** ADJECTIVE ❶ If you are able to do something, you can do it ❷ Someone who is able is very clever or talented

**abnormal** ADJECTIVE not normal or usual

**aboard** PREPOSITION OR ADVERB on a ship or plane

**abolish**, abolishes, abolishing, abolished VERB To abolish something is to do away with it **abolition** NOUN

**about** PREPOSITION OR ADVERB ❶ of or concerning ❷ approximately and not exactly ❋ ADVERB ❸ in different directions ❋ ADJECTIVE ❹ present or in a place ❋ PHRASE ❺ If you are **about to** do something, you are just going to do it

**above** PREPOSITION OR ADVERB ❶ directly over or higher than something ❷ greater than a level or amount

**abroad** ADVERB in a foreign country

**abrupt** ADJECTIVE ❶ sudden and quick ❷ not friendly or polite **abruptly** ADVERB

**absent** ADJECTIVE Something that is absent is not present in a place or situation **absence** NOUN

**absent-minded** ADJECTIVE forgetful

**absolute** ADJECTIVE ❶ total and complete ❷ having total power **absolutely** ADVERB

**absorb** VERB If something absorbs liquid or gas, it soaks it up

**absorbent** ADJECTIVE Absorbent materials soak up liquid easily

**abstract** ADJECTIVE [*ab-strakt*] ❶ An abstract idea is based on thoughts and ideas rather than physical objects or events, for example 'bravery' ❷ Abstract art is a style of art

## how English works

### Hello Kitty...

knows that **a** is called 'the indefinite article' and you put it in front of a noun when you are not talking about a particular person or thing. If the noun begins with a vowel, you use **an** instead.

# abuse - according to

which uses shapes rather than images of people or objects ❸ Abstract nouns refer to qualities or ideas rather than to physical objects, for example 'happiness' or 'a question'

**abuse**, abuses [ab-**yoose**] NOUN ❶ cruel treatment of someone ❷ rude and unkind remarks directed towards someone ❸ the wrong use of something

**abuse**, abuses, abusing, abused [ab-**yooze**] VERB ❶ If you abuse someone, you speak insultingly to them ❷ To abuse someone also means to treat them cruelly ❸ If you abuse something, you use it wrongly or for a bad purpose

## how to say it

### Helpful hints...

**Abuse** should be said ab-**yoose** when it is a noun and ab-**yooze** when it is a verb.

**academic** ADJECTIVE ❶ Academic work is work done in a school, college, or university ✿ NOUN ❷ someone who teaches or does research in a college or university

**academy**, academies NOUN ❶ a school or college, usually one that specializes in one particular subject ❷ an organization of scientists, artists, writers, or musicians

**accelerate**, accelerates, accelerating, accelerated VERB To accelerate is to go faster

**accelerator** NOUN the pedal in a vehicle which you press to make it go faster

**accent** NOUN ❶ a way of pronouncing a language ❷ a mark placed above or below a letter in some languages, which affects the way the letter is pronounced ❸ stress placed on a particular word, syllable, or note ❹ an emphasis on something

**accept** VERB ❶ If you accept something, you say yes to it or take it from someone ❷ If you accept a situation, you realize that it cannot be changed ❸ If you accept a statement or story, you believe it is true ❹ If a group accepts you, they treat you as one of the group  **acceptance** NOUN

**acceptable** ADJECTIVE good enough to be accepted  **acceptably** ADVERB

**access**, accesses, accessing, accessed NOUN ❶ the right or opportunity to enter a place or to use something ✿ VERB ❷ If you access information from a computer, you get it

**accessible** ADJECTIVE ❶ easily reached or seen ❷ easily understood or used

**accessory**, accessories NOUN ❶ an extra part ❷ someone who helps another person commit a crime

**accident** NOUN ❶ an unexpected event in which people are injured or killed ❷ Something that happens by accident happens by chance

**accidental** ADJECTIVE happening by chance  **accidentally** ADVERB

**accommodation** NOUN a place provided for someone to sleep, live, or work in

**accompany**, accompanies, accompanying, accompanied VERB ❶ If you accompany someone, you go with them ❷ If one thing accompanies another, the two things exist at the same time ❸ If you accompany a singer or musician, you play an instrument while they sing or play the main tune

**accomplish**, accomplishes, accomplishing, accomplished VERB If you accomplish something, you succeed in doing it

**accomplishment** NOUN Someone's accomplishments are the skills they have gained

**accord** VERB ❶ If you accord someone or something a particular treatment, you treat them in that way ✿ NOUN ❷ agreement ✿ PHRASE ❸ If you do something **of your own accord**, you do it willingly and not because you have been forced to do it

**according to** PREPOSITION ❶ If something is true according to a particular person, that

**accordion - action**

person says that it is true ❷ If something is done according to a principle or plan, that principle or plan is used as the basis for it

**accordion** NOUN a musical instrument like an expanding box. It is played by squeezing the two sides together while pressing the keys on it

**account** NOUN ❶ a written or spoken report of something ❷ If you have a bank account, you can leave money in the bank and take it out when you need it ❸ IN PLURAL Accounts are records of money spent and received by a person or business ❀ PHRASE ❹ If you **take something into account**, you include it in your planning ❺ **On account of** means because of ❀ VERB ❻ To account for something is to explain it ❼ If something accounts for a particular amount of something, it is that amount

**accountant** NOUN a person whose job is to keep or inspect financial accounts

**accurate** ADJECTIVE completely correct or precise **accurately** ADVERB **accuracy** NOUN

**accuse**, accuses, accusing, accused VERB If you accuse someone of doing something wrong, you say they have done it

**ache**, aches, aching, ached VERB ❶ If you ache, you feel a continuous dull pain in a part of your body ❷ If you are aching for something, you want it very much ❀ NOUN ❸ a continuous dull pain

**achieve**, achieves, achieving, achieved VERB If you achieve something, you successfully do it or cause it to happen

**achievement** NOUN something which you succeed in doing, especially after a lot of effort

**acid** NOUN ❶ a chemical liquid with a pH value of less than 7 and which turns litmus paper red. Strong acids can damage skin, cloth, and metal ❀ ADJECTIVE ❷ Acid tastes are sharp or sour

**acid rain** NOUN rain polluted by acid in the atmosphere which has come from factories

**acknowledge**, acknowledges, acknowledging, acknowledged VERB ❶ If you acknowledge a fact or situation, you agree or admit it is true ❷ If you acknowledge someone, you show that you have seen and recognized them ❸ If you acknowledge a message, you tell the person who sent it that you have received it

**acquaintance** NOUN someone you know slightly but not well

**acquire**, acquires, acquiring, acquired VERB If you acquire something, you obtain it

**acre** NOUN a unit for measuring areas of land. One acre is equal to 4840 square yards or about 4047 square metres

**across** PREPOSITION OR ADVERB ❶ going from one side of something to the other ❷ on the other side of a road or river

**acrylic** [a-**kril**-lik] or **acrylics** NOUN ❶ Acrylic is a type of man-made cloth ❷ Acrylics, or acrylic paints, are thick artists' paints which can be used like oil paints or thinned down with water

**act** VERB ❶ If you act, you do something ❷ If you act in a particular way, you behave in that way ❸ If a person or thing acts as something else, it has the function or does the job of that thing ❹ If you act in a play or film, you play a part ❀ NOUN ❺ a single thing someone does ❻ An Act of Parliament is a law passed by the government ❼ In a play, ballet, or opera, an act is one of the main parts it is divided into

**acting** NOUN the profession of performing in plays or films

**action** NOUN ❶ the process of doing something ❷ something that is done

---

**how to remember**

*Hello Kitty...*

remembers that if it can **acceler**ate, **a** **c**ar **c**an **e**asily l**e**ad **e**very **r**ace.

# active – adjective

❸ a physical movement ❹ In law, an action is a legal proceeding

**active** ADJECTIVE ❶ full of energy ❷ busy and hardworking ❸ In grammar, a verb in the active voice is one where the subject does the action, rather than having it done to them

### how English works

**Hello Kitty...**

knows that an **active** verb is when the subject of a sentence does the action, like *lost* in *The boy lost his bicycle.*

**activity**, activities NOUN ❶ Activity is a situation in which a lot of things are happening at the same time ❷ something you do for pleasure

**actor** NOUN a man or woman whose profession is acting

**actress**, actresses NOUN a woman whose profession is acting

**actual** ADJECTIVE real, rather than imaginary or guessed at **actually** ADVERB

**acute** ADJECTIVE ❶ severe or intense ❷ very intelligent ❸ An acute angle is less than 90° ❹ In French and some other languages, an acute accent is a line sloping upwards from left to right placed over a vowel to indicate a change in pronunciation, as in the word *café*

**ad** NOUN INFORMAL an advertisement

**AD** You use 'AD' in dates to indicate the number of years after the birth of Jesus Christ

**adapt** VERB ❶ If you adapt to a new situation, you change so you can deal with it successfully ❷ If you adapt something, you change it so it is suitable for a new purpose or situation ❸ If a plant or animal adapts, it gradually changes over generations to become better suited to its environment **adaptable** ADJECTIVE

**add** VERB ❶ If you add something to a number of things, you put it with the things ❷ If you add numbers together or add them up, you work out the total

**addict** NOUN someone who cannot stop taking harmful drugs **addicted** ADJECTIVE **addiction** NOUN

**addition** NOUN ❶ something that has been added to something else ❷ the process of adding numbers together

**address**, addresses, addressing, addressed NOUN ❶ the number of the house where you live, together with the name of the street and the town or village ❷ a speech given to a group of people ✿ VERB ❸ If a letter is addressed to you, it has your name and address written on it ❹ If you address a problem or task, you start to deal with it

**adequate** ADJECTIVE enough in amount or good enough for a purpose

**adhesive** NOUN ❶ any substance used to stick two things together, for example glue ✿ ADJECTIVE ❷ Adhesive substances are sticky and able to stick to things

**adjective** NOUN a word that adds to the description given by a noun. For example, in

### how English works

**Hello Kitty...**

knows that an **adjective** is a word that describes a person or thing, like *tall* or *silly*. Adjectives are sometimes called 'describing words'.

**adjust - advertisement**

'They live in a large white Georgian house', 'large', 'white', and 'Georgian' are all adjectives

**adjust** VERB ❶ If you adjust something, you change its position or alter it in some other way ❷ If you adjust to a new situation, you get used to it

**administration** NOUN ❶ Administration is the work of organizing and supervising an organization ❷ Administration is also the process of administering something ❸ The administration is the group of people that manages an organization or a country **administrative** ADJECTIVE **administrator** NOUN

**admiration** NOUN a feeling of great liking and respect

**admire**, admires, admiring, admired VERB If you admire someone or something, you respect and approve of them **admirer** NOUN

**admission** NOUN ❶ If you are allowed admission to a place, you are allowed to go in ❷ If you make an admission of something, you agree, often reluctantly, it is true

**admit**, admits, admitting, admitted VERB ❶ If you admit something, you agree, often reluctantly, it is true ❷ To admit someone or something to a place or organization is to allow them to enter it ❸ If you are admitted to hospital, you are taken there to stay until you are better

**adolescent** NOUN a young person who is no longer a child but who is not yet an adult **adolescence** NOUN

**adopt** VERB ❶ If you adopt a child that is not your own, you take him or her into your family as your son or daughter ❷ FORMAL If you adopt a particular attitude, you start to have it **adoption** NOUN

**adore**, adores, adoring, adored VERB If you adore someone, you feel deep love and admiration for them

**adult** NOUN a mature and fully developed person or animal

**advance**, advances, advancing, advanced VERB ❶ To advance is to move forward ❷ To advance a cause or interest is to help it to be successful ❸ If you advance someone a sum of money, you lend it to them ❀ NOUN ❹ Advance in something is progress in it ❺ a sum of money lent to someone ❀ ADJECTIVE ❻ happening before an event ❀ PHRASE ❼ If you do something **in advance**, you do it before something else happens

**advantage** NOUN ❶ a benefit or something that puts you in a better position ❀ PHRASE ❷ If you **take advantage of** someone, you treat them unfairly for your own benefit ❸ If you **take advantage of** something, you make use of it

**adventure** NOUN a series of events that are unusual and exciting

**adverb** NOUN a word that adds information about a verb or a following adjective or other adverb, for example, 'slowly', 'now', and 'here' which say how, when, or where something is done

### how English works

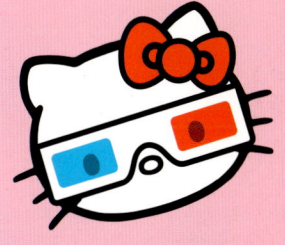

*Hello Kitty...* knows that an **adverb** is a word that tells you how something is done, like *quickly* or *cheerfully*.

**advert** NOUN INFORMAL an advertisement

**advertise**, advertises, advertising, advertised VERB ❶ If you advertise something, you tell people about it in a newspaper or poster, or on TV ❷ To advertise is to make an announcement in a newspaper or poster, or on TV **advertising** NOUN

**advertisement** [ad-**ver**-tiss-ment] NOUN an announcement about something in a newspaper or poster, or on TV

**advice** NOUN a suggestion from someone about what you should do

**don't mix up**

Hello Kitty... never mixes up **advice** (the noun) and **advise** (the verb).

**advise**, advises, advising, advised VERB ❶ If you advise someone to do something, you tell them you think they should do it ❷ FORMAL If you advise someone of something, you inform them of it

**adviser** NOUN a person whose job is to give advice

**aerial** [*air-ee-al*] ADJECTIVE ❶ Aerial means happening in the air ✿ NOUN ❷ a piece of wire for receiving television or radio signals

**aerobics** NOUN a type of fast physical exercise, which increases the oxygen in your blood and strengthens your heart and lungs

**aeroplane** NOUN a vehicle with wings and engines that enable it to fly

**aerosol** NOUN a small metal container in which liquid is kept under pressure so that it can be forced out as a spray

**aesthetic** or **esthetic** [*eess-thet-ik*] ADJECTIVE FORMAL relating to the appreciation of beauty or art  **aesthetically** ADVERB

**affair** NOUN ❶ an event or series of events ❷ To have an affair is to have a secret sexual or romantic relationship, especially when one of the people is married ❸ IN PLURAL Your affairs are your private and personal life

**affect** VERB ❶ If something affects you, it influences you in some way ❷ FORMAL If you affect a particular way of behaving, you behave in that way

**affection** NOUN ❶ a feeling of love and fondness for someone ❷ IN PLURAL Your affections are feelings of love you have for someone

**affectionate** ADJECTIVE full of fondness for someone  **affectionately** ADVERB

**afford** VERB ❶ If you can afford to do something, you have enough money or time to do it ❷ If you cannot afford something to happen, it would be harmful or embarrassing for you if it happened

**afloat** ADVERB OR ADJECTIVE ❶ floating on water ❷ successful and making enough money

**afraid** ADJECTIVE ❶ If you are afraid, you are very frightened ❷ If you are afraid something might happen, you are worried it might happen

**after** PREPOSITION OR ADVERB ❶ later than a particular time, date, or event ❷ behind and following someone or something

**afternoon** NOUN the part of the day between noon and about six o'clock

**aftershave** NOUN a pleasant-smelling liquid men put on their faces after shaving

**afterwards** ADVERB after an event or time

**again** ADVERB ❶ happening one more time ❷ returning to the same state or place as before

**against** PREPOSITION ❶ touching and leaning on ❷ in opposition to ❸ in preparation for or in case of something ❹ in comparison with

**age**, ages, ageing or aging, aged NOUN ❶ The age of something or someone is the number of years they have lived or existed ❷ Age is the quality of being old ❸ a particular period in history ❹ IN PLURAL; INFORMAL Ages means a very long time ✿ VERB ❺ To age is to grow old or to appear older

**aged** [*rhymes with raged*] ADJECTIVE having a particular age

**aged** [*ay-dgid*] ADJECTIVE very old

**agency**, agencies NOUN an organization or business which provides certain services

**agenda** NOUN a list of items to be discussed at a meeting

**agent** NOUN ❶ someone who arranges work or business for other people, especially

## aggressive - all

actors or singers ❷ someone who works for their country's secret service

**aggressive** ADJECTIVE full of hostility and violence **aggressively** ADVERB

**ago** ADVERB in the past

**agony** NOUN very great physical or mental pain

**agree**, agrees, agreeing, agreed VERB ❶ If you agree with someone, you have the same opinion as them ❷ If you agree to do something, you say you will do it ❸ If two stories or totals agree, they are the same ❹ Food that doesn't agree with you makes you ill

**agreement** NOUN ❶ a decision that has been reached by two or more people ❷ Two people who are in agreement have the same opinion about something

**agriculture** NOUN Agriculture is farming **agricultural** ADJECTIVE

**ahead** ADVERB ❶ in front ❷ more advanced than someone or something else ❸ in the future

**aid** NOUN ❶ Aid is money, equipment, or services provided for people in need ❷ something that makes a task easier ✿ VERB ❸ FORMAL If you aid a person or an organization, you help or support them

**AIDS** NOUN a disease which destroys the body's natural system of immunity to diseases. AIDS is an abbreviation for 'acquired immune deficiency syndrome'

**aim** VERB ❶ If you aim an object or weapon at someone or something, you point it at them ❷ If you aim to do something, you are planning or hoping to do it ✿ NOUN ❸ Your aim is what you intend to achieve ❹ If you take aim, you point an object or weapon at someone or something

**air** NOUN ❶ Air is the mixture of oxygen and other gases which we breathe and which forms the earth's atmosphere ❷ An air someone or something has is the impression they give ❸ 'Air' is used to refer to travel in aircraft ✿ VERB ❹ If you air your opinions, you talk about them to other people

**air-conditioning** NOUN a system of providing cool, clean air in buildings **air-conditioned** ADJECTIVE

**aircraft** NOUN any vehicle which can fly

**air force** NOUN the part of a country's armed services that fights using aircraft

**airline** NOUN a company which provides air travel

**airport** NOUN a place where people go to catch planes

**aisle** [rhymes with **mile**] NOUN a long narrow gap that people can walk along between rows of seats or shelves

**alarm** NOUN ❶ a feeling of fear and worry ❷ an automatic device used to warn people of something ✿ VERB ❸ If something alarms you, it makes you worried and anxious

**album** NOUN ❶ a CD, cassette, or record with a number of songs on it ❷ a book in which you keep a collection of things such as photographs or stamps

**alcohol** NOUN Alcohol is any drink that can make people drunk; also the colourless flammable liquid found in these drinks, produced by fermenting sugar

**alcoholic** ADJECTIVE ❶ An alcoholic drink contains alcohol ✿ NOUN ❷ someone who is addicted to alcohol

**alert** ADJECTIVE ❶ paying full attention to what is happening ✿ NOUN ❷ a situation in which people prepare themselves for danger ✿ VERB ❸ If you alert someone to a problem or danger, you warn them of it

**A level** NOUN an advanced exam taken by students in many British schools and colleges, usually following GCSEs

**algebra** NOUN a branch of mathematics in which symbols and letters are used instead of numbers to express relationships between quantities

**alien** [ay-lee-an] ADJECTIVE ❶ not normal to you ✿ NOUN ❷ someone who is not a citizen of the country in which he or she lives ❸ In science fiction, an alien is a creature from outer space

**alike** ADJECTIVE ❶ Things that are alike are similar in some way ✿ ADVERB ❷ If people or things are treated alike, they are treated in a similar way

**alive** ADJECTIVE ❶ living ❷ lively and active

**alkali** [al-kal-eye] NOUN a chemical substance that turns litmus paper blue

**all** ADJECTIVE, PRONOUN, OR ADVERB ❶ used when referring to the whole of something ✿ ADVERB ❷ 'All' is also used when saying the two sides in a game or contest have the same score

**Allah** PROPER NOUN the Muslim name for God

**allergy**, allergies [*al-er-jee*] NOUN a sensitivity someone has to something, so that they become ill when they eat it or touch it

**alley**, alleys NOUN a narrow passage between buildings

**alliance** NOUN a group of people, organizations, or countries working together for similar aims

**alligator** NOUN a large animal, similar to a crocodile

**allocate**, allocates, allocating, allocated VERB If you allocate something, you decide it should be given to a person or place, or used for a particular purpose

**allow** VERB ❶ If you allow something, you say it is all right or let it happen ❷ If you allow a period of time or an amount of something, you set it aside for a particular purpose

**all right** or **alright** ADJECTIVE ❶ If something is all right, it is acceptable ❷ If someone is all right, they are safe and not harmed ❸ You say 'all right' to agree to something

**ally**, allies, allying, allied NOUN ❶ a person or country that helps and supports another ✿ VERB ❷ If you ally yourself with someone, you agree to help and support each other

**almond** NOUN a pale brown oval nut

**almost** ADVERB very nearly

**alone** ADJECTIVE OR ADVERB not with other people or things

**along** PREPOSITION ❶ moving, happening, or existing continuously from one end to the other of something, or at various points beside it ✿ ADVERB ❷ moving forward ❸ with someone ✿ PHRASE ❹ All along means from the beginning of a period of time right up to now

**alongside** PREPOSITION OR ADVERB ❶ next to something ✿ PREPOSITION ❷ If you work alongside other people, you are working in the same place and cooperating with them

**aloud** ADVERB When you read or speak aloud, you speak loudly enough for other people to hear you

**alphabet** NOUN a set of letters in a fixed order that is used in writing a language

**alphabetical** ADJECTIVE

**already** ADVERB having happened before the present time or earlier than expected

**also** ADVERB in addition to something that has just been mentioned

**alter** VERB If something alters or if you alter it, it changes

**alternate**, alternates, alternating, alternated VERB [*ol-tern-ate*] ❶ If one thing alternates with another, the two things regularly occur one after the other ✿ ADJECTIVE [*ol-tern-at*] ❷ If something happens on alternate days, it happens on the first day but not the second, and happens again on the third day but not the fourth, and so on ❸ Alternate angles are two angles on opposite sides of a line that crosses two other lines

**alternative** NOUN ❶ something you can do or have instead of something else ✿ ADJECTIVE ❷ Alternative plans or actions can happen or be done instead of what is already happening or being done

**alternatively** ADVERB

**although** CONJUNCTION in spite of the fact that

**altitude** NOUN The altitude of something is its height above sea level

**altogether** ADVERB ❶ entirely ❷ in total; used of amounts

**aluminium** NOUN Aluminium is a light silvery-white metallic element. It is used to make aircraft and other equipment, usually in the form of aluminium alloys

**always** ADVERB all the time or for ever

### don't mix up

**Hello Kitty...** never mixes up **aloud** (able to be heard) and **allowed** (the past form of allow).

**am – ankle**

**am** the first person singular, present tense of **be**

**a.m.** used to specify times between 12 midnight and 12 noon, eg *I get up at 6 a.m.* It is an abbreviation for the Latin phrase 'ante meridiem', which means 'before noon'

**amateur** NOUN someone who does something as a hobby rather than as a job

**amaze**, amazes, amazing, amazed VERB If something amazes you, it surprises you very much

**amazement** NOUN complete surprise

**amazing** ADJECTIVE very surprising or remarkable  **amazingly** ADVERB

**ambassador** NOUN a person sent to a foreign country as the representative of his or her own government

**ambition** NOUN ❶ If you have an ambition to achieve something, you want very much to achieve it ❷ a great desire for success, power, and wealth

**ambitious** ADJECTIVE ❶ Someone who is ambitious has a strong desire for success, power, and wealth ❷ An ambitious plan is a large one and requires a lot of work

**ambulance** NOUN a vehicle for taking sick and injured people to hospital

**among** or **amongst** PREPOSITION ❶ surrounded by ❷ in the company of ❸ between more than two

**amount** NOUN ❶ An amount of something is how much there is of it ❀ VERB ❷ If something amounts to a particular total, all the parts of it add up to that total

**amplifier** NOUN a piece of equipment in a radio or stereo system which causes sounds or signals to become louder

**amuse**, amuses, amusing, amused VERB ❶ If something amuses you, you think it is funny ❷ If you amuse yourself, you find things to do which stop you from being bored
**amused** ADJECTIVE   **amusing** ADJECTIVE

**amusement** NOUN ❶ Amusement is the state of thinking something is funny ❷ Amusement is also the pleasure you get from being entertained or from doing something interesting ❸ Amusements are ways of passing the time pleasantly

**an** ADJECTIVE 'An' is used instead of 'a' in front of words that begin with a vowel sound

**anaesthetic** [an-niss-**thet**-ik] NOUN a substance that stops you feeling pain. A general anaesthetic stops you from feeling pain in the whole of your body by putting you to sleep, and a local anaesthetic makes just one part of your body go numb

**analyse**, analyses, analysing, analysed VERB To analyse something is to break it down into parts, or investigate it carefully, so that you can describe its main aspects, or find out what it consists of

**analysis**, analyses NOUN the process of investigating something in order to understand it or find out what it consists of

**ancestor** NOUN Your ancestors are the members of your family who lived many years ago and from whom you are descended

**anchor** NOUN ❶ a heavy, hooked object at the end of a chain, dropped from a boat into the water to keep the boat in one place ❀ VERB ❷ To anchor a boat or another object is to stop it from moving by dropping an anchor or attaching it to something solid

**ancient** [ayn-shent] ADJECTIVE ❶ existing or happening in the distant past ❷ very old or having a very long history

**and** CONJUNCTION You use 'and' to link two or more words or phrases together

**angel** NOUN Angels are spiritual beings some people believe live in heaven and act as messengers for God

**anger** NOUN ❶ the strong feeling you get when you feel someone has behaved in an unfair or cruel way ❀ VERB ❷ If something angers you, it makes you feel angry

**angle** NOUN ❶ the distance between two lines at the point where they join together. Angles are measured in degrees ❷ the direction from which you look at something ❸ An angle on something is a particular way of considering it

**angry**, angrier, angriest ADJECTIVE very cross or annoyed

**animal** NOUN any living being except a plant, or any mammal except a human being

**animation** NOUN ❶ a method of film-making in which a series of drawings are photographed. When the film is projected, the characters in the drawings appear to move ❷ Someone who has animation shows liveliness in the way they speak and act

**ankle** NOUN the joint which connects your foot to your leg

13

# anniversary - apologize

**anniversary**, anniversaries NOUN a date which is remembered because something special happened on that date in a previous year

**announce**, announces, announcing, announced VERB If you announce something, you tell people about it publicly or officially

**announcement** NOUN a statement giving information about something

**announcer** NOUN someone who introduces programmes on radio and television

**annoy** VERB If someone or something annoys you, they irritate you and make you fairly angry  **annoyed** ADJECTIVE

**annual** ADJECTIVE ❶ happening or done once a year ❷ happening or calculated over a period of one year ❀ NOUN ❸ a book or magazine published once a year ❹ a plant that grows, flowers, and dies within one year  **annually** ADVERB

**anonymous** ADJECTIVE If something is anonymous, nobody knows who is responsible for it  **anonymously** ADVERB

**another** ADJECTIVE OR PRONOUN Another thing or person is an additional thing or person

**answer** VERB ❶ If you answer someone, you reply to them using words or actions or in writing ❀ NOUN ❷ the reply you give when you answer someone ❸ a solution to a problem

**answering machine** NOUN a machine which records telephone calls while you are out

**ant** NOUN Ants are small insects that live in large groups

**antenna**, antennae or antennas NOUN ❶ The antennae of insects and certain other animals are the two long, thin parts attached to their heads which they use to feel with. The plural is 'antennae' ❷ In Australian, New Zealand, and American English, an antenna is a radio or television aerial. The plural is 'antennas'

**antibiotic** NOUN a drug or chemical used in medicine to kill bacteria and cure infections

**anticipate**, anticipates, anticipating, anticipated VERB If you anticipate an event, you are expecting it and are prepared for it  **anticipation** NOUN

**anticlockwise** ADJECTIVE OR ADVERB moving in the opposite direction to the hands of a clock

**antiperspirant** NOUN a substance which stops you sweating when you put it on your skin

**antique** [an-**teek**] NOUN ❶ an object from the past that is collected because of its value or beauty ❀ ADJECTIVE ❷ from or concerning the past

**antisocial** ADJECTIVE ❶ An antisocial person is unwilling to meet and be friendly with other people ❷ Antisocial behaviour is annoying or upsetting to other people

**antler** NOUN A male deer's antlers are the branched horns on its head

**antonym** NOUN a word which means the opposite of another word. For example, 'hot' is the antonym of 'cold'

**anus**, anuses NOUN the hole between the buttocks

**anxiety**, anxieties NOUN nervousness or worry

**anxious** ADJECTIVE ❶ If you are anxious, you are nervous or worried ❷ If you are anxious to do something or anxious that something should happen, you very much want to do it or want it to happen  **anxiously** ADVERB

**any** ADJECTIVE OR PRONOUN ❶ one, some, or several ❷ even the smallest amount or even one ❸ whatever or whichever, no matter what or which

**anybody** PRONOUN any person

**anyhow** ADVERB ❶ in any case ❷ in a careless way

**anyone** PRONOUN any person

**anything** PRONOUN any object, event, situation, or action

**anyway** ADVERB in any case

**anywhere** ADVERB in, at, or to any place

**apart** ADVERB OR ADJECTIVE ❶ When something is apart from something else, there is a space or a distance between them ❀ ADVERB ❷ If you take something apart, you separate it into pieces

**apartment** NOUN a set of rooms for living in, usually on one floor of a building

**ape**, apes, aping, aped NOUN ❶ Apes are animals with a very short tail or no tail. They are closely related to man. Apes include chimpanzees, gorillas, and gibbons ❀ VERB ❷ If you ape someone's speech or behaviour, you imitate it

**apologize**, apologizes, apologizing, apologized (also **apologise**) VERB When you apologize to someone, you say you are sorry for something you have said or done

14

## apology – appreciate

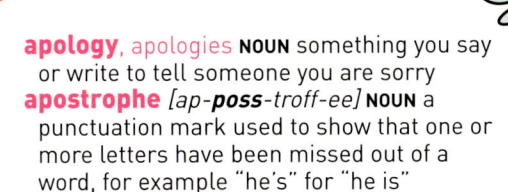

**apology**, apologies NOUN something you say or write to tell someone you are sorry

**apostrophe** [ap-*poss*-troff-ee] NOUN a punctuation mark used to show that one or more letters have been missed out of a word, for example "he's" for "he is"

### punctuation
### Hello Kitty…
knows that you put an **apostrophe** (') to show that a letter is missing (he's). An **apostrophe** s ('s) shows that something belongs to someone (*Hello Kitty's new shoes*).

**apparent** ADJECTIVE ❶ seeming real rather than actually being real ❷ obvious **apparently** ADVERB

**appeal** VERB ❶ If you appeal for something, you make an urgent request for it ❷ If you appeal to someone in authority against a decision, you formally ask them to change it ❸ If something appeals to you, you find it attractive or interesting ❀ NOUN ❹ a formal or serious request ❺ The appeal of something is the quality it has which people find attractive or interesting **appealing** ADJECTIVE

**appear** VERB ❶ When something which you could not see appears, it moves (or you move) so that you can see it ❷ When something new appears, it begins to exist ❸ When an actor or actress appears in a film or show, they take part in it ❹ If something appears to be a certain way, it seems or looks that way

**appearance** NOUN ❶ The appearance of someone in a place is their arrival there, especially when it is unexpected ❷ The appearance of something new is the time when it begins to exist ❸ Someone's or something's appearance is the way they look to other people

**appendix**, appendices or appendixes NOUN ❶ a small closed tube forming part of your digestive system ❷ An appendix to a book is extra information placed after the end of the main text

**appetite** NOUN ❶ Your appetite is your desire to eat ❷ If you have an appetite for something, you have a strong desire for it and enjoyment of it

**applaud** VERB ❶ When a group of people applaud, they clap their hands in approval or praise ❷ When an action or attitude is applauded, people praise it

**applause** NOUN Applause is clapping by a group of people

**apple** NOUN a round fruit with smooth skin and firm white flesh

**appliance** NOUN any machine in your home you use to do a job like cleaning or cooking

**applicant** NOUN someone who is applying for something

**application** NOUN ❶ a formal request for something, usually in writing ❷ The application of a rule, system, or skill is the use of it in a particular situation

**apply**, applies, applying, applied VERB ❶ If you apply for something, you formally ask for it, usually by writing a letter ❷ If you apply a rule or skill, you use it in a situation ❸ If something applies to a person or a situation, it is relevant to that person or situation ❹ If you apply something to a surface, you put it on

**appoint** VERB ❶ If you appoint someone to a job or position, you formally choose them for it ❷ If you appoint a time or place for something to happen, you decide when or where it will happen

**appointment** NOUN ❶ an arrangement you have with someone to meet them ❷ The appointment of a person to do a particular job is the choosing of that person to do it ❸ a job or a position of responsibility

**appreciate**, appreciates, appreciating, appreciated VERB ❶ If you appreciate

15

# apprentice - argue

something, you like it because you recognize its good qualities ❷ If you appreciate a situation or problem, you understand it and know what it involves ❸ If you appreciate something someone has done for you, you are grateful to them for it ❹ If something appreciates over a period of time, its value increases **appreciation** NOUN

**apprentice** NOUN a person who works for a period of time with a skilled craftsman in order to learn a skill or trade

**approach** VERB ❶ To approach something is to come near or nearer to it ❷ When a future event approaches, it gradually gets nearer ❸ If you approach someone about something, you ask them about it ❹ If you approach a situation or problem in a particular way, you think about it or deal with it in that way ✿ NOUN ❺ The approach of something is the process of it coming closer ❻ An approach to a situation or problem is a way of thinking about it or dealing with it ❼ a road or path that leads to a place

**appropriate**, appropriates, appropriating, appropriated ADJECTIVE ❶ suitable or acceptable for a particular situation ✿ VERB ❷ FORMAL If you appropriate something which does not belong to you, you take it without permission **appropriately** ADVERB

**approval** NOUN ❶ Approval is agreement given to a plan or request ❷ Approval is also admiration

**approve**, approves, approving, approved VERB ❶ If you approve of something or someone, you think that thing or person is acceptable or good ❷ If someone in a position of authority approves a plan or idea, they formally agree to it

**approximate** ADJECTIVE almost exact **approximately** ADVERB

**apricot** NOUN a small, soft, yellowish-orange fruit

**April** NOUN the fourth month of the year. April has 30 days

**apron** NOUN a piece of clothing worn over the front of normal clothing to protect it

**aquarium**, aquaria or aquariums NOUN a glass tank filled with water in which fish are kept

**arch**, arches, arching, arched NOUN ❶ a structure that has a curved top supported on either side by a pillar or wall ❷ the curved part of bone at the top of the foot ✿ VERB ❸ When something arches, it forms a curved line or shape ✿ ADJECTIVE ❹ most important

**archaeology** or **archeology** [ar-kee-ol-loj-ee] NOUN the study of the past by digging up and examining the remains of buildings, tools, and other things **archaeologist** NOUN

### how to say it

### Tips and tricks...

Archaeology should be said *ar-kee-**ol**-oj-ee*, with most force on ol.

**architect** [ar-kit-tekt] NOUN a person who designs buildings

**architecture** NOUN the art or practice of designing buildings

**are** the plural form of the present tense of **be**

**area** NOUN ❶ a particular part of a place, country, or the world ❷ The area of a piece of ground or a surface is the amount of space it covers, measured in square metres or square feet ❸ The area of a geometric object is the amount of space enclosed within its lines

**arena** NOUN ❶ a place where sports and other public events take place ❷ A particular arena is the centre of attention or activity in a particular situation

**argue**, argues, arguing, argued VERB ❶ If you argue with someone about something, you disagree with them about it, sometimes in

16

an angry way ❷ If you argue that something is the case, you give reasons why you think it is so

**argument** NOUN ❶ a disagreement between two people which causes a quarrel ❷ a point or a set of reasons you use to try to convince people about something

**arise**, arises, arising, arose, arisen VERB ❶ When something such as an opportunity or problem arises, it begins to exist ❷ FORMAL To arise also means to stand up from a sitting, kneeling, or lying position

**arithmetic** NOUN the part of mathematics which is to do with the addition, subtraction, multiplication, and division of numbers

**arm** NOUN ❶ Your arms are the part of your body between your shoulder and your wrist ❷ The arms of a chair are the parts on which you rest your arms ❸ An arm of an organization is a section of it ❹ IN PLURAL Arms are weapons used in a war ✿ VERB ❺ To arm someone is to provide them with weapons

**armchair** NOUN a comfortable chair with a support on each side for your arms

**armed** ADJECTIVE A person who is armed is carrying a weapon or weapons

**armour** NOUN In the past, armour was metal clothing worn for protection in battle

**armpit** NOUN the area under your arm where your arm joins your shoulder

**army**, armies NOUN a large group of soldiers organized into divisions for fighting on land

**around** PREPOSITION ❶ placed at various points in a place or area ❷ from place to place inside an area ❸ at approximately the time or place mentioned ✿ ADVERB ❹ here and there

**arrange**, arranges, arranging, arranged VERB ❶ If you arrange to do something, you make plans for it ❷ If you arrange something for someone, you make it possible for them to have it or do it ❸ If you arrange objects, you set them out in a particular position **arrangement** NOUN

**arrest** VERB ❶ If the police arrest someone, they take them into custody to decide whether to charge them with an offence ✿ NOUN ❷ An arrest is the act of taking a person into custody

**arrival** NOUN ❶ the act or time of arriving ❷ something or someone that has arrived

**arrive**, arrives, arriving, arrived VERB ❶ When you arrive at a place, you reach it at the end of your journey ❷ When a letter or a piece of news arrives, it is brought to you ❸ When you arrive at an idea or decision you reach it ❹ When a moment, event, or new thing arrives, it begins to happen

**arrogant** ADJECTIVE Someone who is arrogant behaves as if they are better than other people **arrogance** NOUN

**arrow** NOUN a long, thin weapon with a sharp point at one end, shot from a bow

**art** NOUN ❶ Art is the creation of objects such as paintings and sculptures, which are thought to be beautiful or which express a particular idea; also used to refer to the objects themselves ❷ An activity is called an art when it requires special skill or ability ❸ IN PLURAL The arts are literature, music, painting, and sculpture, considered together

**artery**, arteries NOUN ❶ Your arteries are the tubes that carry blood from your heart to the rest of your body ❷ a main road or major section of any system of communication or transport

**arthritis** NOUN a condition in which the joints in someone's body become swollen and painful

**artichoke** NOUN ❶ the round green partly edible flower head of a thistle-like plant; the flower head is made up of clusters of leaves that have a soft fleshy part that is eaten as a vegetable ❷ A Jerusalem artichoke is a small yellowish-white vegetable that grows underground and looks like a potato

**article** NOUN ❶ a piece of writing in a newspaper or magazine ❷ a particular item ❸ In English grammar, 'a' and 'the' are sometimes called articles: 'a' (or 'an') is the indefinite article; 'the' is the definite article

**artificial** ADJECTIVE ❶ created by people rather than occurring naturally ❷ pretending to have attitudes and feelings which other people realize are not real **artificially** ADVERB

**artist** NOUN ❶ a person who draws or paints or produces other works of art ❷ a person who is very skilled at a particular activity

**artistic** ADJECTIVE ❶ able to create good paintings, sculpture, or other works of art ❷ concerning or involving art or artists

# as - at

**as** CONJUNCTION ❶ at the same time that ❷ in the way that ❸ because ❹ You use the structure **as ... as** when you are comparing things that are similar ✿ PREPOSITION ❺ You use 'as' when you are saying what role someone or something has ❻ You use **as if** or **as though** when you are giving a possible explanation for something

**ash**, ashes NOUN ❶ the grey or black powdery remains of anything that has been burnt ❷ a tree with grey bark and hard tough wood

**ashamed** ADJECTIVE ❶ feeling embarrassed or guilty ❷ If you are ashamed of someone, you feel embarrassed to be connected with them

**ashore** ADVERB on land or onto the land

**ashtray** NOUN a small dish for ash from cigarettes and cigars

**aside** ADVERB If you move something aside, you move it to one side

**ask** VERB ❶ If you ask someone a question, you put a question to them for them to answer ❷ If you ask someone to do something or give you something, you tell them you want them to do it or to give it to you ❸ If you ask someone's permission or forgiveness, you try to obtain it ❹ If you ask someone somewhere, you invite them there

**asleep** ADJECTIVE sleeping

**asparagus** NOUN a vegetable that has long shoots which are cooked and eaten

**aspect** NOUN ❶ An aspect of something is one of its features ❷ The aspect of a building is the direction it faces

**aspirin** NOUN ❶ a white drug used to relieve pain, fever, and colds ❷ a tablet of this drug

**assassinate**, assassinates, assassinating, assassinated VERB To assassinate a political or religious leader is to murder him or her **assassination** NOUN

**assault** NOUN ❶ a violent attack on someone ✿ VERB ❷ To assault someone is to attack them violently

**assemble**, assembles, assembling, assembled VERB ❶ To assemble is to gather together ❷ If you assemble something, you fit the parts of it together

**assembly**, assemblies NOUN ❶ a group of people who have gathered together for a meeting ❷ The assembly of an object is the fitting together of its parts

**assess**, assesses, assessing, assessed VERB If you assess something, you consider it carefully and make a judgment about it **assessment** NOUN

**asset** NOUN a person or thing considered useful

**assignment** NOUN a job someone is given to do

**assist** VERB To assist someone is to help them do something **assistance** NOUN

**assistant** NOUN someone whose job is to help another person in their work

**associate**, associates, associating, associated VERB ❶ If you associate one thing with another, you connect the two things in your mind ❷ If you associate with a group of people, you spend a lot of time with them ✿ NOUN ❸ Your associates are the people you work with or spend a lot of time with

**association** NOUN an organization for people who have similar interests, jobs, or aims

**assorted** ADJECTIVE Assorted things are different in size and colour

**assortment** NOUN a group of similar things that are different sizes and colours

**assume**, assumes, assuming, assumed VERB ❶ If you assume that something is true, you accept it is true even though you have not thought about it ❷ To assume responsibility for something is to put yourself in charge of it

**assure**, assures, assuring, assured VERB If you assure someone that something is true, you tell them it is true

**asterisk** NOUN the symbol (*) used in printing and writing

**asthma** [ass-ma] NOUN a disease of the chest which causes difficulty in breathing

**astonish**, astonishes, astonishing, astonished VERB If something astonishes you, it surprises you very much **astonished** ADJECTIVE **astonishing** ADJECTIVE **astonishingly** ADVERB **astonishment** NOUN

**astronaut** NOUN a person who operates a spacecraft

**astronomy** NOUN the scientific study of stars and planets **astronomer** NOUN

**at** PREPOSITION ❶ used to say where someone or something is ❷ used to mention the direction something is going in ❸ used to say when something happens

**athlete** NOUN someone who is good at sport and takes part in sporting events
**athletic** ADJECTIVE ❶ strong, healthy, and good at sports ❷ involving athletes or athletics
**atlas**, atlases NOUN a book of maps

### where does the word come from?

*Did you know…*

that *Atlas* was a giant in Greek legend who held the sky on his shoulders? The earliest collections of maps had pictures of this on them and that is how they got the name *atlas*.

**atmosphere** NOUN ❶ the air and other gases that surround a planet; also the air in a particular place ❷ the general mood of a place
**atom** NOUN the smallest part of an element that can take part in a chemical reaction
**atomic** ADJECTIVE relating to atoms or to the power released by splitting atoms
**attach**, attaches, attaching, attached VERB If you attach something to something else, you join or fasten the two things together
**attached** ADJECTIVE If you are attached to someone, you are very fond of them
**attachment** NOUN ❶ Attachment to someone is a feeling of love and affection for them ❷ a file that is attached to an e-mail
**attack** VERB ❶ To attack someone is to use violence against them so as to hurt or kill them ❷ If you attack someone or their ideas, you criticize them strongly ✿ NOUN ❸ An attack is violent physical action against someone

**attempt** VERB ❶ If you attempt to do something, you try to do it or achieve it, but may not succeed ✿ NOUN ❷ an act of trying to do something
**attend** VERB ❶ If you attend an event, you are present at it ❷ To attend school, church, or hospital is to go there regularly ❸ If you attend to something, you deal with it
**attendance** NOUN
**attendant** NOUN someone whose job is to serve people in a place such as a garage or cloakroom
**attention** NOUN Attention is the thought or care you give to something
**attic** NOUN a room at the top of a house immediately below the roof
**attitude** NOUN Your attitude to someone or something is the way you think about them and behave towards them
**attract** VERB ❶ If something attracts people, it interests them and makes them want to go to it ❷ If someone attracts you, you like and admire them ❸ If something attracts support or publicity, it gets it
**attraction** NOUN ❶ Attraction is a feeling of liking someone or something very much ❷ something people visit for interest or pleasure ❸ a quality that attracts someone or something
**attractive** ADJECTIVE ❶ interesting and possibly advantageous ❷ pleasant to look at or be with

### how to remember

*Hello Kitty…*

remembers that you must att**ach** a **c**oat **h**ook to the wall.

# aubergine – axis

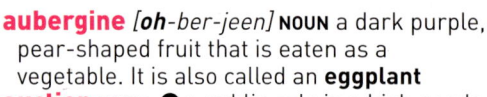

**aubergine** [oh-ber-jeen] NOUN a dark purple, pear-shaped fruit that is eaten as a vegetable. It is also called an **eggplant**

**auction** NOUN ❶ a public sale in which goods are sold to the person who offers the highest price ✿ VERB ❷ To auction something is to sell it in an auction

**audience** NOUN ❶ the group of people who are watching or listening to a performance ❷ a private or formal meeting with an important person

**audio** ADJECTIVE used in recording and reproducing sound

**audition** NOUN a short performance given by an actor or musician, so that a director can decide whether they are suitable for a part in a play or film or for a place in an orchestra

**August** NOUN the eighth month of the year. August has 31 days

**aunt** NOUN Your aunt is the sister of your mother or father, or the wife of your uncle

**authentic** ADJECTIVE real and genuine

**author** NOUN The author of a book is the person who wrote it

**authority**, authorities NOUN ❶ Authority is the power to control people ❷ In Britain, an authority is a local government department ❸ Someone who is an authority on something knows a lot about it

**authorize**, authorizes, authorizing, authorized (also **authorise**) VERB To authorize something is to give official permission for it to happen  **authorization** NOUN

**autobiography**, autobiographies NOUN Someone's autobiography is an account of their life which they have written themselves  **autobiographical** ADJECTIVE

**autograph** NOUN the signature of a famous person

**automatic** ADJECTIVE ❶ An automatic machine is programmed to perform tasks without needing a person to operate it ❷ Automatic actions or reactions take place without involving conscious thought  **automatically** ADVERB

**automobile** NOUN FORMAL OR AMERICAN a car

**autumn** NOUN the season between summer and winter

**auxiliary verb** NOUN In grammar, an auxiliary verb is a verb which forms tenses of other verbs or questions. For example in 'He has gone', 'has' is the auxiliary verb and in 'Do you understand?', 'do' is the auxiliary verb

**available** ADJECTIVE ❶ Something that is available can be obtained ❷ Someone who is available is ready for work or free for people to talk to

**avalanche** [av-a-lahnsh] NOUN a huge mass of snow and ice that falls down a mountain side

**avenue** NOUN a street, especially one with trees along it

**average** NOUN ❶ a result obtained by adding several amounts together and then dividing the total by the number of different amounts ✿ ADJECTIVE ❷ Average means standard

**avocado**, avocados NOUN a pear-shaped fruit, with dark green skin, soft greenish yellow flesh, and a large stone

**avoid** VERB ❶ If you avoid doing something, you make a deliberate effort not to do it ❷ If you avoid someone, you keep away from them

**awake**, awakes, awaking, awoke, awoken ADJECTIVE ❶ Someone who is awake is not sleeping ✿ VERB ❷ When you awake, you wake up ❸ If you are awoken by something, it wakes you up

**award** NOUN ❶ a prize or certificate for doing something well ❷ a sum of money an organization gives to students for training or study ✿ VERB ❸ If you award someone something, you give it to them formally or officially

**aware** ADJECTIVE ❶ If you are aware of something, you realize it is there ❷ If you are aware of something, you know about it  **awareness** NOUN

**away** ADVERB ❶ moving from a place ❷ at a distance from a place ❸ in its proper place

**awesome** ADJECTIVE ❶ Something that is awesome is very impressive and frightening ❷ INFORMAL Awesome also means excellent

**awful** ADJECTIVE ❶ very unpleasant or very bad ✿ ADVERB ❷ INFORMAL very great

**awkward** ADJECTIVE ❶ clumsy and uncomfortable ❷ embarrassed or nervous ❸ difficult to deal with

**axe** NOUN a tool with a handle and a sharp blade, used for chopping wood

**axis**, axes [ak-siss] NOUN ❶ an imaginary line through the centre of something, around which it moves ❷ one of the two sides of a graph

baby – backwards

**baby**, babies NOUN a child in the first year or two of its life

**bachelor** NOUN a man who has never been married

### how to remember
Hello Kitty... remembers **Bach** was a **bach**elor.

**back** ADVERB ❶ When people or things move back, they move in the opposite direction from the one they are facing ❷ When people or things go back to a place or situation, they return to it ❸ If you get something back, it is returned to you ❹ If you do something back to someone, you do to them what they have done to you ❺ Back also means in the past ✿ NOUN ❻ the rear part of your body ❼ the part of something that is behind the front ✿ ADJECTIVE ❽ The back parts of something are the ones near the rear ✿ VERB ❾ If a building backs onto something, its back faces in that direction ❿ To back a person or organization means to support or finance that person or organization

**back down** ✿ VERB If you back down on a demand or claim, you withdraw and give up

**back out** ✿ VERB If you back out of a promise or commitment, you decide not to do what you had promised to do

**back up** ✿ VERB ❶ If you back up a claim or story, you produce evidence to show that it is true ❷ If you back someone up, you help and support them

**backbone** NOUN ❶ the column of linked bones along the middle of a person's or animal's back ❷ the strength of a person's character

**background** NOUN ❶ the circumstances which help to explain an event or caused it to happen ❷ the kind of home you come from and your education and experience ❸ If sounds are in the background, they are there but no one really pays very much attention to them

**backpack** NOUN a large bag that hikers or campers carry on their backs

**backstroke** NOUN Backstroke is a swimming stroke in which you lie on your back, kick your legs, and move your arms back over your head

**backward** ADJECTIVE ❶ Backward means directed behind you ❷ A backward country or society is one that does not have modern industries or technology

**backwards** ADVERB ❶ Backwards means behind you ❷ If you do something backwards, you do it the opposite of the usual way

**bacon - bamboo**

**bacon** NOUN meat from the back or sides of a pig, which has been salted or smoked

**bacteria** PLURAL NOUN Bacteria are very tiny organisms which can cause disease
**bacterial** ADJECTIVE

**bad**, worse, worst ADJECTIVE ❶ Anything harmful or upsetting can be described as bad ❷ insufficient or of poor quality ❸ evil or immoral in character or behaviour ❹ lacking skill in something ❺ Bad language consists of swearwords ❻ If you have a bad temper, you become angry easily

*some other words to use*

**Hello Kitty...**

knows you should try not to use **bad** too much when you are writing. Some other words you can use are: *poor, inferior, unsatisfactory* and *faulty.*

**badge** NOUN a piece of plastic or metal with a design or message on it that you can pin to your clothes

**badger** NOUN a wild animal that has a white head with two black stripes on it

**badly** ADVERB in an inferior or unimpressive way

**badminton** NOUN Badminton is a game in which two or four players use rackets to hit a shuttlecock over a high net. It was first played at Badminton House in Gloucestershire

**bag** NOUN ❶ a container for carrying things in ❷ IN PLURAL; INFORMAL Bags of something is a lot of it

**baggage** NOUN the suitcases and bags that you take on a journey

**baggy**, baggier, baggiest ADJECTIVE Baggy clothing hangs loosely

**bait** NOUN ❶ a small amount of food placed on a hook or in a trap, to attract a fish or wild animal so that it gets caught ❷ something used to tempt a person to do something ❀ VERB ❸ If you bait a hook or trap, you put some food on it to catch a fish or wild animal

**bake**, bakes, baking, baked VERB ❶ To bake food means to cook it in an oven without using liquid or fat ❷ To bake earth or clay means to heat it until it becomes hard

**baker**, bakers NOUN a person who makes and sells bread and cakes

**bakery** NOUN a building where bread and cakes are baked and sold

**balance**, balances, balancing, balanced VERB ❶ When someone or something balances, they remain steady and do not fall over ❀ NOUN ❷ Balance is the state of being upright and steady ❸ Balance is also a situation in which all the parts involved have a stable relationship with each other ❹ The balance in someone's bank account is the amount of money in it

**balcony**, balconies NOUN ❶ a platform on the outside of a building with a wall or railing round it ❷ an area of upstairs seats in a theatre or cinema

**bald** ADJECTIVE A bald person has little or no hair on their head

**ball** NOUN ❶ a round object, especially one used in games such as cricket and soccer ❷ The ball of your foot or thumb is the rounded part where your toes join your foot or your thumb joins your hand ❸ a large formal social event at which people dance

**ballerina**, ballerinas NOUN a woman ballet dancer

**ballet** [*bal-lay*] NOUN Ballet is a type of artistic dancing based on precise steps

**balloon** NOUN ❶ a small bag made of thin rubber that you blow into until it becomes larger and rounder ❷ a large, strong bag filled with gas or hot air, which travels through the air carrying passengers in a compartment underneath

**bamboo** NOUN Bamboo is a tall tropical plant with hard, hollow stems used for making furniture. It is a species of giant grass. The young shoots can be eaten

**ban**, bans, banning, banned VERB ❶ If something is banned, or if you are banned from doing it or using it, you are not allowed to do it or use it ✿ NOUN ❷ If there is a ban on something, it is not allowed

**banana** NOUN a long curved fruit with a yellow skin

**band** NOUN ❶ a group of musicians who play jazz or pop music together, or a group who play brass instruments together ❷ a group of people who share a common purpose ❸ a narrow strip of something used to hold things together or worn as a decoration

**bandage**, bandages, bandaging, bandaged NOUN ❶ a strip of cloth wrapped round a wound to protect it ✿ VERB ❷ If you bandage a wound, you tie a bandage round it

**bang** VERB ❶ If you bang something, you hit it or put it somewhere violently, so that it makes a loud noise ❷ If you bang a part of your body against something, you accidentally bump it ✿ NOUN ❸ a sudden, short, loud noise ❹ a hard or painful bump against something

**banister** or **bannister** NOUN a rail supported by posts along the side of a staircase

**banjo**, banjos or banjoes NOUN a musical instrument, like a small guitar with a round body

**bank** NOUN ❶ a business that looks after people's money ❷ a bank of something is a store of it kept ready for use ❸ the raised ground along the edge of a river or lake ❹ the sloping side of an area of raised ground ✿ VERB ❺ When you bank money, you pay it into a bank ❻ If you bank on something happening, you expect it and rely on it

**bankrupt** ADJECTIVE ❶ People or organizations that go bankrupt do not have enough money to pay their debts ✿ NOUN ❷ someone who has been declared bankrupt ✿ VERB ❸ To bankrupt someone means to make them bankrupt

**banner** NOUN a long strip of cloth with a message or slogan on it

**baptism** NOUN a ceremony in which someone is baptized

**baptize**, baptizes, baptizing, baptized (also **baptise**) VERB When someone is baptized water is sprinkled on them, or they are immersed in water, as a sign that they have become a Christian

**bar**, bars, barring, barred NOUN ❶ a counter or room where alcoholic drinks are served ❷ a long, straight piece of metal ❸ a piece of something made in a rectangular shape ❹ The bars in a piece of music are the many short parts of equal length that the piece is divided into ✿ VERB ❺ If you bar a door, you place something across it to stop it being opened ❻ If you bar someone's way, you stop them going somewhere by standing in front of them

**barbecue**, barbecues, barbecuing, barbecued NOUN ❶ a grill with a charcoal fire on which you cook food, usually outdoors; also an outdoor party where you eat food cooked on a barbecue ✿ VERB ❷ When food is barbecued, it is cooked over a charcoal grill

**barber** NOUN a man who cuts men's hair

**bare**, barer, barest; bares, baring, bared ADJECTIVE ❶ If a part of your body is bare, it is not covered by any clothing ❷ If something is bare, it has nothing on top of it or inside it ❸ When trees are bare, they have no leaves on them ❹ The bare minimum or bare essentials means the very least that is needed ✿ VERB ❺ If you bare something, you uncover or show it

## don't mix up

**Hello Kitty...**

never mixes up **bare** (not having any clothes on) and **bear** (the wild animal with thick fur).

# barefoot – bat

**barefoot** ADJECTIVE OR ADVERB not wearing anything on your feet

**barely** ADVERB only just

**bargain** NOUN ❶ an agreement in which two people or groups discuss and agree what each will do, pay, or receive in a matter which involves them both ❷ something which is sold at a low price and which is good value ✿ VERB ❸ When people bargain with each other, they discuss and agree terms about what each will do, pay, or receive in a matter which involves both

**barge**, barges, barging, barged NOUN ❶ a boat with a flat bottom used for carrying heavy loads, especially on canals ✿ VERB ❷ INFORMAL If you barge into a place, you push into it in a rough or rude way

**bark** VERB ❶ When a dog barks, it makes a short, loud noise, once or several times ✿ NOUN ❷ the short, loud noise that a dog makes ❸ the tough material that covers the outside of a tree

**barn** NOUN a large farm building used for storing crops or animal food

**barracks** PLURAL NOUN a building where soldiers live

**barrel** NOUN ❶ a wooden container with rounded sides and flat ends ❷ The barrel of a gun is the long tube through which the bullet is fired

**barricade**, barricades, barricading, barricaded NOUN ❶ a temporary barrier put up to stop people getting past ✿ VERB ❷ If you barricade yourself inside a room or building, you put something heavy against the door to stop people getting in

**barrier** NOUN ❶ a fence or wall that prevents people or animals getting from one area to another ❷ If something is a barrier, it prevents two people or groups from agreeing or communicating, or prevents something from being achieved

**base**, bases, basing, based NOUN ❶ the lowest part of something, which often supports the rest ❷ A place which part of an army, navy, or air force works from ❸ In chemistry, a base is any compound that reacts with an acid to form a salt ✿ VERB ❹ To base something on something else means to use the second thing as a foundation or starting point of the first ❺ If you are based somewhere, you live there or work from there

**baseball** NOUN Baseball is a team game played with a bat and a ball, similar to rounders

**basement** NOUN a floor of a building built completely or partly below the ground

**bases** PLURAL NOUN ❶ [*bay-seez*] the plural of **basis** ❷ [*bay-siz*] the plural of **base**

**bash**, bashes, bashing, bashed VERB INFORMAL If you bash someone or bash into them, you hit them hard

**bashful** ADJECTIVE shy and easily embarrassed

**basic** ADJECTIVE ❶ The basic aspects of something are the most necessary ones ❷ Something that is basic has only the necessary features without any extras or luxuries **basically** ADVERB

**basin** NOUN ❶ a round wide container which is open at the top ❷ The basin of a river is a bowl of land from which water runs into the river

**basis**, bases NOUN ❶ The basis of something is the essential main principle from which it can be developed ❷ The basis for a belief is the facts that support it

**basket** NOUN a container made of thin strips of cane woven together

**basketball** NOUN Basketball is a game in which two teams try to score goals by throwing a large ball through one of two circular nets suspended high up at each end of the court

**bass**, basses [*rhymes with lace*] NOUN ❶ A bass is a man who sings the lowest part in four-part harmony ❷ A bass is also a musical instrument that provides the rhythm and lowest part in the harmonies. A bass may be either a large guitar or a very large member of the violin family: see **double bass**

**bass**, basses [*rhymes with gas*] NOUN a type of edible sea fish

**bassoon** NOUN a large woodwind instrument

**bat**, bats, batting, batted NOUN ❶ a specially shaped piece of wood with a handle, used for hitting the ball in a game such as cricket or table tennis ❷ a small flying animal, active at night, that looks like a mouse with wings ✿ VERB ❸ In certain sports, when someone

24

**batch – beat**

is batting, it is their turn to try to hit the ball and score runs

**batch**, batches NOUN a group of things of the same kind produced or dealt with together

**bath** NOUN a long container which you fill with water and sit in to wash yourself

**bathe**, bathes, bathing, bathed VERB ❶ When you bathe, you swim or play in open water ❷ When you bathe a wound, you wash it gently ❸ LITERARY If a place is bathed in light, a lot of light reaches it

**bathroom** NOUN a room with a bath or shower, a washbasin, and often a toilet in it

**baton** NOUN ❶ a light, thin stick that a conductor uses to direct an orchestra or choir ❷ In athletics, the baton is a short stick passed from one runner to another in a relay race ❸ A baton is also a short stick used by policemen in some countries as a weapon, lighter than a truncheon

**batter** VERB ❶ To batter someone or something means to hit them many times ❖ NOUN ❷ Batter is a mixture of flour, eggs, and milk, used to make pancakes, or to coat food before frying it

**battery**, batteries NOUN ❶ a device, containing two or more cells, for storing and producing electricity, for example in a torch or a car ❷ a large group of things or people ❖ ADJECTIVE ❸ A battery hen is one of a large number of hens kept in small cages for the mass production of eggs

**battle**, battles NOUN ❶ a fight between armed forces or a struggle between two people or groups with conflicting aims ❷ A battle for something difficult is a determined attempt to obtain or achieve it

**bay**, bays, baying, bayed NOUN ❶ a part of a coastline where the land curves inwards ❷ a space or area used for a particular purpose ❸ Bay is a kind of tree similar to the laurel, with leaves used for flavouring in cooking ❖ PHRASE ❹ If you **keep something at bay**, you prevent it from reaching you ❖ VERB ❺ When a hound or wolf bays, it makes a deep howling noise

**BC** BC means 'before Christ'. You use 'BC' in dates to indicate the number of years before the birth of Jesus Christ

**be** AUXILIARY VERB ❶ 'Be' is used with a present participle to form the continuous tense ❷ 'Be' is also used to say that something will happen ❸ 'Be' is used to form the passive voice ❖ VERB ❹ 'Be' is used to give more information about the subject of a sentence

**beach**, beaches NOUN an area of sand or pebbles beside the sea

**bead** NOUN ❶ Beads are small pieces of coloured glass or wood with a hole through the middle, strung together to make jewellery ❷ Beads of liquid are drops of it

**beak** NOUN A bird's beak is the hard part of its mouth that sticks out

**beam** NOUN ❶ a broad smile ❷ A beam of light is a band of light that shines from something such as a torch ❸ a long, thick bar of wood or metal, especially one that supports a roof ❖ VERB ❹ If you beam, you smile because you are happy

**bean** NOUN Beans are the seeds or pods of a climbing plant, which are eaten as a vegetable; also used of some other seeds, for example the seeds from which coffee is made

**bear**, bears, bearing, bore, borne NOUN ❶ a large, strong wild animal with thick fur and sharp claws ❖ VERB ❷ FORMAL To bear something means to carry it or support its weight ❸ If something bears a mark or typical feature, it has it ❹ If you bear something difficult, you accept it and are able to deal with it ❺ If you can't bear someone or something, you dislike them very much ❻ FORMAL When a plant or tree bears flowers, fruit, or leaves, it produces them **bearable** ADJECTIVE

**beard** NOUN the hair that grows on the lower part of a man's face

**beast** NOUN ❶ OLD-FASHIONED a large wild animal ❷ INFORMAL If you call someone a beast, you mean that they are cruel or spiteful

**beat**, beats, beating, beat, beaten VERB ❶ To beat someone or something means to hit them hard and repeatedly ❷ If you beat someone in a race or game, you defeat them or do better than them ❸ When a bird or insect beats its wings, it moves them up and down ❹ When your heart is beating, it is pumping blood with a regular rhythm ❺ If you beat eggs, cream, or butter, you mix

25

them vigorously using a fork or a whisk ❂ **NOUN** ❻ The beat of your heart is its regular pumping action ❼ The beat of a piece of music is its main rhythm ❽ A police officer's beat is the area which he or she patrols

**beat up** ❂ **VERB** To beat someone up means to hit or kick them repeatedly

**beautiful** **ADJECTIVE** very attractive or pleasing **beautifully** **ADVERB**

**beauty**, beauties **NOUN** ❶ Beauty is the quality of being beautiful ❷ OLD-FASHIONED a very attractive woman ❸ The beauty of an idea or plan is what makes it attractive or worthwhile

**beaver** **NOUN** an animal with a big, flat tail and webbed hind feet. Beavers build dams

**because** **CONJUNCTION** ❶ 'Because' is used with a clause that gives the reason for something ❂ **PHRASE** ❷ **Because of** is used with a noun that gives the reason for something

## how to remember

Hello Kitty...

knows how to spell **because** by remembering **b**ig **e**lephants **c**an **a**lways **u**nderstand **s**mall **e**lephants.

**become**, becomes, becoming, became, become **VERB** To become something means to start feeling or being that thing

**bed** **NOUN** ❶ a piece of furniture that you lie on when you sleep ❷ A bed in a garden is an area of ground in which plants are grown ❸ The bed of a sea or river is the ground at the bottom of it

**bedroom** **NOUN** a room used for sleeping in

**bedspread** **NOUN** a cover put over a bed, on top of the sheets and blankets

**bee** **NOUN** a winged insect that makes honey and lives in large groups

**beef** **NOUN** Beef is the meat of a cow, bull, or ox

**beehive** **NOUN** a container in which bees live and make their honey

**been** the past participle of **be**

**beer** **NOUN** an alcoholic drink made from malt and flavoured with hops

**beetle** **NOUN** a flying insect with hard wings which cover its body when it is not flying

**beetroot** **NOUN** the round, dark red root of a type of beet, eaten as a vegetable

**before** **ADVERB, PREPOSITION, OR CONJUNCTION** ❶ 'Before' is used to refer to a previous time ❂ **ADVERB** ❷ If you have done something before, you have done it on a previous occasion ❂ **PREPOSITION** ❸ FORMAL Before also means in front of

**beforehand** **ADVERB** before

**beg**, begs, begging, begged **VERB** ❶ When people beg, they ask for food or money, because they are very poor ❷ If you beg someone to do something, you ask them very anxiously to do it

**beggar** **NOUN** someone who lives by asking people for money or food

**begin**, begins, beginning, began, begun **VERB** If you begin to do something, you start doing it. When something begins, it starts

**beginner** **NOUN** someone who has just started learning to do something and cannot do it very well yet

**beginning** **NOUN** The beginning of something is the first part of it or the time when it starts

**behalf** **PHRASE** To do something **on behalf of** someone or something means to do it for their benefit or as their representative

**behave**, behaves, behaving, behaved **VERB** ❶ If you behave in a particular way, you act in that way ❷ To behave yourself means to act correctly or properly

**behaviour** **NOUN** Your behaviour is the way in which you behave

**behind** **PREPOSITION** ❶ at the back of ❷ responsible for or causing ❸ supporting someone ❂ **ADVERB** ❹ If you stay behind,

## beige – between

you remain after other people have gone ❺ If you leave something behind, you do not take it with you

**beige** [bayj] NOUN OR ADJECTIVE pale creamy-brown

**being** ❶ Being is the present participle of **be** ✿ NOUN ❷ Being is the state of existing ❸ a living creature, either real or imaginary

**belief** NOUN ❶ a feeling of certainty that something exists or is true ❷ one of the principles of a religion or moral system

**believable** ADJECTIVE possible or likely to be the case

**believe**, believes, believing, believed VERB ❶ If you believe that something is true, you accept that it is true ❷ If you believe someone, you accept that they are telling the truth ❸ If you believe in things such as God and miracles, you accept that they exist or happen ❹ If you believe in something such as a plan or system, you are in favour of it

**bell** NOUN ❶ a cup-shaped metal object with a piece inside that swings and hits the sides, producing a ringing sound ❷ an electrical device that rings or buzzes in order to attract attention

**belly**, bellies NOUN ❶ Your belly is your stomach or the front of your body below your chest ❷ An animal's belly is the underneath part of its body

**belong** VERB ❶ If something belongs to you, it is yours and you own it ❷ To belong to a group means to be a member of it ❸ If something belongs in a particular place, that is where it should be

**belongings** PLURAL NOUN Your belongings are the things that you own

**below** PREPOSITION OR ADVERB ❶ If something is below a line or the surface of something else, it is lower down ❷ Below also means at or to a lower point, level, or rate

**belt** NOUN ❶ a strip of leather or cloth that you fasten round your waist to hold your trousers or skirt up ❷ In a machine, a belt is a circular strip of rubber that drives moving parts or carries objects along ❸ a specific area of a country ✿ VERB ❹ INFORMAL To belt someone means to hit them very hard

**bench**, benches NOUN a long seat that two or more people can sit on

**bend**, bends, bending, bent VERB ❶ When you bend something, you use force to make it curved or angular ❷ When you bend, you move your head and shoulders forwards and downwards ✿ NOUN ❸ a curved part of something

**beneath** PREPOSITION, ADJECTIVE OR ADVERB ❶ an old-fashioned word for **underneath** ✿ PREPOSITION ❷ If someone thinks something is beneath them, they think that it is too unimportant for them to bother with it

**benefit** NOUN ❶ The benefits of something are the advantages that it brings to people ❷ Benefit is money given by the government to people who are unemployed or ill ✿ VERB ❸ If you benefit from something or something benefits you, it helps you

**bent** ❶ Bent is the past participle and past tense of **bend** ✿ PHRASE ❷ If you are **bent on** doing something, you are determined to do it

**berry**, berries NOUN Berries are small, round fruits that grow on bushes or trees

**beside** PREPOSITION If one thing is beside something else, they are next to each other

**best** ADJECTIVE OR ADVERB ❶ the superlative of **good** and **well** ✿ ADVERB ❷ The thing that you like best is the thing that you prefer to everything else ✿ NOUN ❸ the thing most preferred

**bet**, bets, betting, bet VERB ❶ If you bet on the result of an event, you will win money if something happens and lose money if it does not ✿ NOUN ❷ the act of betting on something, or the amount of money that you agree to risk ✿ PHRASE ❸ You say **I bet** to indicate that you are sure that something is or will be so **betting** NOUN

**better** ADJECTIVE OR ADVERB ❶ the comparative of **good** and **well** ✿ ADVERB ❷ If you like one thing better than another, you like it more than the other thing ✿ ADJECTIVE ❸ If you are better after an illness, you are no longer ill

**between** PREPOSITION OR ADVERB ❶ If something is between two other things, it is situated or happens in the space or time that separates them ❷ A relationship or difference between two people or things involves only those two

# beware – bitter

**beware** VERB If you tell someone to beware of something, you are warning them that it might be dangerous or harmful

**beyond** PREPOSITION ❶ If something is beyond a certain place, it is on the other side of it ❷ If something continues beyond a particular point, it continues further than that point ❸ If someone or something is beyond understanding or help, they cannot be understood or helped

**biceps** NOUN the large muscle on your upper arms

**bicycle** NOUN a two-wheeled vehicle which you ride by pushing two pedals with your feet

**bid**, bids, bidding, bade, bidden, bid NOUN ❶ an attempt to obtain or do something ❷ an offer to buy something for a certain sum of money ✿ VERB ❸ If you bid for something, you offer to pay a certain sum of money for it ❹ OLD-FASHIONED If you bid someone a greeting or a farewell, you say it to them

**big**, bigger, biggest ADJECTIVE ❶ of a large size ❷ of great importance

some other words to use

## Tips and tricks...

Try not to use **big** too much when you are writing. Some other words you can use are: *gigantic, immense, vast* and *massive*.

**bike** NOUN INFORMAL a bicycle or motorcycle
**bikini**, bikinis NOUN a small two-piece swimming costume worn by women
**bilingual** ADJECTIVE involving or using two languages

**bill** NOUN ❶ a written statement of how much is owed for goods or services ❷ a formal statement of a proposed new law that is discussed and then voted on in Parliament ❸ a notice or a poster ❹ A bird's bill is its beak

**billboard** NOUN a large board on which advertisements are displayed

**billion** NOUN a thousand million. Formerly, a billion was a million million

**bin** NOUN a container, especially one that you put rubbish in

**bind**, binds, binding, bound VERB ❶ If you bind something, you tie rope or string round it so that it is held firmly ❷ If something binds you to a course of action, it makes you act in that way

**binoculars** PLURAL NOUN Binoculars are an instrument with lenses for both eyes, which you look through in order to see objects far away

**biography**, biographies NOUN the history of someone's life, written by someone else

**biology** NOUN Biology is the study of living things **biological** ADJECTIVE **biologist** NOUN

**bird** NOUN an animal with two legs, two wings, and feathers

**birth** NOUN ❶ The birth of a baby is when it comes out of its mother's womb at the beginning of its life ❷ The birth of something is its beginning

**birthday**, birthdays NOUN Your birthday is the anniversary of the date on which you were born

**biscuit** NOUN a small flat cake made of baked dough

**bishop** NOUN ❶ a high-ranking clergyman in some Christian churches ❷ In chess, a bishop is a piece that is moved diagonally across the board

**bit** ❶ Bit is the past tense of **bite** ✿ NOUN ❷ A bit of something is a small amount of it ✿ PHRASE ❸ **A bit** means slightly or to a small extent

**bite**, bites, biting, bit, bitten VERB ❶ To bite something or someone is to cut it or cut through it with the teeth ✿ NOUN ❷ a small amount that you bite off something with your teeth ❸ the injury you get when an animal or insect bites you

**bitter** ADJECTIVE ❶ If someone is bitter, they feel angry and resentful ❷ A bitter disappointment or experience makes people feel angry or unhappy for a long time afterwards ❸ In a bitter argument or war, people argue or fight fiercely and angrily ❹ A bitter wind is an extremely cold wind ❺ Something that tastes bitter has a sharp, unpleasant taste **bitterly** ADVERB

**bizarre** [biz-*zahr*] ADJECTIVE very strange or eccentric

**black** NOUN OR ADJECTIVE ❶ Black is the darkest possible colour, like tar or soot ❷ Someone who is Black is a member of a dark-skinned race ❸ Black coffee or tea has no milk or cream added to it ❹ Black humour involves jokes about death or suffering

**blackberry**, blackberries NOUN Blackberries are small black fruits that grow on prickly bushes called brambles

**blackboard** NOUN a dark-coloured board in a classroom, which teachers write on using chalk

**blackmail** VERB ❶ If someone blackmails another person, they threaten to reveal an unpleasant secret about them unless that person gives them money or does something for them ✿ NOUN ❷ Blackmail is the action of blackmailing people

**blacksmith** NOUN a person whose job is making things out of iron, such as horseshoes

**bladder** NOUN the part of your body where urine is held until it leaves your body

**blade** NOUN ❶ The blade of a weapon or cutting tool is the sharp part of it ❷ The blades of a propeller are the thin, flat parts that turn round ❸ A blade of grass is a single piece of it

**blame**, blames, blaming, blamed VERB ❶ If someone blames you for something bad that has happened, they believe you caused it ✿ NOUN ❷ The blame for something bad that happens is the responsibility for letting it happen

**bland** ADJECTIVE tasteless, dull or boring

**blank** ADJECTIVE ❶ Something that is blank has nothing on it ❷ If you look blank, your face shows no feeling or interest ✿ NOUN ❸ If your mind is a blank, you cannot think of anything or remember anything

**blanket** NOUN ❶ a large rectangle of thick cloth that is put on a bed to keep people warm ❷ A blanket of something such as snow is a thick covering of it

**blast** VERB ❶ When people blast a hole in something they make a hole with an explosion ✿ NOUN ❷ a big explosion, especially one caused by a bomb ❸ a sudden strong rush of wind or air

**blaze**, blazes, blazing, blazed NOUN ❶ a large, hot fire ❷ A blaze of light or colour is a great or strong amount of it ❸ A blaze of publicity or attention is a lot of it ✿ VERB ❹ If something blazes it burns or shines brightly

**blazer** NOUN a kind of jacket, often in the colours of a school or sports team

**bleach**, bleaches, bleaching, bleached VERB ❶ To bleach material or hair means to make it white, usually by using a chemical ✿ NOUN ❷ Bleach is a chemical that is used to make material white or to clean thoroughly and kill germs

**bleak** ADJECTIVE ❶ If a situation is bleak, it is bad and seems unlikely to improve ❷ If a place is bleak, it is cold, bare, and exposed to the wind

**bleed**, bleeds, bleeding, bled VERB When you bleed, you lose blood as a result of an injury

**blend** VERB ❶ When you blend substances, you mix them together to form a single substance ❷ When colours or sounds blend, they combine in a pleasing way ✿ NOUN ❸ A blend of things is a mixture of them, especially one that is pleasing

**bless**, blesses, blessing, blessed or blest VERB When a priest blesses people or things, he or she asks for God's protection for them

**blew** the past tense of **blow**

**blind** ADJECTIVE ❶ Someone who is blind cannot see ❷ If someone is blind to a particular fact, they do not understand it ✿ VERB ❸ If something blinds you, you become unable to see, either for a short time or permanently ✿ NOUN ❹ a roll of cloth or paper that you pull down over a window to keep out the light

**blindfold** NOUN ❶ a strip of cloth tied over someone's eyes so that they cannot see ✿ VERB ❷ To blindfold someone means to cover their eyes with a strip of cloth

**blink** VERB When you blink, you close your eyes quickly for a moment

# blister – board

**blister** NOUN ❶ a small bubble on your skin containing watery liquid, caused by a burn or rubbing ✿ VERB ❷ If someone's skin blisters, blisters appear on it as result of burning or rubbing

**blizzard** NOUN a heavy snowstorm with strong winds

**blob** NOUN a small amount of a thick or sticky substance

**block** NOUN ❶ A block of flats or offices is a large building containing flats or offices ❷ In a town, a block is an area of land with streets on all its sides ❸ A block of something is a large rectangular piece of it ✿ VERB ❹ To block a road or channel means to put something across it so that nothing can get through ❺ If something blocks your view, it is in the way and prevents you from seeing what you want to see ❻ If someone blocks something, they prevent it from happening

**blog** NOUN INFORMAL short for **weblog**: a person's online diary that he or she puts on the internet so that other people can read it

**blogger** NOUN INFORMAL a person who keeps a blog

**blonde** or **blond** ADJECTIVE ❶ Blonde hair is pale yellow in colour. The spelling 'blond' is used when referring to men ✿ NOUN ❷ A blonde, or blond, is a person with light-coloured hair

**blood** NOUN Blood is the red liquid that is pumped by the heart round the bodies of human beings and other mammals

**blood vessel** NOUN Blood vessels are the narrow tubes in your body through which your blood flows

**bloom** NOUN ❶ a flower on a plant ✿ VERB ❷ When a plant blooms, it produces flowers ❸ When something like a feeling blooms, it grows

**blossom** NOUN ❶ Blossom is the growth of flowers that appears on a tree before the fruit ✿ VERB ❷ When a tree blossoms, it produces blossom

**blouse** NOUN a light shirt, worn by a girl or a woman

**blow**, blows, blowing, blew, blown VERB ❶ When the wind blows, the air moves ❷ If something blows or is blown somewhere, the wind moves it there ❸ If you blow a whistle or horn, you make a sound by blowing into it ✿ NOUN ❹ If you receive a blow, someone or something hits you ❺ A blow is something that makes you very disappointed or unhappy

**blow up** ✿ VERB ❶ To blow something up means to destroy it with an explosion ❷ To blow up a balloon or a tyre means to fill it with air

**blue**, bluer, bluest; blues ADJECTIVE OR NOUN ❶ Blue is the colour of the sky on a clear, sunny day ✿ PHRASE ❷ If something happens **out of the blue**, it happens suddenly and unexpectedly ✿ ADJECTIVE ❸ Blue films and jokes are about sex

**blunt** ADJECTIVE ❶ A blunt object has a rounded point or edge, rather than a sharp one ❷ If you are blunt, you say exactly what you think, without trying to be polite

**blush**, blushes, blushing, blushed VERB ❶ If you blush, your face becomes red, because you are embarrassed or ashamed ✿ NOUN ❷ the red colour on someone's face when they are embarrassed or ashamed

**board** NOUN ❶ a long, flat piece of wood ❷ the group of people who control a company or organization ❸ Board is the meals provided when you stay somewhere ✿ VERB ❹ If you board a ship or aircraft, you get on it or in it

---

**don't mix up**

*Hello Kitty...*

never mixes up **board** (a piece of wood) and **bored** (not interested).

**boast** VERB ❶ If you boast about your possessions or achievements, you talk about them proudly ✿ NOUN ❷ something that you say which shows that you are proud of what you own or have done

**boat** NOUN a small vehicle for travelling across water

**body**, bodies NOUN ❶ Your body is either all your physical parts, or just the main part not including your head, arms, and legs ❷ a person's dead body ❸ the main part of a car or aircraft, not including the engine ❹ A body of people is also an organized group

**bodyguard** NOUN a person employed to protect someone

**boil** VERB ❶ When a hot liquid boils, bubbles appear in it and it starts to give off steam ❷ When you boil a kettle, you heat it until the water in it boils ❸ When you boil food, you cook it in boiling water ✿ NOUN ❹ a red swelling on your skin

**boiling** ADJECTIVE INFORMAL very hot

**boiling point** NOUN the temperature at which a liquid starts to boil and turn to vapour

**bold** ADJECTIVE ❶ confident and not shy or embarrassed ❷ not afraid of risk or danger ❸ clear and noticeable

**bolt** NOUN ❶ a metal bar that you slide across a door or window in order to fasten it ❷ a metal object which screws into a nut and is used to fasten things together ✿ VERB ❸ If you bolt a door or window, you fasten it using a bolt. If you bolt things together, you fasten them together using a bolt ❹ To bolt means to escape or run away ❺ To bolt food means to eat it very quickly

**bomb** NOUN ❶ a container filled with material that explodes when it hits something or is set off by a timer ✿ VERB ❷ When a place is bombed, it is attacked with bombs

**bond** NOUN ❶ a close relationship between people ❷ LITERARY Bonds are chains or ropes used to tie a prisoner up ❸ a certificate which records that you have lent money to a business and that it will repay you the loan with interest ❹ In chemistry, a bond is the means by which atoms or groups of atoms are combined in molecules ❺ Bonds are also feelings or obligations that force you to behave in a particular way ✿ VERB ❻ When two things bond or are bonded, they become closely linked or attached

**bone** NOUN Bones are the hard parts that form the framework of a person's or animal's body

**bonfire** NOUN a large fire made outdoors, often to burn rubbish

**bonnet** NOUN ❶ the metal cover over a car's engine ❷ a baby's or woman's hat tied under the chin

**bonus**, bonuses NOUN ❶ an amount of money added to your usual pay ❷ Something that is a bonus is a good thing that you get in addition to something else

**book** NOUN ❶ a number of pages held together inside a cover ✿ VERB ❷ When you book something such as a room, you arrange to have it or use it at a particular time

**bookcase** NOUN a piece of furniture with shelves for books

**booklet** NOUN a small book with a paper cover

**bookmark** NOUN a piece of card which you put between the pages of a book to mark your place

**boom** NOUN ❶ a rapid increase in something ❷ a loud deep echoing sound ✿ VERB ❸ When something booms, it increases rapidly ❹ To boom means to make a loud deep echoing sound

**boost** VERB ❶ To boost something means to cause it to improve or increase ✿ NOUN ❷ an improvement or increase

**boot** NOUN ❶ Boots are strong shoes that come up over your ankle and sometimes your calf ❷ the covered space in a car, usually at the back, for carrying things in ✿ VERB ❸ INFORMAL If you boot something, you kick it ✿ PHRASE ❹ To boot means also or in addition

**border** NOUN ❶ the dividing line between two places or things ❷ a strip or band round the edge of something ❸ a long flower bed in a garden ✿ VERB ❹ To border something means to form a boundary along the side of it

**bore**, bores, boring, bored VERB ❶ If something bores you, you find it dull and not at all interesting ❷ If you bore a hole in something, you make it using a tool such as a drill ✿ NOUN ❸ someone or something that bores you

# bored – bow

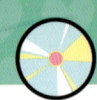

**bored** ADJECTIVE If you are bored, you are impatient because you do not find something interesting or because you have nothing to do

**boring** ADJECTIVE dull and lacking interest

**born** VERB ❶ When a baby is born, it comes out of its mother's womb at the beginning of its life ✿ ADJECTIVE ❷ You use 'born' to mean that someone has a particular quality from birth

**borne** the past participle of **bear**

**borrow** VERB If you borrow something that belongs to someone else, they let you have it for a period of time

**boss**, bosses, bossing, bossed NOUN ❶ Someone's boss is the person in charge of the place where they work ✿ VERB ❷ If someone bosses you around, they keep telling you what to do

**bossy**, bossier, bossiest ADJECTIVE A bossy person enjoys telling other people what to do

**botany** NOUN Botany is the scientific study of plants

**both** ADJECTIVE OR PRONOUN 'Both' is used when saying something about two things or people

**bother** VERB ❶ If you do not bother to do something, you do not do it because it takes too much effort or it seems unnecessary ❷ If something bothers you, you are worried or concerned about it. If you do not bother about it, you are not concerned about it ❸ If you bother someone, you interrupt them when they are busy ✿ NOUN ❹ Bother is trouble, fuss, or difficulty

**bottle**, bottles, bottling, bottled NOUN ❶ a glass or plastic container for keeping liquids in ✿ VERB ❷ To bottle something means to store it in bottles

**bottom** NOUN ❶ The bottom of something is its lowest part ❷ Your bottom is your buttocks ✿ ADJECTIVE ❸ The bottom thing in a series of things is the lowest one

**bought** the past tense and past participle of **buy**

**bounce**, bounces, bouncing, bounced VERB ❶ When an object bounces, it springs back from something after hitting it ❷ To bounce also means to move up and down ❸ If a cheque bounces, the bank refuses to accept it because there is not enough money in the account

**bound** ADJECTIVE ❶ If you say that something is bound to happen, you mean that it is certain to happen ❷ If a person or a vehicle is bound for a place, they are going there ❸ If someone is bound by an agreement or regulation, they must obey it ✿ NOUN ❹ a large leap ❺ IN PLURAL Bounds are limits which restrict or control something ✿ PHRASE ❻ If a place is **out of bounds**, you are forbidden to go there ✿ VERB ❼ When animals or people bound, they move quickly with large leaps ❽ Bound is also the past tense and past participle of **bind**

**boundary**, boundaries NOUN something that indicates the farthest limit of anything

**bouquet** [boo-**kay**] NOUN an attractively arranged bunch of flowers

**boutique** [boo-**teek**] NOUN a small shop that sells fashionable clothes

**bow** [rhymes with **now**] VERB ❶ When you bow, you bend your body or lower your head as a sign of respect or greeting ❷ If you bow to something, you give in to it ✿ NOUN ❸ the movement you make when you bow ❹ the front part of a ship

**bow** [rhymes with **low**] NOUN ❶ a knot with two loops and two loose ends ❷ a long thin piece of wood with horsehair stretched along it, which you use to play a violin ❸ a long flexible piece of wood used for shooting arrows

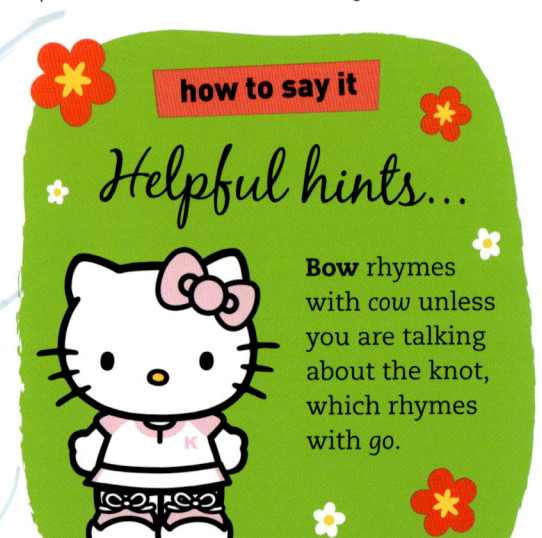

## how to say it

### Helpful hints...

**Bow** rhymes with *cow* unless you are talking about the knot, which rhymes with *go*.

**bowl** [rhymes with **mole**] NOUN ❶ a round container with a wide uncovered top, used for holding liquid or for serving food ❷ the hollow, rounded part of something ❸ a large heavy ball used in the game of bowls or tenpin bowling

**bowling** NOUN Bowling is a game in which you roll a heavy ball down a narrow track towards a group of wooden objects called pins and try to knock them down

**bow tie** [rhymes with **low**] NOUN a man's tie in the form of a bow, often worn at formal occasions

**box**, boxes, boxing, boxed NOUN ❶ a container with a firm base and sides and usually a lid ❷ On a form, a box is a rectangular space which you have to fill in ❸ In a theatre, a box is a small separate area where a few people can watch the performance together ✿ VERB ❹ To box means to fight someone according to the rules of boxing

**boxer** NOUN ❶ a person who boxes ❷ a type of medium-sized, smooth-haired dog with a flat face

**boxing** NOUN Boxing is a sport in which two people fight using their fists, wearing padded gloves

**box office** NOUN the place where tickets are sold in a theatre or cinema

**boy** NOUN a male child

**boycott** VERB ❶ If you boycott an organization or event, you refuse to have anything to do with it ✿ NOUN ❷ the boycotting of an organization or event

**boyfriend** NOUN Someone's boyfriend is the man or boy with whom they are having a romantic relationship

**bra** NOUN a piece of underwear worn by a woman to support her breasts

**bracelet** NOUN a chain or band worn around someone's wrist as an ornament

**bracket** NOUN ❶ Brackets are a pair of written marks, ( ), [ ], or { }, placed round a word or sentence that is not part of the main text, or to show that the items inside the brackets belong together ❷ a range between two limits, for example of ages or prices ❸ a piece of metal or wood fastened to a wall to support something such as a shelf

**brain** NOUN ❶ Your brain is the mass of nerve tissue inside your head that controls your body and enables you to think and feel; also used to refer to your mind and the way that you think ❷ IN PLURAL If you say that someone has brains, you mean that they are very intelligent

**brake**, brakes, braking, braked NOUN ❶ a device for making a vehicle stop or slow down ✿ VERB ❷ When a driver brakes, he or she makes a vehicle stop or slow down by using its brakes

**branch**, branches, branching, branched NOUN ❶ The branches of a tree are the parts that grow out from its trunk ❷ A branch of an organization is one of a number of its offices or shops ❸ A branch of a subject is one of its areas of study or activity ✿ VERB ❹ A road that branches off from another road splits off from it to lead in a different direction

**brand** NOUN ❶ A brand of something is a particular kind or make of it ✿ VERB ❷ When an animal is branded, a mark is burned on its skin to show who owns it

**brand-new** ADJECTIVE completely new

**brandy** NOUN a strong alcoholic drink, usually made from wine

**brass** NOUN OR ADJECTIVE ❶ Brass is a yellow-coloured metal made from copper and zinc ❷ In an orchestra, the brass section consists of brass wind instruments such as trumpets and trombones

### punctuation

*Hello Kitty...*

You put **brackets** (which can look like (), [] or {}) round something to show that it is extra information that is being given.

# brave – bring

**brave**, braver, bravest; braves, braving, braved ADJECTIVE ❶ A brave person is willing to do dangerous things and does not show any fear ✿ VERB ❷ If you brave an unpleasant or dangerous situation, you face up to it in order to do something **bravely** ADVERB

**bravery** NOUN the quality of being courageous

**bread** NOUN a food made from flour and water, usually raised with yeast, and then baked

**break**, breaks, breaking, broke, broken VERB ❶ When an object breaks, it is damaged and separates into pieces ❷ If you break a rule or promise you fail to keep it ❸ When a boy's voice breaks, it becomes permanently deeper ❹ When a wave breaks, it falls and becomes foam ✿ NOUN ❺ a short period during which you rest or do something different

**breakdown** NOUN ❶ The breakdown of something such as a system is its failure ❷ If a driver has a breakdown, their car stops working ❸ A breakdown of something complicated is a summary of its important points

**breakfast** NOUN the first meal of the day

**breakthrough** NOUN a sudden important development

**breast** NOUN A woman's breasts are the two soft, fleshy parts on her chest, which produce milk after she has had a baby

**breaststroke** NOUN Breaststroke is a swimming stroke in which you lie on your front, moving your arms horizontally through the water and kicking both legs at the same time

**breath** NOUN ❶ Your breath is the air you take into your lungs and let out again when you breathe ✿ PHRASE ❷ If you are **out of breath**, you are breathing with difficulty after doing something energetic

**breathe**, breathes, breathing, breathed VERB When you breathe, you take air into your lungs and let it out again

**breathless** ADJECTIVE If you are breathless, you are breathing fast or with difficulty

**breed**, breeds, breeding, bred NOUN ❶ A breed of a species of domestic animal is a particular type of it ✿ VERB ❷ Someone who breeds animals or plants keeps them in order to produce more animals or plants with particular qualities ❸ When animals breed, they mate and produce offspring

**breeze** NOUN a gentle wind

**bribe**, bribes, bribing, bribed NOUN ❶ a gift or money given to an official to persuade them to make a favourable decision ✿ VERB ❷ To bribe someone means to give them a bribe **bribery** NOUN

**brick** NOUN Bricks are rectangular blocks of baked clay used in building

**bride** NOUN a woman who is getting married or who has just got married

**bridegroom** NOUN a man who is getting married or who has just got married

**bridesmaid** NOUN a woman who helps and accompanies a bride on her wedding day

**bridge** NOUN ❶ a structure built over a river, road, or railway so that vehicles and people can cross ❷ the platform from which a ship is steered and controlled ❸ the hard ridge at the top of your nose ❹ Bridge is a card game for four players

**brief** ADJECTIVE ❶ Something that is brief lasts only a short time ✿ VERB ❷ When you brief someone on a task, you give them all the necessary instructions and information about it **briefly** ADVERB

**briefcase** NOUN a small flat case for carrying papers

**bright** ADJECTIVE ❶ strong and startling ❷ clever ❸ cheerful **brightly** ADVERB

**brighten** VERB ❶ If something brightens, it becomes brighter ❷ If someone brightens, they suddenly look happier

**brighten up** ✿ VERB To brighten something up means to make it more attractive and cheerful

**brilliant** ADJECTIVE ❶ A brilliant light or colour is extremely bright ❷ A brilliant person is extremely clever ❸ A brilliant career is extremely successful **brilliantly** ADVERB

**brim**, brims NOUN ❶ the wide part of a hat is the part that sticks outwards at the bottom ✿ PHRASE ❷ If a container is filled **to the brim**, it is filled right to the top

**bring**, brings, bringing, brought VERB ❶ If you bring something or someone with you when you go to a place, you take them with

you ❷ To bring something to a particular state means to cause it to be like that
**bring about** ✿ VERB To bring something about means to cause it to happen
**bring up** ✿ VERB ❶ To bring up children means to look after them while they grow up ❷ If you bring up a subject, you introduce it into the conversation
**brisk** ADJECTIVE ❶ A brisk action is done quickly and energetically ❷ If someone's manner is brisk, it shows that they want to get things done quickly and efficiently **briskly** ADVERB
**bristle**, bristles, bristling, bristled NOUN ❶ Bristles are strong animal hairs used to make brushes ✿ VERB ❷ If the hairs on an animal's body bristle, they rise up, because it is frightened
**brittle** ADJECTIVE An object that is brittle is hard but breaks easily
**broad** ADJECTIVE ❶ wide ❷ having many different aspects or concerning many different people ❸ general rather than detailed ❹ If someone has a broad accent, the way that they speak makes it very clear where they come from
**broadband** NOUN Broadband is a digital system used on the internet and in other forms of telecommunication which can process and transfer information input from various sources
**broadcast**, broadcasts, broadcasting, broadcast NOUN ❶ a programme or announcement on radio or television ✿ VERB ❷ To broadcast something means to send it out by radio waves, so that it can be seen on television or heard on radio
**broccoli** NOUN Broccoli is a green vegetable, similar to cauliflower
**brochure** [broh-sher] NOUN a booklet which gives information about a product or service
**broke** ❶ the past tense of **break** ✿ ADJECTIVE ❷ INFORMAL If you are broke, you have no money
**broken** ❶ the past participle of **break** ✿ ADJECTIVE ❷ in pieces ❸ not kept
**bronze** NOUN Bronze is a yellowish-brown metal which is a mixture of copper and tin; also the yellowish-brown colour of this metal
**brooch**, brooches [rhymes with coach] NOUN a piece of jewellery with a pin at the back for attaching to clothes

**brood** NOUN ❶ a family of baby birds ✿ VERB ❷ If you brood about something, you keep thinking about it in a serious or unhappy way
**broom** NOUN ❶ a long-handled brush ❷ Broom is a shrub with yellow flowers
**brother** NOUN Your brother is a boy or man who has the same parents as you
**brother-in-law**, brothers-in-law NOUN Someone's brother-in-law is the brother of their husband or wife, or their sister's husband
**brought** the past tense and past participle of **bring**
**brow** NOUN ❶ Your brow is your forehead ❷ Your brows are your eyebrows ❸ The brow of a hill is the top of it
**brown** ADJECTIVE OR NOUN Brown is the colour of earth or wood
**brownie** NOUN a junior member of the Guides
**browse**, browses, browsing, browsed VERB ❶ If you browse through a book, you look through it in a casual way ❷ If you browse in a shop, you look at the things in it for interest rather than because you want to buy something
**browser** NOUN a piece of computer software that lets you look at websites on the World Wide Web
**bruise**, bruises, bruising, bruised NOUN ❶ a purple mark that appears on your skin after something has hit it ✿ VERB ❷ If something bruises you, it hits you so that a bruise appears on your skin
**brush**, brushes, brushing, brushed NOUN ❶ an object with bristles which you use for cleaning things, painting, or tidying your hair ✿ VERB ❷ If you brush something, you clean it or tidy it with a brush ❸ To brush against something means to touch it while passing it
**brussels sprout** NOUN Brussels sprouts are vegetables that look like tiny cabbages
**brutal** ADJECTIVE Brutal behaviour is cruel and violent **brutally** ADVERB
**bubble**, bubbles, bubbling, bubbled NOUN ❶ a ball of air in a liquid ❷ a hollow, delicate ball of soapy liquid ✿ VERB ❸ When a liquid bubbles, bubbles form in it ❹ If you are bubbling with something like excitement, you are full of it **bubbly** ADJECTIVE
**bucket** NOUN a deep round container with an open top and a handle

# buckle – bumper

**buckle**, buckles, buckling, buckled NOUN ❶ a fastening on the end of a belt or strap ✿ VERB ❷ If you buckle a belt or strap, you fasten it ❸ If something buckles, it becomes bent because of severe heat or pressure

**bud**, buds, budding, budded NOUN ❶ a small, tight swelling on a tree or plant, which develops into a flower or a cluster of leaves ✿ VERB ❷ When a tree or plant buds, new buds appear on it

**Buddhism** NOUN Buddhism is a religion, founded by the Buddha, which teaches that the way to end suffering is by overcoming your desires  **Buddhist** NOUN OR ADJECTIVE

**budge**, budges, budging, budged VERB If something will not budge, you cannot move it

**budget** NOUN ❶ a plan showing how much money will be available and how it will be spent ✿ VERB ❷ If you budget for something, you plan your money carefully, so that you are able to afford it

**buffalo**, buffaloes NOUN a wild animal like a large cow with long curved horns

**buffet** [*boof*-ay] NOUN ❶ a café at a station ❷ a meal at which people serve themselves

**buffet** [*buff*-it] VERB If the wind or sea buffets a place or person, it strikes them violently and repeatedly

**bug**, bugs, bugging, bugged NOUN ❶ an insect, especially one that causes damage ❷ a small error in a computer program which means that the program will not work properly ❸ INFORMAL a virus or minor infection ✿ VERB ❹ If a place is bugged, tiny microphones are hidden there to pick up what people are saying

**build**, builds, building, built VERB ❶ To build something such as a house means to make it from its parts ❷ To build something such as an organization means to develop it gradually ✿ NOUN ❸ Your build is the shape and size of your body  **builder** NOUN

**building** NOUN a structure with walls and a roof

**bulb** NOUN ❶ the glass part of an electric lamp ❷ an onion-shaped root that grows into a flower or plant

**bulge**, bulges, bulging, bulged VERB ❶ If something bulges, it swells out from a surface ✿ NOUN ❷ a lump on a normally flat surface

**bulk** NOUN ❶ a large mass of something ❷ The bulk of something is most of it ✿ PHRASE ❸ To buy something **in bulk** means to buy it in large quantities

**bulky**, bulkier, bulkiest ADJECTIVE large and heavy

**bull** NOUN the male of some species of animals, including the cow family, elephants, and whales

**bulldog** NOUN a squat dog with a broad head and muscular body

**bulldozer** NOUN a powerful tractor with a broad blade in front, which is used for moving earth or knocking things down

**bullet** NOUN a small piece of metal fired from a gun

**bully**, bullies, bullying, bullied NOUN ❶ someone who uses their strength or power to hurt or frighten other people ✿ VERB ❷ If you bully someone, you frighten or hurt them deliberately ❸ If someone bullies you into doing something, they make you do it by using force or threats

**bump** VERB ❶ If you bump or bump into something, you knock it with a jolt ✿ NOUN ❷ a soft or dull noise made by something knocking into something else ❸ a raised, uneven part of a surface  **bumpy** ADJECTIVE

**bumper** NOUN ❶ Bumpers are bars on the front and back of a vehicle which protect it if

## how to say it

### Helpful hints ...

Buffet should be said **boof**-ay for the café and meal, and **buff**-it for the wind sense.

**bun - byte**

there is a collision ✿ ADJECTIVE ❷ A bumper crop or harvest is larger than usual

**bun** NOUN a small, round cake

**bunch**, bunches, bunching, bunched NOUN ❶ a group of people ❷ a number of flowers held or tied together ❸ a group of things ❹ a group of bananas or grapes growing on the same stem ✿ VERB ❺ When people bunch together or bunch up, they stay very close to each other

**bundle** NOUN a number of things tied together or wrapped up in a cloth

**bungalow** NOUN a one-storey house

**bunk** NOUN a bed fixed to a wall in a ship or caravan

**buoy**, buoys [boy] NOUN a floating object anchored to the bottom of the sea, marking a channel or warning of danger

**burden** NOUN ❶ a heavy load ❷ If something is a burden to you, it causes you a lot of worry or hard work

**burglar**, burglars NOUN a thief who breaks into a building **burglary** NOUN

**burgle**, burgles, burgling, burgled VERB If your house is burgled, someone breaks into it and steals things

**burial** NOUN a ceremony held when a dead person is buried

**burn**, burns, burning, burned or burnt VERB ❶ If something is burning, it is on fire ❷ To burn something means to destroy it with fire ❸ If you burn yourself or are burned, you are injured by fire or by something hot ✿ NOUN ❹ an injury caused by fire or by something hot

**burp** VERB ❶ If you burp, you make a noise because air from your stomach has been forced up through your throat ✿ NOUN ❷ the noise that you make when you burp

**burst**, bursts, bursting, burst VERB ❶ When something bursts, it splits open because of pressure from inside it ❷ If you burst into a room, you enter it suddenly ✿ NOUN ❸ A burst of something is a short period of it

**bury**, buries, burying, buried VERB ❶ When a dead person is buried, their body is put into a grave and covered with earth ❷ To bury something means to put it in a hole in the ground and cover it up ❸ If something is buried under something, it is covered by it

**bus**, buses NOUN a large motor vehicle that carries passengers

**bush**, bushes NOUN ❶ a thick plant with many stems branching out from ground level ❷ In Australia and South Africa, an area of land in its natural state is called the bush ❸ In New Zealand, the bush is land covered with rainforest

**business**, businesses NOUN ❶ Business is work relating to the buying and selling of goods and services ❷ an organization which produces or sells goods or provides a service ❸ You can refer to any event, situation, or activity as a business

**businessman** NOUN **businesswoman** NOUN

**busy**, busier, busiest; busies, busying, busied ADJECTIVE ❶ If you are busy, you are in the middle of doing something ❷ A busy place is full of people doing things or moving about ✿ VERB ❸ If you busy yourself with something, you occupy yourself by doing it **busily** ADVERB

**but** CONJUNCTION ❶ used to introduce an idea that is opposite to what has gone before ❷ used when apologizing ❸ except

**butcher** NOUN a shopkeeper who sells meat

**butter** NOUN ❶ Butter is a soft fatty food made from cream, which is spread on bread and used in cooking ✿ VERB ❷ To butter bread means to spread butter on it

**butterfly**, butterflies NOUN a type of insect with large colourful wings

**button** NOUN ❶ Buttons are small, hard objects sewn on to clothing, and used to fasten two surfaces together ❷ a small object on a piece of equipment that you press to make it work ✿ VERB ❸ If you button a piece of clothing, you fasten it using its buttons

**buy**, buys, buying, bought VERB If you buy something, you obtain it by paying money for it **buyer** NOUN

**buzz**, buzzes, buzzing, buzzed VERB ❶ If something buzzes, it makes a humming sound, like a bee ✿ NOUN ❷ the sound something makes when it buzzes

**by** PREPOSITION ❶ used to indicate who or what has done something ❷ used to indicate how something is done ❸ located next to ❹ before a particular time ✿ PREPOSITION OR ADVERB ❺ going past

**byte** NOUN a unit of storage in a computer

# cab – call

**cab** NOUN ❶ a taxi ❷ In a lorry, bus, or train, the cab is where the driver sits

**cabbage** NOUN a large green or reddish purple leafy vegetable

**cabin** NOUN ❶ a room in a ship where a passenger sleeps ❷ a small house, usually in the country and often made of wood ❸ the area where the passengers or the crew sit in a plane

**cabinet** NOUN ❶ a small cupboard ❷ The cabinet in a government is a group of ministers who advise the leader and decide policies

**cable** NOUN ❶ a strong, thick rope or chain ❷ a bundle of wires with a rubber covering, which carries electricity

**cable television** NOUN a television service people can receive from underground wires which carry the signals

**cactus**, cacti or **cactuses** NOUN a thick, fleshy plant that grows in deserts and is usually covered in spikes

**café** [*kaf*-fay] NOUN ❶ a place where you can buy light meals and drinks ❷ In South African English, a café is a corner shop or grocer's shop

**cafeteria** [*kaf-fit-ee-ree-ya*] NOUN a restaurant where you serve yourself

**caffeine** or **caffein** [*kaf-feen*] NOUN Caffeine is a chemical in coffee and tea which makes you more active

**cage** NOUN a box made of wire or bars in which birds or animals are kept

**cake**, cakes, caking, caked NOUN ❶ a sweet food made by baking flour, eggs, fat, and sugar ❷ a block of a hard substance such as soap ✿ VERB ❸ If something cakes or is caked, it forms or becomes covered with a solid layer

**calculate**, calculates, calculating, calculated VERB If you calculate something, you work it out, usually by doing some arithmetic **calculation** NOUN

**calculator** NOUN a small electronic machine used for doing mathematical calculations

**calendar** NOUN ❶ a chart showing the date of each day in a particular year ❷ a system of dividing time into fixed periods of days, months, and years

**calf**, calves NOUN ❶ a young cow, bull, elephant, whale, or seal ❷ the thick part at the back of your leg below your knee

**call** VERB ❶ If someone or something is called

Hello Kitty... knows that some words that sound as if they begin with s actually begin with c, like *centre*.

### call off - capacity

a particular name, that is their name ❷ If you call people or situations something, you use words to describe your opinion of them ❸ If you call someone, you telephone them ❹ If you call or call out something, you say it loudly ❺ If you call on someone, you pay them a short visit ✿ NOUN ❻ If you get a call from someone, they telephone you or pay you a visit ❼ a cry or shout ❽ a demand for something

**call off** ✿ VERB If you call something off, you cancel it

**calm**, calmer, calmest; calms, calming, calmed ADJECTIVE ❶ Someone who is calm is quiet and does not show any worry or excitement ❷ If the weather or the sea is calm, it is still because there is no strong wind ✿ NOUN ❸ Calm is a state of quietness and peacefulness ✿ VERB ❹ To calm someone means to make them less upset or excited

**calmly** ADVERB

**calorie** NOUN a unit of measurement for the energy food and drink gives you

**camel** NOUN a large mammal with either one or two humps on its back. Camels live in hot desert areas

**camera** NOUN a piece of equipment used for taking photographs or for filming

**camp** NOUN ❶ a place where people live in tents or stay in tents on holiday ❷ a collection of buildings for a particular group of people such as soldiers or prisoners ❸ a group of people who support a particular idea or belief ✿ VERB ❹ If you camp, you stay in a tent

**camper** NOUN **camping** NOUN

**campaign** [kam-*pane*] NOUN ❶ a set of actions aiming to achieve a particular result ✿ VERB ❷ To campaign means to carry out a campaign

**campus**, campuses NOUN the area of land and the buildings that make up a university or college

**can**, could VERB ❶ If you can do something, it is possible for you to do it or you are allowed to do it ❷ If you can do something, you have the ability to do it

**can**, cans, canning, canned NOUN ❶ a metal container, often a sealed one with food or drink inside ✿ VERB ❷ To can food or drink is to seal it in cans

**canal** NOUN a long, narrow man-made stretch of water

**cancel**, cancels, cancelling, cancelled VERB ❶ If you cancel something that has been arranged, you stop it from happening ❷ If you cancel a cheque or an agreement, you make sure that it is no longer valid

**cancellation** NOUN

**cancer** NOUN a serious disease in which abnormal cells in a part of the body increase rapidly, causing growths

**candidate** NOUN ❶ a person who is being considered for a job ❷ a person taking an examination

**candle** NOUN a stick of hard wax with a wick through the middle. The lighted wick gives a flame that provides light

**candlestick** NOUN a holder for a candle

**candy**, candies NOUN In America, candy is sweets

**cane**, canes, caning, caned NOUN ❶ Cane is the long, hollow stems of a plant such as bamboo ❷ Cane is also strips of cane used for weaving things such as baskets ❸ a long narrow stick, often one used to beat people as a punishment ✿ VERB ❹ To cane someone means to beat them with a cane as a punishment

**cannon**, cannons or cannon NOUN a large gun, usually on wheels, used in battles to fire heavy metal balls

**cannot** VERB Cannot is the same as can not

**canoe** [ka-*noo*] NOUN a small, narrow boat that you row using a paddle

**canteen** NOUN the part of a workplace where the workers can go to eat

**canvas**, canvases NOUN ❶ Canvas is strong, heavy cloth used for making things such as sails and tents ❷ a piece of canvas on which an artist does a painting

**canyon** NOUN a narrow river valley with steep sides

**cap**, caps, capping, capped NOUN ❶ a soft, flat hat, often with a peak at the front ❷ the top of a bottle ✿ VERB ❸ To cap something is to cover it with something ❹ If you cap a story or a joke that someone has just told, you tell a better one

**capable** ADJECTIVE ❶ able to do something ❷ skilful or talented

**capacity**, capacities [kap-*pas*-sit-tee] NOUN ❶ the maximum amount that something can hold or produce ❷ a person's power or

# cape – carpenter

ability to do something ❸ someone's role or position

**cape** NOUN ❶ a short cloak with no sleeves ❷ a large piece of land sticking out into the sea

**capital** NOUN ❶ The capital of a country is the city where the government meets ❷ Capital is the amount of money or property owned or used by a business ❸ Capital is also a sum of money that you save or invest in order to gain interest ❹ A capital or capital letter is a larger letter used at the beginning of a sentence or a name

**capitalism** NOUN Capitalism is an economic and political system where businesses and industries are not owned and run by the government, but by individuals who can make a profit from them **capitalist** ADJECTIVE OR NOUN

**capital punishment** NOUN Capital punishment is legally killing someone as a punishment for a crime they have committed

**captain** NOUN ❶ the officer in charge of a ship or aeroplane ❷ an army officer of the rank immediately above lieutenant ❸ a navy officer of the rank immediately above commander ❹ the leader of a sports team ✿ VERB ❺ If you captain a group of people, you are their leader

**caption** NOUN a title printed underneath a picture or photograph

**captive** NOUN ❶ a person who has been captured and kept prisoner ✿ ADJECTIVE ❷ imprisoned or enclosed **captivity** NOUN

**capture**, captures, capturing, captured VERB ❶ To capture someone is to take them prisoner ❷ To capture a quality or mood means to succeed in representing or describing it ✿ NOUN ❸ The capture of someone or something is the action of taking them prisoner

**car** NOUN ❶ a four-wheeled road vehicle with room for a small number of people ❷ a railway carriage used for a particular purpose

**caramel** NOUN ❶ a chewy sweet made from sugar, butter, and milk ❷ Caramel is burnt sugar used for colouring or flavouring food

**caravan** NOUN ❶ a vehicle pulled by a car in which people live or spend their holidays ❷ a group of people and animals travelling together, usually across a desert

**carbohydrate** NOUN Carbohydrate is a substance that gives you energy. It is found in foods like sugar and bread

**card** NOUN ❶ a piece of stiff paper or plastic with information or a message on it ❷ Cards can mean playing cards ❸ When you play cards, you play any game using playing cards ❹ Card is strong, stiff paper

**cardboard** NOUN Cardboard is thick, stiff paper

**cardigan** NOUN a knitted jacket that fastens up the front

**care**, cares, caring, cared VERB ❶ If you care about something, you are concerned about it and interested in it ❷ If you care about someone, you feel affection towards them ❸ If you care for someone, you look after them ✿ NOUN ❹ Care is concern or worry ❺ Care of someone or something is treatment for them or looking after them ❻ If you do something with care, you do it with close attention

**career** NOUN ❶ the series of jobs that someone has in life, usually in the same occupation ✿ VERB ❷ To career somewhere is to move very quickly, often out of control

**careful** ADJECTIVE ❶ acting sensibly and with care ❷ complete and well done **carefully** ADVERB

**careless** ADJECTIVE ❶ done badly without enough attention ❷ relaxed and unconcerned

**caretaker** NOUN ❶ a person who looks after a large building such as a school ✿ ADJECTIVE ❷ having an important position for a short time until a new person is appointed

**cargo**, cargoes NOUN the goods carried on a ship or plane

**carnation** NOUN a plant with a long stem and white, pink, or red flowers

**carnival** NOUN a public festival with music, processions, and dancing

**carnivore** NOUN an animal that eats meat

**carol** NOUN a religious song sung at Christmas time

**carpenter** NOUN a person who makes and repairs wooden structures

A B **C** D E F G H I J K L M N O P Q R S T U V W X Y Z

40

## carpet - catalogue

**carpet** NOUN ❶ a thick covering for a floor, usually made of a material like wool ✿ VERB ❷ To carpet a floor means to cover it with a carpet

**carriage** NOUN ❶ one of the separate sections of a passenger train ❷ an old-fashioned vehicle for carrying passengers, usually pulled by horses ❸ a machine part that moves and supports another part

**carrier bag** NOUN a bag made of plastic or paper, which is used for carrying shopping

**carrot** NOUN a long, thin, orange root vegetable

**carry**, carries, carrying, carried VERB ❶ To carry something is to hold it and take it somewhere ❷ When a vehicle carries people, they travel in it ❸ A person or animal that carries a germ can pass it on to other people or animals ❹ If a sound carries, it can be heard far away ❺ In a meeting, if a proposal is carried, it is accepted by a majority of the people there

**carry away** ✿ VERB If you are carried away, you are so excited by something that you do not behave sensibly

**carry on** ✿ VERB To carry on doing something means to continue doing it

**carry out** ✿ VERB To carry something out means to do it and complete it

**cart** NOUN a vehicle with wheels, used to carry goods and often pulled by horses or cattle

**carton** NOUN a cardboard or plastic container

**cartoon** NOUN ❶ a drawing or a series of drawings which are funny or make a point ❷ a film in which the characters and scenes are drawn

**carve**, carves, carving, carved VERB ❶ To carve an object means to cut it out of a substance such as stone or wood ❷ To carve meat means to cut slices from it

**case** NOUN ❶ a particular situation, event, or example ❷ a container for something, or a suitcase ❸ Doctors sometimes refer to a patient as a case ❹ Police detectives refer to a crime they are investigating as a case ❺ In an argument, the case for an idea is the reasons used to support it ❻ In law, a case is a trial or other inquiry ❼ In grammar, the case of a noun or pronoun is the form of it which shows its relationship with other words in a sentence ✿ PHRASE ❽ You say **in that case** to show that you are assuming something said before is true

**cash**, cashes, cashing, cashed NOUN ❶ Cash is money in notes and coins rather than cheques ✿ VERB ❷ If you cash a cheque, you take it to a bank and exchange it for money

**cashew** [kash-oo] NOUN a curved, edible nut

**cashier** NOUN the person that customers pay in a shop or get money from in a bank

**casino**, casinos [kass-ee-noh] NOUN a place where people go to play gambling games

**cassette** NOUN a small flat container with magnetic tape inside, which is used for recording and playing back sounds

**cast**, casts, casting, cast NOUN ❶ all the people who act in a play or film ❷ an object made by pouring liquid into a mould and leaving it to harden ❸ a stiff plaster covering put on broken bones to keep them still so that they heal properly ✿ VERB ❹ To cast actors is to choose them for roles in a play or film ❺ When people cast their votes in an election, they vote ❻ To cast something is to throw it ❼ If you cast your eyes somewhere, you look there ❽ To cast an object is to make it by pouring liquid into a mould and leaving it to harden

**cast off** ✿ VERB If you cast off, you untie the rope fastening a boat to a harbour or shore

**castle** NOUN ❶ a large building with walls or ditches round it to protect it from attack ❷ a chess piece which can move any number of squares in a straight but not diagonal line

**casual** ADJECTIVE ❶ happening by chance without planning ❷ careless or without interest ❸ Casual clothes are suitable for informal occasions ❹ Casual work is not regular or permanent **casually** ADVERB

**casualty**, casualties NOUN a person killed or injured in an accident or war

**cat** NOUN ❶ a small furry animal with whiskers, a tail, and sharp claws, often kept as a pet ❷ any of the family of mammals that includes lions and tigers

**catalogue**, catalogues, cataloguing, catalogued NOUN ❶ a book containing pictures and descriptions of goods that you can buy in a shop or through the post ❷ a list of things such as the objects in a museum or the books in a library ✿ VERB ❸ To catalogue a collection of things means to list them in a catalogue

A B C D E F G H I J K L M N O P Q R S T U V W X Y Z

41

# catastrophe – cease-fire

**catastrophe** [kat-*tass*-trif-fee] NOUN a terrible disaster **catastrophic** ADJECTIVE

**catch**, catches, catching, caught VERB ❶ If you catch a ball moving in the air, you grasp hold of it when it comes near you ❷ To catch an animal means to trap it ❸ When the police catch criminals, they find them and arrest them ❹ If you catch someone doing something they should not be doing, you discover them doing it ❺ If you catch a bus or train, you get on it and travel somewhere ❻ If you catch a cold or a disease, you become infected with it ❼ If something catches on an object, it sticks to it or gets trapped ✿ NOUN ❽ a device that fastens something ❾ a problem or hidden complication in something

**catch on** ✿ VERB ❶ If you catch on to something, you understand it ❷ If something catches on, it becomes popular

**catch out** ✿ VERB To catch someone out is to trick them or trap them

**catch up** ✿ VERB ❶ To catch up with someone in front of you is to reach the place where they are by moving slightly faster than them ❷ To catch up with someone is also to reach the same level or standard as them

**categorize**, categorizes, categorizing, categorized (also **categorise**) VERB To categorize things is to arrange them in different categories

**category**, categories NOUN a set of things with a particular characteristic in common

**caterpillar** NOUN the larva of a butterfly or moth. It looks like a small coloured worm and feeds on plants

**cathedral** NOUN an important church with a bishop in charge of it

**Catholic** NOUN OR ADJECTIVE ❶ (a) Roman Catholic ✿ ADJECTIVE ❷ If a person has catholic interests, they have a wide range of interests

**cattle** PLURAL NOUN Cattle are cows and bulls kept by farmers

**caught** the past tense and past participle of **catch**

**cauliflower** NOUN a large, round, white vegetable surrounded by green leaves

**cause**, causes, causing, caused NOUN ❶ The cause of something is the thing that makes it happen ❷ an aim or principle which a group of people are working for ❸ If you have cause for something, you have a reason for it ✿ VERB ❹ To cause something is to make it happen

**caution** NOUN ❶ Caution is great care which you take to avoid danger ❷ a warning ✿ VERB ❸ If someone cautions you, they warn you, usually not to do something again

**cautious** ADJECTIVE acting very carefully to avoid danger **cautiously** ADVERB

**cave**, caves, caving, caved NOUN ❶ a large hole in rock, that is underground or in the side of a cliff ✿ VERB ❷ If a roof caves in, it collapses inwards

**caveman**, cavemen NOUN Cavemen were people who lived in caves in prehistoric times

**CD** an abbreviation for 'compact disc'

**CD-ROM** CD-ROM is a method of storing video, sound, or text on a compact disc which can be played on a computer using a laser. CD-ROM is an abbreviation for 'Compact Disc Read-Only Memory'

**cease**, ceases, ceasing, ceased VERB ❶ If something ceases, it stops happening ❷ If you cease to do something, or cease doing it, you stop doing it

**cease-fire** NOUN an agreement between groups that are fighting each other to stop for a period and discuss peace

**where does the word come from?**

*Did you know...*

that the word **caterpillar** comes from an old French word *catepelose* which means 'hairy cat'?

**ceiling - certificate**

**ceiling** NOUN the top inside surface of a room

**celebrate**, celebrates, celebrating, celebrated VERB ❶ If you celebrate or celebrate something, you do something special and enjoyable because of it ❷ When a priest celebrates Mass, he performs the ceremonies of the Mass

**celebration** NOUN an event in honour of a special occasion

**celebrity**, celebrities NOUN a famous person

**celery** NOUN Celery is a vegetable with long pale green stalks

**cell** NOUN ❶ In biology, a cell is the smallest part of an animal or plant that can exist by itself. Each cell contains a nucleus ❷ a small room where a prisoner is kept in a prison or police station ❸ a small group of people set up to work together as part of a larger organization ❹ a device that converts chemical energy to electricity

**cellar** NOUN a room underneath a building, often used to store wine

**cello**, cellos [*chel-loh*] NOUN a large musical stringed instrument which you play sitting down, holding the instrument upright with your knees  **cellist** NOUN

**cellphone** NOUN a small portable telephone

**Celsius** [*sel-see-yuss*] NOUN Celsius is a scale for measuring temperature in which water freezes at 0 degrees (0°C) and boils at 100 degrees (100°C). Celsius is the same as 'Centigrade'

**cement** NOUN ❶ Cement is a fine powder made from limestone and clay, which is mixed with sand and water to make concrete ✿ VERB ❷ To cement things is to stick them together with cement or cover them with cement ❸ Something that cements a relationship makes it stronger

**cemetery**, cemeteries NOUN an area of land where dead people are buried

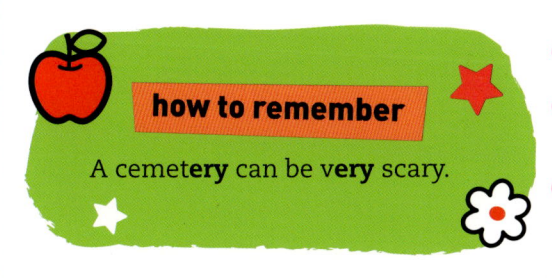

**how to remember**

A cemet**ery** can be **very** scary.

**census**, censuses NOUN an official survey of the population of a country

**cent** NOUN a unit of currency. In the USA, a cent is worth one hundredth of a dollar; in Europe, it is worth one hundredth of a euro

**centilitre** NOUN a unit of liquid volume equal to one hundredth of a litre

**centimetre** NOUN a unit of length equal to ten millimetres or one hundredth of a metre

**central** ADJECTIVE ❶ in or near the centre of an object or area ❷ main or most important

**central heating** NOUN Central heating is a system of heating a building in which water or air is heated in a tank and travels through pipes and radiators round the building

**centre**, centres, centring, centred NOUN ❶ the middle of an object or area ❷ a building where people go for activities, meetings, or help ❸ Someone or something that is the centre of attention attracts a lot of attention ✿ VERB ❹ To centre something is to move it so that it is balanced or at the centre of something else ❺ If something centres on or around a particular thing, that thing is the main subject of attention

**century**, centuries NOUN a period of one hundred years

**ceramic** [*sir-ram-mik*] NOUN Ceramic is a hard material made by baking clay to a very high temperature

**cereal** NOUN ❶ a food made from grain, often eaten with milk for breakfast ❷ a plant that produces edible grain, such as wheat or oats

**ceremonial** ADJECTIVE relating to a ceremony

**ceremony**, ceremonies NOUN ❶ a set of formal actions performed at a special occasion or important public event ❷ Ceremony is very formal and polite behaviour

**certain** ADJECTIVE ❶ definite or reliable ❷ having no doubt in your mind ❸ You use 'certain' to refer to a specific person or thing ❹ You use 'certain' to suggest that a quality is noticeable but not obvious

**certainly** ADVERB ❶ without doubt ❷ of course

**certainty**, certainties NOUN ❶ Certainty is the state of being certain ❷ something that is known without doubt

**certificate** NOUN a document stating particular facts, for example of someone's birth or death

A B C D E F G H I J K L M N O P Q R S T U V W X Y Z

# chain - chaos

**chain** NOUN ❶ a number of metal rings connected together in a line ❷ a number of things in a series or connected to each other ✿ VERB ❸ If you chain one thing to another, you fasten them together with a chain

**chair** NOUN ❶ a seat with a back and four legs for one person ❷ the person in charge of a meeting who decides when each person may speak ✿ VERB ❸ The person who chairs a meeting is in charge of it

**chairman**, chairmen NOUN ❶ the person in charge of a meeting who decides when each person may speak ❷ the head of a company or committee **chairperson** NOUN **chairwoman** NOUN

**chalk** NOUN ❶ Chalk is a soft white rock. Small sticks of chalk are used for writing or drawing on a blackboard ✿ VERB ❷ To chalk up a result is to achieve it

**challenge**, challenges, challenging, challenged NOUN ❶ something that is new and exciting but requires a lot of effort ❷ a suggestion from someone to compete with them ❸ A challenge to something is a questioning of whether it is correct or true ✿ VERB ❹ If someone challenges you, they suggest that you compete with them in some way ❺ If you challenge something, you question whether it is correct or true

**champagne** [sham-**pain**] NOUN Champagne is a sparkling white wine made in France

**champion** NOUN ❶ a person who wins a competition ❷ someone who supports or defends a cause or principle ✿ VERB ❸ Someone who champions a cause or principle supports or defends it

**championship** NOUN a competition to find the champion of a sport

**chance**, chances, chancing, chanced NOUN ❶ The chance of something happening is how possible or likely it is ❷ an opportunity to do something ❸ a possibility that something dangerous or unpleasant may happen ❹ Chance is also the way things happen unexpectedly without being planned ✿ VERB ❺ If you chance something, you try it although you are taking a risk

**change**, changes, changing, changed NOUN ❶ a difference or alteration in something ❷ a replacement of something by something else ❸ Change is money you get back when you have paid more than the actual price of something ✿ VERB ❹ When something changes or when you change it, it becomes different ❺ If you change something, you exchange it for something else ❻ When you change, you put on different clothes ❼ To change money means to exchange it for smaller coins of the same total value, or to exchange it for foreign currency

**channel**, channels, channelling, channelled NOUN ❶ a wavelength used to receive programmes broadcast by a television or radio station; also the station itself ❷ a passage along which water flows or along which something is carried ❸ The Channel or the English Channel is the stretch of sea between England and France ❹ a method of achieving something ✿ VERB ❺ To channel something such as money or energy means to direct it in a particular way

**chant** NOUN ❶ a group of words repeated over and over again ❷ a religious song sung on only a few notes ✿ VERB ❸ If people chant a group of words, they repeat them over and over again

**chaos** [**kay**-oss] NOUN Chaos is a state of complete disorder and confusion **chaotic** ADJECTIVE

## how to say it

Hello Kitty...

knows that **chaos** should be said **kay**-oss, with most force on *kay*.

44

**chapel** NOUN ❶ a section of a church or cathedral with its own altar ❷ a type of small church

**chapter** NOUN ❶ one of the parts into which a book is divided ❷ a particular period in someone's life or in history

**character** NOUN ❶ all the qualities which combine to form the personality or atmosphere of a person or place ❷ A person or place that has character has an interesting, attractive, or admirable quality ❸ The characters in a film, play, or book are the people in it ❹ a person ❺ a letter, number, or other written symbol

**characteristic** NOUN ❶ a quality that is typical of a particular person or thing ❷ a feature that is typical of a particular living thing ❀ ADJECTIVE ❸ Characteristic means typical of a particular person or thing

**charcoal** NOUN Charcoal is a black form of carbon made by burning wood without air, used as a fuel and also for drawing

**charge**, charges, charging, charged VERB ❶ If someone charges you money, they ask you to pay it for something you have bought or received ❷ To charge someone means to accuse them formally of having committed a crime ❸ To charge a battery means to pass an electrical current through it to make it store electricity ❹ To charge somewhere means to rush forward, often to attack someone ❀ NOUN ❺ the price that you have to pay for something ❻ a formal accusation that a person is guilty of a crime and has to go to court ❼ To have charge or be in charge of someone or something means to be responsible for them and be in control of them ❽ an explosive put in a gun or other weapon ❾ An electrical charge is the amount of electricity that something carries

**charity**, charities NOUN ❶ an organization that raises money to help people who are ill, poor, or disabled ❷ Charity is money or other help given to poor, disabled, or ill people ❸ Charity is also a kind, sympathetic attitude towards people

**charm** NOUN ❶ Charm is an attractive and pleasing quality that some people and things have ❷ a small ornament worn on a bracelet ❸ a magical spell or an object that is supposed to bring good luck ❀ VERB ❹ If you charm someone, you use your charm to please them

**charming** ADJECTIVE very pleasant and attractive

**chart** NOUN ❶ a diagram or table showing information ❷ a map of the sea or stars ❀ VERB ❸ If you chart something, you observe and record it carefully

**charter** NOUN ❶ a document stating the rights or aims of a group or organization, often written by the government ❀ VERB ❷ To charter transport such as a plane or boat is to hire it for private use

**chase**, chases, chasing, chased VERB ❶ If you chase someone or something, you run after them in order to catch them ❷ If you chase someone, you force them to go somewhere else ❀ NOUN ❸ the activity of chasing or hunting someone or something

**chat**, chats, chatting, chatted NOUN ❶ a friendly talk with someone, usually about things that are not very important ❀ VERB ❷ When people chat, they talk to each other in a friendly way

**chat up** ❀ VERB INFORMAL If you chat someone up, you talk to them in a friendly way, because you are attracted to them

**chatroom** NOUN an internet site where users have group discussions using e-mail

**chatter** VERB ❶ When people chatter, they talk very fast ❷ If your teeth are chattering, they are knocking together and making a clicking noise because you are cold ❀ NOUN ❸ Chatter is a lot of fast unimportant talk

**chauffeur** [*show-fur*] NOUN a person whose job is to drive another person's car

**cheap** ADJECTIVE ❶ costing very little money ❷ inexpensive but of poor quality ❸ A cheap joke or cheap remark is unfair and unkind
**cheaply** ADVERB

**cheat** VERB ❶ If someone cheats, they do wrong or unfair things to win or get something that they want ❷ If you are cheated of or out of something, you do not get what you are entitled to ❀ NOUN ❸ a person who cheats

**check** VERB ❶ To check something is to examine it in order to make sure that everything is all right ❷ To check the growth or spread of something is to make it stop ❀ NOUN ❸ an inspection to make sure

# check out – chip

that everything is all right ❹ Checks are different coloured squares which form a pattern ✿ PHRASE ❺ If you keep something **in check**, you keep it under control ✿ ADJECTIVE ❻ Check or checked means marked with a pattern of squares

**check out** ✿ VERB If you check something out, you inspect it and find out whether everything about it is right

**checkout** NOUN a counter in a supermarket where the customers pay for their goods

**cheek** NOUN ❶ Your cheeks are the sides of your face below your eyes ❷ Cheek is speech or behaviour that is rude or disrespectful

**cheeky**, cheekier, cheekiest ADJECTIVE rather rude and disrespectful

**cheer** VERB ❶ When people cheer, they shout with approval or in order to show support for a person or team ✿ NOUN ❷ a shout of approval or support

**cheer up** ✿ VERB When you cheer up, you feel more cheerful

**cheerful** ADJECTIVE ❶ happy and in good spirits ❷ bright and pleasant-looking **cheerfully** ADVERB **cheerfulness** NOUN

**cheese** NOUN a hard or creamy food made from milk

**chef** NOUN a head cook in a restaurant or hotel

**chemical** NOUN ❶ Chemicals are substances manufactured by chemistry ✿ ADJECTIVE ❷ involved in chemistry or using chemicals

**chemist** NOUN ❶ a person who is qualified to make up drugs and medicines prescribed by a doctor ❷ a shop where medicines and cosmetics are sold ❸ a scientist who does research in chemistry

**chemistry** NOUN Chemistry is the scientific study of substances and the ways in which they change when they are combined with other substances

**cheque** NOUN a printed form on which you write an amount of money that you have to pay. You sign the cheque and your bank pays the money from your account

**cherry**, cherries NOUN ❶ a small, juicy fruit with a red or black skin and a hard stone in the centre ❷ a tree that produces cherries

**chess** NOUN Chess is a board game for two people in which each player has 16 pieces and tries to move his or her pieces so that the other player's king cannot escape

**chest** NOUN ❶ the front part of your body between your shoulders and your waist ❷ a large wooden box with a hinged lid

**chest of drawers**, chests of drawers NOUN a piece of furniture with drawers in it, used for storing clothes

**chew** VERB When you chew something, you use your teeth to break it up in your mouth before swallowing it

**chewing gum** NOUN Chewing gum is a kind of sweet that you chew for a long time, but which you do not swallow

**chick** NOUN a young bird

**chicken** NOUN a bird kept on a farm for its eggs and meat; also the meat of this bird

**chief** NOUN ❶ the leader of a group or organization ✿ ADJECTIVE ❷ most important **chiefly** ADVERB

**child**, children NOUN ❶ a young person who is not yet an adult ❷ Someone's child is their son or daughter

**childhood** NOUN Someone's childhood is the time when they are a child

**childish** ADJECTIVE immature and foolish

**chill** VERB ❶ To chill something is to make it cold ❷ If something chills you, it makes you feel worried or frightened ✿ NOUN ❸ a feverish cold ❹ a feeling of cold

**chilli**, chillies NOUN the red or green seed pod of a type of pepper which has a very hot, spicy taste

**chilly**, chillier, chilliest ADJECTIVE ❶ rather cold ❷ unfriendly and without enthusiasm

**chimney**, chimneys NOUN a vertical pipe or other hollow structure above a fireplace or furnace through which smoke from a fire escapes

**chimpanzee** NOUN a small ape with dark fur that lives in forests in Africa

**chin** NOUN the part of your face below your mouth

**china** NOUN ❶ China is items like cups, saucers, and plates made from very fine clay ❷ INFORMAL In South African English, a china is a friend

**chip**, chips, chipping, chipped NOUN ❶ Chips are thin strips of fried potato ❷ In electronics, a chip is a tiny piece of silicon inside a computer which is used to form

**chocolate - circuit**

electronic circuits ❸ a small piece broken off an object, or the mark made when a piece breaks off ❹ In some gambling games, chips are counters used to represent money ✿ **VERB** ❺ If you chip an object, you break a small piece off it

**chocolate** **NOUN** ❶ Chocolate is a sweet food made from cacao seeds ❷ a sweet made of chocolate ✿ **ADJECTIVE** ❸ dark brown

**choice** **NOUN** ❶ a range of different things that are available to choose from ❷ something that you choose ❸ Choice is the power or right to choose

**choir** [*kwire*] **NOUN** a group of singers, for example in a church

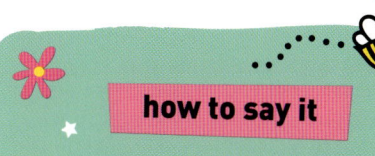

### how to say it
**Choir** should be said **kwire**.

**choke**, chokes, choking, choked **VERB** ❶ If you choke, you stop being able to breathe properly, usually because something is blocking your windpipe ❷ If things choke a place, they fill it so much that it is blocked or clogged up

**cholesterol** [*kol-less-ter-rol*] **NOUN** Cholesterol is a substance found in all animal fats, tissues, and blood

**choose**, chooses, choosing, chose, chosen **VERB** To choose something is to decide to have it or do it

**chop**, chops, chopping, chopped **VERB** ❶ To chop something is to cut it with quick, heavy strokes using an axe or a knife ✿ **NOUN** ❷ a small piece of lamb or pork containing a bone, usually cut from the ribs

**chord** **NOUN** a group of three or more musical notes played together

**chore** **NOUN** an uninteresting job that has to be done

**chorus** **NOUN** ❶ a large group of singers; also a piece of music for a large group of singers ❷ a part of a song which is repeated after each verse ✿ **VERB** ❸ If people chorus something, they all say or sing it at the same time

**christen** **VERB** When a baby is christened, it is named by a member of the clergy in a religious ceremony

**Christian** **NOUN** ❶ a person who believes in Jesus Christ and his teachings ✿ **ADJECTIVE** ❷ relating to Christ and his teachings ❸ good, kind, and considerate **Christianity** **NOUN**

**Christmas**, Christmases **NOUN** the Christian festival celebrating the birth of Christ, falling on December 25th

**chromosome** **NOUN** In biology, a chromosome is a part of a cell which contains genes that determine the characteristics of an animal or plant

**chubby**, chubbier, chubbiest **ADJECTIVE** plump and round

**chuckle**, chuckles, chuckling, chuckled **VERB** When you chuckle, you laugh quietly

**chunk** **NOUN** a thick piece of something

**chunky**, chunkier, chunkiest **ADJECTIVE** Someone who is chunky is broad and heavy but usually short

**church**, churches **NOUN** ❶ a building where Christians go for religious services and worship ❷ In the Christian religion, a church is one of the groups with their own particular beliefs, customs, and clergy

**cider** **NOUN** Cider is an alcoholic drink made from apples

**cigar** **NOUN** a roll of dried tobacco leaves which people smoke

**cigarette** **NOUN** a thin roll of tobacco covered in thin paper which people smoke

**cinema** **NOUN** ❶ a place where people go to watch films ❷ Cinema is the business of making films

**cinnamon** **NOUN** Cinnamon is a sweet spice which comes from the bark of an Asian tree

**circle**, circles, circling, circled **NOUN** ❶ a completely regular round shape. Every point on its edge is the same distance from the centre ❷ a group of people with the same interest or profession ❸ an area of seats on an upper floor of a theatre ✿ **VERB** ❹ To circle is to move round and round as though going round the edge of a circle

**circuit** [*sir-kit*] **NOUN** ❶ any closed line or path, often circular, for example a racing track; also the distance round this path ❷ An electrical circuit is a complete route around which an electric current can flow

**circular** ADJECTIVE ❶ in the shape of a circle ❷ A circular argument or theory is not valid because it uses a statement to prove a conclusion and the conclusion to prove the statement ✿ NOUN ❸ a letter or advert sent to a lot of people at the same time

**circulate**, circulates, circulating, circulated VERB ❶ When something circulates or when you circulate it, it moves easily around an area ❷ When you circulate something among people, you pass it round or tell it to all the people

**circulation** NOUN ❶ The circulation of something is the act of circulating it or the action of it circulating ❷ The circulation of a newspaper or magazine is the number of copies that are sold of each issue ❸ Your circulation is the movement of blood through your body

**circumference** NOUN The circumference of a circle is its outer line or edge; also the length of this line

**circumstance** NOUN ❶ The circumstances of a situation or event are the conditions that affect what happens ❷ Someone's circumstances are their position and conditions in life

**circus**, circuses NOUN a show given by a travelling group of entertainers such as clowns, acrobats, and specially trained animals

**citizen** NOUN The citizens of a country or city are the people who live in it or belong to it

**city**, cities NOUN a large town where many people live and work

**civil** ADJECTIVE ❶ relating to the citizens of a country ❷ relating to people or things that are not connected with the armed forces ❸ polite

**civilian** NOUN a person who is not in the armed forces

**civilization** or **civilisation** NOUN ❶ a society which has a highly developed organization and culture ❷ Civilization is an advanced state of social organization and culture

**civilized** ADJECTIVE ❶ A civilized society is one with a developed social organization and way of life ❷ A civilized person is polite and reasonable

**civil war** NOUN a war between groups of people who live in the same country

**claim** VERB ❶ If you claim that something is the case, you say that it is the case ❷ If you claim something, you ask for it because it belongs to you or you have a right to it ✿ NOUN ❸ a statement that something is the case, or that you have a right to something

**clam** NOUN a kind of shellfish

**clamp** NOUN ❶ an object with movable parts that are used to hold two things firmly together ✿ VERB ❷ To clamp things together is to fasten them or hold them firmly with a clamp

**clamp down on** ✿ VERB To clamp down on something is to become stricter in controlling it

**clap**, claps, clapping, clapped VERB ❶ When you clap, you hit your hands together loudly to show your appreciation ❷ If you clap someone on the back or shoulder, you hit them in a friendly way ❸ If you clap something somewhere, you put it there quickly and firmly ✿ NOUN ❹ a sound made by clapping your hands ❺ A clap of thunder is a sudden loud noise of thunder

**clarify**, clarifies, clarifying, clarified VERB To clarify something is to make it clear and easier to understand

**clarinet** NOUN a woodwind instrument with a straight tube and a single reed in its mouthpiece

**clarity** NOUN The clarity of something is its clearness

**clash**, clashes, clashing, clashed VERB ❶ If people clash with each other, they fight or argue ❷ Ideas or styles that clash are so different that they do not go together ❸ If two events clash, they happen at the same time so you cannot go to both ❹ When metal objects clash, they hit each other with a loud noise ✿ NOUN ❺ a fight or argument ❻ A clash of ideas, styles, or events is a situation in which they do not go together ❼ a loud noise made by metal objects when they hit each other

**clasp** VERB ❶ To clasp something means to hold it tightly or fasten it ✿ NOUN ❷ a fastening such as a hook or catch

**class**, classes, classing, classed NOUN ❶ A class of people or things is a group of them of a particular type or quality ❷ a group of pupils or students taught

## classic - climate

together, or a lesson that they have together ❸ Someone who has class is elegant in appearance or behaviour ✿ **VERB** ❹ To class something means to arrange it in a particular group or to consider it as belonging to a particular group

**classic** ADJECTIVE ❶ typical and therefore a good model or example of something ❷ of very high quality ❸ simple in style and form ✿ **NOUN** ❹ something of the highest quality ❺ Classics is the study of Latin and Greek, and the literature of ancient Greece and Rome

**classical** ADJECTIVE ❶ traditional in style, form, and content ❷ Classical music is serious music considered to be of lasting value ❸ characteristic of the style of ancient Greece and Rome

**classify**, classifies, classifying, classified VERB To classify things is to arrange them into groups with similar characteristics

**classroom** NOUN a room in a school where pupils have lessons

**clause** NOUN ❶ a section of a legal document ❷ In grammar, a clause is a group of words with a subject and a verb, which may be a complete sentence or one of the parts of a sentence

### how English works

### Tips and tricks...

A **clause** is a group of words which make up part of a sentence and can sometimes be a sentence in its own right.

**claw** NOUN ❶ An animal's claws are hard, curved nails at the end of its feet ❷ The claws of a crab or lobster are the two jointed parts, used for grasping things ✿ **VERB** ❸ If an animal claws something, it digs its claws into it

**clay** NOUN Clay is a type of earth that is soft and sticky when wet and hard when baked dry. It is used to make pottery and bricks

**clean** ADJECTIVE ❶ free from dirt or marks ❷ clean from germs or infection ❸ If humour is clean it is not rude and does not involve bad language ❹ A clean movement is skilful and accurate ❺ Clean also means free from fault or error ✿ **VERB** ❻ To clean something is to remove dirt from it **cleaner** NOUN

**clear**, clearer, clearest; clears, clearing, cleared ADJECTIVE ❶ easy to understand, see, or hear ❷ easy to see through ❸ free from obstructions or unwanted things ✿ **VERB** ❹ To clear an area is to remove unwanted things from it ❺ If you clear a fence or other obstacle, you jump over it without touching it ❻ When fog or mist clears, it disappears ❼ If someone is cleared of a crime, they are proved to be not guilty **clearly** ADVERB

**clear up** ✿ **VERB** ❶ If you clear up, you tidy a place and put things away ❷ When a problem or misunderstanding is cleared up, it is solved or settled

**clerk** [klahrk] NOUN a person who keeps records or accounts in an office, bank, or law court

**clever**, cleverer, cleverest ADJECTIVE ❶ intelligent and quick to understand things ❷ very effective or skilful **cleverly** ADVERB

**click** VERB ❶ When something clicks or when you click it, it makes a short snapping sound ❷ When you click on an area of a computer screen, you point the cursor at it and press one of the buttons on the mouse in order to make something happen ✿ **NOUN** ❸ a sound of something clicking

**client** NOUN someone who pays a professional person or company for a service

**cliff** NOUN a steep high rock face by the sea

**climate** NOUN ❶ The climate of a place is the typical weather conditions there ❷ the general attitude and opinion of people at a particular time

A B C D E F G H I J K L M N O P Q R S T U V W X Y Z

# climax – club together

**climax**, climaxes NOUN The climax of a process, story, or piece of music is the most exciting moment in it, usually near the end

**climb** VERB ❶ To climb is to move upwards ❷ If you climb somewhere, you move there with difficulty ❀ NOUN ❸ a movement upwards **climber** NOUN

**cling**, clings, clinging, clung VERB To cling to something is to hold onto it or stay closely attached to it

**clinic** NOUN a building where people go for medical treatment

**clinical** ADJECTIVE ❶ relating to the medical treatment of patients ❷ Clinical behaviour or thought is logical and unemotional

**clip**, clips, clipping, clipped NOUN ❶ a small metal or plastic object used for holding things together ❷ a short piece of a film shown by itself ❀ VERB ❸ If you clip things together, you fasten them with clips ❹ If you clip something, you cut bits from it to shape it

**cloakroom** NOUN a room for coats or a room with toilets and washbasins in a public building

**clock** NOUN ❶ a device that measures and shows the time ❀ PHRASE ❷ If you work **round the clock**, you work all day and night

**clockwise** ADJECTIVE OR ADVERB in the same direction as the hands on a clock

**close**, closes, closing, closed; closer, closest VERB ❶ To close something is to shut it ❷ To close a road or entrance is to block it so that no-one can go in or out ❸ If a shop closes at a certain time, then it does not do business after that time ❀ ADJECTIVE OR ADVERB ❹ near to something ❀ ADJECTIVE ❺ People who are close to each other are very friendly and know each other well ❻ You say the weather is close when it is uncomfortably warm and there is not enough air **closely** ADVERB **closed** ADJECTIVE

**close down** ❀ VERB If a business closes down, all work stops there permanently

**closet** NOUN ❶ a cupboard ❀ VERB ❷ If you are closeted somewhere, you shut yourself away alone or in private with another person ❀ ADJECTIVE ❸ Closet beliefs or habits are kept private and secret

**cloth** NOUN ❶ Cloth is fabric made by a process such as weaving ❷ a piece of material used for wiping or protecting things

**clothes** PLURAL NOUN the things people wear on their bodies

**clothing** NOUN the clothes people wear

**cloud** NOUN ❶ a mass of water vapour, smoke, or dust that forms in the air and is seen floating in the sky ❀ VERB ❷ If something clouds or is clouded, it becomes cloudy or difficult to see through ❸ Something that clouds an issue makes it more confusing

**cloudy**, cloudier, cloudiest ADJECTIVE ❶ full of clouds ❷ difficult to see through

**clown** NOUN ❶ a circus performer who wears funny clothes and make-up and does silly things to make people laugh ❀ VERB ❷ If you clown, you do silly things to make people laugh

**club**, clubs, clubbing, clubbed NOUN ❶ an organization of people with a particular interest, who meet regularly; also the place where they meet ❷ a thick, heavy stick used as a weapon ❸ a stick with a shaped head that a golf player uses to hit the ball ❹ Clubs is one of the four suits in a pack of playing cards. It is marked by a black symbol in the shape of a clover leaf ❀ VERB ❺ To club someone is to hit them hard with a heavy object

**club together** ❀ VERB If people club together, they all join together to give money to buy something

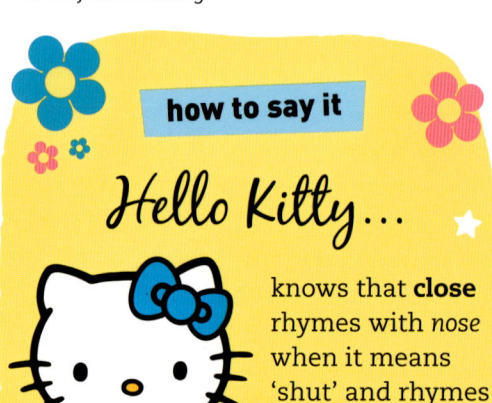

## how to say it

Hello Kitty... knows that **close** rhymes with *nose* when it means 'shut' and rhymes with *dose* when it means 'near'.

# clue - collapse

**clue** NOUN something that helps to solve a problem or mystery

**clumsy**, clumsier, clumsiest ADJECTIVE ❶ moving awkwardly and carelessly ❷ said or done without thought or tact **clumsily** ADVERB

**cluster** NOUN ❶ A cluster of things is a group of them together ✿ VERB ❷ If people cluster together, they stay together in a close group

**clutch**, clutches, clutching, clutched VERB ❶ If you clutch something, you hold it tightly or seize it ✿ NOUN ❷ IN PLURAL If you are in someone's clutches, they have power or control over you

**clutter** NOUN ❶ Clutter is an untidy mess ✿ VERB ❷ Things that clutter a place fill it and make it untidy

**coach**, coaches, coaching, coached NOUN ❶ a long motor vehicle used for taking passengers on long journeys ❷ a section of a train that carries passengers ❸ a four-wheeled vehicle with a roof pulled by horses, which people used to travel in ❹ a person who coaches a sport or a subject ✿ VERB ❺ If someone coaches you, they teach you and help you to get better at a sport or a subject

**coal** NOUN ❶ Coal is a hard black rock obtained from under the earth and burned as a fuel ❷ Coals are burning pieces of coal

**coarse**, coarser, coarsest ADJECTIVE ❶ Something that is coarse is rough in texture, often consisting of large particles ❷ Someone who is coarse talks or behaves in a rude or rather offensive way

**coast** NOUN ❶ the edge of the land where it meets the sea ✿ VERB ❷ A vehicle that is coasting is moving without engine power **coastal** ADJECTIVE

**coastline** NOUN the outline of a coast, especially its appearance as seen from the sea or air

**coat** NOUN ❶ a piece of clothing with sleeves which you wear over your other clothes ❷ An animal's coat is the fur or hair on its body ❸ A coat of paint or varnish is a layer of it ✿ VERB ❹ To coat something means to cover it with a thin layer of a something

**cobweb** NOUN the very thin net that a spider spins for catching insects

**cockpit** NOUN The place in a plane where the pilot sits

**cockroach**, cockroaches NOUN a large dark-coloured insect often found in dirty rooms

**cocoa** NOUN Cocoa is a brown powder made from the seeds of a tropical tree and used for making chocolate; also a hot drink made from this powder

**coconut** NOUN a very large nut with white flesh, milky juice, and a hard hairy shell

**cocoon** NOUN a silky covering over the larvae of moths and some other insects

**cod** NOUN a large edible fish

**code** NOUN ❶ a system of replacing the letters or words in a message with other letters or words, so that nobody can understand the message unless they know the system ❷ a group of numbers and letters which is used to identify something

**coffee** NOUN Coffee is a substance made by roasting and grinding the beans of a tropical shrub; also a hot drink made from this substance

**coffin** NOUN a box in which a dead body is buried or cremated

**coil** NOUN ❶ a length of rope or wire wound into a series of loops; also one of the loops ✿ VERB ❷ If something coils, it turns into a series of loops

**coin** NOUN ❶ a small metal disc which is used as money ✿ VERB ❷ If you coin a word or a phrase, you invent it

**coincidence** NOUN ❶ what happens when two similar things occur at the same time by chance ❷ the fact that two things are surprisingly the same

**cold** ADJECTIVE ❶ having a low temperature ❷ Someone who is cold does not show much affection ✿ NOUN ❸ You can refer to cold weather as the cold ❹ a minor illness in which you sneeze and may have a sore throat

**coleslaw** NOUN Coleslaw is a salad of chopped cabbage and other vegetables in mayonnaise

**collage** [*kol-lahj*] NOUN a picture made by sticking pieces of paper or cloth onto a surface

**collapse**, collapses, collapsing, collapsed VERB ❶ If something such as a building collapses, it falls down suddenly. If a person collapses, they fall down suddenly because

# collar – come

A B C D E F G H I J K L M N O P Q R S T U V W X Y Z

they are ill ❷ If something such as a system or a business collapses, it suddenly stops working ✿ NOUN ❸ The collapse of something is what happens when it stops working

**collar** NOUN ❶ The collar of a shirt or coat is the part round the neck which is usually folded over ❷ a leather band round the neck of a dog or cat

**collarbone** NOUN Your collarbones are the two long bones which run from the base of your neck to your shoulders

**colleague** NOUN A person's colleagues are the people he or she works with

**collect** VERB ❶ To collect things is to gather them together for a special purpose or as a hobby ❷ If you collect someone or something from a place, you call there and take them away ❸ When things collect in a place, they gather there over a period of time  **collector** NOUN

**collection** NOUN ❶ a group of things acquired over a period of time ❷ Collection is the collecting of something ❸ the organized collecting of money, for example for charity, or the sum of money collected

**college** NOUN ❶ a place where students study after they have left school ❷ a name given to some secondary schools ❸ one of the institutions into which some universities are divided ❹ In New Zealand English, a college can also refer to a teacher training college

**collide**, collides, colliding, collided VERB If a moving object collides with something, it hits it

**collie** NOUN a dog that is used for rounding up sheep

**collision** NOUN A collision occurs when a moving object hits something

**colon** NOUN ❶ the punctuation mark (:) ❷ part of your intestine

## what does the colon do?

You put a **colon** (:) before a list, a quotation or an explanation.

**colony**, colonies NOUN ❶ a country controlled by a more powerful country ❷ a group of people who settle in a country controlled by their homeland

**colour** NOUN ❶ the appearance something has as a result of reflecting light ❷ a substance used to give colour ❸ Someone's colour is the normal colour of their skin ❹ Colour is also a quality that makes something interesting or exciting ✿ VERB ❺ If you colour something, you give it a colour ❻ If something colours your opinion, it affects the way you think about something  **coloured** ADJECTIVE

**colourful** ADJECTIVE ❶ full of colour ❷ interesting or exciting

**column** NOUN ❶ a tall solid upright cylinder, especially one supporting a part of a building ❷ a group of people moving in a long line

**coma** NOUN Someone who is in a coma is in a state of deep unconsciousness

**comb** NOUN ❶ a flat object with pointed teeth used for tidying your hair ✿ VERB ❷ When you comb your hair, you tidy it with a comb ❸ If you comb a place, you search it thoroughly to try to find someone or something

**combat** NOUN ❶ Combat is fighting ✿ VERB ❷ To combat something means to try to stop it happening or developing

**combination** NOUN ❶ a mixture of things ❷ a series of letters or numbers used to open a special lock

**combine**, combines, combining, combined VERB ❶ To combine things is to cause them to exist together ❷ To combine things also means to join them together to make a single thing ❸ If something combines two qualities or features, it has them both

**come**, comes, coming, came, come VERB ❶ To come to a place is to move there or arrive there ❷ To come to a place also means to reach as far as that place ❸ 'Come' is used to say that someone or something reaches a particular state ❹ When a particular time or event comes, it happens ❺ If you come from a place, you were born there or it is your home ✿ PHRASE ❻ A time or event **to come** is a future time or event

52

**come about** VERB The way something comes about is the way it happens

**come across** VERB If you come across something, you find it by chance

**come off** VERB If something comes off, it succeeds

**come on** VERB If something is coming on, it is making progress

**come up** VERB If something comes up in a conversation or meeting, it is mentioned or discussed

**come up with** VERB If you come up with a plan or idea, you suggest it

**comedian** NOUN an entertainer whose job is to make people laugh

**comedy**, comedies NOUN a light-hearted play or film with a happy ending

**comet** NOUN an object that travels around the sun leaving a bright trail behind it

**comfort** NOUN ❶ Comfort is the state of being physically relaxed ❷ Comfort is also a feeling of relief from worries or unhappiness ❸ IN PLURAL Comforts are things which make your life easier and more pleasant VERB ❹ To comfort someone is to make them less worried or unhappy

**comfortable** ADJECTIVE ❶ If you are comfortable, you are physically relaxed ❷ Something that is comfortable makes you feel relaxed ❸ If you feel comfortable in a particular situation, you are not afraid or embarrassed **comfortably** ADVERB

**comic** ADJECTIVE ❶ funny NOUN ❷ someone who tells jokes ❸ a magazine that contains stories told in pictures

**comical** ADJECTIVE funny

**comma** NOUN the punctuation mark (,)

**command** VERB ❶ To command someone to do something is to order them to do it ❷ If you command something such as respect, you receive it because of your personal qualities ❸ An officer who commands part of an army or navy is in charge of it NOUN ❹ an order to do something ❺ Your command of something is your knowledge of it and your ability to use this knowledge

**commence**, commences, commencing, commenced VERB FORMAL To commence is to begin

**comment** VERB ❶ If you comment on something, you make a remark about it NOUN ❷ a remark about something

**commerce** NOUN Commerce is the buying and selling of goods

**commercial** ADJECTIVE ❶ relating to commerce ❷ Commercial activities involve producing goods on a large scale in order to make money NOUN ❸ an advertisement on television or radio

**commit**, commits, committing, committed VERB ❶ To commit a crime or sin is to do it ❷ If you commit yourself, you state an opinion or state that you will do something ❸ If someone is committed to hospital or prison, they are officially sent there

**commitment** NOUN ❶ Commitment is a strong belief in an idea or system ❷ something that regularly takes up some of your time

**committee** NOUN a group of people who make decisions on behalf of a larger group

**common** ADJECTIVE ❶ Something that is common exists in large numbers or happens often ❷ If something is common to two or more people, they all have it or use it ❸ 'Common' is used to indicate that something is of the ordinary kind and not special ❹ If you describe someone as common, you mean they do not have good taste or good manners NOUN ❺ an area of grassy land where everyone can go

**commonly** ADVERB

### punctuation

### Helpful hints...

You put a **comma** (,) between words or clauses to show that there is a pause between them. You also put it between the things in a list.

# common sense – competent

**A B C D E F G H I J K L M N O P Q R S T U V W X Y Z**

**common sense** NOUN Your common sense is your natural ability to behave sensibly and make good judgments

**communicate**, communicates, communicating, communicated VERB ❶ If you communicate with someone, you keep in touch with them ❷ If you communicate information or a feeling to someone, you make them aware of it

**communication** NOUN ❶ Communication is the process by which people or animals exchange information ❷ Communications are the systems by which people communicate or broadcast information, especially using electricity or radio waves

**communism** NOUN Communism is the doctrine that the state should own the means of production and that there should be no private property **communist** ADJECTIVE OR NOUN

**community**, communities NOUN all the people living in a particular area; also used to refer to particular groups within a society

**commute**, commutes, commuting, commuted VERB People who commute travel a long distance to work every day **commuter** NOUN

**compact** ADJECTIVE taking up very little space

**compact disc** NOUN a music or video recording in the form of a plastic disc which is played using a laser on a special machine, and gives good quality sound or pictures

**companion** NOUN someone you travel or spend time with

**company**, companies NOUN ❶ a business that sells goods or provides a service ❷ a group of actors, opera singers, or dancers ❸ If you have company, you have a friend or visitor with you

**comparable** [kom-pra-bl] ADJECTIVE If two things are comparable, they are similar in size or quality

**comparative** ADJECTIVE ❶ You add comparative to indicate that something is true only when compared with what is normal ❀ NOUN ❷ In grammar, the comparative is the form of an adjective which indicates that the person or thing described has more of a particular quality than someone or something else. For example, 'quicker', 'better', and 'easier' are all comparatives

**compare**, compares, comparing, compared VERB ❶ When you compare things, you look at them together and see in what ways they are different or similar ❷ If you compare one thing to another, you say it is like the other thing

**comparison** NOUN When you make a comparison, you consider two things together and see in what ways they are different or similar

**compartment** NOUN ❶ a section of a railway carriage ❷ one of the separate parts of an object

**compass**, compasses NOUN ❶ an instrument with a magnetic needle for finding directions ❷ IN PLURAL Compasses are a hinged instrument for drawing circles

**compatible** ADJECTIVE If people or things are compatible, they can live or work together successfully

**compete**, competes, competing, competed VERB ❶ When people or firms compete, each tries to prove that they or their products are the best ❷ If you compete in a contest or game, you take part in it

**competent** ADJECTIVE Someone who is competent at something can do it satisfactorily **competence** NOUN

## how English works

### Helpful hints...

A **comparative** adjective shows that the noun has more of a certain quality than another noun, like *taller* and *more interesting*.

54

**competition — concentrate**

**competition** NOUN ❶ When there is competition between people or groups, they are all trying to get something that not everyone can have ❷ an event in which people take part to find who is best at something ❸ When there is competition between firms, each firm is trying to get people to buy its own goods

**competitive** ADJECTIVE ❶ A competitive situation is one in which people or firms are competing with each other ❷ A competitive person is eager to be more successful than others ❸ Goods sold at competitive prices are cheaper than other goods of the same kind

**competitor** NOUN a person or firm that is competing to become the most successful

**complain** VERB ❶ If you complain, you say that you are not satisfied with something ❷ If you complain of pain or illness, you say that you have it

**complaint** NOUN If you make a complaint, you complain about something

**complete**, completes, completing, completed ADJECTIVE ❶ to the greatest degree possible ❷ If something is complete, none of it is missing ❸ When a task is complete, it is finished ✿ VERB ❹ If you complete something, you finish it ❺ If you complete a form, you fill it in **completely** ADVERB

**complex**, complexes ADJECTIVE ❶ Something that is complex has many different parts ✿ NOUN ❷ A complex is a group of buildings, roads, or other things connected with each other in some way

**complexion** NOUN the quality of the skin on your face

**complicate**, complicates, complicating, complicated VERB To complicate something is to make it more difficult to understand or deal with

**complicated** ADJECTIVE Something that is complicated has so many parts or aspects that it is difficult to understand or deal with

**complication** NOUN something that makes a situation more difficult to deal with

**compliment** NOUN ❶ If you pay someone a compliment, you tell them you admire something about them ✿ VERB ❷ If you compliment someone, you pay them a compliment

**compose**, composes, composing, composed VERB ❶ If something is composed of particular things or people, it is made up of them ❷ To compose a piece of music, letter, or speech means to write it ❸ If you compose yourself, you become calm after being excited or upset

**composer** NOUN someone who writes music

**composition** NOUN ❶ The composition of something is the things it consists of ❷ The composition of a poem or piece of music is the writing of it ❸ a piece of music or writing

**compound** NOUN ❶ an enclosed area of land with buildings used for a particular purpose ❷ In chemistry, a compound is a substance consisting of two or more different substances or chemical elements ✿ VERB ❸ To compound something is to put together different parts to make a whole ❹ To compound a problem is to make it worse by adding to it

**comprehend** VERB FORMAL To comprehend something is to understand or appreciate it **comprehension** NOUN

**compromise**, compromises, compromising, compromised NOUN ❶ an agreement in which people accept less than they originally wanted ✿ VERB ❷ When people compromise, they agree to accept less than they originally wanted

**compulsory** ADJECTIVE If something is compulsory, you have to do it

**computer** NOUN an electronic machine that can make calculations quickly or store and find information

**computing** NOUN Computing is the use of computers and the writing of programs for them

**conceal** VERB To conceal something is to hide it

**conceive**, conceives, conceiving, conceived VERB ❶ If you can conceive of something, you can imagine it or believe it ❷ If you conceive something such as a plan, you think of it and work out how it could be done ❸ When a woman conceives, she becomes pregnant

**concentrate**, concentrates, concentrating, concentrated VERB ❶ If you concentrate on something, you give it all your attention

55

# concept – confine

❷ When something is concentrated in one place, it is all there rather than in several places **concentration** NOUN

**concept** NOUN an abstract or general idea

**concern** NOUN ❶ Concern is a feeling of worry about something or someone ❷ If something is your concern, it is your responsibility ❸ a business ✿ VERB ❹ If something concerns you or if you are concerned about it, it worries you ❺ You say that something concerns you if it affects or involves you **concerned** ADJECTIVE

**concerning** PREPOSITION You use 'concerning' to show what something is about

**concert** NOUN a public performance by musicians

**conclude**, concludes, concluding, concluded VERB ❶ If you conclude something, you decide that it is so because of the other things that you know ❷ When you conclude something, you finish it

**conclusion** NOUN ❶ a decision made after thinking carefully about something ❷ the finish or ending of something

**concrete** NOUN ❶ Concrete is a solid building material made by mixing cement, sand, and water ✿ ADJECTIVE ❷ definite, rather than general or vague ❸ real and physical, rather than abstract

**condemn** VERB ❶ If you condemn something, you say it is bad and unacceptable ❷ If someone is condemned to a punishment, they are given it ❸ If you are condemned to something unpleasant, you must suffer it ❹ When a building is condemned, it is going to be pulled down because it is unsafe

**condition** NOUN ❶ the state someone or something is in ❷ IN PLURAL The conditions in which something is done are the location and other factors likely to affect it ❸ a requirement that must be met for something else to be possible ❹ You can refer to an illness or other medical problem as a condition ✿ PHRASE ❺ If you are **out of condition**, you are unfit ✿ VERB ❻ If someone is conditioned to behave or think in a certain way, they do it as a result of their upbringing or training

**conditional** ADJECTIVE If one thing is conditional on another, it can only happen if the other thing happens

**conduct** VERB ❶ To conduct an activity or task is to carry it out ❷ FORMAL The way you conduct yourself is the way you behave ❸ When someone conducts an orchestra or choir, they stand in front of it and direct it ❹ If something conducts heat or electricity, heat or electricity can pass through it ✿ NOUN ❺ If you take part in the conduct of an activity or task, you help to carry it out ❻ Your conduct is your behaviour

**conductor** NOUN ❶ someone who conducts an orchestra or choir ❷ someone who moves round a bus or train selling tickets ❸ a substance that conducts heat or electricity

**cone** NOUN ❶ a regular three-dimensional shape with a circular base and a point at the top ❷ A fir cone or pine cone is the fruit of a fir or pine tree

**conference** NOUN a meeting at which formal discussions take place

**confess**, confesses, confessing, confessed VERB If you confess to something, you admit it

**confession** NOUN ❶ If you make a confession, you admit you have done something wrong ❷ Confession is the act of confessing something, especially a religious act in which people confess their sins to a priest

**confidence** NOUN ❶ If you have confidence in someone, you feel you can trust them ❷ Someone who has confidence is sure of their own abilities or qualities ❸ a secret you tell someone

**confident** ADJECTIVE ❶ If you are confident about something, you are sure it will happen the way you want it to ❷ People who are confident are sure of their own abilities or qualities **confidently** ADVERB

**confidential** ADJECTIVE Confidential information is meant to be kept secret **confidentially** ADVERB

**confine**, confines, confining, confined VERB ❶ If something is confined to one place, person, or thing, it exists only in that place or affects only that person or thing ❷ If you confine yourself to doing or saying something, it is the only thing you do or say ❸ If you are confined to a place, you cannot

**confirm - conservative**

leave it ✿ PLURAL NOUN ❹ The confines of a place are its boundaries  **confinement** NOUN

**confirm** VERB ❶ To confirm something is to say or show that it is true ❷ If you confirm an arrangement or appointment, you say it is definite ❸ When someone is confirmed, they are formally accepted as a member of a Christian church  **confirmation** NOUN

**conflict** NOUN [kon-flikt] ❶ Conflict is disagreement and argument ❷ a war or battle ❸ When there is a conflict of ideas or interests, people have different ideas or interests which cannot all be satisfied ✿ VERB [kon-flikt] ❹ When ideas or interests conflict, they are different and cannot all be satisfied

**conform** VERB ❶ If you conform, you behave the way people expect you to ❷ If something conforms to a law or to someone's wishes, it is what is required or wanted

**confuse**, confuses, confusing, confused VERB ❶ It you confuse two things, you mix them up and think one of them is the other ❷ To confuse someone means to make them uncertain about what is happening or what to do ❸ To confuse a situation means to make it more complicated

**confused** ADJECTIVE ❶ uncertain about what is happening or what to do ❷ in an untidy mess

**confusing** ADJECTIVE puzzling or bewildering

**confusion** NOUN a bewildering state or untidy mess

**congratulate**, congratulates, congratulating, congratulated VERB If you congratulate someone, you express pleasure at something good that has happened to them, or praise them for something they have achieved  **congratulation** NOUN

**conjunction** NOUN ❶ In grammar, a conjunction is a word that links two other words or two clauses, for example 'and', 'but', 'while', and 'that' ✿ PHRASE ❷ If two or more things are done **in conjunction**, they are done together

**connect** VERB ❶ To connect two things is to join them together ❷ If you connect something with something else, you think of them as being linked

**connection** or **connexion** NOUN ❶ a link or relationship between things ❷ the point where two wires or pipes are joined together ❸ IN PLURAL Someone's connections are the people they know

**conquer** VERB ❶ To conquer people is to take control of their country by force ❷ If you conquer something difficult or dangerous, you succeed in controlling it

**conscience** NOUN the part of your mind that tells you what is right and wrong

**conscientious** [kon-shee-**en**-shus] ADJECTIVE Someone who is conscientious is very careful to do their work properly  **conscientiously** ADVERB

**conscious** ADJECTIVE ❶ If you are conscious of something, you are aware of it ❷ A conscious action or effort is done deliberately ❸ Someone who is conscious is awake, rather than asleep or unconscious

**consent** NOUN ❶ Consent is permission to do something ❷ Consent is also agreement between two or more people ✿ VERB ❸ If you consent to something, you agree to it or allow it

**consequence** NOUN ❶ The consequences of something are its results or effects ❷ FORMAL If something is of consequence, it is important  **consequently** ADVERB

**conservation** NOUN Conservation is the preservation of the environment

**conservative** NOUN ❶ In Britain, a Conservative is a member or supporter of

### how English works

*Hello Kitty...*

knows that a **conjunction** is a word that joins two parts of a sentence together, like *but* and *because*. Conjunctions are sometimes called 'joining words'.

# conserve – consumer

the Conservative Party, a political party that believes that the government should interfere as little as possible in the running of the economy ❁ **ADJECTIVE** ❷ In Britain, Conservative views and policies are those of the Conservative Party ❸ Someone who is conservative is not willing to accept changes or new ideas ❹ A conservative estimate or guess is a cautious or moderate one

**conserve**, conserves, conserving, conserved **VERB** If you conserve a supply of something, you make it last

**consider VERB** ❶ If you consider something to be the case, you think or judge it to be so ❷ To consider something is to think about it carefully ❸ If you consider someone's needs or feelings, you take account of them

**considerable ADJECTIVE** A considerable amount of something is a lot of it **considerably ADVERB**

**considerate ADJECTIVE** Someone who is considerate pays attention to other people's needs and feelings

**consideration NOUN** ❶ Consideration is careful thought about something ❷ If you show consideration for someone, you take account of their needs and feelings ❸ something that has to be taken into account

**consist VERB** What something consists of is its different parts or members

**consistency**, consistencies **NOUN** ❶ Consistency is the quality of being consistent ❷ The consistency of a substance is how thick or smooth it is

**consistent ADJECTIVE** ❶ If you are consistent, you keep doing something the same way ❷ If something such as a statement or argument is consistent, there are no contradictions in it **consistently ADVERB**

**console**, consoles, consoling, consoled **VERB** [con-**sole**] ❶ To console someone who is unhappy is to make them more cheerful ❁ **NOUN** [con-sole] ❷ a panel with switches or knobs for operating a machine

**consonant NOUN** a sound such as 'p' or 'm' which you make by stopping the air flowing freely through your mouth

**constant ADJECTIVE** ❶ Something that is constant happens all the time or is always there ❷ If an amount or level is constant, it stays the same ❸ People who are constant stay loyal to a person or idea **constantly ADVERB**

**constituency**, constituencies **NOUN** a town or area represented by an MP

**constitution NOUN** ❶ The constitution of a country is the system of laws which formally states people's rights and duties ❷ Your constitution is your health

**construct VERB** To construct something is to build or make it

**construction NOUN** ❶ The construction of something is the building or making of it ❷ something built or made

**consult VERB** ❶ If you consult someone, you ask for their opinion or advice ❷ When people consult each other, they exchange ideas and opinions ❸ If you consult a book or map, you look at it for information

**consultant NOUN** ❶ an experienced doctor who specializes in one type of medicine ❷ someone who gives expert advice

**consultation NOUN** ❶ a meeting held to discuss something ❷ Consultation is discussion or the seeking of advice

**consume**, consumes, consuming, consumed **VERB** ❶ FORMAL If you consume something, you eat or drink it ❷ To consume fuel or energy is to use it up

**consumer NOUN** someone who buys things or uses services

## help with spelling

Hello Kitty... knows that these letters are all **consonants**: b, c, d, f, g, h, j, k, l, m, n, p, q, r, s, t, v, w, x and z.

**contact – contribute**

**contact** NOUN ❶ If you are in contact with someone, you regularly talk to them or write to them ❷ When things are in contact, they are touching each other ❸ someone you know in a place or organization from whom you can get help or information ✿ VERB ❹ If you contact someone, you telephone them or write to them

**contact lens**, contact lenses NOUN Contact lenses are small plastic lenses that you put in your eyes instead of wearing glasses, to help you see better

**contagious** ADJECTIVE A contagious disease can be caught by touching people or things infected with it

**contain** VERB ❶ If a substance contains something, that thing is a part of it ❷ The things a box or room contains are the things inside it ❸ FORMAL To contain something also means to stop it increasing or spreading

**container** NOUN ❶ something such as a box or a bottle that you keep things in ❷ a large sealed metal box for transporting things

**contemporary**, contemporaries ADJECTIVE ❶ produced or happening now ❷ produced or happening at the time you are talking about ✿ NOUN ❸ Someone's contemporaries are other people living or active at the same time as them

**content** NOUN [*con*-tent] ❶ IN PLURAL The contents of something are the things inside it ❷ The content of an article or speech is what is expressed in it ❸ Content is the proportion of something that a substance contains ✿ ADJECTIVE [*con*-**tent**] ❹ happy and satisfied with your life ❺ willing to do or have something ✿ VERB [*con*-**tent**] ❻ If you content yourself with doing something, you do it and do not try to do anything else

**contented** ADJECTIVE happy and satisfied with your life

**contest** NOUN [*con*-test] ❶ a competition or game ❷ a struggle for power ✿ VERB [*con*-**test**] ❸ If you contest a statement or decision, you object to it formally

**contestant** NOUN someone taking part in a competition

**context** NOUN ❶ The context of something consists of matters related to it which help to explain it ❷ The context of a word or sentence consists of the words or sentences before and after it

**continent** NOUN ❶ a very large area of land, such as Africa or Asia ❷ The Continent is the mainland of Europe **continental** ADJECTIVE

**continual** ADJECTIVE ❶ happening all the time without stopping ❷ happening again and again **continually** ADVERB

**continuation** NOUN ❶ The continuation of something is the continuing of it ❷ Something that is a continuation of an event follows it and seems like a part of it

**continue**, continues, continuing, continued VERB ❶ If you continue to do something, you keep doing it ❷ If something continues, it does not stop ❸ You also say something continues when it starts again after stopping

**continuous** ADJECTIVE ❶ Continuous means happening or existing without stopping ❷ A continuous line or surface has no gaps or holes in it. A continuous set of data has an unlimited amount of numbers or items in it **continuously** ADVERB

**contract** NOUN [*con*-trakt] ❶ a written legal agreement about the sale of something or work done for money ✿ VERB [*con*-**trakt**] ❷ When something contracts, it gets smaller or shorter ❸ FORMAL If you contract an illness, you get it

**contraction** NOUN ❶ contracting ❷ a shortened form of a word or words, for example *I'm* for *I am*

**contradict** VERB If you contradict someone, you say that what they have just said is not true, and that something else is

**contrary** ADJECTIVE ❶ Contrary ideas or opinions are opposed to each other and cannot be held by the same person ✿ PHRASE ❷ You say **on the contrary** when you are contradicting what someone has just said

**contrast** NOUN ❶ a great difference between things ❷ If one thing is a contrast to another, it is very different from it

**contrast** VERB ❶ If you contrast things, you describe or emphasize the differences between them ❷ If one thing contrasts with another, it is very different from it

**contribute**, contributes, contributing, contributed VERB ❶ If you contribute to something, you do things to help it succeed ❷ If you contribute money, you give it to help to pay for something ❸ If something

# control – cope

contributes to an event or situation, it is one of its causes **contribution** NOUN **contributor** NOUN

**control**, controls, controlling, controlled NOUN ❶ Control of a country or organization is the power to make the important decisions about how it is run ❷ Your control over something is your ability to make it work the way you want it to ❸ The controls on a machine are knobs or other devices used to work it ✿ VERB ❹ To control a country or organization means to have the power to make decisions about how it is run ❺ To control something such as a machine or system means to make it work the way you want it to ❻ If you control yourself, you make yourself behave calmly when you are angry or upset ✿ PHRASE ❼ If something is **out of control**, nobody has any power over it **controller** NOUN

**controversial** ADJECTIVE Something that is controversial causes a lot of discussion and argument, because many people disapprove of it

**controversy**, controversies [**kon**-triv-ver-see or kon-**trov**-ver-see] NOUN discussion and argument because many people disapprove of something

**convenience** NOUN ❶ The convenience of something is the fact that it is easy to use or that it makes something easy to do ❷ something useful

**convenient** ADJECTIVE If something is convenient, it is easy to use or it makes something easy to do **conveniently** ADVERB

**conventional** ADJECTIVE ❶ You say that people are conventional when there is nothing unusual about their way of life ❷ Conventional methods are the ones that are usually used

**conversation** NOUN If you have a conversation with someone, you spend time talking to them

**convert** VERB [con-**vert**] ❶ To convert one thing into another is to change it so that it becomes the other thing ❷ If you convert a unit or measurement, you express it in terms of another unit or scale of measurement. For example, you can convert inches to centimetres by multiplying by 2.54 ❸ If someone converts you, they persuade you to change your religious or political beliefs ✿ NOUN [**con**-vert] ❹ someone who has changed their religious or political beliefs

**convict** VERB [kon-**vikt**] ❶ To convict someone of a crime is to find them guilty ✿ NOUN [**kon**-vikt] ❷ someone serving a prison sentence

**convince**, convinces, convincing, convinced VERB To convince someone of something is to persuade them that it is true

**cook** VERB ❶ To cook food is to prepare it for eating by heating it ✿ NOUN ❷ someone who prepares and cooks food, often as their job

**cooker** NOUN a device for cooking food

**cookery** NOUN Cookery is the activity of preparing and cooking food

**cookie** NOUN ❶ a sweet biscuit ❷ a small file placed on a user's computer by a website, containing information about the user's preferences that will be used on any future visits he or she may make to the site

**cool** ADJECTIVE ❶ Something cool has a low temperature but is not cold ❷ If you are cool in a difficult situation, you stay calm and unemotional ✿ VERB ❸ When something cools or when you cool it, it becomes less warm

**cooperate**, cooperates, cooperating, cooperated [koh-**op**-er-rate] VERB ❶ When people cooperate, they work or act together ❷ To cooperate also means to do what someone asks **cooperation** NOUN

**cooperative** [koh-**op**-er-ut-tiv] NOUN ❶ a business or organization run by the people who work for it, and who share its benefits or profits ✿ ADJECTIVE ❷ A cooperative activity is done by people working together ❸ Someone who is cooperative does what you ask them to

**coordinate** [koh-**or**-din-ate] VERB ❶ To coordinate an activity is to organize the people or things involved in it ❷ IN PLURAL Coordinates are a pair of numbers or letters which tell you how far along and up or down a point is on a grid **coordination** NOUN

**cop** NOUN INFORMAL a policeman

**cope**, copes, coping, coped VERB If you cope with a problem or task, you deal with it successfully

**copper** NOUN ❶ Copper is a reddish-brown metallic element ❷ Coppers are brown metal coins of low value

**copy**, copies, copying, copied NOUN ❶ something made to look like something else ❷ A copy of a book, newspaper, or record is one of many identical ones produced at the same time ✿ VERB ❸ If you copy what someone does, you do the same thing ❹ If you copy something, you make a copy of it

**coral** NOUN Coral is a hard substance that forms in the sea from the skeletons of tiny animals called corals

**cord** NOUN ❶ Cord is strong, thick string ❷ Electrical wire covered in rubber or plastic is also called cord

### don't mix up

Don't mix up **cord** (thick string) and **chord** (notes played together).

**core** NOUN ❶ the hard central part of a fruit such as an apple ❷ the most central part of an object or place ❸ the most important part of something

**cork** NOUN ❶ Cork is the very light, spongelike bark of a Mediterranean tree ❷ a piece of cork pushed into the end of a bottle to close it

**corkscrew** NOUN a device for pulling corks out of bottles

**corn** NOUN ❶ Corn refers to crops such as wheat and barley and to their seeds ❷ a small painful area of hard skin on your foot

**corner** NOUN ❶ a place where two sides or edges of something meet ✿ VERB ❷ To corner a person or animal is to get them into a place they cannot escape from

**corporate** ADJECTIVE FORMAL belonging to or done by all members of a group together

**corporation** NOUN ❶ a large business ❷ a group of people responsible for running a city

**corpse** NOUN a dead body

**correct** ADJECTIVE ❶ If something is correct, there are no mistakes in it ❷ The correct thing in a particular situation is the right one ❸ Correct behaviour is considered to be socially acceptable ✿ VERB ❹ If you correct something which is wrong, you make it right

**correctly** ADVERB

**correction** NOUN the act of making something right

**correspond** VERB ❶ If one thing corresponds to another, it has a similar purpose, function, or status ❷ If numbers or amounts correspond, they are the same ❸ When people correspond, they write to each other

**correspondence** NOUN ❶ Correspondence is the writing of letters; also the letters written ❷ If there is a correspondence between two things, they are closely related or very similar

**correspondent** NOUN a newspaper, television, or radio reporter

**corridor** NOUN a passage in a building or train

**corrupt** ADJECTIVE ❶ Corrupt people act dishonestly or illegally in return for money or power ✿ VERB ❷ To corrupt someone means to make them dishonest ❸ To corrupt someone also means to make them immoral

**cost**, costs, costing, cost NOUN ❶ The cost of something is the amount of money needed to buy it, do it, or make it ❷ The cost of achieving something is the loss or injury in achieving it ✿ VERB ❸ You use 'cost' to talk about the amount of money you have to pay for things ❹ If a mistake costs you something, you lose that thing because of the mistake

**costly**, costlier, costliest ADJECTIVE expensive

**costume** NOUN ❶ a set of clothes worn by an actor ❷ Costume is the clothing worn in a particular place or during a particular period

**cosy**, cosier, cosiest; cosies ADJECTIVE ❶ warm and comfortable ❷ Cosy activities are pleasant and friendly ✿ NOUN ❸ a soft cover put over a teapot to keep the tea warm

**cot** NOUN a small bed for a baby, with bars or panels round it to stop the baby falling out

**cottage** NOUN a small house in the country

**cotton** NOUN ❶ Cotton is cloth made from the soft fibres of the cotton plant ❷ Cotton is also thread used for sewing

# cotton wool – court

**cotton wool** NOUN Cotton wool is soft fluffy cotton, often used for dressing wounds

**couch**, couches, couching, couched NOUN ❶ a long, soft piece of furniture which more than one person can sit on ✿ VERB ❷ If a statement is couched in a particular type of language, it is expressed in that language

**cough** [koff] VERB ❶ When you cough, you force air out of your throat with a sudden harsh noise ✿ NOUN ❷ an illness that makes you cough a lot; also the noise you make when you cough

**could** VERB ❶ You use 'could' to say that you were able or allowed to do something ❷ You also use 'could' to say that something might happen or might be the case ❸ You use 'could' when you are asking for something politely

**council** NOUN ❶ a group of people elected to look after the affairs of a town, district, or county ❷ Some other groups have Council as part of their name

**count** VERB ❶ To count is to say all the numbers in order up to a particular number ❷ If you count all the things in a group, you add them up to see how many there are ❸ What counts in a situation is whatever is most important ❹ To count as something means to be regarded as that thing ❺ If you can count on someone or something, you can rely on them ✿ NOUN ❻ a number reached by counting ❼ FORMAL If something is wrong on a particular count, it is wrong in that respect ❽ a European nobleman

**counter** NOUN ❶ a long, flat surface over which goods are sold in a shop ❷ a small, flat, round object used in board games ✿ VERB ❸ If you counter something that is being done, you take action to make it less effective

**counterfeit** [kown-ter-fit] ADJECTIVE ❶ Something counterfeit is not genuine but has been made to look genuine to deceive people ✿ VERB ❷ To counterfeit something is to make a counterfeit version of it

**country**, countries NOUN ❶ one of the political areas the world is divided into ❷ The country is land away from towns and cities ❸ 'Country' is used to refer to an area with particular features or associations

**countryside** NOUN The countryside is land away from towns and cities

**county**, counties NOUN a region with its own local government

**couple**, couples, coupling, coupled NOUN ❶ two people who are married or having a sexual or romantic relationship ❷ A couple of things or people means two of them ✿ VERB ❸ If one thing is coupled with another, the two things are done or dealt with together

**coupon** NOUN ❶ a piece of printed paper which, when you hand it in, entitles you to pay less than usual for something ❷ a form you fill in to ask for information or to enter a competition

**courage** NOUN Courage is the quality shown by people who do things knowing they are dangerous or difficult **courageous** ADJECTIVE

**courgette** [koor-jet] NOUN a type of small marrow with dark green skin. Courgettes are also called **zucchini**

**course**, courses NOUN ❶ a series of lessons or lectures ❷ a series of medical treatments ❸ one of the parts of a meal ❹ A course or a course of action is one of the things you can do in a situation ❺ a piece of land where a sport such as golf is played ❻ the route a ship or aircraft takes ❼ If something happens in the course of a period of time, it happens during that period ✿ PHRASE ❽ If you say **of course**, you are showing that something is totally expected or that you are sure about something

### don't mix up

Don't mix up **course** (a set of lessons) and **coarse** (rough).

**court** NOUN ❶ a place where legal matters are decided by a judge and jury or a magistrate. The judge and jury or magistrate can also be referred to as the court ❷ a place where a game such as tennis or

**courteous - cream**

badminton is played ❸ the place where a king or queen lives and carries out ceremonial duties

**courteous** [*kur-tee-yuss*] **ADJECTIVE** Courteous behaviour is polite and considerate

**courtesy** **NOUN** Courtesy is polite, considerate behaviour

**courtyard** **NOUN** a flat area of ground surrounded by buildings or walls

**cousin** **NOUN** Your cousin is the child of your uncle or aunt

**cover** **VERB** ❶ If you cover something, you put something else over it to protect it or hide it ❷ If something covers something else, it forms a layer over it ❸ If you cover a particular distance, you travel that distance ✿ **NOUN** ❹ something put over an object to protect it or keep it warm ❺ The cover of a book or magazine is its outside ❻ Insurance cover is a guarantee that money will be paid if something is lost or harmed ❼ In the open, cover consists of trees, rocks, or other places where you can shelter or hide

**cover up** ✿ **VERB** If you cover up something you do not want people to know about, you hide it from them

**cow** **NOUN** a large animal kept on farms for its milk

**coward** **NOUN** someone who is easily frightened and who avoids dangerous or difficult situations

**cowardly** **ADJECTIVE** easily scared

**cowboy** **NOUN** a man employed to look after cattle in America

**crab** **NOUN** a sea creature with four pairs of legs, two pincers, and a flat, round body covered by a shell

**crack** **VERB** ❶ If something cracks, it becomes damaged, with lines appearing on its surface ❷ If you crack a joke, you tell it ❸ If you crack a problem or code, you solve it ✿ **NOUN** ❹ one of the lines appearing on something when it cracks ❺ a narrow gap ✿ **ADJECTIVE** ❻ A crack soldier or sportsman is highly trained and skilful

**cracker** **NOUN** ❶ a thin, crisp biscuit that is often eaten with cheese ❷ a paper-covered tube that pulls apart with a bang and usually has a toy and paper hat inside

**crackle**, crackles, crackling, crackled **VERB** ❶ If something crackles, it makes a rapid series of short, harsh noises ✿ **NOUN** ❷ a short, harsh noise

**cradle**, cradles, cradling, cradled **NOUN** ❶ a box-shaped bed for a baby ✿ **VERB** ❷ If you cradle something in your arms or hands, you hold it there carefully

**craft** **NOUN** ❶ an activity such as weaving, carving, or pottery ❷ a skilful occupation ❸ a boat, plane, or spacecraft

**crafty**, craftier, craftiest **ADJECTIVE** Someone who is crafty gets what they want by tricking people in a clever way

**cramp** **NOUN** Cramp or cramps is a pain caused by a muscle contracting

**crane**, cranes, craning, craned **NOUN** ❶ a machine that moves heavy things by lifting them in the air ❷ a large bird with a long neck and long legs ✿ **VERB** ❸ If you crane your neck, you extend your head in a particular direction to see or hear something better

**crash**, crashes, crashing, crashed **NOUN** ❶ an accident in which a moving vehicle hits something violently ❷ a sudden loud noise ❸ the sudden failure of a business or financial institution ✿ **VERB** ❹ When a vehicle crashes, it hits something and is badly damaged

**crate** **NOUN** a large box used for transporting or storing things

**crater** **NOUN** a wide hole in the ground caused by something hitting it or by an explosion

**crawl** **VERB** ❶ When you crawl, you move forward on your hands and knees ❷ When a vehicle crawls, it moves very slowly ❸ **INFORMAL** If a place is crawling with people or things, it is full of them

**crayon** **NOUN** a coloured pencil or a stick of coloured wax

**crazy**, crazier, craziest **ADJECTIVE** **INFORMAL** ❶ very strange or foolish ❷ If you are crazy about something, you are very keen on it

**crazily** **ADVERB**

**creak** **VERB** ❶ If something creaks, it makes a harsh sound when it moves or when you stand on it ✿ **NOUN** ❷ a harsh squeaking noise

**cream** **NOUN** ❶ Cream is a thick, yellowish-white liquid taken from the top of milk ❷ Cream is also a substance people can rub

A B C D E F G H I J K L M N O P Q R S T U V W X Y Z

63

# crease - crop

on their skin to make it soft ✿ **ADJECTIVE** ❸ yellowish-white **creamy** ADJECTIVE

**crease**, creases, creasing, creased NOUN ❶ an irregular line that appears on cloth or paper when it is crumpled ❷ a straight line on something that has been pressed or folded neatly ✿ **VERB** ❸ To crease something is to make lines appear on it **creased** ADJECTIVE

**create**, creates, creating, created VERB ❶ To create something is to cause it to happen or exist ❷ When someone creates a new product or process, they invent it **creator** NOUN **creation** NOUN

**creative** ADJECTIVE ❶ Creative people are able to invent and develop original ideas ❷ Creative activities involve the inventing and developing of original ideas

**creature** NOUN any living thing that moves about

**credit** NOUN ❶ If you are allowed credit, you can take something and pay for it later ❷ If you get the credit for something, people praise you for it ❸ If you say someone is a credit to their family or school, you mean that their family or school should be proud of them ❹ IN PLURAL The list of people who helped make a film, record, or television programme is called the credits ✿ **VERB** ❺ If you are credited with an achievement, people believe that you were responsible for it

**credit card** NOUN a plastic card that allows someone to buy goods on credit

**creep**, creeps, creeping, crept VERB To creep is to move quietly and slowly

**creepy**, creepier, creepiest ADJECTIVE INFORMAL strange and frightening

**crescent** NOUN a curved shape that is wider in its middle than at the ends, which are pointed

**crew** NOUN ❶ The crew of a ship, aeroplane, or spacecraft are the people who operate it ❷ people with special technical skills who work together

**crib**, cribs, cribbing, cribbed VERB ❶ INFORMAL If you crib, you copy what someone else has written and pretend it is your own work ✿ **NOUN** ❷ OLD-FASHIONED a baby's cot

**cricket** NOUN ❶ Cricket is an outdoor game played by two teams who take turns at scoring runs by hitting a ball with a bat ❷ a small jumping insect that produces sounds by rubbing its wings together

**crime** NOUN an action for which you can be punished by law

**criminal** NOUN ❶ someone who has committed a crime ✿ **ADJECTIVE** ❷ involving or related to crime

**cripple**, cripples, crippling, crippled VERB ❶ To cripple someone is to injure them severely ❷ To cripple a company or country is to prevent it from working

**crisis**, crises [kry-seez in the plural] NOUN a serious or dangerous situation

**crisp** ADJECTIVE ❶ Something that is crisp is pleasantly fresh and firm ❷ If the air or the weather is crisp, it is pleasantly fresh, cold, and dry ✿ **NOUN** ❸ Crisps are thin slices of potato fried until they are hard and crunchy

**critic** NOUN ❶ someone who writes reviews of books, films, plays, or musical performances ❷ A critic of a person or system is someone who criticizes them publicly

**critical** ADJECTIVE ❶ A critical time is one which is very important in determining what happens in the future ❷ A critical situation is a very serious one ❸ If an ill or injured person is critical, they are in danger of dying ❹ If you are critical of something or someone, you express severe judgments or opinions about them ❺ If you are critical, you examine and judge something carefully **critically** ADVERB

**criticism** NOUN ❶ When there is criticism of someone or something, people express disapproval of them ❷ If you make a criticism, you point out a fault you think someone or something has

**criticize**, criticizes, criticizing, criticized (also **criticise**) VERB If you criticize someone or something, you say what you think is wrong with them

**crocodile** NOUN a large scaly meat-eating reptile which lives in tropical rivers

**crooked** [kroo-kid] ADJECTIVE ❶ bent or twisted ❷ Someone who is crooked is dishonest

**crop**, crops, cropping, cropped NOUN ❶ Crops are plants such as wheat and potatoes that are grown for food ❷ the plants collected at

**cross – crust**

### help with spelling

**Hello Kitty...** remembers that **i** comes before **e** except after **c** when they make the sound 'ee'. Some examples of this are *chief* and *ceiling*.

harvest time ✿ VERB ❸ To crop someone's hair is to cut it very short

**cross**, crosses, crossing, crossed; crosser, crossest VERB ❶ If you cross something such as a room or a road, you go to the other side of it ❷ Lines or roads that cross meet and go across each other ❸ If a thought crosses your mind, you think of it ❹ If you cross your arms, legs, or fingers, you put one on top of the other ✿ NOUN ❺ a vertical bar or line crossed by a shorter horizontal bar or line; also used to describe any object shaped like this ❻ The Cross is the cross-shaped structure on which Jesus Christ was crucified. A cross is also any symbol representing Christ's Cross ❼ a written mark shaped like an X ❽ Something that is a cross between two things is neither one thing nor the other, but a mixture of both ✿ ADJECTIVE ❾ Someone who is cross is rather angry **crossly** ADVERB

**crossword** NOUN a puzzle in which you work out the answers to clues and write them in the white squares of a pattern of black and white squares

**crouch**, crouches, crouching, crouched VERB If you are crouching, you are leaning forward with your legs bent under you

**crow** NOUN ❶ a large black bird which makes a loud, harsh noise ✿ VERB ❷ When a cock crows, it utters a loud squawking sound

**crowd** NOUN ❶ a large group of people gathered together ✿ VERB ❷ When people crowd somewhere, they gather there close together or in large numbers

**crowded** ADJECTIVE A crowded place is full of people

**crown** NOUN ❶ a circular ornament worn on a royal person's head ❷ The crown of something such as your head is the top part of it ✿ VERB ❸ When a king or queen is crowned, a crown is put on their head during their coronation ceremony ❹ When something crowns an event, it is the final part of it

**crude** ADJECTIVE ❶ rough and simple ❷ A crude person speaks or behaves in a rude and offensive way **crudely** ADVERB

**cruel**, crueller, cruellest ADJECTIVE Cruel people deliberately cause pain or distress to other people or to animals **cruelly** ADVERB

**cruelty** NOUN cruel behaviour

**cruise**, cruises, cruising, cruised NOUN ❶ a holiday in which you travel on a ship and visit places ✿ VERB ❷ When a vehicle cruises, it moves at a constant moderate speed

**crumb** NOUN Crumbs are very small pieces of bread or cake

**crumble**, crumbles, crumbling, crumbled VERB When something crumbles, it breaks into small pieces

**crumple**, crumples, crumpling, crumpled VERB To crumple paper or cloth is to squash it so that it is full of creases and folds

**crunch**, crunches, crunching, crunched VERB If you crunch something, you crush it noisily, for example between your teeth or under your feet

**crunchy**, crunchier, crunchiest ADJECTIVE Crunchy food is hard or crisp and makes a noise when you eat it

**crush**, crushes, crushing, crushed VERB ❶ To crush something is to destroy its shape by squeezing it ❷ To crush a substance is to turn it into liquid or powder by squeezing or grinding it ❸ To crush an army or political organization is to defeat it completely ✿ NOUN ❹ a dense crowd of people

**crust** NOUN ❶ the hard outside part of a loaf ❷ a hard layer on top of something

# crutch – current

**crutch**, crutches NOUN a support like a long stick which you lean on to help you walk when you have an injured foot or leg

**cry**, cries, crying, cried VERB ❶ When you cry, tears appear in your eyes ❷ To cry something is to shout it or say it loudly ❀ NOUN ❸ If you have a cry, you cry for a period of time ❹ a shout or other loud sound made with your voice ❺ a loud sound made by some birds

**crystal** NOUN ❶ a piece of a mineral that has formed naturally into a regular shape ❷ Crystal is a type of transparent rock, used in jewellery ❸ Crystal is also a kind of very high quality glass

**cub** NOUN ❶ Some young wild animals are called cubs ❷ The Cubs is an organization for young boys before they join the Scouts

**cube**, cubes, cubing, cubed NOUN ❶ a three-dimensional shape with six equally-sized square surfaces ❷ If you multiply a number by itself twice, you get its cube ❀ VERB ❸ To cube a number is to multiply it by itself twice

**cubic** ADJECTIVE used in measurements of volume

**cucumber** NOUN a long, thin, green-skinned fruit eaten raw in salads

**cuddle**, cuddles, cuddling, cuddled VERB ❶ If you cuddle someone, you hold them affectionately in your arms ❀ NOUN ❷ If you give someone a cuddle, you hold them affectionately in your arms

**cuddly**, cuddlier, cuddliest ADJECTIVE Cuddly people, animals, or toys are soft or pleasing in some way so that you want to cuddle them

**cue**, cues NOUN ❶ something said or done by a performer that is a signal for another performer to begin ❷ a long stick used to hit the balls in snooker and billiards

**cuff** NOUN the end part of a sleeve

**cultivate**, cultivates, cultivating, cultivated VERB ❶ To cultivate land is to grow crops on it ❷ If you cultivate a feeling or attitude, you try to develop it in yourself or other people

**culture** NOUN ❶ Culture refers to the arts and to people's appreciation of them ❷ The culture of a particular society is its ideas, customs, and art **cultural** ADJECTIVE

**cunning** ADJECTIVE ❶ Someone who is cunning uses clever and deceitful methods to get what they want ❀ NOUN ❷ Cunning is the ability to get what you want using clever and deceitful methods

**cup**, cups, cupping, cupped NOUN ❶ a small, round container with a handle, which you drink out of ❷ a large metal container with two handles, given as a prize ❀ VERB ❸ If you cup your hands, you put them together to make a shape like a cup

**cupboard** NOUN a piece of furniture with doors and shelves

**cure**, cures, curing, cured VERB ❶ To cure an illness is to end it ❷ To cure a sick or injured person is to make them well ❸ If something cures you of a habit or attitude, it stops you having it ❹ To cure food, tobacco, or animal skin is to treat it in order to preserve it ❀ NOUN ❺ A cure for an illness is something that cures it

**curiosity** NOUN Curiosity is the desire to know about something or about many things

**curious** ADJECTIVE ❶ Someone who is curious wants to know more about something ❷ Something that is curious is unusual and hard to explain **curiously** ADVERB

**curl** NOUN ❶ Curls are lengths of hair shaped in tight curves and circles ❷ a curved or spiral shape ❀ VERB ❸ If something curls, it moves in a curve or spiral **curly** ADJECTIVE

**currency**, currencies NOUN A country's currency is its coins and banknotes, or its monetary system generally

**current** NOUN ❶ a strong continuous movement of the water in a river or in the sea ❷ An air current is a flowing movement in the air ❸ An electric current is a flow of electricity through a wire or circuit ❀ ADJECTIVE ❹ Something that is current is happening, being done, or being used now **currently** ADVERB

## don't mix up

Don't mix up **cue** (a sign to speak) and **queue** (people lined up).

# curriculum – cynical

**curriculum** [kur-*rik*-yoo-lum], **curriculums** or **curricula** NOUN the different courses taught at a school or university

**curriculum vitae** [*vee*-tie] NOUN Someone's curriculum vitae is a written account of their personal details, education, and work which they send when they apply for a job

**curry**, curries, currying, curried NOUN ❶ Curry is an Indian dish made with hot spices ✿ PHRASE ❷ To **curry favour** with someone means to try to please them by flattering them or doing things to help them

### Did you know…
that the word **curry** comes from a Tamil word *kari* which means 'sauce'? Tamil is a language spoken in southern India.

**curse**, curses, cursing, cursed VERB ❶ To curse is to swear because you are angry ❷ If you curse someone or something, you say angry things about them using rude words ✿ NOUN ❸ what you say when you curse ❹ something supernatural that is supposed to cause unpleasant things to happen to someone

**cursor** NOUN an arrow or box on a computer monitor which indicates where the next letter or symbol is

**curtain** NOUN a hanging piece of material which can be pulled across a window for privacy or to keep out the light

**curve**, curves, curving, curved NOUN ❶ a smooth, gradually bending line ✿ VERB ❷ When something curves, it moves in a curve or has the shape of a curve **curved** ADJECTIVE

**cushion** NOUN a soft object put on a seat to make it more comfortable

**custard** NOUN Custard is a sweet yellow sauce made from milk and eggs or milk and a powder

**custom** NOUN ❶ a traditional activity ❷ something usually done at a particular time or in particular circumstances by a person or by the people in a society ❸ Customs is the place at a border, airport, or harbour where you have to declare any goods you are bringing into a country

**customer** NOUN A shop's or firm's customers are the people who buy its goods

**cut**, cuts, cutting, cut VERB ❶ If you cut something, you use a knife, scissors, or some other sharp tool to mark it or remove parts of it ❷ If you cut yourself, you injure yourself on a sharp object ❸ If you cut the amount of something, you reduce it ✿ NOUN ❹ a mark or injury made with a knife or other sharp tool ❺ a reduction ✿ ADJECTIVE ❻ Well cut clothes have been well designed and made

**cut back** ✿ VERB To cut back or cut back on spending means to reduce it

**cute**, cuter, cutest ADJECTIVE pretty or attractive

**cutlery** NOUN Cutlery is knives, forks, and spoons

**CV** an abbreviation for **curriculum vitae**

**cyberspace** NOUN all of the data stored in a large computer

**cycle**, cycles, cycling, cycled VERB ❶ When you cycle, you ride a bicycle ✿ NOUN ❷ a bicycle or a motorcycle ❸ a series of events which is repeated again and again in the same order ❹ a single complete series of movements or events in process

**cyclist** NOUN someone who rides a bicycle

**cylinder** NOUN a regular three-dimensional shape with two equally-sized flat circular ends joined by a curved surface

**cymbal** NOUN a circular brass plate used as a percussion instrument. Cymbals are clashed together or hit with a stick

**cynical** ADJECTIVE believing that people always behave selfishly or dishonestly **cynically** ADVERB

# dad - dare

**dad** or **daddy** NOUN INFORMAL Your dad or your daddy is your father

**daffodil** NOUN a plant with a yellow trumpet-shaped flower

**daft**, dafter, daftest ADJECTIVE stupid and not sensible

**daily** ADJECTIVE ❶ occurring every day ❷ of or relating to a single day or to one day at a time

**dainty**, daintier, daintiest ADJECTIVE very delicate and pretty **daintily** ADVERB

**dairy**, dairies NOUN ❶ a shop or company that supplies milk and milk products ❋ ADJECTIVE ❷ Dairy products are foods made from milk, such as butter, cheese, cream, and yogurt ❸ A dairy farm is one which keeps cattle to produce milk ❹ in New Zealand, a small shop selling groceries, often outside usual opening hours

**daisy**, daisies NOUN a small wild flower with a yellow centre and small white petals

**dam** NOUN a barrier built across a river to hold back water

**damage**, damages, damaging, damaged VERB ❶ To damage something means to harm or spoil it ❋ NOUN ❷ Damage to something is injury or harm done to it ❸ Damages is the money awarded by a court to compensate someone for loss or harm **damaging** ADJECTIVE

**damp** ADJECTIVE ❶ slightly wet ❋ NOUN ❷ Damp is slight wetness, especially in the air or in the walls of a building

**dance**, dances, dancing, danced VERB ❶ To dance means to move your feet and body rhythmically in time to music ❋ NOUN ❷ a series of rhythmic movements or steps in time to music ❸ a social event where people dance with each other **dancer** NOUN **dancing** NOUN

**dandelion** NOUN a wild plant with yellow flowers which form a ball of fluffy seeds

**danger** NOUN ❶ Danger is the possibility that someone may be harmed or killed ❷ something or someone that can hurt or harm you

**dangerous** ADJECTIVE able to or likely to cause hurt or harm **dangerously** ADVERB

**dare**, dares, daring, dared VERB ❶ To dare someone means to challenge them to do something in order to prove their courage ❷ To dare to do something means to have the courage to do it ❋ NOUN ❸ a challenge to do something dangerous

*Hello Kitty... knows that some words that sound as if they begin with di actually begin with de, like defend.*

**daring - dead**

**daring** ADJECTIVE ❶ bold and willing to take risks ❖ NOUN ❷ the courage required to do things which are dangerous

**dark** ADJECTIVE ❶ If it is dark, there is not enough light to see properly ❷ Dark colours or surfaces reflect little light and so look deep-coloured or dull ❸ 'Dark' is also used to describe thoughts or ideas which are sinister or unpleasant ❖ NOUN ❹ The dark is the lack of light in a place **darkly** ADVERB **darkness** NOUN

**darling** NOUN ❶ Someone who is lovable or a favourite may be called a darling ❖ ADJECTIVE ❷ much admired or loved

**dart** NOUN ❶ a small pointed arrow ❷ Darts is a game in which the players throw darts at a round board divided into numbered sections ❖ VERB ❸ To dart about means to move quickly and suddenly from one place to another

**dash**, dashes, dashing, dashed VERB ❶ To dash somewhere means to rush there ❷ If something is dashed against something else, it strikes it or is thrown violently against it ❸ If hopes or ambitions are dashed, they are ruined or frustrated ❖ NOUN ❹ a sudden movement or rush ❺ a small quantity of something ❻ the punctuation mark (—) which shows a change of subject, or which may be used instead of brackets

**dashboard** NOUN the instrument panel in a motor vehicle

**data** NOUN ❶ information, usually in the form of facts or statistics ❷ any information put into a computer and which the computer works on or processes

**database** NOUN a collection of information stored in a computer

**date**, dates, dating, dated NOUN ❶ a particular day or year that can be named ❷ If you have a date, you have an appointment to meet someone; also used to refer to the person you are meeting ❸ a small dark-brown sticky fruit with a stone inside, which grows on palm trees ❖ VERB ❹ If you are dating someone, you have a romantic relationship with them ❺ If you date something, you find out the time when it began or was made ❻ If something dates from a particular time, that is when it happened or was made ❖ PHRASE ❼ If something is **out of date**, it is old-fashioned or no longer valid

**daughter** NOUN Someone's daughter is their female child

**daughter-in-law**, daughters-in-law NOUN Someone's daughter-in-law is the wife of their son

**dawn** NOUN ❶ the time in the morning when light first appears in the sky ❷ the beginning of something ❖ VERB ❸ If day is dawning, morning light is beginning to appear ❹ If an idea or fact dawns on you, you realize it

**day** NOUN ❶ one of the seven 24-hour periods of time in a week, measured from one midnight to the next ❷ Day is the period of light between sunrise and sunset ❸ You can refer to a particular day or days meaning a particular period in history

**daydream** NOUN ❶ a series of pleasant thoughts about things that you would like to happen ❖ VERB ❷ When you daydream, you drift off into a daydream

**daylight** NOUN ❶ Daylight is the period during the day when it is light ❷ Daylight is also the light from the sun

**dead** ADJECTIVE ❶ no longer living or supporting life ❷ no longer used or no longer functioning ❸ If part of your body goes dead, it loses sensation and feels numb ❖ NOUN

---

**punctuation**

## Tips and tricks...

You put a **dash** (—) to show a change of subject in a sentence or to mark off extra information.

A B C D E F G H I J K L M N O P Q R S T U V W X Y Z

# deadline - decorate

❹ the middle part of night or winter, when it is most quiet and at its darkest or coldest

**deadline** NOUN a time or date before which something must be completed

**deadly**, deadlier, deadliest ADJECTIVE ❶ likely or able to cause death ✿ ADVERB OR ADJECTIVE ❷ 'Deadly' is used to emphasize how serious or unpleasant a situation is

**deaf** ADJECTIVE ❶ partially or totally unable to hear ❷ refusing to listen or pay attention to something

**deafen** VERB If you are deafened by a noise, it is so loud that you cannot hear anything else

**deafening** ADJECTIVE If a noise is deafening, it is so loud that you cannot hear anything else

**deal**, deals, dealing, dealt NOUN ❶ an agreement or arrangement, especially in business ✿ VERB ❷ If you deal with something, you do what is necessary to sort it out ❸ If you deal in a particular type of goods, you buy and sell those goods ❹ If you deal someone or something a blow, you hurt or harm them

**dealer** NOUN a person or firm whose business involves buying or selling things

**dear** NOUN ❶ 'Dear' is used as a sign of affection ✿ ADJECTIVE ❷ much loved ❸ Something that is dear is very expensive ❹ You use 'dear' at the beginning of a letter before the name of the person you are writing to

**death** NOUN Death is the end of the life of a person or animal

**debate** NOUN ❶ Debate is argument or discussion ❷ a formal discussion in which opposing views are expressed ✿ VERB ❸ When people debate something, they discuss it in a fairly formal manner ❹ If you are debating whether or not to do something, you are considering it

**debris** [day-bree] NOUN Debris is fragments or rubble left after something has been destroyed

**debt** [det] NOUN ❶ a sum of money that is owed to one person by another ❷ Debt is the state of owing money

**decade** NOUN a period of ten years

**decay** VERB ❶ When things decay, they rot or go bad ✿ NOUN ❷ Decay is the process of decaying

**deceive**, deceives, deceiving, deceived VERB If you deceive someone, you make them believe something that is not true

**December** NOUN December is the twelfth and last month of the year. It has 31 days

**decent** ADJECTIVE ❶ of an acceptable standard or quality ❷ Decent people are honest and respectable  **decently** ADVERB

**deception** NOUN ❶ something that is intended to trick or deceive someone ❷ Deception is the act of deceiving someone

**deceptive** ADJECTIVE likely to make people believe something that is not true
**deceptively** ADVERB

**decide**, decides, deciding, decided VERB If you decide to do something, you choose to do it

**decimal** ADJECTIVE ❶ The decimal system expresses numbers using all the digits from 0 to 9 ✿ NOUN ❷ a fraction in which a dot called a decimal point is followed by numbers representing tenths, hundredths, and thousandths. For example, 0.5 represents $^5/_{10}$ (or $^1/_2$); 0.05 represents $^5/_{100}$ (or $^1/_{20}$)

**decision** NOUN a choice or judgment that is made about something

**deck** NOUN ❶ a floor or platform built into a ship, or one of the two floors on a bus ❷ a pack of cards

**declaration** NOUN a firm, forceful statement, often an official announcement

**declare**, declares, declaring, declared VERB ❶ If you declare something, you state it forcefully or officially ❷ If you declare goods or earnings, you state what you have bought or earned, in order to pay tax or duty

**decline**, declines, declining, declined VERB ❶ If something declines, it becomes smaller or weaker ❷ If you decline something, you politely refuse to accept it or do it ✿ NOUN ❸ a gradual weakening or decrease

**decorate**, decorates, decorating, decorated VERB ❶ If you decorate something, you make

## how to say it

**Debt** should be said *det* because you do not say the *b*.

**decoration - defy**

it more attractive by adding some ornament or colour to it ❷ If you decorate a room or building, you paint or wallpaper it

**decoration** NOUN ❶ Decorations are features added to something to make it more attractive ❷ The decoration in a building or room is the style of the furniture and wallpaper

**decorative** ADJECTIVE intended to look attractive

**decrease**, decreases, decreasing, decreased VERB ❶ If something decreases or if you decrease it, it becomes less in quantity or size ❀ NOUN ❷ a lessening in the amount of something; also the amount by which something becomes less

**dedicate**, dedicates, dedicating, dedicated VERB If you dedicate yourself to something, you devote your time and energy to it **dedication** NOUN

**deduct** VERB To deduct an amount from a total amount means to subtract it from the total

**deed** NOUN ❶ something that is done ❷ a legal document, especially concerning the ownership of land or buildings

**deep** ADJECTIVE ❶ situated or extending a long way down from the top surface of something, or a long way inwards ❷ great or intense ❸ low in pitch ❹ strong and fairly dark in colour **deeply** ADVERB

**deepen** VERB If something deepens or is deepened, it becomes deeper or more intense

**deer** NOUN a large, hoofed mammal that lives wild in parts of Britain

### don't mix up
Don't mix up **deer** (the animal) and **dear** (much loved).

**default** VERB ❶ If someone defaults on something they have legally agreed to do, they fail to do it ❀ PHRASE ❷ If something happens **by default**, it happens because something else which might have prevented it has failed to happen

**defeat** VERB ❶ If you defeat someone or something, you win a victory over them, or cause them to fail ❀ NOUN ❷ the state of being beaten or of failing or an occasion on which someone is beaten or fails to achieve something

**defective** ADJECTIVE imperfect or faulty

**defence** NOUN ❶ Defence is action that is taken to protect someone or something from attack ❷ any arguments used in support of something that has been criticized or questioned ❸ the case presented, in a court of law, by a lawyer for the person on trial; also the person on trial and his or her lawyers ❹ A country's defences are its military resources, such as its armed forces and weapons

**defend** VERB ❶ To defend someone or something means to protect them from harm or danger ❷ If you defend a person or their ideas and beliefs, you argue in support of them ❸ To defend someone in court means to represent them and argue their case for them ❹ In a game such as football or hockey, to defend means to try to prevent goals being scored by your opponents

**defender** NOUN ❶ a person who protects someone or something from harm or danger ❷ a person who argues in support of something ❸ a person who tries to stop goals being scored in certain sports **defiant** ADJECTIVE **defiantly** ADVERB

**deficit** [*def-iss-it*] NOUN the amount by which money received by an organization is less than money spent

**define** VERB If you define something, you say clearly what it is or what it means

**definite** ADJECTIVE ❶ firm and unlikely to be changed ❷ certain or true rather than guessed or imagined **definitely** ADVERB

**definition** NOUN a statement explaining the meaning of a word or idea

**deform** VERB To deform something means to put it out of shape or spoil its appearance

**deformed** ADJECTIVE disfigured or abnormally shaped

**defy**, defies, defying, defied VERB ❶ If you defy a person or a law, you openly refuse to obey ❷ FORMAL If you defy someone to do something that you think is impossible, you challenge them to do it

A B C D E F G H I J K L M N O P Q R S T U V W X Y Z

71

# degree – dental

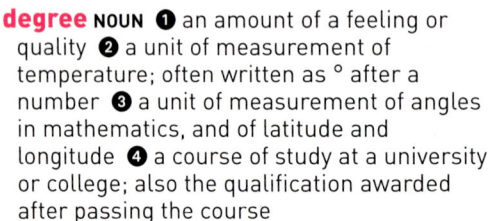

**degree** NOUN ❶ an amount of a feeling or quality ❷ a unit of measurement of temperature; often written as ° after a number ❸ a unit of measurement of angles in mathematics, and of latitude and longitude ❹ a course of study at a university or college; also the qualification awarded after passing the course

**delay** VERB ❶ If you delay doing something, you put it off until a later time ❷ If something delays you, it hinders you or slows you down ✿ NOUN ❸ Delay is time during which something is delayed

**delegate**, delegates, delegating, delegated NOUN ❶ a person appointed to vote or to make decisions on behalf of a group of people ✿ VERB ❷ If you delegate duties, you give them to someone who can then act on your behalf

**delete**, deletes, deleting, deleted VERB To delete something means to cross it out or remove it

**deliberate**, deliberates, deliberating, deliberated ADJECTIVE [di-**lib**-er-at] ❶ done on purpose or planned in advance ❷ careful and not hurried in speech and action ✿ VERB [di-**lib**-er-ayt] ❸ If you deliberate about something, you think about it seriously and carefully **deliberately** ADVERB

**delicate** ADJECTIVE ❶ fine, graceful, or subtle in character ❷ fragile and needing to be handled carefully ❸ precise or sensitive, and able to notice very small changes

**delicatessen** NOUN a shop selling unusual or imported foods

**delicious** ADJECTIVE very pleasing, especially to taste **deliciously** ADVERB

**delight** NOUN ❶ Delight is great pleasure or joy ✿ VERB ❷ If something delights you or if you are delighted by it, it gives you a lot of pleasure **delighted** ADJECTIVE

**deliver** VERB ❶ If you deliver something to someone, you take it to them and give them it ❷ To deliver a lecture or speech means to give it

**delivery**, deliveries NOUN ❶ Delivery or a delivery is the bringing of letters or goods to a person or firm ❷ Someone's delivery is the way in which they give a speech

**demand** VERB ❶ If you demand something, you ask for it forcefully and urgently ❷ If a job or situation demands a particular quality, it needs it ✿ NOUN ❸ a forceful request for something ❹ If there is a demand for something, a lot of people want to buy it or have it

**democracy**, democracies NOUN Democracy is a system of government in which the people choose their leaders by voting for them in elections

**democrat** NOUN a person who believes in democracy, personal freedom, and equality

**democratic** ADJECTIVE having representatives elected by the people

**demolish**, demolishes, demolishing, demolished VERB To demolish a building means to pull it down or break it up **demolition** NOUN

**demonstrate**, demonstrates, demonstrating, demonstrated VERB ❶ To demonstrate a fact or theory means to prove or show it to be true ❷ If you demonstrate something to somebody, you show and explain it by using or doing the thing itself ❸ If people demonstrate, they take part in a march or rally to show their opposition or support for something

**demonstration** NOUN ❶ a talk or explanation to show how to do or use something ❷ Demonstration is proof that something exists or is true ❸ a public march or rally in support of or opposition to something **demonstrator** NOUN

**den** NOUN ❶ the home of some wild animals such as lions or foxes ❷ a secret place where people meet

**denial** NOUN ❶ A denial of something is a statement that it is untrue ❷ The denial of a request or something to which you have a right is the refusal of it

**denim** NOUN ❶ Denim is strong cotton cloth, used for making clothes ❷ IN PLURAL Denims are jeans made from denim

**dense** ADJECTIVE ❶ thickly crowded or packed together ❷ difficult to see through **densely** ADVERB

**density**, densities NOUN the degree to which something is filled or occupied

**dent** VERB ❶ To dent something means to damage it by hitting it and making a hollow in its surface ✿ NOUN ❷ a hollow in the surface of something

**dental** ADJECTIVE relating to the teeth

**dentist – design**

**dentist** NOUN a person who is qualified to treat people's teeth

**deny**, denies, denying, denied VERB ❶ If you deny something that has been said, you state that it is untrue ❷ If you deny that something is the case, you refuse to believe it ❸ If you deny someone something, you refuse to give it to them

**deodorant** NOUN a substance or spray used to hide the smell of perspiration

**depart** VERB When you depart, you leave **departure** NOUN

**department** NOUN one of the sections into which an organization is divided

**depend** VERB ❶ If you depend on someone or something, you trust them and rely on them ❷ If one thing depends on another, it is influenced by it

**dependable** ADJECTIVE reliable and trustworthy

**dependence** NOUN Dependence is a constant need that someone has for something or someone in order to survive or operate properly

**dependent** ADJECTIVE reliant on someone or something

**deposit** VERB ❶ If you deposit something, you put it down or leave it somewhere ❷ If you deposit money or valuables, you put them somewhere for safekeeping ❸ If something is deposited on a surface, a layer of it is left there as a result of chemical or geological action ✿ NOUN ❹ a sum of money given in part payment for goods or services

**depot** [dep-oh] NOUN a place where large supplies of materials or equipment may be stored

**depress**, depresses, depressing, depressed VERB If something depresses you, it makes you feel sad and gloomy

**depressed** ADJECTIVE ❶ unhappy and gloomy ❷ A place that is depressed has little economic activity and therefore low incomes and high unemployment

**depression** NOUN ❶ a state of mind in which someone feels unhappy and has no energy or enthusiasm ❷ a time of industrial and economic decline ❸ A depression is a mass of air that has low pressure and often causes rain ❹ A depression in the surface of something is a part which is lower than the rest

**deprive**, deprives, depriving, deprived VERB If you deprive someone of something, you take it away or prevent them from having it **deprived** ADJECTIVE

**depth** NOUN ❶ The depth of something is the measurement or distance between its top and bottom, or between its front and back ❷ The depth of something such as emotion is its intensity

**deputy**, deputies NOUN Someone's deputy is a person appointed to act in their place

**descend** VERB ❶ To descend means to move downwards ❷ If you descend on people or on a place, you arrive unexpectedly

**describe**, describes, describing, described VERB To describe someone or something means to give an account or a picture of them in words

**description** NOUN an account or picture of something in words

**desert** [dez-ert] NOUN a region of land with very little plant life, usually because of low rainfall

### how to say it

In **desert**, the force is on *dez* for the noun and on *ert* for the verb.

**desert** [dez-zert] VERB To desert a person means to leave or abandon them

**deserve**, deserves, deserving, deserved VERB If you deserve something, you are entitled to it or earn it because of your qualities, achievements, or actions

**design** VERB ❶ To design something means to plan it, especially by preparing a detailed sketch or drawings from which it can be built or made ✿ NOUN ❷ a drawing or plan from which something can be built or made ❸ The design of something is its shape and style **designer** NOUN

73

## desirable – determine

**desirable** ADJECTIVE ❶ worth having or doing ❷ sexually attractive

**desire**, desires, desiring, desired VERB ❶ If you desire something, you want it very much ✿ NOUN ❷ a strong feeling of wanting something

**desk** NOUN ❶ a piece of furniture designed for working at or writing on ❷ a counter or table in a public building behind which a receptionist sits

**desktop** ADJECTIVE of a convenient size to be used on a desk or table

**despair** NOUN ❶ Despair is a total loss of hope ✿ VERB ❷ If you despair, you lose hope

**desperate** ADJECTIVE ❶ If you are desperate, you are so worried or frightened that you will try anything to improve your situation ❷ A desperate person is violent and dangerous ❸ A desperate situation is extremely dangerous or serious **desperately** ADVERB **desperation** NOUN

**despise**, despises, despising, despised VERB If you despise someone or something, you dislike them very much

**despite** PREPOSITION in spite of

**dessert** [diz-ert] NOUN a sweet food served after the main course of a meal

**destination** NOUN a place to which someone or something is going or is being sent

**destiny**, destinies NOUN ❶ Your destiny is all the things that happen to you in your life, especially when they are considered to be outside human control ❷ Destiny is the force which some people believe controls everyone's life

**destroy** VERB ❶ To destroy something means to damage it so much that it is completely ruined ❷ To destroy something means to put an end to it

**destruction** NOUN Destruction is the act of destroying something or the state of being destroyed

**destructive** ADJECTIVE causing or able to cause great harm, damage, or injury

**detach**, detaches, detaching, detached VERB To detach something means to remove it

**detached** ADJECTIVE ❶ separate or standing apart ❷ having no real interest or emotional involvement in something

**detail** NOUN ❶ an individual fact or feature of something ❷ Detail is all the small features that make up the whole of something **detailed** ADJECTIVE

**detect** VERB ❶ If you detect something, you notice it ❷ To detect something means to find it

**detection** NOUN ❶ Detection is the act of noticing, discovering, or sensing something ❷ Detection is also the work of investigating crime

**detective** NOUN a person, usually a police officer, whose job is to investigate crimes

**detergent** NOUN a chemical substance used for washing or cleaning things

**deteriorate**, deteriorates, deteriorating, deteriorated VERB If something deteriorates, it gets worse **deterioration** NOUN

**determination** NOUN Determination is great firmness, after you have made up your mind to do something

**determine**, determines, determining, determined VERB ❶ If something determines a situation or result, it causes it or controls it ❷ To determine something means to decide or settle it firmly ❸ To determine something means to find out or calculate the facts about it

### don't mix up

Hello Kitty... never mixes up **dessert** (the sweet food at the end of a meal) and **desert** (to leave without warning).

**determined – die**

**determined** ADJECTIVE firmly decided

**detest** VERB If you detest someone or something, you strongly dislike them

**devastate**, devastates, devastating, devastated VERB To devastate an area or place means to damage it severely or destroy it  **devastation** NOUN

**develop** VERB ❶ When something develops or is developed, it grows or becomes more advanced ❷ To develop an area of land means to build on it ❸ To develop an illness or a fault means to become affected by it

**development** NOUN ❶ Development is gradual growth or progress ❷ The development of land or water is the process of making it more useful or profitable by the expansion of industry or housing ❸ a new stage in a series of events

**device** NOUN ❶ a machine or tool that is used for a particular purpose ❷ a plan or scheme

**devil** NOUN ❶ In Christianity and Judaism, the Devil is the spirit of evil and enemy of God ❷ an evil spirit

**devise**, devises, devising, devised VERB To devise something means to work it out

**devote**, devotes, devoting, devoted VERB If you devote yourself to something, you give all your time, energy, or money to it

**devoted** ADJECTIVE very loving and loyal

**dew** NOUN Dew is drops of moisture that form on the ground and other cool surfaces at night

**diagnose**, diagnoses, diagnosing, diagnosed VERB To diagnose an illness or problem means to identify exactly what is wrong

**diagnosis**, diagnoses NOUN the identification of what is wrong with someone who is ill

**diagonal** ADJECTIVE in a slanting direction  **diagonally** ADVERB

**diagram** NOUN a drawing that shows or explains something

**dial**, dials, dialling, dialled NOUN ❶ the face of a clock or meter, with divisions marked on it so that a time or measurement can be recorded and read ❷ a part of a device, such as a radio, used to control or tune it ✿ VERB ❸ To dial a telephone number means to press the number keys to select the required number

**dialect** NOUN a form of a language spoken in a particular geographical area

**dialogue** NOUN ❶ In a novel, play, or film, dialogue is conversation ❷ Dialogue is communication or discussion between people or groups of people

**diameter** NOUN The diameter of a circle is the length of a straight line drawn across it through its centre

**diamond** NOUN ❶ a precious stone made of pure carbon ❷ a shape with four straight sides of equal length forming two opposite angles less than 90° and two opposite angles greater than 90° ❸ Diamonds is one of the four suits in a pack of playing cards. It is marked by a red diamond-shaped symbol ✿ ADJECTIVE ❹ A diamond anniversary is the 60th anniversary of an event

**diarrhoea** [dy-a-**ree**-a] NOUN Diarrhoea is a condition in which the faeces are more liquid and frequent than usual

**diary**, diaries NOUN a book which has a separate space or page for each day of the year on which to keep a record of appointments

**dice**, dices, dicing, diced NOUN ❶ a small cube which has each side marked with dots representing the numbers one to six ✿ VERB ❷ To dice food means to cut it into small cubes

**dictate**, dictates, dictating, dictated VERB ❶ If you dictate something, you say or read it aloud for someone else to write down ❷ To dictate something means to command or state what must happen  **dictation** NOUN

**dictator** NOUN A dictator is a ruler who has complete power in a country, especially one who has taken power by force

**dictionary**, dictionaries NOUN a book in which words are listed alphabetically and explained, or equivalent words are given in another language

**die**, dies, dying, died VERB ❶ When people, animals, or plants die, they stop living ❷ When something dies, dies away, or dies down, it gradually fades away ✿ NOUN ❸ a dice

### don't mix up

Don't mix up **die** (to stop living) and **dye** (to change the colour).

75

**die out – diplomacy**

**die out** VERB When something dies out, it ceases to exist

**diesel** [*dee-zel*] NOUN ❶ a heavy fuel used in trains, buses, and lorries ❷ a vehicle with a diesel engine

**diet** NOUN ❶ Someone's diet is the usual food that they eat ❷ a special restricted selection of foods that someone eats to improve their health or regulate their weight

**differ** VERB ❶ If two or more things differ, they are unlike each other ❷ If people differ, they have opposing views or disagree about something

**difference** NOUN ❶ The difference between things is the way in which they are unlike each other ❷ The difference between two numbers is the amount by which one is less than another ❸ A difference in someone or something is a significant change in them

**different** ADJECTIVE ❶ unlike something else ❷ unusual and out of the ordinary ❸ distinct and separate, although of the same kind **differently** ADVERB

**difficult** ADJECTIVE ❶ not easy to do, understand, or solve ❷ hard to deal with, especially because of being unreasonable or unpredictable

**difficulty**, difficulties NOUN ❶ a problem ❷ Difficulty is the fact or quality of being difficult

**dig** VERB ❶ If you dig, you break up soil or sand, especially with a spade or garden fork ❷ To dig something into an object means to push, thrust, or poke it in NOUN ❸ a prod or jab, especially in the ribs ❹ INFORMAL A dig at someone is a spiteful or unpleasant remark intended to hurt or embarrass them

**digest** VERB ❶ To digest food means to break it down in the gut so that it can be easily absorbed and used by the body ❷ If you digest information or a fact, you understand it and take it in

**digestion** NOUN ❶ Digestion is the process of digesting food ❷ Your digestion is your ability to digest food

**digit** [*dij-it*] NOUN a written symbol for any of the numbers from 0 to 9

**digital** ADJECTIVE displaying information, especially time, by numbers, rather than by a pointer moving round a dial

**dignified** ADJECTIVE full of dignity

**dignity** NOUN Dignity is behaviour which is serious, calm, and controlled

**dilemma** NOUN a situation in which a choice has to be made between alternatives that are equally difficult or unpleasant

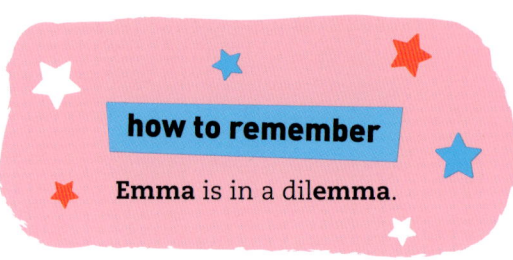

### how to remember

**Emma** is in a dil**emma**.

**diligent** ADJECTIVE hard-working, and showing care and perseverance **diligently** ADVERB **diligence** NOUN

**dilute**, dilutes, diluting, diluted VERB To dilute a liquid means to add water or another liquid to it to make it less concentrated

**dim**, dimmer, dimmest; dims, dimming, dimmed ADJECTIVE ❶ badly lit and lacking in brightness ❷ very vague and unclear in your mind ❸ INFORMAL stupid or mentally dull VERB ❹ If lights dim or are dimmed, they become less bright **dimly** ADVERB

**dine**, dines, dining, dined VERB FORMAL To dine means to eat dinner in the evening

**dinner** NOUN ❶ the main meal of the day, eaten either in the evening or at lunchtime ❷ a formal social occasion in the evening, at which a meal is served

**dinosaur** [*dy-no-sor*] NOUN a large reptile which lived in prehistoric times

**dip**, dips, dipping, dipped VERB ❶ If you dip something into a liquid, you lower it or plunge it quickly into the liquid ❷ If something dips, it slopes downwards or goes below a certain level ❸ To dip also means to make a quick, slight downward movement NOUN ❹ a rich creamy mixture which you scoop up with biscuits or raw vegetables and eat

**diploma** NOUN a certificate awarded to a student who has successfully completed a course of study

**diplomacy** NOUN ❶ Diplomacy is the managing of relationships between countries ❷ Diplomacy is also skill in

76

**diplomat – disco**

dealing with people without offending or upsetting them **diplomatic** ADJECTIVE **diplomatically** ADVERB

**diplomat** NOUN an official who negotiates and deals with another country on behalf of his or her own country

**direct** ADJECTIVE ❶ moving or aimed in a straight line or by the shortest route ❷ straightforward, and without delay or evasion ❸ without anyone or anything intervening ❹ exact ✿ VERB ❺ To direct something means to guide and control it ❻ To direct people or things means to send them, tell them, or show them the way ❼ To direct a film, a play, or a television programme means to organize the way it is made and performed

**direction** NOUN ❶ the general line that someone or something is moving or pointing in ❷ Direction is the controlling and guiding of something ❸ IN PLURAL Directions are instructions that tell you how to do something or how to get somewhere

**directly** ADVERB in a straight line or immediately

**director** NOUN ❶ a member of the board of a company or institution ❷ the person responsible for the making and performance of a programme, play, or film

**directory**, directories NOUN ❶ a book which gives lists of facts, such as names and addresses, and is usually arranged in alphabetical order ❷ another name for **folder**

**dirt** NOUN ❶ Dirt is any unclean substance, such as dust, mud, or stains ❷ Dirt is also earth or soil

**dirty**, dirtier, dirtiest ADJECTIVE ❶ marked or covered with dirt ❷ unfair or dishonest ❸ about sex in a way that many people find offensive

**disability**, disabilities NOUN a physical or mental condition or illness that restricts someone's way of life

**disabled** ADJECTIVE lacking one or more physical powers, such as the ability to walk or to coordinate one's movements

**disadvantage** NOUN an unfavourable or harmful circumstance

**disagree**, disagrees, disagreeing, disagreed VERB ❶ If you disagree with someone, you have a different view or opinion from theirs ❷ If you disagree with an action or proposal, you disapprove of it and believe it is wrong ❸ If food or drink disagrees with you, it makes you feel unwell

**disagreement** NOUN ❶ a dispute about something ❷ an objection to something

**disappear**, disappears, disappearing, disappeared VERB ❶ If something or someone disappears, they go out of sight or become lost ❷ To disappear also means to stop existing or happening **disappearance** NOUN

**disappoint** VERB If someone or something disappoints you, it fails to live up to what you expected of it

**disappointed** ADJECTIVE sad because something has not happened

**disappointment** NOUN ❶ a feeling of being disappointed ❷ something that disappoints you

**disapproval** NOUN the belief that something is wrong or inappropriate

**disapprove**, disapproves, disapproving, disapproved VERB To disapprove of something or someone means to believe they are wrong or bad

**disaster** NOUN ❶ an event or accident that causes great distress or destruction ❷ a complete failure **disastrous** ADJECTIVE

**disc** or **disk** NOUN ❶ a flat round object ❷ in computing, another spelling of **disk**

**discard** VERB To discard something means to get rid of it, because you no longer want it or find it useful

**discipline**, disciplines, disciplining, disciplined NOUN ❶ Discipline is making people obey rules and punishing them when they break them ❷ Discipline is the ability to behave and work in a controlled way ✿ VERB ❸ If you discipline yourself, you train yourself to behave and work in an ordered way ❹ To discipline someone means to punish them

**disc jockey**, disc jockeys NOUN someone who introduces and plays pop records on the radio or at a night club

**disclose**, discloses, disclosing, disclosed VERB To disclose something means to make it known or allow it to be seen

**disco**, discos NOUN a party or a club where people go to dance to pop records

## discomfort – dismiss

**discomfort** NOUN ❶ Discomfort is distress or slight pain ❷ Discomfort is also a feeling of worry or embarrassment ❸ Discomforts are things that make you uncomfortable

**disconnect** VERB ❶ To disconnect something means to detach it from something else ❷ If someone disconnects your fuel supply or telephone, they cut you off

**discount** NOUN ❶ a reduction in the price of something ✿ VERB ❷ If you discount something, you reject it or ignore it

**discourage**, discourages, discouraging, discouraged VERB To discourage someone means to take away their enthusiasm to do something

**discover** VERB When you discover something, you find it or find out about it **discovery** NOUN

**discreet** ADJECTIVE If you are discreet, you avoid causing embarrassment when dealing with secret or private matters

**discriminate**, discriminates, discriminating, discriminated VERB ❶ To discriminate between things means to recognize and understand the differences between them ❷ To discriminate against a person or group means to treat them unfairly, usually because of their race, colour, or sex ❸ To discriminate in favour of a person or group means to treat them more favourably than others **discrimination** NOUN

**discus**, discuses NOUN a disc-shaped object with a heavy middle, thrown by athletes

**discuss**, discusses, discussing, discussed VERB ❶ When people discuss something, they talk about it in detail ❷ To discuss a question is to look at the points or arguments of both sides and try to reach your own opinion

**discussion** NOUN a conversation or piece of writing in which a subject is considered in detail

**disease** NOUN an unhealthy condition in people, animals, or plants

**disgrace**, disgraces, disgracing, disgraced NOUN ❶ Disgrace is a state in which people disapprove of someone ❷ If something is a disgrace, it is unacceptable ❸ If someone is a disgrace to a group of people, their behaviour makes the group feel ashamed ✿ VERB ❹ If you disgrace yourself or disgrace someone else, you cause yourself or them to be strongly disapproved of by other people

**disgraceful** ADJECTIVE If something is disgraceful, people disapprove of it strongly and think that those who are responsible for it should be ashamed **disgracefully** ADVERB

**disguise**, disguises, disguising, disguised VERB ❶ To disguise something means to change its appearance so that people do not recognize it ❷ To disguise a feeling means to hide it ✿ NOUN ❸ something you wear or something you do to alter your appearance so that you cannot be recognized by other people

**disgust** NOUN ❶ Disgust is a strong feeling of dislike or disapproval ✿ VERB ❷ To disgust someone means to make them feel a strong sense of dislike or disapproval **disgusted** ADJECTIVE

**disgusting** ADJECTIVE very unpleasant and offensive

**dish**, dishes NOUN ❶ a shallow container for cooking or serving food ❷ food of a particular kind or food cooked in a particular way

**dishonest** ADJECTIVE not truthful or able to be trusted

**dishonesty** NOUN Dishonesty is behaviour which is meant to deceive people, either by not telling the truth or by cheating

**disinfectant** NOUN a chemical substance that kills germs

**disk** NOUN ❶ In a computer, the disk is the part where information is stored ❷ another spelling of **disc**

**dislike**, dislikes, disliking, disliked VERB ❶ If you dislike something or someone, you think they are unpleasant and do not like them ✿ NOUN ❷ Dislike is a feeling that you have when you do not like someone or something

**dismay** NOUN ❶ Dismay is a feeling of fear and worry ✿ VERB ❷ If someone or something dismays you, it fills you with alarm and worry

**dismiss**, dismisses, dismissing, dismissed VERB ❶ If you dismiss something, you decide to ignore it because it is not important enough for you to think about ❷ To dismiss an employee means to ask that person to leave their job ❸ If someone in authority dismisses you, they tell you to leave

**disobey** VERB To disobey a person or an order means to refuse deliberately to do what you are told

**disorganized** or **disorganised** ADJECTIVE If something is disorganized, it is confused and badly prepared or badly arranged

**dispenser** NOUN a machine or container from which you can get things

**display**, displays, displaying, displayed VERB ❶ If you display something, you show it or make it visible to people ❷ If you display something such as an emotion, you behave in a way that shows you feel it ✿ NOUN ❸ an arrangement of things designed to attract people's attention

**disposable** ADJECTIVE designed to be thrown away after use

**disposal** NOUN Disposal is the act of getting rid of something that is no longer wanted or needed

**dispose**, disposes, disposing, disposed VERB ❶ To dispose of something means to get rid of it ❷ If you are not disposed to do something, you are not willing to do it

**dispute**, disputes, disputing, disputed NOUN ❶ an argument ✿ VERB ❷ To dispute a fact or theory means to question the truth of it

**disqualify**, disqualifies, disqualifying, disqualified VERB If someone is disqualified from a competition or activity, they are officially stopped from taking part in it

**disrupt** VERB To disrupt something such as an event or system means to break it up or throw it into confusion **disruption** NOUN **disruptive** ADJECTIVE

**dissatisfied** ADJECTIVE not pleased or not contented

**dissect** VERB To dissect a plant or a dead body means to cut it up so that it can be scientifically examined **dissection** NOUN

**dissolve**, dissolves, dissolving, dissolved VERB ❶ If you dissolve something or if it dissolves in a liquid, it becomes mixed with and absorbed in the liquid ❷ To dissolve an organization or institution means to end it officially

**distance**, distances, distancing, distanced NOUN ❶ The distance between two points is how far it is between them ❷ Distance is the fact of being far away in space or time ✿ VERB ❸ If you distance yourself from someone or something or are distanced from them, you become less involved with them

**distant** ADJECTIVE ❶ far away in space or time ❷ A distant relative is one who is not closely related to you ❸ Someone who is distant is cold and unfriendly

**distinct** ADJECTIVE ❶ If one thing is distinct from another, it is recognizably different from it ❷ If something is distinct, you can hear, smell, or see it clearly and plainly ❸ If something such as a fact, idea, or intention is distinct, it is clear and definite

**distinction** NOUN ❶ a difference between two things ❷ Distinction is a quality of excellence and superiority ❸ a special honour or claim

**distinguish**, distinguishes, distinguishing, distinguished VERB ❶ To distinguish between things means to recognize the difference between them ❷ To distinguish something means to make it out by seeing, hearing, or tasting it ❸ If you distinguish yourself, you do something that makes people think highly of you

**distract** VERB If something distracts you, your attention is taken away from what you are doing

**distraction** NOUN ❶ something that takes people's attention away from something ❷ an activity that is intended to amuse or relax someone

**distress**, distresses, distressing, distressed NOUN ❶ Distress is great suffering caused by pain or sorrow ❷ Distress is also the state of needing help because of difficulties or danger ✿ VERB ❸ To distress someone means to make them feel alarmed or unhappy

**how to say it**

**Dissect** should be said *die-***sekt** with most force on *sekt*.

# distressing – document

**distressing** ADJECTIVE very worrying or upsetting

**distribute**, distributes, distributing, distributed VERB ❶ To distribute something such as leaflets means to hand them out or deliver them ❷ If things are distributed, they are spread throughout an area or space ❸ To distribute something means to divide it and share it out among a number of people

**distribution** NOUN ❶ Distribution is the delivering of something to various people or organizations ❷ Distribution is the sharing out of something to various people

**district** NOUN an area of a town or country

**disturb** VERB ❶ If you disturb someone, you break their peace or privacy ❷ If something disturbs you, it makes you feel upset or worried ❸ If something is disturbed, it is moved out of position or meddled with **disturbing** ADJECTIVE

**disturbance** NOUN ❶ Disturbance is the state of being disturbed ❷ a violent or unruly incident in public **disused** ADJECTIVE

**ditch**, ditches NOUN a channel at the side of a road or field, to drain away excess water

**dive**, dives, diving, dived VERB ❶ To dive means to jump into water with your arms held straight above your head ❷ If you go diving, you go down under the surface of the sea or a lake using special breathing equipment ❸ If an aircraft or bird dives, it flies in a steep downward path, or drops sharply **diver** NOUN **diving** NOUN

**diverse** ADJECTIVE ❶ If a group of things is diverse, it is made up of different kinds of things ❷ People, ideas, or objects that are diverse are very different from each other

**diversion** NOUN ❶ a special route arranged for traffic when the usual route is closed ❷ something that takes your attention away from what you should be concentrating on ❸ a pleasant or amusing activity

**divert** VERB To divert something means to change the course or direction it is following

**divide**, divides, dividing, divided VERB ❶ When something divides or is divided, it is split up and separated into two or more parts ❷ If something divides two areas, it forms a barrier between them ❸ If people divide over something or if something divides them, it causes strong disagreement between them ❹ In mathematics, when you divide, you calculate how many times one number contains another ✿ NOUN ❺ a separation

**division** NOUN ❶ Division is the separation of something into two or more distinct parts ❷ Division is also the process of dividing one number by another ❸ a difference of opinion that causes separation between ideas or groups of people ❹ any one of the parts or groups into which something is split

**divorce**, divorces, divorcing, divorced NOUN ❶ Divorce is the formal and legal ending of a marriage ✿ VERB ❷ When a married couple divorce, their marriage is legally ended **divorced** ADJECTIVE

**DIY** NOUN DIY is the activity of making or repairing things yourself. DIY is an abbreviation for 'do-it-yourself'

**dizzy**, dizzier, dizziest ADJECTIVE having or causing a whirling sensation **dizziness** NOUN

**do**, does, doing, did, done VERB ❶ Do is an auxiliary verb, which is used to form questions, negatives, and to give emphasis to the main verb of a sentence ❷ If someone does a task or activity, they perform it and finish it ❸ If you ask what people do, you want to know what their job is ❹ If you do well at something, you are successful. If you do badly, you are unsuccessful ❺ If something will do, it is adequate but not the most suitable option

**do up** ✿ VERB To do up something old means to repair and decorate it

**dock** NOUN ❶ an enclosed area in a harbour where ships go to be loaded, unloaded, or repaired ❷ In a court of law, the dock is the place where the accused person stands or sits ✿ VERB ❸ When a ship docks, it is brought into dock at the end of its voyage ❹ To dock someone's wages means to deduct an amount from the sum they would normally receive ❺ To dock an animal's tail means to cut part of it off

**doctor** NOUN ❶ a person who is qualified in medicine and treats people who are ill ❷ A doctor of an academic subject is someone who has been awarded the highest academic degree ✿ VERB ❸ To doctor something means to alter it in order to deceive people

**document** NOUN ❶ a piece of paper which

# documentary – down

provides an official record of something ❷ a piece of text or graphics stored in a computer as a file that can be amended or altered by document processing software ✿ **VERB** ❸ If you document something, you make a detailed record of it

**documentary**, documentaries **NOUN** ❶ a radio or television programme, or a film, which gives information on real events ✿ **ADJECTIVE** ❷ Documentary evidence is made up of written or official records

**dodge**, dodges, dodging, dodged **VERB** ❶ If you dodge or dodge something, you move suddenly to avoid being seen, hit, or caught ❷ If you dodge something such as an issue or accusation, you avoid dealing with it

**does** the third person singular of the present tense of **do**

**dog**, dogs, dogging, dogged **NOUN** ❶ a four-legged, meat-eating animal, kept as a pet, or to guard property or go hunting ✿ **VERB** ❷ If you dog someone, you follow them very closely and never leave them

**doll NOUN** a child's toy which looks like a baby or person

**dollar NOUN** the main unit of currency in Australia, New Zealand, the USA, Canada, and some other countries. A dollar is worth 100 cents

**dolphin NOUN** a mammal which lives in the sea and looks like a large fish with a long snout

**dome NOUN** a round roof

**domestic ADJECTIVE** ❶ happening or existing within one particular country ❷ involving or concerned with the home and family

**dominate**, dominates, dominating, dominated **VERB** ❶ If something or someone dominates a situation or event, they are the most powerful or important thing in it and have control over it ❷ If a person or country dominates other people or places, they have power or control over them ❸ If something dominates an area, it towers over it

**donate**, donates, donating, donated **VERB** To donate something to a charity or organization means to give it as a gift **donation NOUN**

**done** the past participle of **do**

**donkey**, donkeys **NOUN** an animal like a horse, but smaller and with longer ears

**donor NOUN** ❶ someone who gives some of their blood while they are alive or an organ after their death to be used to help someone who is ill ❷ someone who gives something such as money to a charity or other organization

**door NOUN** a swinging or sliding panel for opening or closing the entrance to something; also the entrance itself

**doorway NOUN** an opening in a wall for a door

**dormitory**, dormitories **NOUN** a large bedroom where several people sleep

**dose**, doses **NOUN** a measured amount of a medicine or drug

**dot**, dots, dotting, dotted **NOUN** ❶ a very small, round mark ✿ **VERB** ❷ If things dot an area, they are scattered all over it

**double**, doubles, doubling, doubled **ADJECTIVE** ❶ twice the usual size ❷ consisting of two parts ✿ **VERB** ❸ If something doubles, it becomes twice as large ❹ To double as something means to have a second job or use as well as the main one ✿ **NOUN** ❺ Your double is someone who looks exactly like you

**double bass**, double basses **NOUN** a musical instrument like a large violin, which you play standing up

**doubt NOUN** ❶ Doubt is a feeling of uncertainty about whether something is true or possible ✿ **VERB** ❷ If you doubt something, you think that it is probably not true or possible

**doubtful ADJECTIVE** unlikely or uncertain

**dough** [rhymes with **go**] **NOUN** Dough is a mixture of flour and water and sometimes other ingredients, used to make bread, pastry, or biscuits

**doughnut NOUN** a ring of sweet dough cooked in hot fat

**dove NOUN** a bird like a small pigeon

**down PREPOSITION OR ADVERB** ❶ Down means towards the ground, towards a lower level, or in a lower place ❷ If you go down a road or river, you go along it ✿ **ADVERB** ❸ If you put something down, you place it on a surface ❹ If an amount of something goes down, it decreases ✿ **ADJECTIVE** ❺ If you feel down, you feel depressed ✿ **VERB** ❻ If you down a drink, you drink it quickly

# downhill - draw

❖ NOUN ❼ Down is the small, soft feathers on young birds

**downhill** ADVERB ❶ moving down a slope ❷ becoming worse

**download** VERB ❶ If you download data you transfer it from the memory of one computer to that of another, especially over the internet ❖ NOUN ❷ a piece of data transferred in this way

**downpour** NOUN a heavy fall of rain

**downstairs** ADVERB ❶ going down a staircase towards the ground floor ❖ ADJECTIVE OR ADVERB ❷ on a lower floor or on the ground floor

**downwards** or **downward** ADVERB OR ADJECTIVE ❶ If you move or look downwards, you move or look towards the ground or towards a lower level ❷ If an amount or rate moves downwards, it decreases

**doze**, dozes, dozing, dozed VERB ❶ When you doze, you sleep lightly for a short period ❖ NOUN ❷ a short, light sleep

**dozen** NOUN A dozen things are twelve of them

**Dr** [*dock-ter*] 'Dr' is short for 'Doctor' and is used before the name of someone with the highest form of academic degree or who practises medicine

**drab**, drabber, drabbest ADJECTIVE dull and unattractive

**draft** NOUN ❶ an early rough version of a document or speech ❖ VERB ❷ When you draft a document or speech, you write the first rough version of it ❸ To draft people somewhere means to move them there so that they can do a specific job ❹ In Australian and New Zealand English, to draft cattle or sheep is to select some from a herd or flock

### don't mix up

Don't mix up **draft** (a rough version) and **draught** (cold air).

**drag**, drags, dragging, dragged VERB ❶ If you drag a heavy object somewhere, you pull it slowly and with difficulty ❷ If you drag someone somewhere, you make them go although they may be unwilling ❸ If things drag behind you, they trail along the ground as you move along ❹ If an event or a period of time drags, it is boring and seems to last a long time ❖ NOUN ❺ Drag is the resistance to the motion of a body passing through air or a fluid

**dragon** NOUN In stories and legends, a dragon is a fierce animal like a large lizard with wings and claws that breathes fire

**dragonfly**, dragonflies NOUN a colourful insect which is often found near water

**drain** VERB ❶ If you drain something, you cause liquid to flow out of it ❷ If you drain a glass, you drink all its contents ❸ If liquid drains somewhere, it flows there ❹ If something drains strength or resources, it gradually uses them up ❖ NOUN ❺ a pipe or channel that carries water or sewage away from a place ❻ a metal grid in a road, through which rainwater flows

**drama** NOUN ❶ a serious play for the theatre, television, or radio ❷ Drama is plays and the theatre in general ❸ You can refer to the exciting events or aspects of a situation as drama

**dramatic** ADJECTIVE A dramatic change or event happens suddenly and is very noticeable **dramatically** ADVERB

**dramatist** NOUN a person who writes plays

**drape**, drapes, draping, draped VERB If you drape a piece of cloth, you arrange it so that it hangs down or covers something in loose folds

**drastic** ADJECTIVE A drastic course of action is very severe and is usually taken urgently

**draught** [*draft*] NOUN ❶ a current of cold air ❷ an amount of liquid that you swallow ❸ Draughts is a game for two people played on a chessboard with round pieces

**draw**, draws, drawing, drew, drawn VERB ❶ When you draw, you use a pen or crayon to make a picture or diagram ❷ To draw near means to move closer. To draw away or draw back means to move away ❸ If you draw something in a particular direction, you pull it there smoothly and gently ❹ If you

**draw up - droop**

draw a deep breath, you breathe in deeply ❺ If you draw the curtains, you pull them so that they cover or uncover the window ❻ If something such as water or energy is drawn from a source, it is taken from it ✿ **NOUN** ❼ the result of a game or competition in which nobody wins

**draw up** ✿ **VERB** To draw up a plan, document, or list means to prepare it and write it out

**drawback** **NOUN** a problem that makes something less acceptable or desirable

**drawer** **NOUN** a sliding box-shaped part of a piece of furniture used for storing things

**drawing** **NOUN** ❶ a picture made with a pencil, pen, or crayon ❷ Drawing is the skill or work of making drawings

**drawn** Drawn is the past participle of **draw**

**dread** **VERB** ❶ If you dread something, you feel very worried and frightened about it ✿ **NOUN** ❷ Dread is a feeling of great fear or anxiety

**dreadful** **ADJECTIVE** very bad or unpleasant

**dream**, dreams, dreaming, dreamed or dreamt **NOUN** ❶ a series of events that you experience in your mind while asleep ❷ a situation or event which you often think about because you would very much like it to happen ✿ **VERB** ❸ When you dream, you see events in your mind while you are asleep ❹ When you dream about something happening, you often think about it because you would very much like it to happen ❺ If someone dreams up a plan or idea, they invent it ✿ **ADJECTIVE** ❻ too good to be true

**dress**, dresses, dressing, dressed **NOUN** ❶ a piece of clothing for women or girls made up of a skirt and top attached ❷ Dress is any clothing worn by men or women ✿ **VERB** ❸ When you dress, you put clothes on ❹ If you dress for a special occasion, you put on formal clothes ❺ To dress a wound means to clean it up and treat it

**dresser** **NOUN** a piece of kitchen or dining room furniture with cupboards or drawers in the lower part and open shelves in the top part

**dressing gown** **NOUN** an item of clothing shaped like a coat and put on over nightwear

**dribble**, dribbles, dribbling, dribbled **VERB** ❶ When liquid dribbles down a surface, it trickles down it in drops or a thin stream ❷ If a person or animal dribbles, saliva trickles from their mouth ❸ In sport, to dribble a ball means to move it along by repeatedly tapping it with your foot or a stick ✿ **NOUN** ❹ a small quantity of liquid flowing in a thin stream or drops

**drift** **VERB** ❶ When something drifts, it is carried along by the wind or by water ❷ When people drift, they move aimlessly from one place or activity to another ❸ If you drift off to sleep, you gradually fall asleep ✿ **NOUN** ❹ A snow drift is a pile of snow heaped up by the wind ❺ The drift of an argument or a speech is its main point

**drill** **NOUN** ❶ a tool for making holes ❷ Drill is a routine exercise or routine training ✿ **VERB** ❸ To drill into something means to make a hole in it using a drill ❹ If you drill people, you teach them to do something by repetition

**drink**, drinks, drinking, drank, drunk **VERB** ❶ When you drink, you take liquid into your mouth and swallow it ❷ To drink also means to drink alcohol ✿ **NOUN** ❸ an amount of liquid suitable for drinking ❹ an alcoholic drink **drinker** **NOUN**

**drip**, drips, dripping, dripped **VERB** ❶ When liquid drips, it falls in small drops ❷ When an object drips, drops of liquid fall from it ✿ **NOUN** ❸ a drop of liquid falling from something ❹ a device for allowing liquid food to enter the bloodstream of a person who cannot eat properly because they are ill

**drive**, drives, driving, drove, driven **VERB** ❶ To drive a vehicle means to operate it and control its movements ❷ If something or someone drives you to do something, they force you to do it ❸ If you drive a post or nail into something, you force it in by hitting it with a hammer ❹ If something drives a machine, it supplies the power that makes it work ✿ **NOUN** ❺ a journey in a vehicle ❻ a private road that leads from a public road to a person's house ❼ Drive is energy and determination **driver** **NOUN** **driving** **NOUN**

**droop** **VERB** If something droops, it hangs or sags downwards with no strength or firmness

A B C D E F G H I J K L M N O P Q R S T U V W X Y Z

83

# drop - duck

**drop**, drops, dropping, dropped VERB ❶ If you drop something, you let it fall ❷ If something drops, it falls straight down ❸ If a level or amount drops, it becomes less ❹ If you drop something that you are doing or dealing with, you stop doing it or dealing with it ❺ If you drop a hint, you give someone a hint in a casual way ❻ If you drop something or someone somewhere, you deposit or leave them there ✿ NOUN ❼ A drop of liquid is a very small quantity of it that forms or falls in a round shape ❽ a decrease ❾ the distance between the top and bottom of something tall, such as a cliff or building

**drought** [rhymes with **shout**] NOUN a long period during which there is no rain

### how to say it

### Helpful hints...

**Drought** should be said so that it rhymes with *shout*.

**drove**, droves, droving, droved ❶ Drove is the past tense of **drive** ✿ VERB ❷ To drove cattle or sheep is to drive them over a long distance

**drown** VERB ❶ When someone drowns or is drowned, they die because they have gone under water and cannot breathe ❷ If a noise drowns a sound, it is louder than the sound and makes it impossible to hear it

**drowsy**, drowsier, drowsiest ADJECTIVE feeling sleepy

**drug**, drugs, drugging, drugged NOUN ❶ a chemical given to people to treat disease ❷ Drugs are chemical substances that some people smoke, swallow, inhale, or inject because of their stimulating effects ✿ VERB ❸ To drug a person or animal means to give them a drug to make them unconscious ❹ To drug food or drink means to add a drug to it in order to make someone unconscious

**drum**, drums, drumming, drummed NOUN ❶ a musical instrument consisting of a skin stretched tightly over a round frame ❷ an object or container shaped like a drum ❸ INFORMAL In Australian English, the drum is information or advice ✿ VERB ❹ If something is drumming on a surface, it is hitting it regularly, making a continuous beating sound ❺ If you drum something into someone, you keep saying it to them until they understand it or remember it

**drummer** NOUN

**drunk** ❶ Drunk is the past participle of **drink** ✿ ADJECTIVE ❷ If someone is drunk, they have drunk so much alcohol that they cannot speak clearly or behave sensibly ✿ NOUN ❸ a person who is drunk, or who often gets drunk

**dry**, drier or dryer, driest; dries, drying, dried ADJECTIVE ❶ Something that is dry contains or uses no water or liquid ❷ Dry bread or toast is eaten without a topping ❸ Dry sherry or wine does not taste sweet ❹ Dry also means plain and sometimes boring ❺ Dry humour is subtle and sarcastic ✿ VERB ❻ When you dry something, or when it dries, liquid is removed from it

**dry up** ✿ VERB If something dries up, it becomes completely dry

**dry-clean** VERB When clothes are dry-cleaned, they are cleaned with a liquid chemical rather than with water

**dryer** or **drier** NOUN a device for removing moisture from something by heating or by hot air

**duck**, ducks, ducking, ducked NOUN ❶ a bird that lives in water and has webbed feet and a large flat bill ✿ VERB ❷ If you duck, you move your head quickly downwards in order to avoid being hit by something ❸ If you

84

**due – dynamic**

duck a duty or responsibility, you avoid it ❹ To duck someone means to push them briefly under water

**due** ADJECTIVE ❶ expected to happen or arrive ❷ If you give something due consideration, you give it the consideration it needs ✿ PHRASE ❸ **Due to** means because of ✿ ADVERB ❹ Due means exactly in a particular direction ✿ NOUN ❺ IN PLURAL Dues are sums of money that you pay regularly to an organization you belong to

**duet** NOUN a piece of music sung or played by two people

**dug** Dug is the past tense and past participle of **dig**

**duke** NOUN a nobleman with a rank just below that of a prince

**dull**, duller, dullest; dulls, dulling, dulled ADJECTIVE ❶ not at all interesting in any way ❷ slow to learn or understand ❸ not bright, sharp, or clear ❹ A dull day or dull sky is very cloudy ❺ Dull feelings are weak and not intense ✿ VERB ❻ If something dulls or is dulled, it becomes less bright, sharp, or clear

**dumb** ADJECTIVE ❶ unable to speak ❷ INFORMAL slow to understand or stupid

**dummy**, dummies NOUN ❶ a rubber teat which a baby sucks or bites on ❷ an imitation or model of something which is used for display ✿ ADJECTIVE ❸ imitation or substitute

**dump** VERB ❶ When unwanted waste is dumped, it is left somewhere ❷ If you dump something, you throw it down or put it down somewhere in a careless way ✿ NOUN ❸ a place where rubbish is left ❹ a storage place, especially used by the military for storing supplies ❺ INFORMAL You refer to a place as a dump when it is unattractive and unpleasant to live in

**dune** NOUN A dune or sand dune is a hill of sand near the sea or in the desert

**duo**, duos NOUN ❶ a pair of musical performers; also a piece of music written for two players ❷ Any two people doing something together can be referred to as a duo

**during** PREPOSITION happening throughout a particular time or at a particular point in time

**dusk** NOUN Dusk is the time just before nightfall when it is not completely dark

**dust** NOUN ❶ Dust is dry fine powdery material such as particles of earth, dirt, or pollen ✿ VERB ❷ When you dust furniture or other objects, you remove dust from them using a duster ❸ If you dust a surface with powder, you cover it lightly with the powder

**dustbin** NOUN a large container for rubbish

**duster** NOUN a cloth used for removing dust from furniture and other objects

**dustman**, dustmen NOUN someone whose job is to collect the rubbish from people's houses

**dusty**, dustier, dustiest ADJECTIVE covered with dust

**duty**, duties NOUN ❶ something you ought to do or feel you should do, because it is your responsibility ❷ a task which you do as part of your job ❸ Duty is tax paid to the government on some goods, especially imports

**duty-free** ADJECTIVE Duty-free goods are sold at airports or on planes or ships at a cheaper price than usual because they are not taxed

**duvet** [doo-vay] NOUN a cotton quilt filled with feathers or other material, used on a bed in place of sheets and blankets

**DVD** NOUN an abbreviation for 'digital versatile disc' or 'digital video disc': a type of compact disc that can store large amounts of video and sound information

**dwarf**, dwarfs, dwarfing, dwarfed VERB ❶ If one thing dwarfs another, it is so much bigger that it makes it look very small ✿ ADJECTIVE ❷ smaller than average ✿ NOUN ❸ a person who is much smaller than average size

**dye**, dyes, dyeing, dyed VERB ❶ To dye something means to change its colour by applying coloured liquid to it ✿ NOUN ❷ a colouring substance which is used to change the colour of something such as cloth or hair

**dynamic** ADJECTIVE ❶ A dynamic person is full of energy, ambition, and new ideas ❷ relating to energy or forces which produce motion

A B C D E F G H I J K L M N O P Q R S T U V W X Y Z

85

# each - eat

A B C D **E** F G H I J K L M N O P Q R S T U V W X Y Z

**each** ADJECTIVE OR PRONOUN ❶ every one taken separately ✿ PHRASE ❷ If people do something to **each other**, each person does it to the other or others

**eager** ADJECTIVE wanting very much to do or have something  **eagerly** ADVERB

**eagle** NOUN a large bird of prey

**ear** NOUN ❶ the parts of your body on either side of your head with which you hear sounds ❷ An ear of corn or wheat is the top part of the stalk which contains seeds

**eardrum** NOUN Your eardrums are thin pieces of tightly stretched skin inside your ears which vibrate so that you can hear sounds

**early**, earlier, earliest ADJECTIVE ❶ before the arranged or expected time ✿ ADVERB ❷ before the arranged or expected time

**earn** VERB ❶ If you earn money, you get it in return for work that you do ❷ If you earn something such as praise, you receive it because you deserve it

**earphones** PLURAL NOUN small speakers which you wear on your ears to listen to a radio or MP3 player

**earring** NOUN Earrings are pieces of jewellery that you wear on your ear lobes

**earth** NOUN ❶ The earth is the planet on which we live ❷ Earth is the dry land on the surface of the earth, especially the soil in which things grow ❸ The earth in a piece of electrical equipment is the wire through which electricity can pass into the ground and so make the equipment safe for use

**earthquake** NOUN a shaking of the ground caused by movement of the earth's crust

**ease**, eases, easing, eased NOUN ❶ lack of difficulty, worry, or hardship ✿ VERB ❷ When something eases, or when you ease it, it becomes less severe or less intense ❸ If you ease something somewhere, you move it there slowly and carefully

**easel** NOUN an upright frame which supports a picture that someone is painting

**easily** ADVERB ❶ without difficulty ❷ without a doubt

**east** NOUN ❶ East is the direction in which you look to see the sun rise ❷ The east of a place is the part which is towards the east when you are in the centre ❸ The East is the countries in the south and east of Asia ✿ ADJECTIVE OR ADVERB ❹ East means in or towards the east ✿ ADJECTIVE ❺ An east wind blows from the east

**Easter** NOUN a Christian religious festival celebrating the resurrection of Christ

**easterly** ADJECTIVE ❶ Easterly means to or towards the east ❷ An easterly wind blows from the east

**eastern** ADJECTIVE in or from the east

**easy**, easier, easiest ADJECTIVE ❶ able to be done without difficulty ❷ comfortable and without any worries

**eat**, eats, eating, ate, eaten VERB ❶ To eat means to chew and swallow food ❷ When you eat, you have a meal

### letter E

Some words that sound like they begin with *e* actually begin with *ae*, like *aesthete*.

**eat away — effect**

**eat away** VERB If something is eaten away, it is slowly destroyed

**echo**, echoes, echoing, echoed NOUN ❶ a sound which is caused by sound waves reflecting off a surface ❷ a repetition, imitation, or reminder of something VERB ❸ If a sound echoes, it is reflected off a surface so that you can hear it again after the original sound has stopped

**eclipse** NOUN An eclipse occurs when one planet passes in front of another and hides it from view for a short time

**ecology** NOUN the relationship between living things and their environment; also used of the study of this relationship **ecological** ADJECTIVE **ecologist** NOUN

**economic** ADJECTIVE ❶ concerning the management of the money, industry, and trade of a country ❷ concerning making a profit

**economical** ADJECTIVE ❶ another word for **economic** ❷ Something that is economical is cheap to use or operate ❸ Someone who is economical spends money carefully and sensibly **economically** ADVERB

**economics** NOUN Economics is the study of the production and distribution of goods, services, and wealth in a society and the organization of its money, industry, and trade

**economist** NOUN a person who studies or writes about economics

**economy**, economies NOUN ❶ The economy of a country is the system it uses to organize and manage its money, industry, and trade; also used of the wealth that a country gets from business and industry ❷ Economy is the careful use of things to save money, time, or energy

**ecosystem** NOUN TECHNICAL the relationship between plants and animals and their environment

**edge**, edges, edging, edged NOUN ❶ The edge of something is a border or line where it ends or meets something else ❷ The edge of a blade is its thin, sharp side ❸ If you have the edge over someone, you have an advantage over them VERB ❹ If you edge something, you make a border for it ❺ If you edge somewhere, you move there very gradually

**edible** ADJECTIVE safe and pleasant to eat

**edit** VERB ❶ If you edit a piece of writing, you correct it so that it is fit for publishing ❷ To edit a film or television programme means to select different parts of it and arrange them in a particular order ❸ Someone who edits a newspaper or magazine is in charge of it

**edition** NOUN ❶ An edition of a book or magazine is a particular version of it printed at one time ❷ An edition of a television or radio programme is a single programme that is one of a series

**editor** NOUN ❶ a person who is responsible for the content of a newspaper or magazine ❷ a person who checks books and makes corrections to them before they are published ❸ a person who selects different parts of a television programme or a film and arranges them in a particular order

**educate**, educates, educating, educated VERB To educate someone means to teach them so that they gain knowledge about something

**educated** ADJECTIVE having a high standard of learning and culture

**education** NOUN the process of gaining knowledge and understanding through learning or the system of teaching people **educational** ADJECTIVE

**eel** NOUN a long, thin, snakelike fish

**effect** NOUN ❶ a direct result of someone or something on another person or thing ❷ An effect that someone or something has is the overall impression or result that they have

**don't mix up**

*Hello Kitty…*

never mixes up **effect** (the result of something) and **affect** (to influence in some way).

## effective - eliminate

❃ PHRASE ❸ If something **takes effect** at a particular time, it starts to happen or starts to produce results at that time
**effective** ADJECTIVE ❶ working well and producing the intended results ❷ coming into operation or beginning officially **effectively** ADVERB
**efficient** ADJECTIVE capable of doing something well without wasting time or energy **efficiently** ADVERB **efficiency** NOUN
**effort** NOUN ❶ Effort is the physical or mental energy needed to do something ❷ an attempt or struggle to do something
**egg** NOUN ❶ an oval or rounded object laid by female birds, reptiles, fishes, and insects. A baby creature develops inside the egg until it is ready to be born ❷ a hen's egg used as food ❸ In a female animal, an egg is a cell produced in its body which can develop into a baby if it is fertilized
**eggplant** NOUN a dark purple pear-shaped fruit eaten as a vegetable. It is also called **aubergine**
**eight** the number 8 **eighth** ADJECTIVE
**eighteen** the number 18 **eighteenth** ADJECTIVE
**eighty**, eighties the number 80 **eightieth** ADJECTIVE
**either** ADJECTIVE, PRONOUN, OR CONJUNCTION ❶ one or the other of two possible alternatives ❃ ADJECTIVE ❷ both one and the other
**eject** VERB If you eject something or someone, you forcefully push or send them out
**elastic** ADJECTIVE ❶ able to stretch easily ❃ NOUN ❷ Elastic is rubber material which stretches and returns to its original shape
**elbow** NOUN ❶ Your elbow is the joint between the upper part of your arm and your forearm ❃ VERB ❷ If you elbow someone aside, you push them away with your elbow
**elderly** ADJECTIVE ❶ Elderly is a polite way to describe an old person ❃ NOUN ❷ The elderly are old people
**elect** VERB ❶ If you elect someone, you choose them to fill a position, by voting ❷ FORMAL If you elect to do something, you choose to do it
**election** NOUN the selection of one or more people for an official position by voting

**electric** ADJECTIVE ❶ powered or produced by electricity ❷ very tense or exciting
**electrical** ADJECTIVE using or producing electricity
**electrician** NOUN a person whose job is to install and repair electrical equipment
**electricity** NOUN Electricity is a form of energy used for heating and lighting, and to provide power for machines
**electronic** ADJECTIVE having transistors or silicon chips which control an electric current **electronically** ADVERB
**elegant** ADJECTIVE attractive and graceful or stylish

### how to remember
What an **el**egant leg **Ant**onia has.

**element** NOUN ❶ a part of something which combines with others to make a whole ❷ In chemistry, an element is a substance that is made up of only one type of atom ❸ A particular element within a large group of people is a section of it which is similar ❹ An element of a quality is a certain amount of it ❺ The elements of a subject are the basic and most important points ❻ The elements are the weather conditions
**elementary** ADJECTIVE simple and basic
**elephant** NOUN a very large four-legged mammal with a long trunk, large ears, and ivory tusks
**eleven** NOUN Eleven is the number 11 **eleventh** ADJECTIVE
**elf** NOUN In folklore, an elf is a small mischievous fairy
**eligible** [*el-lij-i-bl*] ADJECTIVE suitable or having the right qualifications for something
**eliminate**, eliminates, eliminating, eliminated VERB ❶ If you eliminate something or someone, you get rid of them ❷ If a team or a person is eliminated from a competition, they can no longer take part

**else** ADVERB ❶ other than this or more than this ✿ PHRASE ❷ You say **or else** to introduce a possibility or an alternative

**elsewhere** ADVERB in or to another place

**e-mail** or **email** NOUN ❶ the sending of messages from one computer to another ❷ a message sent in this way ✿ VERB ❸ If you e-mail someone, you send an e-mail to them

**embarrass**, embarrasses, embarrassing, embarrassed VERB If you embarrass someone, you make them feel ashamed or awkward **embarrassing** ADJECTIVE

**embarrassed** ADJECTIVE ashamed or awkward

**embarrassment** NOUN shame and awkwardness

**embrace**, embraces, embracing, embraced VERB ❶ If you embrace someone, you hug them to show affection or as a greeting ❷ If you embrace a belief or cause you accept it and believe in it ✿ NOUN ❸ a hug

**embroider** VERB If you embroider fabric, you sew a decorative design onto it

**embroidery** NOUN Embroidery is decorative designs sewn onto fabric; also the art or skill of embroidery

**embryo** [em-bree-oh] NOUN an animal or human being in the very early stages of development in the womb

**emerald** NOUN ❶ a bright green precious stone ✿ NOUN OR ADJECTIVE ❷ bright green

**emerge**, emerges, emerging, emerged VERB ❶ If someone emerges from a place, they come out of it so that they can be seen ❷ If something emerges, it becomes known or begins to be recognized as existing

**emergency**, emergencies NOUN an unexpected and serious event which needs immediate action to deal with it

**emigrate**, emigrates, emigrating, emigrated VERB If you emigrate, you leave your native country and go to live permanently in another one

**emotion** NOUN a strong feeling, such as love or fear

**emotional** ADJECTIVE ❶ causing strong feelings ❷ to do with feelings rather than your physical condition ❸ showing your feelings openly **emotionally** ADVERB

**emperor** NOUN a male ruler of an empire

**emphasis**, emphases NOUN Emphasis is special importance or extra stress given to something

**emphasize**, emphasizes, emphasizing, emphasized (also **emphasise**) VERB If you emphasize something, you make it known that it is very important

**empire** NOUN ❶ a group of countries controlled by one country ❷ a powerful group of companies controlled by one person

**employ** VERB ❶ If you employ someone, you pay them to work for you ❷ If you employ something for a particular purpose, you make use of it

**employee** NOUN a person who is paid to work for another person or for an organization

**employer** NOUN Someone's employer is the person or organization that they work for

**employment** NOUN Employment is the state of having a paid job, or the activity of recruiting people for a job

**empty**, emptier, emptiest; empties, emptying, emptied ADJECTIVE ❶ having nothing or nobody inside ❷ without purpose, value, or meaning ✿ VERB ❸ If you empty something, or empty its contents, you remove the contents

**enable**, enables, enabling, enabled VERB To enable something to happen means to make it possible

**enclose**, encloses, enclosing, enclosed VERB To enclose an object or area means to surround it with something solid

**encourage**, encourages, encouraging, encouraged VERB ❶ If you encourage someone, you give them courage and confidence to do something ❷ If someone or something encourages a particular activity, they support it **encouraging** ADJECTIVE **encouragement** NOUN

**encyclopedia** or **encyclopaedia** [en-sigh-klop-ee-dee-a] NOUN a book or set of books giving information about many different subjects

**end** NOUN ❶ The end of a period of time or an event is the last part ❷ The end of something is the farthest point of it ❸ the purpose for which something is done

# endless – enrol

✿ **VERB** ❹ If something ends or if you end it, it comes to a finish

### some other words to use

### Tips and tricks...

You should try not to use **end** too much when you are writing. Some other words you can use are: *finish, close, conclusion* and *finale*.

**endless** ADJECTIVE having or seeming to have no end  **endlessly** ADVERB

**endurance** NOUN Endurance is the ability to put up with a difficult situation for a period of time

**endure**, endures, enduring, endured VERB ❶ If you endure a difficult situation, you put up with it calmly and patiently ❷ If something endures, it lasts or continues to exist

**enemy**, enemies NOUN a person or group that is hostile or opposed to another person or group

**energetic** ADJECTIVE having or showing energy or enthusiasm

**energy** NOUN ❶ the physical strength to do active things ❷ the power which drives machinery ❸ In physics, energy is the capacity of a body or system to do work. It is measured in joules

**engaged** ADJECTIVE ❶ When two people are engaged, they have agreed to marry each other ❷ If someone or something is engaged, they are occupied or busy

**engagement** NOUN ❶ an appointment that you have with someone ❷ an agreement that two people have made with each other to get married

**engine** NOUN ❶ a machine designed to convert heat or other kinds of energy into mechanical movement ❷ a railway locomotive

**engineer** NOUN ❶ a person trained in designing and building machinery and electrical devices, or roads and bridges ❷ a person who repairs mechanical or electrical devices ✿ VERB ❸ If you engineer an event or situation, you arrange it cleverly, usually for your own advantage

**engineering** NOUN Engineering is the profession of designing and constructing machinery and electrical devices, or roads and bridges

**English** ADJECTIVE ❶ belonging or relating to England ✿ NOUN ❷ English is the main language spoken in the United Kingdom, the USA, Canada, Australia, New Zealand, and many other countries

**enhance**, enhances, enhancing, enhanced VERB To enhance something means to make it more valuable or attractive

**enjoy** VERB ❶ If you enjoy something, you find pleasure and satisfaction in it ❷ If you enjoy something, you are lucky to have it or experience it

**enjoyable** ADJECTIVE giving pleasure or satisfaction

**enjoyment** NOUN Enjoyment is the feeling of pleasure or satisfaction you get from something you enjoy

**enlarge**, enlarges, enlarging, enlarged VERB ❶ When you enlarge something, it gets bigger ❷ If you enlarge on a subject, you give more details about it

**enormous** ADJECTIVE very large in size or amount  **enormously** ADVERB

**enough** ADJECTIVE OR ADVERB ❶ as much or as many as required ✿ NOUN ❷ Enough is the quantity necessary for something ✿ ADVERB ❸ very or fairly

**enquire**, enquires, enquiring, enquired (also **inquire**) VERB If you enquire about something or someone, you ask about them

**enquiry**, enquiries or **inquiry**, inquiries NOUN ❶ a question that you ask in order to find something out ❷ an investigation into something that has happened and that needs explaining

**enrol**, enrols, enrolling, enrolled VERB If you

**ensure – equation**

enrol for something such as a course or a college, you register to join or become a member of it

**ensure**, ensures, ensuring, ensured **VERB** To ensure that something happens means to make certain that it happens

**enter** **VERB** ❶ To enter a place means to go into it ❷ If you enter an organization or institution, you join and become a member of it ❸ If you enter a competition or examination, you take part in it ❹ If you enter something in a diary or a list, you write it down

**enterprise** **NOUN** ❶ a business or company ❷ a project or task, especially one that involves risk or difficulty

**entertain** **VERB** ❶ If you entertain people, you keep them amused or interested ❷ If you entertain guests, you receive them into your house and give them food and hospitality

**entertainer** **NOUN** someone whose job is to amuse and please audiences, for example a comedian or singer

**entertainment** **NOUN** anything people watch or do for pleasure

**enthusiasm** **NOUN** Enthusiasm is interest, eagerness, or delight in something that you enjoy

**enthusiastic** **ADJECTIVE** showing great excitement, eagerness, or approval for something

**entire** **ADJECTIVE** all of something

**entirely** **ADVERB** wholly and completely

**entitle**, entitles, entitling, entitled **VERB** If something entitles you to have or do something, it gives you the right to have or do it

**entrance** **NOUN** ❶ The entrance of a building or area is its doorway or gate ❷ A person's entrance is their arrival in a place, or the way in which they arrive ❸ In the theatre, an actor makes his or her entrance when he or she comes on to the stage ❹ Entrance is the right to enter a place

**entrance**, entrances, entrancing, entranced [en-**trahnss**] **VERB** If something entrances you, it gives you a feeling of wonder and delight

**entry**, entries **NOUN** ❶ Entry is the act of entering a place ❷ a place through which you enter somewhere ❸ anything which is entered or recorded

**envelope** **NOUN** a flat covering of paper with a flap that can be folded over to seal it, which is used to hold a letter

**envious** **ADJECTIVE** full of envy **enviously** **ADVERB**

**environment** **NOUN** ❶ Your environment is the circumstances and conditions in which you live or work ❷ The environment is the natural world around us **environmental** **ADJECTIVE** **environmentally** **ADVERB**

**how to remember**

There is **iron** in the env**iron**ment.

**envy**, envies, envying, envied **NOUN** ❶ Envy is a feeling of resentment you have when you wish you could have what someone else has ✿ **VERB** ❷ If you envy someone, you wish that you had what they have

**epic** **NOUN** ❶ a long story of heroic events and actions ✿ **ADJECTIVE** ❷ very impressive or ambitious

**epidemic** **NOUN** ❶ an occurrence of a disease in one area, spreading quickly and affecting many people ❷ a rapid development or spread of something

**epilogue** [ep-ill-og] **NOUN** An epilogue is a passage added to the end of a book or play as a conclusion

**episode** **NOUN** ❶ an event or period ❷ one of several parts of a novel or drama appearing for example on television

**equal**, equals, equalling, equalled **ADJECTIVE** ❶ having the same size, amount, value, or standard ❷ If you are equal to a task, you have the necessary ability to deal with it ✿ **NOUN** ❸ Your equals are people who have the same ability, status, or rights as you ✿ **VERB** ❹ If one thing equals another, it is as good or remarkable as the other **equally** **ADVERB** **equality** **NOUN**

**equation** **NOUN** a mathematical formula stating that two amounts or values are the same

# equator – eternal

**equator** [ik-*way*-tor] NOUN an imaginary line drawn round the middle of the earth, lying halfway between the North and South poles
**equatorial** ADJECTIVE

**equip**, equips, equipping, equipped VERB If a person or thing is equipped with something, they have it or are provided with it

**equipment** NOUN Equipment is all the things that are needed or used for a particular job or activity

**equivalent** ADJECTIVE ❶ equal in use, size, value, or effect ✿ NOUN ❷ something that has the same use, value, or effect as something else

**era** [*ear*-a] NOUN a period of time distinguished by a particular feature

**erase**, erases, erasing, erased VERB To erase something means to remove it

**erect** VERB ❶ To erect something means to put it up or construct it ✿ ADJECTIVE ❷ in a straight and upright position

**erode**, erodes, eroding, eroded VERB If something erodes or is eroded, it is gradually worn or eaten away and destroyed

**erosion** NOUN the gradual wearing away and destruction of something

**errand** NOUN a short trip you make in order to do a job for someone

**error** NOUN a mistake or something which you have done wrong

**erupt** VERB ❶ When a volcano erupts, it violently throws out a lot of hot lava and ash ❷ When a situation erupts, it starts up suddenly and violently **eruption** NOUN

**escalate**, escalates, escalating, escalated VERB If a situation escalates, it becomes greater in size, seriousness, or intensity

**escalator** NOUN a mechanical moving staircase

**escape**, escapes, escaping, escaped VERB ❶ To escape means to get free from someone or something ❷ If you escape something unpleasant or difficult, you manage to avoid it ❸ If something escapes you, you cannot remember it ✿ NOUN ❹ an act of escaping from a particular place or situation ❺ a situation or activity which distracts you from something unpleasant

**especially** ADVERB You say especially to show that something applies more to one thing, person, or situation than to any other

**essay**, essays NOUN a short piece of writing on a particular subject, for example one done as an exercise by a student

**essential** ADJECTIVE ❶ vitally important and absolutely necessary ❷ very basic, important, and typical

**establish**, establishes, establishing, established VERB ❶ To establish something means to set it up in a permanent way ❷ If you establish yourself or become established as something, you achieve a strong reputation for a particular activity ❸ If you establish a fact or establish the truth of something, you discover it and can prove it

**establishment** NOUN ❶ The establishment of an organization or system is the act of setting it up ❷ a shop, business, or some other sort of organization or institution ❸ The Establishment is the group of people in a country who have power and influence

**estate** NOUN ❶ a large area of privately owned land in the country, together with all the property on it ❷ an area of land, usually in or near a city, which has been developed for housing or industry ❸ LEGAL A person's estate consists of all the possessions they leave behind when they die

**estate agent** NOUN a person who works for a company that sells houses and land

**estimate** VERB ❶ If you estimate an amount or quantity, you calculate it approximately ❷ If you estimate something, you make a guess about it based on the evidence you have available ✿ NOUN ❸ a guess at an amount, quantity, or outcome, based on the evidence you have available ❹ a formal statement from a company who may do some work for you, telling you how much it is likely to cost

**estuary**, estuaries [*est*-yoo-ree] NOUN the wide part of a river near where it joins the sea and where fresh water mixes with salt water

**etc.** a written abbreviation for **et cetera**

**et cetera** [it *set*-ra] 'Et cetera' is used at the end of a list to indicate that other items of the same type you have mentioned could have been mentioned if there had been time or space

**eternal** ADJECTIVE lasting forever, or seeming to last forever

# ethical – exact

**ethical** ADJECTIVE in agreement with accepted principles of behaviour that are thought to be right

**ethnic** ADJECTIVE ❶ involving different racial groups of people ❷ relating to a particular racial or cultural group, especially when very different from modern western culture

**euro**, euros NOUN the official unit of currency in some countries of the European Union, replacing their old currencies at the beginning of January 2002

**European** ADJECTIVE ❶ belonging or relating to Europe ✿ NOUN ❷ someone who comes from Europe

**evacuate**, evacuates, evacuating, evacuated VERB If someone is evacuated, they are removed from a place of danger to a place of safety

**evaluate**, evaluates, evaluating, evaluated VERB If you evaluate something, you assess its strengths and weaknesses

**evaluation** NOUN ❶ Evaluation is assessing the strengths and weaknesses of something ❷ To carry out an evaluation of a design, product or system is to do an assessment to find out how well it works or will work

**evaporate**, evaporates, evaporating, evaporated VERB ❶ When a liquid evaporates, it gradually becomes less and less because it has changed from a liquid into a gas ❷ If a substance has been evaporated, all the liquid has been taken out so that it is dry or concentrated

**eve** NOUN the evening or day before an event or occasion

**even** ADJECTIVE ❶ flat and level ❷ regular and without variation ❸ In maths, numbers that are even can be divided exactly by two ❹ Scores that are even are exactly the same ✿ ADVERB ❺ 'Even' is used to suggest that something is unexpected or surprising ❻ 'Even' is also used to say that something is greater in degree than something else ✿ PHRASE ❼ **Even if** or **even though** is used to introduce something that is surprising in relation to the main part of the sentence

**evening** NOUN the part of the day between late afternoon and the time you go to bed

**event** NOUN ❶ something that happens, especially when it is unusual or important ❷ one of the competitions that are part of an organized occasion, especially in sports ✿ PHRASE ❸ If you say **in any event**, you mean whatever happens

**eventually** ADVERB in the end

**ever** ADVERB ❶ at any time ❷ all the time ❸ 'Ever' is used to give emphasis to what you are saying

**every** ADJECTIVE ❶ 'Every' is used to refer to all the members of a particular group, separately and one by one ❷ 'Every' is used to mean the greatest or the best possible degree of something ❸ 'Every' is also used to indicate that something happens at regular intervals ✿ PHRASE ❹ **Every other** means each alternate

**everybody** PRONOUN ❶ all the people in a group ❷ all the people in the world

**everyday** ADJECTIVE usual or ordinary

**everyone** PRONOUN ❶ all the people in a group ❷ all the people in the world

**everything** PRONOUN ❶ all or the whole of something ❷ the most important thing

**everywhere** ADVERB in or to all places

**evidence** NOUN ❶ Evidence is anything you see, read, or are told which gives you reason to believe something ❷ Evidence is the information used in court to attempt to prove or disprove something

**evident** ADJECTIVE easily noticed or understood **evidently** ADVERB

**evil** NOUN ❶ Evil is a force or power that is believed to cause wicked or bad things to happen ❷ a very unpleasant or harmful situation or activity ✿ ADJECTIVE ❸ Someone or something that is evil is morally wrong or bad

**evolution** [ee-vol-**oo**-shn] NOUN ❶ Evolution is a process of gradual change taking place over many generations during which living things slowly change as they adapt to different environments ❷ Evolution is also any process of gradual change and development over a period of time

**evolve**, evolves, evolving, evolved VERB ❶ If something evolves or if you evolve it, it develops gradually over a period of time ❷ When living things evolve, they gradually change and develop into different forms over a period of time

**exact** ADJECTIVE ❶ correct and complete in every detail ❷ accurate and precise, as

# exactly - excuse

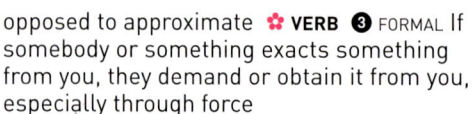

opposed to approximate ✿ **VERB** ❸ FORMAL If somebody or something exacts something from you, they demand or obtain it from you, especially through force

**exactly** ADVERB ❶ with complete accuracy and precision ❷ You can use 'exactly' to emphasize the truth of a statement, or a similarity or close relationship between one thing and another ✿ **INTERJECTION** ❸ an expression implying total agreement

**exaggerate**, exaggerates, exaggerating, exaggerated VERB ❶ If you exaggerate, you make the thing you are describing seem better, worse, bigger, or more important than it really is ❷ To exaggerate something means to make it more noticeable than usual **exaggeration** NOUN

**exam** NOUN an official test set to find out your knowledge or skill in a subject

**examination** NOUN ❶ an exam ❷ If you make an examination of something, you inspect it very carefully ❸ A medical examination is a check by a doctor to find out the state of your health

**examine**, examines, examining, examined VERB ❶ If you examine something, you inspect it very carefully ❷ To examine a subject is to look closely at the issues involved and form your own opinion ❸ To examine someone means to find out their knowledge or skill in a particular subject by testing them ❹ If a doctor examines you, he or she checks your body to find out the state of your health

**example** NOUN ❶ something which represents or is typical of a group or set ❷ If you say someone or something is an example to people, you mean that people can imitate and learn from them ✿ **PHRASE** ❸ You use **for example** to give an example of something you are talking about

**exceed** VERB To exceed something such as a limit means to go beyond it or to become greater than it

**excellent** ADJECTIVE very good indeed **excellence** NOUN

**except** PREPOSITION Except or except for means other than or apart from

**exception** NOUN somebody or something that is not included in a general statement or rule

**exceptional** ADJECTIVE ❶ unusually talented or clever ❷ unusual and likely to happen very rarely **exceptionally** ADVERB

**excess**, excesses NOUN ❶ Excess is behaviour which goes beyond normally acceptable limits ❷ a larger amount of something than is needed, usual, or healthy ✿ **ADJECTIVE** ❸ more than is needed, allowed, or healthy ✿ **PHRASE** ❹ **In excess of** a particular amount means more than that amount ❺ If you do something **to excess**, you do it too much

**excessive** ADJECTIVE too great in amount or degree

**exchange**, exchanges, exchanging, exchanged VERB ❶ To exchange things means to give or receive one thing in return for another ✿ **NOUN** ❷ the act of giving or receiving something in return for something else ❸ a place where people trade and do business

**excited** ADJECTIVE happy and unable to relax

**excitement** NOUN interest and enthusiasm

**exciting** ADJECTIVE making you feel happy and enthusiastic

**exclaim** VERB When you exclaim, you cry out suddenly or loudly because you are excited or shocked

**exclamation** NOUN a word or phrase spoken suddenly to express a strong feeling

**exclamation mark** NOUN a punctuation mark (!) used in writing to express a strong feeling

**exclude**, excludes, excluding, excluded VERB ❶ If you exclude something, you deliberately do not include it or do not consider it ❷ If you exclude somebody from a place or an activity, you prevent them from entering the place or taking part in the activity

**exclusive** ADJECTIVE ❶ available to or for the use of a small group of rich or privileged people ❷ belonging to a particular person or group only ✿ **NOUN** ❸ a story or interview which appears in only one newspaper or on only one television programme **exclusively** ADVERB

**excuse**, excuses, excusing, excused NOUN ❶ a reason which you give to explain why something has been done, has not been done, or will not be done ✿ **VERB** ❷ If you excuse yourself or something that you have

## executive - expense

done, you give reasons defending your actions ❸ If you excuse somebody for something wrong they have done, you forgive them for it ❹ If you excuse somebody from a duty or responsibility, you free them from it ✿ **PHRASE** ❺ You say **excuse me** to try to catch somebody's attention or to apologize for an interruption or for rude behaviour

**executive** NOUN ❶ a person who is employed by a company at a senior level ❷ The executive of an organization is a committee which has the authority to make decisions and ensure that they are carried out ✿ **ADJECTIVE** ❸ concerned with making important decisions and ensuring that they are carried out

**exempt** ADJECTIVE ❶ excused from a rule or duty ✿ **VERB** ❷ To exempt someone from a rule, duty, or obligation means to excuse them from it

**exercise**, exercises, exercising, exercised NOUN ❶ Exercise is any activity which you do to get fit or remain healthy ❷ Exercises are also activities which you do to practise and train for a particular skill ✿ **VERB** ❸ When you exercise, you do activities which help you to get fit and remain healthy ❹ If you exercise your rights or responsibilities, you use them

**exhaust** VERB ❶ To exhaust somebody means to make them very tired ❷ If you exhaust a supply of something such as money or food, you use it up completely ❸ If you exhaust a subject, you talk about it so much that there is nothing else to say about it ✿ **NOUN** ❹ a pipe which carries the gas or steam out of the engine of a vehicle ❺ Exhaust is the gas or steam produced by the engine of a vehicle **exhaustion** NOUN

**exhibit** VERB ❶ To exhibit things means to show them in a public place for people to see ❷ If you exhibit your feelings or abilities, you display them so that other people can see them ✿ **NOUN** ❸ anything which is put on show for the public to see

**exhibition** NOUN a public display of works of art, products, or skills

**exist** VERB If something exists, it is present in the world as a real or living thing

**existence** NOUN ❶ Existence is the state of being or existing ❷ a way of living or being

**exit** NOUN ❶ a way out of a place ❷ If you make an exit, you leave a place ✿ **VERB** ❸ To exit means to go out ❹ An actor exits when he or she leaves the stage

**exotic** ADJECTIVE ❶ attractive or interesting through being unusual ❷ coming from a foreign country

**expand** VERB ❶ If something expands or you expand it, it becomes larger in number or size ❷ If you expand on something, you give more details about it **expansion** NOUN

**expect** VERB ❶ If you expect something to happen, you believe that it will happen ❷ If you are expecting somebody or something, you believe that they are going to arrive or to happen ❸ If you expect something, you believe that it is your right to get it or have it

**expectation** NOUN Expectation or an expectation is a strong belief or hope that something will happen

**expel**, expels, expelling, expelled VERB ❶ If someone is expelled from a school or club, they are officially told to leave because they have behaved badly ❷ If a gas or liquid is expelled from a place, it is forced out of it

**expense** NOUN ❶ Expense is the money that something costs ❷ IN PLURAL Expenses are

---

**punctuation**

Hello Kitty...

You put an **exclamation mark** (!) at the end of a sentence or phrase that shows strong feeling or excitement.

the money somebody spends while doing something connected with their work, which is paid back to them by their employer

**expensive** ADJECTIVE costing a lot of money

**experience**, experiences, experiencing, experienced NOUN ❶ Experience consists of all the things that you have done or that have happened to you ❷ the knowledge or skill you have in a particular activity ❸ something that you do or something that happens to you, especially something new or unusual ✿ VERB ❹ If you experience a situation or feeling, it happens to you or you are affected by it

**experienced** ADJECTIVE skilled or knowledgeable through doing something for a long time

**experiment** NOUN ❶ the testing of something, either to find out its effect or to prove something ✿ VERB ❷ If you experiment with something, you do a scientific test on it to prove or discover something  **experimental** ADJECTIVE

**expert** NOUN ❶ a person who is very skilled at doing something or very knowledgeable about a particular subject ✿ ADJECTIVE ❷ having or requiring special skill or knowledge

**expertise** [eks-per-*teez*] NOUN Expertise is special skill or knowledge

**expire**, expires, expiring, expired VERB When something expires, it reaches the end of the period of time for which it is valid

**explain** VERB If you explain something, you give details about it or reasons for it so that it can be understood

**explanation** NOUN a helpful or clear description

**explicit** ADJECTIVE shown or expressed clearly and openly

**explode**, explodes, exploding, exploded VERB ❶ If something such as a bomb explodes, it bursts loudly and with great force, often causing damage ❷ If somebody explodes, they express strong feelings suddenly or violently ❸ When something increases suddenly and rapidly, it can be said to explode

**exploit** VERB ❶ If somebody exploits a person or a situation, they take advantage of them for their own ends ❷ If you exploit something, you make the best use of it, often for profit ✿ NOUN ❸ something daring or interesting that somebody has done

**explore**, explores, exploring, explored VERB ❶ If you explore a place, you travel in it to find out what it is like ❷ If you explore an idea, you think about it carefully

**exploration** NOUN  **explorer** NOUN

**explosion** NOUN a sudden violent burst of energy, for example one caused by a bomb

**explosive** ADJECTIVE ❶ capable of exploding or likely to explode ❷ happening suddenly and making a loud noise ❸ An explosive situation is one which is likely to have serious or dangerous effects ✿ NOUN ❹ a substance or device that can explode

**export** VERB ❶ To export goods means to send them to another country and sell them there ✿ NOUN ❷ Exports are goods which are sent to another country and sold

**exporter** NOUN

**expose**, exposes, exposing, exposed VERB ❶ To expose something means to uncover it and make it visible ❷ To expose a person to something dangerous means to put them in a situation in which it might harm them ❸ To expose a person or situation means to reveal the truth about them

**express**, expresses, expressing, expressed VERB ❶ When you express an idea or feeling, you show what you think or feel by saying or doing something ❷ If you express a quantity in a particular form, you write it down in that form ✿ ADJECTIVE ❸ very fast ✿ NOUN ❹ a fast train or coach which stops at only a few places

**expression** NOUN ❶ Your expression is the look on your face which shows what you are thinking or feeling ❷ The expression of ideas or feelings is the showing of them through words, actions, or art ❸ a word or phrase used in communicating

**expressive** ADJECTIVE ❶ showing feelings clearly ❷ full of expression

**extend** VERB ❶ If something extends for a distance, it continues and stretches into the distance ❷ If something extends from a

**extension - eyesight**

surface or an object, it sticks out from it ❸ If you extend something, you make it larger or longer

### how to remember

**Hello Kitty...** remembers that **extraordinary** is made from *extra* and *ordinary* so there are two *a*'s in it.

**extension** NOUN ❶ a room or building which is added to an existing building ❷ an extra period of time for which something continues to exist or be valid ❸ an additional telephone connected to the same line as another telephone

**extensive** ADJECTIVE ❶ covering a large area ❷ very great in effect

**extent** NOUN The extent of something is its length, area, or size

**exterior** NOUN ❶ The exterior of something is its outside ❷ Your exterior is your outward appearance

**external** ADJECTIVE existing or happening on the outside or outer part of something

**extinct** ADJECTIVE ❶ An extinct species of animal or plant is no longer in existence ❷ An extinct volcano is no longer likely to erupt **extinction** NOUN

**extinguish**, extinguishes, extinguishing, extinguished VERB To extinguish a light or fire means to put it out

**extra** ADJECTIVE ❶ more than is usual, necessary, or expected ✿ NOUN ❷ anything which is additional ❸ a person who is hired to play a very small and unimportant part in a film

**extract** VERB ❶ To extract something from a place means to take it out or get it out, often by force ❷ If you extract information from someone, you get it from them with difficulty ✿ NOUN ❸ a small section taken from a book or piece of music

**extraordinary** ADJECTIVE unusual or surprising

**extravagant** ADJECTIVE ❶ spending or costing more money than is reasonable or affordable ❷ going beyond reasonable limits

**extreme** ADJECTIVE ❶ very great in degree or intensity ❷ going beyond what is usual or reasonable ❸ at the furthest point or edge of something ✿ NOUN ❹ the highest or furthest degree of something **extremely** ADVERB

**eye**, eyes, eyeing or eying, eyed NOUN ❶ the organ of sight ❷ the small hole at the end of a needle through which you pass the thread ✿ VERB ❸ To eye something means to look at it carefully or suspiciously

**eyeball** NOUN the whole of the ball-shaped part of the eye

**eyebrow** NOUN Your eyebrows are the lines of hair which grow on the ridges of bone above your eyes

**eyelash**, eyelashes NOUN Your eyelashes are hairs that grow on the edges of your eyelids

**eyelid** NOUN Your eyelids are the folds of skin which cover your eyes when they are closed

**eyesight** NOUN Your eyesight is your ability to see

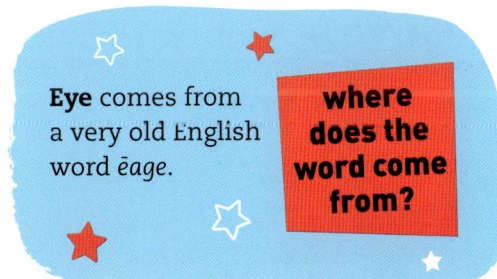

**where does the word come from?**

**Eye** comes from a very old English word *ēage*.

# F f

**fable** NOUN a story intended to teach a moral lesson

**fabric** NOUN ❶ cloth ❷ The fabric of a building is its walls, roof, and other parts ❸ The fabric of a society or system is its structure, laws, and customs

**fabulous** ADJECTIVE ❶ wonderful or very impressive ❷ not real, but happening in stories and legends

**face**, faces, facing, faced NOUN ❶ the front part of your head from your chin to your forehead ❷ the expression someone has or is making ❸ a surface or side of something, especially the most important side ❹ the main aspect or general appearance of something ✿ VERB ❺ To face something or someone is to be opposite them or to look at them or towards them ❻ If you face something difficult or unpleasant, you have to deal with it ✿ PHRASE ❼ **On the face of it** means judging by the appearance of something or your initial reaction to it

**fact** NOUN ❶ a piece of knowledge or information that is true or something that has actually happened ✿ PHRASES ❷ **In fact**, **as a matter of fact**, and **in point of fact** mean 'actually' or 'really' and are used for emphasis or when making an additional comment

**factor** NOUN ❶ something that helps to cause a result ❷ The factors of a number are the whole numbers that will divide exactly into it. For example, 2 and 5 are factors of 10 ❸ If something increases by a particular factor, it is multiplied that number of times

**factory**, factories NOUN a building or group of buildings where goods are made in large quantities

**fade**, fades, fading, faded VERB If something fades, the intensity of its colour, brightness, or sound is gradually reduced

**Fahrenheit** [*far-ren-hite*] NOUN a scale of temperature in which the freezing point of water is 32° and the boiling point is 212°

**fail** VERB ❶ If someone fails to achieve something, they are not successful ❷ If you fail an exam, your marks are too low and you do not pass ❸ If you fail to do something that you should have done, you do not do it ❹ If something fails, it becomes less effective or stops working properly ✿ NOUN ❺ In an exam, a fail is a piece of work that is

*Hello Kitty... knows that some words that sound as if they begin with f actually begin with ph, like phrase.*

**failure – fancy**

not good enough to pass ❃ PHRASE ❻ **Without fail** means definitely or regularly

**failure** NOUN ❶ lack of success ❷ an unsuccessful person, thing, or action ❸ Your failure to do something is not doing something that you were expected to do ❹ a weakness in something

**faint** ADJECTIVE ❶ A sound, colour, or feeling that is faint is not very strong or intense ❷ If you feel faint, you feel weak, dizzy, and unsteady ❃ VERB ❸ If you faint, you lose consciousness for a short time  **faintly** ADVERB

**fair** ADJECTIVE ❶ reasonable and just ❷ quite large ❸ moderately good or likely to be correct ❹ having light coloured hair or pale skin ❺ with pleasant and dry weather ❃ NOUN ❻ a form of entertainment that takes place outside, with stalls, sideshows, and machines to ride on ❼ an exhibition of goods produced by a particular industry  **fairly** ADVERB  **fairness** NOUN

**fairy**, fairies NOUN In stories, fairies are small, supernatural creatures with magical powers

**fairy tale** NOUN a story of magical events

**faith** NOUN ❶ Faith is a feeling of confidence, trust or optimism about something ❷ someone's faith is their religion

**faithful** ADJECTIVE ❶ loyal to someone or something and remaining firm in support of them ❷ accurate and truthful  **faithfully** ADVERB

**fake**, fakes, faking, faked NOUN ❶ an imitation of something made to trick people into thinking that it is genuine ❃ ADJECTIVE ❷ imitation and not genuine ❃ VERB ❸ If you fake a feeling, you pretend that you are experiencing it

**fall**, falls, falling, fell, fallen VERB ❶ If someone or something falls or falls over, they drop towards the ground ❷ If something falls somewhere, it lands there ❸ If something falls in amount or strength, it becomes less ❹ If a person or group in a position of power falls, they lose their position and someone else takes control ❺ Someone who falls in battle is killed ❻ If, for example, you fall asleep, fall ill, or fall in love, you change quite quickly to that new state ❼ If you fall for someone, you become strongly attracted to them and fall in love ❽ If you fall for a trick or lie, you are deceived by it ❾ Something that falls on a particular date occurs on that date ❃ NOUN ❿ If you have a fall, you accidentally fall over ⓫ A fall of snow, soot, or other substance is a quantity of it that has fallen to the ground ⓬ A fall in something is a reduction in its amount or strength

**fall down** ❃ VERB An argument or idea that falls down on a particular point is weak on that point and as a result will be unsuccessful

**fall out** ❃ VERB If people fall out, they disagree and quarrel

**fall through** ❃ VERB If an arrangement or plan falls through, it fails or is abandoned

**false** ADJECTIVE ❶ untrue or incorrect ❷ not real or genuine but intended to seem real ❸ unfaithful or deceitful  **falsely** ADVERB

**fame** NOUN the state of being very well-known

**familiar** ADJECTIVE ❶ well-known or easy to recognize ❷ knowing or understanding something well

**family**, families NOUN ❶ a group consisting of parents and their children; also all the people who are related to each other, including aunts and uncles, cousins, and grandparents ❷ a group of related species of animals or plants. It is smaller than an order and larger than a genus

**famine** NOUN a serious shortage of food which may cause many deaths

**famous** ADJECTIVE very well-known

**fan**, fans, fanning, fanned NOUN ❶ If you are a fan of someone or something, you like them very much and are very enthusiastic about them ❷ a hand-held or mechanical object which creates a draught of cool air when it moves ❃ VERB ❸ To fan someone or something is to create a draught in their direction

**fan out** ❃ VERB If things or people fan out, they move outwards in different directions

**fanatic** NOUN a person who is very extreme in their support for a cause or in their enthusiasm for a particular activity

**fancy**, fancies, fancying, fancied; fancier, fanciest VERB ❶ If you fancy something, you want to have it or do it ❃ ADJECTIVE ❷ special and elaborate

# fantastic - fatality

*Fozen* (handwritten)

**fantastic** ADJECTIVE ❶ wonderful and very pleasing ❷ extremely large in degree or amount ❸ strange and difficult to believe

**fantasy**, fantasies NOUN ❶ an imagined story or situation ❷ Fantasy is the activity of imagining things or the things that you imagine ❸ In books and films, fantasy is the people or situations which are created in the writer's imagination and which are not real or realistic

**far**, farther, farthest; further, furthest ADVERB ❶ If something is far away from other things, it is a long distance away ❷ Far also means very much or to a great extent or degree ✿ ADJECTIVE ❸ Far means very distant ❹ Far also describes the more distant of two things rather than the nearer one ✿ PHRASE ❺ By **far** and **far and away** are used to say that something is the best ❻ **So far** means up to the present moment ❼ **As far as, so far as**, and **in so far as** mean to the degree or extent that something is true

**fare**, fares, faring, fared NOUN ❶ the amount charged for a journey on a bus, train, or plane ✿ VERB ❷ How someone fares in a particular situation is how they get on

**don't mix up**

**Hello Kitty...**

never mixes up **fair** (an event with machines to ride on) and **fare** (the cost of a journey).

**farewell** INTERJECTION ❶ Farewell means goodbye ✿ ADJECTIVE ❷ A farewell act is performed by or for someone who is leaving a particular job or career

**farm** NOUN ❶ an area of land together with buildings, used for growing crops and raising animals ✿ VERB ❷ Someone who farms uses land to grow crops and raise animals **farmer** NOUN **farming** NOUN

**farmhouse** NOUN the main house on a farm

**fascinate**, fascinates, fascinating, fascinated VERB If something fascinates you, it interests you so much that you think about it and nothing else **fascinating** ADJECTIVE

**fashion** NOUN ❶ a style of dress or way of behaving that is popular at a particular time ❷ The fashion in which someone does something is the way in which they do it ✿ VERB ❸ If you fashion something, you make or shape it

**fashionable** ADJECTIVE Something that is fashionable is very popular with a lot of people at the same time **fashionably** ADVERB

**fast** ADJECTIVE ❶ moving or done at great speed ❷ If a clock is fast, it shows a time that is later than the real time ✿ ADVERB ❸ quickly and without delay ❹ Something that is held fast is firmly fixed ✿ PHRASE ❺ If you are **fast asleep**, you are in a deep sleep ✿ VERB ❻ If you fast, you eat no food at all for a period of time, usually for religious reasons ✿ NOUN ❼ a period of time during which someone does not eat food

**fasten** VERB ❶ To fasten something is to close it or attach it firmly to something else ❷ If you fasten your hands or teeth around or onto something, you hold it tightly with them

**fast food** NOUN hot food that is prepared and served quickly after you have ordered it

**fat**, fatter, fattest; fats ADJECTIVE ❶ Someone who is fat has too much weight on their body ❷ large or great ✿ NOUN ❸ Fat is the greasy, cream-coloured substance that animals and humans have under their skin, which is used to store energy and to help keep them warm ❹ Fat is also the greasy solid or liquid substance obtained from animals and plants and used in cooking

**fatal** ADJECTIVE ❶ causing death ❷ very important or significant and likely to have an undesirable effect **fatally** ADVERB

**fatality**, fatalities NOUN a death caused by accident or violence

100

**fate - feel**

**fate** NOUN ❶ Fate is a power that is believed to control events ❷ Someone's fate is what happens to them

**father** NOUN ❶ A person's father is their male parent ❷ The father of something is the man who invented or started it ❸ 'Father' is used to address a priest in some Christian churches ❹ Father is another name for God ✿ VERB ❺ LITERARY When a man fathers a child, he makes a woman pregnant

**father-in-law**, fathers-in-law NOUN A person's father-in-law is the father of their husband or wife

**fatigue**, fatigues, fatiguing, fatigued [fat-**eeg**] NOUN ❶ Fatigue is extreme tiredness ✿ VERB ❷ If you are fatigued by something, it makes you extremely tired

**fault** NOUN ❶ If something bad is your fault, you are to blame for it ❷ a weakness or imperfection in someone or something ❸ a large crack in rock caused by movement of the earth's crust ✿ PHRASE ❹ If you are **at fault**, you are mistaken or are to blame for something ✿ VERB ❺ If you fault someone, you criticize them for what they are doing because they are not doing it well

**faulty** ADJECTIVE containing flaws or errors

**favour** NOUN ❶ If you regard someone or something with favour, you like or support them ❷ If you do someone a favour, you do something helpful for them ✿ PHRASE ❸ Something that is **in someone's favour** is a help or advantage to them ❹ If you are **in favour of** something, you agree with it and think it should happen ✿ VERB ❺ If you favour something or someone, you prefer that person or thing

**favourable** ADJECTIVE ❶ of advantage or benefit to someone ❷ positive and expressing approval

**favourite** ADJECTIVE ❶ Your favourite person or thing is the one you like best ✿ NOUN ❷ Someone's favourite is the person or thing they like best ❸ the animal or person expected to win in a race or contest

**fax**, faxes NOUN an exact copy of a document sent electronically along a telephone line

**fear** NOUN ❶ Fear is an unpleasant feeling of danger ❷ a thought that something undesirable or unpleasant might happen ✿ VERB ❸ If you fear someone or something, you are frightened of them ❹ If you fear something unpleasant, you are worried that it is likely to happen **fearless** ADJECTIVE

**fearful** ADJECTIVE ❶ afraid and full of fear ❷ extremely unpleasant or worrying

**feast** NOUN a large and special meal for many people

**feat** NOUN an impressive and difficult achievement

**feather** NOUN one of the light fluffy things covering a bird's body

**feature**, features, featuring, featured NOUN ❶ an interesting or important part or characteristic of something ❷ Someone's features are the various parts of their face ❸ a characteristic that is typical of a particular living thing ❹ a special article or programme dealing with a particular subject ❺ the main film in a cinema programme ✿ VERB ❻ To feature something is to include it or emphasize it as an important part or subject

**February** NOUN February is the second month of the year. It has 28 days, except in a leap year, when it has 29 days

**fed** the past tense and past participle of **feed**

**fed up** ADJECTIVE INFORMAL unhappy or bored

**fee** NOUN a charge or payment for a job, service, or activity

**feeble**, feebler, feeblest ADJECTIVE weak or lacking in power or influence

**feed**, feeds, feeding, fed VERB ❶ To feed a person or animal is to give them food ❷ When an animal or baby feeds, it eats ❸ To feed something is to supply what is needed for it to operate or exist ✿ NOUN ❹ Feed is food for animals or babies

**feedback** NOUN ❶ Feedback is comments and information about the quality or success of something ❷ Feedback is also a condition in which some of the power, sound, or information produced by electronic equipment goes back into it

**feel**, feels, feeling, felt VERB ❶ If you feel an emotion or sensation, you experience it ❷ If you feel that something is the case, you believe it to be so ❸ If you feel something, you touch it ❹ If something feels warm or cold, for example, you experience its warmth or coldness through the sense of touch ❺ To feel

# feeling – fibre

the effect of something is to be affected by it ❀ NOUN ❻ The feel of something is how it feels to you when you touch it ❀ PHRASE ❼ If you **feel like** doing something, you want to do it
**feeling** NOUN ❶ an emotion or reaction ❷ a physical sensation ❸ Feeling is the ability to experience the sense of touch in your body ❹ IN PLURAL Your feelings about something are your general attitudes or thoughts about it
**feet** the plural of **foot**
**fell** ❶ the past tense of **fall** ❀ VERB ❷ To fell a tree is to cut it down
**fellow** NOUN ❶ OLD-FASHIONED a man ❷ a senior member of a learned society or a university college ❸ Your fellows are the people who share work or an activity with you ❀ ADJECTIVE ❹ You use 'fellow' to describe people who have something in common with you
**felt** ❶ the past tense and past participle of **feel** ❀ NOUN ❷ Felt is a thick cloth made by pressing short threads together
**female** NOUN ❶ a person or animal that belongs to the sex that can have babies or young ❀ ADJECTIVE ❷ concerning or relating to females
**feminine** ADJECTIVE ❶ relating to women or considered to be typical of women ❷ belonging to a particular class of nouns in some languages, such as French, German, and Latin
**feminism** NOUN Feminism is the belief that women should have the same rights and opportunities as men **feminist** NOUN OR ADJECTIVE
**fence**, fences, fencing, fenced NOUN ❶ a wooden or wire barrier between two areas of land ❷ a barrier or hedge for the horses to jump over in horse racing or show jumping ❀ VERB ❸ To fence an area of land is to surround it with a fence ❹ When two people fence, they use special swords to fight each other as a sport
**fern** NOUN a plant with long feathery leaves and no flowers
**ferry**, ferries, ferrying, ferried NOUN ❶ a boat that carries people and vehicles across short stretches of water ❀ VERB ❷ To ferry people or goods somewhere is to transport them there, usually on a short, regular journey
**fertile** ADJECTIVE ❶ capable of producing offspring or plants ❷ creative **fertility** NOUN

**fertilizer** or **fertiliser** NOUN a substance put onto soil to improve plant growth
**festival** NOUN ❶ an organized series of events and performances ❷ a day or period of religious celebration
**fetch**, fetches, fetching, fetched VERB ❶ If you fetch something, you go to where it is and bring it back ❷ If something fetches a particular sum of money, it is sold for that amount
**fever** NOUN ❶ Fever is a condition occurring during illness, in which the patient has a very high body temperature ❷ A fever is extreme excitement or agitation
**feverish** ADJECTIVE ❶ in a state of extreme excitement or agitation ❷ suffering from a high body temperature
**few** ADJECTIVE OR NOUN ❶ used to refer to a small number of things ❀ PHRASES ❷ **Quite a few** or **a good few** means quite a large number of things
**fiancé** [fee-**on**-say] NOUN A woman's fiancé is the man to whom she is engaged
**fiancée** NOUN A man's fiancée is the woman to whom he is engaged
**fibre** NOUN ❶ a thin thread of a substance used to make cloth ❷ Fibre is also a part of plants that can be eaten but not digested; it helps food pass quickly through the body

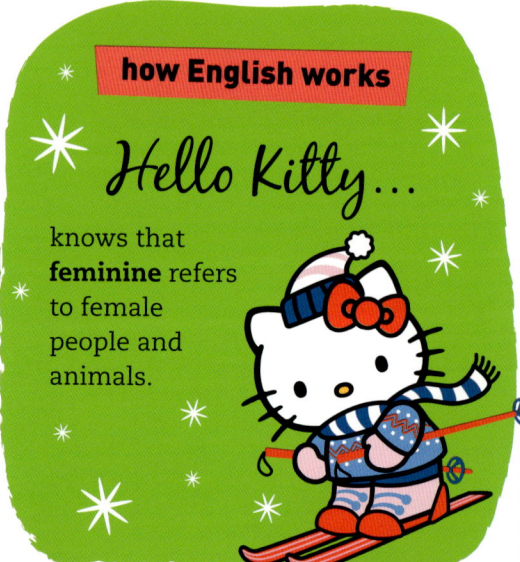

## how English works

Hello Kitty...

knows that **feminine** refers to female people and animals.

**fiction** NOUN ❶ Fiction is stories about people and events that have been invented by the author ❷ something that is not true **fictional** ADJECTIVE

**fidget** VERB ❶ If you fidget, you keep changing your position because of nervousness or boredom ✿ NOUN ❷ someone who fidgets

**field** NOUN ❶ an area of land where crops are grown or animals are kept ❷ an area of land where sports are played ❸ A coal field, oil field, or gold field is an area where coal, oil, or gold is found ❹ a particular subject or area of interest ✿ ADJECTIVE ❺ A field trip or a field study involves research or activity in the natural environment rather than theoretical or laboratory work ❻ In an athletics competition, the field events are the events such as the high jump and the javelin which do not take place on a running track ✿ VERB ❼ To field questions is to answer or deal with them skilfully

**fielder** NOUN In cricket, the fielders are the team members who stand at various parts of the pitch and try to get the batsmen out or to prevent runs from being scored

**fierce**, fiercer, fiercest ADJECTIVE ❶ very aggressive or angry ❷ extremely strong or intense **fiercely** ADVERB

**fifteen** the number 15 **fifteenth** ADJECTIVE

**fifth** ADJECTIVE ❶ The fifth item in a series is the one counted as number five ✿ NOUN ❷ one of five equal parts

**fifty**, fifties the number 50 **fiftieth** ADJECTIVE

**fig** NOUN a soft, sweet fruit full of tiny seeds. It grows in hot countries and is often eaten dried

**fight**, fights, fighting, fought VERB ❶ When people fight, they take part in a battle, a war, a boxing match, or in some other attempt to hurt or kill someone ❷ To fight for something is to try in a very determined way to achieve it ✿ NOUN ❸ a situation in which people hit or try to hurt each other ❹ a determined attempt to prevent or achieve something ❺ an angry disagreement

**fighter** NOUN someone who physically fights another person

**figure**, figures, figuring, figured NOUN ❶ a written number or the amount a number stands for ❷ a geometrical shape ❸ a diagram or table in a written text ❹ the shape of a human body, sometimes one that you cannot see properly ❺ a person ✿ VERB ❻ To figure in something is to appear or be included in it ❼ INFORMAL If you figure that something is the case, you guess or conclude this

**file**, files, filing, filed NOUN ❶ a box or folder in which a group of papers or records is kept; also used of the information kept in the file ❷ In computing, a file is a stored set of related data with its own name ❸ a long steel tool with a rough surface, used for smoothing and shaping hard materials ✿ VERB ❹ When someone files a document, they put it in its correct place with similar documents ❺ When a group of people file somewhere, they walk one behind the other in a line ❻ If you file something, you smooth or shape it with a file

**fill** VERB ❶ If you fill something or if it fills up, it becomes full ❷ If something fills a need, it satisfies the need ❸ To fill a job vacancy is to appoint someone to do that job

**fill in** ✿ VERB ❶ If you fill in a form, you write information in the appropriate spaces ❷ If you fill someone in, you give them information to bring them up to date

**filling** NOUN ❶ the soft food mixture inside a sandwich, cake, or pie ❷ a small amount of metal or plastic put into a hole in a tooth by a dentist

**film** NOUN ❶ a series of moving pictures projected onto a screen and shown at the cinema or on television ❷ a thin flexible strip of plastic used in a camera to record images when exposed to light ❸ a very thin layer of powder or liquid on a surface ❹ Plastic film is a very thin sheet of plastic used for wrapping things ✿ VERB ❺ If you film someone, you use a video camera to record their movements on film

**filter** NOUN ❶ a device that allows some substances, lights, or sounds to pass through it, but not others ✿ VERB ❷ To filter a substance is to pass it through a filter ❸ If something filters somewhere, it gets there slowly or faintly

**fin** NOUN a thin, flat structure on the body of a fish, used to help guide it through the water

**final** ADJECTIVE ❶ last in a series or happening at the end of something ❷ A

# finalist - first

decision that is final cannot be changed or questioned ❖ NOUN ❸ the last game or contest in a series which decides the overall winner ❹ IN PLURAL Finals are the last and most important examinations of a university or college course

**finalist** NOUN a person taking part in the final of a competition

**finally** ADVERB If something finally happens, it happens after a long delay

**finance**, finances, financing, financed VERB ❶ To finance a project or a large purchase is to provide the money for it ❖ NOUN ❷ Finance for something is the money or loans used to pay for it ❸ Finance is also the management of money, loans, and investments

**financial** ADJECTIVE relating to or involving money

**find**, finds, finding, found VERB ❶ If you find someone or something, you discover them, either as a result of searching or by coming across them unexpectedly ❷ If you find that something is the case, you become aware of it or realize it ❸ Something that is found in a particular place typically lives or exists there ❹ When a court or jury finds a person guilty or not guilty, they decide that the person is guilty or innocent ❖ NOUN ❺ If you describe something or someone as a find, you mean that you have recently discovered them and they are valuable or useful

**fine**, finer, finest; fines, fining, fined ADJECTIVE ❶ very good or very beautiful ❷ satisfactory or suitable ❸ very narrow or thin ❹ A fine detail, adjustment, or distinction is very delicate, exact, or subtle ❺ When the weather is fine, it is not raining and is bright or sunny ❖ NOUN ❻ a sum of money paid as a punishment ❖ VERB ❼ Someone who is fined has to pay a sum of money as a punishment

**finger** NOUN ❶ Your fingers are the four long jointed parts of your hands, sometimes including the thumbs ❖ VERB ❷ If you finger something you feel it with your fingers

**fingernail** NOUN Your fingernails are the hard coverings at the ends of your fingers

**fingerprint** NOUN a mark made showing the pattern on the skin at the tip of a person's finger

**finish** VERB ❶ When you finish something, you reach the end of it and complete it ❷ When something finishes, it ends or stops ❖ NOUN ❸ The finish of something is the end or last part of it ❹ The finish that something has is the texture or appearance of its surface

**fir** NOUN a tall pointed evergreen tree that has thin needle-like leaves and produces cones

**fire**, fires, firing, fired NOUN ❶ Fire is the flames produced when something burns ❷ a pile or mass of burning material ❸ a piece of equipment that is used as a heater ❖ VERB ❹ If you fire a weapon or fire a bullet, you operate the weapon so that the bullet or missile is released ❺ If you fire questions at someone, you ask them a lot of questions very quickly ❻ INFORMAL If an employer fires someone, he or she dismisses that person from their job ❖ PHRASE ❼ If someone **opens fire**, they start shooting

**firearm** NOUN a gun

**fire brigade** NOUN the organization which has the job of putting out fires

**fire engine** NOUN a large vehicle that carries equipment for putting out fires

**fire extinguisher** NOUN a metal cylinder containing water or foam for spraying onto a fire

**firefighter** NOUN a person whose job is to put out fires and rescue trapped people

**fireplace** NOUN the opening beneath a chimney where a fire can be lit

**firework** NOUN a small container of gunpowder and other chemicals which explodes and produces coloured sparks or smoke when lit

**firm** ADJECTIVE ❶ Something that is firm does not move easily when pressed or pushed, or when weight is put on it ❷ A firm grasp or push is one with controlled force or pressure ❸ A firm decision is definite ❹ Someone who is firm behaves with authority that shows they will not change their mind ❖ NOUN ❺ a business selling or producing something **firmly** ADVERB **firmness** NOUN

**first** ADJECTIVE ❶ done or in existence before anything else ❷ more important than anything else ❖ ADVERB ❸ done or occurring before anything else ❖ NOUN

**first aid - flatten**

❹ something that has never happened or been done before  **firstly** ADVERB

**first aid** NOUN First aid is medical treatment given to an injured person

**first class** ADJECTIVE ❶ Something that is first class is of the highest quality or standard ❷ First-class accommodation on a train, aircraft, or ship is the best and most expensive type of accommodation ❸ First-class postage is quick but more expensive

**fish**, fishes, fishing, fished NOUN ❶ a cold-blooded creature living in water that has a spine, gills, fins, and a scaly skin ❷ Fish is the flesh of fish eaten as food ✿ VERB ❸ To fish is to try to catch fish for food or sport  **fishing** NOUN  **fisherman** NOUN

**fist** NOUN a hand with the fingers curled tightly towards the palm

**fit**, fits, fitting, fitted; fitter, fittest VERB ❶ Something that fits is the right shape or size for a particular person or position ❷ If you fit something somewhere, you put it there carefully or securely ❸ If something fits a particular situation, person, or thing, it is suitable or appropriate ✿ NOUN ❹ The fit of something is how it fits ❺ If someone has a fit, their muscles suddenly start contracting violently and they may lose consciousness ❻ A fit of laughter, coughing, anger, or panic is a sudden uncontrolled outburst ✿ ADJECTIVE ❼ good enough or suitable ❽ Someone who is fit is healthy and has strong muscles as a result of regular exercise  **fitness** NOUN

**five** the number 5

**fix**, fixes, fixing, fixed VERB ❶ If you fix something somewhere, you attach it or put it there securely ❷ If you fix something broken, you mend it ❸ If you fix your attention on something, you concentrate on it ❹ If you fix something, you make arrangements for it ❺ INFORMAL To fix something is to arrange the outcome unfairly or dishonestly ✿ NOUN ❻ INFORMAL something that has been unfairly or dishonestly arranged ❼ INFORMAL If you are in a fix, you are in a difficult situation

**fizzy**, fizzier, fizziest ADJECTIVE Fizzy drinks have carbon dioxide in them to make them bubbly

**flag**, flags, flagging, flagged NOUN ❶ a rectangular or square cloth which has a particular colour and design, and is used as the symbol of a nation or as a signal ✿ VERB ❷ If you or your spirits flag, you start to lose energy or enthusiasm

**flake**, flakes, flaking, flaked NOUN ❶ a small thin piece of something ✿ VERB ❷ When something such as paint flakes, small thin pieces of it come off

**flame**, flames NOUN ❶ a flickering tongue or blaze of fire ❷ A flame of passion, desire, or anger is a sudden strong feeling

**flammable** ADJECTIVE likely to catch fire and burn easily

**flap**, flaps, flapping, flapped VERB ❶ Something that flaps moves up and down or from side to side with a snapping sound ✿ NOUN ❷ a loose piece of something such as paper or skin that is attached at one edge

**flash**, flashes, flashing, flashed NOUN ❶ a sudden short burst of light ✿ VERB ❷ If a light flashes, it shines for a very short period, often repeatedly ❸ Something that flashes past moves or happens so fast that you almost miss it ❹ If you flash something, you show it briefly ✿ PHRASE ❺ Something that happens **in a flash** happens suddenly and lasts a very short time

**flat**, flats, flatting, flatted; flatter, flattest NOUN ❶ a self-contained set of rooms, usually on one level, for living in ❷ In music, a flat is a note or key a semitone lower than that described by the same letter. It is represented by the symbol (♭) ✿ VERB ❸ In Australian and New Zealand English, to flat is to live in a flat ✿ ADJECTIVE ❹ Something that is flat is level and smooth ❺ A flat object is not very tall or deep ❻ A flat tyre or ball has not got enough air in it ❼ A flat battery has lost its electrical charge ❽ A flat refusal or denial is complete and firm ❾ Something that is flat is without emotion or interest ❿ A flat rate or price is fixed and the same for everyone ⓫ A musical instrument or note that is flat is slightly too low in pitch ✿ ADVERB ⓬ Something that is done in a particular time flat, takes exactly that time

**flatten** VERB If you flatten something or if it flattens, it becomes flat or flatter

105

# flatter - float

**flatter** VERB ❶ If you flatter someone, you praise them in an exaggerated way, either to please them or to persuade them to do something ❷ If you are flattered by something, it makes you feel pleased and important ❸ If you flatter yourself that something is the case, you believe, perhaps mistakenly, something good about yourself or your abilities ❹ Something that flatters you makes you appear more attractive **flattering** ADJECTIVE

**flavour** NOUN ❶ The flavour of food is its taste ❷ The flavour of something is its distinctive characteristic or quality ✿ VERB ❸ If you flavour food with a spice or herb, you add it to the food to give it a particular taste

**flaw** NOUN ❶ a fault or mark in a piece of fabric or glass, or in a decorative pattern ❷ a weak point or undesirable quality in a theory, plan, or person's character

**flea** NOUN a small wingless jumping insect which feeds on blood

### don't mix up

**Hello Kitty...** never mixes up **flea** (the small biting insect) and **flee** (to run away).

**fled** the past tense and past participle of **flee**

**flee**, flees, fleeing, fled VERB To flee from someone or something is to run away from them

**fleece**, fleeces, fleecing, fleeced NOUN ❶ A sheep's fleece is its coat of wool ✿ VERB ❷ To fleece someone is to swindle them or charge them too much money

**fleet** NOUN a group of ships or vehicles owned by the same organization or travelling together

**flesh** NOUN ❶ Flesh is the soft part of the body ❷ The flesh of a fruit or vegetable is the soft inner part that you eat

**flew** the past tense of **fly**

**flexible** ADJECTIVE ❶ able to be bent easily without breaking ❷ able to adapt to changing circumstances **flexibility** NOUN

**flick** VERB ❶ If you flick something, you move it sharply with your finger ❷ If something flicks somewhere, it moves with a short sudden movement ✿ NOUN ❸ a sudden quick movement or sharp touch with the finger

**flicker** VERB ❶ If a light or a flame flickers, it shines and moves unsteadily ✿ NOUN ❷ a short unsteady light or movement of light ❸ A flicker of a feeling is a very brief experience of it

**flight** NOUN ❶ a journey made by aeroplane ❷ Flight is the action of flying or the ability to fly ❸ Flight is also the act of running away ❹ A flight of stairs or steps is a set running in a single direction

**fling**, flings, flinging, flung VERB ❶ If you fling something, you throw it with a lot of force ✿ NOUN ❷ a short period devoted to pleasure and free from any restrictions or rules

**flip**, flips, flipping, flipped VERB ❶ If you flip something, you turn or move it quickly and sharply ❷ If you flip something, you hit it sharply with your finger or thumb

**flipper** NOUN ❶ one of the broad, flat limbs of sea animals, for example seals or penguins, used for swimming ❷ Flippers are broad, flat pieces of rubber that you can attach to your feet to help you swim

**flirt** VERB ❶ If you flirt with someone, you behave as if you are sexually attracted to them but without serious intentions ❷ If you flirt with an idea, you consider it without seriously intending to do anything about it ✿ NOUN ❸ someone who often flirts with people

**float** VERB ❶ Something that floats is supported by water ❷ Something that floats through the air moves along gently, supported by the air ❸ If a company is floated, shares are sold to the public for the first time and the company gains a listing on the stock exchange ✿ NOUN ❹ a light object that floats and either supports something or someone or regulates the level of liquid in a tank or cistern ❺ In Australian English, a float is also a vehicle for transporting horses

**flock** NOUN ❶ a group of birds, sheep, or goats ✿ VERB ❷ If people flock somewhere, they go there in large numbers

**flood** NOUN ❶ a large amount of water covering an area that is usually dry ❷ A flood of something is a large amount of it suddenly occurring ✿ VERB ❸ If liquid floods an area, or if a river floods, the liquid or water overflows, covering the surrounding area ❹ If people or things flood into a place, they come there in large numbers

**floodlight** NOUN a very powerful outdoor lamp used to light up public buildings and sports grounds

**floor** NOUN ❶ the part of a room you walk on ❷ one of the levels in a building ❸ the ground at the bottom of a valley, forest, or the sea ✿ VERB ❹ If a remark or question floors you, you are completely unable to deal with it or answer it

**flop**, flops, flopping, flopped VERB ❶ If someone or something flops, they fall loosely and rather heavily ❷ INFORMAL Something that flops fails ✿ NOUN ❸ INFORMAL something that is completely unsuccessful

**floppy**, floppier, floppiest ADJECTIVE tending to hang downwards in a rather loose way

**florist** NOUN a person or shop selling flowers

**flour** NOUN Flour is a powder made from finely ground grain, usually wheat, and used for baking and cooking

**flourish**, flourishes, flourishing, flourished VERB ❶ Something that flourishes develops or functions successfully or healthily ❷ If you flourish something, you wave or display it so that people notice it ✿ NOUN ❸ a bold sweeping or waving movement

**flow** VERB ❶ If something flows, it moves or happens in a steady continuous stream ✿ NOUN ❷ A flow of something is a steady continuous movement of it; also the rate at which it flows

**flower** NOUN ❶ the part of a plant containing the reproductive organs from which the fruit or seeds develop ✿ VERB ❷ When a plant flowers, it produces flowers

**flown** the past participle of **fly**

**flu** NOUN Flu is an illness similar to a very bad cold, which causes headaches, sore throat, weakness, and aching muscles. Flu is short for 'influenza'

**fluent** ADJECTIVE ❶ able to speak a foreign language correctly and without hesitation ❷ able to express yourself clearly and without hesitation **fluently** ADVERB

**fluff** NOUN ❶ Fluff is soft, light, woolly threads or fibres bunched together ✿ VERB ❷ If you fluff something up or out, you brush or shake it to make it seem larger and lighter **fluffy** ADJECTIVE

**fluid** NOUN ❶ a liquid ✿ ADJECTIVE ❷ Fluid movement is smooth and flowing ❸ A fluid arrangement or plan is flexible and without a fixed structure

**flung** the past tense of **fling**

**flush**, flushes, flushing, flushed; flusher, flushest NOUN ❶ A flush is a rosy red colour ✿ VERB ❷ If you flush, your face goes red ❸ If you flush a toilet or something such as a pipe, you force water through it to clean it ✿ ADJECTIVE ❹ INFORMAL Someone who is flush has plenty of money ❺ Something that is flush with a surface is level with it or flat against it

**flute** NOUN a musical wind instrument consisting of a long metal tube with holes and keys. It is held sideways to the mouth and played by blowing across a hole in its side

**flutter** VERB ❶ If something flutters, it flaps or waves with small, quick movements ✿ NOUN ❷ If you are in a flutter, you are excited and nervous

**fly**, flies, flying, flew, flown NOUN ❶ an insect with two pairs of wings ❷ The front opening on a pair of trousers is the fly or the flies ❸ The fly or fly sheet of a tent is either a flap at the entrance or an outer layer providing protection from rain ✿ VERB ❹ When a bird, insect, or aircraft flies, it moves through the

# foam – forbid

air ❺ If someone or something flies, they move or go very quickly ❻ If you fly at someone or let fly at them, you attack or criticize them suddenly and aggressively

**foam** NOUN ❶ Foam is a mass of tiny bubbles ❷ Foam is light spongy material used, for example, in furniture or packaging ✿ VERB ❸ When something foams, it forms a mass of small bubbles

**focus**, focuses or focusses, focusing or focussing, focused or focussed; focuses or foci VERB ❶ If you focus your eyes or an instrument on an object, you adjust them so that the image is clear ✿ NOUN ❷ The focus of something is its centre of attention

**foetus**, foetuses or **fetus**, fetuses [*fee-tus*] NOUN an unborn child or animal in the womb

**fog**, fogs, fogging, fogged NOUN ❶ Fog is a thick mist of water droplets suspended in the air ✿ VERB ❷ If glass fogs up, it becomes clouded with steam or condensation **foggy** ADJECTIVE

**foil**, foils, foiling, foiled VERB ❶ If you foil someone's attempt at something, you prevent them from succeeding ✿ NOUN ❷ Foil is thin, paper-like sheets of metal used to wrap food ❸ Something that is a good foil for something else contrasts with it and makes its good qualities more noticeable

**fold** VERB ❶ If you fold something, you bend it so that one part lies over another ❷ INFORMAL If a business folds, it fails and closes down ❸ In cooking, if you fold one ingredient into another, you mix it in gently ✿ NOUN ❹ a crease or bend in paper or cloth ❺ a small enclosed area for sheep

**folder** NOUN ❶ a thin piece of folded cardboard for keeping loose papers together ❷ In computing, a folder is a named area of computer disk where you can group together files and subdirectories. It is also called a **directory**

**folk** NOUN ❶ Folk or folks are people ✿ ADJECTIVE ❷ Folk music, dance, or art is traditional or representative of the ordinary people of an area

**follow** VERB ❶ If you follow someone, you move along behind them. If you follow a path or a sign, you move along in that direction ❷ Something that follows a particular thing happens after it ❸ Something that follows is true or logical as a result of something else being the case ❹ If you follow instructions or advice, you do what you are told ❺ If you follow an explanation or the plot of a story, you understand each stage of it

**fond** ADJECTIVE ❶ If you are fond of someone or something, you like them ❷ A fond hope or belief is thought of with happiness but is unlikely to happen

**font** NOUN a large stone bowl in a church that holds the water for baptisms

**food** NOUN Food is any substance consumed by an animal or plant to provide energy

**food chain** NOUN a series of living things which are linked because each one feeds on the next one in the series. For example, a plant may be eaten by a rabbit which may be eaten by a fox

**fool** NOUN ❶ someone who behaves in a silly or stupid way ❷ a dessert made from fruit, eggs, cream, and sugar whipped together ✿ VERB ❸ If you fool someone, you deceive or trick them

**foolish** ADJECTIVE very silly or unwise **foolishly** ADVERB

**foot**, feet NOUN ❶ the part of your body at the end of your leg ❷ the bottom, base, or lower end of something ❸ a unit of length equal to 12 inches or about 30.5 centimetres ✿ ADJECTIVE ❹ A foot brake, pedal, or pump is operated by your foot

**football** NOUN ❶ Football is any game in which the ball can be kicked, such as soccer, Australian Rules, rugby union, and American football ❷ a ball used in any of these games **footballer** NOUN

**footpath** NOUN a path for people to walk on
**footprint** NOUN a mark left by a foot or shoe
**footstep** NOUN the sound or mark made by someone walking

**for** PREPOSITION ❶ meant to be given to or used by a particular person, or done in order to help or benefit them ❷ 'For' is used when explaining the reason, cause, or purpose of something ❸ You use 'for' to express a quantity, time, or distance ❹ If you are for something, you support it or approve of it

**forbid**, forbids, forbidding, forbade, forbidden VERB If you forbid someone to do something, you order them not to do it **forbidden** ADJECTIVE

**force - formula**

**force**, forces, forcing, forced VERB ❶ To force someone to do something is to make them do it ❷ To force something is to use violence or great strength to move or open it ✿ NOUN ❸ a pressure to do something, sometimes with the use of violence or great strength ❹ The force of something is its strength or power ❺ a person or thing that has a lot of influence or effect ❻ an organized group of soldiers or police ❼ In physics, force is a pushing or pulling influence that changes a body from a state of rest to one of motion, or changes its rate of motion ✿ PHRASE ❽ A law or rule that is **in force** is currently valid and must be obeyed

**forecast**, forecasts, forecasting, forecast or forecasted NOUN ❶ a prediction of what will happen, especially a statement about what the weather will be like ✿ VERB ❷ To forecast an event is to predict what will happen

**foreground** NOUN In a picture, the foreground is the part that seems nearest to you

**forehead** NOUN the area at the front of your head, above your eyebrows and below your hairline

**foreign** ADJECTIVE ❶ belonging to or involving countries other than your own ❷ unfamiliar or uncharacteristic ❸ A foreign object has got into something, usually by accident, and should not be there **foreigner** NOUN

**foresee**, foresees, foreseeing, foresaw, foreseen VERB If you foresee something, you predict or expect that it will happen

**forest** NOUN a large area of trees growing close together

**forever** ADVERB permanently or continually

**foreword** NOUN an introduction in a book

**forge**, forges, forging, forged NOUN ❶ a place where a blacksmith works making metal goods by hand ✿ VERB ❷ To forge metal is to hammer and bend it into shape while hot ❸ To forge a relationship is to create a strong and lasting relationship ❹ Someone who forges money, documents, or paintings makes illegal copies of them ❺ To forge ahead is to progress quickly

**forgery**, forgeries NOUN Forgery is the crime of forging money, documents, or paintings; also something that has been forged **forger** NOUN

**forget**, forgets, forgetting, forgot, forgotten VERB ❶ If you forget something, you fail to remember or think about it ❷ If you forget yourself, you behave in an unacceptable, uncontrolled way **forgetful** ADJECTIVE

**forgive**, forgives, forgiving, forgave, forgiven VERB If you forgive someone for doing something bad, you stop feeling angry and resentful towards them

**fork** NOUN ❶ a pronged instrument used for eating food ❷ a large garden tool with three or four prongs ❸ a y-shaped junction or division in a road, river, or branch ✿ VERB ❹ To fork something is to move or turn it with a fork

**fork out** ✿ VERB INFORMAL If you fork out for something, you pay for it, often unwillingly

**form** NOUN ❶ A particular form of something is a type or kind of it ❷ The form of something is the shape or pattern of something ❸ a sheet of paper with questions and spaces for you to fill in the answers ❹ a class in a school ✿ VERB ❺ The things that form something are the things it consists of ❻ When someone forms something or when it forms, it is created, organized, or started

**formal** ADJECTIVE ❶ correct, serious, and conforming to accepted conventions ❷ official and publicly recognized **formally** ADVERB

**formality**, formalities NOUN an action or process that is carried out as part of an official procedure

**format** NOUN the way in which something is arranged or presented

**formation** NOUN ❶ The formation of something is the process of developing and creating it ❷ the pattern or shape of something

**former** ADJECTIVE ❶ happening or existing before now or in the past ✿ NOUN ❷ You use 'the former' to refer to the first of two things just mentioned **formerly** ADVERB

**formidable** ADJECTIVE very difficult to deal with or overcome, and therefore rather frightening or impressive

**formula**, formulae or formulas NOUN ❶ a group of letters, numbers, and symbols which stand for a mathematical or scientific rule ❷ a list of quantities of

109

# fort - fracture

substances that make another substance when mixed, for example in chemistry ❸ a plan or set of rules for dealing with a particular problem or situation

**fort** NOUN a strong building built for defence

**fortnight** NOUN a period of two weeks

**fortress**, fortresses NOUN a castle or well-protected town built for defence

**fortunate** ADJECTIVE ❶ Someone who is fortunate is lucky ❷ Something that is fortunate brings success or advantage

**fortunately** ADVERB

**fortune** NOUN ❶ Fortune or good fortune is good luck ❷ A fortune is a large amount of money ❀ PHRASE ❸ If someone **tells your fortune**, they predict your future

**forty**, forties the number 40  **fortieth** ADJECTIVE

**forward** ADVERB OR ADJECTIVE ❶ Forward or forwards means in the front or towards the front ❷ Forward means in or towards a future time ❸ Forward or forwards also means developing or progressing ❀ ADVERB ❹ If someone or something is put forward, they are suggested as being suitable for something ❀ VERB ❺ If you forward a letter that you have received, you send it on to the person to whom it is addressed at their new address ❀ NOUN ❻ In a game such as football or hockey, a forward is a player in an attacking position

**fossil** NOUN the remains or impression of an animal or plant from a previous age, preserved in rock

**fossil fuel** NOUN Fossil fuels are fuels such as coal, oil, and natural gas, which have been formed by rotting animals and plants from millions of years ago

**foster** VERB ❶ If someone fosters a child, they are paid to look after the child for a period, but do not become its legal parent ❷ If you foster something such as an activity or an idea, you help its development and growth by encouraging people to do or think it

**fought** the past tense and past participle of **fight**

**foul** ADJECTIVE ❶ Something that is foul is very unpleasant, especially because it is dirty, wicked, or obscene ❀ VERB ❷ To foul something is to make it dirty, especially with faeces ❀ NOUN ❸ In sport, a foul is an act of breaking the rules

**found** ❶ Found is the past tense and past participle of **find** ❀ VERB ❷ If someone founds an organization or institution, they start it and set it up

**foundation** NOUN ❶ The foundation of a belief or way of life is the basic ideas or attitudes on which it is built ❷ A foundation is also a solid layer of concrete or bricks in the ground, on which a building is built to give it a firm base

**founder** NOUN ❶ The founder of an institution or organization is the person who sets it up ❀ VERB ❷ If something founders, it fails

**fountain** NOUN an ornamental structure consisting of a jet of water forced into the air by a pump

**four** ❶ the number 4 ❀ PHRASE ❷ If you are **on all fours**, you are on your hands and knees

**fourteen** the number 14  **fourteenth** ADJECTIVE

**fourth** The fourth item in a series is the one counted as number four

**fowl** NOUN a bird such as chicken or duck that is kept or hunted for its meat or eggs

## how to remember

An **owl** is not a **fowl**.

**fox** NOUN a dog-like wild animal with reddish-brown fur, a pointed face and ears, and a thick tail

**fraction** NOUN ❶ In arithmetic, a fraction is a part of a whole number. A **proper fraction** is a fraction in which the number above the line is lower than the number below it; an **improper fraction** has the greater number above the line ❷ a tiny proportion or amount of something

**fracture**, fractures, fracturing, fractured NOUN ❶ a crack or break in something, especially a bone ❀ VERB ❷ If something fractures, it breaks

**fragile – friendly**

**fragile** ADJECTIVE easily broken or damaged

**fragment** NOUN ❶ a small piece or part of something ✿ VERB ❷ If something fragments, it breaks into small pieces or different parts

**fragrance** NOUN a sweet or pleasant smell

**frail** ADJECTIVE ❶ Someone who is frail is not strong or healthy ❷ Something that is frail is easily broken or damaged

**frame**, frames, framing, framed NOUN ❶ the structure surrounding a door, window, or picture ❷ an arrangement of connected bars over which something is built ❸ The frames of a pair of glasses are the wire or plastic parts that hold the lenses ❹ Your frame is your body ❺ one of the many separate photographs of which a cinema film is made up ✿ VERB ❻ To frame a picture is to put it into a frame

**framework** NOUN ❶ a structure acting as a support or frame ❷ a set of rules, beliefs, or ideas which you use to decide what to do

**frank** ADJECTIVE If you are frank, you say things in an open and honest way **frankly** ADVERB

**frantic** ADJECTIVE If you are frantic, you behave in a wild, desperate way because you are anxious or frightened **frantically** ADVERB

**fraud** NOUN ❶ Fraud is the crime of getting money by deceit or trickery ❷ something that deceives people in an illegal or immoral way

**freak** NOUN ❶ someone whose appearance or behaviour is very unusual ✿ ADJECTIVE OR NOUN ❷ A freak event is very unusual and unlikely to happen

**freckle** NOUN Freckles are small, light brown spots on someone's skin, especially their face

**free**, freer, freest; frees, freeing, freed ADJECTIVE ❶ not controlled or limited ❷ Someone who is free is no longer a prisoner ❸ To be free of something unpleasant is not to have it ❹ If someone is free, they are not busy or occupied. If a place, seat, or machine is free, it is not occupied or not being used ❺ If something is free, you can have it without paying for it ✿ VERB ❻ If you free someone or something that is imprisoned, fastened, or trapped, you release them

**freedom** NOUN ❶ If you have the freedom to do something, you have the scope or are allowed to do it ❷ When prisoners gain their freedom, they escape or are released

**freely** ADVERB Freely means without restriction

**freeze**, freezes, freezing, froze, frozen VERB ❶ When a liquid freezes, it becomes solid because it is very cold ❷ If you freeze, you suddenly become very still and quiet ❸ If you freeze food, you put it in a freezer to preserve it ✿ NOUN ❹ a period of freezing weather

**freezer** NOUN a large refrigerator which freezes and stores food for a long time

**freezing** ADJECTIVE extremely cold

**freight** NOUN Freight is goods moved by lorries, ships, or other transport

**French horn** NOUN a brass musical wind instrument consisting of a tube wound in a circle

**frequency**, frequencies NOUN ❶ The frequency of an event is how often it happens ❷ The frequency of a sound or radio wave is the rate at which it vibrates

**frequent** ADJECTIVE *[free-kwuhnt]* ❶ often happening ✿ VERB *[free-kwent]* ❷ If you frequent a place, you go there often **frequently** ADVERB

**fresh** ADJECTIVE ❶ A fresh thing replaces a previous one, or is added to it ❷ Fresh food is newly made or obtained, and not tinned or frozen ❸ Fresh water is not salty, for example the water in a stream **freshly** ADVERB

**Friday**, Fridays NOUN the day between Thursday and Saturday

**fridge** NOUN the same as a **refrigerator**

**friend** NOUN Your friends are people you know well and like to spend time with

### how to remember
Her **frie**nd likes **frie**d eggs.

**friendly**, friendlier, friendliest ADJECTIVE ❶ If you are friendly to someone, you behave in a kind and pleasant way to them ❷ People who are friendly with each other like each other and enjoy spending time together

A B C D E F G H I J K L M N O P Q R S T U V W X Y Z

111

# friendship - full-time

A B C D E F G H I J K L M N O P Q R S T U V W X Y Z

**friendship** NOUN ❶ Your friendships are the special relationships that you have with your friends ❷ Friendship is the state of being friends with someone

**fright** NOUN Fright is a sudden feeling of fear

**frighten** VERB If something frightens you, it makes you afraid

**frightened** ADJECTIVE having feelings of fear about something

**frightening** ADJECTIVE causing someone to feel fear

**frill** NOUN a strip of cloth with many folds, attached to something as a decoration

**fringe** NOUN ❶ the hair that hangs over a person's forehead ❷ a decoration on clothes and other objects, consisting of a row of hanging strips or threads

**frog** NOUN a small amphibious creature with smooth skin, prominent eyes, and long back legs which it uses for jumping

**from** PREPOSITION ❶ You use 'from' to say what the source, origin, or starting point of something is ❷ If you take something from an amount, you reduce the amount by that much ❸ You also use 'from' when stating the range of something

**front** NOUN ❶ The front of something is the part that faces forward ✿ PHRASE ❷ In front means ahead or further forward ❸ If you do something in front of someone, you do it when they are present

**frontier** NOUN a border between two countries

**frost** NOUN When there is a frost, the temperature outside falls below freezing

**frosty**, frostier, frostiest ADJECTIVE If it is frosty, the temperature outside is below freezing point

**frown** VERB ❶ If you frown, you move your eyebrows closer together, because you are annoyed, worried, or concentrating ✿ NOUN ❷ a cross expression on someone's face

**froze** the past tense of **freeze**

**frozen** ❶ Frozen is the past participle of **freeze** ✿ ADJECTIVE ❷ If you say are frozen, you mean you are extremely cold

**fruit** NOUN the part of a plant that develops after the flower and contains the seeds. Many fruits are edible

**frustrate**, frustrates, frustrating, frustrated VERB If something frustrates you, it prevents you doing what you want and makes you upset and angry  **frustrated** ADJECTIVE **frustrating** ADJECTIVE **frustration** NOUN

**fry**, fries, frying, fried VERB When you fry food, you cook it in a pan containing hot fat or oil

**fuel**, fuels, fuelling, fuelled NOUN ❶ Fuel is a substance such as coal or petrol that is burned to provide heat or power ✿ VERB ❷ A machine or vehicle that is fuelled by a substance works by burning the substance as a fuel

**fulfil**, fulfils, fulfilling, fulfilled VERB ❶ If you fulfil a promise, hope, or duty, you carry it out or achieve it ❷ If something fulfils you, it gives you satisfaction

**full** ADJECTIVE ❶ containing or having as much as it is possible to hold ❷ complete or whole ❸ loose and made from a lot of fabric ❹ rich and strong ✿ ADVERB ❺ completely and directly ✿ PHRASE ❻ Something that has been done or described **in full** has been dealt with completely  **fully** ADVERB

**full stop** NOUN the punctuation mark (.) used at the end of a sentence and after an abbreviation or initial

## punctuation

### Hello Kitty...

You put a **full stop** (.) at the end of a sentence when you are writing, but not if there is already a question mark or exclamation mark there.

**full-time** ADJECTIVE ❶ involving work for the whole of each normal working week ✿ NOUN

**fun - future**

❷ In games such as football, full time is the end of the match

**fun** NOUN ❶ Fun is pleasant, enjoyable and light-hearted activity ❀ PHRASE ❷ If you **make fun** of someone, you tease them or make jokes about them

**function** NOUN ❶ The function of something or someone is their purpose or the job they have to do ❷ a large formal dinner, reception, or party ❸ A function is a variable whose value depends on the value of other independent variables. 'y is a function of x' is written y = f(x) ❀ VERB ❹ When something functions, it operates or works

**functional** ADJECTIVE ❶ relating to the way something works ❷ designed for practical use rather than for decoration or attractiveness ❸ working properly

**fund** NOUN ❶ an amount of available money, usually for a particular purpose ❷ A fund of something is a lot of it ❀ VERB ❸ Someone who funds something provides money for it

**fundamental** ADJECTIVE ❶ basic and central ❀ NOUN ❷ The fundamentals of something are its most basic and important parts

**funeral** [fyoo-ner-al] NOUN a ceremony or religious service for the burial or cremation of a dead person

**fungus**, fungi or funguses NOUN a plant such as a mushroom or mould that does not have leaves and grows on other living things

**funnel**, funnels, funnelling, funnelled NOUN ❶ an open cone narrowing to a tube, used to pour substances into containers ❷ a metal chimney on a ship or steam engine ❀ VERB ❸ If something is funnelled somewhere, it is directed through a narrow space into that place

**funny**, funnier, funniest ADJECTIVE ❶ strange or puzzling ❷ causing amusement or laughter

**fur** NOUN ❶ Fur is the soft thick body hair of many animals ❷ a coat made from an animal's fur **furry** ADJECTIVE

**furious** ADJECTIVE ❶ extremely angry ❷ involving great energy, effort, or speed

**furnace** NOUN a container for a very large, hot fire used, for example, in the steel industry for melting ore

**furniture** NOUN Furniture is movable objects such as tables, chairs and wardrobes

**further** ❶ a comparative form of **far** ❀ ADJECTIVE ❷ additional or more

**furthest** a superlative form of **far**

**fury** NOUN Fury is violent or extreme anger

**fuse**, fuses, fusing, fused NOUN ❶ a safety device in a plug or electrical appliance consisting of a piece of wire which melts to stop the electric current if a fault occurs ❷ a long cord attached to some types of simple bomb which is lit to detonate ❀ VERB ❸ When an electrical appliance fuses, it stops working because the fuse has melted to protect it ❹ If two things fuse, they join or become combined

**fuss**, fusses, fussing, fussed NOUN ❶ Fuss is unnecessarily anxious or excited behaviour ❀ VERB ❷ If someone fusses, they behave with unnecessary anxiety and concern for unimportant things

**fussy**, fussier, fussiest ADJECTIVE ❶ likely to fuss a lot ❷ with too much elaborate detail or decoration

**future** NOUN ❶ The future is the period of time after the present ❷ Something that has a future is likely to succeed ❀ ADJECTIVE ❸ The future tense of a verb is the form used to express something that will happen in the future

**how English works**

Hello Kitty...

knows that the **future tense** shows that something is going to happen, like *I will paint a picture.*

A B C D E **F** G H I J K L M N O P Q R S T U V W X Y Z

# gadget – garden

A B C D E F G H I J K L M N O P Q R S T U V W X Y Z

**gadget** NOUN a small machine or tool

**gain** VERB ❶ If you gain something, you get it gradually ❷ If you gain from a situation, you get some advantage from it ❸ If you gain on someone, you gradually catch them up ✿ NOUN ❹ an increase ❺ an advantage that you get for yourself

**galaxy**, galaxies NOUN an enormous group of stars that extends over many millions of miles

**gale** NOUN an extremely strong wind

**gallery**, galleries NOUN ❶ a building or room where works of art are shown ❷ In a theatre or large hall, the gallery is a raised area at the back or sides

**gallon** NOUN a unit of liquid volume equal to eight pints or about 4.55 litres

**gallop** VERB ❶ When a horse gallops, it runs very fast, so that during each stride all four feet are off the ground at the same time ✿ NOUN ❷ a very fast run

**gamble**, gambles, gambling, gambled VERB ❶ When people gamble, they bet money on the result of a game or race ❷ If you gamble something, you risk losing it in the hope of gaining an advantage ✿ NOUN ❸ If you take a gamble, you take a risk in the hope of gaining an advantage **gambler** NOUN **gambling** NOUN

**game** NOUN ❶ an enjoyable activity with a set of rules which is played by individuals or teams against each other ❷ an enjoyable imaginative activity played by small children ❸ You might describe something as a game when it is designed to gain advantage ❹ Game is wild animals or birds that are hunted for sport or for food ❺ IN PLURAL Games are sports played at school or in a competition ✿ ADJECTIVE ❻ INFORMAL Someone who is game is willing to try something unusual or difficult

**gang** NOUN ❶ a group of people who join together for some purpose, for example to commit a crime ✿ VERB ❷ INFORMAL If people gang up on you, they join together to oppose you

**gap** NOUN ❶ a space between two things or a hole in something solid ❷ a period of time ❸ A gap between things, people, or ideas is a great difference between them

**garage** NOUN ❶ a building where a car can be kept ❷ a place where cars are repaired and where petrol is sold

**garbage** NOUN ❶ Garbage is rubbish, especially household rubbish ❷ If you say something is garbage, you mean it is nonsense

**garden** NOUN ❶ an area of land next to a house, where flowers, fruit, or vegetables are grown ❷ IN PLURAL Gardens are a type of park in a town or around a large house **gardening** NOUN

### letter G

Some words that sound like they begin with *g* actually begin with *gh*, like *ghost*.

114

## gardener - general

**gardener** NOUN a person who looks after a garden as a job or as a hobby

**garlic** NOUN Garlic is the small white bulb of an onion-like plant which has a strong taste and smell and is used in cooking

**garment** NOUN a piece of clothing

**gas**, gases; gasses, gassing, gassed NOUN ❶ any airlike substance that is not liquid or solid, such as oxygen or the gas used as a fuel in heating ✿ VERB ❷ To gas people or animals means to kill them with poisonous gas

**gasoline** NOUN In American English, gasoline is petrol

**gasp** VERB ❶ If you gasp, you quickly draw in your breath through your mouth because you are surprised or in pain ✿ NOUN ❷ a sharp intake of breath through the mouth

**gate** NOUN ❶ a barrier which can open and shut and is used to close the entrance to a garden or field ❷ The gate at a sports event is the number of people who have attended it

**gather** VERB ❶ When people gather, they come together in a group ❷ If you gather a number of things, you bring them together in one place ❸ If something gathers speed or strength, it gets faster or stronger ❹ If you gather something, you learn it, often from what someone says

**gathering** NOUN a meeting of people who have come together for a particular purpose

**gauge**, gauges, gauging, gauged [*gayj*] VERB ❶ If you gauge something, you estimate it or calculate it ✿ NOUN ❷ a piece of equipment that measures the amount of something ❸ On railways, the gauge is the distance between the two rails on a railway line

**gave** the past tense of **give**

**gay** ADJECTIVE ❶ Someone who is gay is homosexual ✿ NOUN ❷ a homosexual person

**gaze**, gazes, gazing, gazed VERB If you gaze at something, you look steadily at it for a long time

**gear** NOUN ❶ a piece of machinery which controls the rate at which energy is converted into movement. Gears in vehicles control the speed and power of the vehicle ❷ The gear for an activity is the clothes and equipment that you need for it ✿ VERB ❸ If someone or something is geared to a particular event or purpose, they are prepared for it

**geese** the plural of **goose**

**gel**, gels, gelling, gelled [*jel*] NOUN ❶ a smooth soft jelly-like substance ✿ VERB ❷ If a liquid gels, it turns into a gel ❸ If a vague thought or plan gels, it becomes more definite

**gem** NOUN ❶ a jewel or precious stone ❷ You can describe something or someone that is extremely good or beautiful as a gem

**gender** NOUN ❶ Gender is the sex of a person or animal ❷ the classification of nouns as masculine, feminine, and neuter in certain languages

### how English works

### Helpful hints...

The **gender** of a noun means whether we talk about it as *he*, *she* or *it*.

**gene** [*jeen*] NOUN one of the parts of a living cell which controls the physical characteristics of an organism and which are passed on from one generation to the next

**general** ADJECTIVE ❶ relating to the whole of something or to most things in a group ❷ true, suitable, or relevant in most situations ❸ including or involving a wide range of different things ❹ having complete responsibility over a wide area of work or a large number of people ✿ NOUN ❺ an army officer of very high rank ✿ PHRASE ❻ **In general** means usually **generally** ADVERB

A B C D E F G H I J K L M N O P Q R S T U V W X Y Z

115

# general election – get on

**general election** NOUN an election for a new government, which all the people of a country may vote in

**generalize**, generalizes, generalizing, generalized (also **generalise**) VERB To generalize means to say that something is true in most cases, ignoring minor details

**general practitioner** NOUN a doctor who works in the community rather than in a hospital

**generate**, generates, generating, generated VERB To generate something means to create or produce it

**generation** NOUN all the people of about the same age; also the period of time between one generation and the next, usually considered to be about 25-30 years

**generator** NOUN a machine which produces electricity from another form of energy such as wind or water power

**generosity** NOUN the willingness to give money, time, or help

**generous** ADJECTIVE ❶ A generous person is very willing to give money or time ❷ Something that is generous is very large **generously** ADVERB **generosity** NOUN

**genetically modified** ADJECTIVE Genetically modified plants and animals have had one or more genes changed, for example so that they grow larger or resist diseases better

**genetics** NOUN Genetics is the science of the way that characteristics are passed on from generation to generation by means of genes **genetic** ADJECTIVE

**genius**, geniuses NOUN ❶ a highly intelligent, creative, or talented person ❷ Genius is great intelligence, creativity, or talent

**gentle**, gentler, gentlest ADJECTIVE mild and calm; not violent or rough **gently** ADVERB

**gentleman**, gentlemen NOUN a man who is polite and well-educated; also a polite way of referring to any man

**genuine** [jen-yoo-in] ADJECTIVE ❶ real and not false or pretend ❷ A genuine person is sincere and honest

**genus**, genera [jee-nuss] NOUN In biology, a genus is a class of animals or closely related plants. It is smaller than a family and larger than a species

**geography** NOUN the study of the physical features of the earth, together with the climate, natural resources and population in different parts of the world

**geology** NOUN the study of the earth's structure, especially the layers of rock and soil that make up the surface of the earth **geologist** NOUN

**geometry** NOUN Geometry is the branch of mathematics that deals with lines, angles, curves, and spaces

**germ** NOUN ❶ a very small organism that causes disease ❷ FORMAL The germ of an idea or plan is the beginning of it

**gesture**, gestures, gesturing, gestured NOUN ❶ a movement of your hands or head that conveys a message or feeling ❷ an action symbolizing something ✿ VERB ❸ If you gesture, you move your hands or head in order to communicate a message or feeling

**get**, gets, getting, got VERB ❶ Get often means the same as become ❷ If you get into a particular situation, you put yourself in that situation ❸ If you get something done, you do it or you persuade someone to do it ❹ If you get somewhere, you go there ❺ If you get something, you fetch it or are given it ❻ If you get a joke or get the point of something, you understand it ❼ If you get a train, bus, or plane, you travel on it

**get across** ✿ VERB If you get an idea across, you make people understand it

**get at** ✿ VERB ❶ If someone is getting at you, they are criticizing you in an unkind way ❷ If you ask someone what they are getting at, you are asking them to explain what they mean

**get away with** ✿ VERB If you get away with something dishonest, you are not found out or punished for doing it

**get by** ✿ VERB If you get by, you have just enough money to live on

**get on** ✿ VERB ❶ If two people get on well together, they like each other's company ❷ If you get on with a task, you do it

## how to say it

**Genus** should be said *jee-nuss*, with most force on *jee*.

**get over with – globalization**

**get over with** VERB If you want to get something unpleasant over with, you want it to be finished quickly

**get through** VERB ❶ If you get through to someone, you make them understand what you are saying ❷ If you get through to someone on the telephone, you succeed in talking to them

**ghetto**, ghettoes or ghettos NOUN a part of a city where many poor people of a particular race live

**ghost** NOUN the spirit of a dead person, believed to haunt people or places

**giant** NOUN ❶ a huge person in a myth or legend ADJECTIVE ❷ much larger than other similar things

**gift** NOUN ❶ a present ❷ a natural skill or ability

**gigantic** ADJECTIVE extremely large

**giggle**, giggles, giggling, giggled VERB ❶ To giggle means to laugh in a nervous or embarrassed way NOUN ❷ a short, nervous laugh

**ginger** NOUN ❶ Ginger is a plant root with a hot, spicy flavour, used in cooking ADJECTIVE ❷ bright orange or red

**giraffe** NOUN a tall, four-legged African mammal with a very long neck

**girl** NOUN a female child

**girlfriend** NOUN Someone's girlfriend is the woman or girl with whom they are having a romantic or sexual relationship

**give**, gives, giving, gave, given VERB ❶ If you give someone something, you hand it to them or provide it for them ❷ 'Give' is also used to express physical actions and speech ❸ If you give a party or a meal, you are the host at it ❹ If something gives, it collapses under pressure NOUN ❺ If material has give, it will bend or stretch when pulled or put under pressure PHRASE ❻ You use **give or take** to indicate that an amount you are mentioning is not exact ❼ If something **gives way** to something else, it is replaced by it ❽ If something **gives way**, it collapses

**give in** VERB If you give in, you admit that you are defeated

**give out** VERB If something gives out, it stops working

**give up** VERB ❶ If you give something up, you stop doing it ❷ If you give up, you admit that you cannot do something ❸ If you give someone up, you let the police know where they are hiding

**given** ❶ the past participle of **give** ADJECTIVE ❷ fixed or specified

**glacier** [*glass*-yer] NOUN a huge frozen river of slow-moving ice

**glad**, gladder, gladdest ADJECTIVE happy and pleased **gladly** ADVERB

**glamour** NOUN The glamour of a fashionable or attractive person or place is the charm and excitement that they have **glamorous** ADJECTIVE

**glance**, glances, glancing, glanced VERB ❶ If you glance at something, you look at it quickly ❷ If one object glances off another, it hits it at an angle and bounces away in another direction NOUN ❸ a quick look

**glare**, glares, glaring, glared VERB ❶ If you glare at someone, you look at them angrily NOUN ❷ a hard, angry look ❸ Glare is extremely bright light

**glass**, glasses NOUN ❶ Glass is a hard, transparent substance that is easily broken, used to make windows and bottles ❷ a container for drinking out of, made from glass

**glasses** PLURAL NOUN Glasses are two lenses in a frame, which some people wear over their eyes to improve their eyesight

**gleam** VERB ❶ If something gleams, it shines and reflects light NOUN ❷ a pale shining light

**glide**, glides, gliding, glided VERB ❶ To glide means to move smoothly ❷ When birds or aeroplanes glide, they float on air currents

**glimmer** NOUN ❶ a faint, unsteady light ❷ A glimmer of a feeling or quality is a faint sign of it

**glimpse**, glimpses, glimpsing, glimpsed NOUN ❶ a brief sight of something VERB ❷ If you glimpse something, you see it very briefly

**glisten** [*gliss*-sn] VERB If something glistens, it shines or sparkles

**glitter** VERB ❶ If something glitters, it shines in a sparkling way NOUN ❷ Glitter is sparkling light

**global** ADJECTIVE concerning the whole world

**globalization** NOUN ❶ the process by which a company expands so that it can do business internationally ❷ the process by

117

# global warming – gobble

which cultures throughout the world become more and more similar for a variety of reasons including increased global business and better international communications

**global warming** NOUN an increase in the world's overall temperature believed to be caused by the greenhouse effect

**globe** NOUN ❶ a ball-shaped object, especially one with a map of the earth on it ❷ You can refer to the world as the globe ❸ In South African, Australian, and New Zealand English, a globe is an electric light bulb

**gloomy** ADJECTIVE ❶ dark and depressing ❷ feeling very sad

**glorious** ADJECTIVE ❶ beautiful and impressive to look at ❷ very pleasant and giving a feeling of happiness ❸ involving great fame and success **gloriously** ADVERB

**glory**, glories, glorying, gloried NOUN ❶ Glory is fame and admiration for an achievement ❷ something considered splendid or admirable ✿ VERB ❸ If you glory in something, you take great delight in it

**glossary**, glossaries NOUN a list of explanations of specialist words, usually found at the back of a book

**glossy**, glossier, glossiest ADJECTIVE smooth and shiny

**glove** NOUN Gloves are coverings which you wear over your hands for warmth or protection

**glow** NOUN ❶ a dull, steady light ❷ a strong feeling of pleasure or happiness ✿ VERB ❸ If something glows, it shines with a dull, steady light ❹ If you are glowing, you look very happy or healthy

**glue**, glues, gluing or glueing, glued NOUN ❶ a substance used for sticking things together ✿ VERB ❷ If you glue one object to another, you stick them together using glue

**go**, goes, going, went, gone VERB ❶ If you go somewhere, you move or travel there ❷ You can use 'go' to mean become ❸ You can use 'go' to describe the state that someone or something is in ❹ If something goes well, it is successful. If it goes badly, it is unsuccessful ❺ If you are going to do something, you will do it ❻ If a machine or clock goes, it works and is not broken ❼ You use 'go' before giving the sound something makes or before quoting a song or saying ❽ If something goes on something or to someone, it is allotted to them ❾ If one thing goes with another, they are appropriate together ❿ If one number goes into another, it can be divided into it ⓫ If you go back on a promise or agreement, you do not do what you promised or agreed ⓬ If someone goes for you, they attack you ⓭ If you go in for something, you decide to do it as your job ⓮ If you go out with someone, you have a romantic relationship with them ⓯ If you go over something, you think about it or discuss it carefully ✿ NOUN ⓰ an attempt at doing something ✿ PHRASE ⓱ If someone is always **on the go**, they are always busy and active ⓲ **To go** means remaining

**go down** ✿ VERB ❶ If something goes down well, people like it. If it goes down badly, they do not like it ❷ If you go down with an illness, you catch it

**go off** ✿ VERB ❶ If you go off someone or something, you stop liking them ❷ If a bomb goes off, it explodes

**go on** ✿ VERB ❶ If you go on doing something, you continue to do it ❷ If you go on about something, you keep talking about it in a rather boring way ❸ Something that is going on is happening

**go through** ✿ VERB ❶ If you go through an unpleasant event, you experience it ❷ If a law or agreement goes through, it is approved and becomes official ❸ If you go through with something, you do it even though it is unpleasant

**goal** NOUN ❶ the space, in games like football or hockey, into which the players try to get the ball in order to score a point ❷ an instance of this ❸ Your goal is something that you hope to achieve

**goalkeeper** NOUN the player, in games like soccer or hockey, who stands in the goal and tries to stop the other team from scoring

**goat** NOUN an animal, like a sheep, with coarse hair, a beard, and horns

**gobble**, gobbles, gobbling, gobbled VERB ❶ If you gobble food, you eat it very quickly ❷ When a turkey gobbles, it makes a loud gurgling sound

# god – grab

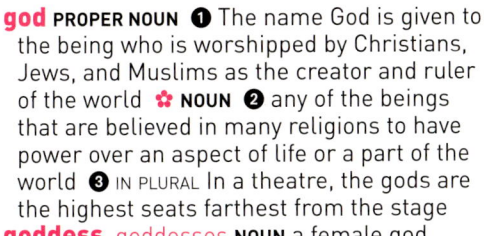

**god** PROPER NOUN ❶ The name God is given to the being who is worshipped by Christians, Jews, and Muslims as the creator and ruler of the world ❋ NOUN ❷ any of the beings that are believed in many religions to have power over an aspect of life or a part of the world ❸ IN PLURAL In a theatre, the gods are the highest seats farthest from the stage

**goddess**, goddesses NOUN a female god

**goggles** PLURAL NOUN Goggles are special glasses that fit closely round your eyes to protect them

**going** NOUN The going is the conditions that affect your ability to do something

**gold** NOUN ❶ Gold is a valuable, yellow-coloured metal. It is used for making jewellery and as an international currency ❷ 'Gold' is also used to mean things that are made of gold ❋ ADJECTIVE ❸ bright yellow

**golden** ADJECTIVE ❶ gold in colour ❷ made of gold ❸ excellent or ideal

**goldfish** NOUN a small orange-coloured fish, often kept in ponds or bowls

**golf** NOUN Golf is a game in which players use special clubs to hit a small ball into holes that are spread out over a large area of grassy land **golfer** NOUN

**golf course** NOUN an area of grassy land where people play golf

**gone** the past participle of **go**

**good**, better, best; goods ADJECTIVE ❶ pleasant, acceptable, or satisfactory ❷ skilful or successful ❸ kind, thoughtful, and loving ❹ well-behaved ❺ used to emphasize something ❋ NOUN ❻ Good is moral and spiritual justice and virtue ❼ Good also refers to anything that is desirable or beneficial as opposed to harmful ❽ IN PLURAL Goods are objects that people own or that are sold in shops ❋ PHRASE ❾ **For good** means for ever ❿ **As good as** means almost

**goodbye** INTERJECTION You say goodbye when you are leaving someone or ending a telephone conversation

**goodness** NOUN ❶ Goodness is the quality of being kind ❋ INTERJECTION ❷ People say 'Goodness!' or 'My goodness!' when they are surprised

**goose**, geese NOUN a fairly large bird with webbed feet and a long neck

**gorgeous** ADJECTIVE extremely pleasant or attractive

**gorilla** NOUN a very large, strong ape with very dark fur

**gossip**, gossips, gossiping, gossiped NOUN ❶ Gossip is informal conversation, often concerning people's private affairs ❷ Someone who is a gossip enjoys talking about other people's private affairs ❋ VERB ❸ If you gossip, you talk informally with someone, especially about other people

**govern** VERB ❶ To govern a country means to control it ❷ Something that governs a situation influences it

**government** NOUN ❶ The government is the group of people who govern a country ❷ Government is the control and organization of a country **governmental** ADJECTIVE

**gown** NOUN ❶ a long, formal dress ❷ a long, dark cloak worn by people such as judges and lawyers

**GP** an abbreviation for **general practitioner**

**grab**, grabs, grabbing, grabbed VERB ❶ If you grab something, you take it or pick it up roughly ❷ If you grab an opportunity, you take advantage of it eagerly ❋ NOUN ❸ A grab at an object is an attempt to grab it

## some other words to use

## Tips and tricks...

You should try not to use **good** too much when you are writing. Some other words you can use are: *excellent*, *first-rate*, *splendid* and *superb*.

# grace – grape

**grace** NOUN ❶ Grace is an elegant way of moving ❷ Grace is also a kind way of behaving ❸ Grace is a short prayer of thanks said before a meal **graceful** ADJECTIVE **gracefully** ADVERB

**grade**, grades, grading, graded VERB ❶ To grade things means to arrange them according to quality ✿ NOUN ❷ The grade of something is its quality ❸ the mark that you get for an exam or piece of written work

**gradual** ADJECTIVE happening or changing slowly over a long period of time

**gradually** ADVERB happening or changing slowly over a long period of time

**graduate**, graduates, graduating, graduated NOUN ❶ a person who has completed a first degree at a university or college ✿ VERB ❷ When students graduate, they complete a first degree at a university or college **graduation** NOUN

**graffiti** [graf-*fee*-tee] NOUN Graffiti is slogans or drawings scribbled on walls

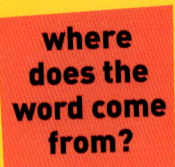

### Did you know...

that the word **graffiti** comes from Italian *graffiare* which means 'to scratch a surface'?

**where does the word come from?**

**grain** NOUN ❶ a cereal plant, such as wheat, that is grown as a crop and used for food ❷ Grains are seeds of a cereal plant ❸ A grain of sand or salt is a tiny particle of it ❹ The grain of a piece of wood is the pattern of lines made by the fibres in it ✿ PHRASE ❺ If something **goes against the grain**, you find it difficult to accept because it is against your principles

**gram** or **gramme** NOUN a unit of weight equal to one thousandth of a kilogram

**grammar** NOUN Grammar is the rules of a language relating to the ways you can combine words to form sentences

**grammatical** ADJECTIVE ❶ relating to grammar ❷ following the rules of grammar correctly

**gran** NOUN INFORMAL Your gran is your grandmother

**grand** ADJECTIVE ❶ magnificent in appearance and size ❷ very important ❸ INFORMAL very pleasant or enjoyable ❹ A grand total is the final complete amount

**grandad** NOUN INFORMAL Your grandad is your grandfather

**grandchild**, grandchildren NOUN Someone's grandchildren are the children of their son or daughter

**granddaughter** NOUN Someone's granddaughter is the daughter of their son or daughter

**grandfather** NOUN Your grandfather is your father's father or your mother's father

**grandmother** NOUN Your grandmother is your father's mother or your mother's mother

**grandparent** NOUN Your grandparents are your parents' parents

**grandson** NOUN Someone's grandson is the son of their son or daughter

**granny**, grannies NOUN INFORMAL Your granny is your grandmother

**grant** NOUN ❶ an amount of money that an official body gives to someone for a particular purpose ✿ VERB ❷ If you grant something to someone, you allow them to have it ❸ If you grant that something is true, you admit that it is true ✿ PHRASES ❹ If you **take something for granted**, you believe it without thinking about it. If you **take someone for granted**, you benefit from them without showing that you are grateful

**grape** NOUN a small green or purple fruit, eaten raw or used to make wine

**grapefruit** NOUN a large, round, yellow citrus fruit

**graph** NOUN a diagram in which a line shows how two sets of numbers or measurements are related

**graphics** PLURAL NOUN Graphics are drawings and pictures composed of simple lines and strong colours

**grasp** VERB ❶ If you grasp something, you hold it firmly ❷ If you grasp an idea, you understand it ❖ NOUN ❸ a firm hold ❹ Your grasp of something is your understanding of it

**grass**, grasses NOUN Grass is the common green plant that grows on lawns and in parks **grassy** ADJECTIVE

**grasshopper** NOUN an insect with long back legs which it uses for jumping and making a high-pitched sound

**grateful** ADJECTIVE If you are grateful for something, you are glad you have it and want to thank the person who gave it to you **gratefully** ADVERB

**gratitude** NOUN Gratitude is the feeling of being grateful

**grave**, graves; graver, gravest [rhymes with save] NOUN ❶ a place where a corpse is buried ❖ ADJECTIVE ❷ FORMAL very serious

**graveyard** NOUN an area of land where corpses are buried

**gravity** NOUN ❶ Gravity is the force that makes things fall when you drop them ❷ FORMAL The gravity of a situation is its seriousness

**gravy** NOUN Gravy is a brown sauce made from meat juices

**grease**, greases, greasing, greased NOUN ❶ Grease is an oily substance used for lubricating machines ❷ Grease is also melted animal fat, used in cooking ❸ Grease is also an oily substance produced by your skin and found in your hair ❖ VERB ❹ If you grease something, you lubricate it with grease **greasy** ADJECTIVE

**great** ADJECTIVE ❶ very large ❷ very important ❸ INFORMAL very good **greatly** ADVERB **greatness** NOUN

**greed** NOUN Greed is a desire for more of something than you really need

**greedy**, greedier, greediest ADJECTIVE wanting more of something than you really need **greedily** ADVERB

**green** ADJECTIVE OR NOUN ❶ Green is a colour between yellow and blue on the spectrum ❖ NOUN ❷ an area of grass in the middle of a village ❸ A putting green or bowling green is a grassy area on which putting or bowls is played ❹ an area of smooth short grass around each hole on a golf course ❺ IN PLURAL Greens are green vegetables ❖ ADJECTIVE ❻ 'Green' is used to describe political movements which are concerned with environmental issues

**greenhouse** NOUN a glass building in which people grow plants that need to be kept warm

**greenhouse effect** NOUN the gradual rise in temperature in the earth's atmosphere due to heat being absorbed from the sun and being trapped by gases such as carbon dioxide in the air around the earth

**greet** VERB ❶ If you greet someone, you say something friendly like 'hello' to them when you meet them ❷ If you greet something in a particular way, you react to it in that way

**greeting** NOUN something friendly that you say to someone when you meet them

**grew** the past tense of **grow**

**grey** ADJECTIVE OR NOUN ❶ Grey is a colour between black and white ❖ VERB ❷ If someone is greying, their hair is going grey

**grid** NOUN ❶ a pattern of lines crossing each other to form squares ❷ The grid is the network of wires and cables by which electricity is distributed throughout a country

**grief** NOUN Grief is extreme sadness, especially when someone dies

**grieve**, grieves, grieving, grieved VERB ❶ If you grieve, you are extremely sad, especially because someone has died ❷ If something grieves you, it makes you feel very sad

**grill** NOUN ❶ a part on a cooker where food is cooked by strong heat from above ❷ a metal frame on which you cook food over a fire ❖ VERB ❸ If you grill food, you cook it on or under a grill

**grin** VERB ❶ If you grin, you smile broadly ❖ NOUN ❷ a broad smile

**grind**, grinds, grinding, ground VERB ❶ If you grind something such as pepper, you crush it into a fine powder ❷ If you grind your teeth, you rub your upper and lower teeth together

# grip – grunt

**grip**, grips, gripping, gripped NOUN ❶ a firm hold ❷ a handle on a bat or a racket ❸ Your grip on a situation is your control over it ✿ VERB ❹ If you grip something, you hold it firmly

**groan** VERB ❶ If you groan, you make a long, low sound of pain, unhappiness, or disapproval ✿ NOUN ❷ the sound you make when you groan

## don't mix up

### Hello Kitty...

never mixes up **groan** (the sound) and **grown** (the past participle of grow).

**groom** NOUN ❶ someone who looks after horses in a stable ❷ At a wedding, the groom is the bridegroom ✿ VERB ❸ To groom an animal means to clean its fur

**groove** NOUN a deep line cut into a surface

**grope**, gropes, groping, groped VERB ❶ If you grope for something you cannot see, you search for it with your hands ❷ If you grope for something such as the solution to a problem, you try to think of it

**ground** NOUN ❶ The ground is the surface of the earth ❷ a piece of land that is used for a particular purpose ❸ The ground covered by a book or course is the range of subjects it deals with ❹ IN PLURAL The grounds of a large building are the land belonging to it and surrounding it ❺ FORMAL The grounds for something are the reasons for it ✿ VERB ❻ If an aircraft is grounded, it has to remain on the ground ❼ Ground is the past tense and past participle of **grind**

**ground floor** NOUN The ground floor of a building is the floor that is approximately level with the ground

**group** NOUN ❶ A group of things or people is a number of them that are linked together in some way ❷ a number of musicians who perform pop music together ✿ VERB ❸ When things or people are grouped together, they are linked together in some way

**grow**, grows, growing, grew, grown VERB ❶ To grow means to increase in size or amount ❷ If a tree or plant grows somewhere, it is alive there ❸ When people grow plants, they plant them and look after them ❹ If a man grows a beard or moustache, he lets it develop by not shaving ❺ To grow also means to pass gradually into a particular state

**grow up** ✿ VERB When a child grows up, he or she becomes an adult

**growl** VERB ❶ When an animal growls, it makes a low rumbling sound, usually because it is angry ✿ NOUN ❷ the sound an animal makes when it growls

**grown-up** NOUN ❶ INFORMAL an adult ✿ ADJECTIVE ❷ Someone who is grown-up is adult, or behaves like an adult

**growth** NOUN ❶ When there is a growth in something, it gets bigger ❷ Growth is the process by which something develops to its full size ❸ an abnormal lump that grows inside or on a person, animal, or plant

**grudge**, grudges, grudging, grudged NOUN ❶ If you have a grudge against someone, you resent them because they have harmed you in the past ✿ VERB ❷ If you grudge someone something, you give it to them unwillingly, or are unhappy that they have it

**grumble**, grumbles, grumbling, grumbled VERB ❶ If you grumble, you complain in a bad-tempered way ✿ NOUN ❷ a bad-tempered complaint

**grumpy**, grumpier, grumpiest ADJECTIVE bad-tempered and fed-up

**grunt** VERB ❶ If a person or a pig grunts, they make a short, low, gruff sound ✿ NOUN

**guarantee – gymnasium**

❷ the sound a person or a pig makes when they grunt

**guarantee**, guarantees, guaranteeing, guaranteed NOUN ❶ If something is a guarantee of something else, it makes it certain that it will happen ❷ a written promise that if a product develops a fault it will be replaced or repaired free ✿ VERB ❸ If something or someone guarantees something, they make certain that it will happen

**guard** VERB ❶ If you guard a person or object, you stay near to them to protect them ❷ If you guard a person, you stop them making trouble or escaping ❸ If you guard against something, you are careful to avoid it happening ✿ NOUN ❹ a person or group of people who guard a person, object, or place ❺ a railway official in charge of a train

**guardian** NOUN ❶ someone who has been legally appointed to look after an orphaned child ❷ A guardian of something is someone who protects it

**guerrilla** or **guerilla** [ger-ril-la] NOUN a member of a small unofficial army fighting an official army

**guess**, guesses, guessing, guessed VERB ❶ If you guess something, you form or express an opinion that it is the case, without having much information ✿ NOUN ❷ an attempt to give the correct answer to something without having much information, or without working it out properly

**guest** NOUN ❶ someone who stays at your home or who attends an occasion because they have been invited ❷ The guests in a hotel are the people staying there

**guidance** NOUN Guidance is help and advice

**guide**, guides, guiding, guided NOUN ❶ someone who shows you round places, or leads the way through difficult country ❷ a book which gives you information or instructions ❸ A Guide is a girl who is a member of an organization that encourages discipline and practical skills ✿ VERB ❹ If you guide someone in a particular direction, you lead them in that direction

**guidebook** NOUN a book which gives information about a place

**guilt** NOUN ❶ Guilt is an unhappy feeling of having done something wrong ❷ Someone's guilt is the fact that they have done something wrong

**guilty**, guiltier, guiltiest ADJECTIVE ❶ If you are guilty of doing something wrong, you did it ❷ If you feel guilty, you are unhappy because you have done something wrong

**guinea pig** NOUN ❶ a small furry animal without a tail, often kept as a pet ❷ a person used to try something out on

**guitar** NOUN a musical instrument with six strings which are strummed or plucked

**guitarist** NOUN

**gulf** NOUN ❶ a very large bay ❷ a wide gap or difference between two things or people

**gulp** VERB ❶ If you gulp food or drink, you swallow large quantities of it ❷ If you gulp, you swallow air, because you are nervous ✿ NOUN ❸ A gulp of food or drink is a large quantity of it swallowed at one time

**gum** NOUN ❶ Gum is a soft flavoured substance that people chew but do not swallow ❷ Gum is also glue for sticking paper ❸ Your gums are the firm flesh in which your teeth are set

**gun** NOUN a weapon which fires bullets or shells

**gush**, gushes, gushing, gushed VERB When liquid gushes from something, it flows out of it in large quantities

**gust** NOUN a sudden rush of wind

**gut**, guts, gutting, gutted NOUN ❶ IN PLURAL Your guts are your internal organs, especially your intestines ❷ IN PLURAL; INFORMAL Guts is courage ✿ VERB ❸ To gut a dead fish means to remove its internal organs ❹ If a building is gutted, the inside of it is destroyed, especially by fire

**gutter** NOUN ❶ the edge of a road next to the pavement, where rain collects and flows away ❷ a channel fixed to the edge of a roof, where rain collects and flows away

**guy** NOUN ❶ INFORMAL a man or boy ❷ a crude model of Guy Fawkes, that is burnt on top of a bonfire on Guy Fawkes Day (November 5)

**gym** NOUN ❶ a gymnasium ❷ Gym is gymnastics

**gymnasium** NOUN a room with special equipment for physical exercises

A B C D E F G H I J K L M N O P Q R S T U V W X Y Z

123

# habit - hamper

**habit** NOUN ❶ something that you do often ❷ something that you keep doing and find it difficult to stop doing ❸ A monk's or nun's habit is a garment like a loose dress

**habitat** NOUN the natural home of a plant or animal

**hail** NOUN ❶ Hail is frozen rain ❷ A hail of things is a lot of them falling together ✿ VERB ❸ When it is hailing, frozen rain is falling ❹ If someone hails you, they call you to attract your attention or greet you

**hair** NOUN Hair consists of the long, threadlike strands that grow from the skin of animals and humans

**haircut** NOUN the cutting of someone's hair; also the style in which it is cut

**hairdresser** NOUN someone who is trained to cut and style people's hair; also a shop where this is done

**hairstyle** NOUN Someone's hairstyle is the way in which their hair is arranged or cut

**hairy**, hairier, hairiest ADJECTIVE ❶ covered in a lot of hair ❷ INFORMAL difficult, exciting, and rather frightening

### letter H

Some words that sound as if they begin with *h* actually begin with *wh*, like *whole*.

**halal** ADJECTIVE Halal meat is from animals that have been killed in the correct way according to Islamic law

**half**, halves NOUN, ADJECTIVE, OR ADVERB ❶ Half refers to one of two equal parts that make up a whole ✿ ADVERB ❷ You can use 'half' to say that something is only partly true

**halfway** ADVERB at the middle of the distance between two points in place or time

**hall** NOUN ❶ the room just inside the front entrance of a house which leads into other rooms ❷ a large room or building used for public events

**Halloween** NOUN Halloween is October 31st, and is celebrated by children dressing up, often as ghosts and witches

**halt** VERB ❶ To halt when moving means to stop ❷ To halt development or action means to stop it ✿ NOUN ❸ a short standstill

**ham** NOUN Ham is meat from the hind leg of a pig, salted and cured

**hamburger** NOUN a flat disc of minced meat, seasoned and fried; often eaten in a bread roll

**hammer** NOUN ❶ a tool consisting of a heavy piece of metal at the end of a handle, used for hitting nails into things ✿ VERB ❷ If you hammer something, you hit it repeatedly, with a hammer or with your fist ❸ If you hammer an idea into someone, you keep repeating it and telling them about it ❹ INFORMAL If you hammer someone, you criticize or attack them severely

**hamper** NOUN ❶ a rectangular wicker basket with a lid, used for carrying food ✿ VERB ❷ If you hamper someone, you make it difficult for them to move or progress

124

**hamster — happy**

**hamster** NOUN a small furry rodent which is often kept as a pet

**hand** NOUN ❶ Your hand is the part of your body beyond the wrist, with four fingers and a thumb ❷ Your hand is also your writing style ❸ The hand of someone in a situation is their influence or the part they play in it ❹ If you give someone a hand, you help them to do something ❺ When an audience gives someone a big hand, they applaud ❻ The hands of a clock or watch are the pointers that point to the numbers ❼ In cards, your hand is the cards you are holding ✿ VERB ❽ If you hand something to someone, you give it to them ✿ PHRASES ❾ Something that is **at hand**, **to hand**, or **on hand** is available, close by, and ready for use ❿ You use **on the one hand** to introduce the first part of an argument or discussion with two different points of view ⓫ You use **on the other hand** to introduce the second part of an argument or discussion with two different points of view ⓬ If you do something **by hand**, you do it using your hands rather than a machine

**hand down** ✿ VERB Something that is handed down is passed from one generation to another

**handbag** NOUN a small bag used mainly by women to carry money and personal items

**handbook** NOUN a book giving information and instructions about something

**handful** NOUN ❶ A handful of something is the amount of it you can hold in your hand ❷ a small quantity ❸ Someone who is a handful is difficult to control

**handkerchief** NOUN a small square of fabric used for blowing your nose

**handle**, handles, handling, handled NOUN ❶ The handle of an object is the part by which it is held or controlled ❷ a small lever used to open and close a door or window ✿ VERB ❸ If you handle an object, you hold it in your hands to examine it ❹ If you handle something, you deal with it or control it

**handout** NOUN ❶ a gift of food, clothing, or money given to a poor person ❷ a piece of paper giving information about something

**handshake** NOUN the grasping and shaking of a person's hand by another person

**handsome** ADJECTIVE ❶ very attractive in appearance ❷ large and generous

**handwriting** NOUN Someone's handwriting is their style of writing as it looks on the page

**handy**, handier, handiest ADJECTIVE ❶ conveniently near ❷ easy to handle or use ❸ skilful

**hang**, hangs, hanging, hung or hanged [for sense 5] VERB ❶ If you hang something somewhere, you attach it to a high point ❷ If something is hanging on something, it is attached by its top to it ❸ If a future event or possibility is hanging over you, it worries or frightens you ❹ When you hang wallpaper, you stick it onto a wall ❺ To hang someone means to kill them by suspending them by a rope around the neck ✿ PHRASE ❻ When you **get the hang of something**, you understand it and are able to do it

**happen** VERB ❶ When something happens, it occurs or takes place ❷ If you happen to do something, you do it by chance

**happiness** NOUN a feeling of great contentment or pleasure

**happy**, happier, happiest ADJECTIVE ❶ feeling, showing, or producing contentment or pleasure ❷ satisfied that something is right ❸ willing ❹ fortunate or lucky
**happily** ADVERB

*some other words to use*

*Tips and tricks...*

You should try not to use **happy** too much when you are writing. Some other words you can use are: *delighted*, *elated*, *joyful* and *thrilled*.

A B C D E F G H I J K L M N O P Q R S T U V W X Y Z

# harbour - head

**harbour** NOUN ❶ a protected area of deep water where boats can be moored ✿ VERB ❷ To harbour someone means to hide them secretly in your house ❸ If you harbour a feeling, you have it for a long time

**hard** ADJECTIVE ❶ Something that is hard is firm, solid, or stiff ❷ requiring a lot of effort ❸ difficult ❹ Someone who is hard has no kindness or pity ❺ A hard colour or voice is harsh and unpleasant ❻ Hard evidence or facts can be proved to be true ❼ Hard water contains a lot of lime and does not easily produce a lather ❽ Hard drugs are very strong illegal drugs ❾ Hard drink is strong alcohol ✿ ADVERB ❿ earnestly or intently ⓫ An event that follows hard upon something takes place immediately afterwards

**hardly** ADVERB ❶ almost not or not quite ❷ certainly not

**hardware** NOUN ❶ Hardware is tools and equipment for use in the home and garden ❷ Hardware is also computer machinery rather than computer programs

**harm** VERB ❶ To harm someone or something means to injure or damage them ✿ NOUN ❷ Harm is injury or damage

**harmful** ADJECTIVE having a bad effect on something

**harmless** ADJECTIVE ❶ safe to use or be near ❷ unlikely to cause problems or annoyance

**harmony**, harmonies NOUN ❶ Harmony is a state of peaceful agreement and cooperation ❷ Harmony is the structure and relationship of chords in a piece of music ❸ Harmony is the pleasant combination of two or more notes played at the same time

**harp** NOUN ❶ a musical instrument consisting of a triangular frame with vertical strings which you pluck with your fingers ✿ VERB ❷ If someone harps on something, they keep talking about it, especially in a boring way

**harsh** ADJECTIVE severe, difficult, and unpleasant **harshly** ADVERB

**harvest** NOUN ❶ the cutting and gathering of a crop; also the ripe crop when it is gathered and the time of gathering ✿ VERB ❷ To harvest food means to gather it when it is ripe

**haste** NOUN Haste is doing something quickly, especially too quickly

**hasty**, hastier, hastiest ADJECTIVE done or happening suddenly and quickly, often without enough care or thought **hastily** ADVERB

**hat** NOUN a covering for the head

**hatch**, hatches, hatching, hatched VERB ❶ When an egg hatches, or when a bird or reptile hatches, the egg breaks open and the young bird or reptile emerges ❷ To hatch a plot means to plan it ✿ NOUN ❸ a covered opening in a floor or wall

**hate**, hates, hating, hated VERB ❶ If you hate someone or something, you have a strong dislike for them ✿ NOUN ❷ Hate is a strong dislike

**haul** VERB ❶ To haul something somewhere means to pull it with great effort ✿ NOUN ❷ a quantity of something obtained

**haunted** ADJECTIVE ❶ regularly visited by a ghost ❷ very worried or troubled

**have**, has, having, had VERB ❶ Have is an auxiliary verb, used to form the past tense or to express completed actions ❷ If you have something, you own or possess it ❸ If you have something, you experience it, it happens to you, or you are affected by it ❹ To have a child or baby animal means to give birth to it ✿ PHRASES ❺ If you **have to** do something, you must do it. If you **had better** do something, you ought to do it

**hawk** NOUN ❶ a bird of prey with short rounded wings and a long tail ✿ VERB ❷ To hawk goods means to sell them by taking them around from place to place

**hay** NOUN Hay is grass which has been cut and dried and is used as animal feed

**hazard** NOUN ❶ a substance, object, or action which could be dangerous to you ✿ VERB ❷ If you hazard something, you put it at risk ✿ PHRASE ❸ If you **hazard a guess**, you make a guess

**he** PRONOUN 'He' is used to refer to a man, boy, or male animal or to any person whose sex is not mentioned

**head** NOUN ❶ Your head is the part of your body which has your eyes, brain, and mouth in it ❷ Your head is also your mind and mental abilities ❸ The head of something is the top, start, or most important end ❹ The head of a group or organization is the person in charge ❺ The head on beer is the layer of

126

## head off - heat

froth on the top ❻ The head on a computer or tape recorder is the part that can read or write information ❼ IN PLURAL When you toss a coin, the side called heads is the one with the head on it ✿ VERB ❽ To head a group or organization means to be in charge ❾ To head in a particular direction means to move in that direction ❿ To head a ball means to hit it with your head ✿ PHRASE ⓫ If you **lose your head**, you panic ⓬ If you say that someone is **off their head**, you mean that they are mad or very stupid ⓭ If something is **over someone's head**, it is too difficult for them to understand ⓮ If you **can't make head nor tail of something**, you cannot understand it

**head off** ✿ VERB If you head off someone or something, you make them change direction or prevent something from happening

**headache** NOUN ❶ a pain in your head ❷ Something that is a headache is causing a lot of difficulty or worry

**heading** NOUN a piece of writing that is written or printed at the top of a page

**headlight** NOUN The headlights on a motor vehicle are the large powerful lights at the front

**headline** NOUN ❶ A newspaper headline is the title of a newspaper article printed in large, bold type ❷ The headlines are the main points of the radio or television news

**headphones** PLURAL NOUN Headphones are a pair of small speakers which you wear over your ears to listen to a radio or MP3 player without other people hearing

**headquarters** NOUN The headquarters of an organization is the main place from which it is run

**head teacher** NOUN the teacher who is in charge of a school

**heal** VERB If something heals or if you heal it, it becomes healthy or normal again

### don't mix up

Don't mix up **heal** (to get better) and **heel** (part of your foot).

**health** NOUN ❶ Your health is the condition of your body ❷ Health is also the state of being free from disease and feeling well

**healthy** ADJECTIVE ❶ Someone who is healthy is fit and strong and does not have any diseases ❷ Something that is healthy is good for you ❸ An organization or system that is healthy is successful

**heap** NOUN ❶ a pile of things ❷ IN PLURAL; INFORMAL Heaps of something means plenty of it ✿ VERB ❸ If you heap things, you pile them up ❹ To heap something such as praise on someone means to give them a lot of it

**hear**, hears, hearing, heard VERB ❶ When you hear sounds, you are aware of them because they reach your ears ❷ When you hear from someone, they write to you, e-mail you, text you, or phone you ❸ When you hear about something, you are informed about it ❹ When a judge hears a case, he or she listens to it in court in order to make a decision on it ✿ PHRASE ❺ If you say that you **won't hear of** something, you mean you refuse to allow it

**hear out** ✿ VERB If you hear someone out, you listen to all they have to say without interrupting

**hearing** NOUN ❶ Hearing is the sense which makes it possible for you to be aware of sounds ❷ a court trial or official meeting to hear facts about an incident ❸ If someone gives you a hearing, they let you give your point of view and listen to you

**heart** NOUN ❶ the organ in your chest that pumps the blood around your body ❷ Your heart is also thought of as the centre of your emotions ❸ Heart is courage, determination, or enthusiasm ❹ The heart of something is the most central and important part of it ❺ a shape similar to a heart, used especially as a symbol of love ❻ Hearts is one of the four suits in a pack of playing cards. It is marked by a red heart-shaped symbol

**heart attack** NOUN a serious medical condition in which the heart suddenly beats irregularly or stops completely

**heat** NOUN ❶ Heat is warmth or the quality of being hot; also the temperature of something that is warm or hot ❷ Heat is

# heating - herbivore

strength of feeling, especially of anger or excitement ❸ a contest or race in a competition held to decide who will play in the final ✿ **VERB** ❹ To heat something means to raise its temperature ✿ **PHRASE** ❺ When a female animal is **on heat**, she is ready for mating  **heater NOUN**

**heating NOUN** Heating is the equipment used to heat a building; also the process and cost of running the equipment to provide heat

**heaven NOUN** ❶ a place of happiness where God is believed to live and where good people are believed to go when they die ❷ If you describe a situation or place as heaven, you mean that it is wonderful

**heavy**, heavier, heaviest **ADJECTIVE** ❶ great in weight or force ❷ great in degree or amount ❸ solid and thick in appearance ❹ using a lot of something quickly ❺ serious and difficult to deal with or understand ❻ Food that is heavy is solid and difficult to digest ❼ When it is heavy, the weather is hot, humid, and still ❽ Someone with a heavy heart is very sad  **heavily ADVERB heaviness NOUN**

**hectic ADJECTIVE** involving a lot of rushed activity

**hedge**, hedges, hedging, hedged **NOUN** ❶ a row of bushes forming a barrier or boundary ✿ **VERB** ❷ If you hedge against something unpleasant happening, you protect yourself ❸ If you hedge, you avoid answering a question or dealing with a problem ✿ **PHRASE** ❹ If you **hedge your bets**, you support two or more people or courses of action to avoid the risk of losing a lot

**hedgehog NOUN** a small, brown animal with sharp spikes covering its back

**heel NOUN** ❶ the back part of your foot ❷ The heel of a shoe or sock is the part that fits over your heel ✿ **VERB** ❸ To heel a pair of shoes means to put a new piece on the heel ✿ **PHRASE** ❹ A person or place that looks **down at heel** looks untidy and in poor condition

**height NOUN** ❶ The height of an object is its measurement from the bottom to the top ❷ a high position or place ❸ The height of something is its peak, or the time when it is most successful or intense

**heir** [air] **NOUN** A person's heir is the person who is entitled to inherit their property or title

### how to say it
**Heir** should be said **air**.

**helicopter NOUN** an aircraft with rotating blades above it which enable it to take off vertically, hover, and fly

**hell NOUN** ❶ Hell is the place where souls of evil people are believed to go to be punished after death ❷ **INFORMAL** If you say that something is hell, you mean it is very unpleasant ✿ **INTERJECTION** ❸ 'Hell' is also a swearword

**hello INTERJECTION** You say 'Hello' as a greeting or when you answer the phone

**helmet NOUN** a hard hat worn to protect the head

**help VERB** ❶ To help someone means to make something easier or better for them ✿ **NOUN** ❷ If you need or give help, you need or give assistance ❸ someone or something that helps you ✿ **PHRASE** ❹ If you **help yourself** to something, you take it ❺ If you **can't help** something, you cannot control it or change it

**helpful ADJECTIVE** ❶ If someone is helpful, they help you by doing something for you ❷ Something that is helpful makes a situation more pleasant or easier to tolerate

**helpless ADJECTIVE** ❶ unable to cope on your own ❷ weak or powerless  **helplessly ADVERB**

**hemisphere** [hem-iss-feer] **NOUN** one half of the earth, the brain, or a sphere

**hen NOUN** a female chicken; also any female bird

**her PRONOUN OR ADJECTIVE** 'Her' is used to refer to a woman, girl, or female animal that has already been mentioned, or to show that something belongs to a particular female

**herb NOUN** a plant whose leaves are used in medicine or to flavour food  **herbal ADJECTIVE**

**herbivore NOUN** an animal that eats only plants

**herd** NOUN ❶ a large group of animals ✿ VERB ❷ To herd animals or people means to make them move together as a group

**here** ADVERB ❶ at, to, or in the place where you are, or the place mentioned or indicated ✿ PHRASE ❷ **Here and there** means in various unspecified places

**hero**, heroes NOUN ❶ the main male character in a book, film, or play ❷ a person who has done something brave or good

**heroic** ADJECTIVE brave, courageous, and determined

**heroin** [herr-oh-in] NOUN Heroin is a powerful drug formerly used as an anaesthetic and now taken illegally by some people for pleasure

**heroine** [herr-oh-in] NOUN ❶ the main female character in a book, film, or play ❷ a woman who has done something brave or good

**hers** PRONOUN 'Hers' refers to something that belongs to or relates to a woman, girl, or female animal

**herself** PRONOUN ❶ 'Herself' is used when the same woman, girl, or female animal does an action and is affected by it ❷ 'Herself' is used to emphasize 'she'

**hesitate**, hesitates, hesitating, hesitated VERB To hesitate means to pause or show uncertainty **hesitation** NOUN

**hexagon** NOUN a shape with six straight sides; a **regular hexagon** has six straight sides of the same length

**hi** INTERJECTION 'Hi!' is an informal greeting

**hibernate**, hibernates, hibernating, hibernated VERB Animals that hibernate spend the winter in a state like deep sleep **hibernation** NOUN

**hiccup**, hiccups, hiccupping, hiccupped [hik-kup] NOUN ❶ Hiccups are short, uncontrolled choking sounds in your throat that you sometimes get if you have been eating or drinking too quickly ❷ INFORMAL a minor problem ✿ VERB ❸ When you hiccup, you make little choking sounds

**hide**, hides, hiding, hid, hidden VERB ❶ To hide something means to put it where it cannot be seen, or to prevent it from being discovered ✿ NOUN ❷ the skin of a large animal

**hideous** [hid-ee-uss] ADJECTIVE extremely ugly or unpleasant **hideously** ADVERB

**high** ADJECTIVE ❶ tall or a long way above the ground ❷ great in degree, quantity, or intensity ❸ towards the top of a scale of importance or quality ❹ close to the top of a range of sound or notes ❺ INFORMAL Someone who is high on a drug is affected by having taken it ✿ ADVERB ❻ at or to a height ✿ NOUN ❼ a high point or level ❽ INFORMAL Someone who is on a high is in a very excited and optimistic mood

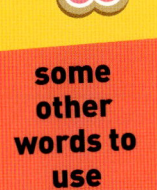

### some other words to use

### Tips and tricks...

You should try not to use **high** too much when you are writing. Some other words you can use are: *tall*, *steep*, *towering* and *lofty*.

**high jump** NOUN The high jump is an athletics event involving jumping over a high bar

**highlight** VERB ❶ If you highlight a point or problem, you emphasize and draw attention to it ✿ NOUN ❷ The highlight of something is the most interesting part of it ❸ Highlights are also light-coloured streaks in someone's hair

**highly** ADVERB ❶ extremely ❷ towards the top of a scale of importance, admiration, or respect

**hijack** VERB If someone hijacks a plane or vehicle, they illegally take control of it during a journey

**hike**, hikes, hiking, hiked NOUN ❶ a long country walk ✿ VERB ❷ To hike means to walk long distances in the country **hiker** NOUN

# hilarious - hoax

**hilarious** ADJECTIVE very funny

**hill** NOUN a rounded area of land higher than the land surrounding it  **hilly** ADJECTIVE

**him** PRONOUN You use 'him' to refer to a man, boy, or male animal that has already been mentioned, or to any person whose sex is not known

**himself** PRONOUN ❶ 'Himself' is used when the same man, boy, or male animal does an action and is affected by it ❷ 'Himself' is used to emphasize 'he'

**Hindu** [*hin-doo*] NOUN a person who believes in Hinduism, an Indian religion which has many gods and believes that people have another life on earth after death  **Hinduism** NOUN

**hinge**, hinges, hinging, hinged NOUN ❶ the movable joint which attaches a door or window to its frame ✿ VERB ❷ Something that hinges on a situation or event depends entirely on that situation or event

**hint** NOUN ❶ an indirect suggestion ❷ a helpful piece of advice ✿ VERB ❸ If you hint at something, you suggest it indirectly

**hip** NOUN Your hips are the two parts at the sides of your body between your waist and your upper legs

**hippo**, hippos NOUN INFORMAL a hippopotamus

**hippopotamus**, hippopotamuses or hippopotami NOUN a large African animal with thick wrinkled skin and short legs, that lives near rivers

**hire**, hires, hiring, hired VERB ❶ If you hire something, you pay money to be able to use it for a period of time ❷ If you hire someone, you pay them to do a job for you ✿ PHRASE ❸ Something that is **for hire** is available for people to hire

**his** ADJECTIVE OR PRONOUN 'His' refers to something that belongs or relates to a man, boy, or male animal that has already been mentioned, and sometimes also to any person whose sex is not known

**hiss**, hisses, hissing, hissed VERB ❶ To hiss means to make a long 's' sound, especially to show disapproval or aggression ✿ NOUN ❷ a long 's' sound

**history**, histories NOUN History is the study of the past. A history is a record of the past

**hit**, hits, hitting, hit VERB ❶ If you hit someone, you strike them forcefully, usually causing hurt or damage ❷ If you hit an object, you collide with it ❸ To hit a ball or other object means to make it move by hitting it with something ❹ If something hits you, it affects you badly and suddenly ❺ If something hits a particular point or place, it reaches it ❻ If you hit on an idea or solution, you suddenly think of it ✿ NOUN ❼ a person or thing that is popular and successful ❽ the action of hitting something ✿ PHRASE ❾ INFORMAL If you **hit it off** with someone, you become friendly with them the first time you meet them

**hi tech** ADJECTIVE designed using the most modern methods and equipment, especially electronic equipment

**HIV** NOUN HIV is a virus that reduces people's resistance to illness and can cause AIDS. HIV is an abbreviation for 'human immunodeficiency virus'

**hive**, hives, hiving, hived NOUN ❶ a beehive ❷ A place that is a hive of activity is very busy with a lot of people working hard ✿ VERB ❸ If part of something such as a business is hived off, it is transferred to new ownership

**hoax**, hoaxes, hoaxing, hoaxed NOUN ❶ a trick or an attempt to deceive someone ✿ VERB ❷ To hoax someone means to trick or deceive them

### some other words to use

### Hello Kitty...

You should try not to use **hit** too much when you are writing. Some other words you can use are: *strike*, *smack*, *bang* and *bash*.

# hob - homophone

**hob** NOUN a surface on top of a cooker which can be heated in order to cook things

**hobby**, hobbies NOUN something that you do for enjoyment in your spare time

**hockey** NOUN Hockey is a game in which two teams use long sticks with curved ends to try to hit a small ball into the other team's goal

**hold**, holds, holding, held VERB ❶ To hold something means to carry or keep it in place, usually with your hand or arms ❷ Someone who holds power, office, or an opinion has it or possesses it ❸ If you hold something such as a meeting or an election, you arrange it and cause it to happen ❹ If something holds, it is still available or valid ❺ If you hold someone responsible for something, you consider them responsible for it ❻ If something holds a certain amount, it can contain that amount ❼ If you hold something such as theatre tickets, a telephone call, or the price of something, you keep or reserve it for a period of time ❽ To hold something down means to keep it or to keep it under control ❾ If you hold on to something, you continue it or keep it even though it might be difficult ❿ To hold something back means to prevent it, keep it under control, or not reveal it ✿ NOUN ⓫ If someone or something has a hold over you, they have power, control, or influence over you ⓬ a way of holding something or the act of holding it ⓭ the place where cargo or luggage is stored in a ship or a plane

**hole**, holes, holing, holed NOUN ❶ an opening or hollow in something ❷ INFORMAL If you are in a hole, you are in a difficult situation ❸ INFORMAL A hole in a theory or argument is a weakness or error in it ❹ In golf, a hole is one of the small holes into which you have to hit the ball ✿ VERB ❺ When you hole the ball in golf, you hit the ball into one of the holes

**holiday**, holidays, holidaying, holidayed NOUN ❶ a period of time spent away from home for enjoyment ❷ a time when you are not working or not at school ✿ VERB ❸ When you holiday somewhere, you take a holiday there

**hollow** ADJECTIVE ❶ Something that is hollow has space inside it rather than being solid ❷ An opinion or situation that is hollow has no real value or worth ❸ A hollow sound is dull and has a slight echo ✿ NOUN ❹ A hollow is a hole in something or a part of a surface that is lower than the rest ✿ VERB ❺ To hollow means to make a hollow

**holly** NOUN Holly is an evergreen tree or shrub with spiky leaves. It often has red berries in winter

**holocaust** [hol-o-kawst] NOUN ❶ a large-scale destruction or loss of life, especially the result of war or fire ❷ The Holocaust was the mass murder of the Jews in Europe by the Nazis during World War II

**holy**, holier, holiest ADJECTIVE ❶ relating to God or to a particular religion ❷ Someone who is holy is religious and leads a pure and good life

**home** NOUN ❶ Your home is the building or place in which you live or feel you belong ❷ a building in which elderly or ill people live and are looked after ✿ ADJECTIVE ❸ connected with or involving your home or country

**homeless** ADJECTIVE ❶ having no home ✿ PLURAL NOUN ❷ The homeless are people who have no home

**homesick** ADJECTIVE unhappy because of being away from home and missing family and friends

**homework** NOUN ❶ Homework is school work given to pupils to be done in the evening at home ❷ Homework is also research and preparation

**homophone** NOUN Homophones are words which are pronounced the same but have different spellings or meanings, like 'right' and 'write'

### did you know?

A **homophone** is a word that sounds like another word with a different spelling or meaning.

# homosexual – hose

**homosexual** NOUN ❶ a person who is sexually attracted to someone of the same sex ❖ ADJECTIVE ❷ sexually attracted to people of the same sex

**honest** ADJECTIVE truthful and trustworthy **honestly** ADVERB

**honesty** NOUN Honesty is the quality of being truthful and trustworthy

**honey** NOUN Honey is a sweet, edible, sticky substance produced by bees

**honeymoon** NOUN a holiday taken by a couple who have just got married

**honour** NOUN ❶ Your honour is your good reputation and the respect that other people have for you ❷ an award or privilege given as a mark of respect ❸ IN PLURAL Honours is a class of university degree which is higher than a pass or ordinary degree ❖ PHRASE ❹ If something is done **in honour of** someone, it is done out of respect for them ❖ VERB ❺ If you honour someone, you give them special praise or attention, or an award ❻ If you honour an agreement or promise, you do what was agreed or promised

**hood** NOUN ❶ a loose covering for the head, usually part of a coat or jacket ❷ a cover on a piece of equipment or vehicle, usually curved and movable

**hoof**, hooves or hoofs NOUN the hard bony part of certain animals' feet

**hook** NOUN ❶ a curved piece of metal or plastic that is used for catching, holding, or hanging things ❖ VERB ❷ If you hook one thing onto another, you attach it there using a hook

**hoop** NOUN A hoop is a large ring which is often used as a toy

**hoot** VERB ❶ To hoot means to make a long 'oo' sound like an owl ❷ If a car horn hoots, it makes a loud honking noise ❖ NOUN ❸ a sound like that made by an owl or a car horn

**hoover** NOUN ❶ TRADEMARK a vacuum cleaner ❖ VERB ❷ When you hoover, you use a vacuum cleaner to clean the floor

**hooves** a plural of **hoof**

**hop**, hops, hopping, hopped VERB ❶ If you hop, you jump on one foot ❷ When animals or birds hop, they jump with two feet together ❸ INFORMAL If you hop into or out of something, you move there quickly and easily ❖ NOUN ❹ a jump on one leg

**hope**, hopes, hoping, hoped VERB ❶ If you hope that something will happen or hope that it is true, you want it to happen or be true ❖ NOUN ❷ Hope is a wish or feeling of desire and expectation **hopeful** ADJECTIVE **hopefully** ADVERB

**hopeless** ADJECTIVE ❶ having no hope ❷ certain to fail or be unsuccessful ❸ bad or inadequate **hopelessly** ADVERB

**horizon** [hor-**eye**-zn] NOUN the distant line where the sky seems to touch the land or sea

**horizontal** [hor-riz-**zon**-tl] ADJECTIVE flat and parallel with the horizon or with a line considered as a base

**hormone** NOUN a chemical made by one part of your body that stimulates or has a specific effect on another part of your body

**horn** NOUN ❶ one of the hard, pointed growths on the heads of animals such as goats ❷ a musical instrument made of brass, consisting of a pipe that is narrow at one end and wide at the other ❸ On vehicles, a horn is a warning device which makes a loud noise

**horoscope** [**hor**-ros-kope] NOUN a prediction about what is going to happen to someone, based on the position of the stars when they were born

**horrible** ADJECTIVE ❶ disagreeable and unpleasant ❷ causing shock, fear, or disgust **horribly** ADVERB

**horrify**, horrifies, horrifying, horrified VERB If something horrifies you, it makes you feel dismay or disgust **horrifying** ADJECTIVE

**horror** NOUN ❶ a strong feeling of alarm, dismay, and disgust ❷ If you have a horror of something, you fear it very much

**horse** NOUN ❶ a large animal with a mane and long tail, on which people can ride ❷ a piece of gymnastics equipment with four legs, used for jumping over

**horseshoe** NOUN a U-shaped piece of metal, nailed to the hard surface of a horse's hoof to protect it; also anything of this shape, often regarded as a good luck symbol

**hose**, hoses, hosing, hosed NOUN ❶ a long flexible tube through which liquid or gas

132

# hospital - humanity

can be passed ✿ **VERB** ❷ If you hose something, you wash or water it using a hose

**hospital** NOUN a place where sick and injured people are treated and cared for

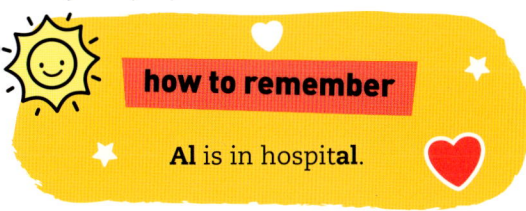

**how to remember**

A**l** is in hospit**al**.

**host** NOUN ❶ The host of an event is the person that welcomes guests and provides food or accommodation for them ❷ a plant or animal with smaller plants or animals living on or in it ❸ A host of things is a large number of them ✿ **VERB** ❹ To host an event means to organize or act as host at it

**hostage** NOUN a person who is illegally held prisoner and threatened with injury or death unless certain demands are met by other people

**hostess**, hostesses NOUN a woman who welcomes guests or visitors and provides food or accommodation for them

**hostile** ADJECTIVE ❶ unfriendly, aggressive, and unpleasant ❷ relating to or involving the enemies of a country

**hot**, hotter, hottest ADJECTIVE ❶ having a high temperature ❷ very spicy and causing a burning sensation in your mouth ❸ new, recent, and exciting

**hot dog** NOUN a sausage served in a roll split lengthways

**hotel** NOUN a building where people stay, paying for their room and meals

**hour** NOUN ❶ a unit of time equal to 60 minutes, of which there are 24 in a day ❷ The hour for something is the time when it happens ❸ The hour is the time of day **hourly** ADJECTIVE OR ADVERB

**house**, houses, housing, housed NOUN [hows] ❶ a building where a person or family lives ❷ a building used for a particular purpose ❸ In a theatre or cinema, the house is the part where the audience sits; also the audience itself ✿ **VERB** [howz] ❹ To house something means to keep it or contain it

**household** NOUN ❶ all the people who live as a group in a house or flat ✿ **PHRASE** ❷ Someone who is **a household name** is very well-known

**housewife**, housewives NOUN a married woman who does the chores in her home, and does not have a paid job

**hover** VERB When a bird, insect, or aircraft hovers, it stays in the same position in the air

**how** ADVERB ❶ 'How' is used to ask about, explain, or refer to the way in which something is done, known, or experienced ❷ 'How' is used to ask about or refer to a measurement or quantity ❸ 'How' is used to emphasize the following word or statement

**however** ADVERB ❶ You use 'however' when you are adding a comment that seems to contradict or contrast with what has just been said ❷ You use 'however' to say that something makes no difference to a situation

**howl** VERB ❶ To howl means to make a long, loud wailing noise such as that made by a dog when it is upset ✿ **NOUN** ❷ a long, loud wailing noise

**hub** NOUN ❶ the centre part of a wheel ❷ the most important or active part of a place or organization

**hug**, hugs, hugging, hugged VERB ❶ If you hug someone, you put your arms round them and hold them close to you ❷ To hug the ground or a stretch of water or land means to keep very close to it ✿ **NOUN** ❸ If you give someone a hug, you hold them close to you

**huge** ADJECTIVE extremely large in amount, size, or degree **hugely** ADVERB

**hum**, hums, humming, hummed VERB ❶ To hum means to make a continuous low noise ❷ If you hum, you sing with your lips closed ✿ **NOUN** ❸ a continuous low noise

**human** ADJECTIVE ❶ relating to, concerning, or typical of people ✿ **NOUN** ❷ a person

**human being** NOUN a person

**humanity** NOUN ❶ Humanity is people in general ❷ Humanity is also the condition of being human ❸ Someone who has humanity is kind and sympathetic

A B C D E F G **H** I J K L M N O P Q R S T U V W X Y Z

133

# human rights - hypnosis

**human rights** PLURAL NOUN Human rights are the rights of individuals to freedom and justice

**humble**, humbler, humblest; humbles, humbling, humbled ADJECTIVE ❶ A humble person is modest and thinks that he or she has very little value ❷ Something that is humble is small or not very important ✿ VERB ❸ To humble someone means to make them feel humiliated

**humid** ADJECTIVE If it is humid, the air feels damp, heavy, and warm

**humidity** NOUN Humidity is the amount of moisture in the air

**humour** NOUN ❶ Humour is the quality of being funny ❷ Humour is also the ability to be amused by certain things ❸ Someone's humour is the mood they are in ✿ VERB ❹ If you humour someone, you are especially kind to them and do whatever they want **humorous** ADJECTIVE

**hump** NOUN a small, rounded lump or mound

**hundred** the number 100 **hundredth** ADJECTIVE

**hunger** NOUN ❶ Hunger is the need to eat or the desire to eat ❷ A hunger for something is a strong need or desire for it

**hungry**, hungrier, hungriest ADJECTIVE needing or wanting to eat **hungrily** ADVERB

**hunt** VERB ❶ To hunt means to chase wild animals to kill them for food or for sport ❷ If you hunt for something, you search for it ✿ NOUN ❸ the act of hunting **hunter** NOUN **hunting** ADJECTIVE OR NOUN

**hurdle** NOUN ❶ one of the frames or barriers that you jump over in an athletics race called hurdles ❷ a problem or difficulty

**hurricane** NOUN A hurricane is a violent wind or storm, usually force 12 or above on the Beaufort scale

**hurry**, hurries, hurrying, hurried VERB ❶ To hurry means to move or do something as quickly as possible ❷ To hurry something means to make it happen more quickly ✿ NOUN ❸ Hurry is the speed with which you do something quickly

**hurt**, hurts, hurting, hurt VERB ❶ To hurt someone means to cause them physical pain ❷ If a part of your body hurts, you feel pain there ❸ If you hurt yourself, you injure yourself ❹ To hurt someone also means to make them unhappy by being unkind or thoughtless towards them ✿ ADJECTIVE ❺ If someone feels hurt, they feel unhappy because of someone's unkindness

**husband** NOUN A woman's husband is the man she is married to

**hush**, hushes, hushing, hushed VERB ❶ If you tell someone to hush, you are telling them to be quiet ❷ To hush something up means to keep it secret, especially something dishonest involving important people ✿ NOUN ❸ If there is a hush, it is quiet

**hut** NOUN a small, simple building, with one or two rooms

**hygiene** [*high-jeen*] NOUN Hygiene is the practice of keeping yourself and your surroundings clean, especially to stop the spread of disease **hygienic** ADJECTIVE

**hymn** NOUN a Christian song in praise of God

**hyperlink** NOUN a word, phrase, or picture in a computer document which a user may click to move to another part of the document, or to another document

**hyphen** NOUN a punctuation mark used to join together words or parts of words, as for example in the word 'left-handed'

## punctuation

### Helpful hints...

You use a **hyphen** (-) to join separate words together, like *duty-free* and *brother-in-law*.

**hypnosis** [*hip-noh-siss*] NOUN Hypnosis is an artificially produced state of relaxation in which the mind is very receptive to suggestion

# I – ignorant

**I** PRONOUN A speaker or writer uses 'I' to refer to himself or herself

**ice**, ices, icing, iced NOUN ❶ water that has frozen solid ❷ an ice cream ✿ VERB ❸ If you ice cakes, you cover them with icing ❹ If something ices over or ices up, it becomes covered with a layer of ice ✿ PHRASE ❺ If you do something to **break the ice**, you make people feel relaxed and comfortable

**iceberg** NOUN a large mass of ice floating in the sea

**ice cream** NOUN a very cold sweet food made from frozen cream

**ice cube** NOUN Ice cubes are small cubes of ice put in drinks to make them cold

**ice hockey** NOUN a type of hockey played on ice, with two teams of six players

**ice-skate**; ice-skates, ice-skating, ice-skated NOUN ❶ a boot with a metal blade on the bottom, which you wear when skating on ice ✿ VERB ❷ If you ice-skate, you move about on ice wearing ice-skates

**icicle** [eye-sik-kl] NOUN a piece of ice shaped like a pointed stick that hangs down from a surface

**icing** NOUN a mixture of powdered sugar and water or egg whites, used to decorate cakes

**icon** [eye-kon] NOUN ❶ a picture on a computer screen representing a program that can be activated by moving the cursor over it ❷ in the Orthodox Churches, a holy picture of Christ, the Virgin Mary, or a saint

**icy**, icier, iciest ADJECTIVE ❶ Something which is icy is very cold ❷ An icy road has ice on it

**idea** NOUN ❶ a plan, suggestion, or thought that you have after thinking about a problem ❷ an opinion or belief ❸ An idea of something is what you know about it

**ideal** NOUN ❶ a principle or idea that you try to achieve because it seems perfect to you ❷ Your ideal of something is the person or thing that seems the best example of it ✿ ADJECTIVE ❸ The ideal person or thing is the best possible person or thing for the situation

**identical** ADJECTIVE exactly the same

**identification** NOUN ❶ The identification of someone or something is the act of identifying them ❷ Identification is a document such as a driving licence or passport, which proves who you are

**identify**, identifies, identifying, identified VERB ❶ To identify someone or something is to recognize them or name them ❷ If you identify with someone, you understand their feelings and ideas

**identity**, identities NOUN the characteristics that make you who you are

**idiom** NOUN a group of words whose meaning together is different from all the words taken individually. For example, 'It is raining cats and dogs' is an idiom

**idiot** NOUN someone who is stupid or foolish

**idol** [eye-doll] NOUN ❶ a famous person who is loved and admired by fans ❷ a picture or statue which is worshipped as if it were a god

**if** CONJUNCTION ❶ on the condition that ❷ whether

**ignorant** ADJECTIVE ❶ If you are ignorant of something, you do not know about it ❷ Someone who is ignorant does not know about things in general **ignorance** NOUN

# ignore – import

**ignore**, ignores, ignoring, ignored VERB If you ignore someone or something, you deliberately do not take any notice of them

**ill** ADJECTIVE ❶ unhealthy or sick ❷ harmful or unpleasant ❖ PLURAL NOUN ❸ Ills are difficulties or problems

**illegal** ADJECTIVE forbidden by the law
**illegally** ADVERB

**illness**, illnesses NOUN ❶ Illness is the experience of being ill ❷ a particular disease

**illusion** NOUN ❶ a false belief which you think is true ❷ a false appearance of reality which deceives the eye

**illustrate**, illustrates, illustrating, illustrated VERB ❶ If you illustrate a point, you explain it or make it clearer, often by using examples ❷ If you illustrate a book, you put pictures in it

**illustration** NOUN ❶ an example or a story which is used to make a point clear ❷ a picture in a book

**image** NOUN ❶ a mental picture of someone or something ❷ the appearance which a person, group, or organization presents to the public

**imaginary** ADJECTIVE Something that is imaginary exists only in your mind, not in real life

**imagination** NOUN the ability to form new and exciting ideas

**imagine**, imagines, imagining, imagined VERB ❶ If you imagine something, you form an idea of it in your mind, or you think you have seen or heard it but you have not really ❷ If you imagine that something is the case, you believe it is the case

**imitate**, imitates, imitating, imitated VERB To imitate someone or something is to copy them

**imitation** NOUN a copy of something else

**immature** ADJECTIVE ❶ Something that is immature has not finished growing or developing ❷ A person who is immature does not behave in a sensible adult way

**immediate** ADJECTIVE ❶ Something that is immediate happens or is done without delay ❷ Your immediate relatives and friends are the ones most closely connected or related to you

**immediately** ADVERB ❶ If something happens immediately it happens right away ❷ Immediately means very near in time or position

**immense** ADJECTIVE very large or huge
**immensely** ADVERB

**immigrant** NOUN someone who has come to live permanently in a new country
**immigration** NOUN

**immoral** ADJECTIVE If you describe someone or their behaviour as immoral, you mean that they do not fit in with most people's idea of what is right and proper

**immortal** ADJECTIVE ❶ Something that is immortal is famous and will be remembered for a long time ❷ In stories, someone who is immortal will never die

**immune** [im-*yoon*] ADJECTIVE ❶ If you are immune to a particular disease, you cannot catch it ❷ If someone or something is immune to something, they are able to avoid it or are not affected by it

**impact** NOUN ❶ The impact that someone or something has is the impression that they make or the effect that they have ❷ Impact is the action of one object hitting another, usually with a lot of force

**impatient** ADJECTIVE ❶ Someone who is impatient becomes annoyed easily or is quick to lose their temper when things go wrong ❷ If you are impatient to do something, you are eager and do not want to wait **impatiently** ADVERB **impatience** NOUN

**imperative** ADJECTIVE ❶ Something that is imperative is extremely urgent or important ❖ NOUN ❷ In grammar, an imperative is the form of a verb that is used for giving orders

**imperfect** ADJECTIVE ❶ Something that is imperfect has faults or problems ❖ NOUN ❷ In grammar, the imperfect is a tense used to describe continuous or repeated actions which happened in the past

**imperialism** NOUN a system of rule in which a rich and powerful nation controls other nations **imperialist** ADJECTIVE OR NOUN

**import** VERB ❶ If you import something from another country, you bring it into your country or have it sent there ❖ NOUN ❷ a product that is made in another country and sent to your own country for use there **importer** NOUN

**important** ADJECTIVE ❶ Something that is important is very valuable, necessary, or significant ❷ An important person has great influence or power **importantly** ADVERB **importance** NOUN

**impossible** ADJECTIVE Something that is impossible cannot happen, be done, or be believed

### Helpful hints...
You can have either **ize** or **ise** at the end of some verbs, but some words must have **ize** (*capsize* and *prize*) and some must have **ise** (*advertise, surprise, exercise* and *revise*).

**impractical** ADJECTIVE not practical, sensible, or realistic

**impress**, impresses, impressing, impressed VERB ❶ If you impress someone, you make them admire or respect you ❷ If you impress something on someone, you make them understand the importance of it

**impression** NOUN ❶ An impression of someone or something is the way they look or seem to you ❷ If you **make an impression**, you have a strong effect on people you meet

**impressive** ADJECTIVE If something is impressive, it impresses you

**improve**, improves, improving, improved VERB If something improves or if you improve it, it gets better or becomes more valuable

**improvement** NOUN the fact or process of getting better

**impulse** NOUN a strong urge to do something

**impulsive** ADJECTIVE If you are impulsive, you do things suddenly, without thinking about them carefully

**in** PREPOSITION OR ADVERB 'In' is used to indicate position, direction, time, and manner

**inability** NOUN a lack of ability to do something

**inaccurate** ADJECTIVE not accurate or correct

**inappropriate** ADJECTIVE not suitable for a particular purpose or occasion

**incapable** ADJECTIVE ❶ Someone who is incapable of doing something is not able to do it ❷ An incapable person is weak and helpless

**incentive** NOUN something that encourages you to do something

**inch**, inches, inching, inched NOUN ❶ a unit of length equal to about 2.54 centimetres ✿ VERB ❷ To inch forward is to move forward slowly

**incident** NOUN an event

**include**, includes, including, included VERB If one thing includes another, it has the second thing as one of its parts **including** PREPOSITION

**income** NOUN the money a person earns

**income tax** NOUN Income tax is a part of someone's salary which they have to pay regularly to the government

**incompetent** ADJECTIVE Someone who is incompetent does not have the ability to do something properly

**incomplete** ADJECTIVE not complete or finished

**incorrect** ADJECTIVE wrong or untrue **incorrectly** ADVERB

**increase**, increases, increasing, increased VERB ❶ If something increases, it becomes larger in amount ✿ NOUN ❷ a rise in the number, level, or amount of something **increasingly** ADVERB

**incredible** ADJECTIVE ❶ totally amazing ❷ impossible to believe **incredibly** ADVERB

**indeed** ADVERB You use 'indeed' to strengthen a point that you are making

**indefinite** ADJECTIVE ❶ If something is indefinite, no time to finish has been decided ❷ Indefinite also means vague or not exact **indefinitely** ADVERB

**indefinite article** NOUN the grammatical term for 'a' and 'an'

# independence - inflation

**independence** NOUN ❶ Independence is not relying on anyone else ❷ A nation or state gains its independence when it stops being ruled or governed by another country and has its own government and laws

**independent** ADJECTIVE ❶ Something that is independent happens or exists separately from other people or things ❷ Someone who is independent does not need other people's help ❸ An independent nation is one that is not ruled or governed by another country **independently** ADVERB

**index**, indices; indexes, indexing, indexed NOUN ❶ An index is an alphabetical list at the back of a book, referring to items in the book ❷ An index is also a set of cards listing all the books in a library, arranged alphabetically ❸ In maths, an index is a small number placed to the right of another number to indicate the number of times the number is to be multiplied by itself ✿ VERB ❹ To index a book or collection of information means to provide an index for it ❺ To index one thing to another means to arrange them so that they increase and decrease at the same rate

**indicate**, indicates, indicating, indicated VERB ❶ If something indicates something, it shows that it is true ❷ If you indicate something to someone, you point to it ❸ If you indicate a fact, you mention it ❹ If the driver of a vehicle indicates, they give a signal to show which way they are going to turn

**indication** NOUN a sign of what someone feels or what is likely to happen

**indicator** NOUN ❶ something which tells you what something is like or what is happening ❷ A car's indicators are the lights at the front and back which are used to show when it is turning left or right

**indifferent** ADJECTIVE ❶ If you are indifferent to something, you have no interest in it ❷ If something is indifferent, it is of a poor quality or low standard

**indigestion** NOUN Indigestion is a pain you get when you find it difficult to digest food

**indirect** ADJECTIVE Something that is indirect is not done or caused directly by a particular person or thing, but by someone or something else  **indirectly** ADVERB

**individual** ADJECTIVE ❶ relating to one particular person or thing ❷ Someone who is individual behaves quite differently from the way other people behave ✿ NOUN ❸ a person, different from any other person **individually** ADVERB

**indoor** ADJECTIVE situated or happening inside a building

**indoors** ADVERB If something happens indoors, it takes place inside a building

**industrial** ADJECTIVE relating to industry

**industry**, industries NOUN ❶ Industry is the work and processes involved in manufacturing things in factories ❷ all the people and processes involved in manufacturing a particular thing

**inefficient** ADJECTIVE badly organized, wasteful, and slow

**inequality**, inequalities NOUN a difference in size, status, wealth, or position, between different things, groups, or people

**inevitable** ADJECTIVE certain to happen **inevitably** ADVERB

**inexperienced** ADJECTIVE lacking experience of a situation or activity

**infant** NOUN ❶ a baby or very young child ✿ ADJECTIVE ❷ designed for young children

**infect** VERB To infect someone or something is to cause disease in them

**infection** NOUN ❶ a disease caused by germs ❷ Infection is the state of being infected

**infectious** ADJECTIVE spreading from one person to another

**inferior** ADJECTIVE ❶ having a lower position than something or someone else ❷ of low quality ✿ NOUN ❸ Your inferiors are people in a lower position than you

**infertile** ADJECTIVE ❶ Infertile soil is of poor quality and plants cannot grow well in it ❷ Someone who is infertile cannot have children

**infinite** ADJECTIVE without any limit or end

**infinitive** NOUN In grammar, the infinitive is the base form of the verb. It often has 'to' in front of it, for example 'to go' or 'to see'

**inflate**, inflates, inflating, inflated VERB When you inflate something, you fill it with air or gas to make it swell  **inflatable** ADJECTIVE

**inflation** NOUN Inflation is an increase in the price of goods and services in a country

**influence**, influences, influencing, influenced NOUN ❶ Influence is power that a person has over other people ❷ An influence is also the effect that someone or something has ❖ VERB ❸ To influence someone or something means to have an effect on them

**influential** ADJECTIVE Someone who is influential has a lot of influence over people

**inform** VERB ❶ If you inform someone of something, you tell them about it ❷ If you inform on a person, you tell the police about a crime they have committed

**informal** ADJECTIVE relaxed and casual **informally** ADVERB

**information** NOUN If you have information on or about something, you know something about it

**informative** ADJECTIVE Something that is informative gives you useful information

**ingredient** NOUN Ingredients are the things that something is made from, especially in cookery

**inhabit** VERB If you inhabit a place, you live there

**inhabitant** NOUN The inhabitants of a place are the people who live there

**inhale**, inhales, inhaling, inhaled VERB When you inhale, you breathe in

**inherit** VERB ❶ If you inherit money or property, you receive it from someone who has died ❷ If you inherit a quality or characteristic from a parent or ancestor, it is passed on to you at birth

**inheritance** NOUN something that is passed on from another person

**initial** [in-nish-l] ADJECTIVE ❶ first, or at the beginning ❖ NOUN ❷ the first letter of a name **initially** ADVERB

**inject** VERB ❶ If a doctor or nurse injects you with a substance, they use a needle and syringe to put the substance into your body ❷ If you inject something new into a situation, you add it **injection** NOUN

**injure**, injures, injuring, injured VERB To injure someone is to damage part of their body

**injury**, injuries NOUN hurt or damage, especially to part of a person's body or to their feelings

**injustice** NOUN ❶ Injustice is lack of justice and fairness ❷ If you do someone an injustice, you judge them too harshly

**ink** NOUN Ink is the coloured liquid used for writing or printing

**inland** ADJECTIVE ❶ near the middle of a country, away from the sea ❖ ADVERB ❷ towards the middle of a country, away from the sea

**inner** ADJECTIVE contained inside a place or object

**innocence** NOUN inexperience of evil or unpleasant things

**innocent** ADJECTIVE ❶ not guilty of a crime ❷ without experience of evil or unpleasant things

**innovation** NOUN a completely new idea, product, or system of doing things

**input** NOUN ❶ Input consists of all the money, information, and other resources that are put into a job, project, or company to make it work ❷ In computing, input is information which is fed into a computer

**inquire**, inquires, inquiring, inquired (also **enquire**) VERB If you inquire about something, you ask for information about it **inquiry** NOUN

**inquisitive** ADJECTIVE Someone who is inquisitive is keen to find out about things

**insane** ADJECTIVE Someone who is insane is mad

**insect** NOUN a small creature with six legs, and usually wings

**insecure** ADJECTIVE ❶ If you are insecure, you feel unsure of yourself and doubt whether other people like you ❷ Something that is insecure is not safe or well protected **insecurity** NOUN

**insensitive** ADJECTIVE If you are insensitive, you do not notice when you are upsetting people **insensitivity** NOUN

**insert** VERB If you insert an object into something, you put it inside

**inside** NOUN ❶ the part of something that is surrounded by the main part and often hidden ❷ IN PLURAL Your insides are the parts inside your body ❖ ADJECTIVE ❸ surrounded by the main part and often hidden ❖ PREPOSITION ❹ in or to the interior of ❖ PHRASE ❺ **Inside out** means with the inside part facing outwards

**insight** NOUN If you gain insight into a problem, you gradually get a deep and accurate understanding of it

# insignificant – insure

**insignificant** ADJECTIVE unimportant and small

**insist** VERB If you insist on something, you demand it forcefully

**inspect** VERB To inspect something is to examine it carefully to check that everything is all right **inspection** NOUN

**inspector** NOUN ❶ someone who inspects things ❷ a police officer just above a sergeant in rank

**inspire**, inspires, inspiring, inspired VERB ❶ If something inspires you, it gives you new ideas and enthusiasm to do something ❷ To inspire an emotion in someone is to make them feel this emotion **inspiring** ADJECTIVE **inspiration** NOUN

**install** VERB ❶ If you install a piece of equipment in a place, you put it there so it is ready to be used ❷ To install someone in an important job is to officially give them that position ❸ If you install yourself in a place, you settle there and make yourself comfortable **installation** NOUN

**instalment** NOUN ❶ If you pay for something in instalments, you pay small amounts of money regularly over a period of time ❷ one of the parts of a story or television series

**instance** NOUN ❶ a particular example or occurrence of an event, situation, or person ✿ PHRASE ❷ You use **for instance** to give an example of something you are talking about

**instant** NOUN ❶ a moment or short period of time ✿ ADJECTIVE ❷ immediate and without delay **instantly** ADVERB

**instead** ADVERB in place of something

**instinct** NOUN a natural tendency to do something **instinctive** ADJECTIVE **instinctively** ADVERB

**institute**, institutes, instituting, instituted NOUN ❶ an organization for teaching or research ✿ VERB ❷ FORMAL If you institute a rule or system, you introduce it

**institution** NOUN ❶ a custom or system regarded as an important tradition within a society ❷ a large, important organization, for example a university or bank

**instruct** VERB ❶ If you instruct someone to do something, you tell them to do it ❷ If someone instructs you in a subject or skill, they teach you about it **instructor** NOUN **instruction** NOUN

## how to remember

### Hello Kitty...

remembers that she can **tell** when a **gent**leman is in**telligent**.

**instrument** NOUN ❶ a tool or device used for a particular job ❷ A musical instrument is an object, such as a piano or flute, played to make music

**instrumental** ADJECTIVE ❶ If you are instrumental in doing something, you help to make it happen ❷ Instrumental music is performed using only musical instruments, and not voices

**insulate**, insulates, insulating, insulated VERB ❶ If you insulate a person from harmful things, you protect them from those things ❷ If materials such as feathers, fur, or foam insulate something, they keep it warm by covering it in a thick layer ❸ You insulate an electrical or metal object by covering it with rubber or plastic. This is to stop electricity passing through it and giving you an electric shock

**insult** VERB ❶ If you insult someone, you offend them by being rude to them ✿ NOUN ❷ a rude remark which offends you **insulting** ADJECTIVE

**insure**, insures, insuring, insured VERB ❶ If you insure yourself or something, you pay money regularly to a company so that if there is an accident or damage, the company will pay for medical treatment or repairs ❷ If you do something to insure

## intellectual – interrogate

against something unpleasant happening, you do it to prevent the unpleasant thing from happening or to protect yourself if it does happen **insurance** NOUN

**intellectual** ADJECTIVE ❶ involving thought, ideas, and understanding ❀ NOUN ❷ someone who enjoys thinking about complicated ideas

**intelligence** NOUN A person's intelligence is their ability to understand and learn things quickly and well

**intelligent** ADJECTIVE able to understand and learn things quickly and well **intelligently** ADVERB

**intend** VERB ❶ If you intend to do something, you have decided or planned to do it ❷ If something is intended for a particular use, you have planned that it should have this use

**intense** ADJECTIVE ❶ very great in strength or amount ❷ If a person is intense, they take things very seriously and have very strong feelings **intensely** ADVERB

**intensive** ADJECTIVE involving a lot of energy or effort over a very short time

**intention** NOUN If you have an intention to do something, you have a plan of what you are going to do

**intentional** ADJECTIVE If something is intentional, it is done on purpose **intentionally** ADVERB

**interactive** ADJECTIVE Interactive television, computers and games react to decisions taken by the viewer, user or player

**interest** NOUN ❶ If you have an interest in something or if something is of interest, you want to learn or hear more about it ❷ Your interests are your hobbies ❸ If you have an interest in something being done, you want it to be done because it will benefit you ❹ Interest is an extra payment made to the lender by someone who has borrowed a sum of money, or by a bank or company to someone who has invested money in them. Interest is worked out as a percentage of the sum of money borrowed or invested ❀ VERB ❺ Something that interests you attracts your attention so that you want to learn or hear more about it **interested** ADJECTIVE

**interesting** ADJECTIVE making you want to know, learn, or hear more **interestingly** ADVERB

**interfere**, interferes, interfering, interfered VERB ❶ If you interfere in a situation, you try to influence it, although it does not really concern you ❷ Something that interferes with a situation has a damaging effect on it **interference** NOUN

**interior** NOUN ❶ the inside part of something ❀ ADJECTIVE ❷ Interior means inside

**interjection** NOUN a word or phrase spoken suddenly to express surprise, pain, or anger

### how English works
### Hello Kitty...
knows that an **interjection** is a word that is a greeting or that shows a strong feeling, like *hello* and *wow*.

**intermediate** ADJECTIVE An intermediate level occurs in the middle, between two other stages

**internal** ADJECTIVE happening inside a person, place, or object

**international** ADJECTIVE ❶ involving different countries ❀ NOUN ❷ a sports match between two countries **internationally** ADVERB

**internet** NOUN The internet is a worldwide communication system which people use through computers

**interpret** VERB ❶ If you interpret what someone says or does, you decide what it means ❷ If you interpret a foreign language that someone is speaking, you translate it **interpreter** NOUN

**interrogate**, interrogates, interrogating, interrogated VERB If you interrogate someone,

# interrupt – iron

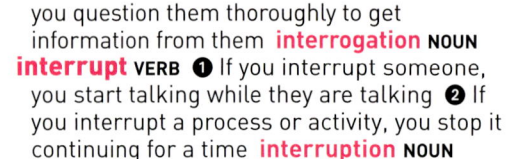

you question them thoroughly to get information from them **interrogation** NOUN

**interrupt** VERB ❶ If you interrupt someone, you start talking while they are talking ❷ If you interrupt a process or activity, you stop it continuing for a time **interruption** NOUN

**interval** NOUN ❶ the period of time between two moments or dates ❷ a short break during a play or concert ❸ In music, an interval is the difference in pitch between two musical notes

**interview** NOUN ❶ a meeting at which someone asks you questions about yourself to see if you are suitable for a particular job ❷ a conversation in which a journalist asks a famous person questions ✿ VERB ❸ If you interview someone, you ask them questions about themselves

**intestine** NOUN Your intestines are a long tube which carries food from your stomach through to your bowels, and in which the food is digested

**intimate** ADJECTIVE ❶ If two people are intimate, there is a close relationship between them ❷ An intimate matter is very private and personal ❸ An intimate knowledge of something is very deep and detailed **intimately** ADVERB

**intimidate**, intimidates, intimidating, intimidated VERB If you intimidate someone, you frighten them in a threatening way **intimidation** NOUN

**into** PREPOSITION ❶ If something goes into something else, it goes inside it ❷ If you bump or crash into something, you hit it

**intransitive** ADJECTIVE An intransitive verb is one that does not have a direct object. For example, 'sings' is intransitive in 'She sings', but not in 'She sings a song'

**introduce**, introduces, introducing, introduced VERB If you introduce one person to another, you tell them each other's name so that they can get to know each other

**introduction** NOUN ❶ The introduction of someone or something is the act of presenting them for the first time ❷ a piece of writing at the beginning of a book, which usually tells you what the book is about

**intuition** [int-yoo-**ish**-n] NOUN Your intuition is a feeling you have about something that you cannot explain

**invade**, invades, invading, invaded VERB If an army invades a country, it enters it by force

**invalid** [**in**-va-lid] NOUN someone who is so ill that they need to be looked after by someone else

**invalid** [in-**val**-id] ADJECTIVE ❶ If an argument or result is invalid, it is not acceptable because it is based on a mistake ❷ If a law, marriage, or election is invalid, it is illegal because it has not been carried out properly

**invasion** NOUN The invasion of a country or territory is the act of entering it by force

**invent** VERB ❶ If you invent a device or process, you are the first person to think of it or to use it ❷ If you invent a story or an excuse, you make it up **inventor** NOUN **invention** NOUN

**invertebrate** NOUN An invertebrate is a creature which does not have a spine

**invest** VERB ❶ If you invest money, you pay it into a bank or buy shares so that you will receive a profit ❷ If you invest in something useful, you buy it because it will help you do something better ❸ If you invest money, time, or energy in something, you try to make it a success **investment** NOUN

**investigate**, investigates, investigating, investigated VERB To investigate something is to try to find out all the facts about it **investigator** NOUN **investigation** NOUN

**invisible** ADJECTIVE If something is invisible, you cannot see it, because it is hidden, very small, or imaginary

**invite**, invites, inviting, invited VERB ❶ If you invite someone to an event, you ask them to come to it ❷ If you invite someone to do something, you ask them to do it **invitation** NOUN

**invoice**, invoices NOUN a bill for services or goods

**involve**, involves, involving, involved VERB If a situation involves someone or something, it includes them as a necessary part **involvement** NOUN

**iris**, irises [**eye**-riss] NOUN ❶ the round, coloured part of your eye ❷ a tall plant with long leaves and large blue, yellow, or white flowers

**iron** NOUN ❶ Iron is a strong hard metallic element found in rocks. It is used in making tools and machines, and is also an important component of blood ❷ An iron is a device which heats up and which you rub over clothes to remove creases ✿ VERB ❸ If you iron clothes, you use a hot iron to remove creases from them **ironing** NOUN

**iron out** ✿ VERB If you iron out difficulties, you solve them

**irony**, ironies [*eye-ron-ee*] NOUN Irony is a form of humour in which you say the opposite of what you really mean **ironic** or **ironical** ADJECTIVE **ironically** ADVERB

**irrational** ADJECTIVE Irrational feelings are not based on logical reasons **irrationally** ADVERB

**irregular** ADJECTIVE ❶ not smooth or even ❷ not forming a regular pattern ❸ Irregular things are uneven or unequal, or are not symmetrical **irregularly** ADVERB

**irrelevant** ADJECTIVE not directly connected with a subject

**irresponsible** ADJECTIVE An irresponsible person does things without considering the consequences

**irritable** ADJECTIVE easily annoyed

**irritate**, irritates, irritating, irritated VERB ❶ If something irritates you, it annoys you ❷ If something irritates part of your body, it makes it sore or itchy **irritation** NOUN

**is** the third person, present tense of **be**

**Islam** [*iz-lahm*] NOUN Islam is the Muslim religion, which teaches that there is only one God, Allah, and Mohammed is his prophet. The holy book of Islam is the Koran **Islamic** ADJECTIVE

**island** [*eye-land*] NOUN a piece of land surrounded on all sides by water

**isle** [*rhymes with* **mile**] NOUN LITERARY an island

**isolate**, isolates, isolating, isolated VERB ❶ If something isolates you or if you isolate yourself, you are set apart from other people ❷ If you isolate something, you separate it from everything else **isolated** ADJECTIVE

**ISP** an abbreviation for 'internet service provider', a company which provides people with access to the internet

**issue**, issues, issuing, issued [*ish-yoo*] NOUN ❶ an important subject that people are talking about ❷ a particular edition of a newspaper or magazine ✿ VERB ❸ If you issue a statement or a warning, you say it formally and publicly

**it** PRONOUN ❶ 'It' is used to refer to something that has already been mentioned, or to a situation or fact ❷ 'It' is used to refer to people or animals whose sex is not known ❸ You use 'it' to make statements about the weather, time, or date

**itch**, itches, itching, itched VERB ❶ When your skin itches, it has an unpleasant feeling and you want to scratch it ❷ If you are itching to do something, you are impatient to do it ✿ NOUN ❸ an unpleasant feeling on your skin that you want to scratch **itchy** ADJECTIVE

**item** NOUN ❶ one of a collection or list of objects ❷ a newspaper or magazine article

**its** ADJECTIVE OR PRONOUN 'Its' refers to something belonging to or relating to things, children, or animals that have already been mentioned

### don't mix up

### Hello Kitty...

never mixes up **its** (belonging to it, as in *The horse broke its leg*) and **it's** (it is or it has, as in *It's Friday* or *It's been a boring week*).

**itself** PRONOUN ❶ 'Itself' is used when the same thing, child, or animal does an action and is affected by it ❷ 'Itself' is used to emphasize 'it'

**ivy** NOUN an evergreen plant which creeps along the ground and up walls

143

# jacket – jelly

A B C D E F G H I J K L M N O P Q R S T U V W X Y Z

**jacket** NOUN ❶ a short coat reaching to the waist or hips ❷ an outer covering for something ❸ The jacket of a baked potato is its skin

**jackpot** NOUN In a gambling game, the jackpot is the top prize

**jagged** ADJECTIVE sharp and spiky

**jail** or **gaol** NOUN ❶ a building where people convicted of a crime are locked up ✿ VERB ❷ To jail someone means to lock them up in a jail

**jam** NOUN ❶ a food, made by boiling fruit and sugar together until it sets ❷ a situation in which it is impossible to move ✿ PHRASE ❸ INFORMAL If someone is **in a jam**, they are in a difficult situation ✿ VERB ❹ If people or things are jammed into a place, they are squeezed together so closely that they can hardly move ❺ To jam something somewhere means to push it there roughly ❻ If something is jammed, it is stuck or unable to work properly ❼ To jam a radio signal means to interfere with it and prevent it from being received clearly

**January** NOUN January is the first month of the year. It has 31 days

**jar**, jars, jarring, jarred NOUN ❶ a glass container with a wide top used for storing food ✿ VERB ❷ If something jars on you, you find it unpleasant or annoying

**javelin** NOUN a long spear that is thrown in sports competitions

**jaw** NOUN ❶ A person's or animal's jaw is the bone in which the teeth are set ❷ A person's or animal's mouth and teeth are their jaws

**jazz**, jazzes, jazzing, jazzed NOUN ❶ Jazz is a style of popular music with a forceful rhythm ✿ VERB ❷ INFORMAL To jazz something up means to make it more colourful or exciting

**jealous** ADJECTIVE ❶ If you are jealous, you feel bitterness towards someone who has something that you would like to have ❷ If you are jealous of something you have, you feel you must try to keep it from other people **jealously** ADVERB **jealousy** NOUN

**jeans** PLURAL NOUN Jeans are casual denim trousers

**jelly**, jellies NOUN ❶ a clear, sweet food eaten as a dessert ❷ a type of clear, set jam

### Hello Kitty...

knows that some words that sound as if they begin with *j* actually begin with *g*, like *giraffe*.

144

## jellyfish - journey

**jellyfish** NOUN a sea animal with a clear soft body and tentacles which may sting

**jerk** VERB ❶ To jerk something means to give it a sudden, sharp pull ❷ If something jerks, it moves suddenly and sharply ✿ NOUN ❸ a sudden sharp movement ❹ INFORMAL If you call someone a jerk, you mean they are stupid **jerky** ADJECTIVE

**jersey**, jerseys NOUN ❶ a knitted garment for the upper half of the body ❷ Jersey is a type of knitted woollen or cotton fabric used to make clothing

**jet**, jets, jetting, jetted NOUN ❶ a plane which is able to fly very fast ❷ a stream of liquid, gas, or flame forced out under pressure ❸ Jet is a hard black stone, usually highly polished and used in jewellery and ornaments ✿ VERB ❹ To jet somewhere means to fly there in a plane, especially a jet

**Jew** [joo] NOUN a person who practises the religion of Judaism, or who is of Hebrew descent **Jewish** ADJECTIVE

**jewel** NOUN a precious stone used to decorate valuable ornaments or jewellery

**jeweller** NOUN a person who makes jewellery or who sells and repairs jewellery and watches

**jewellery** NOUN Jewellery consists of ornaments that people wear, such as rings or necklaces, made of valuable metals and sometimes decorated with precious stones

**jigsaw** NOUN a puzzle consisting of a picture on cardboard that has been cut up into small pieces, which have to be put together again

**jingle**, jingles, jingling, jingled NOUN ❶ a short, catchy phrase or rhyme set to music and used to advertise something on radio or television ❷ the sound of something jingling ✿ VERB ❸ When something jingles, it makes a tinkling sound like small bells

**job** NOUN ❶ the work that someone does to earn money ❷ a duty or responsibility

**jobless** ADJECTIVE without any work

**jockey** NOUN ❶ someone who rides a horse in a race ✿ VERB ❷ To jockey for a position means to manoeuvre in order to gain an advantage over other people

**jog**, jogs, jogging, jogged VERB ❶ To jog means to run slowly and rhythmically, often as a form of exercise ❷ If you jog something, you knock it slightly so that it shakes or moves ❸ If someone or something jogs your memory, they remind you of something ✿ NOUN ❹ a slow run **jogger** NOUN **jogging** NOUN

**join** VERB ❶ When two things join, or when one thing joins another, they come together ❷ If you join a club or organization, you become a member of it or start taking part in it ❸ To join two things means to fasten them ✿ NOUN ❹ a place where two things are fastened together

**join up** ✿ VERB If someone joins up, they become a member of the armed forces

**joint** ADJECTIVE ❶ shared by or belonging to two or more people ✿ NOUN ❷ a part of the body where two bones meet and are joined together so that they can move, for example a knee or hip ❸ a place where two things are fixed together ❹ a large piece of meat suitable for roasting ✿ VERB ❺ To joint meat means to cut it into large pieces according to where the bones are

**joke**, jokes, joking, joked NOUN ❶ something that you say or do to make people laugh, such as a funny story ❷ anything that you think is ridiculous and not worthy of respect ✿ VERB ❸ If you are joking, you are teasing someone

**jolly**, jollier, jolliest ADJECTIVE ❶ happy, cheerful, and pleasant ✿ ADVERB ❷ INFORMAL Jolly also means very

**jolt** VERB ❶ To jolt means to move or shake roughly and violently ❷ If you are jolted by something, it gives you an unpleasant surprise ✿ NOUN ❸ a sudden jerky movement ❹ an unpleasant shock or surprise

**jot**, jots, jotting, jotted VERB ❶ If you jot something down, you write it quickly in the form of a short informal note ✿ NOUN ❷ a very small amount

**journal** NOUN ❶ a magazine that deals with a particular subject, trade, or profession ❷ a diary which someone keeps regularly

**journalism** NOUN Journalism is the work of collecting, writing, and publishing news in newspapers, magazines, and on television and radio **journalist** NOUN

**journey**, journeys, journeying, journeyed NOUN ❶ the act of travelling from one place

A B C D E F G H I J K L M N O P Q R S T U V W X Y Z

# joy – justify

to another ✿ **VERB** ❷ FORMAL To journey somewhere means to travel there

**joy**, joys **NOUN** ❶ Joy is a feeling of great happiness ❷ something that makes you happy or gives you pleasure

**joyful ADJECTIVE** ❶ causing pleasure and happiness ❷ Someone who is joyful is extremely happy **joyfully ADVERB**

**Judaism** [joo-day-i-zm] **NOUN** Judaism is the religion of the Jewish people. It is based on a belief in one God, and draws its laws and authority from the Old Testament

**judge**, judges, judging, judged **NOUN** ❶ the person in a law court who decides how the law should be applied to people who appear in the court ❷ someone who decides the winner in a contest or competition ✿ **VERB** ❸ If you judge someone or something, you form an opinion about them based on the evidence that you have ❹ To judge a contest or competition means to decide on the winner

**judgment** or **judgement NOUN** an opinion or decision based on evidence

**judo NOUN** Judo is a sport in which two people try to force each other to the ground using special throwing techniques

**jug NOUN** a container with a lip or spout used for holding or serving liquids

**juggle**, juggles, juggling, juggled **VERB** To juggle means to throw objects into the air, catching them in sequence, and tossing them up again so there are several in the air at one time **juggler NOUN**

**juice**, juices **NOUN** ❶ Juice is the liquid that can be squeezed or extracted from fruit or other food ❷ Juices in the body are fluids

**juicy**, juicier, juiciest **ADJECTIVE** ❶ Juicy food has a lot of juice in it ❷ Something that is juicy is interesting, exciting, or scandalous

**July NOUN** July is the seventh month of the year. It has 31 days

**jump VERB** ❶ To jump means to spring off the ground using your leg muscles ❷ To jump something means to spring off the ground and move over or across it ❸ If you jump at something such as an opportunity, you accept it eagerly ❹ If you jump on someone, you criticize them suddenly and forcefully ❺ If someone jumps, they make a sudden sharp movement of surprise ❻ If an amount or level jumps, it suddenly increases ✿ **NOUN** ❼ a spring into the air, sometimes over an object

**jumper NOUN** a knitted garment for the top half of the body

**June NOUN** June is the sixth month of the year. It has 30 days

**jungle NOUN** ❶ a dense tropical forest ❷ a tangled mass of plants or other objects

**junior ADJECTIVE** ❶ Someone who is junior to other people has a lower position in an organization ❷ Junior also means younger ❸ relating to childhood ✿ **NOUN** ❹ someone who holds an unimportant position in an organization

**junk NOUN** ❶ Junk is old or second-hand articles which are sold cheaply or thrown away ❷ If you think something is junk, you think it is worthless rubbish ❸ a Chinese sailing boat with a flat bottom and square sails

**jury**, juries **NOUN** a group of people in a court of law who have been selected to listen to the facts of a case on trial, and to decide whether the accused person is guilty or not

**just ADJECTIVE** ❶ fair and impartial ❷ morally right or proper ✿ **ADVERB** ❸ If something has just happened, it happened a very short time ago ❹ If you just do something, you do it by a very small amount ❺ simply or only ❻ exactly ✿ **PHRASE** ❼ In South African English, **just now** means in a little while

**justice NOUN** ❶ Justice is fairness and reasonableness ❷ The system of justice in a country is the way in which laws are maintained by the courts ❸ a judge or magistrate

**justify**, justifies, justifying, justified **VERB** If you justify an action or idea, you prove or explain why it is reasonable or necessary

---

**where does the word come from?**

**Jungle** comes from a word meaning 'wilderness' in an old language called Sanskrit.

# kangaroo - key

**kangaroo**, kangaroos NOUN a large Australian animal with very strong back legs which it uses for jumping

**karate** [kar-*rat*-ee] NOUN Karate is a sport in which people fight each other using only their hands, elbows, feet, and legs

**keen** ADJECTIVE ❶ Someone who is keen shows great eagerness and enthusiasm ❷ If you are keen on someone or something, you are attracted to or fond of them ❸ quick to notice or understand things ❹ Keen senses let you see, hear, smell, and taste things very clearly or strongly

**keep**, keeps, keeping, kept VERB ❶ To keep someone or something in a particular condition means to make them stay in that condition ❷ If you keep something, you have it and look after it ❸ To keep something also means to store it in the usual place ❹ If you keep doing something, you do it repeatedly or continuously ❺ If you keep a promise, you do what you promised to do ❻ If you keep a secret, you do not tell anyone else ❼ If you keep a diary, you write something in it every day ❽ If you keep someone from going somewhere, you delay them so that they are late ✿ NOUN ❾ Your keep is the cost of the food you eat, your housing, and your clothing ❿ the main tower inside the walls of a castle

**keep up** ✿ VERB If you keep up with other people, you move or work at the same speed as they do

**kennel** NOUN ❶ a shelter for a dog ❷ IN PLURAL A kennels is a place where dogs can be kept for a time, or where they are bred

**kerb** NOUN the raised edge at the point where a pavement joins onto a road

**ketchup** NOUN Ketchup is a cold sauce, usually made from tomatoes

**kettle** NOUN a metal container with a spout, in which you boil water

**key**, keys, keying, keyed NOUN ❶ a shaped piece of metal that fits into a hole so that you can unlock a door, wind something that is clockwork, or start a car ❷ The keys on a typewriter, piano, or cash register are the buttons that you press to use it ❸ an explanation of the symbols used in a map or diagram ❹ In music, a key is a scale of notes ✿ VERB ❺ If you key in information on a computer keyboard, you type it

*Hello Kitty...*

knows that some words that sound as if they begin with *k* actually begin with *ch*, like *choir* or *q*, like *quick*.

# keyboard - km

**keyboard** NOUN a row of levers or buttons on a piano, typewriter, or computer

**kg** an abbreviation for 'kilograms'

**khaki** [*kah-kee*] NOUN ❶ Khaki is a strong yellowish-brown material, used especially for military uniforms ❀ NOUN OR ADJECTIVE ❷ yellowish-brown

**kick** VERB ❶ If you kick something, you hit it with your foot ❀ NOUN ❷ If you give something a kick, you hit it with your foot ❸ INFORMAL If you get a kick out of doing something, you enjoy doing it very much

**kick off** ❀ VERB When players kick off, they start a soccer or rugby match

**kid**, kids, kidding, kidded NOUN ❶ INFORMAL a child ❷ a young goat ❀ VERB ❸ If you kid people, you tease them by deceiving them in fun

**kidnap**, kidnaps, kidnapping, kidnapped VERB To kidnap someone is to take them away by force and demand a ransom in exchange for returning them **kidnapper** NOUN **kidnapping** NOUN

**kidney**, kidneys NOUN Your kidneys are two organs in your body that remove waste products from your blood

**kill** VERB ❶ To kill a person, animal, or plant is to make them die ❷ If something is killing you, it is causing you severe pain or discomfort ❀ NOUN ❸ The kill is the moment when a hunter kills an animal **killer** NOUN

**kilo**, kilos NOUN a kilogram

**kilogram** NOUN A kilogram is a unit of weight equal to 1000 grams

**kilometre** NOUN a unit of distance equal to 1000 metres

**kind** NOUN ❶ A particular kind of thing is something of the same type or sort as other things ❀ ADJECTIVE ❷ Someone who is kind is considerate and generous towards other people **kindly** ADVERB

**kindness** NOUN the quality of being considerate towards other people

**king** NOUN ❶ a man who is the head of state in a country, and who inherited his position from his parents ❷ a chess piece which can only move one square at a time ❸ In a pack of cards, a king is a card with a picture of a king on it

**kingdom** NOUN ❶ a country that is governed by a king or queen ❷ The largest divisions of the living organisms in the natural world are called kingdoms

**kiosk** [*kee-osk*] NOUN a covered stall on a street where you can buy newspapers, sweets, or cigarettes

**kiss**, kisses, kissing, kissed VERB ❶ When you kiss someone, you touch them with your lips as a sign of love or affection ❀ NOUN ❷ When you give someone a kiss, you kiss them

**kit** NOUN ❶ a collection of things that you use for a sport or other activity ❷ a set of parts that you put together to make something

**kitchen** NOUN a room used for cooking and preparing food

**kite** NOUN ❶ a frame covered with paper or cloth which is attached to a piece of string, and which you fly in the air ❷ a shape with four sides, with two pairs of the same length, and none of the sides parallel to each other ❸ a large bird of prey with a long tail and long wings

**kitten** NOUN a young cat

**kiwi fruit** NOUN a fruit with a brown hairy skin and green flesh

**km** an abbreviation for 'kilometres'

## how to say it

### Hello Kitty ...

knows that words that begin with *kn*, like *knee*, sound as if they start with *n*. But originally the *k* was pronounced so *knee* was said *k-nee*.

148

## knead - knuckle

**knead** VERB If you knead dough, you press it and squeeze it with your hands before baking it

**knee** NOUN the joint in your leg between your ankle and your hip

**kneel**, kneels, kneeling, knelt VERB When you kneel, you bend your legs and lower your body until your knees are touching the ground

**knickers** PLURAL NOUN Knickers are underpants worn by women and girls

**knife**, knives; knifes, knifing, knifed NOUN ❶ a sharp metal tool that you use to cut things ✿ VERB ❷ To knife someone is to stab them with a knife

**knight** NOUN ❶ a man who has been given the title 'Sir' by the King or Queen ❷ In medieval Europe, a knight was a man who served a monarch or lord as a mounted soldier ❸ a chess piece that is usually in the shape of a horse's head ✿ VERB ❹ To knight a man is to give him the title 'Sir'

**knit**, knits, knitting, knitted VERB If you knit a piece of clothing, you make it by working lengths of wool together, either using needles held in the hand, or with a machine

**knitting** NOUN

**knob** NOUN ❶ a round handle ❷ a round switch on a machine

**knock** VERB ❶ If you knock on something, you strike it with your hand or fist ❷ If you knock a part of your body against something, you bump into it quite forcefully ❸ INFORMAL To knock someone is to criticize them ✿ NOUN ❹ a firm blow on something solid

**knock out** ✿ VERB To knock someone out is to hit them so hard that they become unconscious

**knot**, knots, knotting, knotted NOUN ❶ a fastening made by looping a piece of string around itself and pulling the ends tight ❷ a small lump visible on the surface of a piece of wood ❸ A knot of people is a small group of them ❹ TECHNICAL a unit of speed used for ships and aircraft ✿ VERB ❺ If you knot a piece of string, you tie a knot in it

**know**, knows, knowing, knew, known VERB ❶ If you know a fact, you have it in your mind and you do not need to learn it ❷ People you know are not strangers because you have met them and spoken to them ✿ PHRASE ❸ INFORMAL If you are **in the know**, you are one of a small number of people who share a secret

**knowledge** NOUN Knowledge is all the information and facts that you know

**knowledgeable** ADJECTIVE Someone who is knowledgeable knows a lot about a subject

**knuckle**, knuckles NOUN Your knuckles are the joints at the end of your fingers where they join your hand

---

**don't mix up**

Hello Kitty...

never mixes up **know** (to have a fact in your mind) and **now** (at this time).

# lab – laid

## L l

**lab** NOUN INFORMAL a laboratory

**label**, labels, labelling, labelled NOUN ❶ a piece of paper or plastic attached to something as an identification ✿ VERB ❷ If you label something, you put a label on it

**laboratory**, laboratories NOUN a place where scientific experiments are carried out

**labour** NOUN ❶ Labour is hard work ❷ The workforce of a country or industry is sometimes called its labour ❸ In Britain, the Labour Party is a political party that traditionally promotes equality and protects the rights of working people ❹ In New Zealand, the Labour Party is one of the main political parties ❺ Labour is also the last stage of pregnancy when a woman gives birth to a baby ✿ VERB ❻ OLD-FASHIONED To labour means to work hard

**lace**, laces, lacing, laced NOUN ❶ Lace is a very fine decorated cloth made with a lot of holes in it ❷ Laces are cords with which you fasten your shoes ✿ VERB ❸ When you lace up your shoes, you tie a bow in the laces ❹ To lace someone's food or drink means to put a small amount of alcohol, a drug, or poison in it

**lack** NOUN ❶ If there is a lack of something, it is not present when or where it is needed ✿ VERB ❷ If something is lacking, it is not present when or where it is needed ❸ If someone or something is lacking something, they do not have it or do not have enough of it

**lad** NOUN a boy or young man

**ladder** NOUN ❶ a wooden or metal frame used for climbing which consists of horizontal steps fixed to two vertical poles ❷ If your stockings or tights have a ladder in them, they have a vertical, ladder-like tear in them ✿ VERB ❸ If you ladder your stockings or tights, you get a ladder in them

**ladle**, ladles, ladling, ladled NOUN ❶ a long-handled spoon with a deep, round bowl, which you use to serve soup ✿ VERB ❷ If you ladle out food, you serve it with a ladle

**lady**, ladies NOUN ❶ a woman, especially one who is considered to be well mannered ❷ Lady is a title used in front of the name of a woman from the nobility, such as a lord's wife

**ladybird** NOUN a small flying beetle with a round red body patterned with black spots

**laid** the past tense and past participle of **lay**

### help with spelling

*Hello Kitty...*

knows that you write **Labour** with a capital letter when you are talking about the political party.

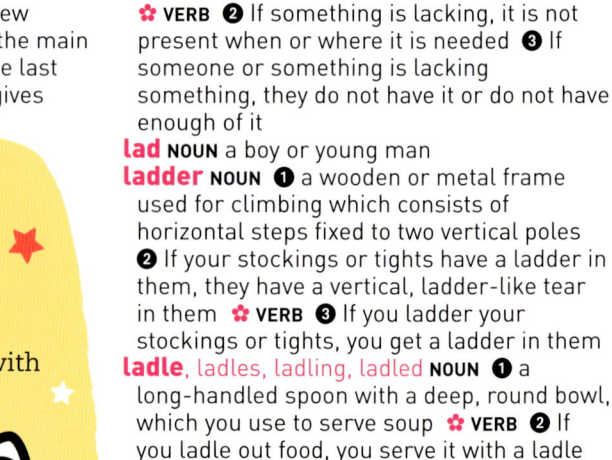

**lain** the past participle of some meanings of **lie**

**lake** NOUN an area of fresh water surrounded by land

**lamb** NOUN ❶ a young sheep ❷ Lamb is the meat from a lamb

**lame** ADJECTIVE ❶ Someone who is lame has an injured leg and cannot walk easily ❷ A lame excuse is not very convincing

**lamp** NOUN a device that produces light

**land** NOUN ❶ Land is an area of ground ❷ Land is also the part of the earth that is not covered by water ❸ a country ✿ VERB ❹ When a plane lands, it arrives back on the ground after a flight ❺ If you land something you have been trying to get, you succeed in getting it ❻ To land a fish means to catch it while fishing ❼ If you land someone with something unpleasant, you cause them to have to deal with it

**landing** NOUN ❶ a flat area in a building at the top of a flight of stairs ❷ The landing of an aeroplane is its arrival back on the ground after a flight

**landlady**, landladies NOUN a woman who owns a house or small hotel and who lets rooms to people

**landlord** NOUN a man who owns a house or small hotel and who lets rooms to people

**landmark** NOUN ❶ a noticeable feature in a landscape, which you can use to check your position ❷ an important stage in the development of something

**landscape** NOUN ❶ The landscape is the view over an area of open land ❷ a painting of the countryside

**lane** NOUN ❶ a narrow road, especially in the country ❷ one of the strips on a road marked with lines to guide drivers

**language** NOUN ❶ the system of words that the people of a country use to communicate with each other ❷ Your language is the style in which you express yourself ❸ Language is the study of the words and grammar of a particular language

**lantern** NOUN a lamp in a metal frame with glass sides

**lap**, laps, lapping, lapped NOUN ❶ Your lap is the flat area formed by your thighs when you are sitting down ❷ one circuit of a running track or racecourse ✿ VERB ❸ When an animal laps up liquid, it drinks using its tongue to get the liquid into its mouth ❹ If you lap someone in a race, you overtake them when they are still on the previous lap ❺ When water laps against something, it gently moves against it in little waves

**lapel** [lap-el] NOUN a flap which is joined on to the collar of a jacket or coat

**large**, larger, largest ADJECTIVE ❶ Someone or something that is large is much bigger than average ✿ PHRASE ❷ If a prisoner is **at large**, he or she has escaped from prison

**largely** ADVERB to a great extent

**laser** NOUN a machine that produces a powerful concentrated beam of light which is used to cut very hard materials and in some kinds of surgery

**last** ADJECTIVE ❶ The last thing or event is the most recent one ❷ The last thing that remains is the only one left after all the others have gone ✿ ADVERB ❸ If you last did something on a particular occasion, you have not done it since then ❹ The thing that happens last in a sequence of events is the final one ✿ VERB ❺ If something lasts, it continues to exist or happen ❻ To last also means to remain in good condition **lastly** ADVERB

**latch**, latches, latching, latched NOUN ❶ a simple door fastening consisting of a metal bar which falls into a hook ❷ a type of door lock which locks automatically when you close the door and which has to be opened with a key

**late**, later, latest ADJECTIVE OR ADVERB ❶ Something that happens late happens towards the end of a period of time ❷ If you arrive late, or do something late, you arrive or do it after the time you were expected to ✿ ADJECTIVE ❸ A late event happens after the time when it usually takes place ❹ FORMAL Late means dead

**lately** ADVERB Events that happened lately happened recently

**latitude** NOUN The latitude of a place is its distance north or south of the equator measured in degrees

**latter** ADJECTIVE OR NOUN ❶ You use 'latter' to refer to the second of two things that are mentioned ✿ ADJECTIVE ❷ 'Latter' also describes the second or end part of something

# laugh – lead

**laugh** VERB ❶ When you laugh, you make a noise which shows that you are amused or happy ✿ NOUN ❷ the noise you make when you laugh **laughter** NOUN

**launch**, launches, launching, launched VERB ❶ To launch a ship means to send it into the water for the first time ❷ To launch a rocket means to send it into space ❸ When a company launches a new product, they have an advertising campaign to promote it as they start to sell it ✿ NOUN ❹ a motorboat

**laundry**, laundries NOUN ❶ a business that washes and irons clothes and sheets ❷ Laundry is also the dirty clothes and sheets that are being washed, or are about to be washed

**lava** NOUN Lava is the very hot liquid rock that comes shooting out of an erupting volcano, and becomes solid as it cools

**lavatory**, lavatories NOUN a toilet

**law** NOUN ❶ The law is the system of rules developed by the government of a country, which regulate what people may and may not do and deals with people who break these rules ❷ The law is also the profession of people such as lawyers, whose job involves the application of the laws of a country ❸ one of the rules established by a government or a religion, which tells people what they may or may not do ❹ a scientific fact which allows you to explain how things work in the physical world **lawful** ADJECTIVE **lawfully** ADVERB

**lawn** NOUN an area of cultivated grass

**lawnmower** NOUN a machine for cutting grass

**lawsuit** NOUN a civil court case between two people, as opposed to the police prosecuting someone for a criminal offence

**lawyer** NOUN a person who is qualified in law, and whose job is to advise people about the law and represent them in court

**lay**, lays, laying, laid VERB ❶ When you lay something somewhere, you put it down so that it lies there ❷ If you lay something, you arrange it or set it out ❸ If you lay the table, you put cutlery on the table ready for a meal ❹ When a bird lays an egg, it produces the egg out of its body ❺ If you lay a trap for someone, you create a situation in which you will be able to catch them out ❻ If you lay odds on something, you bet that it will happen ✿ ADJECTIVE ❼ You use 'lay' to describe people who are involved with a Christian church but are not members of the clergy ❽ Lay is the past tense of some senses of **lie**

**lay off** ✿ VERB ❶ When workers are laid off, their employers tell them not to come to work for a while because there is a shortage of work ❷ INFORMAL If you tell someone to lay off, you want them to stop doing something annoying

**lay on** ✿ VERB If you lay on a meal or entertainment, you provide it

**layer** NOUN a single thickness of something

**layout** NOUN The layout of something is the pattern in which it is arranged

**lazy**, lazier, laziest ADJECTIVE idle and unwilling to work **laziness** NOUN

**lead**, leads, leading, led [rhymes with **feed**] VERB ❶ If you lead someone somewhere, you go in front of them in order to show them the way ❷ If one thing leads to another, it causes the second thing to happen ❸ a person who leads a group of people is in charge of them ✿ NOUN ❹ a length of leather or chain attached to a dog's collar, so that the dog can be kept under control ❺ If the police have a lead, they have a clue which might help them to solve a crime

### how to say it

## Tips and tricks...

**Lead** rhymes with *feed* unless you are talking about the metal, and then it rhymes with *fed*.

152

# lead - ledge

**lead** [rhymes with **fed**] NOUN Lead is a soft, grey, heavy metal

**leader** NOUN ❶ someone who is in charge of a country, an organization, or a group of people ❷ the person who is winning in a competition or race ❸ a newspaper article that expresses the newspaper's opinions

**leadership** NOUN ❶ the group of people in charge of an organization ❷ Leadership is the ability to be a good leader

**leading** ADJECTIVE particularly important, respected, or advanced

**leaf**, leaves; leafs, leafing, leafed NOUN ❶ the flat green growth on the end of a twig or branch of a tree or other plant ✿ VERB ❷ If you leaf through a book, magazine, or newspaper, you turn the pages over quickly

**leaflet** NOUN a piece of paper with information or advertising printed on it

**league** [leeg] NOUN ❶ a group of countries, clubs, or people who have joined together for a particular purpose or because they share a common interest ❷ a unit of distance used in former times, equal to about 3 miles

**leak** VERB ❶ If a pipe or container leaks, it has a hole which lets gas or liquid escape ❷ If liquid or gas leaks, it escapes from a pipe or container ❸ If someone in an organization leaks information, they give the information to someone who is not supposed to have it ✿ NOUN ❹ If a pipe or container has a leak, it has a hole which lets gas or liquid escape ❺ If there is a leak in an organization, someone inside the organization is giving information to people who are not supposed to have it

**lean**, leans, leaning, leant or leaned VERB ❶ When you lean in a particular direction, you bend your body in that direction ❷ When you lean on something, you rest your body against it for support ❸ If you lean on someone, you depend on them ❹ If you lean towards particular ideas, you approve of them and follow them ✿ ADJECTIVE ❺ having little or no fat ❻ A lean period is a time when food or money is in short supply

**leap**, leaps, leaping, leapt or leaped VERB ❶ If you leap somewhere, you jump over a long distance or high in the air ✿ NOUN ❷ a jump over a long distance or high in the air

**learn**, learns, learning, learnt or learned VERB ❶ When you learn something, you gain knowledge or a skill through studying or training ❷ If you learn of something, you find out about it **learner** NOUN

**lease**, leases, leasing, leased NOUN ❶ an agreement which allows someone to use a house or flat in return for rent ✿ VERB ❷ To lease property to someone means to allow them to use it in return for rent

**least** NOUN ❶ The least is the smallest possible amount of something ✿ ADJECTIVE ❷ as small or as few as possible ✿ ADVERB ❸ Least is a superlative form of **little** ✿ PHRASE ❹ You use **at least** to show that you are referring to the minimum amount of something, and that you think the true amount is greater

**leather** NOUN Leather is the tanned skin of some animals, used to make shoes and clothes

**leave**, leaves, leaving, left VERB ❶ When you leave a place, you go away from it ❷ If you leave someone somewhere, they stay behind after you go away ❸ If you leave a job or organization, you stop being part of it ❹ If someone leaves money or possessions to someone, they arrange for them to be given to them after their death ❺ In subtraction, when you take one number from another, it leaves a third number ✿ NOUN ❻ a period of holiday or absence from a job

**lecture**, lectures, lecturing, lectured NOUN ❶ a formal talk intended to teach people about a particular subject ❷ a talk intended to tell someone off ✿ VERB ❸ Someone who lectures teaches in a college or university

**lecturer** NOUN a teacher in a college or university

**led** the past tense and past participle of **lead**

### don't mix up

Don't mix up **led** (the past form of lead) and **lead** (a type of metal).

**ledge** NOUN a narrow shelf on the side of a cliff or rock face, or on the outside of a building, directly under a window

# leek – leopard

**leek** NOUN a long vegetable of the onion family, which is white at one end and has green leaves at the other

**left** NOUN ❶ The left is one of two sides of something. For example, on a page, English writing begins on the left ❷ People and political groups who hold socialist or communist views are referred to as the Left ❸ Left is the past tense and past participle of **leave** ✿ ADJECTIVE OR ADVERB ❹ Left means on or towards the left side of something

**left-handed** ADJECTIVE OR ADVERB Someone who is left-handed does things such as writing with their left hand

**leftovers** PLURAL NOUN the bits of food which have not been eaten at the end of the meal

**left-wing** ADJECTIVE believing more strongly in socialism, or less strongly in capitalism or conservatism, than other members of the same party or group

**leg** NOUN ❶ Your legs are the two limbs which stretch from your hips to your feet ❷ The legs of a pair of trousers are the parts that cover your legs ❸ The legs of an object such as a table are the parts which rest on the floor and support the object's weight ❹ A leg of a journey is one part of it ❺ one of two matches played between two sports teams

**legal** ADJECTIVE ❶ relating to the law ❷ allowed by the law

**legalize**, legalizes, legalizing, legalized (also **legalise**) VERB To legalize something that is illegal means to change the law so that it becomes legal

**legend** NOUN ❶ an old story which was once believed to be true, but which is probably untrue ❷ If you refer to someone or something as a legend, you mean they are very famous

**leisure** [rhymes with **measure**] NOUN ❶ Leisure is time during which you do not have to work, and can do what you enjoy doing ✿ PHRASES ❷ If you do something **at leisure**, or **at your leisure**, you do it at a convenient time

**leisurely** ADJECTIVE OR ADVERB A leisurely action is done in an unhurried and calm way

**lemon** NOUN ❶ a yellow citrus fruit with a sour taste ✿ ADJECTIVE ❷ pale yellow

**lemonade** NOUN a sweet, fizzy drink made from lemons, water, and sugar

**lend**, lends, lending, lent VERB ❶ If you lend someone something, you give it to them for a period of time and then they give it back to you ❷ If a bank lends money, it gives the money to someone and the money has to be repaid in the future, usually with interest ✿ PHRASE ❸ If you **lend someone a hand**, you help them

**length** NOUN ❶ The length of something is the horizontal distance from one end to the other ❷ The length of an event or activity is the amount of time it lasts for ❸ The length of something is also the fact that it is long rather than short ❹ a long piece of something

**lengthen** VERB To lengthen something means to make it longer

**lengthy**, lengthier, lengthiest ADJECTIVE Something that is lengthy lasts for a long time

**lens**, lenses NOUN ❶ a curved piece of glass designed to focus light in a certain way, for example in a camera, telescope, or pair of glasses ❷ The lens in your eye is the part behind the iris, which focuses light

**lent** ❶ the past tense and past participle of **lend** ✿ NOUN ❷ Lent is the period of forty days leading up to Easter, during which Christians give up something they enjoy

**lentil** NOUN Lentils are small dried red or brown seeds which are cooked and eaten in soups and curries

**leopard** NOUN a wild Asian or African big cat, with yellow fur and black or brown spots

### how to say it

*Tips and tricks...*

**Leopard** should be said **lep**-ird, with most force on **lep**.

154

# leotard – licence

**leotard** [*lee*-eh-tard] NOUN a tight-fitting costume covering the body and legs, which is worn for dancing or exercise

**lesbian** NOUN a homosexual woman

**less** ADJECTIVE OR ADVERB ❶ Less means a smaller amount, or not as much in quality ❷ Less is a comparative form of **little** ✿ PREPOSITION ❸ You use 'less' to show that you are subtracting one number from another

**lessen** VERB If something lessens, it is reduced in amount, size, or quality

**lesson** NOUN ❶ a fixed period of time during which a class of pupils is taught by a teacher ❷ an experience that makes you understand something important which you had not realized before

**let**, lets, letting, let VERB ❶ If you let someone do something, you allow them to do it ❷ If someone lets a house or flat that they own, they rent it out ❸ You can say 'let's' or 'let us' when you want to suggest doing something with someone else ❹ If you let yourself in for something, you agree to do it although you do not really want to

**let off** ✿ VERB ❶ If someone in authority lets you off, they do not punish you for something you have done wrong ❷ If you let off a firework or explosive, you light it or detonate it

**lethal** [*lee*-thal] ADJECTIVE able to kill someone

**letter** NOUN ❶ Letters are written symbols which go together to make words ❷ a piece of writing addressed to someone, and usually sent through the post

**letter box**, letter boxes NOUN ❶ an oblong gap in the front door of a house or flat, through which letters are delivered ❷ a large metal container in the street, where you post letters

**lettering** NOUN Lettering is writing, especially when you are describing the type of letters used

**lettuce** NOUN a vegetable with large green leaves eaten raw in salad

**level**, levels, levelling, levelled ADJECTIVE ❶ A surface that is level is smooth, flat, and parallel to the ground ✿ VERB ❷ To level a piece of land means to make it flat ❸ If you level a criticism at someone, you say or write something critical about them ✿ ADVERB ❹ If you draw level with someone, you get closer to them so that you are moving next to them ✿ NOUN ❺ a point on a scale which measures the amount, importance, or difficulty of something ❻ The level of a liquid is the height it comes up to in a container

**level off** or **level out** ✿ VERB If something levels off or levels out, it stops increasing or decreasing

**lever** NOUN ❶ a handle on a machine that you pull in order to make the machine work ❷ a long bar that you wedge underneath a heavy object and press down on to make the object move

**liable** ADJECTIVE ❶ If you say that something is liable to happen, you mean that you think it will probably happen ❷ If you are liable for something you have done, you are legally responsible for it

**liar** NOUN a person who tells lies

**liberal** NOUN ❶ someone who believes in political progress, social welfare, and individual freedom ✿ ADJECTIVE ❷ Someone who is liberal is tolerant of a wide range of behaviour, standards, or opinions ❸ To be liberal with something means to be generous with it ❹ A liberal quantity of something is a large amount of it

**liberty** NOUN Liberty is the freedom to choose how you want to live, without government restrictions

**librarian** NOUN a person who works in, or is in charge of, a library

**library**, libraries NOUN ❶ a building in which books are kept for people to come and read or borrow ❷ a collection of books, music, or films

**lice** the plural of **louse**

**licence** NOUN ❶ an official document which entitles you to carry out a particular activity, for example to drive a car ❷ Licence is the

### don't mix up

**Licence** is the noun and **license** is the verb.

# license – lily

freedom to do what you want, especially when other people consider that it is being used irresponsibly

**license**, licenses, licensing, licensed VERB To license an activity means to give official permission for it to be carried out

**lick** VERB ❶ If you lick something, you move your tongue over it ✿ NOUN ❷ the action of licking

**lid** NOUN the top of a container, which you open in order to reach what is inside

**lie**, lies, lying, lay, lain VERB ❶ To lie somewhere means to rest there horizontally ❷ If you say where something lies, you are describing where it is

**lie**, lies, lying, lied VERB ❶ To lie means to say something that is not true ✿ NOUN ❷ something you say which is not true

**lieutenant** [lef-**ten**-ent] NOUN a junior officer in the army or navy

**life**, lives NOUN ❶ Life is the quality of being able to grow and develop, which is present in people, plants, and animals ❷ Your life is your existence from the time you are born until the time you die ❸ The life of a machine is the period of time for which it is likely to work ❹ If you refer to the life in a place, you are talking about the amount of activity there ❺ If criminals are sentenced to life, they are sent to prison for the rest of their lives, or until they are granted parole

**lifeboat** NOUN ❶ a boat kept on shore, which is sent out to rescue people who are in danger at sea ❷ a small boat kept on a ship, which is used if the ship starts to sink

**lifeguard** NOUN a person whose job is to rescue people who are in difficulty in the sea or in a swimming pool

**life jacket** NOUN a sleeveless inflatable jacket that keeps you afloat in water

**lifetime** NOUN Your lifetime is the period of time during which you are alive

**lift** VERB ❶ To lift something means to move it to a higher position ❷ When fog or mist lifts, it clears away ❸ To lift a ban on something means to remove it ✿ NOUN ❹ a machine like a large box which carries passengers from one floor to another in a building ❺ If you give someone a lift, you drive them somewhere in a car or on a motorcycle

**light**, lights, lighting, lighted or lit NOUN ❶ Light is brightness from the sun, fire, or lamps, that enables you to see things ❷ a lamp or other device that gives out brightness ❸ If you give someone a light, you give them a match or lighter to light their cigarette ✿ ADJECTIVE ❹ A place that is light is bright because of the sun or the use of lamps ❺ A light colour is pale ❻ A light object does not weigh much ❼ A light task is fairly easy ❽ Light books or music are entertaining and are not intended to be serious ✿ VERB ❾ To light a place means to cause it to be filled with light ❿ To light a fire means to make it start burning ⓫ To light upon something means to find it by accident

**lighten** VERB ❶ When something lightens, it becomes less dark ❷ To lighten a load means to make it less heavy

**lighter** NOUN a device for lighting a cigarette or cigar

**lighthouse** NOUN a tower by the sea, which sends out a powerful light to guide ships and warn them of danger

**lighting** NOUN The lighting in a room or building is the way that it is lit

**lightning** NOUN Lightning is the bright flashes of light in the sky which are produced by natural electricity during a thunder storm

**likable** or **likeable** ADJECTIVE Someone who is likable is very pleasant and friendly

**like**, likes, liking, liked PREPOSITION ❶ If one thing is like another, it is similar to it ✿ NOUN ❷ 'The like' means other similar things of the sort just mentioned ✿ PHRASE ❸ If you **feel like** something, you want to do it or have it ✿ VERB ❹ If you like something or someone, you find them pleasant

**likelihood** NOUN If you say that there is a likelihood that something will happen, you mean that you think it will probably happen

**likely**, likelier, likeliest ADJECTIVE Something that is likely will probably happen or is probably true

**likewise** ADVERB Likewise means similarly

**liking** NOUN If you have a liking for someone or something, you like them

**lilac** NOUN ❶ a shrub with large clusters of pink, white, or mauve flowers ✿ ADJECTIVE ❷ pale mauve

**lily**, lilies NOUN a plant with trumpet-shaped flowers of various colours

# limb - little

**limb** NOUN ❶ Your limbs are your arms and legs ❷ The limbs of a tree are its branches ✿ PHRASE ❸ If you have gone **out on a limb**, you have said or done something risky

**lime** NOUN ❶ a small, green citrus fruit, rather like a lemon ❷ A lime tree is a large tree with pale green leaves ❸ Lime is a chemical substance that is used in cement and as a fertilizer

**limit** NOUN ❶ a boundary or an extreme beyond which something cannot go ✿ VERB ❷ To limit something means to prevent it from becoming bigger, spreading, or making progress

**limousine** [lim-o-zeen] NOUN a large, luxurious car, usually driven by a chauffeur

**limp** VERB ❶ If you limp, you walk unevenly because you have hurt your leg or foot ✿ NOUN ❷ an uneven way of walking ✿ ADJECTIVE ❸ Something that is limp is soft and floppy, and not stiff or firm

**line**, lines, lining, lined NOUN ❶ a long, thin mark ❷ a number of people or things positioned one behind the other ❸ a route along which someone or something moves ❹ In a piece of writing, a line is a number of words together ❺ In maths, a line is the straight, one-dimensional space between two points ❻ The line someone takes is the attitude they have towards something ❼ In a shop or business, a line is a type of product ✿ VERB ❽ To line something means to cover its inside surface or edge with something

**line up** ✿ VERB When people line up, they stand in a line

**linen** NOUN ❶ Linen is a type of cloth made from a plant called flax ❷ Linen is also household goods made of cloth, such as sheets and tablecloths

**liner** NOUN a large passenger ship that makes long journeys

**lingerie** [lan-jer-ee] NOUN Lingerie is women's nightclothes and underclothes

**lining** NOUN any material used to line the inside of something

**link** NOUN ❶ a relationship or connection between two things ❷ a physical connection between two things or places ❸ one of the rings in a chain ✿ VERB ❹ To link people, places, or things means to join them together

**lion** NOUN a large member of the cat family which comes from Africa. Lions have light brown fur, and the male has a long mane. A female lion is called a lioness

**lip** NOUN ❶ Your lips are the edges of your mouth ❷ The lip of a jug is the slightly pointed part through which liquids are poured out

**lipstick** NOUN a coloured substance which women wear on their lips

**liquid** NOUN ❶ any substance which is not a solid or a gas, and which can be poured ✿ ADJECTIVE ❷ Something that is liquid is in the form of a liquid

**list** NOUN ❶ a set of words or items written one below the other ✿ VERB ❷ If you list a number of things, you make a list of them

**listen** VERB If you listen to something, you hear it and pay attention to it  **listener** NOUN

**lit** a past tense and past participle of **light**

**literacy** NOUN Literacy is the ability to read and write

**literature** NOUN ❶ Literature consists of novels, plays, and poetry ❷ The literature on a subject is everything that has been written about it

**litre** NOUN a unit of liquid volume equal to about 1.76 pints

**litter** NOUN ❶ Litter is rubbish in the street and other public places ❷ Cat litter is a gravelly substance you put in a container where you want your cat to urinate and defecate ❸ a number of baby animals born at the same time to the same mother ✿ VERB ❹ If things litter a place, they are scattered all over it

**little**, less, lesser, least ADJECTIVE ❶ small in size or amount ✿ NOUN ❷ A little is a small

### some other words to use

You should try not to use **little** too much when you are writing. Some other words you can use are: *miniature*, *tiny*, *wee* and *mini*.

157

# live - logical

amount or degree ❸ Little also means not much ✿ ADVERB ❹ to a small amount or degree

**live**, lives, living, lived VERB ❶ If you live in a place, that is where your home is ❷ To live means to be alive ❸ If something lives up to your expectations, it is as good as you thought it would be ✿ ADJECTIVE OR ADVERB ❹ Live television or radio is broadcast while the event is taking place ✿ ADJECTIVE ❺ Live animals or plants are alive, rather than dead or artificial ❻ Something is live if it is directly connected to an electricity supply ❼ Live bullets or ammunition have not yet been exploded

**live down** ✿ VERB If you cannot live down a mistake or failure, you cannot make people forget it

**lively** ADJECTIVE full of life and enthusiasm

**liver** NOUN ❶ Your liver is a large organ in your body which cleans your blood and helps digestion ❷ Liver is also the liver of some animals, which may be cooked and eaten

**living** ADJECTIVE ❶ If someone is living, they are alive ✿ NOUN ❷ The work you do for a living is the work you do in order to earn money to live

**living room** NOUN the room where people relax and entertain in their homes

**lizard** NOUN a long, thin, dry-skinned reptile found in hot, dry countries

**load** NOUN ❶ something being carried ❷ INFORMAL Loads means a lot ✿ VERB ❸ To load a vehicle or animal means to put a large number of things into it or onto it

**loaf**, loaves; loafs, loafing, loafed NOUN ❶ a large piece of bread baked in a shape that can be cut into slices ✿ VERB ❷ To loaf around means to be lazy and not do any work

**loan** NOUN ❶ a sum of money that you borrow ❷ the act of borrowing or lending something ✿ VERB ❸ If you loan something to someone, you lend it to them

**loathe**, loathes, loathing, loathed VERB To loathe someone or something means to feel strong dislike for them

**lobby** NOUN ❶ The lobby in a building is the main entrance area with corridors and doors leading off it ❷ a group of people trying to persuade an organization that something should be done

**lobster** NOUN an edible shellfish with two front claws and eight legs

**local** ADJECTIVE ❶ Local means in, near, or belonging to the area in which you live ✿ NOUN ❷ The locals are the people who live in a particular area **locally** ADVERB

**location** NOUN ❶ a place, or the position of something ❷ In South Africa, a location was a small town where only Black people were allowed to live

**lock** VERB ❶ If you lock something, you close it and fasten it with a key ❷ If something locks into place, it moves into place and becomes firmly fixed there ✿ NOUN ❸ a device on something which fastens it and prevents it from being opened except with a key ❹ A lock on a canal is a place where the water level can be raised or lowered to allow boats to go between two parts of the canal which have different water levels ❺ A lock of hair is a small bunch of hair

**locker** NOUN a small cupboard for your personal belongings, for example in a changing room

**loft** NOUN the space immediately under the roof of a house, often used for storing things

**log**, logs, logging, logged NOUN ❶ a thick branch or piece of tree trunk which has fallen or been cut down ❷ the captain's official record of everything that happens on board a ship ✿ VERB ❸ If you log something, you officially make a record of it, for example in a ship's log ❹ To log into a computer system means to gain access to it, usually by giving your name and password. To log out means to finish using the system

**logic** NOUN Logic is a way of reasoning involving a series of statements, each of which must be true if the statement before it is true

**logical** ADJECTIVE ❶ A logical argument uses logic ❷ A logical course of action or decision is sensible or reasonable in the circumstances

158

**logo**, logos [loh-goh] NOUN The logo of an organization is a special design that is put on all its products

**lollipop** NOUN a hard sweet on the end of a stick

**lonely**, lonelier, loneliest ADJECTIVE ❶ If you are lonely, you are unhappy because you are alone ❷ A lonely place is an isolated one which very few people visit **loneliness** NOUN

**long** ADJECTIVE ❶ continuing for a great amount of time ❖ ADJECTIVE ❷ great in length or distance ❖ ADVERB ❸ for a certain period of time ❹ for an extensive period of time ❖ VERB ❺ If you long for something, you want it very much

**longitude** NOUN The longitude of a place is its distance east or west of a line passing through Greenwich, measured in degrees

**loo** NOUN INFORMAL a toilet

**look** VERB ❶ If you look at something, you turn your eyes towards it so that you can see it ❷ If you look at a subject or situation, you study it or judge it ❸ If you look down on someone, you think that they are inferior to you ❹ If you are looking forward to something, you want it to happen because you think you will enjoy it ❺ If you look up to someone, you admire and respect them ❻ If you describe the way that something or someone looks, you are describing the appearance of it or them ❖ NOUN ❼ If you have a look at something, you look at it ❽ The look of someone or something is the way they appear, especially the expression on a person's face ❖ INTERJECTION ❾ You say 'look out' to warn someone of danger

**look after** ❖ VERB If you look after someone or something, you take care of them

**look for** ❖ VERB If you look for someone or something, you try to find them

**look up** ❖ VERB ❶ To look up information means to find it out in a book ❷ If you look someone up, you go to see them after not having seen them for a long time

**loom** NOUN a machine for weaving cloth

**loop** NOUN a curved or circular shape in something long such as a piece of string

**loose**, looser, loosest ADJECTIVE ❶ If something is loose, it is not firmly held, fixed, or attached ❷ Loose clothes are rather large and do not fit closely ❖ ADVERB ❸ To set animals loose means to set them free after they have been tied up or kept in a cage **loosely** ADVERB

**loosen** VERB To loosen something means to make it looser

**lord** NOUN ❶ a nobleman ❷ Lord is a title used in front of the names of some noblemen, and of bishops, archbishops, judges, and some high-ranking officials ❸ In Christianity, Lord is a name given to God and Jesus Christ

**lorry**, lorries NOUN a large vehicle for transporting goods by road

**lose**, loses, losing, lost VERB ❶ If you lose something, you cannot find it, or you no longer have it because it has been taken away from you ❷ If you lose a relative or friend, they die ❸ If you lose a fight or an argument, you are beaten ❹ If a business loses money, it is spending more money than it is earning **loser** NOUN

**loss**, losses NOUN ❶ The loss of something is the losing of it ❖ PHRASE ❷ If you are **at a loss**, you do not know what to do

**lost** ADJECTIVE ❶ If you are lost, you do not know where you are ❷ If something is lost,

---

## Helpful hints...

You should try not to use **look** too much when you are writing. Some other words you can use are: *regard*, *observe*, *scan* and *view*.

*some other words to use*

# lot – lying

*MiKX*

you cannot find it ❸ Lost is the past tense and past participle of **lose**

**lot** NOUN ❶ A lot of something, or lots of something, is a large amount of it ❷ A lot means very much or very often ❸ an amount of something or a number of things ❹ In an auction, a lot is one of the things being sold

**lotion** NOUN a liquid that you put on your skin to protect or soften it

**lottery**, lotteries NOUN a method of raising money by selling tickets by which a winner is selected at random

**loud** ADJECTIVE OR ADVERB ❶ A loud noise has a high volume of sound ❷ If you describe clothing as loud, you mean that it is too bright **loudly** ADVERB

**lounge** NOUN a room in a house or hotel with comfortable chairs where people can relax

**louse**, lice NOUN Lice are small insects that live on people's bodies

**lousy**, lousier, lousiest ADJECTIVE INFORMAL ❶ of bad quality or very unpleasant ❷ ill or unhappy

**lovable** or **loveable** ADJECTIVE having very attractive qualities

**love**, loves, loving, loved VERB ❶ If you love someone, you have strong emotional feelings of affection for them ❷ If you love something, you like it very much ❸ If you would love to do something, you want very much to do it ✿ NOUN ❹ Love is a strong emotional feeling of affection for someone or something ❺ a strong liking for something ❻ In tennis, love is a score of zero ✿ PHRASE ❼ If you are **in love** with someone, you feel strongly attracted to them romantically or sexually

**lovely**, lovelier, loveliest ADJECTIVE very beautiful, attractive, and pleasant

**lover** NOUN ❶ A person's lover is someone that they have a sexual relationship with but are not married to ❷ Someone who is a lover of something, for example art or music, is very fond of it

**loving** ADJECTIVE feeling or showing love **lovingly** ADVERB

**low** ADJECTIVE ❶ Something that is low is close to the ground, or measures a short distance from the ground to the top ❷ Low means small in value or amount ✿ ADVERB ❸ in a low position, level, or degree ✿ NOUN ❹ a level or amount that is less than before

**lower** VERB To lower something means to move it downwards

**lower case** ADJECTIVE Lower case letters are the small letters used in printing or on a typewriter or computer

**loyal** ADJECTIVE firm in your friendship or support for someone or something **loyally** ADVERB **loyalty** NOUN

**Ltd** an abbreviation for 'limited'; used after the names of limited companies

**luck** NOUN Luck is anything that seems to happen by chance and not through your own efforts

**lucky**, luckier, luckiest ADJECTIVE ❶ Someone who is lucky has a lot of good luck ❷ Something that is lucky happens by chance and has good effects or consequences **luckily** ADVERB

**luggage** NOUN Your luggage is the bags and suitcases that you take with you when you travel

**lukewarm** ADJECTIVE ❶ slightly warm ❷ not very enthusiastic or interested

**lullaby**, lullabies NOUN a song used for sending a baby or child to sleep

**lump** NOUN ❶ A lump of something is a solid piece of it, of any shape or size ❷ a bump on the surface of something **lumpy** ADJECTIVE

**lunch**, lunches, lunching, lunched NOUN ❶ a meal eaten in the middle of the day ✿ VERB ❷ When you lunch, you eat lunch

**lung** NOUN Your lungs are the two organs inside your ribcage with which you breathe

**lush** ADJECTIVE In a lush field or garden, the grass or plants are healthy and growing thickly

**luxurious** ADJECTIVE very expensive and full of luxury

**luxury** NOUN Luxury is great comfort in expensive and beautiful surroundings

**lying** NOUN ❶ Lying is telling lies ✿ ADJECTIVE ❷ A lying person often tells lies ❸ Lying is also the present participle of **lie**

**macaroni** NOUN Macaroni is short hollow tubes of pasta

**machine**, machines, machining, machined NOUN ❶ a piece of equipment which uses electricity or power from an engine to make it work ✿ VERB ❷ If you machine something, you make it or work on it using a machine

**machinery** NOUN Machinery is machines in general

**mad**, madder, maddest ADJECTIVE ❶ Someone who is mad has a mental illness which often causes them to behave in strange ways ❷ If you describe someone as mad, you mean that they are very foolish ❸ INFORMAL Someone who is mad is angry ❹ If you are mad about someone or something, you like them very much

**don't mix up**

Hello Kitty...

never mixes up **main** (most important) and **mane** (the hair on the neck of a horse or lion).

**madam** NOUN 'Madam' is a very formal way of addressing a woman

**madly** ADVERB If you do something madly, you do it in a fast, excited way

**magazine** NOUN ❶ a weekly or monthly publication with articles and photographs ❷ a compartment in a gun for cartridges

**magic** NOUN ❶ In fairy stories, magic is a special power that can make impossible things happen ❷ Magic is the art of performing tricks to entertain people

**magical** ADJECTIVE wonderful and exciting

**magician** NOUN ❶ a person who performs tricks as entertainment ❷ In fairy stories, a magician is a man with magical powers

**magnet** NOUN a piece of iron which attracts iron or steel towards it, and which points towards north if allowed to swing freely

**magnetic** ADJECTIVE

**magnificent** ADJECTIVE extremely beautiful or impressive

**magnify**, magnifies, magnifying, magnified VERB When a microscope or lens magnifies something, it makes it appear bigger than it actually is

**magnifying glass**, magnifying glasses NOUN a lens which makes things appear bigger than they really are

**maid** NOUN a female servant

**mail** NOUN ❶ Your mail is the letters and parcels delivered to you by the post office ✿ VERB ❷ If you mail a letter, you send it by post

**mail order** NOUN Mail order is a system of buying goods by post

**main** ADJECTIVE ❶ most important ✿ NOUN ❷ The mains are large pipes or wires that carry gas, water or electricity

# mainland - manner

**mainland** NOUN The mainland is the main part of a country in contrast to islands around its coast

**mainly** ADVERB true in most cases

**maintain** VERB ❶ If you maintain something, you keep it going or keep it at a particular rate or level ❷ If you maintain someone, you provide them regularly with money for what they need ❸ To maintain a machine or a building is to keep it in good condition ❹ If you maintain that something is true, you believe it is true and say so

**maintenance** NOUN ❶ Maintenance is the process of keeping something in good condition ❷ Maintenance is also money that a person sends regularly to someone to provide for the things they need

**majesty**, majesties ❶ You say 'His Majesty' when you are talking about a king, and 'Her Majesty' when you are talking about a queen NOUN ❷ Majesty is great dignity and impressiveness **majestic** ADJECTIVE

**major** ADJECTIVE ❶ more important or more significant than other things ❷ A major key is one of the keys in which most European music is written ✿ NOUN ❸ an army officer of the rank immediately above captain

**majority**, majorities NOUN ❶ The majority of people or things in a group is more than half of the group ❷ In an election, the majority is the difference between the number of votes gained by the winner and the number gained by the runner-up

**make**, makes, making, made VERB ❶ To make something is to produce or construct it, or to cause it to happen ❷ To make something is to do it ❸ To make something is to prepare it ❹ If someone makes you do something, they force you to do it ✿ NOUN ❺ The make of a product is the name of the company that manufactured it

**make up** ✿ VERB ❶ If a number of things make up something, they form that thing ❷ If you make up a story, you invent it ❸ If you make yourself up, you put make-up on ❹ If two people make it up, they become friends again after a quarrel

**make-up** NOUN ❶ Make-up is coloured creams and powders which women put on their faces to make themselves look more attractive ❷ Someone's make-up is their character or personality

**malaria** [mal-**lay**-ree-a] NOUN Malaria is a tropical disease caught from mosquitoes which causes fever and shivering

**male** NOUN ❶ a person or animal belonging to the sex that cannot give birth or lay eggs ✿ ADJECTIVE ❷ concerning or affecting men rather than women

**mammal** NOUN Animals that give birth to live babies and feed their young with milk from the mother's body are called mammals. Human beings, dogs, and whales are all mammals

**man**, men; mans, manning, manned NOUN ❶ an adult male human being ✿ PLURAL NOUN ❷ Human beings in general are sometimes referred to as men ✿ VERB ❸ To man something is to be in charge of it or operate it

**manage**, manages, managing, managed VERB ❶ If you manage to do something, you succeed in doing it ❷ If you manage an organization or business, you control it

**management** NOUN ❶ The management of a business is the controlling and organizing of it ❷ The people who control an organization are called the management

**manager** NOUN a person responsible for running a business or organization

**mane** NOUN the long hair growing from the neck of a lion or horse

**mango**, mangoes or mangos NOUN a sweet yellowish fruit which grows in tropical countries

**manicure**, manicures, manicuring, manicured VERB ❶ If you manicure your hands, you care for them by softening the skin and shaping and polishing the nails ✿ NOUN ❷ A manicure is a special treatment for the hands and nails

**manipulate**, manipulates, manipulating, manipulated VERB ❶ To manipulate people or events is to control or influence them to produce a particular result ❷ If you manipulate a piece of equipment, you control it in a skilful way

**mankind** NOUN 'Mankind' is used to refer to all human beings

**manner** NOUN ❶ The manner in which you do something is the way you do it ❷ Your manner is the way in which you behave and

**manoeuvre – marketing**

talk ❸ IN PLURAL If you have good manners, you behave very politely

**manoeuvre**, manoeuvres, manoeuvring, manoeuvred [man-**noo**-ver] VERB If you manoeuvre something into a place, you skilfully move it there

**mansion** NOUN a very large house

**mantelpiece** NOUN a shelf over a fireplace

**manual** ADJECTIVE ❶ Manual work involves physical strength rather than mental skill ❷ operated by hand rather than by electricity or by motor ✿ NOUN ❸ an instruction book which tells you how to use a machine

**manufacture**, manufactures, manufacturing, manufactured VERB ❶ To manufacture goods is to make them in a factory ✿ NOUN ❷ The manufacture of goods is the making of them in a factory **manufacturer** NOUN

**many** ADJECTIVE ❶ If there are many people or things, there is a large number of them ❷ You also use 'many' to ask how great a quantity is or to give information about it ✿ PRONOUN ❸ a large number of people or things

**map**, maps, mapping, mapped NOUN ❶ a detailed drawing of an area as it would appear if you saw it from above ✿ VERB ❷ If you map out a plan, you work out in detail what you will do

**marathon** NOUN ❶ a race in which people run 26 miles along roads ✿ ADJECTIVE ❷ A marathon task is a large one that takes a long time

**marble** NOUN ❶ Marble is a very hard, cold stone which is often polished to show the coloured patterns in it ❷ Marbles is a children's game played with small coloured glass balls. These balls are also called marbles

**march**, marches, marching, marched NOUN ❶ March is the third month of the year. It has 31 days ❷ an organized protest in which a large group of people walk somewhere together ✿ VERB ❸ When soldiers march, they walk with quick regular steps in time with each other ❹ To march somewhere is to walk quickly in a determined way

**margarine** [mar-jar-reen] NOUN Margarine is a substance that is similar to butter but is made from vegetable oil and animal fats

**margin** NOUN ❶ If you win a contest by a large or small margin, you win it by a large or small amount ❷ an extra amount that allows you more freedom in doing something ❸ the blank space at each side on a written or printed page

**marine** NOUN ❶ a soldier who serves with the navy ✿ ADJECTIVE ❷ relating to or involving the sea

**marital** ADJECTIVE relating to or involving marriage

**mark** NOUN ❶ a small stain or damaged area on a surface ❷ a written or printed symbol ❸ a letter or number showing how well you have done in homework or in an exam ✿ VERB ❹ If something marks a surface, it damages it in some way ❺ If you mark something, you write a symbol on it or identify it in some other way ❻ When a teacher marks your work, he or she decides how good it is and gives it a mark ❼ To mark something is to be a sign of it

*some other words to use*

*Helpful hints...*

You should try not to use **mark** too much when you are writing. Some other words you can use are: *smudge, spot, stain* and *streak*.

**market** NOUN ❶ a place where goods or animals are bought and sold ❷ The market for a product is the number of people who want to buy it ✿ VERB ❸ To market a product is to sell it in an organized way

**marketing** NOUN Marketing is the part of a business concerned with the way a product is sold

# marmalade - mate

**marmalade** NOUN Marmalade is a jam made from citrus fruit, usually eaten at breakfast

**marriage** NOUN ❶ the relationship between a husband and wife ❷ Marriage is the act of marrying someone

**marry**, marries, marrying, married VERB ❶ When a man and a woman marry, they become each other's husband and wife during a special ceremony ❷ When a clergyman or registrar marries a couple, he or she is in charge of their marriage ceremony  **married** ADJECTIVE

**marsh**, marshes NOUN an area of land which is permanently wet

**marshmallow** NOUN a soft, spongy, pink or white sweet made using gelatine

**marvellous** ADJECTIVE wonderful or excellent

**masculine** ADJECTIVE ❶ typical of men, rather than women ❷ belonging to a particular class of nouns in some languages, such as French, German, and Latin

## how English works

### Hello Kitty...

knows that **masculine** refers to male people and animals.

**mash**, mashes, mashing, mashed VERB If you mash vegetables, you crush them after they have been cooked

**mask** NOUN ❶ something you wear over your face for protection or disguise ❀ VERB ❷ If you mask something, you cover it so that it is protected or cannot be seen

**mass**, masses, massing, massed NOUN ❶ a large amount of something ❷ The masses are the ordinary people in society considered as a group ❸ In physics, the mass of an object is the amount of physical matter that it has ❹ In the Roman Catholic Church, Mass is a religious service in which people share bread and wine in remembrance of the death and resurrection of Jesus Christ ❀ ADJECTIVE ❺ involving a large number of people ❀ VERB ❻ When people mass, they gather together in a large group

**massacre**, massacres, massacring, massacred [*mass-ik-ker*] NOUN ❶ the killing of a very large number of people in a violent and cruel way ❀ VERB ❷ To massacre people is to kill large numbers of them in a violent and cruel way

**massage**, massages, massaging, massaged VERB ❶ To massage someone is to rub their body in order to help them relax or to relieve pain ❀ NOUN ❷ A massage is treatment which involves rubbing the body

**massive** ADJECTIVE extremely large

**mast** NOUN the tall upright pole that supports the sails of a boat

**master** NOUN ❶ a man who has authority over others, such as the employer of servants, or the owner of slaves or animals ❷ If you are master of a situation, you have control over it ❸ a male teacher at some schools ❀ VERB ❹ If you master a difficult situation, you succeed in controlling it ❺ If you master something, you learn how to do it properly

**masterpiece** NOUN an extremely good painting or other work of art

**mat** NOUN ❶ a small round or square piece of cloth, card, or plastic that is placed on a table to protect it from plates or glasses ❷ a small piece of carpet or other thick material that is placed on the floor

**match**, matches, matching, matched NOUN ❶ an organized game of football, cricket, or some other sport ❷ a small, thin stick of wood that produces a flame when you strike it against a rough surface ❀ VERB ❸ If one thing matches another, the two things look the same or have similar qualities

**mate**, mates, mating, mated NOUN ❶ INFORMAL Your mates are your friends ❷ An animal's mate is its sexual partner ❀ VERB ❸ When a

# material - measure

male and female animal mate, they come together sexually in order to breed

**material** NOUN ❶ Material is cloth ❷ a substance from which something is made ❸ The equipment for a particular activity can be referred to as materials ❹ Material for a book, play, or film is the information or ideas on which it is based ✿ ADJECTIVE ❺ involving possessions and money

**maternal** ADJECTIVE relating to or involving a mother

**mathematics** NOUN Mathematics is the study of numbers, quantities, and shapes
**mathematical** ADJECTIVE

**maths** NOUN Maths is mathematics

**matinee** or **matinée** [mat-in-nay] NOUN an afternoon performance of a play or film

**matter** NOUN ❶ something that you have to deal with ❷ Matter is any substance ❸ Books and magazines are reading matter ✿ VERB ❹ If something matters to you, it is important ✿ PHRASE ❺ If you ask **What's the matter?**, you are asking what is wrong

**mattress**, mattresses NOUN a large thick pad filled with springs or feathers that is put on a bed to make it comfortable

**mature**, matures, maturing, matured VERB ❶ When a child or young animal matures, it becomes an adult ❷ When something matures, it reaches complete development ✿ ADJECTIVE ❸ Mature means fully developed and emotionally balanced
**maturity** NOUN

**maximum** ADJECTIVE ❶ The maximum amount is the most that is possible ✿ NOUN ❷ The maximum is the most that is possible

**may** VERB ❶ If something may happen, it is possible that it will happen ❷ If someone may do something, they are allowed to do it ❸ You can use 'may' when saying that, although something is true, something else is also true ❹ FORMAL You also use 'may' to express a wish that something will happen ✿ NOUN ❺ May is the fifth month of the year. It has 31 days

**maybe** ADVERB You use 'maybe' when you are stating a possibility that you are not certain about

**mayonnaise** [may-on-**nayz**] NOUN Mayonnaise is a thick salad dressing made with egg yolks and oil

**mayor** NOUN a person who has been elected to lead and represent the people of a town or city

**maze** NOUN a system of complicated passages which it is difficult to find your way through

**me** PRONOUN A speaker or writer uses 'me' to refer to himself or herself

**meadow** NOUN a field of grass

**meal** NOUN an occasion when people eat, or the food they eat at that time

**mean**, means, meaning, meant VERB ❶ If you ask what something means, you want to know what it refers to or what its message is ❷ If you mean what you say, you are serious ❸ If something means a lot to you, it is important to you ❹ If one thing means another, it shows that the second thing is true or will happen ❺ If you mean to do something, you intend to do it ❻ If something is meant to be true, it is supposed to be true ✿ ADJECTIVE ❼ Someone who is mean is unwilling to spend much money ❽ Someone who is mean is unkind or cruel ✿ NOUN ❾ IN PLURAL A means of doing something is a method or object which makes it possible ❿ IN PLURAL Someone's means are their money and income ⓫ The mean is the average of a set of numbers

**meaning** NOUN ❶ The meaning of a word is what it refers to or expresses ❷ The meaning of what someone says, or of a book or a film, is the thoughts or ideas that it is intended to express ❸ If something has meaning, it seems to be worthwhile and to have real purpose **meaningless** ADJECTIVE

**meantime** PHRASE **In the meantime** means in the period of time between two events

**meanwhile** ADVERB ❶ Meanwhile means while something else is happening ✿ NOUN ❷ The meanwhile means the time between two events

**measles** NOUN Measles is an infectious illness in which you have red spots on your skin

**measure**, measures, measuring, measured VERB ❶ When you measure something, you find out how big it is ❷ If something measures a particular distance, its length or depth is that distance ✿ NOUN ❸ A measure of something is a certain amount of it ❹ a unit in which size, speed, or depth is

165

# measurement – memorize

**A B C D E F G H I J K L M N O P Q R S T U V W X Y Z**

expressed ❺ Measures are actions carried out to achieve a particular result

**measurement** NOUN ❶ the result that you obtain when you measure something ❷ Measurement is the activity of measuring something ❸ Your measurements are the sizes of your chest, waist, and hips that you use to buy the correct size of clothes

**meat** NOUN Meat is the flesh of animals that is cooked and eaten

**mechanic** NOUN ❶ a person who repairs and maintains engines and machines ❷ IN PLURAL The mechanics of something are the way in which it works or is done ❸ IN PLURAL Mechanics is also the scientific study of movement and the forces that affect objects

**mechanical** ADJECTIVE ❶ A mechanical device has moving parts and is used to do a physical task ❷ A mechanical action is done automatically without thinking about it

**mechanism** NOUN ❶ a part of a machine that does a particular task ❷ part of your behaviour that is automatic

**medal** NOUN a small disc of metal given as an award for bravery or as a prize for sport

**media** PLURAL NOUN You can refer to the television, radio, and newspapers as the media

**median** [mee-dee-an] ADJECTIVE ❶ The median value of a set is the middle value when the set is arranged in order ✿ NOUN ❷ In geometry, a straight line drawn from one of the angles of a triangle to the middle point of the opposite side

**medical** ADJECTIVE ❶ relating to the prevention and treatment of illness and injuries ✿ NOUN ❷ a thorough examination of your body by a doctor

**medication** NOUN Medication is a substance that is used to treat illness

**medicine** NOUN ❶ Medicine is the treatment of illness and injuries by doctors and nurses ❷ a substance that you drink or swallow to help cure an illness

**medieval** or **mediaeval** [med-dee-ee-vul] ADJECTIVE relating to the period between about 1100 AD and 1500 AD, especially in Europe

**medium**, mediums or media ADJECTIVE ❶ If something is of medium size or degree, it is neither large nor small ✿ NOUN ❷ a means that you use to communicate something ❸ a person who claims to be able to speak to the dead and to receive messages from them

**meet**, meets, meeting, met VERB ❶ If you meet someone, you happen to be in the same place as them ❷ If you meet a visitor you go to be with them when they arrive ❸ When a group of people meet, they gather together for a purpose ❹ If something meets a need, it can fulfil it ❺ If something meets with a particular reaction, it gets that reaction from people

**meeting** NOUN ❶ an event in which people discuss proposals and make decisions together ❷ what happens when you meet someone

**megabyte** NOUN a unit of storage in a computer, equal to 1 048 576 bytes

**melody**, melodies NOUN a tune

**melon** NOUN a large, juicy fruit with a green or yellow skin and many seeds inside

**melt** VERB ❶ When something melts or when you melt it, it changes from a solid to a liquid because it has been heated ❷ If something melts, it disappears

**member** NOUN ❶ A member of a group is one of the people or things belonging to the group ❷ A member of an organization is a person who has joined the organization ✿ ADJECTIVE ❸ A country belonging to an international organization is called a member country

**Member of Parliament**, Members of Parliament NOUN a person who has been elected to represent people in a country's parliament

**membership** NOUN ❶ Membership of an organization is the state of being a member of it ❷ The people who belong to an organization are its membership

**memo**, memos NOUN a note from one person to another within the same organization. Memo is short for 'memorandum'

**memorable** ADJECTIVE If something is memorable, it is likely to be remembered because it is special or unusual

**memorize**, memorizes, memorizing, memorized (also **memorise**) VERB If you memorize something, you learn it thoroughly so you can remember it exactly

166

**memory – microphone**

**memory**, memories NOUN ❶ Your memory is your ability to remember things ❷ something you remember about the past ❸ the part in which information is stored in a computer

**men** the plural of **man**

**mend** VERB If you mend something that is broken, you repair it

**mental** ADJECTIVE ❶ relating to the process of thinking or intelligence ❷ relating to the health of the mind **mentally** ADVERB

**mention** VERB ❶ If you mention something, you talk about it briefly ✿ NOUN ❷ a brief comment about someone or something

**menu** NOUN ❶ a list of the foods you can eat in a restaurant ❷ a list of different options shown on a computer screen which the user must choose from

**merchandise** NOUN FORMAL Merchandise is goods that are sold

**mercury** NOUN Mercury is a silver-coloured metallic element that is liquid at room temperature. It is used in thermometers

**mercy**, mercies NOUN If you show mercy, you show forgiveness and do not punish someone as severely as you could **merciful** ADJECTIVE

**mere**, merest ADJECTIVE used to emphasize how unimportant or small something is **merely** ADVERB

**merge**, merges, merging, merged VERB When two things merge, they combine together to make one thing

**merit** NOUN ❶ If something has merit, it is good or worthwhile ❷ The merits of something are its advantages or good qualities ✿ VERB ❸ If something merits a particular treatment, it deserves that treatment

**mermaid** NOUN In stories, a mermaid is a woman with a fish's tail instead of legs, who lives in the sea

**merry**, merrier, merriest ADJECTIVE happy and cheerful

**mess**, messes, messing, messed NOUN ❶ something untidy ❷ a situation which is full of problems and trouble ❸ The mess is a room or building in which members of the armed forces eat ✿ VERB ❹ If you mess about or mess around, you do things without any particular purpose ❺ If you mess something up, you spoil it or do it wrong **messy** ADJECTIVE

**message** NOUN ❶ a piece of information or a request that you send someone or leave for them ❷ an idea that someone tries to communicate to people

**met** the past tense and past participle of **meet**

**metal** NOUN Metal is a chemical element such as iron, steel, copper, or lead. Metals are good conductors of heat and electricity

**metaphor** NOUN an imaginative way of describing something as another thing, and so suggesting that it has the typical qualities of that other thing. For example, if you wanted to say that someone is shy, you might say they are a mouse

**meteor** NOUN a piece of rock or metal that burns very brightly when it enters the earth's atmosphere from space

**meter** NOUN a device that measures and records something

### don't mix up

Don't mix up **meter** (a measuring instrument) and **metre** (100 centimetres).

**method** NOUN ❶ a particular way of doing something ❷ a way that an experiment or test is carried out

**metre** NOUN ❶ The metre is the SI unit of length. One metre is equal to 100 centimetres ❷ In poetry, metre is the regular and rhythmic arrangement of words and syllables

**metric** ADJECTIVE relating to the system of measurement that uses metres, grams, and litres

**mice** the plural of **mouse**

**microchip** NOUN a small piece of silicon on which electronic circuits for a computer are printed

**microphone** NOUN a device that is used to

A B C D E F G H I J K L M N O P Q R S T U V W X Y Z

167

# microscope - mimic

make sounds louder or to record them on a tape recorder

**microscope** NOUN a piece of equipment which magnifies very small objects so that you can study them

**microwave** NOUN A microwave or microwave oven is a type of oven which cooks food very quickly by radiation

**midday** NOUN Midday is twelve o'clock in the middle of the day

**middle** NOUN ❶ The middle of something is the part furthest from the edges, ends, or outside surface ❖ ADJECTIVE ❷ The middle one in a series or a row is the one that has an equal number of people or things each side of it

**middle age** NOUN Middle age is the period of your life when you are between about 40 and 60 years old  **middle-aged** ADJECTIVE

**Middle Ages** PLURAL NOUN In European history, the Middle Ages were the period between about 1100 AD and 1500 AD

**middle class**, middle classes NOUN The middle classes are the people in the middle range of a society, for example managers and lawyers

**midnight** NOUN Midnight is twelve o'clock at night

**midway** ADVERB in the middle of a distance or period of time

**might** VERB ❶ If you say something might happen, you mean that it is possible that it will happen ❷ If you say that someone might do something, you are suggesting that they do it ❸ Might is also the past tense of may ❖ NOUN ❹ LITERARY Might is strength or power

**mighty**, mightier, mightiest ADJECTIVE LITERARY very powerful or strong

**migraine** [*mee*-grane or *my*-grane] NOUN a severe headache that makes you feel very ill

**migrate**, migrates, migrating, migrated VERB ❶ If people migrate, they move from one place to another, especially to find work ❷ When birds or animals migrate, they move at a particular season to a different place, usually to breed or to find new feeding grounds  **migration** NOUN  **migrant** NOUN OR ADJECTIVE

**mild** ADJECTIVE ❶ Something that is mild is not strong and does not have any powerful or damaging effects ❷ Someone who is mild is gentle and kind ❸ Mild weather is warmer than usual ❹ Mild emotions or attitudes are not very great or extreme

**mile** NOUN a unit of distance equal to 1760 yards or about 1.6 kilometres

**mileage** NOUN ❶ Your mileage is the distance that you have travelled, measured in miles ❷ The amount of mileage that you get out of something is how useful it is to you

**military** ADJECTIVE ❶ related to or involving the armed forces of a country ❖ NOUN ❷ The military are the armed forces of a country

**milk** NOUN ❶ Milk is the white liquid produced by female cows, goats, and some other animals to feed their young. People drink milk and use it to make butter, cheese, and yogurt ❷ Milk is also the white liquid that a baby drinks from its mother's breasts ❖ VERB ❸ When someone milks a cow or a goat, they get milk from it by pulling its udders

**milky**, milkier, milkiest ADJECTIVE ❶ pale creamy white ❷ containing a lot of milk

**mill** NOUN ❶ a building where grain is crushed to make flour ❷ a factory for making materials such as steel, wool, or cotton ❸ a small device for grinding coffee or spices into powder

**milligram** NOUN a unit of weight equal to one thousandth of a gram

**millilitre** NOUN a unit of liquid volume equal to one thousandth of a litre

**millimetre** NOUN a unit of length equal to one tenth of a centimetre or one thousandth of a metre

**million** the number 1000000

**millionaire** NOUN a very rich person who has property worth millions of pounds or dollars

**mime**, mimes, miming, mimed NOUN ❶ Mime is the use of movements and gestures to express something or to tell a story without using speech ❖ VERB ❷ If you mime something, you describe or express it using mime

**mimic**, mimics, mimicking, mimicked VERB ❶ If you mimic someone's actions or voice, you imitate them in an amusing way ❖ NOUN ❷ a person who can imitate other people

**mince**, minces, mincing, minced NOUN ❶ Mince is meat which has been chopped into very small pieces in a special machine ✿ VERB ❷ If you mince meat, you chop it into very small pieces ❸ To mince about is to walk with small quick steps in an affected, effeminate way

**mind** NOUN ❶ Your mind is your ability to think, together with all the thoughts you have and your memory ✿ PHRASE ❷ If you **change your mind**, you change a decision that you have made or an opinion that you have ✿ VERB ❸ If you do not mind something, you are not annoyed by it or bothered about it ❹ If you say that you wouldn't mind something, you mean that you would quite like it ❺ If you mind a child or mind something for someone, you look after it for a while

**mine**, mines, mining, mined PRONOUN ❶ 'Mine' refers to something belonging or relating to the person who is speaking or writing ✿ NOUN ❷ a series of holes or tunnels in the ground from which diamonds, coal, or other minerals are dug out ❸ a bomb hidden in the ground or underwater, which explodes when people or things touch it ✿ VERB ❹ To mine diamonds, coal, or other minerals is to obtain these substances from underneath the ground **miner** NOUN

**mineral** NOUN a substance such as tin, salt, or coal that is formed naturally in rocks and in the earth

**mineral water** NOUN Mineral water is water which comes from a natural spring

**miniature** [*min-nit-cher*] ADJECTIVE ❶ copying something on a much smaller scale ✿ NOUN ❷ a very small detailed painting, often of a person

**minimal** ADJECTIVE very small in quality, quantity, or degree

**minimize**, minimizes, minimizing, minimized (also **minimise**) VERB If you minimize something, you reduce it to the smallest amount possible

**minimum** ADJECTIVE ❶ The minimum amount is the smallest amount that is possible ✿ NOUN ❷ The minimum is the smallest amount that is possible

**minister** NOUN ❶ A minister is a person who is in charge of a particular government department ❷ A minister in a Protestant church is a member of the clergy

**ministry**, ministries NOUN ❶ a government department that deals with a particular area of work ❷ Members of the clergy can be referred to as the ministry

**minor** ADJECTIVE ❶ not as important or serious as other things ❷ A minor key is one of the keys in which most European music is written ✿ NOUN ❸ FORMAL a young person under the age of 18

**don't mix up**

**Hello Kitty...**

never mixes up **miner** (someone who works in a mine) and **minor** (not important).

**minority**, minorities NOUN ❶ The minority of people or things in a group is a number of them forming less than half of the whole ❷ A minority is a group of people of a particular race or religion living in a place where most people are of a different race or religion

**mint** NOUN ❶ Mint is a herb used for flavouring in cooking ❷ a peppermint-flavoured sweet ❸ The mint is the place where the official coins of a country are made ✿ VERB ❹ When coins or medals are minted, they are made ✿ ADJECTIVE ❺ If something is in mint condition, it is in very good condition, like new

**minus** ❶ You use 'minus' to show that one number is being subtracted from another ADJECTIVE ❷ 'Minus' is used when talking about temperatures below 0°C or 0°F

# minute - mixed

**minute**, minutes, minuting, minuted [*min-nit*] NOUN ❶ a unit of time equal to sixty seconds ❷ IN PLURAL The minutes of a meeting are the written records of what was said and decided ✿ VERB ❸ To minute a meeting is to write the official notes of it

**minute** [*my-nyoot*] ADJECTIVE extremely small

**miracle** NOUN ❶ a wonderful and surprising event, believed to have been caused by God ❷ any very surprising and fortunate event

**mirror** NOUN ❶ a piece of glass which reflects light and in which you can see your reflection ✿ VERB ❷ To mirror something is to have similar features to it

**misbehave**, misbehaves, misbehaving, misbehaved VERB If a child misbehaves, he or she is naughty or behaves badly
**misbehaviour** NOUN

**mischief** NOUN Mischief is eagerness to have fun by teasing people or playing tricks
**mischievous** ADJECTIVE

**miserable** ADJECTIVE ❶ If you are miserable, you are very unhappy ❷ If a place or a situation is miserable, it makes you feel depressed **miserably** ADVERB

**misery**, miseries NOUN Misery is great unhappiness

**misfortune** NOUN an unpleasant occurrence that is regarded as bad luck

**mislead**, misleads, misleading, misled VERB To mislead someone is to make them believe something which is not true

**miss**, misses, missing, missed VERB ❶ If you miss something, you do not notice it ❷ If you miss someone or something, you feel sad that they are no longer with you ❸ If you miss a chance or opportunity, you fail to take advantage of it ❹ If you miss a bus, plane, or train, you arrive too late to catch it ❺ If you miss something, you fail to hit it when you aim at it ✿ NOUN ❻ an act of missing something that you were aiming at ❼ 'Miss' is used before the name of a woman or girl who is not married as a form of address

**missile** NOUN a weapon that moves long distances through the air and explodes when it reaches its target; also used of any object thrown as a weapon

**mission** NOUN ❶ an important task that you have to do ❷ a group of people who have been sent to a foreign country to carry out an official task ❸ a journey made by a military aeroplane or space rocket to carry out a task ❹ If you have a mission, there is something that you believe it is your duty to try to achieve ❺ the workplace of a group of Christians who are working for the Church

**mist** NOUN ❶ Mist consists of a large number of tiny drops of water in the air, which make it hard to see clearly ✿ VERB ❷ If your eyes mist, you cannot see very far because there are tears in your eyes ❸ If glass mists over or mists up, it becomes covered with condensation so that you cannot see through it

**mistake**, mistakes, mistaking, mistook, mistaken NOUN ❶ an action or opinion that is wrong or is not what you intended ✿ VERB ❷ If you mistake someone or something for another person or thing, you wrongly think that they are the other person or thing

**mistaken** ADJECTIVE ❶ If you are mistaken about something, you are wrong about it ❷ If you have a mistaken belief or opinion, you believe something which is not true
**mistakenly** ADVERB

**mistook** the past tense of **mistake**

**mistrust** VERB ❶ If you mistrust someone, you do not feel that you can trust them ✿ NOUN ❷ Mistrust is a feeling that you cannot trust someone

**misty**, mistier, mistiest ADJECTIVE full of or covered with mist

**misunderstand**, misunderstands, misunderstanding, misunderstood VERB If you misunderstand someone, you do not understand properly what they say or do

**misunderstanding** NOUN If two people have a misunderstanding, they have a slight quarrel or disagreement

**mitten** NOUN Mittens are gloves which have one section that covers your thumb and another section for the rest of your fingers together

**mix**, mixes, mixing, mixed VERB If you mix things, you combine them or shake or stir them together

**mix up** ✿ VERB If you mix up two things or people, you cannot tell which one is which, and you often confuse them

**mixed** ADJECTIVE ❶ consisting of several things of the same general kind ❷ involving

# mixer – monarchy

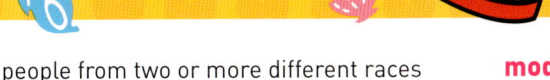

people from two or more different races ❸ Mixed education or accommodation is for both males and females

**mixer** NOUN a machine used for mixing things together

**mixture** NOUN several different things mixed or shaken together

**mnemonic** [*nim-on-nik*] NOUN A mnemonic is a word or rhyme that helps you to remember things such as scientific facts or spelling rules. 'I before e, except after c' is an example of a mnemonic

**moan** VERB ❶ If you moan, you make a low, miserable sound because you are in pain or suffering ❷ INFORMAL If you moan about something, you complain about it ✿ NOUN ❸ a low cry of pain or misery

**mobile** ADJECTIVE ❶ able to move or be moved freely and easily ❷ If you are mobile, you are able to travel or move about from one place to another ✿ NOUN ❸ A mobile is a mobile phone ❹ A mobile is also a decoration consisting of several small objects which hang from threads and move around when a breeze blows

**mobile phone** NOUN a small portable telephone

**mock** VERB ❶ If you mock someone, you say something scornful or imitate their foolish behaviour ✿ ADJECTIVE ❷ not genuine ❸ A mock examination is one that you do as a practice before the real examination

**model**, models, modelling, modelled NOUN OR ADJECTIVE ❶ a copy of something that shows what it looks like or how it works ✿ NOUN ❷ Something that is described as, for example, a model of clarity or a model of perfection, is extremely clear or absolutely perfect ❸ a type or version of a machine ❹ a person who poses for a painter or a photographer ❺ a person who wears the clothes that are being displayed at a fashion show ✿ ADJECTIVE ❻ Someone who is described as, for example, a model wife or a model student is an excellent wife or student ✿ VERB ❼ If you model yourself on someone, you copy their behaviour because you admire them ❽ To model clothes is to display them by wearing them ❾ To model shapes or figures is to make them out of clay or wood

**modem** [*moe-dem*] NOUN a piece of equipment that links a computer to the telephone system so that data can be transferred from one machine to another via the telephone line

**moderate**, moderates, moderating, moderated ADJECTIVE ❶ Moderate views are not extreme, and usually favour gradual changes rather than major ones ❷ A moderate amount of something is neither large nor small ✿ NOUN ❸ a person whose political views are not extreme ✿ VERB ❹ If you moderate something or if it moderates, it becomes less extreme or violent **moderately** ADVERB

**modern** ADJECTIVE ❶ relating to the present time ❷ new and involving the latest ideas and equipment

**modernize**, modernizes, modernizing, modernized (also **modernise**) VERB To modernize something is to introduce new methods or equipment to it

**modest** ADJECTIVE ❶ quite small in size or amount ❷ Someone who is modest does not boast about their abilities or possessions ❸ shy and easily embarrassed **modestly** ADVERB **modesty** NOUN

**modification** NOUN a small change made to improve something

**modify**, modifies, modifying, modified VERB If you modify something, you change it slightly in order to improve it

**moist** ADJECTIVE slightly wet

**moisture** NOUN Moisture is tiny drops of water in the air or on the ground

**mole** NOUN ❶ a dark, slightly raised spot on your skin ❷ a small animal with black fur. Moles live in tunnels underground ❸ INFORMAL a member of an organization who is working as a spy for a rival organization

**molecule** NOUN the smallest amount of a substance that can exist

**moment** NOUN ❶ a very short period of time ❷ The moment at which something happens is the point in time at which it happens ✿ PHRASE ❸ If something is happening **at the moment**, it is happening now

**monarchy**, monarchies NOUN a system in which a queen or king reigns in a country

A B C D E F G H I J K L M N O P Q R S T U V W X Y Z

171

# Monday – morning

**Monday**, Mondays NOUN Monday is the day between Sunday and Tuesday

**money** NOUN Money is the coins or banknotes that you use to buy something

**monitor** VERB ❶ If you monitor something, you regularly check its condition and progress ✿ NOUN ❷ a machine used to check or record things ❸ the visual display unit of a computer

**monk** NOUN a member of a male religious community

**monkey**, monkeys NOUN an animal which has a long tail and climbs trees. Monkeys live in hot countries

**monopoly**, monopolies NOUN control of most of an industry by one or a few large firms

**monotonous** ADJECTIVE having a regular pattern which is very dull and boring

**monsoon** NOUN the season of very heavy rain in South-east Asia

**monster** NOUN ❶ a large, imaginary creature that looks very frightening ❷ a cruel or frightening person ✿ ADJECTIVE ❸ extremely large

**where does the word come from?**

*Did you know…*

that the word **monster** comes from the Latin word *monstrum* which means 'warning'? That's because a *monster* is something scary.

**month** NOUN one of the twelve periods that a year is divided into

**monthly** ADJECTIVE Monthly describes something that happens or appears once a month

**monument** NOUN a large stone structure built to remind people of a famous person or event

**moo**, moos, mooing, mooed VERB When a cow moos, it makes a long, deep sound

**mood** NOUN the way you are feeling at a particular time

**moody**, moodier, moodiest ADJECTIVE ❶ Someone who is moody is depressed or unhappy ❷ Someone who is moody often changes their mood for no apparent reason

**moon** NOUN The moon is an object moving round the earth which you see as a shining circle or crescent in the sky at night. Some other planets have moons

**moonlight**, moonlights, moonlighting, moonlighted NOUN ❶ Moonlight is the light that comes from the moon at night ✿ VERB ❷ INFORMAL If someone is moonlighting, they have a second job that they have not informed the tax office about so that they are not paying tax on the money they earn

**moose** NOUN a large North American deer with flat antlers

**mop**, mops, mopping, mopped NOUN ❶ a tool for washing floors, consisting of a sponge or string head attached to a long handle ❷ a large amount of loose or untidy hair ✿ VERB ❸ To mop a floor is to clean it with a mop ❹ To mop a surface is to wipe it with a dry cloth to remove liquid

**moral** NOUN ❶ IN PLURAL Morals are values based on beliefs about the correct and acceptable way to behave ✿ ADJECTIVE ❷ concerned with whether behaviour is right or acceptable **morally** ADVERB

**more** ADJECTIVE ❶ More means a greater number or extent than something else ❷ used to refer to an additional thing or amount of something ✿ PRONOUN ❸ a greater number or extent ✿ ADVERB ❹ to a greater degree or extent ❺ You can use 'more' in front of adjectives and adverbs to form comparatives

**moreover** ADVERB used to introduce a piece of information that supports or expands the previous statement

**morning** NOUN ❶ the early part of the day until lunchtime ❷ the part of the day between midnight and noon

# mortgage – mould

**mortgage**, mortgages, mortgaging, mortgaged [*mor*-gijj] NOUN ❶ a loan which you get from a bank or a building society in order to buy a house ✿ VERB ❷ If you mortgage your house, you use it as a guarantee to a company in order to borrow money from them. They can take the house from you if you do not pay back the money you have borrowed

## how to say it

### Helpful hints...

**Mortgage** should be said ***mor**-gijj*, with most force on *mor* and without saying the *t*.

**mosaic** [moe-*zay*-yik] NOUN a design made of small coloured stones or pieces of coloured glass set into concrete or plaster

**Moslem** another spelling of **Muslim**

**mosque** [*mosk*] NOUN a building where Muslims go to worship

**mosquito**, mosquitoes or mosquitos [moss-*skee*-toe] NOUN Mosquitoes are small insects which bite people in order to suck their blood

**moss**, mosses NOUN Moss is a soft, low-growing, green plant which grows on damp soil or stone

**most** ADJECTIVE OR PRONOUN ❶ Most of a group of things or people means nearly all of them ❷ The most means a larger amount than anyone or anything else ✿ ADVERB ❸ You can use 'most' in front of adjectives or adverbs to form superlatives

**mostly** ADVERB 'Mostly' is used to show that a statement is generally true

**motel** NOUN a hotel providing overnight accommodation for people in the middle of a car journey

**moth** NOUN an insect like a butterfly which usually flies at night

**mother** NOUN ❶ Your mother is the woman who gave birth to you ❷ Your mother could also be the woman who has looked after you and brought you up ✿ VERB ❸ To mother someone is to look after them and bring them up

**motherhood** NOUN Motherhood is the state of being a mother

**mother-in-law**, mothers-in-law NOUN Someone's mother-in-law is the mother of their husband or wife

**motion** NOUN ❶ Motion is the process of continually moving or changing position ❷ an action or gesture ❸ a proposal which people discuss and vote on at a meeting ✿ VERB ❹ If you motion to someone, you make a movement with your hand in order to show them what they should do

**motionless** ADJECTIVE not moving at all

**motivate**, motivates, motivating, motivated VERB ❶ If you are motivated by something, it makes you behave in a particular way ❷ If you motivate someone, you make them feel determined to do something  **motivated** ADJECTIVE  **motivation** NOUN

**motive** NOUN a reason or purpose for doing something

**motor** NOUN ❶ a part of a vehicle or a machine that uses electricity or fuel to produce movement so that the machine can work ✿ ADJECTIVE ❷ concerned with or relating to vehicles with a petrol or diesel engine

**motorist** NOUN a person who drives a car

**motorway** NOUN a wide road built for fast travel over long distances

**motto**, mottoes or mottos NOUN a short sentence or phrase that is a rule for good or sensible behaviour

**mould** VERB ❶ To mould someone or something is to influence and change them so they develop in a particular way ❷ To mould a substance is to make it into a particular shape ✿ NOUN ❸ a container

173

# mound – mug

A B C D E F G H I J K L M N O P Q R S T U V W X Y Z

used to make something into a particular shape ❹ Mould is a soft grey or green substance that can form on old food or damp walls

**mound** NOUN ❶ a small man-made hill ❷ a large, untidy pile

**mountain** NOUN ❶ a very high piece of land with steep sides ❷ a large amount of something

**mountaineer** NOUN a person who climbs mountains

**mountainous** ADJECTIVE A mountainous area has a lot of mountains

**mourn** VERB ❶ If you mourn for someone who has died, you are very sad and think about them a lot ❷ If you mourn something, you are sad because you no longer have it

**mourner** NOUN a person who attends a funeral

**mourning** NOUN If someone is in mourning, they wear special black clothes or behave in a quiet and restrained way because a member of their family has died

**mouse**, mice NOUN ❶ a small rodent with a long tail ❷ a small device moved by hand to control the position of the cursor on a computer screen

**mousse**, mousses [*moos*] NOUN Mousse is a light, fluffy food made from whipped eggs and cream

**moustache**, moustaches [*mus-stahsh*] NOUN A man's moustache is hair growing on his upper lip

**mouth** NOUN ❶ your lips, or the space behind them where your tongue and teeth are ❷ The mouth of a cave or a hole is the entrance to it ❸ The mouth of a river is the place where it flows into the sea ✿ VERB ❹ If you mouth something, you form words with your lips without making any sound

**mouthful** NOUN

**move**, moves, moving, moved VERB ❶ To move means to go to a different place or position. To move something means to change its place or position ❷ If you move, or move house, you go to live in a different house ❸ If something moves you, it causes you to feel a deep emotion ✿ NOUN ❹ a change from one place or position to another ❺ an act of moving house ❻ the act of putting a piece or counter in a game in a different position

**movement** NOUN ❶ Movement involves changing position or going from one place to another ❷ IN PLURAL; FORMAL Your movements are everything you do during a period of time ❸ a group of people who share the same beliefs or aims ❹ one of the major sections of a piece of classical music

**moving** ADJECTIVE Something that is moving makes you feel deep sadness or emotion

**mow**, mows, mowing, mowed, mown VERB ❶ To mow grass is to cut it with a lawnmower ❷ To mow down a large number of people is to kill them all violently

**MP**, MPs NOUN a person who has been elected to represent people in a country's parliament. MP is an abbreviation for 'Member of Parliament'

**MP3 player** NOUN a device that plays audio or video files, often used for listening to music downloaded from the internet

**mph** an abbreviation for 'miles per hour'

**Mr** [*miss-ter*] NOUN 'Mr' is used before a man's name when you are speaking or referring to him

**Mrs** [*miss-iz*] NOUN 'Mrs' is used before the name of a married woman when you are speaking or referring to her

**Ms** [*miz*] NOUN 'Ms' is used before a woman's name when you are speaking or referring to her. Ms does not specify whether a woman is married or not

**much** ADVERB ❶ You use 'much' to emphasize that something is true to a great extent ❷ If something does not happen much, it does not happen very often ✿ ADJECTIVE OR PRONOUN ❸ You use 'much' to ask questions or give information about the size or amount of something

**mud** NOUN Mud is wet, sticky earth

**muddle**, muddles, muddling, muddled NOUN ❶ A muddle is a state of disorder or untidiness ✿ VERB ❷ If you muddle things, you mix them up

**muddy**, muddier, muddiest ADJECTIVE ❶ covered in mud ❷ A muddy colour is dull and not clear

**muffin** NOUN a small, round cake which you eat hot

**mug**, mugs, mugging, mugged NOUN ❶ a large, deep cup ❷ INFORMAL someone who is stupid and easily deceived ✿ VERB

**multimedia – myth**

❸ INFORMAL If someone mugs you, they attack you in order to steal your money  **mugger** NOUN

**multimedia** NOUN ❶ In computing, you use multimedia to refer to products which use sound, pictures, film, and ordinary text to convey information ❷ In the classroom, all the things like TV, computers, and books which are used as teaching aids are called multimedia

**multinational** NOUN a very large company with branches in many countries

**multiple** ADJECTIVE ❶ having or involving many different functions or things ✿ NOUN ❷ The multiples of a number are other numbers that it will divide into exactly. For example, 6, 9, and 12 are multiples of 3

**multiplication** NOUN Multiplication is the process of multiplying one number by another

**multiply**, multiplies, multiplying, multiplied VERB ❶ When something multiplies, it increases greatly in number ❷ When you multiply one number by another, you calculate the total you would get if you added the first number to itself a particular number of times. For example, two multiplied by three is equal to two plus two plus two, which equals six

**mum** NOUN INFORMAL Your mum is your mother

**mumble**, mumbles, mumbling, mumbled VERB If you mumble, you speak very quietly and indistinctly

**mummy**, mummies NOUN ❶ INFORMAL Your mummy is your mother ❷ a dead body which was preserved long ago by being rubbed with special oils and wrapped in cloth

**murder** NOUN ❶ Murder is the deliberate killing of a person ✿ VERB ❷ To murder someone is to kill them deliberately  **murderer** NOUN

**murmur** VERB ❶ If you murmur, you say something very softly ✿ NOUN ❷ something that someone says which can hardly be heard

**muscle**, muscles, muscling, muscled NOUN ❶ Your muscles are pieces of flesh which you can expand or contract in order to move parts of your body ✿ VERB ❷ If you muscle in on something, you force your way into a situation in which you are not welcome

**muscular** [musk-yool-lar] ADJECTIVE ❶ involving or affecting your muscles ❷ Someone who is muscular has strong, firm muscles

**museum** NOUN a building where many interesting or valuable objects are kept and displayed

**mushroom** NOUN a fungus with a short stem and a round top. Some types of mushroom are edible

**music** NOUN ❶ Music is a pattern of sounds performed by people singing or playing instruments ❷ Music is also the written symbols that represent musical sounds

**musical** ADJECTIVE ❶ relating to playing or studying music ✿ NOUN ❷ a play or film that uses songs and dance to tell the story

**musician** NOUN a person who plays a musical instrument as their job or hobby

**Muslim** NOUN ❶ a person who believes in Islam and lives according to its rules ✿ ADJECTIVE ❷ relating to Islam

**must** VERB ❶ If something must happen, it is very important or necessary that it happens ❷ If you tell someone they must do something, you are suggesting that they do it ✿ NOUN ❸ something that is absolutely necessary

**mustard** NOUN Mustard is a spicy-tasting yellow or brown paste made from seeds

**mutter** VERB To mutter is to speak in a very low and perhaps cross voice

**mutual** ADJECTIVE used to describe something that two or more people do to each other or share

**my** ADJECTIVE 'My' refers to something belonging or relating to the person speaking or writing

**myself** PRONOUN ❶ 'Myself' is used when the person speaking or writing does an action and is affected by it ❷ 'Myself' is also used to emphasize 'I'

**mysterious** ADJECTIVE ❶ strange and not well understood ❷ secretive about something  **mysteriously** ADVERB

**mystery**, mysteries NOUN something that is not understood or known about

**myth** NOUN ❶ an untrue belief or explanation ❷ a story which was made up long ago to explain natural events and religious beliefs

# nag - national

**nag**, nags, nagging, nagged VERB ❶ If you nag someone, you keep complaining to them about something ❷ If something nags at you, it keeps worrying you

**nail** NOUN ❶ a small piece of metal with a sharp point at one end, which you hammer into objects to hold them together ❷ Your nails are the thin hard areas covering the ends of your fingers and toes ✿ VERB ❸ If you nail something somewhere, you fit it there using a nail

**naive** or **naïve** [ny-*eev*] ADJECTIVE foolishly believing that things are easier or less complicated than they really are  **naivety** NOUN

**naked** ADJECTIVE ❶ not wearing any clothes or not covered by anything ❷ shown openly

**name**, names, naming, named NOUN ❶ a word that you use to identify a person, place, or thing ❷ Someone's name is also their reputation ✿ VERB ❸ If you name someone or something, you give them a name or you say their name ❹ If you name a price or a date, you say what you want it to be

**nanny**, nannies NOUN a woman whose job is looking after young children

**nap**, naps, napping, napped NOUN ❶ a short sleep ✿ VERB ❷ When you nap, you have a short sleep

**napkin** NOUN a small piece of cloth or paper used to wipe your hands and mouth after eating

**nappy**, nappies NOUN a piece of towelling or paper worn round a baby's bottom

**narrator** NOUN ❶ a person who is reading or telling a story out loud ❷ a character in a novel who tells the story

**narrow** ADJECTIVE ❶ having a small distance from one side to the other ❷ concerned only with a few aspects of something and ignoring the important points ❸ A narrow escape or victory is one that you only just achieve ✿ VERB ❹ To narrow means to become less wide

**nasty**, nastier, nastiest ADJECTIVE very unpleasant

**nation** NOUN a large group of people sharing the same history and language and usually inhabiting a particular country

**national** ADJECTIVE ❶ relating to the whole of a country ❷ typical of a particular country ✿ NOUN ❸ A national of a country is a citizen of that country

## Hello Kitty…

knows that some words that sound as if they begin with *n* actually begin with *gn*, like *gnaw*, or with *kn*, like *knife*, with *mn*, like *mnemonic*, or with *pn*, like *pneumonia*.

## national anthem - needle

**national anthem** NOUN A country's national anthem is its official song

**nationality**, nationalities NOUN Nationality is the fact of belonging to a particular country

**nationwide** ADJECTIVE OR ADVERB happening all over a country

**native** ADJECTIVE ❶ Your native country is the country where you were born ❷ Your native language is the language that you first learned to speak ❸ Animals or plants that are native to a place live or grow there naturally and have not been brought there by people ✿ NOUN ❹ A native of a place is someone who was born there

**natural** ADJECTIVE ❶ normal and to be expected ❷ not trying to pretend or hide anything ❸ existing or happening in nature ❹ A natural ability is one you were born with ❺ Your natural mother or father is your biological mother or father and not someone who has adopted you ✿ NOUN ❻ someone who is born with a particular ability ❼ In music, a natural is a note that is not a sharp or a flat. It is represented by the symbol (♮) **naturally** ADVERB

**nature** NOUN ❶ Nature is animals, plants, and all the other things in the world not made by people ❷ The nature of a person or thing is their basic character

### where does the word come from?

Nature comes from a Latin word *natura* which means 'birth'.

**naughty**, naughtier, naughtiest ADJECTIVE ❶ behaving badly ❷ rude or indecent

**nausea** [naw-zee-ah] NOUN Nausea is a feeling in your stomach that you are going to be sick

**naval** ADJECTIVE relating to or having a navy

**navigate**, navigates, navigating, navigated VERB ❶ When someone navigates, they work out the direction in which a ship, plane, or car should go, using maps and sometimes instruments ❷ To navigate a stretch of water means to travel safely across it **navigation** NOUN

**navy**, navies NOUN ❶ the part of a country's armed forces that fights at sea ✿ ADJECTIVE ❷ dark blue

**near** PREPOSITION ❶ not far from ✿ ADJECTIVE ❷ not far away in distance ❸ not far away in time ❹ You can also use 'near' to mean almost ✿ VERB ❺ When you are nearing something, you are approaching it and will soon reach it

**nearby** ADJECTIVE ❶ only a short distance away ✿ ADVERB ❷ only a short distance away

**nearly** ADVERB not completely but almost

**neat** ADJECTIVE ❶ tidy and smart ❷ A neat alcoholic drink does not have anything added to it **neatly** ADVERB

**necessary** ADJECTIVE ❶ Something that is necessary is needed or must be done ❷ FORMAL Necessary also means certain or inevitable

### how to remember

It is ne**cess**ary to wear one **c**ardigan but two **s**ocks.

**necessity**, necessities NOUN ❶ Necessity is the need to do something ❷ Necessities are things needed in order to live

**neck** NOUN ❶ the part of your body which joins your head to the rest of your body ❷ the long narrow part at the top of a bottle

**necklace** NOUN ❶ a piece of jewellery which a woman wears around her neck ❷ In South Africa, a name for a tyre filled with petrol which is placed round a person's neck and set on fire in order to kill that person

**nectarine** NOUN a kind of peach with a smooth skin

**need** VERB ❶ If you need something, you believe that you must have it or do it ✿ NOUN ❷ Your needs are the things that you need to have ❸ a strong feeling that you must have or do something

**needle** NOUN ❶ a small thin piece of metal with a pointed end and a hole at the other, which is used for sewing ❷ Needles are also long thin pieces of steel or plastic, used

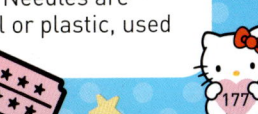

A B C D E F G H I J K L M N O P Q R S T U V W X Y Z

# needless – network

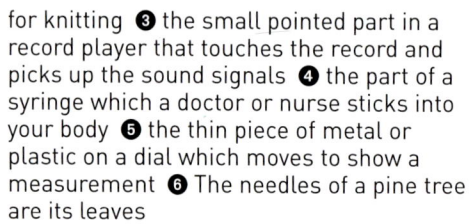

for knitting ❸ the small pointed part in a record player that touches the record and picks up the sound signals ❹ the part of a syringe which a doctor or nurse sticks into your body ❺ the thin piece of metal or plastic on a dial which moves to show a measurement ❻ The needles of a pine tree are its leaves

**needless** ADJECTIVE unnecessary **needlessly** ADVERB

**needy**, needier, neediest ADJECTIVE very poor

**negative** ADJECTIVE ❶ A negative answer means 'no' ❷ Someone who is negative sees only problems and disadvantages ❸ If a medical or scientific test is negative, it shows that something has not happened or is not present ❹ A negative number is less than zero ❺ In physics, a negative electric charge has the same polarity as the charge of an electron ✿ NOUN ❻ the image that is first produced when you take a photograph **negatively** ADVERB

**neglect** VERB ❶ If you neglect something, you do not look after it properly ❷ FORMAL If you neglect to do something, you fail to do it ✿ NOUN ❸ Neglect is failure to look after something or someone properly

**negligent** ADJECTIVE not taking enough care **negligence** NOUN

**negotiate**, negotiates, negotiating, negotiated VERB ❶ When people negotiate, they have formal discussions in order to reach an agreement about something ❷ If you negotiate an obstacle, you manage to get over it or round it

**neigh** [rhymes with day] VERB ❶ When a horse neighs, it makes a loud high-pitched sound ✿ NOUN ❷ a loud sound made by a horse

**neighbour** NOUN ❶ Your neighbour is someone who lives next door to you or near you ❷ Your neighbour is also someone standing or sitting next to you

**neighbourhood** NOUN a district where people live

**neither** ADJECTIVE OR PRONOUN used to indicate that a negative statement refers to two or more things or people

**nephew** NOUN Someone's nephew is the son of their sister or brother

**nerve** NOUN ❶ a long thin fibre that sends messages between your brain and other parts of your body ❷ If you talk about someone's nerves, you are referring to how able they are to remain calm in a difficult situation ❸ Nerve is courage ❹ INFORMAL Nerve is boldness or rudeness

**nervous** ADJECTIVE ❶ worried and frightened ❷ A nervous illness affects your emotions and mental health **nervously** ADVERB **nervousness** NOUN

**nest** NOUN ❶ a place that a bird makes to lay its eggs in; also a place that some insects and other animals make to rear their young in ✿ VERB ❷ When birds nest, they build a nest and lay eggs in it

**net** NOUN ❶ a piece of material made of threads woven together with small spaces in between ❷ The net is the same as the **internet** ✿ ADJECTIVE ❸ A net result or amount is final, after everything has been considered ❹ The net weight of something is its weight without its wrapping

**netball** NOUN Netball is a game played by two teams of seven players in which each team tries to score goals by throwing a ball through a net at the top of a pole

**network** NOUN ❶ a large number of lines or roads which cross each other at many points ❷ A network of people or organizations is a large number of them that work together as a system ❸ A television network is a group

---

**how English works**

**Hello Kitty...**

knows that you can say **neither** as **nye**-thuh or as **nee**-thuh because both are correct

of broadcasting stations that all transmit the same programmes at the same time ❹ a group of computers connected to each other

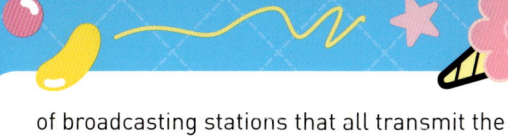

**neuter** [*nyoo-ter*] **VERB** ❶ When an animal is neutered, its reproductive organs are removed ✿ **ADJECTIVE** ❷ In some languages, a neuter noun or pronoun is one which is not masculine or feminine

**neutral ADJECTIVE** ❶ People who are neutral do not support either side in a disagreement or war ❷ The neutral wire in an electric plug is the one that is not earth or live ❸ A neutral colour is not definite or striking, for example pale grey ❹ In chemistry, a neutral substance is neither acid nor alkaline ✿ **NOUN** ❺ a person or country that does not support either side in a disagreement or war ❻ Neutral is the position between the gears of a vehicle in which the gears are not connected to the engine and so the vehicle cannot move

**never ADVERB** at no time in the past, present, or future

**nevertheless ADVERB** in spite of what has just been said

**new ADJECTIVE** ❶ recently made, created, or discovered ❷ not used or owned before ❸ different or unfamiliar

**newborn ADJECTIVE** born recently

**newcomer NOUN** someone who has recently arrived in a place

**newly ADVERB** recently

**news NOUN** News is information about things that have happened

**newsagent NOUN** a person or shop that sells newspapers and magazines

**newspaper NOUN** a publication, on large sheets of paper, that is produced regularly and contains news and articles

**next ADJECTIVE** ❶ coming immediately after something else ❷ in a position nearest to something ✿ **ADVERB** ❸ coming immediately after something else

**next door ADJECTIVE OR ADVERB** in the house next to yours

**nibble**, nibbles, nibbling, nibbled **VERB** ❶ When you nibble something, you take small bites of it ✿ **NOUN** ❷ a small bite of something

**nice**, nicer, nicest **ADJECTIVE** pleasant or attractive **nicely ADVERB**

**nickname NOUN** an informal name given to someone

**niece NOUN** Someone's niece is the daughter of their sister or brother

**night NOUN** Night is the time between sunset and sunrise when it is dark

**nightclub NOUN** a place where people go late in the evening to drink and dance

**nightdress NOUN** a loose dress that a woman or girl wears to sleep in

**nightly ADJECTIVE OR ADVERB** happening every night

**nightmare NOUN** a very frightening dream; also used of any very unpleasant or frightening situation

**nil NOUN** Nil means zero or nothing. It is used especially in sports scores

**nine** the number 9 **ninth ADJECTIVE**

**nineteen** the number 19 **nineteenth ADJECTIVE**

**ninety** the number 90 **ninetieth ADJECTIVE**

**no INTERJECTION** ❶ used to say that something is not true or to refuse something ✿ **ADJECTIVE** ❷ none at all or not at all ✿ **ADVERB** ❸ used with a comparative to mean 'not'

**nobody**, nobodies **PRONOUN** ❶ not a single person ✿ **NOUN** ❷ Someone who is a nobody is not at all important

**nod**, nods, nodding, nodded **VERB** ❶ When you nod, you move your head up and down,

## Helpful hints...

You should try not to use **nice** too much when you are writing. Some other words you can use are: *pleasant, delightful, charming* and *enjoyable*.

# nod off - notify

**A B C D E F G H I J K L M N O P Q R S T U V W X Y Z**

usually to show agreement ✿ **NOUN** ❷ a movement of your head up and down
**nod off** ✿ **VERB** If you nod off, you fall asleep
**noise** **NOUN** a sound, especially one that is loud or unpleasant
**noisy**, noisier, noisiest **ADJECTIVE** making a lot of noise or full of noise **noisily ADVERB**
**nominate**, nominates, nominating, nominated **VERB** If you nominate someone for a job or position, you formally suggest that they have it **nomination NOUN**
**none PRONOUN** not a single thing or person, or not even a small amount of something
**nonfiction NOUN** Nonfiction is writing that gives facts and information rather than telling a story
**nonsense NOUN** Nonsense is foolish and meaningless words or behaviour
**noon NOUN** Noon is midday
**nor CONJUNCTION** used after 'neither' or after a negative statement, to add something else that the negative statement applies to
**normal ADJECTIVE** usual and ordinary **normality NOUN**
**normally ADVERB** ❶ usually ❷ in a way that is normal
**north NOUN** ❶ The north is the direction to your left when you are looking towards the place where the sun rises ❷ The north of a place or country is the part which is towards the north when you are in the centre ✿ **ADVERB OR ADJECTIVE** ❸ North means towards the north ✿ **ADJECTIVE** ❹ A north wind blows from the north
**north-east NOUN, ADVERB, OR ADJECTIVE** North-east is halfway between north and east
**north-eastern ADJECTIVE** in or from the north-east
**northerly ADJECTIVE** ❶ Northerly means to or towards the north ❷ A northerly wind blows from the north
**northern ADJECTIVE** in or from the north
**north-west NOUN, ADVERB, OR ADJECTIVE** North-west is halfway between north and west
**north-western ADJECTIVE** in or from the north-west
**nose NOUN** ❶ the part of your face above your mouth which you use for smelling and breathing ❷ the front part of a car or plane

## how English works

### Hello Kitty...

knows that a **noun** is a word that gives a name to a person, a place or a thing, like *Sally*, *Japan* or *cake*. Nouns are sometimes called 'naming words'.

**nostril NOUN** Your nostrils are the two openings in your nose which you breathe through
**not ADVERB** used to make a sentence negative, to refuse something, or to deny something
**note**, notes, noting, noted **NOUN** ❶ a short letter ❷ a written piece of information that helps you to remember something ❸ In music, a note is a musical sound of a particular pitch, or a written symbol that represents it ❹ a banknote ❺ an atmosphere, feeling, or quality ✿ **VERB** ❻ If you note a fact, you become aware of it or you mention it
**notebook NOUN** a small book for writing notes in
**nothing PRONOUN** not anything
**notice**, notices, noticing, noticed **VERB** ❶ If you notice something, you become aware of it ✿ **NOUN** ❷ Notice is attention or awareness ❸ a written announcement ❹ Notice is also advance warning about something ✿ **PHRASE** ❺ If you **hand in your notice**, you tell your employer that you intend to leave your job after a fixed period of time
**noticeable ADJECTIVE** obvious and easy to see
**noticeboard NOUN** a board for notices
**notify**, notifies, notifying, notified **VERB** To notify someone of something means to officially inform them of it

**nought** the number 0

**noun** NOUN a word which refers to a person, thing, or idea. Examples of nouns are 'president', 'table', 'sun', and 'beauty'

**nourish** [*nur-rish*] VERB To nourish people or animals means to provide them with food

**nourishing** ADJECTIVE Food that is nourishing makes you strong and healthy

**nourishment** NOUN Nourishment is food that your body needs in order to remain healthy

**novel** NOUN ❶ a book that tells an invented story ✿ ADJECTIVE ❷ new and interesting

**novelist** NOUN a person who writes novels

**novelty**, novelties NOUN ❶ Novelty is the quality of being new and interesting ❷ something new and interesting ❸ a small, unusual object sold as a gift or souvenir

**November** NOUN November is the eleventh month of the year. It has 30 days

**now** ADVERB ❶ at the present time or moment ✿ CONJUNCTION ❷ as a result or consequence of a particular fact ✿ PHRASE ❸ **Just now** means very recently ❹ If something happens **now and then**, it happens sometimes but not regularly

**nowadays** ADVERB at the present time

**nowhere** ADVERB not anywhere

**nuclear** ADJECTIVE ❶ relating to the energy produced when the nuclei of atoms are split ❷ relating to weapons that explode using the energy released by atoms ❸ relating to the structure and behaviour of the nuclei of atoms

**nucleus**, nuclei [*nyoo-klee-uss*] NOUN ❶ The nucleus of an atom is the central part of it. It is positively charged and is made up of protons and neutrons ❷ The nucleus of a cell is the part that contains the chromosomes and controls the growth and reproduction of the cell

**nude** ADJECTIVE ❶ naked ✿ NOUN ❷ a picture or statue of a naked person

**nudge**, nudges, nudging, nudged VERB ❶ If you nudge someone, you push them gently, usually with your elbow ✿ NOUN ❷ a gentle push

**nuisance** NOUN someone or something that is annoying or inconvenient

**numb** ADJECTIVE ❶ unable to feel anything ✿ VERB ❷ If something numbs you, it makes you unable to feel anything at all

**number** NOUN ❶ a word or a symbol used for counting or calculating ❷ Someone's number is the series of numbers that you dial when you telephone them ❸ A number of things is a quantity of them ❹ a song or piece of music ✿ VERB ❺ If things number a particular amount, there are that many of them ❻ If you number something, you give it a number ❼ To be numbered among a particular group means to belong to it

**numeral** NOUN a symbol that represents a number

**numerous** ADJECTIVE existing or happening in large numbers

**nun** NOUN a woman who has taken religious vows and lives in a convent

**nurse**, nurses, nursing, nursed NOUN ❶ a person whose job is to look after people who are ill ✿ VERB ❷ If you nurse someone, you look after them when they are ill ❸ If you nurse a feeling, you feel it strongly for a long time

**nursery**, nurseries NOUN ❶ a place where young children are looked after while their parents are working ❷ a room in which young children sleep and play ❸ a place where plants are grown and sold

**nursery rhyme** NOUN A nursery rhyme is a short poem or song for young children

**nursing home** NOUN a privately run hospital, especially for old people

**nut** NOUN ❶ a fruit with a hard shell and an edible centre that grows on certain trees ❷ a piece of metal with a hole in the middle which a bolt screws into

**nutrient** NOUN Nutrients are substances that help plants or animals to grow

**nutritious** ADJECTIVE containing substances that help you to grow and remain healthy

**nylon** NOUN ❶ Nylon is a type of strong artificial material ❷ Nylons are stockings or tights

### how to say it

**Nuclear** should be said ***new**-clear* with most force on *new*.

# oak - observe

**oak** NOUN a large tree which produces acorns. It has a hard wood which is often used to make furniture

**oar** NOUN a wooden pole with a wide, flat end, used for rowing a boat

**oasis**, oases [oh-**ay**-siss] NOUN a small area in a desert where water and plants are found

**oatmeal** NOUN Oatmeal is a rough flour made from oats

**obedient** ADJECTIVE If you are obedient, you do what you are told to do  **obediently** ADVERB  **obedience** NOUN

**obese** [oh-**bees**] ADJECTIVE extremely fat

**obey** VERB If you obey a person or an order, you do what you are told to do

**object** NOUN ❶ anything solid that you can touch or see, and that is not alive ❷ an aim or purpose ❸ The object of your feelings or actions is the person that they are directed towards ❹ In grammar, the object of a verb or preposition is the word or phrase which follows it and describes the person or thing affected ✿ VERB ❺ If you object to something, you dislike it or disapprove of it

**objection** NOUN If you have an objection to something, you dislike it or disapprove of it

**objective** NOUN ❶ an aim ✿ ADJECTIVE ❷ If you are objective, you are not influenced by personal feelings or prejudices

**obligation** NOUN something that you must do because it is your duty

**obligatory** [ob-**lig**-a-tree] ADJECTIVE required by a rule or law

**oblige**, obliges, obliging, obliged VERB ❶ If you are obliged to do something, you have to do it ❷ If you oblige someone, you help them

**oblong** NOUN ❶ a four-sided shape with two parallel short sides, two parallel long sides, and four right angles ✿ ADJECTIVE ❷ shaped like an oblong

**oboe** NOUN a woodwind musical instrument with a double reed

**obscene** ADJECTIVE indecent and likely to upset people

**observe**, observes, observing, observed VERB ❶ To observe something is to watch it carefully ❷ To observe something is to notice it ❸ If you observe that something is the case, you make a comment about it ❹ To observe a law or custom is to obey or follow it

## how English works

### Helpful hints...

The **object** of a sentence is the person or thing that has something done to it, like squirrels in My dog chases squirrels.

# obsession - offer

**obsession** NOUN If someone has an obsession about something, they cannot stop thinking about that thing

**obstacle** NOUN something which is in your way and makes it difficult to do something

**obstinate** ADJECTIVE Someone who is obstinate is stubborn and unwilling to change their mind

**obstruct** VERB If something obstructs a road or path, it blocks it **obstruction** NOUN

**obtain** VERB If you obtain something, you get it

**obvious** ADJECTIVE easy to see or understand **obviously** ADVERB

**occasion** NOUN ❶ a time when something happens ❷ an important event ❸ An occasion for doing something is an opportunity for doing it

**occasional** ADJECTIVE happening sometimes but not often **occasionally** ADVERB

**occupant** NOUN The occupants of a building are the people who live or work in it

**occupation** NOUN ❶ a job or profession ❷ a hobby or something you do for pleasure ❸ The occupation of a country is the act of invading it and taking control of it

**occupy**, occupies, occupying, occupied VERB ❶ The people who occupy a building are the people who live or work there ❷ When people occupy a place, they move into it and take control of it ❸ To occupy a position in a system or plan is to have that position ❹ If something occupies you, you spend your time doing it

**occur**, occurs, occurring, occurred VERB ❶ If something occurs, it happens or exists ❷ If something occurs to you, you suddenly think of it

**occurrence** NOUN ❶ an event ❷ The occurrence of something is the fact that it happens or exists

### letter O

Some words that sound like they begin with o actually begin with au, like author.

**ocean** NOUN The five oceans are the five very large areas of sea on earth

**o'clock** ADVERB You use 'o'clock' after the number of the hour to say what the time is

**octave** NOUN ❶ the difference in pitch between the first note and the eighth note of a musical scale ❷ eight lines of poetry together

**October** NOUN October is the tenth month of the year. It has 31 days

**octopus**, octopuses NOUN a sea creature with eight long tentacles which it uses to catch food

**odd** ADJECTIVE ❶ Something odd is strange or unusual ❷ Odd things do not match each other ❸ Odd numbers are numbers that cannot be divided exactly by two ✿ ADVERB ❹ You use 'odd' after a number to say that it is approximate **oddly** ADVERB

**odds** PLURAL NOUN In gambling, the probability of something happening is called the odds

**odour** NOUN FORMAL a strong smell

**of** PREPOSITION ❶ consisting of or containing ❷ used when naming something or describing a characteristic of something ❸ belonging to or connected with

**off** PREPOSITION OR ADVERB ❶ indicating movement away from or out of a place ❷ indicating separation or distance from a place ❸ not working ✿ ADVERB OR ADJECTIVE ❹ not switched on ✿ ADJECTIVE ❺ cancelled or postponed ❻ Food that is off has gone sour or bad ✿ PREPOSITION ❼ not liking or not using something

**offence** NOUN ❶ a crime ✿ PHRASES ❷ If something **gives offence**, it upsets people. If you **take offence**, you are upset by someone or something

**offend** VERB ❶ If you offend someone, you upset them ❷ FORMAL To offend or to offend a law is to commit a crime

**offensive** ADJECTIVE ❶ Something offensive is rude and upsetting ❷ Offensive actions or weapons are used in attacking someone ✿ NOUN ❸ an attack

**offer** VERB ❶ If you offer something to someone, you ask them if they would like it ✿ NOUN ❷ something that someone says they will give you or do for you if you want them to ❸ a specially low price for a product in a shop

# office - once

**office** NOUN ❶ a room where people work at desks ❷ a government department ❸ a place where people can go for information, tickets, or other services ❹ Someone who holds office has an important job or position in government or in an organization

**officer** NOUN a person with a position of authority in the armed forces, the police, or a government organization

**official** ADJECTIVE ❶ approved by the government or by someone in authority ❷ done or used by someone in authority as part of their job ❀ NOUN ❸ a person who holds a position of authority in an organization **officially** ADVERB

**offline** ADJECTIVE ❶ If a computer is offline, it is switched off or not connected to the internet ❀ ADVERB ❷ If you do something offline, you do it while not connected to the internet

**often** ADVERB happening many times or a lot of the time

**oil** NOUN ❶ Oil is a thick, sticky liquid used as a fuel and for lubrication ❷ Oil is also a thick, greasy liquid made from plants or animals ❀ VERB ❸ If you oil something, you put oil in it or on it

**oil painting** NOUN a picture that has been painted with thick paints made from coloured powder and a kind of oil

**oily** ADJECTIVE Something that is oily is covered with or contains oil

**ointment** NOUN a smooth, thick substance that you put on sore skin to heal it

**okay** or **OK** ADJECTIVE INFORMAL Okay means all right

**old** ADJECTIVE ❶ having lived or existed for a long time ❷ 'Old' is used to give the age of someone or something ❸ 'Old' also means former

**old-fashioned** ADJECTIVE ❶ Something which is old-fashioned is no longer fashionable ❷ Someone who is old-fashioned believes in the values and standards of the past

**olive** NOUN ❶ a small green or black fruit containing a stone. Olives are usually pickled and eaten as a snack or crushed to produce oil ❀ ADJECTIVE OR NOUN ❷ dark yellowish-green

**Olympic Games** [ol-*lim*-pik] PLURAL NOUN The Olympic Games are a set of sporting contests held in a different city every four years

**omelette** [om-*lit*] NOUN a dish made by beating eggs together and cooking them in a flat pan

**omit**, omits, omitting, omitted VERB ❶ If you omit something, you do not include it ❷ FORMAL If you omit to do something, you do not do it

**omnivore** NOUN An omnivore is an animal that eats all kinds of food, including meat and plants

**on** PREPOSITION ❶ touching or attached to something ❷ If you are on a bus, plane, or train, you are inside it ❸ If something happens on a particular day, that is when it happens ❹ If something is done on an instrument or machine, it is done using that instrument or machine ❺ A book or talk on a particular subject is about that subject ❀ ADVERB ❻ If you have a piece of clothing on, you are wearing it ❀ ADJECTIVE ❼ A machine or switch that is on is working ❽ If an event is on, it is happening or taking place

**once** ADVERB ❶ If something happens once, it happens one time only ❷ If something was once true, it was true in the past, but is no longer true ❀ CONJUNCTION ❸ If something happens once another thing has happened, it happens immediately afterwards

---

**some other words to use**

*Helpful hints...*

You should try not to use **old** too much when you are writing. Some other words you can use are: *aged*, *elderly* and *ancient*.

184

**one** ❶ One is the number 1 ❀ **ADJECTIVE** ❷ If you refer to the one person or thing of a particular kind, you mean the only person or thing of that kind ❸ One also means 'a'; used when emphasizing something ❀ **PRONOUN** ❹ One refers to a particular thing or person ❺ One also means people in general

**oneself** **PRONOUN** 'Oneself' is used when you are talking about people in general

**one-way** **ADJECTIVE** ❶ One-way streets are streets along which vehicles can drive in only one direction ❷ A one-way ticket is one that you can use to travel to a place, but not to travel back again

**onion** **NOUN** a small, round vegetable with a brown skin like paper and a very strong taste

**online** **ADJECTIVE** ❶ If a computer is online, it is switched on or connected to the internet ❀ **ADVERB** ❷ If you do something online, you do it while connected to the internet

**onlooker** **NOUN** someone who is watching an event

**only** **ADVERB** ❶ You use 'only' to indicate the one thing or person involved ❷ You use 'only' to emphasize that something is unimportant or small ❸ You can use 'only' to introduce something which happens immediately after something else ❀ **ADJECTIVE** ❹ If you talk about the only thing or person, you mean that there are no others ❺ If you are an only child, you have no brothers or sisters ❀ **CONJUNCTION** ❻ 'Only' also means but or except ❀ **PHRASE** ❼ Only too means extremely

**onto** or **on to** **PREPOSITION** If you put something onto an object, you put it on it

**ooze**, oozes, oozing, oozed **VERB** When a thick liquid oozes, it flows slowly

**open** **VERB** ❶ When you open something, or when it opens, you move it so that it is no longer closed ❷ When a shop or office opens, people are able to go in ❸ To open something also means to start it ❀ **ADJECTIVE** ❹ Something that is open is not closed or fastened ❺ If you have an open mind, you are willing to consider new ideas or suggestions ❻ Someone who is open is honest and frank ❼ When a shop or office is open, people are able to go in ❽ An open area of sea or land is a large, empty area ❾ If something is open to you, it is possible for you to do it ❿ If a situation is still open, it is still being considered ❀ **PHRASE** ⓫ In the open means outside ⓬ In the open also means not secret

**opening** **ADJECTIVE** ❶ Opening means coming first ❀ **NOUN** ❷ The opening of a book or film is the first part of it ❸ a hole or gap ❹ an opportunity

**open-minded** **ADJECTIVE** willing to consider new ideas and suggestions

**opera** **NOUN** a play in which the words are sung rather than spoken **operatic** **ADJECTIVE**

**operate**, operates, operating, operated **VERB** ❶ To operate is to work ❷ When you operate a machine, you make it work ❸ When surgeons operate, they cut open a patient's body to remove or repair a damaged part

**operation** **NOUN** ❶ a complex, planned event ❷ a form of medical treatment in which a surgeon cuts open a patient's body to remove or repair a damaged part ❸ any process in which a number or quantity is operated on according to a set of rules, for example addition, subtraction, multiplication, and division ❀ **PHRASE** ❹ If something is **in operation**, it is working or being used

**operator** **NOUN** ❶ someone who works at a telephone exchange or on a switchboard ❷ someone who operates a machine ❸ someone who runs a business

**opinion** **NOUN** a belief or view

**opponent** **NOUN** someone who is against you in an argument or a contest

**opportunity**, opportunities **NOUN** a chance to do something

**oppose**, opposes, opposing, opposed **VERB** If you oppose something, you disagree with it and try to prevent it

**opposed** **ADJECTIVE** ❶ If you are opposed to something, you disagree with it ❷ Opposed also means opposite or very different ❀ **PHRASE** ❸ If you refer to one thing **as opposed to** another, you are emphasizing that it is the first thing rather than the second which concerns you

**opposite** **PREPOSITION OR ADVERB** ❶ If one thing is opposite another, it is facing it ❀ **ADJECTIVE** ❷ The opposite part of something is the part farthest away from you ❸ If things are opposite, they are completely different ❀ **NOUN** ❹ If two things are completely different, they are opposites

# opposition - original

**opposition** NOUN ❶ If there is opposition to something, people disagree with it and try to prevent it ❷ The political parties who are not in power are referred to as the Opposition ❸ In a game or sports event, the opposition is the person or team that you are competing against

**optician** NOUN someone who tests people's eyes, and makes and sells glasses and contact lenses

**optimism** NOUN Optimism is a feeling of hopefulness about the future **optimist** NOUN

**optimistic** ADJECTIVE hopeful about the future

**option** NOUN a choice between two or more things **optional** ADJECTIVE

**or** CONJUNCTION ❶ used to link two different things ❷ used to introduce a warning

**oral** ADJECTIVE ❶ spoken rather than written ❷ Oral describes things that are used in your mouth or done with your mouth ✿ NOUN ❸ an examination that is spoken rather than written

**orange** NOUN ❶ a round citrus fruit that is juicy and sweet and has a thick reddish-yellow skin ✿ ADJECTIVE OR NOUN ❷ reddish-yellow

**orbit** NOUN ❶ the curved path followed by an object going round a planet or the sun ✿ VERB ❷ If something orbits a planet or the sun, it goes round and round it

**orchard** NOUN a piece of land where fruit trees are grown

**orchestra** [or-kess-tra] NOUN a large group of musicians who play musical instruments together

**ordeal** NOUN a difficult and extremely unpleasant experience

**order** NOUN ❶ a command given by someone in authority ❷ If things are arranged or done in a particular order, they are arranged or done in that sequence ❸ Order is a situation in which everything is in the correct place or done at the correct time ❹ something that you ask to be brought to you or sent to you ❺ An order is a division of living organisms that is smaller than a class and larger than a family ✿ VERB ❻ To order someone to do something is to tell them firmly to do it ❼ When you order something, you ask for it to be brought or sent to you

**ordinary** ADJECTIVE Ordinary means not special or different in any way

**organ** NOUN ❶ Your organs are parts of your body that have a particular function, for example your heart or lungs ❷ a large musical instrument with pipes of different lengths through which air is forced. It has various keyboards which are played like a piano

**organic** ADJECTIVE ❶ Something that is organic is produced by or found in plants or animals ❷ Organic food is produced without the use of artificial fertilizers or pesticides

**organism** NOUN any living animal, plant, fungus, or bacterium

**organization** or **organisation** NOUN ❶ any group or business ❷ The organization of something is the act of planning and arranging it

**organize**, organizes, organizing, organized (also **organise**) VERB ❶ If you organize an event, you plan and arrange it ❷ If you organize things, you arrange them in a sensible order **organized** ADJECTIVE **organizer** NOUN

**oriental** ADJECTIVE relating to eastern or south-eastern Asia

**origin** NOUN ❶ You can refer to the beginning or cause of something as its origin or origins ❷ You can refer to someone's family background as their origin or origins

**original** ADJECTIVE ❶ Original describes things that existed at the beginning, rather than being added later, or things that were

### how to remember

Hello Kitty... remembers that she originally asked for **gin**ger beer.

**ornament – outside**

the first of their kind to exist ❷ Original means imaginative and clever ❖ NOUN ❸ a work of art or a document that is the one that was first produced, and not a copy **originally** ADVERB

**ornament** NOUN a small, attractive object that you display in your home or that you wear in order to look attractive

**orphan** NOUN ❶ a child whose parents are dead ❖ VERB ❷ If a child is orphaned, its parents die

**orphanage** NOUN a place where orphans are looked after

**ostrich**, ostriches NOUN The ostrich is the largest bird in the world. It cannot fly

**other** ADJECTIVE OR PRONOUN ❶ Other people or things are different people or things ❖ PHRASES ❷ **The other day** or **the other week** means recently

**otherwise** ADVERB ❶ You use 'otherwise' to say a different situation would exist if a particular fact or occurrence was not the case ❷ 'Otherwise' means apart from the thing mentioned ❸ 'Otherwise' also means in a different way

**ouch** INTERJECTION You say ouch when you suddenly feel pain

**ought** [awt] VERB If you say that someone ought to do something, you mean that they should do it

**ounce** NOUN a unit of weight equal to one sixteenth of a pound or about 28.35 grams

**our** ADJECTIVE 'Our' refers to something belonging or relating to the speaker or writer and one or more other people

### don't mix up

Don't mix up **our** (belonging to us) and **hour** (sixty minutes).

**ours** PRONOUN 'Ours' refers to something belonging or relating to the speaker or writer and one or more other people

**ourselves** PRONOUN ❶ 'Ourselves' is used when the same speaker or writer and one or more other people do an action and are affected by it ❷ 'Ourselves' is used to emphasize 'we'

**out** ADVERB ❶ towards the outside of a place ❷ not at home ❸ in the open air ❹ no longer shining or burning ❖ ADJECTIVE ❺ on strike ❻ unacceptable or unfashionable ❼ incorrect

**outbreak** NOUN If there is an outbreak of something unpleasant, such as war, it suddenly occurs

**outcome** NOUN a result

**outdoor** ADJECTIVE happening or used outside

**outdoors** ADVERB outside

**outer** ADJECTIVE The outer parts of something are the parts furthest from the centre

**outfit** NOUN ❶ a set of clothes ❷ INFORMAL an organization

**outing** NOUN a trip made for pleasure

**outline**, outlines, outlining, outlined VERB ❶ If you outline a plan or idea, you explain it in a general way ❷ You say that something is outlined when you can see its shape because there is a light behind it ❖ NOUN ❸ a general explanation or description of something ❹ The outline of something is its shape

**outlook** NOUN ❶ Your outlook is your general attitude towards life ❷ The outlook of a situation is the way it is likely to develop

**out of** PREPOSITION ❶ If you do something out of a particular feeling, you are motivated by that feeling ❷ 'Out of' also means from ❸ If you are out of something, you no longer have any of it ❹ If you are out of the rain, sun, or wind, you are sheltered from it ❺ You also use 'out of' to indicate proportion. For example, one out of five means one in every five

**out of date** ADJECTIVE old-fashioned and no longer useful

**output** NOUN ❶ Output is the amount of something produced by a person or organization ❷ The output of a computer is the information that it produces

**outrage**, outrages, outraging, outraged VERB ❶ If something outrages you, it angers and shocks you ❖ NOUN ❷ Outrage is a feeling of anger and shock ❸ something very shocking or violent **outrageous** ADJECTIVE

**outside** NOUN ❶ The outside of something is the part which surrounds or encloses the rest of it ❖ PREPOSITION ❷ on or to the exterior of ❸ Outside also means not included in something ❖ ADJECTIVE ❹ Outside means not inside ❖ ADVERB ❺ out of doors

187

# outskirts – oyster

**outskirts** PLURAL NOUN The outskirts of a city or town are the parts around the edge of it

**outstanding** ADJECTIVE ❶ extremely good ❷ Money that is outstanding is still owed

**oval** NOUN ❶ a round shape, similar to a circle but wider in one direction than the other ❈ ADJECTIVE ❷ shaped like an oval

**oven** NOUN the part of a cooker that you use for baking or roasting food

**over** PREPOSITION ❶ Over something means directly above it or covering it ❷ A view over an area is a view across that area ❸ If something is over a road or river, it is on the opposite side of the road or river ❹ Something that is over a particular amount is more than that amount ❺ 'Over' indicates a topic which is causing concern ❻ If something happens over a period of time, it happens during that period ❈ ADVERB OR PREPOSITION ❼ If you lean over, you bend your body in a particular direction ❈ ADVERB ❽ 'Over' is used to indicate a position ❾ If something rolls or turns over, it is moved so that its other side is facing upwards ❈ ADJECTIVE ❿ Something that is over is completely finished

**overcast** ADJECTIVE If it is overcast, the sky is covered by cloud

**overcome**, overcomes, overcoming, overcame, overcome VERB ❶ If you overcome a problem or a feeling, you manage to deal with it or control it ❈ ADJECTIVE ❷ If you are overcome by a feeling, you feel it very strongly

**overcrowded** ADJECTIVE If a place is overcrowded, there are too many things or people in it

**overdue** ADJECTIVE If someone or something is overdue, they are late

**overflow**, overflows, overflowing, overflowed, overflown VERB If a liquid overflows, it spills over the edges of its container. If a river overflows, it flows over its banks

**overhead** ADJECTIVE ❶ Overhead means above you ❈ ADVERB ❷ Overhead means above you

**overhear**, overhears, overhearing, overheard VERB If you overhear someone's conversation, you hear what they are saying to someone else

**overlap**, overlaps, overlapping, overlapped VERB If one thing overlaps another, one part of it covers part of the other thing

**overlook** VERB ❶ If a building or window overlooks a place, it has a view over that place ❷ If you overlook something, you ignore it or do not notice it

**overnight** ADVERB ❶ for the duration of the night ❷ suddenly ❈ ADJECTIVE ❸ during the night ❹ sudden ❺ for use when you go away for one or two nights

**overseas** ADVERB ❶ abroad ❈ ADJECTIVE ❷ abroad ❸ from abroad

**overtake**, overtakes, overtaking, overtook, overtaken VERB If you overtake someone, you pass them because you are moving faster than them

**overtime** NOUN ❶ Overtime is time that someone works in addition to their normal working hours ❈ ADVERB ❷ If someone works overtime, they do work in addition to their normal working hours

**overweight** ADJECTIVE too fat, and therefore unhealthy **overwhelming** ADJECTIVE

**owe**, owes, owing, owed VERB ❶ If you owe someone money, they have lent it to you and you have not yet paid it back ❷ If you owe a quality or skill to someone, they are responsible for giving it to you ❸ If you say that you owe someone gratitude or loyalty, you mean that they deserve it from you

**owl** NOUN Owls are birds of prey that hunt at night. They have large eyes and short, hooked beaks

**own** ADJECTIVE ❶ If something is your own, it belongs to you or is associated with you ❈ VERB ❷ If you own something, it belongs to you

**owner** NOUN The owner of something is the person it belongs to

**ownership** NOUN If you have ownership of something, you own it

**oxygen** NOUN Oxygen is a chemical element in the form of a colourless gas. It makes up about 21% of the Earth's atmosphere. With an extremely small number of exceptions, living things need oxygen to live, and things cannot burn without it

**oyster** NOUN Oysters are large, flat shellfish. Some oysters can be eaten, and others produce pearls

# pace - pair

**pace**, paces, pacing, paced NOUN ❶ The pace of something is the speed at which it moves or happens ❷ a step; also used as a measurement of distance ✿ VERB ❸ If you pace up and down, you continually walk around because you are anxious or impatient

**pack** VERB ❶ If you pack, you put things neatly into a suitcase, bag, or box ❷ If people pack into a place, it becomes crowded with them ✿ NOUN ❸ a bag or rucksack carried on your back ❹ a packet or collection of something ❺ A pack of playing cards is a complete set ❻ A pack of dogs or wolves is a group of them

**pack up** ✿ VERB If you pack up your belongings, you put them in a bag because you are leaving

**package** NOUN ❶ a small parcel ❷ a set of proposals or offers presented as a whole

**packaging** NOUN Packaging is the container or wrapping in which an item is sold or sent

**packed** ADJECTIVE very full

**packet** NOUN a thin cardboard box or paper container in which something is sold

**pad**, pads, padding, padded NOUN ❶ a thick, soft piece of material ❷ a number of pieces of paper fixed together at one end ❸ The pads of an animal such as a cat or dog are the soft, fleshy parts on the bottom of its paws ❹ a flat surface from which helicopters take off or rockets are launched ✿ VERB ❺ If you pad something, you put a pad inside it or over it to protect it or change its shape ❻ If you pad around, you walk softly **padding** NOUN

**paddle**, paddles, paddling, paddled NOUN ❶ a short pole with a broad blade at one or both ends, used to move a small boat or a canoe ✿ VERB ❷ If someone paddles a boat, they move it using a paddle ❸ If you paddle, you walk in shallow water

**padlock** NOUN a lock made up of a metal case with a U-shaped bar attached to it, which can be put through a metal loop and then closed. It is unlocked by turning a key in the lock on the case

**page**, pages, paging, paged NOUN ❶ one side of one of the pieces of paper in a book or magazine; also the sheet of paper itself ❷ In medieval times, a page was a young boy servant who was learning to be a knight ✿ VERB ❸ To page someone is to send a signal or message to a small electronic device which they are carrying

**pain** NOUN ❶ Pain is an unpleasant feeling of physical hurt ❷ Pain is also an unpleasant feeling of deep unhappiness ✿ VERB ❸ If something pains you, it makes you very unhappy **painless** ADJECTIVE

**painful** ADJECTIVE ❶ causing emotional pain ❷ causing physical pain **painfully** ADVERB

**painkiller** NOUN a drug that reduces or stops pain

**paint** NOUN ❶ Paint is a coloured liquid used to decorate buildings, or to make a picture ✿ VERB ❷ If you paint something or paint a picture of it, you make a picture of it using paint ❸ When you paint something such as a wall, you cover it with paint **painter** NOUN **painting** NOUN

**pair** NOUN ❶ A pair is two things of the same type or that do the same thing ❷ You use 'pair' when referring to certain objects which have two main matching parts ✿ VERB

# pal - parcel

❸ If you pair up with someone, you agree to do something together
**pal** NOUN INFORMAL a friend
**palace** NOUN a large, grand house, especially the official home of a king or queen
**pale**, paler, palest ADJECTIVE rather white and without much colour or brightness
**palm** NOUN ❶ A palm or palm tree is a tropical tree with no branches and a crown of long leaves ❷ the flat surface of your hand which your fingers bend towards
**pamphlet** NOUN a very thin book in paper covers giving information about something
**pan**, pans, panning, panned NOUN ❶ a round metal container with a long handle, used for cooking things in on top of a cooker ✿ VERB ❷ When a film camera pans, it moves in a wide sweep ❸ INFORMAL To pan something is to criticize it strongly
**pancake** NOUN a thin, flat piece of fried batter which can be served with savoury or sweet fillings
**panda** NOUN A panda or giant panda is a large animal rather like a bear that lives in China. It has black fur with large patches of white
**pane** NOUN a sheet of glass in a window or door
**panel**, panels NOUN ❶ a small group of people who are chosen to do something ❷ a flat piece of wood that is part of a larger object ❸ A control panel is a surface containing switches and instruments to operate a machine
**panic**, panics, panicking, panicked NOUN ❶ Panic is a sudden overwhelming feeling of fear or anxiety ✿ VERB ❷ If you panic, you become so afraid or anxious that you cannot act sensibly
**pant** VERB If you pant, you breathe quickly and loudly through your mouth
**pants** PLURAL NOUN ❶ Pants are a piece of underwear with holes for your legs and elastic around the waist or hips ❷ Pants are also trousers
**paper** NOUN ❶ Paper is a material made from wood pulp and used for writing on or wrapping things ❷ a newspaper ❸ IN PLURAL Papers are official documents, for example a passport for identification ❹ part of a written examination ✿ VERB ❺ If you paper a wall, you put wallpaper on it
**paperback** NOUN a book with a thin cardboard cover

### don't mix up

### Hello Kitty...

never mixes up **pair** (two matching things) and **pear** (the fruit).

**paperwork** NOUN Paperwork is the part of a job that involves dealing with letters and records
**parachute** [*par-rash-oot*] NOUN a circular piece of fabric attached by lines to a person or package so that they can fall safely to the ground from an aircraft
**parade**, parades, parading, paraded NOUN ❶ a line of people or vehicles standing or moving together as a display ✿ VERB ❷ When people parade, they walk together in a group as a display
**paraffin** NOUN Paraffin is a strong-smelling liquid which is used as a fuel
**paragraph** NOUN a section of a piece of writing. Paragraphs begin on a new line
**parallel** NOUN ❶ Something that is a parallel to something else has similar qualities or features to it ✿ ADJECTIVE ❷ If two lines are parallel, they are the same distance apart along the whole of their length
**paralyse**, paralyses, paralysing, paralysed VERB If something paralyses you, it causes loss of feeling and movement in your body
**parcel**, parcels, parcelling, parcelled NOUN ❶ something wrapped up in paper ✿ VERB ❷ If you parcel something up, you make it into a parcel

**pardon – part of speech**

**pardon** INTERJECTION ❶ You say **pardon** or **I beg your pardon** to express surprise or apology, or when you have not heard what someone has said ✿ VERB ❷ If you pardon someone, you forgive them for doing something wrong

**parent** NOUN Your parents are your father and mother

**park** NOUN ❶ a public area with grass and trees ❷ a private area of grass and trees around a large country house ✿ VERB ❸ When someone parks a vehicle, they drive it into a position where it can be left **parking** NOUN

**parliament** NOUN the group of elected representatives who make the laws of a country

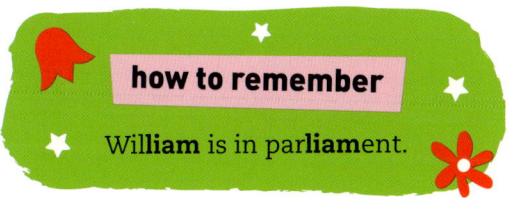

### how to remember
Wi**lliam** is in par**liam**ent.

**parody**, parodies, parodying, parodied NOUN ❶ an amusing imitation of the style of an author or of a familiar situation ✿ VERB ❷ If you parody something, you make a parody of it

**parrot** NOUN a brightly coloured tropical bird with a curved beak

**parsley** NOUN Parsley is a herb with curly leaves used for flavouring in cooking

**part** NOUN ❶ one of the pieces or aspects of something ❷ one of the roles in a play or film, played by an actor or actress ❸ Someone's part in something is their involvement in it ✿ PHRASE ❹ If you **take part** in an activity, you do it together with other people ✿ VERB ❺ If things that are next to each other part, they move away from each other ❻ If two people part, they leave each other

**partial** ADJECTIVE ❶ not complete or whole ❷ liking something very much ❸ supporting one side in a dispute, rather than being fair and without bias **partially** ADVERB

**participate**, participates, participating, participated VERB If you participate in an activity, you take part in it **participant** NOUN **participation** NOUN

**participle** NOUN In grammar, a participle is a form of a verb used with an auxiliary verb in compound tenses and often as an adjective. English has two participles: the past participle, which describes a completed action, and the present participle, which describes a continuing action. For example in 'He has gone', 'gone' is a past participle and in 'She was winning', 'winning' is a present participle

**particular** ADJECTIVE ❶ relating or belonging to only one thing or person ❷ especially great or intense ❸ Someone who is particular has high standards and is not easily satisfied **particularly** ADVERB

**partly** ADVERB to some extent but not completely

**partner** NOUN ❶ Someone's partner is the person they are married to or are living with ❷ Your partner is the person you are doing something with, for example in a dance or a game ❸ Business partners are joint owners of their business ✿ VERB ❹ If you partner someone, you are their partner for a game or social occasion **partnership** NOUN

**part of speech**, parts of speech NOUN a particular grammatical class of word, such as 'noun' or 'adjective'

### how English works

**Hello Kitty...**

knows that a word's **part of speech** is the grammatical group it belongs to, like *noun*, *verb* or *adjective*.

A B C D E F G H I J K L M N O P Q R S T U V W X Y Z

# part-time – paste

**part-time** ADJECTIVE involving work for only a part of the working day or week

**party**, parties NOUN ❶ a social event held for people to enjoy themselves ❷ an organization whose members share the same political beliefs and campaign for election to government ❸ a group who are doing something together ❹ FORMAL one of the people involved in a legal agreement or dispute

**pass**, passes, passing, passed VERB ❶ To pass something is to move past it ❷ To pass in a particular direction is to move in that direction ❸ If you pass something to someone, you hand it to them or transfer it to them ❹ If you pass a period of time doing something, you spend it that way ❺ When a period of time passes, it happens and finishes ❻ If you pass a test, you are considered to be of an acceptable standard ❼ When a new law or proposal is passed, it is formally approved ❽ When a judge passes sentence on someone, the judge states what the punishment will be ❾ If you pass the ball in a ball game, you throw, kick, or hit it to another player in your team ✤ NOUN ❿ the transfer of the ball in a ball game to another player in the same team ⓫ an official document that allows you to go somewhere ⓬ a narrow route between mountains

**pass away** or **pass on** ✤ VERB Someone who has passed away has died

**pass out** ✤ VERB If someone passes out, they faint

**passage** NOUN ❶ a space that connects two places ❷ a long narrow corridor ❸ a section of a book or piece of music

**passenger** NOUN a person travelling in a vehicle, aircraft, or ship

**passion** NOUN ❶ Passion is a very strong feeling of physical attraction ❷ Passion is also any strong emotion

**passionate** ADJECTIVE expressing very strong feelings about something

**passive** ADJECTIVE ❶ remaining calm and showing no feeling when provoked ✤ NOUN ❷ In grammar, the passive or passive voice is the form of the verb in which the person or thing to which an action is being done is the grammatical subject of the sentence, and is given more emphasis as a result. For example, the passive of *The committee rejected your application* is *Your application was rejected by the committee* **passively** ADVERB

### how English works

### Hello Kitty...

knows that a **passive** verb is when the action is done to the subject of a sentence, like *was given* in *The boy was given a new bicycle.*

**passport** NOUN an official identification document which you need to show when you travel abroad

**password** NOUN ❶ a secret word known to only a few people. It allows people on the same side to recognize a friend ❷ a word you need to know to get into some computers or computer files

**past** NOUN ❶ The past is the period of time before the present ✤ ADJECTIVE ❷ Past things are things that happened or existed before the present ❸ The past tense of a verb is the form used to express something that happened in the past ✤ PREPOSITION OR ADVERB ❹ You use 'past' when you are telling the time ❺ If you go past something, you move towards it and continue until you are on the other side ✤ PREPOSITION ❻ Something that is past a place is situated on the other side of it

**pasta** NOUN Pasta is a dried mixture of flour, eggs, and water, formed into shapes

**paste**, pastes, pasting, pasted NOUN ❶ Paste is a soft, rather sticky mixture that can be easily spread ✤ VERB ❷ If you paste something onto a surface, you stick it with glue

**pastel** ADJECTIVE ❶ Pastel colours are pale and soft ✿ NOUN ❷ Pastels are small sticks of coloured crayon, used for drawing

**pastry**, pastries NOUN ❶ Pastry is a mixture of flour, fat, and water, rolled flat and used for making pies ❷ a small cake

**past tense** NOUN In grammar, the past tense is the tense of a verb that you use mainly to refer to things that happened or existed before the time of writing or speaking

### how English works

The **past tense** shows that something has already happened, like *I was here*.

**pat**, pats, patting, patted VERB ❶ If you pat something, you tap it lightly with your hand held flat ✿ NOUN ❷ a small lump of butter

**patch**, patches, patching, patched NOUN ❶ a piece of material used to cover a hole in something ❷ an area of a surface that is different in appearance from the rest ✿ VERB ❸ If you patch something, you mend it by fixing a patch over the hole

**patch up** ✿ VERB If you patch something up, you mend it hurriedly or temporarily

**path** NOUN ❶ a strip of ground for people to walk on ❷ Your path is the area ahead of you and the direction in which you are moving

**pathetic** ADJECTIVE ❶ If something is pathetic, it makes you feel pity ❷ Pathetic also means very poor or unsuccessful

**patience** NOUN Patience is the ability to stay calm in a difficult or irritating situation

**patient** ADJECTIVE ❶ If you are patient, you stay calm in a difficult or irritating situation ✿ NOUN ❷ a person receiving medical treatment from a doctor or in a hospital **patiently** ADVERB

**patio**, patios NOUN a paved area close to a house

**patriot** NOUN someone who loves their country and feels very loyal towards it **patriotic** ADJECTIVE

**patrol**, patrols, patrolling, patrolled VERB ❶ When soldiers, police, or guards patrol an area, they walk or drive around to make sure there is no trouble ✿ NOUN ❷ a group of people patrolling an area

**pattern** NOUN ❶ a decorative design of repeated shapes ❷ The pattern of something is the way it is usually done or happens ❸ a diagram used as a guide for making something, for example clothes

**pause**, pauses, pausing, paused VERB ❶ If you pause, you stop what you are doing for a short time ✿ NOUN ❷ a short period when you stop what you are doing ❸ a short period of silence

**pavement** NOUN a path with a hard surface at the side of a road

**paw** NOUN The paws of an animal such as a cat or bear are its feet with claws and soft pads

**pay**, pays, paying, paid VERB ❶ When you pay money to someone, you give it to them because you are buying something or owe it to them ❷ If it pays to do something, it is to your advantage to do it ❸ If you pay for something that you have done, you suffer as a result ❹ If you pay attention to something, you give it your attention ❺ If you pay a visit to someone, you visit them ✿ NOUN ❻ Someone's pay is their salary or wages

**payment** NOUN ❶ Payment is the act of paying money ❷ a sum of money paid

**PC**, PCs NOUN ❶ in Britain, a police constable ❷ a personal computer

**PE** NOUN PE is a lesson in which gymnastics or sports are taught. PE is an abbreviation for 'physical education'

**pea** NOUN Peas are small round green seeds that grow in pods and are eaten as a vegetable

**peace** NOUN ❶ Peace is a state of calm and quiet when there is no disturbance of any kind ❷ When a country is at peace, it is not at war

**peaceful** ADJECTIVE quiet and calm **peacefully** ADVERB

**peach**, peaches NOUN ❶ a soft, round fruit with yellow flesh and a yellow and red skin ✿ ADJECTIVE ❷ pale pink with a hint of orange

# peak – penetrate

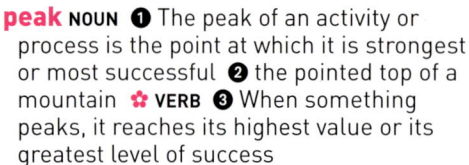

**peak** NOUN ❶ The peak of an activity or process is the point at which it is strongest or most successful ❷ the pointed top of a mountain ✿ VERB ❸ When something peaks, it reaches its highest value or its greatest level of success

**peanut** NOUN Peanuts are small oval nuts that grow under the ground

**pear** NOUN a fruit which is narrow at the top and wide and rounded at the bottom

**pearl** NOUN a hard, round, creamy-white object used in jewellery. Pearls grow inside the shell of an oyster

**peasant** NOUN a person who works on the land, especially in a poor country

**pebble** NOUN a smooth, round stone

**peculiar** ADJECTIVE ❶ strange and perhaps unpleasant ❷ relating or belonging only to a particular person or thing

**pedal**, pedals, pedalling, pedalled NOUN ❶ a control lever on a machine or vehicle that you press with your foot ✿ VERB ❷ When you pedal a bicycle, you push the pedals round with your feet to move along

**pedestrian** NOUN ❶ someone who is walking ✿ ADJECTIVE ❷ Pedestrian means ordinary and rather dull

**pedestrian crossing** NOUN a specially marked place where you can cross the road safely

**peek** VERB ❶ If you peek at something, you have a quick look at it ✿ NOUN ❷ a quick look at something

**peel** NOUN ❶ The peel of a fruit is the skin when it has been removed ✿ VERB ❷ When you peel fruit or vegetables, you remove the skin ❸ If a surface is peeling, it is coming off in thin layers

**peep** VERB ❶ If you peep at something, you have a quick look at it ❷ If something peeps out from behind something else, a small part of it becomes visible ✿ NOUN ❸ a quick look at something

**peer** VERB ❶ If you peer at something, you look at it very hard ✿ NOUN ❷ a member of the nobility ❸ Your peers are the people who are of the same age and social status as yourself

**peg**, pegs, pegging, pegged NOUN ❶ a plastic or wooden clip used for hanging wet clothes on a line ❷ a hook on a wall where you can hang things ✿ VERB ❸ If you peg clothes on a line, you fix them there with pegs ❹ If a price is pegged at a certain level, it is fixed at that level

**pelvis**, pelvises NOUN the wide, curved group of bones at hip-level at the base of your spine

**pen**, pens, penning, penned NOUN ❶ a long, thin instrument used for writing with ink ❷ a small fenced area in which farm animals are kept for a short time ✿ VERB ❸ LITERARY If someone pens a letter or article, they write it ❹ If you are penned in or penned up, you have to remain in an uncomfortably small area

*where does the word come from?*

*Did you know…*

that the word **pen** comes from Latin *penna* which means 'feathers'? That's because *pens* were originally made from birds' feathers.

**penalty**, penalties NOUN ❶ a punishment or disadvantage that someone is made to suffer ❷ In soccer, a penalty is a free kick at goal that is given to the attacking team if the defending team have committed a foul near their goal

**pence** a plural form of **penny**

**pencil** NOUN a long thin stick of wood with graphite in the centre, used for drawing or writing

**penetrate**, penetrates, penetrating, penetrated VERB To penetrate an area that is difficult to get into is to succeed in getting into it

194

**penguin - person**

**penguin** NOUN a black and white bird with webbed feet and small wings like flippers

**peninsula** NOUN an area of land almost surrounded by water

**penis**, penises NOUN A man's penis is the part of his body that he uses when urinating and having sexual intercourse

**penknife**, penknives NOUN a small knife with a blade that folds back into the handle

**penny**, pennies or pence NOUN a unit of currency in Britain and some other countries. In Britain a penny is worth one hundredth of a pound

**pension** [pen-shn] NOUN a regular sum of money paid to an old or retired person

**pensioner** NOUN an old or retired person who gets a pension paid by the state

**pentagon** NOUN a shape with five straight sides; a **regular pentagon** is a shape with five straight sides of the same length

**people**, peoples, peopling, peopled PLURAL NOUN ❶ People are men, women, and children ✿ NOUN ❷ all the men, women, and children of a particular country or race ✿ VERB ❸ If an area is peopled by a particular group, that group of people live there

**pepper** NOUN ❶ a hot-tasting powdered spice used for flavouring in cooking ❷ a hollow green, orange, red, or yellow fruit eaten as a vegetable, with sweet-flavoured flesh

**peppermint** NOUN Peppermint is a plant with a strong taste. It is used for making sweets and in medicine

**per** PREPOSITION 'Per' is used to mean 'each' when expressing rates and ratios

**perceive**, perceives, perceiving, perceived VERB If you perceive something that is not obvious, you see it or realize it

**per cent** PHRASE You use **per cent** to talk about amounts as a proportion of a hundred. An amount that is ten per cent (10%) of a larger amount is equal to ten hundredths of the larger amount

**percentage** NOUN a fraction expressed as a number of hundredths

**perch** VERB ❶ If you perch on something, you sit on the edge of it ❷ When a bird perches on something, it stands on it ✿ NOUN ❸ a short rod for a bird to stand on ❹ an edible freshwater fish

**percussion** NOUN OR ADJECTIVE Percussion instruments are musical instruments that you hit to produce sounds

**perfect** ADJECTIVE ❶ of the highest standard and without fault ❷ complete or absolute ❸ In English grammar, the perfect tense of a verb is formed with the present tense of 'have' and the past participle of the main verb ✿ VERB ❹ If you perfect something, you make it as good as it can possibly be **perfectly** ADVERB **perfection** NOUN

**perform** VERB ❶ To perform a task or action is to do it ❷ To perform is to act, dance, or play music in front of an audience **performer** NOUN

**performance** NOUN ❶ an entertainment provided for an audience ❷ The performance of a task or action is the doing of it ❸ Someone's or something's performance is how successful they are

**perfume** NOUN ❶ Perfume is a pleasant-smelling liquid which women put on their bodies ❷ The perfume of something is its pleasant smell

**perhaps** ADVERB You use 'perhaps' when you are not sure whether something is true or possible

**perimeter** NOUN The perimeter of an area or figure is the whole of its outer edge

**period** NOUN ❶ a particular length of time ❷ one of the parts the day is divided into at school ❸ A woman's period is the monthly bleeding from her womb ✿ ADJECTIVE ❹ relating to a historical period of time

**permanent** ADJECTIVE lasting for ever, or present all the time **permanently** ADVERB

**permission** NOUN If you have permission to do something, you are allowed to do it

**permit**, permits, permitting, permitted VERB ❶ To permit something is to allow it or make it possible ✿ NOUN ❷ an official document which says that you are allowed to do something

**persevere**, perseveres, persevering, persevered VERB If you persevere, you keep trying to do something and do not give up

**person**, people or persons NOUN ❶ a man, woman, or child ❷ In grammar, the first person is the speaker (I), the second person

# personal – phrasal verb

is the person being spoken to (you), and the third person is anyone else being referred to (he, she, they)

**personal** ADJECTIVE ❶ Personal means belonging or relating to a particular person rather than to people in general ❷ Personal matters relate to your feelings, relationships, and health which you may not wish to discuss with other people
**personally** ADVERB

**personality**, personalities NOUN ❶ Your personality is your character and nature ❷ a famous person in entertainment or sport

**personnel** [per-son-nell] NOUN The personnel of an organization are the people who work for it

**perspective** NOUN ❶ A particular perspective is one way of thinking about something ❷ Perspective is a method artists use to make some people and things seem further away than others

**perspiration** NOUN Perspiration is the moisture that appears on your skin when you are hot or frightened

**persuade**, persuades, persuading, persuaded VERB If someone persuades you to do something or persuades you that something is true, they make you do it or believe it by giving you very good reasons
**persuasion** NOUN

**pessimism** NOUN Pessimism is the tendency to believe that bad things will happen
**pessimist** NOUN

**pessimistic** ADJECTIVE believing that bad things will happen

**pest** NOUN ❶ an insect or small animal which damages plants or food supplies ❷ someone who keeps bothering or annoying you

**pet**, pets, petting, petted NOUN ❶ a tame animal kept at home ✿ ADJECTIVE ❷ Someone's pet theory or pet project is something that they particularly support or feel strongly about ✿ VERB ❸ If you pet a person or animal, you stroke them affectionately

**petal** NOUN The petals of a flower are the coloured outer parts

**petition** NOUN ❶ a document demanding official action which is signed by a lot of people ❷ a formal request to a court for legal action to be taken ✿ VERB ❸ If you petition someone in authority, you make a formal request to them

**petrol** NOUN Petrol is a liquid obtained from petroleum and used as a fuel for motor vehicles

**pharmacist** NOUN a person who is qualified to prepare and sell medicines

**pharmacy**, pharmacies NOUN a shop where medicines are sold

**phase**, phases, phasing, phased NOUN ❶ a particular stage in the development of something ✿ VERB ❷ To phase something is to cause it to happen gradually in stages

**philosophical** or **philosophic** ADJECTIVE Someone who is philosophical does not get upset when disappointing things happen

**philosophy**, philosophies NOUN ❶ Philosophy is the study or creation of ideas about existence, knowledge, or beliefs ❷ a set of beliefs that a person has
**philosopher** NOUN

**phone**, phones, phoning, phoned NOUN ❶ a piece of electronic equipment which allows you to speak to someone in another place by keying in or dialling their number ✿ VERB ❷ If you phone someone, you key in or dial their number and speak to them using a phone

**photo**, photos NOUN INFORMAL a photograph

**photocopier** NOUN a machine which makes instant copies of documents by photographing them

**photocopy**, photocopies, photocopying, photocopied NOUN ❶ a copy of a document produced by a photocopier ✿ VERB ❷ If you photocopy a document, you make a copy of it using a photocopier

**photograph** NOUN ❶ a picture made using a camera ✿ VERB ❷ When you photograph someone, you take a picture of them by using a camera **photographer** NOUN
**photography** NOUN

**photosynthesis** NOUN Photosynthesis is the process by which the action of sunlight on the chlorophyll in plants produces the substances that keep the plants alive

**phrasal verb** NOUN a verb such as 'take over' or 'break in', which is made up of a verb and an adverb or preposition

**phrase - pile**

**phrase**, phrases, phrasing, phrased NOUN ❶ a group of words considered as a unit ✿ VERB ❷ If you phrase something in a particular way, you choose those words to express it

**how English works**

**Hello Kitty...**

knows that a **phrase** is a group of words which go together but need other words to be a proper sentence.

**physical** ADJECTIVE ❶ concerning the body rather than the mind ❷ relating to things that can be touched or seen, especially with regard to their size or shape **physically** ADVERB

**physical education** NOUN Physical education consists of the sport that you do at school

**physics** NOUN Physics is the scientific study of matter, energy, gravity, electricity, heat, and sound **physicist** NOUN

**piano**, pianos NOUN ❶ a large musical instrument with a row of black and white keys. When the keys are pressed, little hammers hit wires to produce the different notes ❷ In music, piano is an instruction to play or sing something quietly **pianist** NOUN

**piccolo**, piccolos NOUN a high-pitched wind instrument like a small flute

**pick** VERB ❶ To pick something is to choose it ❷ If you pick a flower or fruit, or pick something from a place, you remove it with your fingers ❸ If someone picks a lock, they open it with a piece of wire instead of a key ✿ NOUN ❹ The pick of a group of people or things are the best ones in it ❺ a pickaxe

**pick on** ✿ VERB If you pick on someone, you criticize them unfairly or treat them unkindly

**pick up** ✿ VERB If you pick someone or something up, you collect them from the place where they are waiting

**pickle**, pickles, pickling, pickled NOUN ❶ Pickle or pickles consists of vegetables or fruit preserved in vinegar or salt water ✿ VERB ❷ To pickle food is to preserve it in vinegar or salt water

**picnic**, picnics, picnicking, picnicked NOUN ❶ a meal eaten out of doors ✿ VERB ❷ People who are picnicking are having a picnic

**picture**, pictures, picturing, pictured NOUN ❶ a drawing, painting, or photograph of someone or something ❷ If you have a picture of something in your mind, you have an idea or impression of it ❸ IN PLURAL If you go to the pictures, you go to see a film at the cinema ✿ VERB ❹ If someone is pictured in a newspaper or magazine, a photograph of them is printed in it ❺ If you picture something, you think of it and imagine it clearly

**pie** NOUN a dish of meat, vegetables, or fruit covered with pastry

**piece**, pieces, piecing, pieced NOUN ❶ a portion or part of something ❷ something that has been written or created, such as a work of art or a musical composition ❸ a coin ✿ VERB ❹ If you piece together a number of things, you gradually put them together to make something complete

**pierce**, pierces, piercing, pierced VERB If a sharp object pierces something, it goes through it, making a hole

**piercing** ADJECTIVE ❶ A piercing sound is high-pitched and unpleasant ❷ Someone with piercing eyes seems to look at you very intensely

**pig** NOUN a farm animal kept for its meat. It has pinkish skin, short legs, and a snout

**pigeon** NOUN a largish bird with grey feathers, often seen in towns

**pigtail** NOUN a length of plaited hair

**pile**, piles, piling, piled NOUN ❶ a quantity of things lying one on top of another ❷ the soft surface of a carpet consisting of many threads standing on end ❸ IN PLURAL Piles

A B C D E F G H I J K L M N O P Q R S T U V W X Y Z

197

# pill – place

are painful swellings that appear in the veins inside or just outside a person's anus ✿ **VERB** ❹ If you pile things somewhere, you put them one on top of the other

**pill** NOUN ❶ a small, hard tablet of medicine that you swallow ❷ The pill is a type of drug that women can take regularly to prevent pregnancy

**pillar** NOUN ❶ a tall, narrow, solid structure, usually supporting part of a building ❷ Someone who is described as a pillar of a particular group is an active and important member of it

**pillow** NOUN a rectangular cushion which you rest your head on when you are in bed

**pillowcase** NOUN a cover for a pillow which can be removed and washed

**pilot** NOUN ❶ a person who is trained to fly an aircraft ❷ a person who goes on board ships to guide them through local waters to a port ✿ **VERB** ❸ To pilot something is to control its movement or to guide it ✿ **ADJECTIVE** ❹ testing of a scheme or product, done to see if it would be successful

**pin**, pins, pinning, pinned NOUN ❶ a thin, pointed piece of metal used to fasten together things such as pieces of fabric or paper ✿ **VERB** ❷ If you pin something somewhere, you fasten it there with a pin or a drawing pin ❸ If someone pins you in a particular position, they hold you there so that you cannot move ❹ If you try to pin something down, you try to get or give a clear and exact description of it or statement about it

**pinch**, pinches, pinching, pinched VERB ❶ If you pinch something, you squeeze it between your thumb and first finger ❷ INFORMAL If someone pinches something, they steal it ✿ NOUN ❸ A pinch of something is the amount that you can hold between your thumb and first finger

**pine**, pines, pining, pined NOUN ❶ A pine or pine tree is an evergreen tree with very thin leaves ✿ **VERB** ❷ If you pine for something, you are sad because you cannot have it

**pineapple** NOUN a large, oval fruit with sweet, yellow flesh and a thick, lumpy brown skin

**pink** ADJECTIVE pale reddish-white

**pint** NOUN a unit of liquid volume equal to one eighth of a gallon or about 0.568 litres

**pioneer** [pie-on-**ear**] NOUN ❶ Someone who is a pioneer in a particular activity is one of the first people to develop it ✿ **VERB** ❷ Someone who pioneers a new process or invention is the first person to develop it

**pip** NOUN Pips are the hard seeds in a fruit

**pipe**, pipes, piping, piped NOUN ❶ a long, hollow tube through which liquid or gas can flow ❷ an object used for smoking tobacco. It consists of a small hollow bowl attached to a tube ✿ **VERB** ❸ To pipe a liquid or gas somewhere is to transfer it through a pipe

**pirate**, pirates NOUN Pirates were sailors who attacked and robbed other ships

**pistol** NOUN a small gun held in the hand

**pit**, pits NOUN ❶ a large hole in the ground ❷ a small hollow in the surface of something ❸ a coal mine

**pitch**, pitches, pitching, pitched NOUN ❶ an area of ground marked out for playing a game such as football ❷ The pitch of a sound is how high or low it is ❸ a black substance used in road tar and also for making boats and roofs waterproof ✿ **VERB** ❹ If you pitch something somewhere, you throw it with a lot of force ❺ If you pitch something at a particular level of difficulty, you set it at that level ❻ When you pitch a tent, you fix it in an upright position

**pity**, pities, pitying, pitied VERB ❶ If you pity someone, you feel very sorry for them ✿ NOUN ❷ Pity is a feeling of being sorry for someone ❸ If you say that it is a pity about something, you are expressing your disappointment about it

**pizza** [peet-sah] NOUN a flat piece of dough covered with cheese, tomato, and other savoury food

**place**, places, placing, placed NOUN ❶ any point, building, or area ❷ the position where something belongs ❸ a space at a table set with cutlery where one person can eat ❹ If you have a place in a group or at a college, you are a member or are accepted as a student ❺ a particular point or stage in a sequence of things ✿ **PHRASE** ❻ When something **takes place**, it happens ✿ **VERB**

**plain – playing card**

❼ If you place something somewhere, you put it there ❽ If you place an order, you order something

**plain** ADJECTIVE ❶ very simple in style with no pattern or decoration ❷ obvious and easy to recognize or understand ❸ A person who is plain is not at all beautiful or attractive ✿ ADVERB ❹ You can use 'plain' before a noun or adjective to emphasize it ✿ NOUN ❺ a large, flat area of land with very few trees

**don't mix up**

Don't mix up **plain** (simply decorated) and **plane** (an aeroplane).

**plait** VERB ❶ If you plait three lengths of hair or rope together, you twist them over each other in turn to make one thick length ✿ NOUN ❷ a length of hair that has been plaited

**plan**, plans, planning, planned NOUN ❶ a method of achieving something that has been worked out beforehand ❷ a detailed diagram or drawing of something that is to be made ✿ VERB ❸ If you plan something, you decide in detail what it is to be and how to do it ❹ If you are planning to do something, you intend to do it

**plane**, planes, planing, planed NOUN ❶ a vehicle with wings and engines that enable it to fly ❷ a flat surface ❸ You can refer to a particular level of something as a particular plane ❹ a tool with a flat bottom with a sharp blade in it. You move it over a piece of wood to remove thin pieces from the surface ✿ VERB ❺ If you plane a piece of wood, you smooth its surface with a plane

**planet** NOUN a round object in space which moves around the sun or a star and is lit by light from it

**plant** NOUN ❶ a living thing that grows in the earth and has stems, leaves, and roots ❷ a factory or power station ✿ VERB ❸ When you plant a seed or plant, you put it into the ground ❹ If you plant something somewhere, you put it there firmly or secretly

**plaster** NOUN ❶ Plaster is a paste made of sand, lime, and water, which is used to form a smooth surface for inside walls and ceilings ❷ a strip of sticky material with a small pad, used for covering cuts on your body ✿ VERB ❸ To plaster a wall is to cover it with a layer of plaster ✿ PHRASE ❹ If your arm or leg is **in plaster**, it has a plaster cast on it to protect a broken bone

**plastic** NOUN ❶ Plastic is a substance made by a chemical process that can be moulded when soft to make a wide range of objects ✿ ADJECTIVE ❷ made of plastic

**plastic surgery** NOUN Plastic surgery is surgery to replace or repair damaged skin or to improve a person's appearance by changing the shape of their features

**plate** NOUN ❶ a flat dish used to hold food ❷ a flat piece of metal or other hard material used for various purposes in machinery or building

**plateau**, plateaus or plateaux [rhymes with snow] NOUN a large area of high and fairly flat land

**platform** NOUN ❶ a raised structure on which someone or something can stand ❷ the raised area in a railway station where passengers get on and off trains

**play**, plays, playing, played VERB ❶ When children play, they take part in games or use toys ❷ When you play a sport or match, you take part in it ❸ If an actor plays a character in a play or film, he or she performs that role ❹ If you play a musical instrument, you produce music from it ❺ If you play a CD, you listen to it ✿ NOUN ❻ a piece of drama performed in the theatre or on television or radio **player** NOUN

**playful** ADJECTIVE ❶ friendly and light-hearted ❷ lively

**playground** NOUN a special area for children to play in

**playgroup** NOUN an informal kind of school for very young children where they learn by playing

**playing card** NOUN Playing cards are cards printed with numbers or pictures which are used to play various games

# playing field - poet

A B C D E F G H I J K L M N O P Q R S T U V W X Y Z

**playing field** NOUN an area of grass where people play sports

**playwright** NOUN a person who writes plays

**plea** NOUN ❶ an emotional request ❷ In a court of law, someone's plea is their statement that they are guilty or not guilty

**plead** VERB ❶ If you plead with someone, you ask them in an intense emotional way to do something ❷ When a person pleads guilty or not guilty, they state in court that they are guilty or not guilty of a crime

**pleasant** ADJECTIVE ❶ enjoyable or attractive ❷ friendly or charming

**please**, pleases, pleasing, pleased INTERJECTION ❶ You say please when you are asking someone politely to do something ✿ VERB ❷ If something pleases you, it makes you feel happy and satisfied

**pleased** ADJECTIVE happy or satisfied

**pleasing** ADJECTIVE attractive, satisfying, or enjoyable

**pleasure** NOUN ❶ Pleasure is a feeling of happiness, satisfaction, or enjoyment ❷ an activity that you enjoy

**plenty** NOUN If there is plenty of something, there is a lot of it

**pliers** PLURAL NOUN Pliers are a small tool with metal jaws for holding small objects and bending wire

**plop**, plops, plopping, plopped NOUN ❶ a gentle sound made by something light dropping into a liquid ✿ VERB ❷ If something plops into a liquid, it drops into it with a gentle sound

**plot**, plots, plotting, plotted NOUN ❶ a secret plan made by a group of people ❷ The plot of a novel or play is the story ❸ a small piece of land ✿ VERB ❹ If people plot to do something, they plan it secretly ❺ If someone plots the course of a plane or ship on a map, or plots a graph, they mark the points in the correct places

**plough** [rhymes with **cow**] NOUN ❶ a large farming tool that is pulled across a field to turn the soil over before planting seeds ✿ VERB ❷ When someone ploughs land, they use a plough to turn over the soil

**pluck** VERB ❶ To pluck a fruit or flower is to remove it with a sharp pull ❷ To pluck a chicken or other dead bird means to pull its feathers out before cooking it ❸ When you pluck a stringed instrument, you pull the strings and let them go ✿ NOUN ❹ Pluck is courage

**plug**, plugs, plugging, plugged NOUN ❶ a plastic object with metal prongs that can be pushed into a socket to connect an appliance to the electricity supply ❷ a disc of rubber or metal with which you block up the hole in a sink or bath ✿ VERB ❸ If you plug a hole, you block it with something

**plum** NOUN a small fruit with a smooth red or yellow skin and a large stone in the middle

**plumber** NOUN a person who connects and repairs water pipes

**plump** ADJECTIVE rather fat

**plunge**, plunges, plunging, plunged VERB ❶ If something plunges, it falls suddenly ❷ If you plunge an object into something, you push it in quickly ❸ If you plunge into an activity or state, you suddenly become involved in it or affected by it ✿ NOUN ❹ a sudden fall

**plural** NOUN the form of a word that is used to refer to two or more people or things, for example the plural of 'chair' is 'chairs', and the plural of 'mouse' is 'mice'

**plus** PREPOSITION ❶ You use 'plus' to show that one number is being added to another ❷ You can use 'plus' when you mention an additional item ✿ ADJECTIVE ❸ slightly more than the number mentioned

**p.m.** used to specify times between 12 noon and 12 midnight, eg *He went to bed at 9 p.m.* It is an abbreviation for the Latin phrase 'post meridiem', which means 'after noon'

**pneumonia** [new-**moan**-ee-ah] NOUN Pneumonia is a serious disease which affects a person's lungs and makes breathing difficult

**pocket** NOUN ❶ a small pouch that forms part of a piece of clothing ❷ A pocket of something is a small area of it

**pocket money** NOUN Pocket money is an amount of money given regularly to children by their parents

**pod** NOUN a long narrow seed container that grows on plants such as peas or beans

**poem** NOUN a piece of writing in which the words are arranged in short rhythmic lines, often with a rhyme

**poet** NOUN a person who writes poems

200

# poetry - political

**poetry** NOUN Poetry is poems, considered as a form of literature

**point** NOUN ❶ an opinion or fact expressed by someone ❷ a quality ❸ the purpose or meaning something has ❹ a position or time ❺ a single mark in a competition ❻ the thin, sharp end of something such as a needle or knife ❼ The points of a compass are the 32 directions indicated on it ❽ The decimal point in a number is the dot separating the whole number from the fraction ❾ On a railway track, the points are the levers and rails which enable a train to move from one track to another ✿ VERB ❿ If you point at something, you stick out your finger to show where it is ⓫ If something points in a particular direction, it faces that way

**pointed** ADJECTIVE ❶ A pointed object has a thin, sharp end ❷ Pointed comments express criticism

**pointless** ADJECTIVE Something that is pointless has no purpose

**point of view**, points of view NOUN Your point of view is your opinion about something or your attitude towards it

**poison** NOUN ❶ Poison is a substance that can kill people or animals if they swallow it or absorb it ✿ VERB ❷ To poison someone is to try to kill them with poison

**poisonous** ADJECTIVE containing something that causes death or illness

**poke**, pokes, poking, poked VERB ❶ If you poke someone or something, you push at them quickly with your finger or a sharp object ❷ Something that pokes out of another thing appears from underneath or behind it ✿ NOUN ❸ a sharp jab or prod

**poker** NOUN ❶ Poker is a card game in which the players make bets on the cards dealt to them ❷ a long metal rod used for moving coals or logs in a fire

**pole** NOUN ❶ a long rounded piece of wood or metal ❷ The earth's poles are the two opposite ends of its axis

**police**, polices, policing, policed PLURAL NOUN ❶ The police are the people who are officially responsible for making sure that people obey the law ✿ VERB ❷ To police an area is to keep law and order there by means of the police or an armed force

**policeman**, policemen NOUN a man who is a member of a police force **policewoman** NOUN

**policy**, policies NOUN ❶ a set of plans, especially in politics or business ❷ An insurance policy is a document which shows an agreement made with an insurance company

**polish**, polishes, polishing, polished VERB ❶ If you polish something, you put polish on it or rub it with a cloth to make it shine ❷ If you polish a skill or technique you have, you work on it in order to improve it ✿ NOUN ❸ Polish is a substance that you put on an object to clean it and make it shine ❹ Something that has polish is elegant and of good quality

**polite** ADJECTIVE ❶ Someone who is polite has good manners and behaves considerately towards other people ❷ Polite society is cultivated and refined **politely** ADVERB

**politeness** NOUN the quality of having good manners and behaving considerately

**political** ADJECTIVE ❶ relating to the state, government, or public administration ❷ relating to or interested in politics **politically** ADVERB

### don't mix up

Hello Kitty... never mixes up **pole** (a long stick) and **poll** (a time when you ask people what they think of something).

# politician - pose

**politician** NOUN a person involved in the government of a country

**politics** NOUN Politics is the activity and planning concerned with achieving power and control in a country or organization

**poll** NOUN ❶ a survey in which people are asked their opinions about something ❷ IN PLURAL A political election can be referred to as the polls ✿ VERB ❸ If you are polled on something, you are asked your opinion about it as part of a survey

**pollen** NOUN Pollen is a fine yellow powder produced by flowers in order to fertilize other flowers of the same species

**pollute**, pollutes, polluting, polluted VERB To pollute water or air is to make it dirty and dangerous to use or live in **polluted** ADJECTIVE

**pollution** NOUN Pollution of the environment happens when dirty or dangerous substances get into the air, water, or soil

**polyester** NOUN a man-made fibre, used especially to make clothes

**pond** NOUN a small, usually man-made area of water

**pony**, ponies NOUN a small horse

**ponytail** NOUN a hairstyle in which long hair is tied at the back of the head and hangs down like a tail

**pool** NOUN ❶ a small area of still water ❷ Pool is a game in which players try to hit coloured balls into pockets around the table using long sticks called cues ❸ A pool of people, money, or things is a group or collection used or shared by several people ❹ IN PLURAL The pools are a competition in which people try to predict the results of football matches ✿ VERB ❺ If people pool their resources, they gather together the things they have so that they can be shared or used by all of them

**poor** ADJECTIVE ❶ Poor people have very little money and few possessions ❷ Poor places are inhabited by people with little money and show signs of neglect ❸ You use 'poor' to show sympathy ❹ 'Poor' also means of a low quality or standard

**poorly** ADJECTIVE ❶ feeling unwell or ill ✿ ADVERB ❷ badly

**pop**, pops, popping, popped NOUN ❶ Pop is modern music played and enjoyed especially by young people ❷ You can refer to fizzy, nonalcoholic drinks as pop ❸ a short, sharp sound ✿ VERB ❹ If something pops, it makes a sudden sharp sound ❺ If you pop something somewhere, you put it there quickly ❻ If you pop somewhere, you go there quickly

**popcorn** NOUN Popcorn is a snack consisting of grains of maize heated until they puff up and burst

**popular** ADJECTIVE ❶ liked or approved of by a lot of people ❷ involving or intended for ordinary people **popularity** NOUN

**population** NOUN The population of a place is the people who live there, or the number of people living there

**porch**, porches NOUN a covered area at the entrance to a building

**pore**, pores, poring, pored NOUN ❶ The pores in your skin or on the surface of a plant are very small holes which allow moisture to pass through ✿ VERB ❷ If you pore over a piece of writing or a diagram, you study it carefully

**pork** NOUN Pork is meat from a pig which has not been salted or smoked

**porridge** NOUN Porridge is a thick, sticky food made from oats cooked in water or milk

**port** NOUN ❶ a town or area which has a harbour or docks ❷ Port is a kind of strong, sweet red wine ✿ ADJECTIVE ❸ The port side of a ship is the left side when you are on board the ship, facing the front

**portable** ADJECTIVE designed to be easily carried

**porter** NOUN ❶ a person whose job is to be in charge of the entrance of a building, greeting and directing visitors ❷ A porter in a railway station or hospital is a person whose job is to carry or move things

**portion** NOUN a part or amount of something

**portrait** NOUN a picture or photograph of someone

**pose**, poses, posing, posed VERB ❶ If something poses a problem, it is the cause of the problem ❷ If you pose a question, you ask it ❸ If you pose as someone else, you pretend to be that person in order to deceive people ✿ NOUN ❹ a way of standing, sitting, or lying

**posh – potential**

**posh** ADJECTIVE INFORMAL ❶ smart, fashionable, and expensive ❷ upper-class

**position** NOUN ❶ The position of someone or something is the place where they are or ought to be ❷ When someone or something is in a particular position, they are sitting or lying in that way ❸ a job or post in an organization ❹ The position that you are in at a particular time is the situation that you are in ✿ VERB ❺ To position something somewhere is to put it there

**positive** ADJECTIVE ❶ completely sure about something ❷ confident and hopeful ❸ showing approval or encouragement ❹ providing definite proof of the truth or identity of something ❺ A positive number is greater than zero ❻ In physics, a positive electric charge has an opposite charge to that of an electron **positively** ADVERB

**possess**, possesses, possessing, possessed VERB ❶ If you possess a particular quality, you have it ❷ If you possess something, you own it ❸ If a feeling or belief possesses you, it strongly influences you

**possession** NOUN ❶ If something is in your possession or if you are in possession of it, you have it ❷ Your possessions are the things that you own or that you have with you

**possessive** ADJECTIVE ❶ A person who is possessive about someone or something wants to keep them to themselves ✿ NOUN ❷ In grammar, the possessive is the form of a noun or pronoun used to show possession

**possibility**, possibilities NOUN something that might be true or might happen

**possible** ADJECTIVE ❶ likely to happen or able to be done ❷ likely or capable of being true or correct **possibly** ADVERB

**post** NOUN ❶ The post is the system by which letters and parcels are collected and delivered ❷ a job or official position in an organization ❸ a strong upright pole fixed into the ground ✿ VERB ❹ If you post a letter, you send it to someone by putting it into a postbox

**postage** NOUN Postage is the money that you pay to send letters and parcels by post

**postbox**, postboxes NOUN a metal box with a hole in it which you put letters into for collection by the postman

**postcard** NOUN a card, often with a picture on one side, which you write on and send without an envelope

**postcode** NOUN a short sequence of letters and numbers at the end of an address which helps the post office to sort the mail

**poster** NOUN a large notice or picture that is stuck on a wall as an advertisement or for decoration

**postman**, postmen NOUN someone who collects and delivers letters and parcels sent by post

**post office** NOUN ❶ The Post Office is the national organization responsible for postal services ❷ a building where you can buy stamps and post letters

**postpone**, postpones, postponing, postponed VERB If you postpone an event, you arrange for it to take place at a later time than was originally planned

**pot**, pots NOUN a deep round container; also used to refer to its contents

**potato**, potatoes NOUN a white vegetable that has a brown or red skin and grows underground

**potential** ADJECTIVE ❶ capable of becoming the thing mentioned ✿ NOUN ❷ Your potential is your ability to achieve success in the future **potentially** ADVERB

**how English works**

Hello Kitty…

knows that the **possessive** shows that something belongs to a person or thing.

# pottery – preface

**pottery** NOUN Pottery is pots, dishes, and items made from clay and fired in a kiln

**poultry** NOUN Chickens, turkeys, and other birds kept for their meat or eggs are referred to as poultry

**pounce**, pounces, pouncing, pounced VERB If an animal or person pounces on something, they leap and grab it

**pound** NOUN ❶ The pound is the main unit of currency in Britain and in some other countries ❷ a unit of weight equal to 16 ounces or about 0.454 kilograms ✿ VERB ❸ If you pound something, you hit it repeatedly with your fist ❹ If your heart is pounding, it is beating very strongly and quickly

**pour** VERB ❶ If you pour a liquid out of a container, you make it flow out by tipping the container ❷ If something pours somewhere, it flows there quickly and in large quantities ❸ When it is raining heavily, you can say that it is pouring

**poverty** NOUN the state of being very poor

**powder** NOUN Powder consists of many tiny particles of a solid substance

**power** NOUN ❶ Someone who has power has a lot of control over people and activities ❷ Someone who has the power to do something has the ability to do it ❸ Power is also the authority to do something ❹ Power is energy obtained, for example, by burning fuel or using the wind or waves

**powerful** ADJECTIVE ❶ able to control people and events ❷ having great physical strength ❸ having a strong effect

**powerless** ADJECTIVE unable to control or influence events

**practical** ADJECTIVE ❶ The practical aspects of something are those that involve experience and real situations rather than ideas or theories ❷ sensible and likely to be effective ❸ Someone who is practical is able to deal effectively with problems

**practically** ADVERB ❶ almost but not completely or exactly ❷ in a practical way

**practice** NOUN ❶ You can refer to something that people do regularly as a practice ❷ Practice is regular training or exercise ❸ A doctor's or lawyer's practice is his or her business

**practise**, practises, practising, practised VERB ❶ If you practise something, you do it regularly in order to improve ❷ People who practise a religion, custom, or craft regularly take part in the activities associated with it ❸ Someone who practises medicine or law works as a doctor or lawyer

**praise**, praises, praising, praised VERB ❶ If you praise someone or something, you express strong approval of their qualities or achievements ✿ NOUN ❷ Praise is what is said or written in approval of someone's qualities or achievements

**pram** NOUN a baby's cot on wheels

**prawn** NOUN a small, pink, edible shellfish with a long tail

**pray** VERB When someone prays, they speak to God to give thanks or to ask for help

**prayer** NOUN ❶ Prayer is the activity of praying ❷ the words said when someone prays

**precaution** NOUN an action that is intended to prevent something from happening

**precede**, precedes, preceding, preceded VERB ❶ Something that precedes another thing happens or occurs before it ❷ If you precede someone somewhere, you go in front of them

**precious** ADJECTIVE Something that is precious is valuable or very important and should be looked after or used carefully

**precise** ADJECTIVE exact and accurate in every detail **precisely** ADVERB **precision** NOUN

**predator** [*pred-dat-tor*] NOUN an animal that kills and eats other animals

**predict** VERB If someone predicts an event, they say that it will happen in the future

**prediction** NOUN something that is forecast in advance

**preface** [*pref-fiss*] NOUN an introduction at the beginning of a book explaining what the book is about or why it was written

---

**don't mix up**

**Practice** is the noun and **practise** is the verb.

**prefer**, prefers, preferring, preferred VERB If you prefer one thing to another, you like it better than the other thing **preferable** ADJECTIVE **preferably** ADVERB

**preference** [pref-fer-enss] NOUN If you have a preference for something, you like it more than other things

**prefix**, prefixes NOUN a letter or group of letters added to the beginning of a word to make a new word, for example 'semi-', 'pre-', and 'un-'

**pregnant** ADJECTIVE A woman who is pregnant has a baby developing in her womb **pregnancy** NOUN

**prejudice**, prejudices NOUN ❶ Prejudice is an unfair dislike or preference formed without carefully examining the facts ❷ Prejudice is a dislike of certain people or groups **prejudiced** ADJECTIVE

**preliminary** ADJECTIVE Preliminary activities take place before something starts

**premature** ADJECTIVE happening too early, or earlier than expected

**prepare**, prepares, preparing, prepared VERB If you prepare something, you make it ready for a particular purpose **preparation** NOUN

**prepared** ADJECTIVE If you are prepared to do something, you are willing to do it

**preposition** NOUN a word such as 'by', 'for', 'into', or 'with', which usually has a noun as its object

### how English works

A **preposition** shows the relation between things, like *on* or *into*.

**prescribe**, prescribes, prescribing, prescribed VERB When a doctor prescribes treatment, he or she states what treatment a patient should have

**prescription** NOUN a piece of paper on which the doctor has written the name of a medicine needed by a patient

**presence** NOUN ❶ Someone's presence in a place is the fact of their being there ❷ If you are in someone's presence, you are in the same place as they are

**present** ADJECTIVE [prez-ent] ❶ If someone is present somewhere, they are there ❷ A present situation is one that exists now rather than in the past or the future ❸ The present tense of a verb is the form used to express something that is happening in the present ❀ NOUN [prez-ent] ❹ The present is the period of time that is taking place now ❺ something that you give to someone for them to keep ❀ VERB [pri-zent] ❻ If you present someone with something, you give it to them

### how English works

The **present tense** shows that something is happening now, like *I am here*.

**presentation** NOUN ❶ the act of presenting or a way of presenting something ❷ To give a presentation is to give a talk on to an audience on something you have been studying or working on

**preservative** NOUN a substance or chemical that stops things decaying

**preserve**, preserves, preserving, preserved VERB ❶ If you preserve something, you take action so that it remains as it is ❷ If you preserve food, you treat it to prevent it from decaying **preservation** NOUN

**preside**, presides, presiding, presided VERB A person who presides over a formal event is in charge of it

**president** NOUN ❶ In a country which has no king or queen, the president is the elected leader ❷ The president of an organization is the person who has the highest position **presidency** NOUN **presidential** ADJECTIVE

**press**, presses, pressing, pressed VERB ❶ If you press something, you push it or hold it

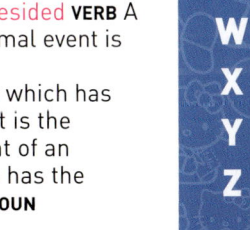

**pressure - prisoner**

firmly against something else ❁ NOUN ❷ Newspapers and the journalists who work for them are called the press

**pressure**, pressures, pressuring, pressured NOUN ❶ Pressure is the force that is produced by pushing on something ❁ VERB ❷ If you pressure someone, you try hard to persuade them to do something

**presumably** ADVERB If you say that something is presumably the case, you mean you assume that it is

**presume**, presumes, presuming, presumed [priz-**yoom**] VERB If you presume something, you think that it is the case although you have no proof

**pretend** VERB If you pretend that something is the case, you try to make people believe that it is, although in fact it is not

**pretty**, prettier, prettiest ADJECTIVE ❶ attractive in a delicate way ❁ ADVERB ❷ INFORMAL quite or rather

**prevent** VERB If you prevent something, you stop it from happening or being done **prevention** NOUN

**previous** ADJECTIVE happening or existing before something else in time or position **previously** ADVERB

**prey** [rhymes with **say**] NOUN ❶ The creatures that an animal hunts and eats are called its prey ❁ VERB ❷ An animal that preys on a particular kind of animal lives by hunting and eating it

**price**, prices, pricing, priced NOUN ❶ The price of something is the amount of money you have to pay to buy it ❁ VERB ❷ To price something at a particular amount is to fix its price at that amount

**priceless** ADJECTIVE Something that is priceless is so valuable that it is difficult to work out how much it is worth

**prick** VERB ❶ If you prick something, you stick a sharp pointed object into it ❁ NOUN ❷ a small, sharp pain caused when something pricks you

**pride**, prides, priding, prided NOUN ❶ Pride is a feeling of satisfaction you have when you have done something well ❷ Pride is also a feeling of being better than other people ❸ A pride of lions is a group of them ❁ VERB ❹ If you pride yourself on a quality or skill, you are proud of it

**priest** NOUN a member of the clergy in some Christian churches

**primarily** ADVERB You use 'primarily' to indicate the main or most important feature of something

**primary** ADJECTIVE 'Primary' is used to describe something that is extremely important for someone or something

**primary colour** NOUN In art, the primary colours are red, yellow, and blue, from which other colours can be obtained by mixing

**primary school** NOUN a school for children aged up to 11

**prime minister** NOUN The prime minister is the leader of the government

**primitive** ADJECTIVE ❶ connected with a society that lives very simply without industries or a writing system ❷ very simple, basic, or old-fashioned

**prince** NOUN a male member of a royal family, especially the son of a king or queen

**princess**, princesses NOUN a female member of a royal family, usually the daughter of a king or queen, or the wife of a prince

**principal** ADJECTIVE ❶ main or most important ❁ NOUN ❷ the person in charge of a school or college

**principle** NOUN ❶ a belief you have about the way you should behave ❷ a general rule or scientific law which explains how something happens or works

**print** VERB ❶ To print a newspaper or book is to reproduce it in large quantities using a mechanical or electronic copying process ❷ If you print when you are writing, you do not join the letters together ❁ NOUN ❸ a photograph, or a printed copy of a painting **printer** NOUN

**print-out** NOUN a printed copy of information from a computer

**prior** ADJECTIVE ❶ planned or done at an earlier time ❁ PHRASE ❷ Something that happens **prior to** a particular time or event happens before it ❁ NOUN ❸ a monk in charge of a small group of monks in a priory

**priority**, priorities NOUN something that needs to be dealt with first

**prison** NOUN a building where criminals are kept in captivity

**prisoner** NOUN someone who is kept in prison or held in captivity against their will

## private – program

**private** ADJECTIVE ❶ for the use of just one person rather than people in general ❷ taking place between a small number of people and kept secret from others ❸ owned or run by individuals or companies rather than by the state ✿ NOUN ❹ a soldier of the lowest rank **privacy** NOUN **privately** ADVERB

**privilege** NOUN a special right or advantage given to a person or group **privileged** ADJECTIVE

**prize**, prizes, prizing, prized NOUN ❶ a reward given to the winner of a competition or game ✿ ADJECTIVE ❷ of the highest quality or standard ✿ VERB ❸ Something that is prized is wanted and admired for its value or quality

**probability**, probabilities NOUN ❶ The probability of something happening is how likely it is to happen ❷ If something is a probability, it is likely to happen

**probable** ADJECTIVE Something that is probable is likely to be true or correct, or likely to happen

**probably** ADVERB Something that is probably the case is likely but not certain

**problem** NOUN ❶ an unsatisfactory situation that causes difficulties ❷ a puzzle or question that you solve using logical thought or mathematics

**procedure** NOUN a way of doing something, especially the correct or usual way

**proceed** VERB If you proceed to do something, you start doing it, or continue doing it

**process**, processes, processing, processed NOUN ❶ a series of actions intended to achieve a particular result or change ✿ PHRASE ❷ If you are **in the process** of doing something, you have started doing it but have not yet finished ✿ VERB ❸ When something such as food or information is processed, it is treated or dealt with

**procession** NOUN a group of people or vehicles moving in a line, often as part of a ceremony

**processor** NOUN In computing, a processor is the central chip in a computer which controls its operations

**produce**, produces, producing, produced VERB ❶ To produce something is to make it or cause it ❷ If you produce something from somewhere, you bring it out so it can be seen ✿ NOUN ❸ Produce is food that is grown to be sold

**producer** NOUN The producer of a record, film, or show is the person in charge of making it or putting it on

**product** NOUN ❶ something that is made to be sold ❷ The product of two or more numbers or quantities is the result of multiplying them together

**production** NOUN ❶ Production is the process of manufacturing or growing something in large quantities ❷ Production is also the amount of goods manufactured or food grown by a country or company

**productive** ADJECTIVE ❶ To be productive means to produce a large number of things ❷ If something such as a meeting is productive, good or useful things happen as a result of it

**profession** NOUN ❶ a type of job that requires advanced education or training ❷ You can use 'profession' to refer to all the people who have a particular profession

**professional** ADJECTIVE ❶ Professional means relating to the work of someone who is qualified in a particular profession ❷ Professional also describes activities when they are done to earn money rather than as a hobby ❸ A professional piece of work is of a very high standard ✿ NOUN ❹ a person who has been trained in a profession ❺ someone who plays a sport to earn money rather than as a hobby

**professor** NOUN the senior teacher in a department of a British university

**profile** NOUN ❶ Your profile is the outline of your face seen from the side ❷ A profile of someone is a short description of their life and character

**profit**, profits, profiting, profited NOUN ❶ When someone sells something, the profit is the amount they gain by selling it for more than it cost them to buy or make ✿ VERB ❷ If you profit from something, you gain or benefit from it **profitable** ADJECTIVE

**program**, programs, programming, programmed NOUN ❶ a set of instructions that a computer follows to perform a particular

# programme - proof

task ✿ VERB ❷ When someone programs a computer, they write a program and put it into the computer  **programmer** NOUN

**programme** NOUN ❶ a planned series of events ❷ a particular piece presented as a unit on television or radio, such as a play, show, or discussion ❸ a booklet giving information about a play, concert, or show that you are attending

**progress**, progresses, progressing, progressed NOUN ❶ Progress is the process of gradually improving or getting near to achieving something ❷ The progress of something is the way in which it develops or continues ✿ PHRASE ❸ Something that is **in progress** is happening ✿ VERB ❹ If you progress, you become more advanced or skilful ❺ To progress is to continue

**prohibit**, prohibits, prohibiting, prohibited VERB If someone prohibits something, they forbid it or make it illegal

**project** NOUN ❶ a carefully planned attempt to achieve something or to study something over a period of time ✿ VERB ❷ Something that is projected is planned or expected to happen in the future ❸ To project an image onto a screen is to make it appear there using equipment such as a projector ❹ Something that projects sticks out beyond a surface or edge

**projector** NOUN a piece of equipment which produces a large image on a screen by shining light through a photographic slide or film strip

**prologue** NOUN a speech or section that introduces a play or book

**prolong** VERB If you prolong something, you make it last longer

**prominent** ADJECTIVE ❶ Prominent people are important ❷ Something that is prominent is very noticeable

**promise**, promises, promising, promised VERB ❶ If you promise to do something, you say that you will definitely do it ❷ Something that promises to have a particular quality shows signs that it will have that quality ✿ NOUN ❸ a statement made by someone that they will definitely do something ❹ Someone or something that shows promise seems likely to be very successful

**promote**, promotes, promoting, promoted VERB ❶ If someone promotes something, they try to make it happen ❷ If someone promotes a product such as a film or a book, they try to make it popular by advertising ❸ If someone is promoted, they are given a more important job at work  **promotion** NOUN

**prompt** VERB ❶ If something prompts someone to do something, it makes them decide to do it ❷ If you prompt someone when they stop speaking, you tell them what to say next or encourage them to continue ✿ ADVERB ❸ exactly at the time mentioned ✿ ADJECTIVE ❹ A prompt action is done without any delay  **promptly** ADVERB

**pronoun** NOUN In grammar, a pronoun is a word that is used to replace a noun. 'He', 'she', and 'them' are all pronouns

## how English works

### Hello Kitty...

knows that a **pronoun** is a word that stands in for a noun, like *she* or *his*.

**pronounce**, pronounces, pronouncing, pronounced VERB When you pronounce a word, you say it

**pronunciation** [pron-nun-see-**ay**-shn] NOUN the way a word is usually said

**proof** NOUN If you have proof of something, you have evidence which shows that it is true or exists

208

**propaganda – provoke**

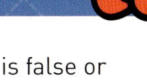

**propaganda** NOUN Propaganda is false or exaggerated information that is meant to influence people

**propeller** NOUN a device on a boat or aircraft with rotating blades which make the boat or aircraft move

**proper** ADJECTIVE ❶ real and satisfactory ❷ correct or suitable ❸ accepted or conventional

**proper noun** NOUN the name of a person, place, or institution

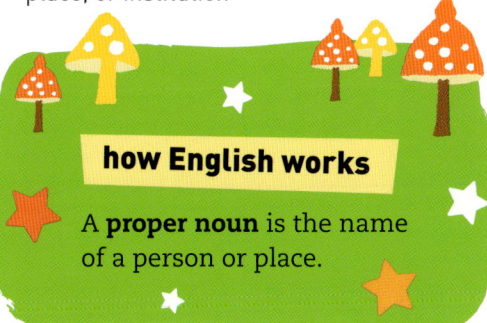

### how English works

A **proper noun** is the name of a person or place.

**property**, properties NOUN ❶ A person's property is the things that belong to them ❷ a building and the land belonging to it

**proportion** NOUN ❶ A proportion of an amount or group is a part of it ❷ The proportion of one amount to another is its size in comparison with the other amount

**proposal** NOUN a plan that has been suggested

**propose**, proposes, proposing, proposed VERB ❶ If you propose a plan or idea, you suggest it ❷ If you propose to do something, you intend to do it ❸ If someone proposes to another person, they ask that person to marry them

**prose** NOUN Prose is ordinary written language in contrast to poetry

**prosecute**, prosecutes, prosecuting, prosecuted VERB If someone is prosecuted, they are charged with a crime and have to stand trial

**prosecution** NOUN The lawyers who try to prove that a person on trial is guilty are called the prosecution

**protect** VERB To protect someone or something is to prevent them from being harmed or damaged **protection** NOUN **protective** ADJECTIVE **protector** NOUN

**protection** NOUN ❶ the act of preventing harm or damage ❷ something that keeps a person or thing safe

**protein** NOUN Protein is a substance that is found in meat, eggs, and milk and that is needed by bodies for growth

**protest** VERB ❶ If you protest about something, you say or demonstrate publicly that you disagree with it ✿ NOUN ❷ a demonstration or statement showing that you disagree with something

**Protestant** NOUN OR ADJECTIVE a member of one of the Christian churches which separated from the Catholic Church in the sixteenth century

**protractor** NOUN a flat, semicircular piece of plastic used for measuring angles

**proud** ADJECTIVE ❶ feeling pleasure and satisfaction at something you own or have achieved ❷ having great dignity and self-respect **proudly** ADVERB

**prove**, proves, proving, proved or proven VERB To prove that something is true is to provide evidence that it is definitely true

**proverb** NOUN a short sentence which gives advice or makes a comment about life

**provide**, provides, providing, provided VERB ❶ If you provide something for someone, you give it to them or make it available for them ❷ If you provide for someone, you give them the things they need

**provided** or **providing** CONJUNCTION If you say that something will happen provided or providing something else happens, you mean that the first thing will happen only if the second thing does

**province** NOUN one of the areas into which some large countries are divided, each province having its own administration

**provision** NOUN ❶ The provision of something is the act of making it available to people ❷ IN PLURAL Provisions are supplies of food

**provisional** ADJECTIVE A provisional arrangement has not yet been made definite and so might be changed

**provoke**, provokes, provoking, provoked VERB ❶ If you provoke someone, you deliberately

A B C D E F G H I J K L M N O P Q R S T U V W X Y Z

# prune - punishment

try to make them angry ❷ If something provokes an unpleasant reaction, it causes it

**prune**, prunes, pruning, pruned NOUN ❶ a dried plum ✿ VERB ❷ When someone prunes a tree or shrub, they cut back some of the branches

**PS** PS is written before an additional message at the end of a letter. PS is an abbreviation for 'postscript'

**psychology** NOUN Psychology is the scientific study of the mind and of the reasons for people's behaviour  **psychological** ADJECTIVE  **psychologist** NOUN

**pub** NOUN a building where people go to buy and drink alcoholic or soft drinks and meet their friends

**public** NOUN ❶ You can refer to people in general as the public ✿ ADJECTIVE ❷ relating to people in general ❸ provided for everyone to use, or open to anyone

**publication** NOUN ❶ The publication of a book is the act of printing it and making it available ❷ a book or magazine

**publicity** NOUN Publicity is information or advertisements about an item or event

**publicize**, publicizes, publicizing, publicized (also **publicise**) VERB When someone publicizes a fact or event, they advertise it and make it widely known

**public school** NOUN In Britain, a public school is a school that is privately run and that charges fees for the pupils to attend

**publish**, publishes, publishing, published VERB When a company publishes a book, newspaper, or magazine, they print copies of it and distribute it

**publisher** NOUN The publisher of a book, newspaper, or magazine is the person or company that prints and distributes it

**pudding** NOUN ❶ a sweet cake mixture cooked with fruit or other flavouring and served hot ❷ You can refer to the sweet course of a meal as the pudding

**puddle** NOUN a small shallow pool of liquid

**puff** VERB ❶ To puff a cigarette or pipe is to smoke it ❷ If you are puffing, you are breathing loudly and quickly with your mouth open ❸ If something puffs out or puffs up, it swells and becomes larger and rounder ✿ NOUN ❹ a small amount of air or smoke that is released

**pull** VERB ❶ When you pull something, you hold it and move it towards you ❷ When something is pulled by a vehicle or animal, it is attached to it and moves along behind it ❸ When you pull a curtain or blind, you move it so that it covers or uncovers the window ❹ If you pull a muscle, you injure it by stretching it too far or too quickly

**pull out** ✿ VERB If you pull out of something, you decide not to continue with it

**pull through** ✿ VERB When someone pulls through, they recover from a serious illness

**pullover** NOUN a woollen piece of clothing that covers the top part of your body

**pulse**, pulses, pulsing, pulsed NOUN ❶ Your pulse is the regular beating of blood through your body, the rate of which you can feel at your wrists and elsewhere ❷ The seeds of beans, peas, and lentils are called pulses when they are used for food ✿ VERB ❸ If something is pulsing, it is moving or vibrating with rhythmic, regular movements

**pump** NOUN ❶ a machine that is used to force a liquid or gas to move in a particular direction ✿ VERB ❷ To pump a liquid or gas somewhere is to force it to flow in that direction, using a pump

**pumpkin** NOUN a very large, round, orange fruit eaten as a vegetable

**pun** NOUN a clever and amusing use of words so that what you say has two different meanings, such as *my dog's a champion boxer*

**punch**, punches, punching, punched VERB ❶ If you punch someone, you hit them hard with your fist ✿ NOUN ❷ a hard blow with the fist

**punctual** ADJECTIVE arriving at the correct time  **punctually** ADVERB

**punctuation** NOUN The marks in writing such as full stops, question marks, and commas are called punctuation or punctuation marks

**puncture**, punctures, puncturing, punctured NOUN ❶ If a tyre has a puncture, a small hole has been made in it and it has become flat ✿ VERB ❷ To puncture something is to make a small hole in it

**punish**, punishes, punishing, punished VERB To punish someone who has done something wrong is to make them suffer because of it

**punishment** NOUN something unpleasant done to someone because they have done something wrong

## pup – python

**pup** NOUN a young dog. Some other young animals such as seals are also called pups

**pupil** NOUN ❶ The pupils at a school are the children who go there ❷ Your pupils are the small, round, black holes in the centre of your eyes

**puppet** NOUN a doll or toy animal that is moved by pulling strings or by putting your hand inside its body

**puppy**, puppies NOUN a young dog

**purchase**, purchases, purchasing, purchased VERB ❶ When you purchase something, you buy it ✿ NOUN ❷ something you have bought

**pure**, purer, purest ADJECTIVE ❶ Something that is pure is not mixed with anything else ❷ Pure also means clean and free from harmful substances ❸ Pure also means complete and total

**purely** ADVERB involving only one feature and not including anything else

**purple** NOUN OR ADJECTIVE reddish-blue

**purpose** NOUN ❶ The purpose of something is the reason for it ❷ If you have a particular purpose, this is what you want to achieve ✿ PHRASE ❸ If you do something **on purpose**, you do it deliberately

**purr**, purrs, purring, purred VERB When a cat purrs, it makes a low vibrating sound because it is contented

**purse**, purses, pursing, pursed NOUN ❶ a small leather or fabric container for carrying money ✿ VERB ❷ If you purse your lips, you move them into a tight, rounded shape

**pursue**, pursues, pursuing, pursued VERB ❶ If you pursue an activity or plan, you do it or make efforts to achieve it ❷ If you pursue someone, you follow them to try to catch them **pursuit** NOUN

**push**, pushes, pushing, pushed VERB When you push something, you press it using force in order to move it

**push off** ✿ VERB INFORMAL If you tell someone to push off, you are telling them rudely to go away

**pushchair** NOUN a small folding chair on wheels in which a baby or toddler can be wheeled around

**put**, puts, putting, put VERB ❶ When you put something somewhere, you move it into that place or position ❷ If you put an idea or remark in a particular way, you express it that way ❸ To put someone or something in a particular state or situation means to cause them to be in it

**put down** ✿ VERB ❶ To put someone down is to criticize them and make them appear foolish ❷ If an animal is put down, it is killed because it is very ill or dangerous

**put off** ✿ VERB ❶ If you put something off, you delay doing it ❷ To put someone off is to discourage them

**put out** ✿ VERB If you put a fire out or put the light out, you make it stop burning or shining

**put up** ✿ VERB If you put up resistance to something, you argue or fight against it

**put up with** ✿ VERB If you put up with something, you tolerate it even though you disagree with it or dislike it

**puzzle**, puzzles, puzzling, puzzled VERB ❶ If something puzzles you, it confuses you and you do not understand it ✿ NOUN ❷ A puzzle is a game or question that requires a lot of thought to solve **puzzled** ADJECTIVE

**pyjamas** PLURAL NOUN Pyjamas are loose trousers and a top that you wear in bed

**pyramid** NOUN a three-dimensional shape with a flat base and flat triangular sides sloping upwards to a point

**python** NOUN a large snake that kills animals by squeezing them with its body

---

### punctuation

### Helpful hints...

**Punctuation** is the set of marks that help to make writing understandable.

---

A B C D E F G H I J K L M N O **P** Q R S T U V W X Y Z

211

# quack - query

**quack** VERB When a duck quacks, it makes a loud harsh sound

**qualification** NOUN ❶ Your qualifications are your skills and achievements, especially as officially recognized at the end of a course of training or study ❷ something you add to a statement to make it less strong

**qualify**, qualifies, qualifying, qualified VERB ❶ When you qualify, you pass the examinations or tests that you need to pass to do a particular job or to take part in a sporting event ❷ If you qualify a statement, you add a detail or explanation to make it less strong ❸ If you qualify for something, you become entitled to have it **qualified** ADJECTIVE

### don't mix up

## Hello Kitty...

never mixes up **quay** (the place where boats are tied) and **key** (the object that unlocks doors).

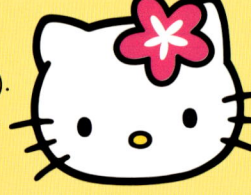

**quality**, qualities NOUN ❶ The quality of something is how good it is ❷ A quality is a characteristic

**quantity**, quantities NOUN ❶ an amount you can measure or count ❷ Quantity is the amount of something that there is

**quarrel**, quarrels, quarrelling, quarrelled NOUN ❶ an angry argument ✿ VERB ❷ If people quarrel, they have an angry argument

**quarry**, quarries, quarrying, quarried [*kwor-ree*] NOUN ❶ a place where stone is removed from the ground by digging or blasting ❷ A person's or animal's quarry is the animal that they are hunting

**quarter** NOUN ❶ one of four equal parts ❷ an American coin worth 25 cents ❸ You can refer to a particular area in a city as a quarter ❹ You can use 'quarter' to refer vaguely to a particular person or group of people ❺ IN PLURAL A soldier's or a servant's quarters are the rooms that they live in

**quartet** [*kwor-tet*] NOUN a group of four musicians who sing or play together; also a piece of music written for four instruments or singers

**quay** [*kee*] NOUN a place where boats are tied up and loaded or unloaded

**queen** NOUN ❶ a female monarch or a woman married to a king ❷ a female bee or ant which can lay eggs ❸ In chess, the queen is the most powerful piece, which can move in any direction ❹ In a pack of cards, a queen is a card with a picture of a queen on it

**query**, queries, querying, queried [*qweer-ree*] NOUN ❶ a question ✿ VERB ❷ If you

212

**question - quote**

query something, you ask about it because you think it might not be right
**question** NOUN ❶ a sentence which asks for information ❷ If there is some question about something, there is doubt about it ❸ a problem that needs to be discussed ❀ VERB ❹ If you question someone, you ask them questions ❺ If you question something, you express doubts about it ❀ PHRASE ❻ If something is **out of the question**, it is impossible

### punctuation

**Hello Kitty...**

knows that you put a **question mark** (?) at the end of a sentence or phrase to show that a question is being asked.

**question mark** NOUN the punctuation mark (?) which is used at the end of a question
**questionnaire** NOUN a list of questions which asks for information for a survey
**queue**, queues, queuing or queueing, queued [kyoo] NOUN ❶ a line of people or vehicles waiting for something ❀ VERB ❷ When people queue, they stand in a line waiting for something
**quick** ADJECTIVE ❶ moving with great speed ❷ lasting only a short time ❸ happening without any delay ❹ intelligent and able to understand things easily
**quickly** ADVERB with great speed

**quiet** ADJECTIVE ❶ Someone or something that is quiet makes very little noise or no noise at all ❷ Quiet also means peaceful ❸ A quiet event happens with very little fuss or publicity ❀ NOUN ❹ Quiet is silence
**quietly** ADVERB
**quilt** NOUN A quilt is a cover for a bed, especially one that is padded
**quit**, quits, quitting, quit VERB If you quit something, you leave it or stop doing it
**quite** ADVERB ❶ fairly but not very ❷ completely ❀ PHRASE ❸ You use **quite a** to emphasize that something is large or impressive
**quiz**, quizzes, quizzing, quizzed NOUN ❶ a game in which the competitors are asked questions to test their knowledge ❀ VERB ❷ If you quiz someone, you question them closely about something
**quotation** NOUN an extract from a book or speech which is quoted
**quote**, quotes, quoting, quoted VERB ❶ If you quote something that someone has written or said, you repeat their exact words ❷ If you quote a fact, you state it because it supports what you are saying ❀ NOUN ❸ an extract from a book or speech ❹ an estimate of how much a piece of work will cost

### remember

**Queuing** and **queueing** are both correct spellings but **queuing** is used more often.

rabbi - radius

**rabbi**, rabbis [*rab-by*] NOUN a Jewish religious leader

**rabbit** NOUN a small animal with long ears

**race**, races, racing, raced NOUN ❶ a competition to see who is fastest, for example in running or driving ❷ one of the major groups that human beings can be divided into according to their physical features ✿ VERB ❸ If you race someone, you compete with them in a race ❹ If you race something or if it races, it goes at its greatest rate ❺ If you race somewhere, you go there as quickly as possible **racing** NOUN

**racecourse** NOUN a grass track, sometimes with jumps, along which horses race

**racial** ADJECTIVE relating to the different races that people belong to **racially** ADVERB

**racism** or **racialism** NOUN Racism or racialism is the treatment of some people as inferior because of their race **racist** NOUN OR ADJECTIVE

**rack** NOUN ❶ a piece of equipment for holding things or hanging things on ✿ VERB ❷ If you are racked by something, you suffer because of it

**racket** NOUN ❶ If someone is making a racket, they are making a lot of noise ❷ an illegal way of making money ❸ Racket is another spelling of **racquet**

**racquet** or **racket** NOUN a bat with strings across it used in tennis and similar games

**radar** NOUN Radar is equipment used to track ships or aircraft that are out of sight by using radio signals that are reflected back from the object and shown on a screen

**radiation** NOUN the stream of particles given out by a radioactive substance

**radiator** NOUN ❶ a hollow metal device for heating a room, usually connected to a central heating system ❷ the part of a car that is filled with water to cool the engine

**radio**, radios, radioing, radioed NOUN ❶ Radio is a system of sending sound over a distance by transmitting electrical signals ❷ Radio is also the broadcasting of programmes to the public by radio ❸ a piece of equipment for listening to radio programmes ✿ VERB ❹ To radio someone means to send them a message by radio

**radius**, radii NOUN The radius of a circle is the length of a straight line drawn from its centre to its circumference

*Hello Kitty...* knows that some words that sound as if they begin with *r* actually begin with *wr*, like *write*, or with *rh*, like *rhino*.

# raffle – ransom

**raffle** NOUN a competition in which people buy numbered tickets and win a prize if they have the ticket that is chosen

**raft** NOUN a floating platform made from long pieces of wood tied together

**rag** NOUN ❶ a piece of old cloth used to clean or wipe things ❷ If someone is dressed in rags, they are wearing old torn clothes

**rage**, rages, raging, raged NOUN ❶ Rage is great anger ✿ VERB ❷ To rage about something means to speak angrily about it ❸ If something such as a storm or battle is raging, it is continuing with great force or violence

**ragged** ADJECTIVE Ragged clothes are old and torn

**raid** VERB ❶ To raid a place means to enter it by force to attack it or steal something ✿ NOUN ❷ the raiding of a building or a place

**rail** NOUN ❶ a fixed horizontal bar used as a support or for hanging things on ❷ Rails are the steel bars which trains run along ❸ Rail is the railway considered as a means of transport

**railing** NOUN Railings are a fence made from metal bars

**railway** NOUN a route along which trains travel on steel rails

**rain** NOUN ❶ water falling from the clouds in small drops ✿ VERB ❷ When it is raining, rain is falling **rainy** ADJECTIVE

**rainbow** NOUN an arch of different colours that sometimes appears in the sky after it has been raining

**raincoat** NOUN a waterproof coat

**rainfall** NOUN the amount of rain that falls in a place during a particular period

**rainforest** NOUN a dense forest of tall trees in a tropical area where there is a lot of rain

**raise**, raises, raising, raised VERB ❶ If you raise something, you make it higher ❷ If you raise your voice, you speak more loudly ❸ To raise money for a cause means to get people to donate money towards it ❹ To raise a child means to look after it until it is grown up ❺ If you raise a subject, you mention it

**raisin** NOUN Raisins are dried grapes

**rake**, rakes, raking, raked NOUN ❶ a garden tool with a row of metal teeth and a long handle

**rake up** ✿ VERB If you rake up something embarrassing from the past, you remind someone about it

**rally**, rallies, rallying, rallied NOUN ❶ a large public meeting held to show support for something ❷ a competition in which vehicles are raced over public roads ❸ In tennis or squash, a rally is a continuous series of shots exchanged by the players ✿ VERB ❹ When people rally to something, they gather together to continue a struggle or to support something

**ram**, rams, ramming, rammed VERB ❶ If one vehicle rams another, it crashes into it ❷ To ram something somewhere means to push it there firmly ✿ NOUN ❸ an adult male sheep

**RAM** NOUN a storage space which can be filled with data but which loses its contents when the machine is switched off. RAM stands for 'random access memory'

**ramp** NOUN a sloping surface connecting two different levels

**ranch**, ranches NOUN a large farm where cattle or horses are reared, especially in the USA

**random** ADJECTIVE ❶ A random choice or arrangement is not based on any definite plan ✿ PHRASE ❷ If you do something **at random**, you do it without any definite plan

**range**, ranges, ranging, ranged NOUN ❶ The range of something is the maximum distance over which it can reach things or detect things ❷ a number of different things of the same kind ❸ a set of values on a scale ❹ A range of mountains is a line of them ❺ A rifle range or firing range is a place where people practise shooting at targets ✿ VERB ❻ When a set of things ranges between two points, they vary within these points on a scale

**rank** NOUN ❶ Someone's rank is their official level in a job or profession ❷ The ranks are the ordinary members of the armed forces, rather than the officers ❸ The ranks of a group are its members ❹ a row of people or things ✿ VERB ❺ To rank as something means to have that status or position on a scale ✿ ADJECTIVE ❻ complete and absolute ❼ having a strong, unpleasant smell

**ransom** NOUN money that is demanded to free someone who has been kidnapped

**rap – read**

**rap**, raps, rapping, rapped VERB ❶ If you rap something, you hit it with a series of quick blows ❋ NOUN ❷ a quick knock or blow on something ❸ Rap is a style of poetry spoken to music with a strong rhythmic beat

**rape**, rapes, raping, raped VERB ❶ If a man rapes a woman, he violently forces her to have sex with him against her will ❋ NOUN ❷ Rape is the act or crime of raping a woman **rapist** NOUN

**rapid** ADJECTIVE happening or moving very quickly **rapidly** ADVERB

**rare** ADJECTIVE ❶ Something that is rare is not common or does not happen often ❷ Rare meat has been lightly cooked **rarely** ADVERB

**rash** ADJECTIVE ❶ If you are rash, you do something hasty and foolish ❋ NOUN ❷ an area of red spots that appear on your skin when you are ill or have an allergy ❸ A rash of events is a lot of them happening in a short time

**raspberry**, raspberries NOUN a small soft red fruit that grows on a bush

**rat** NOUN a long-tailed animal which looks like a large mouse

**rate**, rates, rating, rated NOUN ❶ The rate of something is the speed or frequency with which it happens ❷ The rate of interest is its level ❸ the cost or charge for something ❋ VERB ❹ The way you rate someone or something is your opinion of them

**rather** ADVERB ❶ Rather means to a certain extent ❋ PHRASE ❷ If you **would rather** do a particular thing, you would prefer to do it ❸ If you do one thing **rather than** another, you choose to do the first thing instead of the second

**ratio**, ratios NOUN a relationship which shows how many times one thing is bigger than another

**ration** NOUN ❶ Your ration of something is the amount you are allowed to have ❷ Rations are the food given each day to a soldier or member of an expedition ❋ VERB ❸ When something is rationed, you are only allowed a limited amount of it, because there is a shortage

**rational** ADJECTIVE When people are rational, their judgments are based on reason rather than emotion **rationally** ADVERB

**rattle**, rattles, rattling, rattled VERB ❶ When something rattles, it makes short, regular knocking sounds ❷ If something rattles you, it upsets you ❋ NOUN ❸ the noise something makes when it rattles ❹ a baby's toy which makes a noise when it is shaken

**rave**, raves, raving, raved VERB ❶ If someone raves, they talk in an angry, uncontrolled way ❷ INFORMAL If you rave about something, you talk about it very enthusiastically ❋ ADJECTIVE ❸ INFORMAL If something gets a rave review, it is praised enthusiastically ❋ NOUN ❹ INFORMAL a large party with electronic dance music

**raw** ADJECTIVE ❶ Raw food has not been cooked ❷ A raw substance is in its natural state ❸ If part of your body is raw, the skin has come off or been rubbed away ❹ Someone who is raw is too young or too new in a job or situation to know how to behave

**ray** NOUN ❶ a beam of light or radiation ❷ a large sea fish with eyes on the top of its body, and a long tail

**razor** NOUN a tool that people use for shaving

**reach**, reaches, reaching, reached VERB ❶ When you reach a place, you arrive there ❷ When you reach for something, you stretch out your arm to it ❸ If something reaches a place or point, it extends as far as that place or point ❹ If something or someone reaches a stage or level, they get to it ❺ To reach an agreement or decision means to succeed in achieving it

**react** VERB ❶ When you react to something, you behave in a particular way because of it ❷ If one substance reacts with another, a chemical change takes place when they are put together

**reaction** NOUN ❶ Your reaction to something is what you feel, say, or do because of it ❷ Your reactions are your ability to move quickly in response to something that happens ❸ If there is a reaction against something, it becomes unpopular ❹ In a chemical reaction, a chemical change takes place when two substances are put together

**read**, reads, reading, read VERB ❶ When you read, you look at something written and follow it or say it aloud ❷ If you can read someone's moods or mind, you can judge

### don't mix up

**Hello Kitty...** never mixes up **read** (to look at and understand writing) and **reed** (a plant that grows in water).

what they are feeling or thinking ❸ When you read a meter or gauge, you look at it and record the figure on it
**reader** NOUN The readers of a newspaper or magazine are the people who read it regularly
**readily** ADVERB ❶ willingly and eagerly ❷ easily done or quickly obtainable
**reading** NOUN ❶ Reading is the activity of reading books ❷ The reading on a meter or gauge is the figure or measurement it shows
**ready** ADJECTIVE ❶ having reached the required stage, or prepared for action or use ❷ willing or eager to do something ❸ If you are ready for something, you need it ❹ easily produced or obtained
**real** ADJECTIVE ❶ actually existing and not imagined or invented ❷ genuine and not imitation ❸ true or actual and not mistaken
**realistic** ADJECTIVE ❶ recognizing and accepting the true nature of a situation ❷ representing things in a way that is true to real life
**reality** NOUN ❶ Reality is the real nature of things, rather than the way someone imagines it ❷ If something has become reality, it actually exists or is actually happening
**realize**, realizes, realizing, realized (also **realise**) VERB ❶ If you realize something, you become aware of it ❷ FORMAL If your hopes or fears are realized, what you hoped for or feared happens **realization** NOUN
**really** ADVERB ❶ used to add emphasis to what is being said ❷ used to indicate that you are talking about the true facts about something
**reappear** VERB When people or things reappear, you can see them again, because they have come back
**rear** NOUN ❶ The rear of something is the part at the back ✿ VERB ❷ To rear children or young animals means to bring them up until they are able to look after themselves ❸ When a horse rears, it raises the front part of its body, so that its front legs are in the air
**rearrange**, rearranges, rearranging, rearranged VERB To rearrange something means to organize or arrange it in a different way
**reason** NOUN ❶ The reason for something is the fact or situation which explains why it happens or which causes it to happen ❷ If you have reason to believe or feel something, there are definite reasons why you believe it or feel it ❸ Reason is the ability to think and make judgments ✿ VERB ❹ If you reason that something is true, you decide it is true after considering all the facts ❺ If you reason with someone, you persuade them to accept sensible arguments
**reasonable** ADJECTIVE ❶ Reasonable behaviour is fair and sensible ❷ If an explanation is reasonable, there are good reasons for thinking it is correct ❸ A reasonable amount is a fairly large amount ❹ A reasonable price is fair and not too high **reasonably** ADVERB
**reassure**, reassures, reassuring, reassured VERB If you reassure someone, you say or do things that make them less worried **reassurance** NOUN
**rebel**, rebels, rebelling, rebelled NOUN ❶ Rebels are people who are fighting their own country's army to change the political system ❷ Someone who is a rebel rejects society's values and behaves differently from other people ✿ VERB ❸ To rebel means to fight against authority and reject accepted values

217

# rebellion - rectangle

**rebellion** NOUN A rebellion is organized and often violent opposition to authority

**recall** VERB ❶ To recall something means to remember it ❷ If you are recalled to a place, you are ordered to return there ❸ If a company recalls products, it asks people to return them because they are faulty

**receipt** [ris-**seet**] NOUN ❶ a piece of paper confirming that money or goods have been received ❷ In a shop or theatre, the money received is often called the receipts

**receive**, receives, receiving, received VERB ❶ When you receive something, someone gives it to you, or you get it after it has been sent to you ❷ To receive something also means to have it happen to you ❸ When you receive visitors or guests, you welcome them ❹ If something is received in a particular way, that is how people react to it

**receiver** NOUN the part of a telephone you hold near to your ear and mouth

**recent** ADJECTIVE Something recent happened a short time ago **recently** ADVERB

**reception** NOUN ❶ In a hotel or office, reception is the place near the entrance where appointments or enquiries are dealt with ❷ a formal party ❸ The reception someone or something gets is the way people react to them ❹ If your radio or television gets good reception, the sound or picture is clear

**receptionist** NOUN The receptionist in a hotel or office deals with people when they arrive, answers the telephone, and arranges appointments

**recession** NOUN a period when a country's economy is less successful and more people become unemployed

**recipe** [res-sip-ee] NOUN a list of ingredients and instructions for cooking something

**recite**, recites, reciting, recited VERB If you recite a poem or something you have learnt, you say it aloud

**reckless** ADJECTIVE showing a complete lack of care about danger or damage

**reckon** VERB ❶ INFORMAL If you reckon that something is true, you think it is true ❷ INFORMAL If someone reckons to do something, they claim or expect to do it ❸ To reckon an amount means to calculate it ❹ If you reckon on something, you rely on it happening when making your plans ❺ If you had not reckoned with something, you had not expected it and therefore were unprepared when it happened

**recognize**, recognizes, recognizing, recognized (also **recognise**) VERB ❶ If you recognize someone or something, you realize that you know who or what they are ❷ To recognize something also means to accept and acknowledge it **recognition** NOUN

**recommend** VERB If you recommend something to someone, you praise it and suggest they try it **recommendation** NOUN

**record** NOUN ❶ If you keep a record of something, you keep a written account or store information in a computer ❷ a round, flat piece of plastic on which music has been recorded ❸ an achievement which is the best of its type ❹ Your record is what is known about your achievements or past activities ✿ VERB ❺ If you record information, you write it down or put it into a computer ❻ To record sound means to put it on tape, record, or compact disc ✿ ADJECTIVE ❼ higher, lower, better, or worse than ever before

**recorder** NOUN a small woodwind instrument

**recording** NOUN A recording of something is a record, CD, or DVD of it

**recount** VERB ❶ If you recount a story, you tell it ✿ NOUN ❷ a second count of votes in an election when the result is very close

**recover** VERB ❶ To recover from an illness or unhappy experience means to get well again or get over it ❷ If you recover a lost object or your ability to do something, you get it back

**recovery** NOUN ❶ the act of getting better again ❷ the act of getting something back

**recreation** [rek-kree-**ay**-shn] NOUN Recreation is all the things that you do for enjoyment in your spare time

**recruit** VERB ❶ To recruit people means to get them to join a group or help with something ✿ NOUN ❷ someone who has joined the army or some other organization **recruitment** NOUN

**rectangle** NOUN a four-sided shape with four right angles **rectangular** ADJECTIVE

**recur**, recurs, recurring, recurred **VERB** If something recurs, it happens or occurs again

**recycle**, recycles, recycling, recycled **VERB** To recycle used products means to process them so that they can be used again

**red**, redder, reddest **NOUN OR ADJECTIVE** ❶ Red is the colour of blood or of a ripe tomato ❀ **ADJECTIVE** ❷ Red hair is between orange and brown in colour

**reduce**, reduces, reducing, reduced **VERB** ❶ To reduce something means to make it smaller in size or amount ❷ You can use 'reduce' to say that someone or something is changed to a weaker or inferior state

**reduction** **NOUN** When there is a reduction in something, it is made smaller

**redundant** **ADJECTIVE** ❶ When people are made redundant, they lose their jobs because there is no more work for them or no money to pay them ❷ When something becomes redundant, it is no longer needed

**reed** **NOUN** ❶ Reeds are hollow stemmed plants that grow in shallow water or wet ground ❷ a thin piece of cane or metal inside some wind instruments which vibrates when air is blown over it

**refer**, refers, referring, referred **VERB** ❶ If you refer to something, you mention it ❷ If you refer to a book or record, you look at it to find something out ❸ When a problem or issue is referred to someone, they are formally asked to deal with it

**referee** **NOUN** ❶ the official who controls a football game or a boxing or wrestling match ❷ someone who gives a reference to a person who is applying for a job

**reference** **NOUN** ❶ A reference to something or someone is a mention of them ❷ Reference is the act of referring to something or someone for information or advice ❸ a number or name that tells you where to find information or identifies a document ❹ If someone gives you a reference when you apply for a job, they write a letter about your abilities

**reflect** **VERB** ❶ If something reflects an attitude or situation, it shows what it is like ❷ If something reflects light or heat, the light or heat bounces off it ❸ When something is reflected in a mirror or water, you can see its image in it ❹ If something reflects, its direction is reversed ❺ When you reflect, you think about something

**reflection** **NOUN** ❶ If something is a reflection of something else, it shows what it is like ❷ an image in a mirror or water ❸ Reflection is the process by which light and heat are bounced off a surface ❹ In maths, reflection is also the turning back of something on itself ❺ Reflection is also thought

**reform** **NOUN** ❶ Reforms are major changes to laws or institutions ❀ **VERB** ❷ When laws or institutions are reformed, major changes are made to them ❸ When people reform, they stop committing crimes or doing other unacceptable things

**refresh**, refreshes, refreshing, refreshed **VERB** If something refreshes you when you are hot or tired, it makes you feel cooler or more energetic

**refreshing** **ADJECTIVE** You say that something is refreshing when it is pleasantly different from what you are used to

**refrigerator** **NOUN** an electrically cooled container in which you store food to keep it fresh

**refuge** **NOUN** ❶ a place where you go for safety ❷ If you take refuge, you go somewhere for safety or behave in a way that will protect you

**refugee** **NOUN** Refugees are people who have been forced to leave their country and live elsewhere

**refund** **NOUN** ❶ money returned to you because you have paid too much for something or because you have returned goods ❀ **VERB** ❷ To refund someone's money means to return it to them after they have paid for something with it

**refusal** **NOUN** A refusal is when someone says firmly that they will not do, allow, or accept something

**refuse**, refuses, refusing, refused [rif-yooz] **VERB** ❶ If you refuse to do something, you say or decide firmly that you will not do it ❷ If someone refuses something, they do not allow it or do not accept it

# refuse - reject

**refuse** [*ref*-yooz] NOUN Refuse is rubbish or waste

### how to say it
### Helpful hints...

**Refuse** is said *ref*-yooz when it means 'to say no' and *ref*-yoos when it means 'rubbish'.

**regard** VERB ❶ To regard someone or something in a particular way means to think of them in that way or have that opinion of them ✿ NOUN ❷ If you have a high regard for someone, you have a very good opinion of them ✿ PHRASES ❸ **Regarding**, **as regards**, **with regard to**, and **in regard to** are all used to indicate what you are talking or writing about ❹ 'Regards' is used in various expressions to express friendly feelings

**regardless** PREPOSITION OR ADVERB done or happening in spite of something else

**reggae** NOUN Reggae is a type of music, originally from the West Indies, with a strong beat

**regiment** NOUN a large group of soldiers commanded by a colonel

**region** NOUN ❶ a large area of land ❷ You can refer to any area or part as a region ✿ PHRASE ❸ **In the region of** means approximately **regional** ADJECTIVE

**register** NOUN ❶ an official list or record of things ❷ TECHNICAL a style of speaking or writing used in particular circumstances or social occasions ✿ VERB ❸ When something is registered, it is recorded on an official list

❹ If an instrument registers a measurement, it shows it ❺ If your face registers a feeling, it expresses it **registration** NOUN

**registration number** NOUN the sequence of letters and numbers on the front and back of a motor vehicle that identify it

**regret**, regrets, regretting, regretted VERB ❶ If you regret something, you are sorry that it happened ❷ You can say that you regret something as a way of apologizing ✿ NOUN ❸ If you have regrets, you are sad or sorry about something

**regular** ADJECTIVE ❶ even and equally spaced ❷ A regular shape has equal angles and equal sides ❸ Regular events or activities happen often and according to a pattern, for example each day or each week ❹ If you are a regular customer or visitor somewhere, you go there often ❺ usual or normal ❻ having a well balanced appearance ✿ NOUN ❼ People who go to a place often are known as its regulars **regularly** ADVERB

**regulation** NOUN ❶ Regulations are official rules ❷ Regulation is the control of something

**rehearsal** NOUN a practice of a performance in preparation for the actual event

**rehearse**, rehearses, rehearsing, rehearsed VERB To rehearse a performance means to practise it in preparation for the actual event

**reign** [*rain*] VERB ❶ When a king or queen reigns, he or she rules a country ❷ You can say that something reigns when it is a noticeable feature of a situation or period of time ✿ NOUN ❸ The reign of a king or queen is the period during which he or she reigns

**rein** NOUN ❶ Reins are the thin leather straps which you hold when you are riding a horse ✿ PHRASE ❷ To **keep a tight rein on** someone or something means to control them firmly

**reindeer** NOUN Reindeer are deer with large antlers, that live in northern regions

**reject** VERB ❶ If you reject a proposal or request, you do not accept it or agree to it ❷ If you reject a belief, political system, or way of life, you decide that it is not for you ✿ NOUN ❸ a product that cannot be used, because there is something wrong with it **rejection** NOUN

# rejoice – reluctantly

**rejoice**, rejoices, rejoicing, rejoiced VERB To rejoice means to be very pleased about something

**relate**, relates, relating, related VERB ❶ If something relates to something else, it is connected or concerned with it ❷ If you can relate to someone, you can understand their thoughts and feelings ❸ To relate a story means to tell it

**relation** NOUN ❶ If there is a relation between two things, they are similar or connected in some way ❷ Your relations are the members of your family ❸ Relations between people are their feelings and behaviour towards each other

**relationship** NOUN ❶ The relationship between two people or groups is the way they feel and behave towards each other ❷ a close friendship, especially one involving romantic or sexual feelings ❸ The relationship between two things is the way in which they are connected

**relative** ADJECTIVE ❶ compared to other things or people of the same kind ❷ You use 'relative' when comparing the size or quality of two things ✿ NOUN ❸ Your relatives are the members of your family

**relative pronoun** NOUN a pronoun that replaces a noun that links two parts of a sentence

## how English works

### Hello Kitty...

knows that a **relative pronoun** is a word that stands in for a noun and connects two parts of a sentence, like *who* and *that*.

**relax**, relaxes, relaxing, relaxed VERB ❶ If you relax, you become calm and your muscles lose their tension ❷ If you relax your hold, you hold something less tightly ❸ To relax something also means to make it less strict or controlled **relaxation** NOUN

**relaxed** ADJECTIVE ❶ calm and not worried or tense ❷ If a place or situation is relaxed, it is calm and peaceful

**relay** NOUN ❶ A relay race or relay is a race between teams, with each team member running one part of the race ✿ VERB ❷ To relay a television or radio signal means to send it on ❸ If you relay information, you tell it to someone else

**release**, releases, releasing, released VERB ❶ To release someone or something means to set them free or remove restraints from them ❷ To release something also means to issue it or make it available ✿ NOUN ❸ When the release of someone or something takes place, they are set free ❹ A press release or publicity release is an official written statement given to reporters ❺ A new release is a new CD or DVD that has just become available

**relevant** ADJECTIVE If something is relevant, it is connected with and is appropriate to what is being discussed

**reliable** ADJECTIVE ❶ Reliable people and things can be trusted to do what you want ❷ If information is reliable, you can assume that it is correct **reliably** ADVERB **reliability** NOUN

**relief** NOUN ❶ If you feel relief, you are glad and thankful because a bad situation is over or has been avoided ❷ Relief is also money, food, or clothing provided for poor or hungry people

**religion** NOUN ❶ Religion is the belief in a god or gods and all the activities connected with such beliefs ❷ a system of religious belief

**religious** ADJECTIVE ❶ connected with religion ❷ Someone who is religious has a strong belief in a god or gods

**reluctant** ADJECTIVE If you are reluctant to do something, you are unwilling to do it **reluctance** NOUN

**reluctantly** ADVERB If you do something reluctantly, you do it although you do not want to

A B C D E F G H I J K L M N O P Q R S T U V W X Y Z

221

# rely – replace

**rely**, relies, relying, relied VERB ❶ If you rely on someone or something, you need them and depend on them ❷ If you can rely on someone to do something, you can trust them to do it

**remain** VERB ❶ If you remain in a particular place, you stay there ❷ If you remain in a particular state, you stay the same and do not change ❸ Something that remains still exists or is left over

**remainder** NOUN The remainder of something is the part that is left

**remains** PLURAL NOUN ❶ The remains of something are the parts that are left after most of it has been destroyed ❷ You can refer to a dead body as remains

**remark** VERB ❶ If you remark on something, you mention it or comment on it ✿ NOUN ❷ something you say, often in a casual way

**remarkable** ADJECTIVE impressive and unexpected **remarkably** ADVERB

**remedy**, remedies, remedying, remedied NOUN ❶ a way of dealing with a problem ✿ VERB ❷ If you remedy something that is wrong, you correct it

**remember** VERB ❶ If you can remember someone or something from the past, you can bring them into your mind or think about them ❷ If you remember to do something, you do it when you intended to

**remind** VERB ❶ If someone reminds you of a fact, they say something to make you think about it ❷ If someone reminds you of another person, they look similar and make you think of them

**reminder** NOUN ❶ If one thing is a reminder of another, the first thing makes you think of the second ❷ a note sent to tell someone they have forgotten to do something

**remorse** NOUN FORMAL Remorse is a strong feeling of guilt

**remote**, remoter, remotest ADJECTIVE ❶ Remote areas are far away from places where most people live ❷ far away in time ❸ If you say a person is remote, you mean they do not want to be friendly ❹ If there is only a remote possibility of something happening, it is unlikely to happen

**remote control** NOUN Remote control is a system of controlling a machine or vehicle from a distance using radio or electronic signals

**remotely** ADVERB used to emphasize a negative statement

**removal** NOUN ❶ The removal of something is the act of taking it away ✿ ADJECTIVE ❷ A removal company transports furniture from one building to another

**remove**, removes, removing, removed VERB ❶ If you remove something from a place, you take it off or away ❷ If you are removed from a position of authority, you are not allowed to continue your job ❸ If you remove an undesirable feeling or attitude, you get rid of it

**renew** VERB ❶ To renew an activity or relationship means to begin it again ❷ To renew a licence or contract means to extend the period of time for which it is valid

**renewable** ADJECTIVE ❶ able to be renewed ✿ NOUN ❷ a renewable form of energy, such as wind power or solar power

**rent** VERB ❶ If you rent something, you pay the owner a regular sum of money in return for being able to use it ✿ NOUN ❷ Rent is the amount of money you pay regularly to rent land or accommodation

**repair** NOUN ❶ something you do to mend something that is damaged or broken ✿ VERB ❷ If you repair something, you mend it

**repay**, repays, repaying, repaid VERB ❶ To repay money means to give it back to the person who lent it ❷ If you repay a favour, you do something to help the person who helped you **repayment** NOUN

**repeat** VERB ❶ If you repeat something, you say, write, or do it again ❷ If you repeat what someone has said, you tell someone else about it ✿ NOUN ❸ something which is done or happens again **repeated** ADJECTIVE **repeatedly** ADVERB

**repetition** NOUN ❶ If there is a repetition of something, it happens again ❷ Repetition is when a word, phrase, or sound is repeated, for example to emphasize a point or to make sure it is understood, or for poetic effect

**repetitive** ADJECTIVE A repetitive activity involves a lot of repetition and is boring

**replace**, replaces, replacing, replaced VERB ❶ When one thing replaces another, the first

# replacement – reserve

thing takes the place of the second ❷ If you replace something that is damaged or lost, you get a new one ❸ If you replace something, you put it back where it was before

**replacement** NOUN ❶ The replacement for someone or something is the person or thing that takes their place ❷ The replacement of a person or thing happens when they are replaced by another person or thing

**replay** VERB ❶ If a match is replayed, the teams play it again ❷ If you replay a tape or film, you play it again ✿ NOUN ❸ a match that is played for a second time

**reply**, replies, replying, replied VERB ❶ If you reply to something, you say or write an answer ✿ NOUN ❷ what you say or write when you answer someone

**report** VERB ❶ If you report that something has happened, you tell someone about it or give an official account of it ❷ To report someone to an authority means to make an official complaint about them ❸ If you report to a person or place, you go there and say you have arrived ✿ NOUN ❹ an account of an event or situation

**reporter** NOUN someone who writes news articles or broadcasts news reports

**represent** VERB ❶ If you represent someone, you act on their behalf ❷ If a sign or symbol represents something, it stands for it ❸ To represent something in a particular way means to describe it in that way

**representative** NOUN ❶ a person chosen to act on behalf of another person or a group ✿ ADJECTIVE ❷ A representative selection is typical of the group it belongs to

**reproduce**, reproduces, reproducing, reproduced VERB ❶ To reproduce something means to make a copy of it ❷ When living things reproduce, they produce more of their own kind

**reproduction** NOUN ❶ a modern copy of a painting or piece of furniture ❷ Reproduction is the process by which a living thing produces more of its kind

**reptile** NOUN a cold-blooded animal, such as a snake or a lizard, which has scaly skin and lays eggs

**republic** NOUN a country which has a president rather than a king or queen

**repulsive** ADJECTIVE horrible and disgusting

**reputation** NOUN The reputation of something or someone is the opinion that people have of them

**request** VERB ❶ If you request something, you ask for it politely or formally ✿ NOUN ❷ If you make a request for something, you request it

**require**, requires, requiring, required VERB ❶ If you require something, you need it ❷ If you are required to do something, you have to do it because someone says you must

**requirement** NOUN something that you must have or must do

**rescue**, rescues, rescuing, rescued VERB ❶ If you rescue someone, you save them from a dangerous or unpleasant situation ✿ NOUN ❷ Rescue is help which saves someone from a dangerous or unpleasant situation

**research**, researches, researching, researched NOUN ❶ Research is work that involves studying something and trying to find out facts about it ✿ VERB ❷ If you research something, you try to discover facts about it

**resemblance** NOUN If there is a resemblance between two things, they are similar to each other

**resemble**, resembles, resembling, resembled VERB To resemble something means to be similar to it

**resent** VERB If you resent something, you feel bitter and angry about it

**resentment** NOUN a feeling of anger or bitterness

**reservation** NOUN ❶ If you have reservations about something, you are not sure that it is right ❷ If you make a reservation, you book a place in advance ❸ an area of land set aside for Native American peoples

**reserve**, reserves, reserving, reserved VERB ❶ If something is reserved for a particular person or purpose, it is kept specially for them ✿ NOUN ❷ a supply of something for future use ❸ In sport, a reserve is someone who is available to play in case one of the team is unable to play ❹ A nature reserve is an area of land where animals, birds, or plants are officially protected ❺ If someone shows reserve, they keep their feelings hidden **reserved** ADJECTIVE

223

# reservoir - restore

**reservoir** [*rez-ev-wahr*] NOUN a lake used for storing water before it is supplied to people

**residence** NOUN FORMAL a house

**resident** NOUN ❶ A resident of a house or area is someone who lives there ❖ ADJECTIVE ❷ If someone is resident in a house or area, they live there

**residential** ADJECTIVE ❶ A residential area contains mainly houses rather than offices or factories ❷ providing accommodation

**resign** VERB ❶ If you resign from a job, you formally announce that you are leaving it ❷ If you resign yourself to an unpleasant situation, you realize that you have to accept it

**resignation** NOUN ❶ Someone's resignation is a formal statement of their intention to leave a job ❷ Resignation is the reluctant acceptance of an unpleasant situation or fact

**resist** VERB ❶ If you resist something, you refuse to accept it and try to prevent it ❷ If you resist someone, you fight back against them

**resistance** NOUN ❶ Resistance to something such as change is a refusal to accept it ❷ Resistance to an attack consists of fighting back ❸ Your body's resistance to germs or disease is its power to not be harmed by them ❹ Resistance is also the power of a substance to resist the flow of an electrical current through it

**resolution** NOUN ❶ Resolution is determination ❷ If you make a resolution, you promise yourself to do something ❸ a formal decision taken at a meeting ❹ The resolution of a problem is the solving of it

**resolve**, resolves, resolving, resolved VERB ❶ If you resolve to do something, you firmly decide to do it ❷ If you resolve a problem, you find a solution to it ❖ NOUN ❸ Resolve is absolute determination

**resort** VERB ❶ If you resort to a course of action, you do it because you have no alternative ❖ NOUN ❷ a place where people spend their holidays ❖ PHRASE ❸ If you do something **as a last resort**, you do it because you can find no other way of solving a problem

**respect** VERB ❶ If you respect someone, you have a good opinion of their character or ideas ❷ If you respect someone's rights or wishes, you do not do things that they would not like, or would consider wrong ❖ NOUN ❸ If you have respect for someone, you have a good opinion of them ❖ PHRASE ❹ You can say **in this respect** to refer to a particular feature

**respectable** ADJECTIVE ❶ considered to be acceptable and morally correct ❷ adequate or reasonable

**respectful** ADJECTIVE showing respect for someone

**respiration** NOUN Your respiration is your breathing

**respond**, responds, responding, responded VERB When you respond to something, you react to it by doing or saying something

**response** NOUN Your response to an event is your reaction or reply to it

**responsibility**, responsibilities NOUN ❶ If you have responsibility for something, it is your duty to deal with it or look after it ❷ If you accept responsibility for something that has happened, you agree that you caused it or were to blame

**responsible** ADJECTIVE ❶ If you are responsible for something, it is your job to deal with it ❷ If you are responsible for something bad that has happened, you are to blame for it ❸ If you are responsible to someone, that person is your boss and tells you what you have to do ❹ A responsible person behaves properly and sensibly without needing to be supervised ❺ A responsible job involves making careful judgments about important matters

**rest** NOUN ❶ The rest of something is all the remaining parts of it ❷ If you have a rest, you sit or lie quietly and relax ❖ VERB ❸ If you rest, you relax and do not do anything active for a while

**restaurant** [*rest-ront*] NOUN a place where you can buy and eat a meal

**restless** ADJECTIVE finding it hard to remain still or relaxed because of boredom or impatience

**restore**, restores, restoring, restored VERB ❶ To restore something means to cause it to exist again or to return to its previous state ❷ To restore an old building or work of art means to clean and repair it

224

**restrain** VERB To restrain someone or something means to hold them back or prevent them from doing what they want to

**restrict** VERB ❶ If you restrict something, you prevent it becoming too large or varied ❷ To restrict people or animals means to limit their movement or actions

**restriction** NOUN a rule or situation that limits what you can do

**result** NOUN ❶ The result of an action or situation is the situation that is caused by it ❷ The result is also the final marks, figures, or situation at the end of an exam, calculation, or contest ✿ VERB ❸ If something results in a particular event, it causes that event to happen ❹ If something results from a particular event, it is caused by that event

**resume**, resumes, resuming, resumed [riz-*yoom*] VERB If you resume an activity or position, you return to it after a break

**retail** ADJECTIVE The retail price is the price at which something is sold in the shops
**retailer** NOUN

**retain** VERB To retain something means to keep it

**rethink**, rethinks, rethinking, rethought VERB If you rethink something, you think about how it should be changed

**retire**, retires, retiring, retired VERB ❶ When older people retire, they give up work ❷ FORMAL If you retire, you leave to go into another room, or to bed **retired** ADJECTIVE
**retirement** NOUN

**retreat** VERB ❶ To retreat means to move backwards away from something or someone ❷ If you retreat from something difficult or unpleasant, you avoid doing it ✿ NOUN ❸ If an army moves away from the enemy, this is referred to as a retreat ❹ a quiet place that you can go to rest or do things in private

**return** VERB ❶ When you return to a place, you go back after you have been away ❷ If you return something to someone, you give it back to them ❸ When you return a ball during a game, you hit it back to your opponent ❹ When a judge or jury returns a verdict, they announce it ✿ NOUN ❺ Your return is your arrival back at a place ❻ The return on an investment is the profit or interest you get from it ❼ a ticket for the journey to a place and back again

**reunion** NOUN a party or meeting for people who have not seen each other for a long time

**reunite**, reunites, reuniting, reunited VERB If people are reunited, they meet again after they have been separated for some time

**reveal** VERB ❶ To reveal something means to tell people about it ❷ If you reveal something that has been hidden, you uncover it

**revenge**, revenges, revenging, revenged NOUN ❶ Revenge involves hurting someone who has hurt you ✿ VERB ❷ If you revenge yourself on someone who has hurt you, you hurt them in return

**revenue** NOUN Revenue is money that a government, company, or organization receives

**Reverend** NOUN Reverend is a title used before the name of a member of the clergy

**reverse**, reverses, reversing, reversed VERB ❶ When someone reverses a process, they change it to the opposite process ❷ If you reverse the order of things, you arrange them in the opposite order ❸ When you reverse a car, you drive it backwards ✿ NOUN ❹ The reverse is the opposite of what has just been said or done ✿ ADJECTIVE ❺ Reverse means opposite to what is usual or to what has just been described

**review** NOUN ❶ an article or an item on television or radio, giving an opinion of a new book or play ❷ When there is a review of a situation or system, it is examined to decide whether changes are needed ✿ VERB ❸ To review a play or book means to write an account expressing an opinion of it ❹ To review something means to examine it to decide whether changes are needed
**reviewer** NOUN

**revise**, revises, revising, revised VERB ❶ If you revise something, you alter or correct it ❷ When you revise for an examination, you go over your work to learn things thoroughly
**revision** NOUN

**revive**, revives, reviving, revived VERB ❶ When a feeling or practice is revived, it becomes active or popular again ❷ When you revive someone who has fainted, they become conscious again

# revolt – right

**revolt** NOUN ❶ a violent attempt by a group of people to change their country's political system ✿ VERB ❷ When people revolt, they fight against the authority that governs them ❸ If something revolts you, it is so horrible that you feel disgust

**revolting** ADJECTIVE horrible and disgusting

**revolution** NOUN ❶ a violent attempt by a large group of people to change the political system of their country ❷ an important change in an area of human activity ❸ one complete turn in a circle

**revolutionary**, revolutionaries ADJECTIVE ❶ involving great changes ✿ NOUN ❷ a person who takes part in a revolution

**revolve**, revolves, revolving, revolved VERB ❶ If something revolves round something else, it centres on that as the most important thing ❷ When something revolves, it turns in a circle around a central point

**revolver** NOUN a small gun held in the hand

**reward** NOUN ❶ something you are given because you have done something good ✿ VERB ❷ If you reward someone, you give them a reward

**rewarding** ADJECTIVE Something that is rewarding gives you a lot of satisfaction

**rhinoceros**, rhinoceroses NOUN a large African or Asian animal with one or two horns on its nose

**rhyme**, rhymes, rhyming, rhymed VERB ❶ If two words rhyme, they have a similar sound ✿ NOUN ❷ a word that rhymes with another ❸ a short poem with rhyming lines

**rhythm** NOUN ❶ Rhythm is a regular movement or beat ❷ a regular pattern of changes, for example, in the seasons

**rhythmic** ADJECTIVE

**rib** NOUN Your ribs are the curved bones that go from your backbone to your chest

**ribbon** NOUN a long, narrow piece of cloth used for decoration

**rice** NOUN Rice is a tall grass that produces edible grains. Rice is grown in warm countries on wet ground

**rich**, richer, richest; riches ADJECTIVE ❶ Someone who is rich has a lot of money and possessions ❷ Something that is rich in something contains a large amount of it ❸ Rich food contains a large amount of fat, oil, or sugar ❹ Rich colours, smells, and sounds are strong and pleasant

**rid**, rids, ridding, rid PHRASE ❶ When you **get rid** of something you do not want, you remove or destroy it ✿ VERB ❷ FORMAL To rid a place of something unpleasant means to succeed in removing it

**riddle**, riddles NOUN ❶ a puzzle which seems to be nonsense, but which has an entertaining solution ❷ Something that is a riddle puzzles and confuses you

**ride**, rides, riding, rode, ridden VERB ❶ When you ride a horse or a bike, you sit on it and control it as it moves along ❷ When you ride in a car, you travel in it ✿ NOUN ❸ a journey on a horse or bike or in a vehicle

**rider** NOUN ❶ a person riding on a horse or bicycle ❷ an additional statement which changes or puts a condition on what has already been said

**ridge** NOUN ❶ a long, narrow piece of high land ❷ a raised line on a flat surface

**ridiculous** ADJECTIVE very foolish

**rifle**, rifles, rifling, rifled NOUN ❶ a gun with a long barrel ✿ VERB ❷ When someone rifles something, they make a quick search through it to steal things

**right** ADJECTIVE OR ADVERB ❶ correct and in accordance with the facts ❷ 'Right' means on or towards the right side of something

## how to remember

Hello Kitty...

knows how to spell **rhythm** by remembering **R**oger **h**ates **y**our **t**errible **h**eavy **m**etal.

226

**right angle - risk**

❀ ADJECTIVE ❸ The right choice or decision is the best or most suitable one ❹ The right people or places are those that have influence or are socially admired ❺ The right side of something is the side intended to be seen and to face outwards ❀ NOUN ❻ 'Right' is used to refer to principles of morally correct behaviour ❼ If you have a right to do something, you are morally or legally entitled to do it ❽ The right is one of the two sides of something. For example, when you look at the word 'to', the 'o' is to the right of the 't' ❾ The Right refers to people who support the political ideas of capitalism and conservatism rather than socialism ❀ ADVERB ❿ 'Right' is used to emphasize a precise place ⓫ 'Right' means immediately ❀ VERB ⓬ If you right something, you correct it or put it back in an upright position

**right angle** NOUN an angle of 90°

**right-handed** ADJECTIVE OR ADVERB Someone who is right-handed does things such as writing and painting with their right hand

**right-wing** ADJECTIVE believing more strongly in capitalism or conservatism, or less strongly in socialism, than other members of the same party or group

**rigid** ADJECTIVE ❶ Rigid laws or systems cannot be changed and are considered severe ❷ A rigid object is stiff and does not bend easily

**rim** NOUN the outside or top edge of an object such as a wheel or a cup

**rind** NOUN Rind is the thick outer skin of fruit, cheese, or bacon

**ring**, rings, ringing, rang or ringed (senses 3 & 4), rung or ringed (senses 3 & 4) VERB ❶ If you ring someone, you phone them ❷ When a bell rings, it makes a clear, loud sound ❸ To ring something means to draw a circle around it ❹ If something is ringed with something else, it has that thing all the way around it ❀ NOUN ❺ the sound made by a bell ❻ a small circle of metal worn on your finger ❼ an object or group of things in the shape of a circle ❽ At a boxing match or circus, the ring is the place where the fight or performance takes place ❾ a group of people who are involved in an illegal activity

**rink** NOUN a large indoor area for ice-skating or roller-skating

**rinse**, rinses, rinsing, rinsed VERB ❶ When you rinse something, you wash it in clean water ❀ NOUN ❷ a liquid you can put on your hair to give it a different colour

**riot** NOUN ❶ When there is a riot, a crowd of people behave noisily and violently ❀ VERB ❷ To riot means to behave noisily and violently ❀ PHRASE ❸ To **run riot** means to behave in a wild and uncontrolled way

**rip**, rips, ripping, ripped VERB ❶ When you rip something, you tear it violently ❷ If you rip something away, you remove it quickly and violently ❀ NOUN ❸ a long split in cloth or paper

**rip off** ❀ VERB INFORMAL If someone rips you off, they cheat you by charging you too much money

**ripe**, riper, ripest ADJECTIVE ❶ When fruit or grain is ripe, it is fully developed and ready to be eaten ❷ If a situation is ripe for something to happen, it is ready for it

**ripple**, ripples, rippling, rippled NOUN ❶ Ripples are little waves on the surface of calm water ❷ If there is a ripple of laughter or applause, people laugh or applaud gently for a short time ❀ VERB ❸ When the surface of water ripples, little waves appear on it

**rise**, rises, rising, rose, risen VERB ❶ If something rises, it moves upwards ❷ FORMAL When you rise, you stand up ❸ To rise also means to get out of bed ❹ When the sun rises, it first appears ❺ The place where a river rises is where it begins ❻ If land rises, it slopes upwards ❼ If a sound or wind rises, it becomes higher or stronger ❽ If an amount rises, it increases ❾ If you rise to a challenge or a remark, you respond to it rather than ignoring it ❿ When people rise up, they start fighting against people in authority ❀ NOUN ⓫ an increase ⓬ Someone's rise is the process by which they become more powerful or successful

**risk** NOUN ❶ a chance that something unpleasant or dangerous might happen ❀ VERB ❷ If you risk something unpleasant, you do something knowing that the unpleasant thing might happen as a result ❸ If you risk someone's life, you put them in a dangerous situation in which they might be killed **risky** ADJECTIVE

# ritual – roll

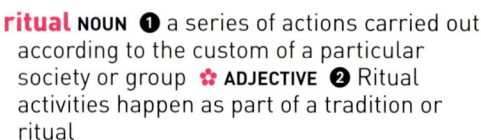

**A B C D E F G H I J K L M N O P Q R S T U V W X Y Z**

**ritual** NOUN ❶ a series of actions carried out according to the custom of a particular society or group ✿ ADJECTIVE ❷ Ritual activities happen as part of a tradition or ritual

**rival**, rivals, rivalling, rivalled NOUN ❶ Your rival is the person you are competing with ✿ VERB ❷ If something rivals something else, it is of the same high standard or quality

**river** NOUN a natural feature consisting of water flowing for a long distance between two banks

**road** NOUN a long piece of hard ground specially surfaced so that people and vehicles can travel along it easily

### don't mix up

Don't mix up **road** (what cars drive on) and **rode** (the past tense of ride).

**roam** VERB If you roam around, you wander around without any particular purpose

**roar** VERB ❶ If something roars, it makes a very loud noise ❷ To roar with laughter or anger means to laugh or shout very noisily ❸ When a lion roars, it makes a loud, angry sound ✿ NOUN ❹ a very loud noise

**roast** VERB ❶ When you roast meat or other food, you cook it using dry heat in an oven or over a fire ✿ ADJECTIVE ❷ Roast meat has been roasted ✿ NOUN ❸ a piece of meat that has been roasted

**rob**, robs, robbing, robbed VERB ❶ If someone robs you, they steal your possessions ❷ If you rob someone of something they need or deserve, you deprive them of it

**robber** NOUN Robbers are people who steal money or property using force or threats **robbery** NOUN

**robe** NOUN a long, loose piece of clothing which covers the body

**robin** NOUN a small bird with a red breast

**robot** NOUN a machine which is programmed to move and perform tasks automatically

**rock** NOUN ❶ Rock is the hard mineral substance that forms the surface of the earth ❷ a large piece of rock ❸ Rock or rock music is music with simple tunes and a very strong beat ❹ Rock is also a sweet shaped into long, hard sticks, sold in holiday resorts ✿ VERB ❺ When something rocks or when you rock it, it moves regularly backwards and forwards or from side to side ❻ If something rocks people, it shocks and upsets them

**rock and roll** NOUN Rock and roll is a style of music with a strong beat that was especially popular in the 1950s

**rocket** NOUN ❶ a space vehicle, usually shaped like a long pointed tube ❷ an explosive missile ❸ a firework that explodes when it is high in the air ✿ VERB ❹ If prices rocket, they increase very quickly

**rocky** ADJECTIVE covered with rocks

**rod** NOUN a long, thin pole or bar, usually made of wood or metal

**rodent** NOUN a small mammal with sharp front teeth which it uses for gnawing

**role** or **rôle** NOUN ❶ Someone's role is their position and function in a situation or society ❷ An actor's role is the character that he or she plays

**roll** VERB ❶ When something rolls or when you roll it, it moves along a surface, turning

### where does the word come from?

### Did you know…

that the word **rodent** comes from the Latin word *rodere* which means 'to gnaw'? That's because *rodents* have sharp teeth for gnawing and biting.

228

**Rollerblade - round**

over and over ❷ When vehicles roll along, they move ❸ If you roll your eyes, you make them turn up or go from side to side ❹ If you roll something flexible into a cylinder or ball, you wrap it several times around itself ✿ NOUN ❺ A roll of paper or cloth is a long piece of it that has been rolled into a tube ❻ a small, rounded, individually baked piece of bread ❼ an official list of people's names ❽ A roll on a drum is a long, rumbling sound made on it

**Rollerblade** NOUN TRADEMARK Rollerblades are roller-skates which have the wheels set in one straight line on the bottom of the boot

**roller-skate**, roller-skates, roller-skating, roller-skated NOUN ❶ Roller-skates are shoes with four small wheels underneath ✿ VERB ❷ If you roller-skate, you move along wearing roller-skates

**Roman Catholic** ADJECTIVE ❶ relating or belonging to the branch of the Christian church that accepts the Pope in Rome as its leader ✿ NOUN ❷ someone who belongs to the Roman Catholic church

**romance** NOUN ❶ a relationship between two people who are in love with each other ❷ Romance is the pleasure and excitement of doing something new and unusual ❸ a novel or film about a love affair

**romantic** ADJECTIVE OR NOUN ❶ A romantic person has ideas that are not realistic, for example about love or about ways of changing society ✿ ADJECTIVE ❷ connected with sexual love ❸ Something that is romantic is beautiful in a way that strongly affects your feelings ❹ Romantic describes a style of music, literature, and art popular in Europe in the late 18th and early 19th centuries, which emphasized feeling and imagination rather than order and form

**roof** NOUN ❶ The roof of a building or car is the covering on top of it ❷ The roof of your mouth or of a cave is the highest part

**room** NOUN ❶ a separate section in a building, divided from other rooms by walls ❷ If there is plenty of room, there is a lot of space

**root** NOUN ❶ The roots of a plant are the parts that grow under the ground ❷ The root of a hair is the part beneath the skin ❸ You can refer to the place or culture that you grew up in as your roots ❹ The root of something is its original cause or basis ✿ VERB ❺ To root through things means to search through them, pushing them aside

**root out** ✿ VERB If you root something or someone out, you find them and force them out

**rope**, ropes, roping, roped NOUN ❶ a thick, strong length of twisted cord ✿ VERB ❷ If you rope one thing to another, you tie them together with rope

**rose** NOUN ❶ a large garden flower which has a pleasant smell and grows on a bush with thorns ✿ NOUN OR ADJECTIVE ❷ reddish-pink

**rot**, rots, rotting, rotted VERB ❶ When food or wood rots, it decays and can no longer be used ❷ When something rots another substance, it causes it to decay ✿ NOUN ❸ Rot is the condition that affects things when they rot

**rotate**, rotates, rotating, rotated VERB When something rotates, it turns with a circular movement **rotation** NOUN

**rotten** ADJECTIVE ❶ decayed and no longer of use ❷ INFORMAL of very poor quality

**rough** [ruff] ADJECTIVE ❶ uneven and not smooth ❷ not using enough care or gentleness ❸ difficult or unpleasant ❹ approximately correct ❺ If the sea is rough, there are large waves because of bad weather ❻ A rough town or area has a lot of crime or violence ✿ NOUN OR ADJECTIVE ❼ A rough or a rough sketch is a drawing or description that shows the main features but does not show the details **roughly** ADVERB

**round** ADJECTIVE ❶ Something round is shaped like a ball or a circle ❷ complete or whole ✿ PREPOSITION OR ADVERB ❸ If something is round something else, it surrounds it ❹ The distance round something is the length of its circumference or boundary ❺ You can refer to an area near a place as the area round it ✿ PREPOSITION ❻ If something moves round you, it keeps moving in a circle with you in the centre ❼ When someone goes to the other side of something, they have gone round it ✿ ADVERB OR PREPOSITION ❽ If you go round

229

# round up - ruin

a place, you go to different parts of it to look at it ✿ **ADVERB** ❾ If you turn or look round, you turn so you are facing in a different direction ❿ When someone comes round, they visit you ✿ **NOUN** ⓫ one of a series of events ⓬ If you buy a round of drinks, you buy a drink for each member of the group you are with

**round up** ✿ **VERB** If you round up people or animals, you gather them together

**roundabout NOUN** ❶ a meeting point of several roads with a circle in the centre which vehicles have to travel around ❷ a circular platform which rotates and which children can ride on in a playground

**rounded ADJECTIVE** curved in shape, without any points or sharp edges

**route** [root] **NOUN** a way from one place to another

**routine ADJECTIVE** ❶ Routine activities are done regularly ✿ **NOUN** ❷ the usual way or order in which you do things ❸ a boring repetition of tasks

**row** [rhymes with *snow*] **NOUN** ❶ A row of people or things is several of them arranged in a line ✿ **VERB** ❷ When you row a boat, you use oars to make it move through the water

**row** [rhymes with *now*] **NOUN** ❶ a serious argument ❷ If someone is making a row, they are making too much noise ✿ **VERB** ❸ If people are rowing, they are quarrelling noisily

**royal ADJECTIVE** ❶ belonging to or involving a queen, a king, or a member of their family ❷ 'Royal' is used in the names of organizations appointed or supported by a member of a royal family ✿ **NOUN** ❸ INFORMAL Members of the royal family are sometimes referred to as the royals

**royalty**, royalties **NOUN** ❶ The members of a royal family are sometimes referred to as royalty ❷ Royalties are payments made to authors and musicians from the sales of their books or music

**rub**, rubs, rubbing, rubbed **VERB** ❶ If you rub something, you move your hand or a cloth backwards and forwards over it

**rub out** ✿ **VERB** To rub out something written means to remove it by rubbing it with a rubber or a cloth

**rubber NOUN** ❶ Rubber is a strong, elastic substance used for making tyres, boots, and other products ❷ a small piece of rubber used to rub out pencil mistakes

**rubbish NOUN** ❶ Rubbish is unwanted things or waste material ❷ You can refer to nonsense or something of very poor quality as rubbish

**ruby**, rubies **NOUN** a type of red jewel

**rucksack NOUN** a bag with shoulder straps for carrying things on your back

**rude**, ruder, rudest **ADJECTIVE** ❶ not polite ❷ embarrassing or offensive because of reference to sex or other bodily functions ❸ unexpected and unpleasant **rudely ADVERB** **rudeness NOUN**

**rug NOUN** ❶ a small, thick carpet ❷ a blanket which you can use to cover your knees or for sitting on outdoors

**rugby NOUN** Rugby is a game played by two teams, who try to kick and throw an oval ball to their opponents' end of the pitch. Rugby League is played with 13 players in each side, Rugby Union is played with 15 players in each side

**ruin VERB** ❶ If you ruin something, you destroy or spoil it completely ❷ If someone is ruined, they have lost all their money ✿ **NOUN** ❸ Ruin is the state of being destroyed or completely spoilt ❹ A ruin or

## how to say it

### Helpful hints...

**Row** rhymes with *snow* when it means 'a line' or 'to use oars', and with *now* when it means 'quarrel'.

the ruins of something refers to the parts that are left after it has been severely damaged

**rule**, rules, ruling, ruled NOUN ❶ Rules are statements which tell you what you are allowed to do ✿ VERB ❷ To rule a country or group of people means to have power over it and be in charge of its affairs ❸ FORMAL When someone in authority rules on a particular matter, they give an official decision about it

**ruler** NOUN ❶ a person who rules a country ❷ a long, flat piece of wood or plastic with straight edges marked in centimetres or inches, used for measuring or drawing straight lines

**rumble**, rumbles, rumbling, rumbled VERB ❶ If something rumbles, it makes a continuous low noise ✿ NOUN ❷ a continuous low noise

**rumour** NOUN ❶ a story that people are talking about, which may or may not be true ✿ VERB ❷ If something is rumoured, people are suggesting that it has happened

**run**, runs, running, ran, run VERB ❶ When you run, you move quickly, leaving the ground during each stride ❷ If you run away from a place, you leave it suddenly and secretly ❸ If you say that a road or river runs in a particular direction, you are describing its course ❹ If you run your hand or an object over something, you move it over it ❺ If you run a business or an activity, you are in charge of it ❻ If you run an experiment, a computer program, or tape, you start it and let it continue ❼ If you run someone somewhere in a car, you drive them there ❽ If you run water, you turn on a tap to make it flow ❾ If your nose is running, it is producing a lot of mucus ❿ If the dye in something runs, the colour comes out when it is washed ✿ NOUN ⓫ If you go for a run, you run for pleasure or exercise ⓬ a journey somewhere ⓭ A run of success or failure is a series of successes or failures ⓮ In cricket or baseball, a player scores one run by running between marked places on the pitch after hitting the ball

**run out** ✿ VERB If you run out of something, you have no more left

**run over** ✿ VERB If someone is run over, they are hit by a moving vehicle

**rung** NOUN The rungs on a ladder are the bars that form the steps

**runner** NOUN ❶ a person who runs, especially as a sport ❷ a person who takes messages or runs errands ❸ A runner on a plant such as a strawberry is a long shoot from which a new plant develops ❹ The runners on drawers and ice-skates are the thin strips on which they move

**runner-up**, runners-up NOUN a person or team that comes second in a race or competition

**running** ADJECTIVE ❶ continuing without stopping over a period of time ❷ Running water is flowing rather than standing still

**runny**, runnier, runniest ADJECTIVE ❶ more liquid than usual ❷ If someone's nose or eyes are runny, liquid is coming out of them

**runway** NOUN a long strip of ground used by aeroplanes for taking off or landing

**rural** ADJECTIVE relating to or involving the countryside

**rush**, rushes, rushing, rushed VERB ❶ To rush means to move fast or do something quickly ✿ NOUN ❷ If you are in a rush, you are busy and do not have enough time to do things

**rush hour** NOUN The rush hour is one of the busy parts of the day when most people are travelling to or from work

**rust** NOUN ❶ Rust is a reddish-brown substance that forms on iron or steel which has been in contact with water and which is decaying gradually ✿ NOUN OR ADJECTIVE ❷ reddish-brown ✿ VERB ❸ When a metal object rusts, it becomes covered in rust

**rustle**, rustles, rustling, rustled VERB When something rustles, it makes soft sounds as it moves

**rusty**, rustier, rustiest ADJECTIVE ❶ affected by rust ❷ If someone's knowledge is rusty, it is not as good as it used to be because they have not used it for a long time

**rut** NOUN a deep, narrow groove in the ground made by the wheels of a vehicle

**ruthless** ADJECTIVE very harsh or cruel

# sack - sake

**sack** NOUN ❶ a large bag made of rough material used for carrying or storing goods ✿ VERB ❷ INFORMAL If someone is sacked, they are dismissed from their job by their employer

**sacred** [*say-krid*] ADJECTIVE holy, or connected with religion or religious ceremonies

**sacrifice**, sacrifices, sacrificing, sacrificed [*sak-riff-ice*] VERB ❶ If you sacrifice something valuable or important, you give it up ❷ To sacrifice an animal means to kill it as an offering to a god ✿ NOUN ❸ the killing of an animal as an offering to a god or gods ❹ the action of giving something up

**sad**, sadder, saddest ADJECTIVE ❶ If you are sad, you feel unhappy ❷ Something sad makes you feel unhappy **sadly** ADVERB

**saddle**, saddles, saddling, saddled NOUN ❶ a leather seat that you sit on when you are riding a horse ❷ The saddle on a bicycle is the seat ✿ VERB ❸ If you saddle a horse, you put a saddle on it

**sadness** NOUN the feeling of being unhappy

**safari**, safaris NOUN an expedition for hunting or observing wild animals

**safe**, safer, safest; safes ADJECTIVE ❶ Something that is safe does not cause harm or danger ❷ If you are safe, you are not in any danger ❸ If it is safe to say something, you can say it with little risk of being wrong ✿ NOUN ❹ a strong metal box with special locks, in which you can keep valuable things **safely** ADVERB

**safety** NOUN the state of being safe from harm or danger

**sag**, sags, sagging, sagged VERB When something sags, it hangs down loosely or sinks downwards in the middle

**sail** NOUN ❶ Sails are large pieces of material attached to a ship's mast. The wind blows against the sail and moves the ship ✿ VERB ❷ When a ship sails, it moves across water ❸ If you sail somewhere, you go there by ship

**sailor** NOUN a member of a ship's crew

**saint** NOUN a person who after death is formally recognized by a Christian church as deserving special honour because of having lived a very holy life

**sake** PHRASE ❶ If you do something **for someone's sake**, you do it to help or please

## Hello Kitty...

knows that some words that sound as if they begin with s actually begin with c, like *city*, or with *ps*, like *psychology*.

232

**salad – satisfy**

them ❷ You use **for the sake of** to say why you are doing something

**salad** NOUN a mixture of raw vegetables

**salary**, salaries NOUN a regular monthly payment to an employee

**sale** NOUN ❶ The sale of goods is the selling of them ❷ an occasion when a shop sells things at reduced prices ❸ IN PLURAL The sales of a product are the numbers that are sold

**salesman** NOUN someone who sells products for a company **saleswoman** NOUN

**saliva** [sal-*live*-a] NOUN Saliva is the watery liquid in your mouth that helps you chew and digest food

**salmon** [*sam*-on] NOUN a large edible silver-coloured fish with pink flesh

**salon** NOUN a place where hairdressers work

**salt** NOUN Salt is a white substance found naturally in sea water. It is used to flavour and preserve food

**salty**, saltier, saltiest ADJECTIVE containing salt or tasting of salt

**salute**, salutes, saluting, saluted NOUN ❶ a formal sign of respect. Soldiers give a salute by raising their right hand to their forehead ✿ VERB ❷ If you salute someone, you give them a salute

**same** ADJECTIVE (USUALLY PRECEDED BY *the*) ❶ If two things are the same, they are like one another ❷ Same means just one thing and not two different ones

**sample**, samples, sampling, sampled NOUN ❶ A sample of something is a small amount of it that you can try or test ✿ VERB ❷ If you sample something, you try it

**sand** NOUN ❶ Sand consists of tiny pieces of stone. Beaches are made of sand ✿ VERB ❷ If you sand something, you rub sandpaper over it to make it smooth

**sandal** NOUN Sandals are light open shoes with straps, worn in warm weather

**sandwich**, sandwiches, sandwiching, sandwiched NOUN ❶ two slices of bread with a filling between them ✿ VERB ❷ If one thing is sandwiched between two others, it is in a narrow space between them

**sandy**, sandier, sandiest ADJECTIVE ❶ A sandy area is covered with sand ❷ Sandy hair is light orange-brown

**sane**, saner, sanest ADJECTIVE ❶ If someone is sane, they have a normal and healthy mind ❷ A sane action is sensible and reasonable

**sarcastic** ADJECTIVE saying or doing the opposite of what you really mean in order to mock or insult someone **sarcasm** NOUN

**sardine** NOUN a small edible sea fish

**satellite** NOUN ❶ an spacecraft sent into orbit round the earth to collect information or as part of a communications system ❷ a natural object in space that moves round a planet or star

**satin** NOUN Satin is a kind of smooth, shiny silk

**satire** NOUN Satire is the use of mocking or ironical humour, especially in literature, to show how foolish or wicked some people are

**satisfaction** NOUN Satisfaction is the feeling of pleasure you get when you do something you wanted or needed to do

**satisfactory** ADJECTIVE acceptable or adequate

**satisfied** ADJECTIVE happy because you have got what you want

**satisfy**, satisfies, satisfying, satisfied VERB ❶ To satisfy someone means to give them enough of something to make them pleased or contented ❷ To satisfy someone that

*where does the word come from?*

*Did you know…*

where the word **sandwich** comes from? It's named after an English lord, the Earl of Sandwich, who had the first sandwich made so that he could eat without having to leave his game of cards.

# satisfying - scarce

something is the case means to convince them of it ❸ To satisfy the requirements for something means to fulfil them

**satisfying** ADJECTIVE Something that is satisfying gives you a feeling of pleasure and fulfilment

**Saturday**, Saturdays NOUN the day between Friday and Sunday

**sauce** NOUN a liquid eaten with food to give it more flavour

**saucepan** NOUN a deep metal cooking pot with a handle and a lid

**saucer** NOUN a small curved plate for a cup

**sauna** [saw-na] NOUN If you have a sauna, you go into a very hot room in order to sweat, then have a cold bath or shower

**sausage** NOUN a mixture of minced meat and herbs formed into a tubular shape and served cooked

**savage**, savages, savaging, savaged ADJECTIVE ❶ cruel and violent ✿ NOUN ❷ If you call someone a savage, you mean that they are violent and uncivilized ✿ VERB ❸ If an animal savages you, it attacks you and bites you

**save**, saves, saving, saved VERB ❶ If you save someone, you rescue them ❷ If you save someone or something, you keep them safe ❸ If you save something, you keep it so that you can use it later ❹ To save time, money, or effort means to prevent it from being wasted ✿ PREPOSITION ❺ FORMAL Save means except

**savoury** ADJECTIVE ❶ Savoury is salty or spicy ❷ Something that is not very savoury is not very pleasant or respectable

**saw**, saws, sawing, sawed, sawn ❶ Saw is the past tense of **see** ✿ NOUN ❷ a tool, with a blade with sharp teeth along one edge, for cutting wood ✿ VERB ❸ If you saw something, you cut it with a saw

**saxophone** NOUN a curved metal wind instrument often played in jazz bands

**say**, says, saying, said VERB ❶ When you say something, you speak words ❷ 'Say' is used to give an example ✿ NOUN ❸ If you have a say in something, you can give your opinion and influence decisions

**saying** NOUN a well-known sentence or phrase that tells you something about human life

**scab** NOUN a hard, dry covering that forms over a wound

**scaffolding** NOUN Scaffolding is a framework of poles and boards that is used by workmen to stand on while they are working on the outside structure of a building

**scald** [skawld] VERB ❶ If you scald yourself, you burn yourself with very hot liquid or steam ✿ NOUN ❷ a burn caused by scalding

**scale**, scales, scaling, scaled NOUN ❶ The scale of something is its size or extent ❷ a set of levels or numbers used for measuring things ❸ The scale of a map, plan, or model is the relationship between the size of something in the map, plan, or model and its size in the real world ❹ an upward or downward sequence of musical notes ❺ The scales of a fish or reptile are the small pieces of hard skin covering its body ❻ IN PLURAL Scales are a piece of equipment used for weighing things ✿ VERB ❼ If you scale something high, you climb it

**scalp** NOUN ❶ Your scalp is the skin under the hair on your head ❷ the piece of skin and hair removed when someone is scalped ✿ VERB ❸ To scalp someone means to remove the skin and hair from their head in one piece

**scan**, scans, scanning, scanned VERB ❶ If you scan something, you look at all of it carefully ❷ If a machine scans something, it examines it by means of a beam of light or X-rays ❸ If the words of a poem scan, they fit into a regular, rhythmical pattern ✿ NOUN ❹ an examination or search by a scanner

**scandal** NOUN a situation or event that people think is shocking and immoral

**scanner** NOUN ❶ a machine which is used to examine, identify, or record things by means of a beam of light or X-rays ❷ a machine which converts text or images into a form that can be stored on a computer

**scar**, scars, scarring, scarred NOUN ❶ a mark left on your skin after a wound has healed ❷ a permanent effect on someone's mind that results from a very unpleasant experience ✿ VERB ❸ If an injury scars you, it leaves a permanent mark on your skin ❹ If an unpleasant experience scars you, it has a permanent effect on you

**scarce**, scarcer, scarcest ADJECTIVE If something is scarce, there is not very much of it

**scarcely - score**

**scarcely** ADVERB Scarcely means hardly

**scare**, scares, scaring, scared VERB ❶ If something scares you, it frightens you ✿ NOUN ❷ If something gives you a scare, it scares you ❸ If there is a scare about something, a lot of people are worried about it **scared** ADJECTIVE

**scarf**, scarfs or scarves NOUN a piece of cloth worn round your neck or head to keep you warm

**scary**, scarier, scariest ADJECTIVE INFORMAL frightening

**scatter** VERB ❶ To scatter things means to throw or drop them all over an area ❷ If people scatter, they suddenly move away in different directions

**scene** NOUN ❶ part of a play or film in which a series of events happen in one place ❷ Pictures and views are sometimes called scenes ❸ The scene of an event is the place where it happened ❹ an area of activity

**don't mix up**

**Hello Kitty...**

never mixes up **scene** (a part of a play) and **seen** (the past participle of see).

**scenery** NOUN ❶ In the countryside, you can refer to everything you see as the scenery ❷ In a theatre, the scenery is the painted cloth on the stage which represents the place where the action is happening

**scent** NOUN ❶ a smell, especially a pleasant one ❷ Scent is perfume ✿ VERB ❸ When an animal scents something, it becomes aware of it by smelling it

**schedule**, schedules, scheduling, scheduled [shed-yool] NOUN ❶ a plan that gives a list of events or tasks, together with the times at which each thing should be done ✿ VERB ❷ If something is scheduled to happen, it has been planned and arranged

**scheme**, schemes, scheming, schemed NOUN ❶ a plan or arrangement ✿ VERB ❷ When people scheme, they make secret plans

**scholar** NOUN ❶ a person who studies an academic subject and knows a lot about it ❷ In South African English, a scholar is a school pupil

**scholarship** NOUN ❶ If you get a scholarship to a school or university, your studies are paid for by the school or university or by some other organization ❷ Scholarship is academic study and knowledge

**school** NOUN ❶ a place where children are educated ❷ University departments and colleges are sometimes called schools ❸ You can refer to a large group of dolphins or fish as a school ✿ VERB ❹ When someone is schooled in something, they are taught it

**science** NOUN ❶ Science is the study of the nature and behaviour of natural things and the knowledge obtained about them ❷ a branch of science, for example physics or biology

**science fiction** NOUN Stories about events happening in the future or in other parts of the universe are called science fiction

**scientific** ADJECTIVE ❶ relating to science or to a particular science ❷ done in a systematic way, using experiments or tests

**scientist** NOUN an expert in one of the sciences who does work connected with it

**scissors** PLURAL NOUN Scissors are a cutting tool with two sharp blades

**scoop** VERB ❶ If you scoop something up, you pick it up using a spoon or the palm of your hand ✿ NOUN ❷ an object like a large spoon which is used for picking up food such as ice cream

**scooter** NOUN ❶ a small, light motorcycle ❷ a simple cycle which a child rides by standing on it and pushing the ground with one foot

**score**, scores, scoring, scored VERB ❶ If you score in a game, you get a goal, run, or point

A B C D E F G H I J K L M N O P Q R S T U V W X Y Z

235

# scorn – seal

❷ To score in a game also means to record the score obtained by the players ❸ If you score a success or victory, you achieve it ❹ To score a surface means to cut a line into it ✿ NOUN ❺ The score in a game is the number of goals, runs, or points obtained by the two teams ❻ Scores of things means very many of them ❼ The score of a piece of music is the written version of it

**scorn** NOUN ❶ Scorn is great contempt ✿ VERB ❷ If you scorn someone, you treat them with great contempt ❸ FORMAL If you scorn something, you refuse to accept it

**scornful** ADJECTIVE showing contempt
**scornfully** ADVERB

**scout** NOUN ❶ a child who is a member of the Scout Association, an organization for children which aims to develop character and responsibility ❷ someone who is sent to an area to find out the position of an enemy army ✿ VERB ❸ If you scout around for something, you look around for it

**scowl** VERB ❶ If you scowl, you frown because you are angry ✿ NOUN ❷ an angry expression

**scramble**, scrambles, scrambling, scrambled VERB If you scramble over something, you climb over it using your hands to help you

**scrap**, scraps, scrapping, scrapped NOUN ❶ A scrap of something is a very small piece of it ❷ IN PLURAL Scraps are pieces of leftover food ✿ ADJECTIVE OR NOUN ❸ Scrap metal or scrap is metal from old machinery or cars that can be re-used ✿ VERB ❹ If you scrap something, you get rid of it

**scrape**, scrapes, scraping, scraped VERB ❶ If you scrape a surface, you rub a rough or sharp object against it ❷ If something scrapes, it makes a harsh noise by rubbing against something

**scratch**, scratches, scratching, scratched VERB ❶ To scratch something means to make a small cut on it accidentally ❷ If you scratch, you rub your skin with your nails because it is itching ✿ NOUN ❸ a small cut

**scream** VERB ❶ If you scream, you shout or cry in a loud, high-pitched voice ✿ NOUN ❷ a loud, high-pitched cry

**screech** VERB ❶ To screech means to make an unpleasant high-pitched noise ✿ NOUN ❷ an unpleasant high-pitched noise

**screen** NOUN ❶ a flat vertical surface on which a picture is shown ❷ a vertical panel used to separate different parts of a room or to protect something ✿ VERB ❸ To screen a film or television programme means to show it ❹ If you screen someone, you put something in front of them to protect them

**screw** NOUN ❶ a small, sharp piece of metal used for fixing things together or for fixing something to a wall ✿ VERB ❷ If you screw things together, you fix them together using screws ❸ If you screw something onto something else, you fix it there by twisting it round and round

**screw up** ✿ VERB If you screw something up, you twist it or squeeze it so that it no longer has its proper shape

**screwdriver** NOUN a tool for turning screws

**scribble**, scribbles, scribbling, scribbled VERB ❶ If you scribble something, you write it quickly and roughly ❷ To scribble also means to make meaningless marks ✿ NOUN ❸ You can refer to something written or drawn quickly and roughly as a scribble

**script** NOUN the written version of a play, film, or television programme

**scroll** NOUN a long roll of paper or parchment with writing on it

**scrub**, scrubs, scrubbing, scrubbed VERB ❶ If you scrub something, you clean it with a stiff brush and water ✿ NOUN ❷ If you give something a scrub, you scrub it ❸ Scrub consists of low trees and bushes

**scruffy**, scruffier, scruffiest ADJECTIVE dirty and untidy

**sculptor** NOUN someone who makes sculptures

**sculpture** NOUN ❶ a work of art produced by carving or shaping stone or clay ❷ Sculpture is the art of making sculptures

**sea** NOUN ❶ The sea is the salty water that covers much of the earth's surface ❷ A sea of people or things is a very large number of them

**seagull** NOUN Seagulls are common white, grey, and black birds that live near the sea

**seal** NOUN ❶ an official mark on a document which shows that it is genuine ❷ a piece of wax fixed over the opening of a container ❸ a large mammal with flippers, that lives partly on land and partly in the sea ✿ VERB

236

**seam – security**

❹ If you seal an envelope, you stick down the flap ❺ If you seal an opening, you cover it securely so that air, gas, or liquid cannot get through

**seam** NOUN ❶ a line of stitches joining two pieces of cloth ❷ A seam of coal is a long, narrow layer of it beneath the ground

**search** VERB ❶ If you search for something, you look for it in several places ❷ If a person is searched their body and clothing are examined to see if they are hiding anything ✿ NOUN ❸ an attempt to find something

**search engine** NOUN a service on the internet which enables users to search for items of interest

**seaside** NOUN The seaside is an area next to the sea

**season** NOUN ❶ The seasons are the periods into which a year is divided and which have their own typical weather conditions. The seasons are spring, summer, autumn, and winter ❷ a period of the year when something usually happens ✿ VERB ❸ If you season food, you add salt, pepper, or spices to it

**seat** NOUN ❶ something you can sit on ❷ The seat of a piece of clothing is the part that covers your bottom ❸ If someone wins a seat in parliament, they are elected ✿ VERB ❹ If you seat yourself somewhere, you sit down ❺ If a place seats a particular number of people, it has enough seats for that number

**seat belt** NOUN a strap that you fasten across your body for safety when travelling in a car or an aircraft

**seaweed** NOUN Plants that grow in the sea are called seaweed

**second** ADJECTIVE ❶ The second item in a series is the one counted as number two ✿ NOUN ❷ one of the sixty parts that a minute is divided into ❸ IN PLURAL Seconds are goods that are sold cheaply because they are slightly faulty ✿ VERB ❹ If you second a proposal, you formally agree with it so that it can be discussed or voted on ❺ If you are seconded somewhere, you are sent there temporarily to work **secondly** ADVERB

**secondary** ADJECTIVE ❶ Something that is secondary is less important than something else ❷ Secondary education is education for pupils between the ages of eleven and eighteen

**secondary school** NOUN a school for pupils between the ages of eleven and eighteen

**second-hand** ADJECTIVE OR ADVERB ❶ Something that is second-hand has already been owned by someone else ❷ If you hear a story second-hand, you hear it indirectly, rather than from the people involved

**secret** ADJECTIVE ❶ Something that is secret is told to only a small number of people and hidden from everyone else ✿ NOUN ❷ a fact told to only a small number of people and hidden from everyone else **secrecy** NOUN

**secretary**, secretaries NOUN ❶ a person employed by an organization to keep records, write letters, and do office work ❷ Ministers in charge of some government departments are also called secretaries **secretarial** ADJECTIVE

### how to remember

A **secret**ary must be able to keep a **secret**.

**secretive** ADJECTIVE Secretive people tend to hide their feelings and intentions

**section** NOUN A section of something is one of the parts it is divided into

**secure**, secures, securing, secured VERB ❶ FORMAL If you secure something, you manage to get it ❷ If you secure a place, you make it safe from attack ❸ To secure something also means to fasten it firmly ✿ ADJECTIVE ❹ If a place is secure, it is tightly locked or well protected ❺ If an object is secure, it is firmly fixed in place ❻ If you feel secure, you feel safe and confident **securely** ADVERB

**security** NOUN OR ADJECTIVE ❶ Security means all the precautions taken to protect a place ✿ NOUN ❷ A feeling of security is a feeling of being safe

237

# see - send

**see**, sees, seeing, saw, seen VERB ❶ If you see something, you are looking at it or you notice it ❷ If you see someone, you visit them or meet them ❸ If you see someone to a place, you accompany them there ❹ To see something also means to realize or understand it ❺ If you say you will see what is happening, you mean you will find out ❻ If you say you will see if you can do something, you mean you will try to do it ❼ If you see that something is done, you make sure that it is done ❽ If you see to something, you deal with it ❾ 'See' is used to say that an event takes place during a particular period of time ✿ NOUN ❿ A bishop's see is his diocese

**seed** NOUN ❶ The seeds of a plant are the small, hard parts from which new plants can grow ❷ The seeds of a feeling or process are its beginning or origins

**seek**, seeks, seeking, sought VERB FORMAL ❶ To seek something means to try to find it, obtain it, or achieve it ❷ If you seek to do something, you try to do it

**seem** VERB If something seems to be the case, it appears to be the case or you think it is the case

**segment** NOUN ❶ A segment of something is one part of it ❷ The segments of an orange or grapefruit are the sections which you can divide it into

**seize**, seizes, seizing, seized VERB ❶ If you seize something, you grab it firmly ❷ To seize a place or to seize control of it means to take control of it quickly and suddenly ❸ If you seize an opportunity, you take advantage of it ❹ If you seize on something, you immediately show great interest in it

**seldom** ADVERB not very often

**select** VERB ❶ If you select something, you choose it ✿ ADJECTIVE ❷ of good quality

**selection** NOUN ❶ Selection is the choosing of people or things ❷ A selection of people or things is a set of them chosen from a larger group ❸ The selection of goods in a shop is the range of goods available

**self**, selves NOUN Your self is your basic personality or nature

**self-confident** ADJECTIVE confident of your own abilities or worth **self-confidence** NOUN

**self-conscious** ADJECTIVE nervous and easily embarrassed, and worried about what other people think of you

**self-control** NOUN Self-control is the ability to restrain yourself and not show your feelings

**self-defence** NOUN Self-defence is the use of special physical techniques to protect yourself when someone attacks you

**selfish** ADJECTIVE caring only about yourself, and not about other people **selfishly** ADVERB **selfishness** NOUN

**self-respect** NOUN Self-respect is a feeling of confidence and pride in your own abilities and worth

**sell**, sells, selling, sold VERB ❶ If you sell something, you let someone have it in return for money ❷ If a shop sells something, it has it available for people to buy ❸ If something sells, people buy it

**sell out** ✿ VERB If a shop has sold out of something, it has sold it all

**Sellotape** NOUN TRADEMARK Sellotape is a transparent sticky tape

**semicircle** NOUN a half of a circle, or something with this shape

**semicolon** NOUN the punctuation mark (;), used to separate different parts of a sentence or to indicate a pause

## What does the semicolon do?

You put a **semicolon** (;) between clauses to show a contrast or balance.

**semifinal** NOUN The semifinals are the two matches in a competition played to decide who plays in the final

**seminar** NOUN a meeting of a small number of university students or teachers to discuss a particular topic

**send**, sends, sending, sent VERB ❶ If you send something to someone, you arrange for it to be delivered to them ❷ To send a radio signal or message means to transmit it ❸ If you send someone somewhere, you tell them to go there or arrange for them to go ❹ If you send for someone, you send a message asking them to come and see you ❺ If you send off for something, you write and ask for it to be sent to you ❻ To send people or things in a particular direction means to make them move in that direction

**senior** ADJECTIVE ❶ The senior people in an organization or profession have the highest and most important jobs ✿ NOUN ❷ Someone who is your senior is older than you

**senior citizen** NOUN an elderly person, especially one receiving an old-age pension

**sensation** NOUN ❶ a feeling, especially a physical feeling ❷ If something is a sensation, it causes great excitement

**sensational** ADJECTIVE ❶ causing great excitement and interest ❷ INFORMAL extremely good

**sense**, senses, sensing, sensed NOUN ❶ Your senses are the physical abilities of sight, hearing, smell, touch, and taste ❷ a feeling ❸ A sense of a word is one of its meanings ❹ Sense is the ability to think and behave sensibly ✿ VERB ❺ If you sense something, you become aware of it

**sensible** ADJECTIVE showing good sense and judgment **sensibly** ADVERB

**sensitive** ADJECTIVE ❶ If you are sensitive to other people's feelings, you understand them ❷ If you are sensitive about something, you are worried or easily upset about it ❸ A sensitive subject or issue needs to be dealt with carefully because it can make people angry or upset ❹ Something that is sensitive to a particular thing is easily affected or harmed by it

**sentence**, sentences, sentencing, sentenced NOUN ❶ a group of words which make a statement, question, or command. When written down a sentence begins with a capital letter and ends with a full stop ❷ In a law court, a sentence is a punishment given to someone who has been found guilty ✿ VERB ❸ When a guilty person is sentenced, they are told officially what their punishment will be

**sentimental** ADJECTIVE ❶ feeling or expressing tenderness or sadness to an exaggerated extent ❷ relating to a person's emotions

**separate**, separates, separating, separated ADJECTIVE ❶ If something is separate from something else, the two things are not connected ✿ VERB ❷ To separate people or things means to cause them to be apart from each other ❸ If a married couple separate, they decide to live apart

**separately** ADVERB

**September** NOUN September is the ninth month of the year. It has 30 days

**sequence** NOUN ❶ A sequence of events is a number of them coming one after the other ❷ The sequence in which things are arranged is the order in which they are arranged

**sergeant** NOUN ❶ a noncommissioned officer of middle rank in the army or air force ❷ a police officer just above a constable in rank

**serial** NOUN a story which is broadcast or published in a number of parts over a period of time

**series** NOUN ❶ A series of things is a number of them coming one after the other ❷ A radio or television series is a set of programmes with the same title

### how English works

Hello Kitty...

knows that a **sentence** is a group of words which make up a statement or question, starting with a capital letter and ending with a full stop.

# serious - settle

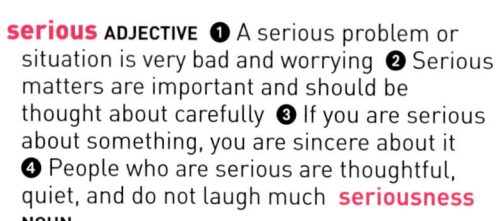

**serious** ADJECTIVE ❶ A serious problem or situation is very bad and worrying ❷ Serious matters are important and should be thought about carefully ❸ If you are serious about something, you are sincere about it ❹ People who are serious are thoughtful, quiet, and do not laugh much **seriousness** NOUN

**seriously** ADVERB You say seriously to emphasize that you mean what you say

**sermon** NOUN a talk on a religious or moral subject given as part of a church service

**servant** NOUN someone who is employed to work in another person's house

**serve**, serves, serving, served VERB ❶ If you serve a country, an organization, or a person, you do useful work for them ❷ To serve as something means to act or be used as that thing ❸ If something serves people in a particular place, it provides them with something they need ❹ If you serve food or drink to people, you give it to them ❺ To serve customers in a shop means to help them and provide them with what they want ❻ To serve a prison sentence or an apprenticeship means to spend time doing it ❼ When you serve in tennis or badminton, you throw the ball or shuttlecock into the air and hit it over the net to start playing ✿ NOUN ❽ the act of serving in tennis or badminton

**server** NOUN a computer or computer program which supplies information or resources to a number of computers on a network

**service**, services, servicing, serviced NOUN ❶ a system organized to provide something for the public ❷ Some government organizations are called services ❸ The services are the army, the navy, and the air force ❹ If you give your services to a person or organization, you work for them or help them in some way ❺ In a shop or restaurant, service is the process of being served ❻ a religious ceremony ❼ When it is your service in a game of tennis or badminton, it is your turn to serve ❽ IN PLURAL Motorway services consist of a petrol station, restaurant, shop, and toilets ✿ VERB ❾ When a machine or vehicle is serviced, it is examined and adjusted so that it will continue working efficiently

**session** NOUN ❶ a meeting of an official group ❷ a period during which meetings are held regularly ❸ The period during which an activity takes place can also be called a session

**set**, sets, setting, set NOUN ❶ Several things make a set when they belong together or form a group ❷ A television set is a television ❸ The set for a play or film is the scenery or furniture on the stage or in the studio ❹ In tennis, a set is a group of six or more games. There are usually several sets in a match ✿ VERB ❺ If something is set somewhere, that is where it is ❻ When the sun sets, it goes below the horizon ❼ When you set the table, you prepare it for a meal by putting plates and cutlery on it ❽ When you set a clock or a control, you adjust it to a particular point or position ❾ If you set someone a piece of work or a target, you give it to them to do or to achieve ❿ When something such as jelly or cement sets, it becomes firm or hard ✿ ADJECTIVE ⓫ Something that is set is fixed and not varying ⓬ If you are set to do something, you are ready or likely to do it ⓭ If you are set on doing something, you are determined to do it ⓮ If a play or story is set at a particular time or in a particular place, the events in it take place at that time or in that place

**set about** ✿ VERB If you set about doing something, you start doing it

**set back** ✿ VERB If something sets back a project or scheme, it delays it

**set off** ✿ VERB ❶ When you set off, you start a journey ❷ To set something off means to cause it to start

**set out** ✿ VERB ❶ When you set out, you start a journey ❷ If you set out to do something, you start trying to do it

**set up** ✿ VERB If you set something up, you make all the necessary preparations for it

**settle**, settles, settling, settled VERB ❶ To settle an argument means to put an end to it ❷ If something is settled, it has all been decided and arranged ❸ If you settle on something or settle for it, you choose it ❹ When you settle a bill, you pay it ❺ If you settle in a place, you make it your

**settle down - shake**

permanent home ❻ If you settle yourself somewhere, you sit down and make yourself comfortable

**settle down** ✿ VERB ❶ When someone settles down, they start living a quiet life in one place, especially when they get married ❷ To settle down means to become quiet or calm

**settlement** NOUN ❶ an official agreement between people who have been involved in a conflict ❷ a place where people have settled and built homes

**seven** the number 7

**seventeen** the number 17   **seventeenth** ADJECTIVE

**seventh** ADJECTIVE ❶ The seventh item in a series is the one counted as number seven ✿ NOUN ❷ one of seven equal parts

**seventy**, seventies the number 70   **seventieth** ADJECTIVE

**several** ADJECTIVE Several people or things means a small number of them

**severe** ADJECTIVE ❶ extremely bad or unpleasant ❷ stern and harsh   **severely** ADVERB

**sew**, sews, sewing, sewed, sewn [so] VERB When you sew things together, you join them using a needle and thread   **sewing** NOUN

**sewer** [sue-uh] NOUN an underground channel that carries sewage to a place where it is treated to make it harmless

**sex** NOUN ❶ The sexes are the two groups, male and female, into which people and animals are divided ❷ The sex of a person or animal is their characteristic of being either male or female ❸ Sex is the physical activity by which people and animals produce young

**sexual** ADJECTIVE ❶ connected with the act of sex or with people's desire for sex ❷ relating to the difference between males and females ❸ relating to the biological process by which people and animals produce young   **sexually** ADVERB

**sexy**, sexier, sexiest ADJECTIVE sexually attractive or exciting

**shabby**, shabbier, shabbiest ADJECTIVE ❶ old and worn in appearance ❷ dressed in old, worn-out clothes ❸ behaving in a mean or unfair way

**shade**, shades, shading, shaded NOUN ❶ Shade is an area of darkness and coolness which the sun does not reach ❷ The shades of a colour are its different forms. For example, olive green is a shade of green ✿ VERB ❸ If a place is shaded by trees or buildings, they prevent the sun from shining on it ❹ If you shade your eyes, you put your hand in front of them to protect them from a bright light

**shadow** NOUN ❶ the dark shape made when an object prevents light from reaching a surface ❷ Shadow is darkness caused by light not reaching a place ✿ VERB ❸ To shadow someone means to follow them and watch them closely

**shady**, shadier, shadiest ADJECTIVE A shady place is sheltered from sunlight by trees or buildings

**don't mix up**

**Hello Kitty...**

never mixes up **sew** (to join using a needle and thread), **so** (the adverb) and **sow** (to plant seeds).

**shake**, shakes, shaking, shook, shaken VERB ❶ To shake something means to move it quickly from side to side or up and down ❷ If something shakes, it moves from side to side or up and down with small, quick movements ❸ If your voice shakes, it trembles because you are nervous or angry ❹ If something shakes you, it shocks and upsets you ❺ When you shake your head,

# shaky - shawl

you move it from side to side in order to say 'no' ✿ NOUN ❻ If you give something a shake, you shake it

**shaky**, shakier, shakiest ADJECTIVE rather weak and unsteady **shakily** ADVERB

**shall** VERB ❶ If I say I shall do something, I mean that I intend to do it ❷ If I say something shall happen, I am emphasizing that it will definitely happen, or I am ordering it to happen ❸ 'Shall' is also used in questions when you are asking what to do, or making a suggestion

**shallow** ADJECTIVE ❶ Shallow means not deep ❷ Shallow also means not involving serious thought or sincere feelings

**shame**, shames, shaming, shamed NOUN ❶ Shame is the feeling of guilt or embarrassment you get when you know you have done something wrong or foolish ❷ Shame is also something that makes people lose respect for you ❸ If you say something is a shame, you mean you are sorry about it ✿ INTERJECTION ❹ INFORMAL In South African English, you say 'Shame!' to show sympathy ✿ VERB ❺ If something shames you, it makes you feel ashamed ❻ If you shame someone into doing something, you force them to do it by making them feel ashamed not to

**shameful** ADJECTIVE If someone's behaviour is shameful, they ought to be ashamed of it

**shampoo** NOUN ❶ Shampoo is a soapy liquid used for washing your hair ✿ VERB ❷ When you shampoo your hair, you wash it with shampoo

**shape**, shapes, shaping, shaped NOUN ❶ The shape of something is the form or pattern of its outline, for example whether it is round or square ❷ something with a definite form, for example a circle or triangle ❸ The shape of something such as an organization is its structure and size ✿ VERB ❹ If you shape an object, you form it into a particular shape ❺ To shape something means to cause it to develop in a particular way

**share**, shares, sharing, shared VERB ❶ If two people share something, they both use it, do it, or have it ❷ If you share an idea or a piece of news with someone, you tell it to them ✿ NOUN ❸ A share of something is a portion of it ❹ The shares of a company are the equal parts into which its ownership is divided. People can buy shares as an investment

**share out** ✿ VERB ❶ If you share something out, you give it out equally among a group of people

**shareholder** NOUN a person who owns shares in a company

**shark** NOUN ❶ Sharks are large, powerful fish with sharp teeth ❷ a person who cheats people out of money

**sharp** ADJECTIVE ❶ A sharp object has a fine edge or point that is good for cutting or piercing things ❷ A sharp outline or distinction is easy to see ❸ A sharp person is quick to notice or understand things ❹ A sharp change is sudden and significant ❺ If you say something in a sharp way, you say it firmly and rather angrily ❻ A sharp sound is short, sudden, and quite loud ❼ A sharp pain is a sudden pain ❽ A sharp taste is slightly sour ❾ A musical instrument or note that is sharp is slightly too high in pitch ✿ ADVERB ❿ If something happens at a certain time sharp, it happens at that time precisely ✿ NOUN ⓫ In music, a sharp is a note or key a semitone higher than that described by the same letter. It is represented by the symbol (#) **sharply** ADVERB

**sharpen**, sharpens, sharpening, sharpened VERB ❶ To sharpen an object means to make its edge or point sharper ❷ If your senses or abilities sharpen, you become quicker at noticing or understanding things

**shatter** VERB ❶ If something shatters, it breaks into a lot of small pieces ❷ If something shatters your hopes or beliefs, it destroys them completely ❸ If you are shattered by an event or piece of news, you are shocked and upset by it

**shave**, shaves, shaving, shaved VERB ❶ When a man shaves, he removes hair from his face with a razor ❷ If you shave off part of a piece of wood, you cut thin pieces from it ✿ NOUN ❸ When a man has a shave, he shaves

**shaver** NOUN an electric razor

**shawl** NOUN a large piece of woollen cloth worn round a woman's head or shoulders or used to wrap a baby in

**she** PRONOUN 'She' is used to refer to a woman or girl whose identity is clear. 'She' is also used to refer to a country, a ship, or a car

**shed**, sheds, shedding, shed NOUN ❶ a small building used for storing things ✿ VERB ❷ When an animal sheds hair or skin, some of its hair or skin drops off. When a tree sheds its leaves, its leaves fall off ❸ FORMAL To shed something also means to get rid of it ❹ If a lorry sheds its load, the load falls off the lorry onto the road ❺ If you shed tears, you cry

**sheep** NOUN A sheep is a farm animal with a thick woolly coat. Sheep are kept for meat and wool

**sheet** NOUN ❶ a large rectangular piece of cloth used to cover a bed ❷ A sheet of paper is a rectangular piece of it ❸ A sheet of glass or metal is a large, flat piece of it

**shelf**, shelves NOUN a flat piece of wood, metal, or glass fixed to a wall and used for putting things on

**shell** NOUN ❶ The shell of an egg or nut is its hard covering ❷ The shell of a tortoise, snail, or crab is the hard protective covering on its back ❸ The shell of a building or other structure is its frame ❹ a container filled with explosives that can be fired from a gun ✿ VERB ❺ If you shell peas or nuts, you remove their natural covering ❻ To shell a place means to fire large explosive shells at it

**shellfish**, shellfish or shellfishes NOUN a small sea creature with a shell

**shelter** NOUN ❶ a small building made to protect people from bad weather or danger ❷ If a place provides shelter, it provides protection from bad weather or danger ✿ VERB ❸ If you shelter in a place, you stay there and are safe ❹ If you shelter someone, you provide them with a place to stay when they are in danger

**shield** NOUN ❶ a large piece of a strong material like metal or plastic which soldiers or policeman carry to protect themselves ❷ If something is a shield against something, it gives protection from it ✿ VERB ❸ To shield someone means to protect them from something

**shift** VERB ❶ If you shift something, you move it. If something shifts, it moves ❷ If an opinion or situation shifts, it changes slightly ✿ NOUN ❸ A shift in an opinion or situation is a slight change ❹ a set period during which people work in a factory

**shin**, shins, shinning, shinned NOUN ❶ Your shin is the front part of your leg between your knee and your ankle ✿ VERB ❷ If you shin up a tree, you climb it quickly by gripping it with your hands and legs

**shine**, shines, shining, shone VERB ❶ When something shines, it gives out or reflects a bright light ❷ If you shine a torch or lamp somewhere, you point it there

**shiny**, shinier, shiniest ADJECTIVE Shiny things are bright and look as if they have been polished

**ship**, ships, shipping, shipped NOUN ❶ a large boat which carries passengers or cargo ✿ VERB ❷ If people or things are shipped somewhere, they are transported there

**shirt** NOUN a piece of clothing worn on the upper part of the body, having a collar, sleeves, and buttons down the front

**shiver** VERB ❶ When you shiver, you tremble slightly because you are cold or scared ✿ NOUN ❷ a slight trembling caused by cold or fear

**shock** NOUN ❶ If you have a shock, you have a sudden upsetting experience ❷ Shock is a person's emotional and physical condition when something very unpleasant or upsetting has happened to them ❸ In medicine, shock is a serious physical condition in which the blood cannot circulate properly because of an injury ❹ a slight movement in something when it is hit by something else ❺ A shock of hair is a thick mass of it ✿ VERB ❻ If something shocks you, it upsets you because it is unpleasant and unexpected ❼ You can say that something shocks you when it offends you because it is rude or immoral **shocked** ADJECTIVE

**shocking** ADJECTIVE ❶ INFORMAL very bad ❷ rude or immoral

**shoe**, shoes, shoeing, shod NOUN ❶ Shoes are strong coverings for your feet. They cover most of your foot, but not your ankle ✿ VERB ❷ To shoe a horse means to fix horseshoes onto its hooves

# shoot - shovel

**shoot**, shoots, shooting, shot **VERB** ❶ To shoot a person or animal means to kill or injure them by firing a gun at them ❷ To shoot an arrow means to fire it from a bow ❸ If something shoots in a particular direction, it moves there quickly and suddenly ❹ When a film is shot, it is filmed ❺ In games such as football or hockey, to shoot means to kick or hit the ball towards the goal ✿ **NOUN** ❻ an occasion when people hunt animals or birds with guns ❼ a plant that is beginning to grow, or a new part growing from a plant

**shop**, shops, shopping, shopped **NOUN** ❶ a place where things are sold ❷ a place where a particular type of work is done ✿ **VERB** ❸ When you shop, you go to the shops to buy things **shopper NOUN**

**shopping NOUN** Your shopping is the goods you have bought from the shops

**shore**, shores, shoring, shored **NOUN** ❶ The shore of a sea, lake, or wide river is the land along the edge of it ✿ **VERB** ❷ If you shore something up, you reinforce it or strengthen it

**short ADJECTIVE** ❶ not lasting very long ❷ small in length, distance, or height ❸ not using many words ❹ If you are short with someone, you speak to them crossly ❺ If you have a short temper, you get angry very quickly ❻ If you are short of something, you do not have enough of it ❼ If a name is short for another name, it is a short version of it ✿ **NOUN** ❽ IN PLURAL Shorts are trousers with short legs ✿ **ADVERB** ❾ If you stop short of a place, you do not quite reach it

**shortage NOUN** If there is a shortage of something, there is not enough of it

**shorten VERB** If you shorten something or if it shortens, it becomes shorter

**shortly ADVERB** ❶ Shortly means soon ❷ If you speak to someone shortly, you speak to them in a cross and impatient way

**short-term ADJECTIVE** happening or having an effect within a short time or for a short time

**shot** ❶ Shot is the past tense and past participle of **shoot** ✿ **NOUN** ❷ the act of firing a gun ❸ Someone who is a good shot can shoot accurately ❹ In football, golf, and tennis, a shot is the act of kicking or hitting the ball ❺ a photograph or short film sequence

**should VERB** ❶ You use 'should' to say that something ought to happen ❷ You also use 'should' to say that you expect something to happen ❸ FORMAL You can use 'should' to announce that you are about to do or say something ❹ 'Should' is used in conditional sentences ❺ 'Should' is sometimes used in 'that' clauses ❻ If you say that you should think something, you mean that it is probably true

**shoulder NOUN** ❶ Your shoulders are the parts of your body between your neck and the tops of your arms ✿ **VERB** ❷ If you shoulder something heavy, you put it across one of your shoulders to carry it ❸ If you shoulder the responsibility or blame for something, you accept it

**shout NOUN** ❶ a loud call or cry ✿ **VERB** ❷ If you shout something, you say it very loudly

**shove**, shoves, shoving, shoved **VERB** ❶ If you shove someone or something, you push them roughly ✿ **NOUN** ❷ a rough push

**shove off** ✿ **VERB** INFORMAL If you tell someone to shove off, you are telling them angrily and rudely to go away

**shovel**, shovels, shovelling, shovelled **NOUN** ❶ a tool like a spade, used for moving earth or snow ✿ **VERB** ❷ If you shovel earth or snow, you move it with a shovel

## some other words to use

## Helpful hints...

You should try not to use **short** too much when you are writing. Some other words you can use are: *brief*, *momentary* and *short-lived*.

**show**, shows, showing, showed, shown VERB ① To show that something exists or is true means to prove it ② If a picture shows something, it represents it ③ If you show someone something, you let them see it ④ If you show someone to a room or seat, you lead them there ⑤ If you show someone how to do something, you demonstrate it to them ⑥ If something shows, it is visible ⑦ If something shows a quality or characteristic, you can see that it has it ⑧ If you show your feelings, you let people see them ⑨ If you show affection or mercy, you behave in an affectionate or merciful way ⑩ To show a film or television programme means to let the public see it ✿ NOUN ⑪ a form of light entertainment at the theatre or on television ⑫ an exhibition ⑬ A show of a feeling or attitude is behaviour in which you show it

**show off** ✿ VERB INFORMAL If someone is showing off, they are trying to impress people

**show up** ✿ VERB ① INFORMAL If you show up, you arrive at a place ② If something shows up, it can be seen clearly

**show business** NOUN Show business is entertainment in the theatre, films, and television

**shower** NOUN ① a device which sprays you with water so that you can wash yourself ② If you have a shower, you wash yourself by standing under a shower ③ a short period of rain ④ You can refer to a lot of things falling at once as a shower ✿ VERB ⑤ If you shower, you have a shower ⑥ If you are showered with a lot of things, they fall on you

**shriek** NOUN ① a high-pitched scream ✿ VERB ② If you shriek, you make a high-pitched scream

**shrimp** NOUN a small edible shellfish with a long tail and many legs

**shrine** NOUN a place of worship associated with a sacred person or object

**shrink**, shrinks, shrinking, shrank, shrunk VERB ① If something shrinks, it becomes smaller ② If you shrink from something, you move away from it because you are afraid of it

**shrub** NOUN a low, bushy plant

**shrug**, shrugs, shrugging, shrugged VERB ① If you shrug your shoulders, you raise them slightly as a sign of indifference ✿ NOUN ② If you give a shrug of your shoulders, you shrug them

**shudder** VERB ① If you shudder, you tremble with fear or horror ② If a machine or vehicle shudders, it shakes violently ✿ NOUN ③ a shiver of fear or horror

**shuffle**, shuffles, shuffling, shuffled VERB ① If you shuffle, you walk without lifting your feet properly off the ground ② If you shuffle about, you move about and fidget because you feel uncomfortable or embarrassed ③ If you shuffle a pack of cards, you mix them up before you begin a game

**shut**, shuts, shutting, shut VERB ① If you shut something, you close it ② When a shop or pub shuts, it is closed and you can no longer go into it ✿ ADJECTIVE ③ If something is shut, it is closed

**shutter** NOUN Shutters are hinged wooden or metal covers fitted on the outside or inside of a window

**shuttle** ADJECTIVE ① A shuttle service is an air, bus, or train service which makes frequent journeys between two places ✿ NOUN ② a plane used in a shuttle service

**shy**, shyer, shyest; shies, shying, shied ADJECTIVE ① A shy person is nervous and uncomfortable in the company of other people ✿ VERB ② When a horse shies, it moves away suddenly because something has frightened it ③ If you shy away from doing something, you avoid doing it because you are afraid or nervous **shyly** ADVERB **shyness** NOUN

**sibling** NOUN FORMAL Your siblings are your brothers and sisters

**sick** ADJECTIVE ① If you are sick, you are ill ② If you feel sick, you feel as if you are going to vomit. If you are sick, you vomit ③ INFORMAL If you are sick of doing something, you feel you have been doing it too long ④ INFORMAL A sick joke or story deals with death or suffering in an unpleasantly frivolous way **sickness** NOUN

**side**, sides, siding, sided NOUN ① Side refers to a position to the left or right of something ② The sides of a boundary or barrier are the two areas it separates ③ Your sides are the

**sidewalk - silk**

parts of your body from your armpits down to your hips ❹ The sides of something are its outside surfaces, especially the surfaces which are not its front or back ❺ The sides of a hill or valley are the parts that slope ❻ The two sides in a war, argument, or relationship are the two people or groups involved ❼ A particular side of something is one aspect of it ✿ **ADJECTIVE** ❽ situated on a side of a building or vehicle ❾ A side road is a small road leading off a larger one ❿ A side issue is an issue that is less important than the main one ✿ **VERB** ⓫ If you side with someone in an argument, you support them

**sidewalk** NOUN In American English, a sidewalk is a pavement

**sideways** ADVERB from or towards the side of something or someone

**siege** [seej] NOUN a military operation in which an army surrounds a place and prevents food or help from reaching the people inside

**sieve**, sieves, sieving, sieved [siv] NOUN ❶ a kitchen tool made of mesh, used for sifting or straining things ✿ **VERB** ❷ If you sieve a powder or liquid, you pass it through a sieve

**sigh** VERB ❶ When you sigh, you let out a deep breath ✿ NOUN ❷ the breath you let out when you sigh

**sight** NOUN ❶ Sight is the ability to see ❷ something you see ❸ IN PLURAL Sights are interesting places which tourists visit ✿ **VERB** ❹ If you sight someone or something, you see them briefly or suddenly

**sightseeing** NOUN Sightseeing is visiting the interesting places that tourists usually visit

**sign** NOUN ❶ a mark or symbol that always has a particular meaning, for example in mathematics or music ❷ a gesture with a particular meaning ❸ A sign can also consist of words, a picture, or a symbol giving information or a warning ❹ A sign is an event or happening that some people believe God has sent as a warning or instruction to an individual or to people in general ❺ If there are signs of something, there is evidence that it exists or is happening ✿ **VERB** ❻ If you sign a document, you write your name on it ❼ If you sign, you use your hands to communicate with a deaf person

**sign on** ✿ **VERB** ❶ If you sign on for a job or course, you officially agree to do it by signing a contract ❷ When people sign on, they officially state that they are unemployed and claim benefit from the state

**sign up** ✿ **VERB** If you sign up for a job or course, you officially agree to do it by signing a contract

**signal**, signals, signalling, signalled NOUN ❶ a gesture, sound, or action intended to give a message to someone ❷ A railway signal is a piece of equipment beside the track which tells train drivers whether to stop or not ✿ **VERB** ❸ If you signal to someone, you make a gesture or sound to give them a message

**signature** NOUN If you write your signature, you write your name the way you usually write it

**significant** ADJECTIVE large or important **significance** NOUN **significantly** ADVERB

**Sikh** [seek] NOUN a person who believes in Sikhism, an Indian religion which separated from Hinduism in the sixteenth century and which teaches that there is only one God

**silence**, silences, silencing, silenced NOUN ❶ Silence is quietness ❷ Someone's silence about something is their failure or refusal to talk about it ✿ **VERB** ❸ To silence someone or something means to stop them talking or making a noise

**silent** ADJECTIVE ❶ If you are silent, you are not saying anything ❷ If you are silent about something, you do not tell people about it ❸ When something is silent, it makes no noise ❹ A silent film has only pictures and no sound **silently** ADVERB

**silhouette** [sil-loo-ett] NOUN the outline of a dark shape against a light background

**silk** NOUN Silk is a fine, soft cloth made from a substance produced by silkworms

### how to say it

**Silhouette** is said sil-loo-ett, without saying the h and with most force on ett.

**silky**, silkier, silkiest ADJECTIVE smooth and soft

**silly**, sillier, silliest ADJECTIVE foolish or childish

**silver** NOUN ❶ Silver is a valuable greyish-white metallic element used for making jewellery and ornaments ❷ Silver is also coins made from silver or from silver-coloured metal ✿ ADJECTIVE OR NOUN ❸ greyish-white

**silver medal** NOUN a medal made from silver awarded to the competitor who comes second in a competition

**similar** ADJECTIVE If one thing is similar to another, or if two things are similar, they are like each other

**similarity**, similarities NOUN If there is a similarity between things, they are alike in some way

**simile** [sim-ill-ee] NOUN an expression in which a person or thing is described as being similar to someone or something else. Examples of similes are *She runs like a deer* and *He's as white as a sheet*

**simmer** VERB When food simmers, it cooks gently at just below boiling point

**simple**, simpler, simplest ADJECTIVE ❶ Something that is simple is uncomplicated and easy to understand or do ❷ Simple also means plain and not elaborate in style ❸ A simple way of life is uncomplicated ❹ You use 'simple' to emphasize that what you are talking about is the only important thing **simplicity** NOUN

**simplify**, simplifies, simplifying, simplified VERB To simplify something means to make it easier to do or understand

**simply** ADVERB ❶ Simply means merely ❷ You use 'simply' to emphasize what you are saying ❸ If you say or write something simply, you do it in a way that makes it easy to understand

**sin**, sins, sinning, sinned NOUN ❶ Sin is wicked and immoral behaviour ✿ VERB ❷ To sin means to do something wicked and immoral

**since** PREPOSITION, CONJUNCTION, OR ADVERB ❶ Since means from a particular time until now ✿ ADVERB ❷ Since also means at some time after a particular time in the past ✿ CONJUNCTION ❸ Since also means because

**sincere** ADJECTIVE If you are sincere, you say things that you really mean

**sincerely** ADVERB ❶ If you say or feel something sincerely, you mean it or feel it genuinely ✿ PHRASE ❷ You write **Yours sincerely** before your signature at the end of a letter in which you have named the person you are writing to in the greeting at the beginning of the letter. For example, if you began your letter 'Dear Mr Brown' you would use 'Yours sincerely'

**sing**, sings, singing, sang, sung VERB ❶ When you sing, you make musical sounds with your voice, usually producing words that fit a tune ❷ When birds or insects sing, they make pleasant sounds **singer** NOUN

**single**, singles, singling, singled ADJECTIVE ❶ Single means only one and not more ❷ People who are single are not married ❸ A single bed or bedroom is for one person ❹ A single ticket is a one-way ticket ✿ NOUN ❺ a recording of one or two short pieces of music

**single out** ✿ VERB If you single someone out from a group, you give them special treatment

**singular** NOUN ❶ In grammar, the singular is the form of a word that refers to just one person or thing ✿ ADJECTIVE ❷ FORMAL unusual and remarkable

### how English works

Hello Kitty...

knows that the **singular** of a word refers to one of that person or thing, like *girl* and *kite*.

# sink - skilled

**sink**, sinks, sinking, sank, sunk NOUN ❶ a basin with taps supplying water, usually in a kitchen or bathroom ✿ VERB ❷ If something sinks, it moves downwards, especially through water ❸ To sink a ship means to cause it to sink by attacking it ❹ If an amount or value sinks, it decreases ❺ If you sink into an unpleasant state, you gradually pass into it ❻ To sink something sharp into an object means to make it go deeply into it

**sink in** ✿ VERB When a fact sinks in, you fully understand it or realize it

**sip**, sips, sipping, sipped VERB ❶ If you sip a drink, you drink it by taking a small amount at a time ✿ NOUN ❷ a small amount of drink that you take into your mouth

**sir** NOUN ❶ Sir is a polite, formal way of addressing a man ❷ Sir is also the title used in front of the name of a knight or baronet

**siren** NOUN a warning device, for example on a police car, which makes a loud, wailing noise

**sister** NOUN ❶ Your sister is a girl or woman who has the same parents as you ❷ a member of a female religious order ❸ In a hospital, a sister is a senior nurse who supervises a ward ✿ ADJECTIVE ❹ Sister means closely related to something or very similar to it

**sister-in-law**, sisters-in-law NOUN Your sister-in-law is the wife of your brother, the sister of your husband or wife, or the woman married to your wife's or husband's brother

**sit**, sits, sitting, sat VERB ❶ If you are sitting, your weight is supported by your buttocks rather than your feet ❷ When you sit or sit down somewhere, you lower your body until you are sitting ❸ If you sit an examination, you take it ❹ FORMAL When a parliament, law court, or other official body sits, it meets and officially carries out its work

**site**, sites, siting, sited NOUN ❶ a piece of ground where a particular thing happens or is situated ✿ VERB ❷ If something is sited in a place, it is built or positioned there

**sitting room** NOUN a room in a house where people sit and relax

**situated** ADJECTIVE If something is situated somewhere, that is where it is

**situation** NOUN ❶ what is happening in a particular place at a particular time ❷ The situation of a building or town is its surroundings

**six** Six is the number 6

**sixteen** the number 16 **sixteenth** ADJECTIVE

**sixth** ADJECTIVE ❶ The sixth item in a series is the one counted as number six ✿ NOUN ❷ one of six equal parts

**sixty**, sixties the number 60 **sixtieth** ADJECTIVE

**size** NOUN ❶ The size of something is how big or small it is ❷ The size of something is also the fact that it is very large ❸ one of the standard graded measurements of clothes and shoes

**skate**, skates, skating, skated NOUN ❶ Skates are ice-skates or roller-skates ❷ a flat edible sea fish ✿ VERB ❸ If you skate, you move about on ice wearing ice-skates ❹ If you skate round a difficult subject, you avoid discussing it

**skateboard** NOUN a narrow board on wheels which you stand on and ride for fun

**skeleton** NOUN Your skeleton is the framework of bones in your body

**sketch**, sketches, sketching, sketched NOUN ❶ a quick, rough drawing ❷ A sketch of a situation or incident is a brief description of it ❸ a short, humorous piece of acting, usually forming part of a comedy show ✿ VERB ❹ If you sketch something, you draw it quickly and roughly

**ski**, skis, skiing, skied NOUN ❶ Skis are long pieces of wood, metal, or plastic that you fasten to special boots so you can move easily on snow ✿ VERB ❷ When you ski, you move on snow wearing skis, especially as a sport

**skid**, skids, skidding, skidded VERB If a vehicle skids, it slides in an uncontrolled way, for example because the road is wet or icy

**skilful** ADJECTIVE If you are skilful at something, you can do it very well **skilfully** ADVERB

**skill** NOUN ❶ Skill is the knowledge and ability that enables you to do something well ❷ a type of work or technique which requires special training and knowledge

**skilled** ADJECTIVE ❶ A skilled person has the knowledge and ability to do something well ❷ Skilled work is work which can only be

248

**skim - sleep**

done by people who have had special training

**skim**, skims, skimming, skimmed VERB ❶ If you skim something from the surface of a liquid, you remove it ❷ If something skims a surface, it moves along just above it

**skin**, skins, skinning, skinned NOUN ❶ Your skin is the natural covering of your body. An animal skin is the skin and fur of a dead animal ❷ The skin of a fruit or vegetable is its outer covering ❸ a solid layer which forms on the surface of a liquid ✿ VERB ❹ If you skin a dead animal, you remove its skin ❺ If you skin a part of your body, you accidentally graze it

**skinny**, skinnier, skinniest ADJECTIVE extremely thin

**skip**, skips, skipping, skipped VERB ❶ If you skip along, you move along jumping from one foot to the other ❷ If you skip something, you miss it out or avoid doing it ✿ NOUN ❸ Skips are the movements you make when you skip ❹ a large metal container for holding rubbish and rubble

**skirt** NOUN ❶ A woman's skirt is a piece of clothing which fastens at her waist and hangs down over her legs ✿ VERB ❷ Something that skirts an area is situated around the edge of it ❸ If you skirt something, you go around the edge of it ❹ If you skirt a problem, you avoid dealing with it

**skull** NOUN Your skull is the bony part of your head which surrounds your brain

**sky**, skies NOUN The sky is the space around the earth which you can see when you look upwards

**skyscraper** NOUN a very tall building

**slab** NOUN a thick, flat piece of something

**slack** ADJECTIVE ❶ Something that is slack is loose and not firmly stretched or positioned ❷ A slack period is one in which there is not much work to do ✿ NOUN ❸ The slack in a rope is the part that hangs loose ❹ IN PLURAL Slacks are casual trousers

**slam**, slams, slamming, slammed VERB ❶ If you slam a door or if it slams, it shuts noisily and with great force ❷ If you slam something down, you throw it down violently

**slang** NOUN Slang consists of very informal words and expressions

**slant** VERB ❶ If something slants, it slopes ❷ If news or information is slanted, it is presented in a biased way ✿ NOUN ❸ a slope ❹ A slant on a subject is one way of looking at it, especially a biased one

**slap**, slaps, slapping, slapped VERB ❶ If you slap someone, you hit them with the palm of your hand ❷ If you slap something onto a surface, you put it there quickly and noisily ✿ NOUN ❸ If you give someone a slap, you slap them

**slash**, slashes, slashing, slashed VERB ❶ If you slash something, you make a long, deep cut in it ❷ INFORMAL To slash money means to reduce it greatly ✿ NOUN ❸ a diagonal line that separates letters, words, or numbers, for example in the number 340/21/K

**slaughter** VERB ❶ To slaughter a large number of people means to kill them unjustly or cruelly ❷ To slaughter farm animals means to kill them for meat ✿ NOUN ❸ Slaughter is the killing of many people

### how to say it

*Helpful hints...*

**Slaughter** should be said so that it rhymes with *daughter*.

**slave**, slaves, slaving, slaved NOUN ❶ someone who is owned by another person and must work for them ✿ VERB ❷ If you slave for someone, you work very hard for them **slavery** NOUN

**sledge** NOUN a vehicle on runners used for travelling over snow

**sleep**, sleeps, sleeping, slept NOUN ❶ Sleep is the natural state of rest in which your eyes

249

# sleeping bag – slow

are closed and you are unconscious ❷ If you have a sleep, you sleep for a while ✿ **VERB** ❸ When you sleep, you rest in a state of sleep ✿ **PHRASE** ❹ If a sick or injured animal **is put to sleep**, it is painlessly killed

**sleeping bag** NOUN a large, warm bag for sleeping in, especially when you are camping

**sleepy**, sleepier, sleepiest ADJECTIVE ❶ tired and ready to go to sleep ❷ A sleepy town or village is very quiet

**sleet** NOUN Sleet is a mixture of rain and snow

**sleeve** NOUN The sleeves of a piece of clothing are the parts that cover your arms

**slice**, slices, slicing, sliced NOUN ❶ A slice of cake, bread, or other food is a piece of it cut from a larger piece ❷ a kitchen tool with a broad, flat blade ❸ In sport, a slice is a stroke in which the player makes the ball go to one side, rather than straight ahead ✿ **VERB** ❹ If you slice food, you cut it into thin pieces ❺ To slice through something means to cut or move through it quickly

**slide**, slides, sliding, slid VERB ❶ When something slides, it moves smoothly over or against something else ✿ **NOUN** ❷ a small piece of photographic film which can be projected onto a screen so that you can see the picture ❸ a small piece of glass on which you put something that you want to examine through a microscope ❹ In a playground, a slide is a structure with a steep, slippery slope for children to slide down

**slight** ADJECTIVE ❶ Slight means small in amount or degree ❷ A slight person has a slim body ✿ **PHRASE** ❸ **Not in the slightest** means not at all ✿ **VERB** ❹ If you slight someone, you insult them by behaving rudely towards them ✿ **NOUN** ❺ A slight is rude or insulting behaviour **slightly** ADVERB

**slim**, slimmer, slimmest; slims, slimming, slimmed ADJECTIVE ❶ A slim person is attractively thin ❷ A slim object is thinner than usual ❸ If there is only a slim chance that something will happen, it is unlikely to happen ✿ **VERB** ❹ If you are slimming, you are trying to lose weight

**slime** NOUN Slime is an unpleasant, thick, slippery substance

**sling**, slings, slinging, slung VERB ❶ INFORMAL If you sling something somewhere, you throw it there ❷ If you sling a rope between two points, you attach it so that it hangs loosely between them ✿ **NOUN** ❸ a piece of cloth tied round a person's neck to support a broken or injured arm ❹ a device made of ropes or cloth used for carrying things

**slip**, slips, slipping, slipped VERB ❶ If you slip, you accidentally slide and lose your balance ❷ If something slips, it slides out of place accidentally ❸ If you slip somewhere, you go there quickly and quietly ❹ If you slip something somewhere, you put it there quickly and quietly ❺ If something slips to a lower level or standard, it falls to that level or standard ✿ **NOUN** ❻ a small mistake ❼ A slip of paper is a small piece of paper ❽ a piece of clothing worn under a dress or skirt

**slipper** NOUN Slippers are loose, soft shoes that you wear indoors

**slippery** ADJECTIVE ❶ smooth, wet, or greasy, and difficult to hold or walk on ❷ You describe a person as slippery when they cannot be trusted

**slit**, slits, slitting, slit VERB ❶ If you slit something, you make a long, narrow cut in it ✿ **NOUN** ❷ a long, narrow cut or opening

**slither** VERB To slither somewhere means to move there by sliding along the ground in an uneven way

**slogan** NOUN a short, easily-remembered phrase used in advertising or by a political party

**slope**, slopes, sloping, sloped NOUN ❶ a flat surface that is at an angle, so that one end is higher than the other ❷ The slope of something is the angle at which it slopes ✿ **VERB** ❸ If a surface slopes, it is at an angle ❹ If something slopes, it leans to one side rather than being upright

**sloppy**, sloppier, sloppiest ADJECTIVE INFORMAL ❶ very messy or careless ❷ foolishly sentimental

**slot**, slots, slotting, slotted NOUN ❶ a narrow opening in a machine or container, for example for putting coins in ✿ **VERB** ❷ When you slot something into something else, you put it into a space where it fits

**slow** ADJECTIVE ❶ moving, happening, or doing something with very little speed

250

## slowly - smelly

❷ Someone who is slow is not very clever ❸ If a clock or watch is slow, it shows a time earlier than the correct one ✿ **VERB** ❹ If something slows, slows down, or slows up, it moves or happens more slowly

**slowly** ADVERB not quickly or hurriedly

**slow motion** NOUN Slow motion is movement which is much slower than normal, especially in a film

**slug** NOUN ❶ a small, slow-moving creative with a slimy body, like a snail without a shell ❷ INFORMAL A slug of a strong alcoholic drink is a mouthful of it

**slum** NOUN a poor, run-down area of a city

**slump** VERB ❶ If an amount or a value slumps, it falls suddenly by a large amount ❷ If you slump somewhere, you fall or sit down heavily ✿ **NOUN** ❸ a sudden, severe drop in an amount or value ❹ a time when there is economic decline and high unemployment

**slur**, slurs, slurring, slurred NOUN ❶ an insulting remark ✿ **VERB** ❷ When people slur their speech, they do not say their words clearly, often because they are drunk or ill

**sly**, slyer or slier, slyest or sliest ADJECTIVE ❶ A sly expression or remark shows that you know something other people do not know ❷ A sly person is cunning and good at deceiving people  **slyly** ADVERB

**smack** VERB ❶ If you smack someone, you hit them with your open hand ❷ If something smacks of something else, it reminds you of it ✿ **NOUN** ❸ If you give someone a smack, you smack them ❹ a loud, sharp noise

**small** ADJECTIVE ❶ Small means not large in size, number, or amount ❷ Small means not important or significant ✿ **NOUN** ❸ The small of your back is the narrow part where your back curves slightly inwards

**smart** ADJECTIVE ❶ A smart person is clean and neatly dressed ❷ Smart means clever ❸ A smart movement is quick and sharp ✿ **VERB** ❹ If a wound smarts, it stings ❺ If you are smarting from criticism or unkindness, you are feeling upset by it **smartly** ADVERB

**smash**, smashes, smashing, smashed VERB ❶ If you smash something, you break it into a lot of pieces by hitting it or dropping it ❷ To smash through something such as a wall means to go through it by breaking it ❸ To smash against something means to hit it with great force ✿ **NOUN** ❹ INFORMAL If a play or film is a smash or a smash hit, it is very successful ❺ a car crash ❻ In tennis, a smash is a stroke in which the player hits the ball downwards very hard

**smear** NOUN ❶ a dirty, greasy mark on a surface ❷ an untrue and malicious rumour ✿ **VERB** ❸ If something smears a surface, it makes dirty, greasy marks on it ❹ If you smear a surface with a greasy or sticky substance, you spread a layer of the substance over the surface

**smell**, smells, smelling, smelled or smelt NOUN ❶ The smell of something is a quality it has which you perceive through your nose ❷ Your sense of smell is your ability to smell things ✿ **VERB** ❸ If something smells, it has a quality you can perceive through your nose, especially an unpleasant quality ❹ If you smell something, you become aware of it through your nose ❺ If you can smell something such as danger or trouble, you feel it is present or likely to happen

**smelly**, smellier, smelliest ADJECTIVE having a strong, unpleasant smell

### some other words to use

### Helpful hints...

You should try not to use **small** too much when you are writing. Some other words you can use are: *diminutive, minuscule, minute* and *petite*.

# smile – sneeze

**smile**, smiles, smiling, smiled VERB ❶ When you smile, the corners of your mouth move outwards and slightly upwards because you are pleased or amused ✿ NOUN ❷ the expression you have when you smile

**smoke**, smokes, smoking, smoked NOUN ❶ Smoke is a mixture of gas and small particles sent into the air when something burns ✿ VERB ❷ If something is smoking, smoke is coming from it ❸ When someone smokes a cigarette or pipe, they suck smoke from it into their mouth and blow it out again ❹ To smoke fish or meat means to hang it over burning wood so that the smoke preserves it and gives it a pleasant flavour

**smoker** NOUN **smoking** NOUN

**smoky**, smokier, smokiest ADJECTIVE A smoky place is full of smoke

**smooth** ADJECTIVE ❶ A smooth surface has no roughness and no holes in it ❷ A smooth liquid or mixture has no lumps in it ❸ A smooth movement or process happens evenly and steadily ❹ Smooth also means successful and without problems ✿ VERB ❺ If you smooth something, you move your hands over it to make it smooth and flat **smoothly** ADVERB

**smother** VERB ❶ If you smother a fire, you cover it with something to put it out ❷ To smother a person means to cover their face with something so that they cannot breathe ❸ To smother someone also means to give them too much love and protection ❹ If you smother an emotion, you control it so that people do not notice it

**smudge**, smudges, smudging, smudged NOUN ❶ a dirty or blurred mark or a smear on something ✿ VERB ❷ If you smudge something, you make it dirty or messy by touching it or marking it

**smug**, smugger, smuggest ADJECTIVE Someone who is smug is very pleased with how good or clever they are **smugly** ADVERB

**smuggle**, smuggles, smuggling, smuggled VERB To smuggle things or people into or out of a place means to take them there illegally or secretly

**smuggler** NOUN someone who smuggles goods illegally into a country

**snack** NOUN a light, quick meal

**snag**, snags, snagging, snagged NOUN ❶ a small problem or disadvantage ❷ INFORMAL in Australian and New Zealand English, a sausage ✿ VERB ❸ If you snag your clothing, you damage it by catching it on something sharp

**snail** NOUN a small, slow-moving creature with a long, shiny body and a shell on its back

**snake**, snakes, snaking, snaked NOUN ❶ a long, thin, scaly reptile with no legs ✿ VERB ❷ Something that snakes moves in long winding curves

**snap**, snaps, snapping, snapped VERB ❶ If something snaps or if you snap it, it breaks with a sharp cracking noise ❷ If you snap something into a particular position, you move it there quickly with a sharp sound ❸ If an animal snaps at you, it shuts its jaws together quickly as if to bite you ❹ If someone snaps at you, they speak in a sharp, unfriendly way ❺ If you snap someone, you take a quick photograph of them ✿ NOUN ❻ the sound of something snapping ❼ INFORMAL a photograph taken quickly and casually ✿ ADJECTIVE ❽ A snap decision or action is taken suddenly without careful thought

**snatch**, snatches, snatching, snatched VERB ❶ If you snatch something, you reach out for it quickly and take it ❷ If you snatch an amount of time or an opportunity, you quickly make use of it ✿ NOUN ❸ If you make a snatch at something, you reach out for it quickly to try to take it ❹ A snatch of conversation or song is a very small piece of it

**sneak** VERB ❶ If you sneak somewhere, you go there quickly trying not to be seen or heard ❷ If you sneak something somewhere, you take it there secretly ✿ NOUN ❸ INFORMAL someone who tells people in authority that someone else has done something wrong

**sneaker** NOUN Sneakers are casual shoes with rubber soles

**sneer** VERB ❶ If you sneer at someone or something, you show by your expression and your comments that you think they are stupid or inferior ✿ NOUN ❷ the expression on someone's face when they sneer

**sneeze**, sneezes, sneezing, sneezed VERB ❶ When you sneeze, you suddenly take in

**sniff - socialism**

breath and blow it down your nose noisily, because there is a tickle in your nose ✿ **NOUN** ❷ an act of sneezing

**sniff** **VERB** ❶ When you sniff, you breathe in air through your nose hard enough to make a sound ❷ If you sniff something, you smell it by sniffing ❸ You can say that a person sniffs at something when they do not think very much of it ✿ **NOUN** ❹ the noise you make when you sniff ❺ A sniff of something is a smell of it

**snigger** **VERB** ❶ If you snigger, you laugh in a quiet, sly way ✿ **NOUN** ❷ a quiet, disrespectful laugh

**snip**, snips, snipping, snipped **VERB** ❶ If you snip something, you cut it with scissors or shears in a single quick action ✿ **NOUN** ❷ a small cut made by scissors or shears

**snob** **NOUN** ❶ someone who admires upper-class people and looks down on lower-class people ❷ someone who believes that they are better than other people

**snooker** **NOUN** Snooker is a game played on a large table covered with smooth green cloth. Players score points by hitting different coloured balls into side pockets using a long stick called a cue

**snore**, snores, snoring, snored **VERB** ❶ When a sleeping person snores, they make a loud noise each time they breathe ✿ **NOUN** ❷ the noise someone makes when they snore

**snorkel** **NOUN** a tube you can breathe through when you are swimming just under the surface of the sea **snorkelling** **NOUN**

**snort** **VERB** ❶ When people or animals snort, they force breath out through their nose in a noisy way ✿ **NOUN** ❷ the noise you make when you snort

**snout** **NOUN** An animal's snout is its nose

**snow** **NOUN** ❶ Snow consists of flakes of ice crystals which fall from the sky in cold weather ✿ **VERB** ❷ When it snows, snow falls from the sky

**snowball** **NOUN** ❶ a ball of snow for throwing ✿ **VERB** ❷ When something such as a project snowballs, it grows rapidly

**snowman**, snowmen **NOUN** a large mound of snow moulded into the shape of a person

**snuggle**, snuggles, snuggling, snuggled **VERB** If you snuggle somewhere, you cuddle up more closely to something or someone

**so** **ADVERB** ❶ 'So' is used to refer back to what has just been mentioned ❷ 'So' is used to mean also ❸ 'So' can be used to mean 'therefore' ❹ 'So' is used when you are talking about the degree or extent of something ❺ 'So' is used before words like 'much' and 'many' to say that there is a definite limit to something ✿ **CONJUNCTION** ❻ 'So that' and 'so as' are used to introduce the reason for doing something

**soak** **VERB** ❶ To soak something or leave it to soak means to put it in a liquid and leave it there ❷ When a liquid soaks something, it makes it very wet ❸ When something soaks up a liquid, the liquid is drawn up into it

**soaked** **ADJECTIVE** extremely wet

**soaking** **ADJECTIVE** If something is soaking, it is very wet

**soap** **NOUN** Soap is a substance made of natural oils and fats and used for washing yourself

**soap opera** **NOUN** a popular television drama serial about people's daily lives

**soar** **VERB** ❶ If an amount soars, it quickly increases by a great deal ❷ If something soars into the air, it quickly goes up into the air

**sob**, sobs, sobbing, sobbed **VERB** ❶ When someone sobs, they cry in a noisy way, breathing in short breaths ✿ **NOUN** ❷ the noise made when you cry

**sober** **ADJECTIVE** ❶ If someone is sober, they are not drunk ❷ Sober also means serious and thoughtful ❸ Sober colours are plain and rather dull ✿ **VERB** ❹ To sober up means to become sober after being drunk

**so-called** **ADJECTIVE** You use 'so-called' to say that the name by which something is called is incorrect or misleading

**soccer** **NOUN** Soccer is a game played by two teams of eleven players kicking a ball in an attempt to score goals

**sociable** **ADJECTIVE** Sociable people are friendly and enjoy talking to other people

**social** **ADJECTIVE** ❶ to do with society or life within a society ❷ to do with leisure activities that involve meeting other people **socially** **ADVERB**

**socialism** **NOUN** Socialism is the political belief that the state should own industries on behalf of the people and that everyone should be equal **socialist** **ADJECTIVE OR NOUN**

A B C D E F G H I J K L M N O P Q R S T U V W X Y Z

# socialize - solitary

**socialize**, socializes, socializing, socialized (also **socialise**) VERB When people socialize, they meet other people socially, for example at parties

**social work**, Social work involves giving help and support to people with serious family problems  social worker NOUN

**society**, societies NOUN ❶ Society is the people in a particular country or region ❷ an organization for people who have the same interest or aim ❸ Society is also rich, upper-class, fashionable people

**sock** NOUN Socks are pieces of clothing covering your foot and ankle

**socket** NOUN ❶ a place on a wall or on a piece of electrical equipment into which you can put a plug or bulb ❷ Any hollow part or opening into which another part fits can be called a socket

**soda** NOUN ❶ Soda is the same as **soda water** ❷ Soda is also sodium in the form of crystals or a powder, and is used for baking or cleaning

**soda water** NOUN Soda water is fizzy water used for mixing with alcoholic drinks

**sodium** NOUN Sodium is a silvery-white chemical element which combines with other chemicals

**sofa** NOUN a long comfortable seat with a back and arms for two or three people

**soft** ADJECTIVE ❶ Something soft is not hard, stiff, or firm ❷ Soft also means very gentle ❸ A soft sound or voice is quiet and not harsh ❹ A soft colour or light is not bright  **softly** ADVERB

**soft drink** NOUN any cold, nonalcoholic drink

**soften** VERB ❶ If something is softened or softens, it becomes less hard, stiff, or firm ❷ If you soften, you become more sympathetic and less critical

**software** NOUN Computer programs are known as software

**soggy**, soggier, soggiest ADJECTIVE unpleasantly wet or full of water

**soil** NOUN ❶ Soil is the top layer on the surface of the earth in which plants grow ❖ VERB ❷ If you soil something, you make it dirty

**solar** ADJECTIVE ❶ relating or belonging to the sun ❷ using the sun's light and heat as a source of energy

**soldier** NOUN a person in an army

**sole**, soles, soling, soled ADJECTIVE ❶ The sole thing or person of a particular type is the only one of that type ❖ NOUN ❷ The sole of your foot or shoe is the underneath part ❸ a flat sea-water fish which you can eat ❖ VERB ❹ When a shoe is soled, a sole is fitted to it

### don't mix up

**Hello Kitty...**

never mixes up **sole** (the bottom of your foot) and **soul** (the part of a person that is not their body).

**solely** ADVERB If something involves solely one thing, it involves that thing and nothing else

**solemn** ADJECTIVE Solemn means serious rather than cheerful or humorous  **solemnly** ADVERB

**solicitor** NOUN a lawyer who gives legal advice and prepares legal documents and cases

**solid** ADJECTIVE ❶ A solid substance or object is hard or firm, and not in the form of a liquid or gas ❷ You say that something is solid when it is not hollow ❸ You say that a structure is solid when it is strong and not likely to fall down ❹ You use 'solid' to say that something happens for a period of time without interruption ❖ NOUN ❺ a solid substance or object

**solitary** ADJECTIVE ❶ A solitary activity is one that you do on your own ❷ A solitary person or animal spends a lot of time alone ❸ If

254

# solo - sound

there is a solitary person, animal, or object somewhere, there is only one

**solo**, solos NOUN ❶ a piece of music played or sung by one person alone ✿ ADJECTIVE ❷ A solo performance or activity is done by one person alone ✿ ADVERB ❸ Solo means alone

**solution** NOUN ❶ a way of dealing with a problem or difficult situation ❷ The solution to a riddle or a puzzle is the answer ❸ a liquid in which a solid substance has been dissolved

**solve**, solves, solving, solved VERB If you solve a problem or a question, you find a solution or answer to it

**some** ❶ You use 'some' to refer to a quantity or number when you are not stating the quantity or number exactly ❷ You use 'some' to emphasize that a quantity or number is fairly large ADVERB ❸ You use 'some' in front of a number to show that it is not exact

**somebody** PRONOUN Somebody means someone

**somehow** ADVERB ❶ You use 'somehow' to say that you do not know how something was done or will be done ❷ You use 'somehow' to say that you do not know the reason for something

**someone** PRONOUN You use 'someone' to refer to a person without saying exactly who you mean

**something** PRONOUN You use 'something' to refer to anything that is not a person without saying exactly what you mean

**sometime** ADVERB ❶ at a time in the future or the past that is unknown or that has not yet been fixed ✿ ADJECTIVE ❷ FORMAL 'Sometime' is used to say that a person had a particular job or role in the past

**sometimes** ADVERB occasionally, rather than always or never

**somewhat** ADVERB to some extent or degree

**somewhere** ADVERB ❶ 'Somewhere' is used to refer to a place without stating exactly where it is ❷ 'Somewhere' is used when giving an approximate amount, number, or time

**son** NOUN Someone's son is their male child

**song** NOUN a piece of music with words that are sung to the music

**son-in-law**, sons-in-law NOUN Someone's son-in-law is the husband of their daughter

**soon** ADVERB If something is going to happen soon, it will happen in a very short time

**soothe**, soothes, soothing, soothed VERB ❶ If you soothe someone who is angry or upset, you make them calmer ❷ Something that soothes pain makes the pain less severe

**soothing** ADJECTIVE

**sophisticated** ADJECTIVE ❶ Sophisticated people have refined or cultured tastes or habits ❷ A sophisticated machine or device is made using advanced and complicated methods

**sore**, sorer, sorest ADJECTIVE ❶ If part of your body is sore, it causes you pain and discomfort ❷ LITERARY 'Sore' is used to emphasize something ✿ NOUN ❸ a painful place where your skin has become infected

**sorrow** NOUN ❶ Sorrow is deep sadness or regret ❷ Sorrows are things that cause sorrow

**sorry**, sorrier, sorriest ADJECTIVE ❶ If you are sorry about something, you feel sadness or regret about it ❷ feeling sympathy for someone ❸ 'Sorry' is used to describe people and things that are in a bad physical or mental state

**sort** NOUN ❶ The different sorts of something are the different types of it ✿ VERB ❷ To sort things means to arrange them into different groups or sorts

**sort out** ✿ VERB If you sort out a problem or misunderstanding, you deal with it and find a solution to it

**sought** the past tense and past participle of seek

**soul** NOUN ❶ A person's soul is the spiritual part of them that is supposed to continue after their body is dead ❷ People also use 'soul' to refer to a person's mind, character, thoughts, and feelings ❸ 'Soul' can be used to mean person ❹ Soul is a type of pop music

**sound** NOUN ❶ Sound is everything that can be heard. It is caused by vibrations travelling through air or water to your ear ❷ A particular sound is something that you hear ❸ The sound of someone or something is the impression you have of them ✿ VERB ❹ If something sounds or if you sound it, it

255

**soup – space shuttle**

makes a noise ❺ To sound something deep, such as a well or the sea, means to measure how deep it is using a weighted line or sonar ✿ **ADJECTIVE** ❻ in good condition ❼ reliable and sensible  **soundly** ADVERB

**soup** NOUN Soup is liquid food made by boiling meat, fish, or vegetables in water

**sour** ADJECTIVE ❶ If something is sour, it has a sharp, acid taste ❷ Sour milk has an unpleasant taste because it is no longer fresh ❸ A sour person is bad-tempered and unfriendly ✿ VERB ❹ If a friendship, situation, or attitude sours or if something sours it, it becomes less friendly, enjoyable, or hopeful

**source** NOUN ❶ The source of something is the person, place, or thing that it comes from ❷ A source is a person or book that provides information for a news story or for research ❸ The source of a river or stream is the place where it begins

**south** NOUN ❶ The south is the direction to your right when you are looking towards the place where the sun rises ❷ The south of a place or country is the part which is towards the south when you are in the centre ✿ ADVERB OR ADJECTIVE ❸ South means towards the south ✿ ADJECTIVE ❹ A south wind blows from the south

**south-east** NOUN, ADVERB, OR ADJECTIVE South-east is halfway between south and east

**south-eastern** ADJECTIVE in or from the south-east

**southerly** ADJECTIVE ❶ Southerly means to or towards the south ❷ A southerly wind blows from the south

**southern** ADJECTIVE in or from the south

**south-west** NOUN, ADVERB, OR ADJECTIVE South-west is halfway between south and west

**south-western** ADJECTIVE in or from the south-west

**souvenir** NOUN something you keep to remind you of a holiday, place, or event

**sovereignty** [*sov-rin-tee*] NOUN Sovereignty is the political power that a country has to govern itself

**sow**, sows, sowing, sowed, sown [*soh*] VERB ❶ To sow seeds or sow an area of land with seeds means to plant them in the ground ❷ To sow undesirable feelings or attitudes means to cause them

**sow** [*rhymes with* **now**] NOUN an adult female pig

### how to say it

*Hello Kitty…* knows that **sow** rhymes with *snow* when it means 'plant', and with *now* when it's a female pig.

**soya** NOUN Soya flour, margarine, oil, and milk are made from soya beans

**soya bean** NOUN Soya beans are a type of edible Asian bean

**spa** NOUN a place where water containing minerals bubbles out of the ground, at which people drink or bathe in the water to improve their health

**space**, spaces, spacing, spaced NOUN ❶ Space is the area that is empty or available in a place, building, or container ❷ Space is the area beyond the earth's atmosphere surrounding the stars and planets ❸ a gap between two things ❹ Space can also refer to a period of time ✿ VERB ❺ If you space a series of things, you arrange them with gaps between them

**spacecraft** NOUN a rocket or other vehicle that can travel in space

**spaceship** NOUN a spacecraft that carries people through space

**space shuttle** NOUN a spacecraft designed to be used many times for travelling out into space and back again

**spacious** ADJECTIVE having or providing a lot of space

**spade** NOUN ❶ a tool with a flat metal blade and a long handle used for digging ❷ Spades is one of the four suits in a pack of playing cards. It is marked by a black symbol like a heart-shaped leaf with a stem

**spaghetti** [spag-*get*-ee] NOUN Spaghetti consists of long, thin pieces of pasta

**spam** NOUN unwanted e-mails, usually containing advertising

**span**, spans, spanning, spanned NOUN ❶ the period of time during which something exists or functions ❷ The span of something is the total length of it from one end to the other ❀ VERB ❸ If something spans a particular length of time, it lasts throughout that time ❹ A bridge that spans something stretches right across it

**spanner** NOUN a tool with a specially shaped end that fits round a nut to turn it

**spare**, spares, sparing, spared ADJECTIVE ❶ extra to what is needed ❀ NOUN ❷ a thing that is extra to what is needed ❀ VERB ❸ If you spare something for a particular purpose, you make it available ❹ If someone is spared an unpleasant experience, they are prevented from suffering it

**spark** NOUN ❶ a tiny, bright piece of burning material thrown up by a fire ❷ a small flash of light caused by electricity ❸ A spark of feeling is a small amount of it ❀ VERB ❹ If something sparks, it throws out sparks ❺ If one thing sparks another thing off, it causes the second thing to start happening

**sparkle**, sparkles, sparkling, sparkled VERB ❶ If something sparkles, it shines with a lot of small, bright points of light ❀ NOUN ❷ Sparkles are small, bright points of light **sparkling** ADJECTIVE

**sparrow** NOUN a common, small bird with brown and grey feathers

**sparse**, sparser, sparsest ADJECTIVE small in number or amount and spread out over an area **sparsely** ADVERB

**speak**, speaks, speaking, spoke, spoken VERB ❶ When you speak, you use your voice to say words ❷ If you speak a foreign language, you know it and can use it

**speak out** ❀ VERB To speak out about something means to state an opinion about it publicly

**speaker** NOUN ❶ a person who is speaking, especially someone making a speech ❷ A speaker on a radio or hi-fi is a loudspeaker

**spear** NOUN ❶ a weapon consisting of a long pole with a sharp point ❀ VERB ❷ To spear something means to push or throw a spear or other pointed object into it

**special** ADJECTIVE ❶ Something special is more important or better than other things of its kind ❷ Special describes someone who is officially appointed, or something that is needed for a particular purpose ❸ Special also describes something that belongs or relates to only one particular person, group, or place

**specialist** NOUN ❶ someone who has a particular skill or who knows a lot about a particular subject ❀ ADJECTIVE ❷ having a skill or knowing a lot about a particular subject

**speciality**, specialities NOUN A person's speciality is something they are especially good at or know a lot about

**specialize**, specializes, specializing, specialized (also **specialise**) VERB If you specialize in something, you make it your speciality

**specially** ADVERB If something has been done specially for a person or purpose, it has been done only for that person or purpose

**species** [*spee*-sheez] NOUN a division of plants or animals whose members have the same characteristics and are able to breed with each other

**specific** ADJECTIVE ❶ particular ❷ precise and exact **specifically** ADVERB

**specify**, specifies, specifying, specified VERB To specify something means to state or describe it precisely

**specimen** NOUN A specimen of something is an example or small amount of it which gives an idea of what the whole is like

**speck** NOUN a very small stain or amount of something

**spectacle** NOUN ❶ a strange or interesting sight or scene ❷ a grand and impressive event or performance

## spectacles – spin

**spectacles** PLURAL NOUN Someone's spectacles are their glasses

**spectacular** ADJECTIVE ❶ Something spectacular is very impressive or dramatic ❀ NOUN ❷ a grand and impressive show or performance

**spectator** NOUN a person who is watching something

**speculate**, speculates, speculating, speculated VERB If you speculate about something, you think about it and form opinions about it **speculation** NOUN

**speech**, speeches NOUN ❶ Speech is the ability to speak or the act of speaking ❷ a formal talk given to an audience ❸ In a play, a speech is a group of lines spoken by one of the characters

**speed**, speeds, speeding, sped or speeded NOUN ❶ The speed of something is the rate at which it moves or happens ❷ Speed is very fast movement or travel ❀ VERB ❸ If you speed somewhere, you move or travel there quickly ❹ Someone who is speeding is driving a vehicle faster than the legal speed limit

**speed limit** NOUN The speed limit is the maximum speed at which vehicles are legally allowed to drive on a particular road

**speedy**, speedier, speediest ADJECTIVE done very quickly

**spell**, spells, spelling, spelt or spelled VERB ❶ When you spell a word, you name or write its letters in order ❷ When letters spell a word, they form that word when put together in a particular order ❸ If something spells a particular result, it suggests that this will be the result ❀ NOUN ❹ A spell of something is a short period of it ❺ a word or sequence of words used to perform magic

**spell out** ❀ VERB If you spell something out, you explain it in detail

**spelling** NOUN The spelling of a word is the correct order of letters in it

**spend**, spends, spending, spent VERB ❶ When you spend money, you buy things with it ❷ To spend time or energy means to use it

**spent** ADJECTIVE ❶ Spent describes things which have been used and therefore cannot be used again ❷ If you are spent, you are exhausted and have no energy left

**sphere** NOUN ❶ a perfectly round object, such as a ball ❷ An area of activity or interest can be referred to as a sphere of activity or interest

**spice**, spices, spicing, spiced NOUN ❶ Spice is powder or seeds from a plant added to food to give it flavour ❷ Spice is something which makes life more exciting ❀ VERB ❸ To spice food means to add spice to it ❹ If you spice something up, you make it more exciting or lively

**spicy**, spicier, spiciest ADJECTIVE strongly flavoured with spices

**spider** NOUN a small insect-like creature with eight legs that spins webs to catch insects for food

### where does the word come from?

## Did you know…

that the word **spider** comes from an Old English word *spinnan* which means 'to spin'? That's because spiders spin webs to catch flies.

**spike** NOUN ❶ a long pointed piece of metal ❷ The spikes on a sports shoe are the pointed pieces of metal attached to the sole

**spill**, spills, spilling, spilled or spilt VERB ❶ If you spill something or if it spills, it accidentally falls or runs out of a container ❷ If people or things spill out of a place, they come out of it in large numbers

**spin**, spins, spinning, spun VERB ❶ If something spins, it turns quickly around a central point ❷ When spiders spin a web, they give out a sticky substance and make it into a web ❸ When people spin, they make thread by twisting together pieces of fibre using a machine ❹ If your head is spinning,

258

## spinach - sponsor

you feel dizzy or confused ❋ NOUN ❺ a rapid turn around a central point

**spinach** [*spin-ij*] NOUN Spinach is a vegetable with large green leaves

**spine** NOUN ❶ Your spine is your backbone ❷ Spines are long, sharp points on an animal's body or on a plant

**spiral**, spirals, spiralling, spiralled NOUN ❶ a continuous curve which winds round and round, with each curve above or outside the previous one ❋ ADJECTIVE ❷ in the shape of a spiral ❋ VERB ❸ If something spirals, it moves up or down in a spiral curve ❹ If an amount or level spirals, it rises or falls quickly at an increasing rate

**spirit**, spirits, spiriting, spirited NOUN ❶ Your spirit is the part of you that is not physical and that is connected with your deepest thoughts and feelings ❷ The spirit of a dead person is a nonphysical part that is believed to remain alive after death ❸ a supernatural being, such as a ghost ❹ Spirit is liveliness, energy, and self-confidence ❺ Spirit can refer to an attitude ❻ IN PLURAL Spirits can describe how happy or unhappy someone is ❼ Spirits are strong alcoholic drinks such as whisky and gin ❋ VERB ❽ If you spirit someone or something into or out of a place, you get them in or out quickly and secretly

**spiritual** ADJECTIVE ❶ to do with people's thoughts and beliefs, rather than their bodies and physical surroundings ❷ to do with people's religious beliefs ❋ NOUN ❸ a religious song originally sung by Black slaves in America

**spit**, spits, spitting, spat NOUN ❶ Spit is saliva ❷ a long stick made of metal or wood which is pushed through a piece of meat so that it can be hung over a fire and cooked ❸ a long, flat, narrow piece of land sticking out into the sea ❋ VERB ❹ If you spit, you force saliva or some other substance out of your mouth ❺ When it is spitting, it is raining very lightly

**spite** PHRASE ❶ **In spite of** is used to introduce a statement which makes the rest of what you are saying seem surprising ❋ VERB ❷ If you do something to spite someone, you do it deliberately to hurt or annoy them ❋ NOUN ❸ If you do something out of spite, you do it to hurt or annoy someone

**splash**, splashes, splashing, splashed VERB ❶ If you splash around in water, your movements disturb the water in a noisy way ❷ If liquid splashes something, it scatters over it in a lot of small drops ❋ NOUN ❸ A splash is the sound made when something hits or falls into water ❹ A splash of liquid is a small quantity of it that has been spilt on something

**splendid** ADJECTIVE ❶ very good indeed ❷ beautiful and impressive

**splinter** NOUN ❶ a thin, sharp piece of wood or glass which has broken off a larger piece ❋ VERB ❷ If something splinters, it breaks into thin, sharp pieces

**split**, splits, splitting, split VERB ❶ If something splits or if you split it, it divides into two or more parts ❷ If something such as wood or fabric splits, a long crack or tear appears in it ❸ If people split something, they share it between them ❋ NOUN ❹ A split in a piece of wood or fabric is a crack or tear ❺ A split between two things is a division or difference between them

**split up** ❋ VERB If two people split up, they end their relationship or marriage

**spoil**, spoils, spoiling, spoiled or spoilt VERB ❶ If you spoil something, you prevent it from being successful or satisfactory ❷ To spoil children means to give them everything they want, with harmful effects on their character ❸ To spoil someone also means to give them something nice as a treat

**spoke** ❶ the past tense of **speak** ❋ NOUN ❷ The spokes of a wheel are the bars which connect the hub to the rim

**spokesperson** NOUN someone who speaks on behalf of another person or a group

**spokesman** NOUN **spokeswoman** NOUN

**sponge**, sponges, sponging, sponged NOUN ❶ a sea creature with a body made up of many cells ❷ part of the very light skeleton of a sponge, used for bathing and cleaning ❸ A sponge or sponge cake is a very light cake ❋ VERB ❹ If you sponge something, you clean it by wiping it with a wet sponge

**sponsor** VERB ❶ To sponsor something, such as an event or someone's training, means to support it financially ❷ If you sponsor someone who is doing something for charity, you agree to give them a sum of money for

# spontaneous - spring

the charity if they manage to do it ❸ If you sponsor a proposal or suggestion, you officially put it forward and support it ✿ **NOUN** ❹ a person or organization sponsoring something or someone

**spontaneous** ADJECTIVE ❶ Spontaneous acts are not planned or arranged, but are done because you feel like it ❷ A spontaneous event happens because of processes within something rather than being caused by things outside it **spontaneously** ADVERB

**spooky**, spookier, spookiest ADJECTIVE eerie and frightening

**spoon** NOUN an object shaped like a small shallow bowl with a long handle, used for eating, stirring, and serving food

**spoonful**, spoonfuls or spoonsful NOUN the amount held by a spoon

**sport** NOUN ❶ Sports are games and other enjoyable activities which need physical effort and skill ❷ You say that someone is a sport when they accept defeat or teasing cheerfully ✿ **VERB** ❸ If you sport something noticeable or unusual, you wear it

**spot**, spots, spotting, spotted NOUN ❶ Spots are small, round, coloured areas on a surface ❷ Spots on a person's skin are small lumps, usually caused by an infection or allergy ❸ A spot of something is a small amount of it ❹ A place can be called a spot ✿ **VERB** ❺ If you spot something, you notice it ✿ **PHRASE** ❻ If you do something **on the spot**, you do it immediately

**spotlight**, spotlights, spotlighting, spotlit or spotlighted NOUN ❶ a powerful light which can be directed to light up a small area ✿ **VERB** ❷ If something spotlights a situation or problem, it draws the public's attention to it

**spotty**, spottier, spottiest ADJECTIVE Someone who is spotty has spots or pimples on their skin, especially on their face

**spouse**, spouses NOUN Someone's spouse is the person they are married to

**spray** NOUN ❶ Spray consists of many drops of liquid splashed or forced into the air ❷ Spray is also a liquid kept under pressure in a can or other container ❸ a piece of equipment for spraying liquid ✿ **VERB** ❹ To spray a liquid over something means to cover it with drops of the liquid

## help with spelling

*Hello Kitty...* knows that you never use an apostrophe and an **s** to make a plural of a normal word.

**spread**, spreads, spreading, spread VERB ❶ If you spread something out, you open it out or arrange it so that it can be seen or used easily ❷ If you spread a substance on a surface, you put a thin layer on the surface ❸ If something spreads, it gradually reaches or affects more people ❹ If something spreads over a period of time, it happens regularly or continuously over that time ❺ If something such as work is spread, it is distributed evenly ✿ **NOUN** ❻ The spread of something is the extent to which it gradually reaches or affects more people ❼ A spread of ideas, interests, or other things is a wide variety of them ❽ soft food put on bread

**spreadsheet** NOUN a computer program that is used for entering and arranging figures, used mainly for financial planning

**spring**, springs, springing, sprang, sprung NOUN ❶ Spring is the season between winter and summer ❷ a coil of wire which returns to its natural shape after being pressed or pulled ❸ a place where water comes up through the ground ❹ an act of springing ✿ **VERB** ❺ To spring means to jump upwards or forwards ❻ If something springs in a particular direction, it moves suddenly and quickly ❼ If one thing springs from another, it is the result of it

**spring onion - stage**

**spring onion** NOUN a small onion with long green shoots, often eaten raw in salads

**sprinkle**, sprinkles, sprinkling, sprinkled VERB If you sprinkle a liquid or powder over something, you scatter it over it

**sprint** NOUN ❶ a short, fast race ✽ VERB ❷ To sprint means to run fast over a short distance

**sprout** VERB ❶ When something sprouts, it grows ❷ If things sprout up, they appear rapidly ✽ NOUN ❸ Sprouts are the same as **brussels sprouts**

**spy**, spies, spying, spied NOUN ❶ a person sent to find out secret information about a country or organization ✽ VERB ❷ Someone who spies tries to find out secret information about another country or organization ❸ If you spy on someone, you watch them secretly ❹ If you spy something, you notice it

**square**, squares, squaring, squared NOUN ❶ a shape with four equal sides and four right angles ❷ In a town or city, a square is a flat, open place, bordered by buildings or streets ❸ The square of a number is the number multiplied by itself. For example, the square of 3, written $3^2$, is 3 x 3 ✽ ADJECTIVE ❹ shaped like a square ❺ 'Square' is used before units of length when talking about the area of something ❻ 'Square' is used after units of length when you are giving the length of each side of something square ✽ VERB ❼ If you square a number, you multiply it by itself

**square root** NOUN A square root of a number is a number that makes the first number when it is multiplied by itself. For example, the square roots of 25 are 5 and -5

**squash**, squashes, squashing, squashed VERB ❶ If you squash something, you press it, so that it becomes flat or loses its shape ✽ NOUN ❷ If there is a squash in a place, there are a lot of people squashed in it ❸ Squash is a game in which two players hit a small rubber ball against the walls of a court using rackets ❹ Squash is a drink made from fruit juice, sugar, and water

**squeak** VERB ❶ If something squeaks, it makes a short high-pitched sound ✽ NOUN ❷ a short, high-pitched sound

**squeal** VERB ❶ When things or people squeal, they make long, high-pitched sounds ✽ NOUN ❷ a long, high-pitched sound

**squeeze**, squeezes, squeezing, squeezed VERB ❶ When you squeeze something, you press it firmly from two sides ❷ If you squeeze something into a small amount of time or space, you manage to fit it in ✽ NOUN ❸ If you give something a squeeze, you squeeze it ❹ If getting into something is a squeeze, it is just possible to fit into it

**squid** NOUN a sea creature with a long soft body and many tentacles

**squirrel** NOUN a small furry animal with a long bushy tail

**squirt** VERB ❶ If a liquid squirts, it comes out of a narrow opening in a thin, fast stream ✽ NOUN ❷ a thin, fast stream of liquid

**stab**, stabs, stabbing, stabbed VERB ❶ To stab someone means to wound them by pushing a knife into their body ❷ To stab at something means to push at it sharply with your finger or with something long and narrow ✽ PHRASE ❸ INFORMAL If you **have a stab** at something, you try to do it ✽ NOUN ❹ You can refer to a sudden unpleasant feeling as a stab of something

**stable** ADJECTIVE ❶ not likely to change or come to an end suddenly ❷ firmly fixed or balanced and not likely to move, wobble, or fall ✽ NOUN ❸ a building in which horses are kept **stability** NOUN

**stack** NOUN ❶ A stack of things is a pile of them, one on top of the other ✽ VERB ❷ If you stack things, you arrange them one on top of the other in a pile

**stadium**, stadiums NOUN a sports ground with rows of seats around it

**staff**, staffs, staffing, staffed NOUN ❶ The staff of an organization are the people who work for it ✽ VERB ❷ To staff an organization means to find and employ people to work in it ❸ If an organization is staffed by particular people, they are the people who work for it

**stag** NOUN an adult male deer

**stage**, stages, staging, staged NOUN ❶ a part of a process that lasts for a period of time ❷ In a theatre, the stage is a raised platform where the actors or entertainers perform ❸ You can refer to the profession of acting

# stagger - stand in

as the stage ❖ VERB ❹ If someone stages a play or event, they organize it and present it or take part in it

**stagger** VERB ❶ If you stagger, you walk unsteadily because you are ill or drunk ❷ If something staggers you, it amazes you ❸ If events are staggered, they are arranged so that they do not all happen at the same time

**stain** NOUN ❶ a mark on something that is difficult to remove ❖ VERB ❷ If a substance stains something, the thing becomes marked or coloured by it

**stair** NOUN Stairs are a set of steps inside a building going from one floor to another

### don't mix up
### Hello Kitty...
never mixes up **stair** (a step) and **stare** (look at for a long time).

**staircase** NOUN a set of stairs

**stale** ADJECTIVE ❶ Stale food or air is no longer fresh ❷ If you feel stale, you have no new ideas and are bored

**stalk** [stawk] NOUN ❶ The stalk of a flower or leaf is its stem ❖ VERB ❷ To stalk a person or animal means to follow them quietly in order to catch, kill, or observe them ❸ If someone stalks into a room, they walk in a stiff, proud, or angry way

**stammer** VERB ❶ When someone stammers, they speak with difficulty, repeating words and sounds and hesitating awkwardly ❖ NOUN ❷ Someone who has a stammer tends to stammer when they speak

**stamp** NOUN ❶ a small piece of gummed paper which you stick on a letter or parcel before posting it ❷ a small block with a pattern cut into it, which you press onto an inky pad and make a mark with it on paper; also the mark made by the stamp ❸ If something bears the stamp of a particular quality or person, it shows clear signs of that quality or of the person's style or characteristics ❖ VERB ❹ If you stamp a piece of paper, you make a mark on it using a stamp ❺ If you stamp, you lift your foot and put it down hard on the ground

**stamp out** ❖ VERB To stamp something out means to put an end to it

**stand**, stands, standing, stood VERB ❶ If you are standing, you are upright, your legs are straight, and your weight is supported by your feet. When you stand up, you get into a standing position ❷ If something stands somewhere, that is where it is ❸ If you stand something somewhere, you put it there in an upright position ❹ If a decision or offer stands, it is still valid ❺ You can use 'stand' when describing the state or condition of something ❻ If a letter stands for a particular word, it is an abbreviation for that word ❼ If you say you will not stand for something, you mean you will not tolerate it ❽ If something can stand a situation or test, it is good enough or strong enough not to be damaged by it ❾ If you cannot stand something, you cannot bear it ❿ If you stand in an election, you are one of the candidates ❖ PHRASE ⓫ When someone **stands trial**, they are tried in a court of law ❖ NOUN ⓬ a stall or very small shop outdoors or in a large public building ⓭ a large structure at a sports ground, where the spectators sit ⓮ a piece of furniture designed to hold something

**stand by** ❖ VERB ❶ If you stand by to provide help or take action, you are ready to do it if necessary ❷ If you stand by while something happens, you do nothing to stop it

**stand down** ❖ VERB If someone stands down, they resign from their job or position

**stand in** ❖ VERB If you stand in for someone, you take their place or do their job while they are ill or away

262

**stand out** ✿ VERB If something stands out, it can be easily noticed or is more important than other similar things

**stand up** ✿ VERB ❶ If something stands up to rough treatment, it is not damaged or harmed ❷ If you stand up to someone who is criticizing or attacking you, you defend yourself

**standard** NOUN ❶ a level of quality or achievement that is considered acceptable ❷ IN PLURAL Standards are moral principles of behaviour ✿ ADJECTIVE ❸ usual, normal, and correct

**staple**, staples, stapling, stapled NOUN ❶ Staples are small pieces of wire that hold sheets of paper firmly together ✿ VERB ❷ If you staple sheets of paper, you fasten them together with staples ✿ ADJECTIVE ❸ A staple food forms a regular and basic part of someone's everyday diet

**star**, stars, starring, starred NOUN ❶ a large ball of burning gas in space that appears as a point of light in the sky at night ❷ a shape with four, five, or more points sticking out in a regular pattern ❸ Famous actors, sports players, and musicians are referred to as stars ❹ IN PLURAL The horoscope in a newspaper or magazine can be referred to as the stars ✿ VERB ❺ If an actor or actress stars in a film or if the film stars that person, he or she has one of the most important parts in it

**stare**, stares, staring, stared VERB ❶ If you stare at something, you look at it for a long time ✿ NOUN ❷ a long fixed look at something

**starfish**, starfishes or starfish NOUN a flat, star-shaped sea creature with five limbs

**start** VERB ❶ If something starts, it begins to take place or comes into existence ❷ If you start to do something, you begin to do it ❸ If you start something, you cause it to begin or to come into existence ❹ If you start a machine or car, you operate the controls to make it work ❺ If you start, your body suddenly jerks because of surprise or fear ✿ NOUN ❻ The start of something is the point or time at which it begins ❼ If you do something with a start, you do it with a sudden jerky movement because of surprise or fear

**starter** NOUN a small quantity of food served as the first part of a meal

**startle**, startles, startling, startled VERB If something sudden and unexpected startles you, it surprises you and makes you slightly frightened **startled** ADJECTIVE

**starve**, starves, starving, starved VERB ❶ If people are starving, they are suffering from a serious lack of food and are likely to die ❷ To starve a person or animal means to prevent them from having any food ❸ INFORMAL If you say you are starving, you mean you are very hungry ❹ If someone or something is starved of something they need, they are suffering because they are not getting enough of it **starvation** NOUN

**state**, states, stating, stated NOUN ❶ The state of something is its condition, what it is like, or its circumstances ❷ Countries are sometimes referred to as states ❸ Some countries are divided into regions called states which make some of their own laws ❹ You can refer to the government or administration of a country as the state ✿ PHRASE ❺ If you are **in a state**, you are nervous or upset and unable to control your emotions ✿ ADJECTIVE ❻ A state ceremony involves the ruler or leader of a country ✿ VERB ❼ If you state something, you say it or write it, especially in a formal way

**statement** NOUN ❶ something you say or write when you give facts or information in a formal way ❷ a document provided by a bank showing all the money paid into and out of an account during a period of time

**static** ADJECTIVE ❶ never moving or changing ✿ NOUN ❷ Static is an electrical charge caused by friction. It builds up in metal objects

**station** NOUN ❶ a building and platforms where trains stop for passengers ❷ A bus or coach station is a place where some buses start their journeys ❸ A radio station is the frequency on which a particular company broadcasts ❹ in Australian and New Zealand English, a large sheep or cattle farm ❺ OLD-FASHIONED A person's station is their position or rank in society ✿ VERB ❻ Someone who is stationed somewhere is sent there to work or do a particular job

**stationary** ADJECTIVE not moving

263

# stationery - step

**stationery** NOUN Stationery is paper, pens, and other writing equipment

### don't mix up

**Hello Kitty...** never mixes up **stationary** (not moving) and **stationery** (paper and pens).

**statistic** NOUN ❶ Statistics are facts obtained by analysing numerical information ❷ Statistics is the branch of mathematics that deals with the analysis of numerical information

**statue** NOUN a sculpture of a person

**status**, statuses [stay-tuss] NOUN ❶ A person's status is their position and importance in society ❷ Status is also the official classification given to someone or something

**stay** VERB ❶ If you stay in a place, you do not move away from it ❷ If you stay at a hotel or a friend's house, you spend some time there as a guest or visitor ❸ If you stay in a particular state, you continue to be in it ❹ In Scottish and South African English, to stay in a place can also mean to live there ❀ NOUN ❺ A stay is a short time spent somewhere

**steady**, steadier, steadiest; steadies, steadying, steadied ADJECTIVE ❶ continuing or developing gradually without major interruptions or changes ❷ firm and not shaking or wobbling ❸ A steady look or voice is calm and controlled ❹ Someone who is steady is sensible and reliable ❀ VERB ❺ When you steady something, you hold on to prevent it from shaking or wobbling ❻ When you steady yourself, you control and calm yourself **steadily** ADVERB

**steak** NOUN ❶ Steak is good-quality beef without much fat ❷ A fish steak is a large piece of fish

**steal**, steals, stealing, stole, stolen VERB ❶ To steal something means to take it without permission and without intending to return it ❷ To steal somewhere means to move there quietly and secretively

**steam** NOUN ❶ Steam is the hot vapour formed when water boils ❀ ADJECTIVE ❷ Steam engines are operated using steam as a means of power ❀ VERB ❸ If something steams, it gives off steam ❹ To steam food means to cook it in steam

**steel** NOUN ❶ Steel is a very strong metal containing mainly iron with a small amount of carbon ❀ VERB ❷ To steel yourself means to prepare to deal with something unpleasant

**steep** ADJECTIVE ❶ A steep slope rises sharply and is difficult to go up ❷ larger than is reasonable ❀ VERB ❸ To steep something in a liquid means to soak it thoroughly **steeply** ADVERB

**steer** VERB ❶ To steer a vehicle or boat means to control it so that it goes in the right direction ❷ To steer someone towards a particular course of action means to influence and direct their behaviour or thoughts ❀ NOUN ❸ A steer is a castrated bull

**stem**, stems, stemming, stemmed NOUN ❶ The stem of a plant is the long thin central part above the ground that carries the leaves and flowers ❷ The stem of a glass is the long narrow part connecting the bowl to the base ❀ VERB ❸ If a problem stems from a particular situation, that situation is the original starting point or cause of the problem ❹ If you stem the flow of something, you restrict it or stop it from spreading

**step**, steps, stepping, stepped NOUN ❶ If you take a step, you lift your foot and put it down somewhere else ❷ one of a series of actions that you take in order to achieve something ❸ a raised flat surface, usually

264

**stereo - stimulate**

one of a series that you can walk up or down ✿ VERB ❹ If you step in a particular direction, you move your foot in that direction ❺ If someone steps down or steps aside from an important position, they resign

**stereo**, stereos ADJECTIVE ❶ A stereo recording or music system is one in which the sound is directed through two speakers ✿ NOUN ❷ a piece of equipment that reproduces sound from records, tapes, or CDs directing the sound through two speakers

**sterile** ADJECTIVE ❶ Sterile means completely clean and free from germs ❷ A sterile person or animal is unable to produce offspring

**stern** ADJECTIVE ❶ very serious and strict ✿ NOUN ❷ The stern of a boat is the back part

**stew** NOUN ❶ a dish of small pieces of savoury food cooked together slowly in a liquid ✿ VERB ❷ To stew meat, vegetables, or fruit means to cook them slowly in a liquid

**steward** NOUN ❶ a man who works on a ship or plane looking after passengers and serving meals ❷ a person who helps to direct the public at a race, march, or other event

**stewardess**, stewardesses NOUN a woman who works on a ship or plane looking after passengers and serving meals

**stick**, sticks, sticking, stuck NOUN ❶ a long, thin piece of wood ❷ A stick of something is a long, thin piece of it ✿ VERB ❸ If you stick a long or pointed object into something, you push it in ❹ If you stick one thing to another, you attach it with glue or sticky tape ❺ If one thing sticks to another, it becomes attached and is difficult to remove ❻ If a movable part of something sticks, it becomes fixed and will no longer move or work properly ❼ INFORMAL If you stick something somewhere, you put it there ❽ If you stick by someone, you continue to help and support them ❾ If you stick to something, you keep to it and do not change to something else ❿ When people stick together, they stay together and support each other

**stick out** ✿ VERB ❶ If something sticks out, it projects from something else ❷ To stick out also means to be very noticeable

**stick up** ✿ VERB ❶ If something sticks up, it points upwards from a surface ❷ INFORMAL If you stick up for a person or principle, you support or defend them

**sticker** NOUN a small piece of paper or plastic with writing or a picture on it, that you stick onto a surface

**sticky**, stickier, stickiest ADJECTIVE ❶ A sticky object is covered with a substance that can stick to other things ❷ Sticky paper or tape has glue on one side so that you can stick it to a surface ❸ INFORMAL A sticky situation is difficult or embarrassing to deal with ❹ Sticky weather is unpleasantly hot and humid

**stiff** ADJECTIVE ❶ Something that is stiff is firm and not easily bent ❷ If you feel stiff, your muscles or joints ache when you move ❸ Stiff behaviour is formal and not friendly or relaxed ❹ Stiff also means difficult or severe ❺ A stiff drink contains a large amount of alcohol ❻ A stiff breeze is blowing strongly ✿ ADVERB ❼ INFORMAL If you are bored stiff or scared stiff, you are very bored or very scared **stiffly** ADVERB **stiffness** NOUN

**stifle**, stifles, stifling, stifled [sty-fl] VERB ❶ If the atmosphere stifles you, you feel you cannot breathe properly ❷ To stifle something means to stop it from happening or continuing

**still** ADVERB ❶ If a situation still exists, it has continued to exist and it exists now ❷ If something could still happen, it might happen although it has not happened yet ❸ 'Still' emphasizes that something is the case in spite of other things ✿ ADVERB OR ADJECTIVE ❹ Still means staying in the same position without moving ✿ ADJECTIVE ❺ A still place is quiet and peaceful with no signs of activity ✿ NOUN ❻ a photograph taken from a cinema film or video

**stimulate**, stimulates, stimulating, stimulated VERB ❶ To stimulate something means to encourage it to begin or develop ❷ If something stimulates you, it gives you new ideas and enthusiasm **stimulating** ADJECTIVE **stimulation** NOUN

265

## sting – stop

**help with spelling**

**Hello Kitty...** knows that you make a plural of a word that ends with a, b, c, d, g, i, k, l, m, n, p, r, t and w by adding s.

**sting**, stings, stinging, stung VERB ❶ If a creature or plant stings you, it pricks your skin and injects a substance which causes pain ❷ If a part of your body stings, you feel a sharp tingling pain there ❸ If someone's remarks sting you, they make you feel upset and hurt ❀ NOUN ❹ A creature's sting is the part it stings you with

**stink**, stinks, stinking, stank, stunk VERB ❶ Something that stinks smells very unpleasant ❀ NOUN ❷ a very unpleasant smell

**stir**, stirs, stirring, stirred VERB ❶ When you stir a liquid, you move it around using a spoon or a stick ❷ To stir means to move slightly ❸ If something stirs you, it makes you feel strong emotions ❀ NOUN ❹ If an event causes a stir, it causes general excitement or shock

**stitch**, stitches, stitching, stitched VERB ❶ When you stitch pieces of material together, you use a needle and thread to sew them together ❷ To stitch a wound means to use a special needle and thread to hold the edges of skin together ❀ NOUN ❸ one of the pieces of thread that can be seen where material has been sewn ❹ one of the pieces of thread that can be seen where a wound has been stitched ❺ If you have a stitch, you feel a sharp pain at the side of your abdomen, usually because you have been running or laughing

**stock** NOUN ❶ Stocks are shares bought as an investment in a company; also the amount of money raised by the company through the issue of shares ❷ A shop's stock is the total amount of goods it has for sale ❸ If you have a stock of things, you have a supply ready for use ❹ The stock an animal or person comes from is the type of animal or person they are descended from ❺ Stock is farm animals ❻ Stock is a liquid made from boiling meat, bones, or vegetables together in water. Stock is used as a base for soups, stews, and sauces ❀ VERB ❼ A shop that stocks particular goods keeps a supply of them to sell ❽ If you stock a shelf or cupboard, you fill it with food or other things ❀ ADJECTIVE ❾ A stock expression or way of doing something is one that is commonly used

**stock up** ❀ VERB If you stock up with something, you buy a supply of it

**stock exchange** NOUN a place where there is trading in stocks and shares

**stocking** NOUN Stockings are long pieces of thin clothing that cover a woman's leg

**stock market** NOUN The stock market is the organization and activity involved in buying and selling stocks and shares

**stomach** NOUN ❶ Your stomach is the organ inside your body where food is digested ❷ You can refer to the front part of your body above your waist as your stomach ❀ VERB ❸ If you cannot stomach something, you strongly dislike it and cannot accept it

**stone**, stones, stoning, stoned NOUN ❶ Stone is the hard solid substance found in the ground and used for building ❷ a small piece of rock ❸ The stone in a fruit such as a plum or cherry is the large seed in the centre ❹ a unit of weight equal to 14 pounds or about 6.35 kilograms ❺ You can refer to a jewel as a stone ❀ VERB ❻ To stone something or someone means to throw stones at them

**stool** NOUN ❶ a seat with legs but no back or arms ❷ a lump of faeces

**stop**, stops, stopping, stopped VERB ❶ If you

266

stop doing something, you no longer do it ❷ If an activity or process stops, it comes to an end or no longer happens ❸ If a machine stops, it no longer functions or it is switched off ❹ To stop something means to prevent it ❺ If people or things that are moving stop, they no longer move ❻ If you stop somewhere, you stay there for a short while ✿ NOUN ❼ a place where a bus, train, or other vehicle stops during a journey ❽ If something that is moving comes to a stop, it no longer moves

**storage** NOUN The storage of something is the keeping of it somewhere until it is needed

**store**, stores, storing, stored NOUN ❶ a shop ❷ A store of something is a supply kept for future use ❸ a place where things are kept while they are not used ✿ VERB ❹ When you store something somewhere, you keep it there until it is needed ✿ PHRASE ❺ Something that is **in store for** you is going to happen to you in the future

**storey**, storeys NOUN A storey of a building is one of its floors or levels

**storm** NOUN ❶ When there is a storm, there is heavy rain, a strong wind, and often thunder and lightning ❷ If something causes a storm, it causes an angry or excited reaction ✿ VERB ❸ If someone storms out, they leave quickly, noisily, and angrily ❹ To storm means to say something in a loud, angry voice ❺ If people storm a place, they attack it **stormy** ADJECTIVE

**story**, stories NOUN ❶ a description of imaginary people and events written or told to entertain people ❷ The story of something or someone is an account of the important events that have happened to them

**stove** NOUN a piece of equipment for heating a room or for cooking

**straight** ADJECTIVE OR ADVERB ❶ continuing in the same direction without curving or bending ❷ upright or level rather than sloping or bent ✿ ADVERB ❸ immediately and directly ✿ ADJECTIVE ❹ neat and tidy ❺ honest, frank, and direct ❻ A straight choice involves only two options

**straighten** VERB ❶ To straighten something means to remove any bends or curves from it ❷ To straighten something also means to make it neat and tidy ❸ To straighten out a confused situation means to organize and deal with it

**strain** NOUN ❶ Strain is worry and nervous tension ❷ If a strain is put on something, it is affected by a strong force which may damage it ❸ You can refer to an aspect of someone's character, remarks, or work as a strain ❹ You can refer to distant sounds of music as strains of music ❺ A particular strain of plant is a variety of it ✿ VERB ❻ To strain something means to force it or use it more than is reasonable or normal ❼ If you strain a muscle, you injure it by moving awkwardly ❽ To strain food means to pour away the liquid from it

**strange**, stranger, strangest ADJECTIVE ❶ unusual or unexpected ❷ not known, seen, or experienced before **strangely** ADVERB

**stranger** NOUN ❶ someone you have never met before ❷ If you are a stranger to a place or situation, you have not been there or experienced it before

**strangle**, strangles, strangling, strangled VERB To strangle someone means to kill them by squeezing their throat

**strap**, straps, strapping, strapped NOUN ❶ a narrow piece of leather or cloth, used to fasten or hold things together ✿ VERB ❷ To strap something means to fasten it with a strap

**strategy**, strategies NOUN ❶ a plan for achieving something ❷ Strategy is the skill of planning the best way to achieve something, especially in war

**straw** NOUN ❶ Straw is the dry, yellowish stalks from cereal crops ❷ a hollow tube of paper or plastic which you use to suck a drink into your mouth ✿ PHRASE ❸ If something is **the last straw**, it is the latest in a series of bad events and makes you feel you cannot stand any more

**strawberry**, strawberries NOUN a small red fruit with tiny seeds in its skin

**stray** VERB ❶ When people or animals stray, they wander away from where they should be ❷ If your thoughts stray, you stop concentrating ✿ ADJECTIVE ❸ A stray dog or cat is one that has wandered away from

# streak – strip

home ❹ Stray things are separated from the main group of things of their kind ✿ NOUN ❺ a stray dog or cat

**streak** NOUN ❶ a long mark or stain ❷ If someone has a particular streak, they have that quality in their character ❸ A lucky or unlucky streak is a series of successes or failures ✿ VERB ❹ If something is streaked with a colour, it has lines of the colour in it

**stream** NOUN ❶ a small river ❷ You can refer to a steady flow of something as a stream ❸ In a school, a stream is a group of children of the same age and ability ✿ VERB ❹ To stream somewhere means to move in a continuous flow in large quantities

**street** NOUN a road in a town or village, usually with buildings along it

**strength** NOUN ❶ Your strength is your physical energy and the power of your muscles ❷ Strength can refer to the degree of someone's confidence or courage ❸ You can refer to power or influence as strength ❹ Someone's strengths are their good qualities and abilities ❺ The strength of an object is the degree to which it can stand rough treatment

**strengthen** VERB ❶ To strengthen something means to give it more power, influence, or support and make it more likely to succeed ❷ To strengthen an object means to improve it or add to its structure so that it can withstand rough treatment

**stress**, stresses, stressing, stressed NOUN ❶ Stress is worry and nervous tension ❷ Stresses are strong physical forces applied to an object ❸ Stress is emphasis put on a word or part of a word when it is pronounced, making it slightly louder ✿ VERB ❹ If you stress a point, you emphasize it and draw attention to its importance **stressful** ADJECTIVE

**stretch**, stretches, stretching, stretched VERB ❶ Something that stretches over an area extends that far ❷ When you stretch, you hold out part of your body as far as you can ❸ To stretch something soft or elastic means to pull it to make it longer or bigger ✿ NOUN ❹ A stretch of land or water is an area of it ❺ A stretch of time is a period of time

**stretcher** NOUN a long piece of material with a pole along each side, used to carry an injured person

**strict** ADJECTIVE ❶ Someone who is strict controls other people very firmly ❷ A strict rule must always be obeyed absolutely

**strictly** ADVERB Strictly means only for a particular purpose

**stride**, strides, striding, strode, stridden VERB ❶ To stride along means to walk quickly with long steps ✿ NOUN ❷ a long step; also the length of a step

**strike**, strikes, striking, struck NOUN ❶ If there is a strike, people stop working as a protest ❷ A hunger strike is a refusal to eat anything as a protest. A rent strike is a refusal to pay rent ❸ a military attack ✿ VERB ❹ To strike someone or something means to hit them ❺ If an illness, disaster, or enemy strikes, it suddenly affects or attacks someone ❻ If a thought strikes you, it comes into your mind ❼ If you are struck by something, you are impressed by it ❽ When a clock strikes, it makes a sound to indicate the time

**strike off** ✿ VERB If a professional person is struck off for bad behaviour, their name is removed from an official register and they are not allowed to practise their profession

**strike up** ✿ VERB To strike up a conversation or friendship means to begin it

**string**, strings, stringing, strung NOUN ❶ String is thin cord made of twisted threads ❷ You can refer to a row or series of similar things as a string of them ❸ The strings of a musical instrument are tightly stretched lengths of wire or nylon which vibrate to produce the notes ❹ IN PLURAL The section of an orchestra consisting of stringed instruments is called the strings

**string along** ✿ VERB INFORMAL To string someone along means to deceive them

**string out** ✿ VERB ❶ If things are strung out, they are spread out in a long line ❷ To string something out means to make it last longer than necessary

**strip**, strips, stripping, stripped NOUN ❶ A strip of something is a long, narrow piece of it ❷ A comic strip is a series of drawings which tell a story ❸ A sports team's strip is the clothes worn by the team when playing a

**stripe - stupidity**

match ✿ **VERB** ❹ If you strip, you take off all your clothes ❺ To strip something means to remove whatever is covering its surface

**stripe NOUN** Stripes are long, thin lines, usually of different colours **striped ADJECTIVE**

**stroke**, strokes, stroking, stroked **VERB** ❶ If you stroke something, you move your hand smoothly and gently over it ✿ **NOUN** ❷ If someone has a stroke, they suddenly lose consciousness as a result of a blockage or rupture in a blood vessel in the brain. A stroke can result in damage to speech and paralysis ❸ A swimming stroke is a particular style of swimming

**stroll VERB** ❶ To stroll along means to walk slowly in a relaxed way ✿ **NOUN** ❷ a slow, pleasurable walk

**strong ADJECTIVE** ❶ Someone who is strong has powerful muscles ❷ You also say that someone is strong when they are confident and have courage ❸ Strong objects are able to withstand rough treatment ✿ **ADVERB** ❹ If someone or something is still going strong, they are still healthy or working well after a long time **strongly ADVERB**

**structure**, structures, structuring, structured **NOUN** ❶ The structure of something is the way it is made, built, or organized ❷ something that has been built or constructed ✿ **VERB** ❸ To structure something means to arrange it into an organized pattern or system

**struggle**, struggles, struggling, struggled **VERB** ❶ If you struggle to do something, you try hard to do it in difficult circumstances ❷ When people struggle, they twist and move violently during a fight ✿ **NOUN** ❸ Something that is a struggle is difficult to achieve and takes a lot of effort ❹ a fight

**stubborn ADJECTIVE** Someone who is stubborn is determined not to change their opinion or course of action **stubbornly ADVERB**

**stuck ADJECTIVE** ❶ If something is stuck in a particular position, it is fixed or jammed and cannot be moved ❷ If you are stuck, you are unable to continue what you were doing because it is too difficult ❸ If you are stuck somewhere, you are unable to get away

**student NOUN** a person studying at university or college

**studio**, studios **NOUN** ❶ a room where a photographer or painter works ❷ a room containing special equipment where records, films, or radio or television programmes are made

**study**, studies, studying, studied **VERB** ❶ If you study a particular subject, you spend time learning about it ❷ If you study something, you look at it carefully ✿ **NOUN** ❸ Study is the activity of studying a subject ❹ Studies are subjects which are studied ❺ A study is also a room used for writing and studying

**stuff**, stuffs, stuffing, stuffed **NOUN** ❶ You can refer to a substance or group of things as stuff ✿ **VERB** ❷ If you stuff something somewhere, you push it there quickly and roughly ❸ If you stuff something with a substance or objects, you fill it with the substance or objects

**stuffy**, stuffier, stuffiest **ADJECTIVE** ❶ very formal and old-fashioned ❷ If it is stuffy in a room, there is not enough fresh air

**stumble**, stumbles, stumbling, stumbled **VERB** ❶ If you stumble while you are walking or running, you trip and almost fall ❷ If you stumble across something or stumble on it, you find it unexpectedly

**stump NOUN** ❶ a small part of something that is left when the rest has been removed ✿ **VERB** ❷ If a question or problem stumps you, you cannot think of an answer or solution

**stun**, stuns, stunning, stunned **VERB** ❶ If you are stunned by something, you are very shocked by it ❷ To stun a person or animal means to knock them unconscious with a blow to the head

**stunning ADJECTIVE** very beautiful or impressive

**stunt NOUN** ❶ an unusual or dangerous and exciting action that someone does to get publicity or as part of a film ✿ **VERB** ❷ To stunt the growth of something means to prevent it from developing as it should

**stupid ADJECTIVE** showing lack of good judgment or intelligence and not at all sensible **stupidly ADVERB**

**stupidity NOUN** a lack of intelligence or good judgment

A B C D E F G H I J K L M N O P Q R **S** T U V W X Y Z

269

# sturdy - subway

**sturdy**, sturdier, sturdiest ADJECTIVE strong and firm and unlikely to be damaged or injured

**stutter** NOUN ❶ Someone who has a stutter finds it difficult to speak smoothly and often repeats sounds through being unable to complete a word ✿ VERB ❷ When someone stutters, they hesitate or repeat sounds when speaking

**style**, styles, styling, styled NOUN ❶ The style of something is the general way in which it is done or presented, often showing the attitudes of the people involved ❷ A person or place that has style is smart, elegant, and fashionable ❸ The style of something is its design ✿ VERB ❹ To style a piece of clothing or a person's hair means to design and create its shape

**stylish** ADJECTIVE smart, elegant, and fashionable

**subject** NOUN ❶ The subject of writing or a conversation is the thing or person being discussed ❷ In grammar, the subject is the word or words representing the person or thing doing the action expressed by the verb. For example, in the sentence 'My cat keeps catching birds', 'my cat' is the subject ❸ an area of study ❹ The subjects of a country are the people who live there ✿ VERB ❺ To subject someone to something means to make them experience it ✿ ADJECTIVE ❻ Someone or something that is subject to something is affected by it

**subjective** ADJECTIVE influenced by personal feelings and opinion rather than based on fact or rational thought

**submarine** NOUN a ship that can travel beneath the surface of the sea

**submit**, submits, submitting, submitted VERB ❶ If you submit to something, you accept it because you are not powerful enough to resist it ❷ If you submit an application or proposal, you send it to someone for consideration

**subscription** NOUN a sum of money that you pay regularly to belong to an organization or to receive regular copies of a magazine

**subsidy**, subsidies NOUN a sum of money paid to help support a company or provide a public service

**substance** NOUN Anything which is a solid, a powder, a liquid, or a paste can be referred to as a substance

**substantial** ADJECTIVE ❶ very large in degree or amount ❷ large and strongly built

**substitute**, substitutes, substituting, substituted VERB ❶ To substitute one thing for another means to use it instead of the other thing or to put it in the other thing's place ✿ NOUN ❷ If one thing is a substitute for another, it is used instead of it or put in its place

**subtle**, subtler, subtlest [sut-tl] ADJECTIVE ❶ very fine, delicate, or small in degree ❷ using indirect methods to achieve something **subtly** ADVERB

**subtract** VERB If you subtract one number from another, you take away the first number from the second

**subtraction** NOUN Subtraction is subtracting one number from another, or a sum in which you do this

**suburb** NOUN an area of a town or city that is away from its centre

**suburban** ADJECTIVE ❶ relating to a suburb or suburbs ❷ dull and conventional

**subway** NOUN ❶ a footpath that goes underneath a road ❷ an underground railway

## how English works

### Helpful hints...

The **subject** of a sentence is the person or thing that is doing something, like *My dog* in *My dog chases squirrels.*

270

**succeed** VERB ❶ To succeed means to achieve the result you intend ❷ To succeed someone means to be the next person to have their job ❸ If one thing succeeds another, it comes after it in time

**success**, successes NOUN ❶ Success is the achievement of something you have been trying to do ❷ Someone who is a success has achieved an important position or made a lot of money

**successful** ADJECTIVE having achieved what you intended to do **successfully** ADVERB

**such** ADJECTIVE OR PRONOUN ❶ You use 'such' to refer to the person or thing you have just mentioned, or to someone or something similar ✿ PHRASE ❷ You can use **such as** to introduce an example of something ❸ You can use **such as it is** to indicate that something is not great in quality or quantity ✿ ADJECTIVE ❹ 'Such' can be used for emphasizing

**suck** VERB ❶ If you suck something, you hold it in your mouth and pull at it with your cheeks and tongue, usually to get liquid out of it ❷ To suck something in a particular direction means to draw it there with a powerful force

**sudden** ADJECTIVE happening quickly and unexpectedly **suddenly** ADVERB

**sue**, sues, suing, sued VERB To sue someone means to start a legal case against them, usually to claim money from them

**suffer** VERB ❶ If someone is suffering pain, or suffering as a result of an unpleasant situation, they are badly affected by it ❷ If something suffers as a result of neglect or a difficult situation, its condition or quality becomes worse **sufferer** NOUN **suffering** NOUN

**sufficient** ADJECTIVE If a supply or quantity is sufficient for a purpose, there is enough of it available **sufficiently** ADVERB

**suffix**, suffixes NOUN a group of letters which is added to the end of a word to form a new word, for example 'ly' or 'ness'

**suffocate**, suffocates, suffocating, suffocated VERB To suffocate means to die as a result of having too little air or oxygen to breathe

**sugar** NOUN Sugar is a sweet substance used to sweeten food and drinks

**suggest** VERB If you suggest a plan or idea to someone, you mention it as a possibility for them to consider

**suggestion** NOUN ❶ a plan or idea that is mentioned as a possibility for someone to consider ❷ A suggestion of something is a very slight indication or faint sign of it

**suicide** NOUN People who commit suicide deliberately kill themselves

**suit** NOUN ❶ a matching jacket and trousers or skirt ❷ In a court of law, a suit is a legal action taken by one person against another ❸ one of four different types of card in a pack of playing cards. The four suits are hearts, clubs, diamonds, and spades ✿ VERB ❹ If a situation or course of action suits you, it is appropriate or acceptable for your purpose ❺ If a piece of clothing or a colour suits you, you look good when you are wearing it

**suitable** ADJECTIVE right or acceptable for a particular purpose or occasion **suitably** ADVERB

**suitcase** NOUN a case in which you carry your clothes when you are travelling

**sulk** VERB Someone who is sulking is showing their annoyance by being silent and moody

**sulky**, sulkier, sulkiest ADJECTIVE showing annoyance by being silent and moody

**sum**, sums, summing, summed NOUN ❶ an amount of money ❷ In arithmetic, a sum is a calculation ❸ The sum of something is the total amount of it

**sum up** ✿ VERB If you sum something up, you briefly describe its main points

**summarize**, summarizes, summarizing, summarized (also **summarise**) VERB To summarize something means to give a short account of its main points

**summary**, summaries NOUN A summary of something is a short account of its main points

**summer** NOUN Summer is the season between spring and autumn

**summit** NOUN ❶ The summit of a mountain is its top ❷ a meeting between leaders of different countries to discuss particular issues

**summon** VERB ❶ If someone summons you, they order you to go to them ❷ If you summon up strength or energy, you make a great effort to be strong or energetic

# sun - supply

**sun**, suns, sunning, sunned NOUN ❶ The sun is the star providing heat and light for the planets revolving around it in our solar system ❷ You refer to heat and light from the sun as sun ✿ VERB ❸ If you sun yourself, you sit in the sunshine

**sunbathe**, sunbathes, sunbathing, sunbathed VERB If you sunbathe, you sit in the sunshine to get a suntan

**sunburn** NOUN Sunburn is sore red skin on someone's body due to too much exposure to the rays of the sun **sunburnt** ADJECTIVE

**sundae** [*sun-day*] NOUN a dish of ice cream with cream and fruit or nuts

**Sunday**, Sundays NOUN Sunday is the day between Saturday and Monday

**sunflower** NOUN a tall plant with very large yellow flowers

**sunglasses** PLURAL NOUN Sunglasses are spectacles with dark lenses that you wear to protect your eyes from the sun

**sunlight** NOUN Sunlight is the bright light produced when the sun is shining

**sunny**, sunnier, sunniest ADJECTIVE When it is sunny, the sun is shining

**sunrise** NOUN Sunrise is the time in the morning when the sun first appears, and the colours produced in the sky at that time

**sunset** NOUN Sunset is the time in the evening when the sun disappears below the horizon, and the colours produced in the sky at that time

**sunshine** NOUN Sunshine is the bright light produced when the sun is shining

**suntan** NOUN If you have a suntan, the sun has turned your skin brown

**super** ADJECTIVE very nice or very good

**superb** ADJECTIVE very good indeed **superbly** ADVERB

**superior** ADJECTIVE ❶ better or of higher quality than other similar things ❷ in a position of higher authority than another person ❸ showing too much pride and self-importance ✿ NOUN ❹ Your superiors are people who are in a higher position than you in society or an organization **superiority** NOUN

**superlative** [*soo-per-lat-tiv*] NOUN ❶ In grammar, the superlative is the form of an adjective which indicates that the person or thing described has more of a particular quality than anyone or anything else. For example, 'quickest', 'best', and 'easiest' are all superlatives ✿ ADJECTIVE ❷ FORMAL very good indeed

**supermarket** NOUN a shop selling food and household goods arranged so that you can help yourself and pay at a till by the exit

**superstition** NOUN Superstition is a belief in things like magic and powers that bring good or bad luck **superstitious** ADJECTIVE

**supervise**, supervises, supervising, supervised VERB To supervise someone means to check and direct what they are doing to make sure that they do it correctly **supervision** NOUN **supervisor** NOUN

**supper** NOUN Supper is a meal eaten in the evening or a snack eaten before you go to bed

**supplement** VERB ❶ To supplement something means to add something to it to improve it ✿ NOUN ❷ something that is added to something else to improve it

**supplier** NOUN a firm which provides particular goods

**supply**, supplies, supplying, supplied VERB ❶ To supply someone with something means to provide it or send it to them ✿ NOUN ❷ A supply of something is an amount available for use ❸ IN PLURAL Supplies are food and equipment for a particular purpose

## how English works

### Helpful hints...

A **superlative** adjective shows that the noun has more of a certain quality than all the others in a group, like *tallest* and *most interesting*.

**support - survey**

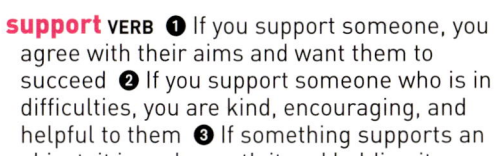

**support** VERB ❶ If you support someone, you agree with their aims and want them to succeed ❷ If you support someone who is in difficulties, you are kind, encouraging, and helpful to them ❸ If something supports an object, it is underneath it and holding it up ❹ To support someone or something means to prevent them from falling by holding them ❺ To support someone financially means to provide them with money ❀ NOUN ❻ an object that is holding something up ❼ Moral support is encouragement given to someone to help them do something difficult ❽ Financial support is money that is provided for someone or something

**supporter** NOUN a person who agrees with or helps someone

**supportive** ADJECTIVE A supportive person is encouraging and helpful to someone who is in difficulties

**suppose**, supposes, supposing, supposed VERB ❶ If you suppose that something is the case, you think that it is likely ❀ CONJUNCTION ❷ You can use 'suppose' or 'supposing' when you are considering or suggesting a possible situation or action

**sure**, surer, surest ADJECTIVE ❶ If you are sure about something, you have no doubts about it ❷ If you are sure of yourself, you are very confident ❸ If something is sure to happen, it will definitely happen ❹ Sure means reliable or accurate ❀ INTERJECTION ❺ Sure is an informal way of saying 'yes'

**surely** ADVERB 'Surely' is used to emphasize the belief that something is the case

**surf** VERB ❶ When you surf, you go surfing ❷ When you surf the internet, you go from website to website reading the information ❀ NOUN ❸ Surf is the white foam that forms on the top of waves when they break near the shore

**surface**, surfaces, surfacing, surfaced NOUN ❶ The surface of something is the top or outside area of it ❀ VERB ❷ If someone surfaces, they come up from under water to the surface

**surfboard** NOUN a long narrow lightweight board used for surfing

**surfing** NOUN Surfing is a sport which involves riding towards the shore on the top of a large wave while standing on a surfboard

**surge**, surges, surging, surged NOUN ❶ a sudden great increase in the amount of something ❀ VERB ❷ If something surges, it moves suddenly and powerfully

**surgeon** NOUN a doctor who performs operations

**surgery**, surgeries NOUN ❶ Surgery is medical treatment involving cutting open part of the patient's body to treat the damaged part ❷ The room or building where a doctor or dentist works is called a surgery

**surgical** ADJECTIVE used in or involving a medical operation

**surname** NOUN Your surname is your last name which you share with other members of your family

**surplus**, surpluses NOUN If there is a surplus of something there is more of it than is needed

**surprise**, surprises, surprising, surprised NOUN ❶ an unexpected event ❷ Surprise is the feeling caused when something unexpected happens ❀ VERB ❸ If something surprises you, it gives you a feeling of surprise ❹ If you surprise someone, you do something they were not expecting **surprising** ADJECTIVE

**surrender** VERB ❶ To surrender means to stop fighting and agree that the other side has won ❷ To surrender something means to give it up to someone else ❀ NOUN ❸ Surrender is a situation in which one side in a fight agrees that the other side has won and gives in

**surround** VERB To surround someone or something means to be situated all around them

**surroundings** PLURAL NOUN You can refer to the area and environment around a place or person as their surroundings

**survey**, surveys, surveying, surveyed VERB ❶ To survey something means to look carefully at the whole of it ❷ To survey a building or piece of land means to examine it carefully in order to make a report or plan of its structure and features ❀ NOUN ❸ A survey of something is a detailed examination of it, often in the form of a report

# survival - swerve

**survival** NOUN Survival is being able to continue living or existing in spite of great danger or difficulties

**survive**, survives, surviving, survived VERB To survive means to continue to live or exist in spite of a great danger or difficulties **survivor** NOUN

**suspect** VERB [sus-**pekt**] ❶ If you suspect something, you think that it is likely or is probably true ❷ If you suspect something, you have doubts about its reliability ❸ If you suspect someone of doing something wrong, you think that they have done it ✿ NOUN [**sus**-pekt] ❹ someone who is thought to be guilty of a crime ✿ ADJECTIVE ❺ If something is suspect, it cannot be trusted

**suspend** VERB ❶ If something is suspended, it is hanging from somewhere ❷ To suspend an activity or event means to delay it or stop it for a while ❸ If someone is suspended from their job, they are told not to do it for a period of time, usually as a punishment

**suspense** NOUN Suspense is a state of excitement or anxiety caused by having to wait for something

**suspicion** NOUN ❶ Suspicion is the feeling of not trusting someone or the feeling that something is wrong ❷ a feeling that something is likely to happen or is probably true

**suspicious** ADJECTIVE If you are suspicious of someone, you do not trust them **suspiciously** ADVERB

**sustain** VERB ❶ To sustain something means to continue it for a period of time ❷ If something sustains you, it gives you energy and strength

**sustainable** ADJECTIVE ❶ capable of being sustained ❷ If economic development or energy resources are sustainable they are capable of being maintained at a steady level without exhausting natural resources or causing ecological damage

**swallow** VERB ❶ If you swallow something, you make it go down your throat and into your stomach ❷ When you swallow, you move your throat muscles as if you were swallowing something, especially when you are nervous ✿ NOUN ❸ a bird with pointed wings and a long forked tail

**swan** NOUN a large, usually white, bird with a long neck that lives on rivers or lakes

**swap**, swaps, swapping, swapped [rhymes with **stop**] VERB To swap one thing for another means to replace the first thing with the second, often by making an exchange with another person

**sway** VERB ❶ To sway means to lean or swing slowly from side to side ❷ If something sways you, it influences your judgment

**swear**, swears, swearing, swore, sworn VERB ❶ To swear means to say words that are considered to be very rude or blasphemous ❷ If you swear to something, you state solemnly that you will do it or that it is true ❸ If you swear by something, you firmly believe that it is a reliable cure or solution

**sweat** NOUN ❶ Sweat is the salty liquid produced by your sweat glands when you are hot or afraid ✿ VERB ❷ When you sweat, sweat comes through the pores in your skin in order to lower the temperature of your body

**sweater** NOUN a knitted piece of clothing covering your upper body and arms

**sweatshirt** NOUN a piece of clothing made of thick cotton, covering your upper body and arms

**sweaty**, sweatier, sweatiest ADJECTIVE covered or soaked with sweat

**sweep**, sweeps, sweeping, swept VERB ❶ If you sweep the floor, you use a brush to gather up dust or rubbish from it ❷ To sweep things off a surface means to push them all off with a quick, smooth movement

**sweet** ADJECTIVE ❶ containing a lot of sugar ❷ pleasant and satisfying ❸ A sweet smell is soft and fragrant ❹ A sweet sound is gentle and tuneful ❺ attractive and delightful ✿ NOUN ❻ Things such as toffees, chocolates, and mints are sweets ❼ a dessert **sweetly** ADVERB

**swell**, swells, swelling, swelled, swollen VERB ❶ If something swells, it becomes larger and rounder ❷ If an amount swells, it increases in number ✿ NOUN ❸ The regular up and down movement of the waves at sea can be called a swell

**swerve**, swerves, swerving, swerved VERB To swerve means to change direction suddenly to avoid colliding with something

274

**swift** ADJECTIVE ❶ happening or moving very quickly ✿ NOUN ❷ a bird with narrow crescent-shaped wings **swiftly** ADVERB

**swim**, swims, swimming, swam, swum VERB ❶ To swim means to move through water using various movements with parts of the body ❷ If things are swimming, it seems as if everything you see is moving and you feel dizzy ✿ NOUN ❸ If you go for a swim, you go into water to swim for pleasure **swimmer** NOUN

**swimming** NOUN Swimming is the activity of moving through water using your arms and legs

**swimming costume** NOUN the clothing worn by a woman when she goes swimming

**swimming pool** NOUN a large hole that has been tiled and filled with water for swimming

**swimming trunks** PLURAL NOUN Swimming trunks are shorts worn by a man when he goes swimming

**swimsuit** NOUN a swimming costume

**swing**, swings, swinging, swung VERB ❶ If something swings, it moves repeatedly from side to side from a fixed point ✿ NOUN ❷ a seat hanging from a frame or a branch, which you sit on and move backwards and forwards

**switch**, switches, switching, switched NOUN ❶ a small control for an electrical device or machine ❷ a change ✿ VERB ❸ To switch to a different task or topic means to change to it ❹ If you switch things, you exchange one for the other

**switch off** ✿ VERB To switch off a light or machine means to stop it working by pressing a switch

**switch on** ✿ VERB To switch on a light or machine means to start it working by pressing a switch

**swollen** ADJECTIVE Something that is swollen has swelled up

**sword** [*sord*] NOUN a weapon consisting of a very long blade with a short handle

**sworn** ADJECTIVE If you make a sworn statement, you swear that everything in it is true

**syllable** NOUN a part of a word that contains a single vowel sound and is pronounced as a unit. For example, 'book' has one syllable and 'reading' has two

**syllabus**, syllabuses or syllabi NOUN the subjects that are studied for a particular course or examination

**symbol** NOUN a shape, design, or idea that is used to represent something

**symmetrical** ADJECTIVE If something is symmetrical, it could be split into two halves, one being the exact reflection of the other

**sympathetic** ADJECTIVE ❶ A sympathetic person shows kindness and understanding to other people ❷ If you are sympathetic to a proposal or an idea, you approve of it

**sympathize**, sympathizes, sympathizing, sympathized (also **sympathise**) VERB To sympathize with someone who is in difficulties means to show them understanding and care

**sympathy**, sympathies NOUN ❶ Sympathy is kindness and understanding towards someone who is in difficulties ❷ If you have sympathy with someone's ideas or actions, you agree with them

**symphony**, symphonies NOUN a piece of music for an orchestra, usually in four movements

**symptom** NOUN something wrong with your body that is a sign of an illness

**synagogue** [*sin-a-gog*] NOUN a building where Jewish people meet for worship and religious instruction

**syndrome** NOUN a medical condition characterized by a particular set of symptoms

**synonym** NOUN If two words have the same or a very similar meaning, they are synonyms

**synthetic** ADJECTIVE made from artificial substances rather than natural ones

**syringe** [*sir-rinj*] NOUN a hollow tube with a part which is pushed down inside and a fine hollow needle at one end, used for injecting or extracting liquids

**syrup** NOUN a thick sweet liquid made by boiling sugar with water

**system** NOUN an organized way of doing or arranging something according to a fixed plan or set of rules

# table - tail

**table**, tables, tabling, tabled **NOUN** ❶ a piece of furniture with a flat horizontal top supported by one or more legs ❷ a set of facts or figures arranged in rows or columns ✿ **VERB** ❸ If you table something such as a proposal, you say formally that you want it to be discussed

**tablecloth**, tablecloths **NOUN** a cloth used to cover a table and keep it clean

**tablespoon NOUN** a large spoon used for serving food; also the amount that a tablespoon contains

**tablet NOUN** ❶ any small, round pill made of powdered medicine ❷ a slab of stone with words cut into it

**table tennis NOUN** Table tennis is a game for two or four people in which you use bats to hit a small hollow ball over a low net across a table

**tabloid NOUN** a newspaper with small pages, short news stories, and lots of photographs

**tackle**, tackles, tackling, tackled **VERB** ❶ If you tackle a difficult task, you start dealing with it in a determined way ❷ If you tackle someone in a game such as soccer, you try to get the ball away from them ❸ If you tackle someone about something, you talk to them about it in order to get something changed or dealt with ✿ **NOUN** ❹ A tackle in sport is an attempt to get the ball away from your opponent ❺ Tackle is the equipment used for fishing

**tactful ADJECTIVE** behaving with or showing tact **tactfully ADVERB**

**tactic NOUN** ❶ Tactics are the methods you use to achieve what you want, especially to win a game ❷ Tactics are also the ways in which troops and equipment are used in order to win a battle

**tadpole NOUN** Tadpoles are the larvae of frogs and toads. They are black with round heads and long tails and live in water

**tag**, tags, tagging, tagged **NOUN** ❶ a small label made of cloth, paper, or plastic ❷ If you tag along with someone, you go with them or behind them

**tail NOUN** ❶ The tail of an animal, bird, or fish is the part extending beyond the end of its body ❷ Tail can be used to mean the end part of something ✿ **VERB** ❸ INFORMAL If you tail someone, you follow them in order to find out where they go and what they do ✿ **ADJECTIVE OR ADVERB** ❹ IN PLURAL The 'tails'

## don't mix up

### Hello Kitty...

never mixes up **tail** (the part at the end of an animal or bird) and **tale** (a story).

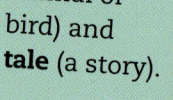

276

**tail off – tank**

side of a coin is the side which does not have a person's head

**tail off** ✿ VERB If something tails off, it becomes gradually less

**tailor** NOUN ❶ a person who makes, alters, and repairs clothes, especially for men ✿ VERB ❷ If something is tailored for a particular purpose, it is specially designed for it

**take**, takes, taking, took, taken VERB ❶ 'Take' is used to show what action or activity is being done ❷ If something takes a certain amount of time, or a particular quality or ability, it requires it ❸ If you take something, you put your hand round it and hold it or carry it ❹ If you take someone somewhere, you drive them there by car or lead them there ❺ If you take something that is offered to you, you accept it ❻ If you take the responsibility or blame for something, you accept responsibility or blame ❼ If you take something that does not belong to you, you steal it ❽ If you take pills or medicine, you swallow them ❾ If you can take something painful, you can bear it ❿ If you take someone's advice, you do what they say you should do ⓫ If you take a person's temperature or pulse, you measure it ⓬ If you take a car or train, or a road or route, you use it to go from one place to another ⓭ If you **take care of** someone or something, you look after them ⓮ If you **take care of** a problem or situation, you deal with it and get it sorted

**take after** ✿ VERB If you take after someone in your family, you look or behave like them

**take down** ✿ VERB If you take down what someone is saying, you write it down

**take in** ✿ VERB ❶ If someone is taken in, they are deceived ❷ If you take something in, you understand it

**take off** ✿ VERB When an aeroplane takes off, it leaves the ground and begins to fly
**takeoff** NOUN

**take over** ✿ VERB To take something over means to start controlling it

**takeaway** NOUN ❶ a shop or restaurant that sells hot cooked food to be eaten elsewhere ❷ a hot cooked meal bought from a takeaway

**tale** NOUN a story

**talent** NOUN Talent is the natural ability to do something well **talented** ADJECTIVE

**talk** VERB ❶ When you talk, you say things to someone ❷ If people talk, especially about other people's private affairs, they gossip about them ❸ If you talk on or about something, you make an informal speech about it ✿ NOUN ❹ Talk is discussion or gossip ❺ an informal speech about something

**talk down** ✿ VERB If you talk down to someone, you talk to them in a way that shows that you think you are more important or clever than them

**tall** ADJECTIVE ❶ of more than average or normal height ❷ having a particular height ✿ PHRASE ❸ If you describe something as **a tall story**, you mean that it is difficult to believe because it is so unlikely

**tambourine** NOUN a percussion instrument made of a skin stretched tightly over a circular frame, with small round pieces of metal around the edge that jingle when the tambourine is beaten or shaken

**tame**, tamer, tamest; tames, taming, tamed ADJECTIVE ❶ A tame animal or bird is not afraid of people and is not violent towards them ❷ Something that is tame is uninteresting and lacks excitement or risk ✿ VERB ❸ If you tame people or things, you bring them under control ❹ To tame a wild animal or bird is to train it to be obedient and live with humans

**tan**, tans, tanning, tanned NOUN ❶ If you have a tan, your skin is darker than usual because you have been in the sun ✿ VERB ❷ To tan an animal's hide is to turn it into leather by treating it with chemicals ✿ ADJECTIVE ❸ Something that is tan is of a light yellowish-brown colour

**tangle**, tangles, tangling, tangled NOUN ❶ a mass of things such as hairs or fibres knotted or coiled together and difficult to separate ✿ VERB ❷ If you are tangled in wires or ropes, you are caught or trapped in them so that it is difficult to get free

**tank** NOUN ❶ a large container for storing liquid or gas ❷ an armoured military vehicle which moves on tracks and is equipped with guns or rockets

**tanker** NOUN a ship or lorry designed to carry large quantities of gas or liquid

**tap**, taps, tapping, tapped NOUN ❶ a device that you turn to control the flow of liquid or gas from a pipe or container ❷ the action of hitting something lightly; also the sound that this action makes ✿ VERB ❸ If you tap something or tap on it, you hit it lightly ❹ If a telephone is tapped, a device is fitted to it so that someone can listen secretly to the calls

**tape**, tapes, taping, taped NOUN ❶ Tape is plastic ribbon covered with a magnetic substance and used to record sounds, pictures, and computer information ❷ a cassette or spool with magnetic tape wound round it ❸ Tape is a long, thin strip of fabric that is used for binding or fastening ❹ Tape is also a strip of sticky plastic which you use for sticking things together ✿ VERB ❺ If you tape sounds or television pictures, you record them using a tape recorder or a video recorder ❻ If you tape one thing to another, you attach them using sticky tape

**tape recorder** NOUN a machine used for recording sounds onto magnetic tape, and for playing these sounds back

**tar** NOUN Tar is a thick, black, sticky substance which is used in making roads

**target** NOUN ❶ something which you aim at when firing weapons ❷ The target of an action or remark is the person or thing at which it is directed ❸ Your target is the result that you are trying to achieve

**tarmac** NOUN Tarmac is a material used for making road surfaces. It consists of crushed stones mixed with tar

**tart** NOUN ❶ a pastry case with a sweet filling ✿ ADJECTIVE ❷ Something that is tart is sour or sharp to taste ❸ A tart remark is unpleasant and cruel

**task** NOUN any piece of work which has to be done

**taste**, tastes, tasting, tasted NOUN ❶ Your sense of taste is your ability to recognize the flavour of things in your mouth ❷ The taste of something is its flavour ❸ If you have a taste of food or drink, you have a small amount of it to see what it is like ❹ If you have a taste for something, you enjoy it ❺ If you have a taste of something, you experience it ❻ A person's taste is their choice in the things they like to buy or have around them ✿ VERB ❼ When you can taste something in your mouth, you are aware of its flavour ❽ If you taste food or drink, you have a small amount of it to see what it is like ❾ If food or drink tastes of something, it has that flavour

**tasteful** ADJECTIVE attractive and elegant **tastefully** ADVERB

**tasteless** ADJECTIVE ❶ vulgar and unattractive ❷ A tasteless remark or joke is offensive ❸ Tasteless food has very little flavour

**tasty**, tastier, tastiest ADJECTIVE having a pleasant flavour

**tattoo**, tattoos, tattooing, tattooed VERB ❶ If someone tattoos you or tattoos a design on you, they draw it on your skin by pricking little holes and filling them with coloured dye ✿ NOUN ❷ a picture or design tattooed on someone's body ❸ a public military display of exercises and music

**taught** the past tense and past participle of **teach**

**tax**, taxes, taxing, taxed NOUN ❶ Tax is an amount of money that the people in a country have to pay to the government so that it can provide public services such as health care and education ✿ VERB ❷ If a sum of money is taxed, a certain amount of it has to be paid to the government ❸ If goods are taxed, a certain amount of their price has to be paid to the government ❹ If a person or company is taxed, they have to pay a certain amount of their income to the government ❺ If something taxes you, it makes heavy demands on you **taxation** NOUN

**taxi**, taxis, taxiing, taxied NOUN ❶ a car with a driver which you hire to take you to where you want to go ✿ VERB ❷ When an aeroplane taxis, it moves slowly along the runway before taking off or after landing

**tea** NOUN ❶ Tea is the dried leaves of an evergreen shrub found in Asia ❷ Tea is a drink made by brewing the leaves of the tea plant in hot water; also a cup of this ❸ Tea is also any drink made with hot water and leaves or flowers ❹ Tea is a meal taken in the late afternoon or early evening

278

**teach**, teaches, teaching, taught VERB ❶ If you teach someone something, you give them instructions so that they know about it or know how to do it ❷ If you teach a subject, you help students learn about a subject at school, college, or university **teaching** NOUN

**teacher** NOUN a person who teaches other people, especially children

**team** NOUN ❶ a group of people who work together or play together against another group in a sport or game ✿ VERB ❷ If you team up with someone, you join them and work together with them

**teamwork** NOUN Teamwork is the ability of a group of people to work well together

**teapot** NOUN a round pot with a handle, a lid, and a spout, used for brewing and pouring tea

**tear**, tears, tearing, tore, torn NOUN ❶ Tears are the drops of salty liquid that come out of your eyes when you cry ✿ NOUN ❷ a hole that has been made in something ✿ VERB ❸ If you tear something, it is damaged by being pulled so that a hole appears in it

### how to say it

**Tear** rhymes with *fear* when it's water from the eye, and with *hair* when it means 'rip'.

**tease**, teases, teasing, teased VERB ❶ If you tease someone, you deliberately make fun of them or embarrass them because it amuses you ✿ NOUN ❷ someone who enjoys teasing people

**teaspoon** NOUN a small spoon used for stirring drinks; also the amount that a teaspoon holds

**technical** ADJECTIVE ❶ involving machines, processes, and materials used in industry, transport, and communications ❷ skilled in practical and mechanical things rather than theories and ideas ❸ involving a specialized field of activity

**technically** ADVERB If something is technically true or correct, it is true or correct when you consider only the facts, rules, or laws, but may not be important or relevant in a particular situation

**technician** NOUN someone whose job involves skilled practical work with scientific equipment

**technique** NOUN ❶ a particular method of doing something ❷ Technique is skill and ability in an activity which is developed through training and practice

**technology** NOUN ❶ Technology is the study of the application of science and scientific knowledge for practical purposes in industry, farming, medicine, or business ❷ a particular area of activity that requires scientific methods and knowledge

**tedious** [tee-dee-uss] ADJECTIVE boring and lasting for a long time

**teenage** ADJECTIVE ❶ aged between thirteen and nineteen ❷ typical of people aged between thirteen and nineteen **teenager** NOUN

**teens** PLURAL NOUN Your teens are the period of your life when you are between thirteen and nineteen years old

**teeth** the plural of **tooth**

**telephone**, telephones, telephoning, telephoned NOUN ❶ a piece of electrical equipment for talking directly to someone who is in a different place ✿ VERB ❷ If you telephone someone, you speak to them using a telephone

**telescope**, telescopes NOUN a long instrument shaped like a tube which has lenses which make distant objects appear larger and nearer

**television** NOUN a piece of electronic equipment which receives pictures and sounds by electrical signals over a distance

**tell**, tells, telling, told VERB ❶ If you tell someone something, you let them know about it ❷ If you tell someone to do something, you order or advise them to do it ❸ If you can tell something, you are able to judge correctly what is happening or what the situation is ❹ If an unpleasant or tiring experience begins to tell, it begins to have a serious effect

# temper - term

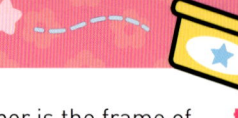

**temper** NOUN ❶ Your temper is the frame of mind or mood you are in ❷ a sudden outburst of anger ❀ PHRASE ❸ If you **lose your temper**, you become very angry ❀ VERB ❹ To temper something is to make it more acceptable or suitable

**temperature** NOUN ❶ The temperature of something is how hot or cold it is ❷ Your temperature is the temperature of your body ❀ PHRASE ❸ If you **have a temperature**, the temperature of your body is higher than it should be, because you are ill

**temple** NOUN ❶ a building used for the worship of a god in various religions ❷ Your temples are the flat parts on each side of your forehead

**temporary** ADJECTIVE lasting for only a short time  **temporarily** ADVERB

**tempt** VERB ❶ If you tempt someone, you try to persuade them to do something by offering them something they want ❷ If you are tempted to do something, you want to do it but you think it might be wrong or harmful

**temptation** NOUN ❶ Temptation is the state you are in when you want to do or have something, even though you know it might be wrong or harmful ❷ something that you want to do or have, even though you know it might be wrong or harmful

**ten** the number 10  **tenth** ADJECTIVE

**tenant** NOUN someone who pays rent for the place they live in, or for land or buildings that they use

**tend** VERB ❶ If something tends to happen, it happens usually or often ❷ If you tend someone or something, you look after them

**tendency**, tendencies NOUN a trend or type of behaviour that happens very often

**tender** ADJECTIVE ❶ Someone who is tender has gentle and caring feelings ❷ If someone is at a tender age, they are young and do not know very much about life ❸ Tender meat is easy to cut or chew ❹ If a part of your body is tender, it is painful and sore ❀ VERB ❺ If someone tenders an apology or their resignation, they offer it ❀ NOUN ❻ a formal offer to supply goods or to do a job for a particular price

**tennis** NOUN Tennis is a game played by two or four players on a rectangular court in which a ball is hit by players over a central net

**tense**, tenser, tensest; tenses, tensing, tensed ADJECTIVE ❶ If you are tense, you are nervous and cannot relax ❷ A tense situation or period of time is one that makes people nervous and worried ❸ If your body is tense, your muscles are tight ❀ VERB ❹ If you tense, or if your muscles tense, your muscles become tight and stiff ❀ NOUN ❺ The tense of a verb is the form which shows whether you are talking about the past, present, or future

## how English works

### Hello Kitty...

knows that **tense** tells us whether something has happened already, is happening now, or is going to happen in the future.

**tension** NOUN ❶ Tension is the feeling of nervousness or worry that you have when something dangerous or important is happening ❷ The tension in a rope or wire is how tightly it is stretched

**tent** NOUN a shelter made of canvas or nylon held up by poles and pinned down with pegs and ropes

**term** NOUN ❶ a fixed period of time ❷ one of the periods of time that each year is divided into at a school or college ❸ a name or word used for a particular thing ❹ IN PLURAL The terms of an agreement are the conditions that have been accepted by the people involved in it ❺ If you express something in particular terms, you express it using a particular type of language or in a way that clearly shows your attitude ❀ PHRASE ❻ If you **come to terms with**

# terminal – thaw

something difficult or unpleasant, you learn to accept it ✿ VERB ❼ To term something is to give it a name or to describe it

**terminal** ADJECTIVE ❶ A terminal illness or disease cannot be cured and causes death gradually ✿ NOUN ❷ a place where vehicles, passengers, or goods begin or end a journey ❸ A computer terminal is a keyboard and a visual display unit that is used to put information into or get information out of a computer ❹ one of the parts of an electrical device through which electricity enters or leaves

**terminate**, terminates, terminating, terminated VERB When you terminate something or when it terminates, it stops or ends

**terrace** NOUN ❶ a row of houses joined together ❷ a flat area of stone next to a building where people can sit

**terrible** ADJECTIVE ❶ serious and unpleasant ❷ INFORMAL very bad or of poor quality

**terribly** ADVERB very or very much

**terrific** ADJECTIVE ❶ INFORMAL very pleasing or impressive ❷ great in amount, degree, or intensity

**terrify**, terrifies, terrifying, terrified VERB If something terrifies you, it makes you feel extremely frightened

**territory**, territories NOUN ❶ The territory of a country is the land that it controls ❷ An animal's territory is an area which it regards as its own and defends when other animals try to enter it

**terror** NOUN ❶ Terror is great fear or panic ❷ something that makes you feel very frightened

**terrorism** NOUN Terrorism is the use of violence for political reasons **terrorist** NOUN OR ADJECTIVE

**test** VERB ❶ When you test something, you try it to find out what it is, what condition it is in, or how well it works ❷ If you test someone, you ask them questions to find out how much they know ✿ NOUN ❸ a deliberate action or experiment to find out whether something works or how well it works ❹ a set of questions or tasks given to someone to find out what they know or can do

**test tube** NOUN a small cylindrical glass container that is used in chemical experiments

**text** NOUN ❶ The text of a book is the main written part of it, rather than the pictures or index ❷ Text is any written material ❸ a book or other piece of writing used for study or an exam at school or college ❹ Text is short for 'text message' ✿ VERB ❺ If you text someone, you send them a text message

**textbook** NOUN a book about a particular subject for students to use

**textile** NOUN a woven cloth or fabric

**text message** NOUN a written message sent using a mobile phone

**texture** NOUN The texture of something is the way it feels when you touch it

**than** PREPOSITION OR CONJUNCTION ❶ You use 'than' to link two parts of a comparison ❷ You use 'than' to link two parts of a contrast

**thank** VERB When you thank someone, you show that you are grateful for something, usually by saying 'thank you'

**thankful** ADJECTIVE happy and relieved that something has happened **thankfully** ADVERB

**thanks** PLURAL NOUN ❶ When you express your thanks to someone, you tell or show them how grateful you are for something ✿ PHRASE ❷ If something happened **thanks to** someone or something, it happened because of them ✿ INTERJECTION ❸ You say 'thanks' to show that you are grateful for something

**thank you** INTERJECTION You say 'thank you' to show that you are grateful to someone for something

**that**, those ADJECTIVE OR PRONOUN ❶ 'That' or 'those' is used to refer to things or people already mentioned or known about ✿ CONJUNCTION ❷ 'That' is used to introduce a clause ✿ PRONOUN ❸ 'That' is also used to introduce a relative clause

**thaw** VERB ❶ When snow or ice thaws, it melts ❷ When you thaw frozen food, or when it thaws, it returns to its normal state in a warmer atmosphere ✿ NOUN ❸ a period of warmer weather in winter when snow or ice melts

# the - thick

**the** ADJECTIVE The definite article 'the' is used when you are talking about something that is known about, that has just been mentioned, or that you are going to give details about

## how English works

### Hello Kitty...

knows **the** is called 'the definite article' and you put it in front of a noun when you are talking about a particular person or thing.

**theatre** [*thee-uh-tuh*] NOUN ❶ a building where plays and other entertainments are performed on a stage ❷ Theatre is work such as writing, producing, and acting in plays ❸ An operating theatre is a room in a hospital designed and equipped for surgical operations

**theft** NOUN Theft is the crime of stealing

**their** ADJECTIVE 'Their' refers to something belonging or relating to people or things, other than yourself or the person you are talking to, which have already been mentioned

**theirs** PRONOUN 'Theirs' refers to something belonging or relating to people or things, other than yourself or the person you are talking to, which have already been mentioned

**them** PRONOUN 'Them' refers to things or people, other than yourself or the people you are talking to, which have already been mentioned

**theme** NOUN ❶ a main idea or topic in a piece of writing, painting, film, or music ❷ a tune, especially one played at the beginning and end of a television or radio programme

**themselves** PRONOUN ❶ 'Themselves' is used when people, other than yourself or the person you are talking to, do an action and are affected by it ❷ 'Themselves' is used to emphasize 'they'

**then** ADVERB at a particular time in the past or future

**theory**, theories NOUN ❶ an idea or set of ideas that is meant to explain something ❷ Theory is the set of rules and ideas that a particular subject or skill is based upon ✿ PHRASE ❸ You use **in theory** to say that although something is supposed to happen, it may not in fact happen

**therapy** NOUN Therapy is the treatment of mental or physical illness, often without the use of drugs or operations **therapist** NOUN

**there** ADVERB ❶ in, at, or to that place, point, or case ✿ PRONOUN ❷ 'There' is used to say that something exists or does not exist, or to draw attention to something

**therefore** ADVERB as a result

**thermometer** NOUN an instrument for measuring the temperature of a room or a person's body

**these** the plural of **this**

**they** PRONOUN ❶ 'They' refers to people or things, other than you or the people you are talking to, that have already been mentioned ❷ 'They' is sometimes used instead of 'he' or 'she' where the sex of the person is unknown or unspecified. Some people consider this to be incorrect

**thick** ADJECTIVE ❶ Something thick has a large distance between its two opposite surfaces ❷ If something is a particular amount thick, it measures that amount

### don't mix up

Don't mix up **their** (belonging to them), **there** (in that place) and **they're** (they are).

between its two sides ❸ Thick means growing or grouped closely together and in large quantities ❹ Thick liquids contain little water and do not flow easily ❺ INFORMAL A thick person is stupid or slow to understand things

**thief**, thieves NOUN a person who steals

**thigh** NOUN Your thighs are the top parts of your legs, between your knees and your hips

**thin**, thinner, thinnest; thins, thinning, thinned ADJECTIVE ❶ Something that is thin is much narrower than it is long ❷ A thin person or animal has very little fat on their body ❸ Thin liquids contain a lot of water ✿ VERB ❹ If you thin something such as paint or soup, you add water or other liquid to it

### some other words to use

### Helpful hints...

You should try not to use **thin** too much when you are writing. Some other words you can use are: *slim*, *slender*, *slight* and *lean*.

**thing** NOUN ❶ an object, rather than a plant, an animal, or a human being ❷ IN PLURAL Your things are your clothes or possessions

**think**, thinks, thinking, thought VERB ❶ When you think about ideas or problems, you use your mind to consider them ❷ If you think something, you have the opinion that it is true or the case ❸ If you think of something, you remember it or it comes into your mind ❹ If you think a lot of someone or something, you admire them or think they are good

**third** ADJECTIVE ❶ The third item in a series is the one counted as number three ✿ NOUN ❷ one of three equal parts

**thirst** NOUN ❶ If you have a thirst, you feel a need to drink something ❷ A thirst for something is a very strong desire for it

**thirsty** ADJECTIVE

**thirteen** the number 13   **thirteenth** ADJECTIVE

**thirty**, thirties the number 30   **thirtieth** ADJECTIVE

**this** ADJECTIVE OR PRONOUN ❶ 'This' is used to refer to something or someone that is nearby or has just been mentioned ❷ 'This' is used to refer to the present time or place

**thorn**, thorns NOUN one of many sharp points growing on some plants and trees

**thorough** [*thur-ruh*] ADJECTIVE ❶ done very carefully and completely ❷ A thorough person is very careful in what they do and makes sure nothing has been missed out

**thoroughly** ADVERB

**those** the plural of **that**

**though** [*rhymes with show*] CONJUNCTION ❶ despite the fact that ❷ if

**thought** ❶ Thought is the past tense and past participle of **think** ✿ NOUN ❷ an idea that you have in your mind ❸ Thought is the activity of thinking ❹ Thought is a particular way of thinking or a particular set of ideas

**thoughtful** ADJECTIVE ❶ When someone is thoughtful, they are quiet and serious because they are thinking about something ❷ A thoughtful person remembers what other people want or need, and tries to be kind to them   **thoughtfully** ADVERB

**thoughtless** ADJECTIVE A thoughtless person forgets or ignores what other people want, need, or feel

**thousand** the number 1000

**thread** NOUN ❶ a long, fine piece of cotton, silk, nylon, or wool ❷ The thread on something such as a screw or the top of a container is the raised spiral line of metal or plastic round it ❸ The thread of an argument or story is an idea or theme that connects the different parts of it ✿ VERB ❹ When you thread something, you pass thread, tape, or cord through it ❺ If you thread your way through people or things, you carefully make your way through them

283

# threat – tick

**threat** NOUN ❶ a statement that someone will harm you, especially if you do not do what they want ❷ anything or anyone that seems likely to harm you ❸ If there is a threat of something unpleasant happening, it is very possible that it will happen

**threaten** VERB ❶ If you threaten to harm someone or threaten to do something that will upset them, you say that you will do it ❷ If someone or something threatens a person or thing, they are likely to harm them

**three** the number 3

**three-dimensional** ADJECTIVE A three-dimensional object or shape is not flat, but has height or depth as well as length and width

**thrill** NOUN ❶ a sudden feeling of great excitement, pleasure, or fear; also any event or experience that gives you such a feeling ✿ VERB ❷ If something thrills you, or you thrill to it, it gives you a feeling of great pleasure and excitement **thrilled** ADJECTIVE **thrilling** ADJECTIVE

**thriller** NOUN a book, film, or play that tells an exciting story about dangerous or mysterious events

**thrive**, thrives, thriving, thrived or throve VERB When people or things thrive, they are healthy, happy, or successful

**throat** NOUN ❶ the back of your mouth and the top part of the passages inside your neck ❷ the front part of your neck

**throb**, throbs, throbbing, throbbed VERB ❶ If a part of your body throbs, you feel a series of strong beats or dull pains ❷ If something throbs, it vibrates and makes a loud, rhythmic noise

**throne** NOUN ❶ a ceremonial chair used by a king or queen on important official occasions ❷ The throne is a way of referring to the position of being king or queen

**through** [threw] PREPOSITION ❶ moving all the way from one side of something to the other ❷ because of ❸ during ❹ If you go through an experience, it happens to you ✿ ADJECTIVE ❺ If you are through with something, you have finished doing it or using it

**throughout** PREPOSITION ❶ during ✿ ADVERB ❷ happening or existing through the whole of a place

**throw**, throws, throwing, threw, thrown VERB ❶ When you throw something you are holding, you move your hand quickly and let it go, so that it moves through the air ❷ If you throw yourself somewhere, you move there suddenly and with force ❸ To throw someone into an unpleasant situation is to put them there ❹ If something throws light or shadow on something else, it makes that thing have light or shadow on it ❺ If you throw yourself into an activity, you become actively and enthusiastically involved in it ❻ If you throw a fit or tantrum, you suddenly begin behaving in an uncontrolled way

**thud**, thuds, thudding, thudded NOUN ❶ a dull sound, usually made by a solid, heavy object hitting something soft ✿ VERB ❷ If something thuds somewhere, it makes a dull sound, usually by hitting something else

**thumb** NOUN ❶ the short, thick finger on the side of your hand ✿ VERB ❷ If someone thumbs a lift, they stand at the side of the road and stick out their thumb until a driver stops and gives them a lift

**thump** VERB ❶ If you thump someone or something, you hit them hard with your fist ❷ If something thumps somewhere, it makes a fairly loud, dull sound, usually when it hits something else ❸ When your heart thumps, it beats strongly and quickly ✿ NOUN ❹ a hard hit ❺ a fairly loud, dull sound

**thunder** NOUN ❶ Thunder is a loud cracking or rumbling noise caused by expanding air which is suddenly heated by lightning ❷ Thunder is any loud rumbling noise ✿ VERB ❸ When it thunders, a loud cracking or rumbling noise occurs in the sky after a flash of lightning ❹ If something thunders, it makes a loud continuous noise

**Thursday**, Thursdays NOUN Thursday is the day between Wednesday and Friday

**tick** NOUN ❶ a written mark (✓) to show that something is correct or has been dealt with ❷ The tick of a clock is the series of short sounds it makes when it is working ❸ a tiny, blood-sucking, insect-like creature that usually lives on the bodies of people or animals ✿ VERB ❹ To tick something written on a piece of paper is to put a tick next to it ❺ When a clock ticks, it makes a regular series of short sounds as it works

284

**ticket** NOUN a piece of paper or card which shows that you have paid for a journey or have paid to enter a place of entertainment

**tickle**, tickles, tickling, tickled VERB ❶ When you tickle someone, you move your fingers lightly over their body in order to make them laugh ❷ If something tickles you, it amuses you or gives you pleasure

**tide**, tides, tiding, tided NOUN ❶ The tide is the regular change in the level of the sea on the shore, caused by the gravitational pull of the sun and the moon ❷ The tide of opinion or fashion is what the majority of people think or do at a particular time ❸ A tide of something is a large amount of it

**tide over** VERB If something will tide someone over, it will help them through a difficult period of time

**tidy**, tidier, tidiest; tidies, tidying, tidied ADJECTIVE ❶ Something that is tidy is neat and arranged in an orderly way ❷ Someone who is tidy always keeps their things neat and arranged in an orderly way ❸ INFORMAL A tidy amount of money is a fairly large amount of it ✿ VERB ❹ To tidy a place is to make it neat by putting things in their proper place

**tie**, ties, tying, tied VERB ❶ If you tie one thing to another or tie it in a particular position, you fasten it using cord of some kind ❷ If you tie a knot or a bow in a piece of cord or cloth, you fasten the ends together to make a knot or bow ❸ Something or someone that is tied to something else is closely linked with it ❹ If you tie with someone in a competition or game, you have the same number of points ✿ NOUN ❺ a long, narrow piece of cloth worn around the neck under a shirt collar and tied in a knot at the front ❻ a connection or feeling that links you with a person, place, or organization

**tiger** NOUN a large meat-eating animal of the cat family. It comes from Asia and has an orange coloured coat with black stripes

**tight** ADJECTIVE ❶ fitting closely ❷ firmly fastened and difficult to move ❸ stretched or pulled so as not to be slack ❹ A tight plan or arrangement allows only the minimum time or money needed to do something ✿ ADVERB ❺ held firmly and securely **tightly** ADVERB

**tighten** VERB ❶ If you tighten your hold on something, you hold it more firmly ❷ If you tighten a rope or chain, or if it tightens, it is stretched or pulled until it is straight ❸ If someone tightens a rule or system, they make it stricter or more efficient

**tights** PLURAL NOUN Tights are a piece of clothing made of thin stretchy material that fit closely round a person's hips, legs, and feet

**tile**, tiles, tiling, tiled NOUN ❶ a small flat square piece of something, for example slate, ceramic, or carpet, that is used to cover surfaces ✿ VERB ❷ To tile a surface is to fix tiles to it

**till** PREPOSITION OR CONJUNCTION ❶ Till means the same as until ✿ NOUN ❷ a drawer or box in a shop where money is kept, usually in a cash register ✿ VERB ❸ To till the ground is to plough it for raising crops

**tilt** VERB ❶ If you tilt an object or it tilts, it changes position so that one end or side is higher than the other ✿ NOUN ❷ a position in which one end or side of something is higher than the other

**timber** NOUN ❶ Timber is wood that has been cut and prepared ready for building and making furniture ❷ The timbers of a ship or house are the large pieces of wood that have been used to build it

**time**, times, timing, timed NOUN ❶ Time is what is measured in hours, days, and years ❷ 'Time' is used to mean a particular period or point ❸ If you say it is time for something or it is time to do it, you mean that it ought to happen or be done now ❹ IN PLURAL 'Times' is used after numbers to indicate how often something happens ❺ IN PLURAL 'Times' is used after numbers when you are saying how much bigger, smaller, better, or worse one thing is compared to another ❻ IN PLURAL 'Times' is used in arithmetic to link numbers that are multiplied together ✿ VERB ❼ If you time something for a particular time, you plan that it should happen then ❽ If you time an activity or action, you measure how long it lasts

**timetable** NOUN ❶ a plan of the times when particular activities or jobs should be done ❷ a list of the times when particular trains, boats, buses, or aeroplanes arrive and leave

# timid - toe

**timid** ADJECTIVE shy and having no courage or self-confidence **timidly** ADVERB

**timing** NOUN ❶ Someone's timing is their skill in judging the right moment at which to do something ❷ The timing of an event is when it actually happens

**tin** NOUN ❶ Tin is a soft silvery-white metal ❷ a metal container which is filled with food and then sealed in order to preserve the food ❸ a small metal container which may have a lid

**tiny**, tinier, tiniest ADJECTIVE extremely small

**tip**, tips, tipping, tipped NOUN ❶ the end of something long and thin ❷ a place where rubbish is dumped ❸ If you give someone such as a waiter a tip, you give them some money to thank them for their services ❹ a useful piece of advice or information ✿ VERB ❺ If you tip an object, you move it so that it is no longer horizontal or upright ❻ If you tip something somewhere, you pour it there quickly or carelessly

**tiptoe**, tiptoes, tiptoeing, tiptoed VERB If you tiptoe somewhere, you walk there very quietly on your toes

**tire**, tires, tiring, tired VERB ❶ If something tires you, it makes you use a lot of energy so that you want to rest or sleep ❷ If you tire of something, you become bored with it

**tired** ADJECTIVE having little energy

**tiring** ADJECTIVE Something that is tiring makes you tired

**tissue** [tiss-yoo] NOUN ❶ The tissue in plants and animals consists of cells that are similar in appearance and function ❷ Tissue is thin paper that is used for wrapping breakable objects ❸ a small piece of soft paper that you use as a handkerchief

**title** NOUN ❶ the name of a book, play, or piece of music ❷ a word that describes someone's rank or job ❸ the position of champion in a sports competition

**to** PREPOSITION ❶ 'To' is used to indicate the place that someone or something is moving towards or pointing at ❷ 'To' is used to indicate the limit of something ❸ 'To' is used in ratios and rates when saying how many units of one type there are for each unit of another ✿ ADVERB ❹ If you push or shut a door to, you close it but do not shut it completely

### don't mix up

## Hello Kitty...

never mixes up **to** (the preposition), **too** (also) and **two** (the number between one and three).

**toad** NOUN an amphibian that looks like a frog but has a drier skin and lives less in the water

**toast** NOUN ❶ Toast is slices of bread made brown and crisp by cooking at a high temperature ❷ To drink a toast to someone is to drink an alcoholic drink in honour of them ✿ VERB ❸ If you toast bread, you cook it at a high temperature so that it becomes brown and crisp ❹ To toast someone is to drink an alcoholic drink in honour of them

**toaster** NOUN a piece of electrical equipment used for toasting bread

**tobacco** NOUN Tobacco is the dried leaves of the tobacco plant which people smoke in pipes, cigarettes, and cigars

**today** ADVERB OR NOUN ❶ Today means the day on which you are speaking or writing ❷ Today also means the present period of history

**toddler**, toddlers NOUN a small child who has just learned to walk

**toe**, toes NOUN ❶ Your toes are the five movable parts at the end of your foot ❷ The toe of a shoe or sock is the part that covers the end of your foot

286

**toffee** NOUN Toffee is a sticky, chewy sweet made by boiling sugar and butter together with water

**together** ADVERB ❶ If people do something together, they do it with each other ❷ If two things happen together, they happen at the same time ❸ If things are joined or fixed together, they are joined or fixed to each other ❹ If things or people are together, they are very near to each other

**toilet** NOUN ❶ a large bowl, connected by a pipe to the drains, which you use when you want to get rid of urine or faeces ❷ a small room containing a toilet

**toiletries** PLURAL NOUN Toiletries are the things you use when cleaning and taking care of your body, such as soap and talc

**token** NOUN ❶ a piece of paper or card that is worth a particular amount of money and can be exchanged for goods ❷ a flat round piece of metal or plastic that can sometimes be used instead of money ❸ If you give something to someone as a token of your feelings for them, you give it to them as a way of showing those feelings ✿ ADJECTIVE ❹ If something is described as token, it shows that it is not being treated as important

**told** Told is the past tense and past participle of **tell**

**tolerance** NOUN ❶ A person's tolerance is their ability to accept or put up with something which may not be enjoyable or pleasant for them ❷ Tolerance is the quality of allowing other people to have their own attitudes or beliefs, or to behave in a particular way, even if you do not agree or approve

**tolerant** ADJECTIVE accepting of different views and behaviour

**tolerate**, tolerates, tolerating, tolerated VERB ❶ If you tolerate things that you do not approve of or agree with, you allow them ❷ If you can tolerate something, you accept it, even though it is unsatisfactory or unpleasant

**tomato**, tomatoes NOUN a small round red fruit, used as a vegetable and often eaten raw in salads

**tomb** NOUN a large grave for one or more corpses

### how to say it

### Helpful hints...

You say **tomb** so that it rhymes with *room*, and you do not say the **b** at the end.

**tomorrow** ADVERB OR NOUN ❶ Tomorrow means the day after today ❷ You can refer to the future, especially the near future, as tomorrow

**ton** NOUN ❶ a unit of weight equal to 2240 pounds or about 1016 kilograms ❷ IN PLURAL; INFORMAL If you have tons of something, you have a lot of it

**tone**, tones, toning, toned NOUN ❶ Someone's tone is a quality in their voice which shows what they are thinking or feeling ❷ The tone of a musical instrument or a singer's voice is the kind of sound it has ❸ The tone of a piece of writing is its style and the ideas or opinions expressed in it ❹ a lighter, darker, or brighter shade of the same colour

**tone down** ✿ VERB If you tone down something, you make it less forceful or severe

**tongue** NOUN ❶ Your tongue is the soft part in your mouth that you can move and use for tasting, licking, and speaking ❷ a language ❸ The tongue of a shoe or boot is the piece of leather underneath the laces

**tonight** ADVERB OR NOUN Tonight is the evening or night that will come at the end of today

**too** ADVERB ❶ also or as well ❷ more than a desirable, necessary, or acceptable amount

**tool** NOUN ❶ any hand-held instrument or piece of equipment that you use to help you do a particular kind of work ❷ an object, skill, or idea that is needed or used for a particular purpose

**toot** VERB If a car horn toots, it produces a short sound

# tooth – tow

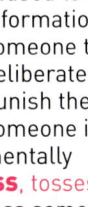

**tooth**, teeth NOUN ❶ Your teeth are the hard enamel-covered objects in your mouth that you use for biting and chewing food ❷ The teeth of a comb, saw, or zip are the parts that stick out in a row on its edge

**toothpaste** NOUN Toothpaste is a substance which you use to clean your teeth

**top**, tops, topping, topped NOUN ❶ The top of something is its highest point, part, or surface ❷ The top of a bottle, jar, or tube is its cap or lid ❸ a piece of clothing worn on the upper half of your body ❹ a toy with a pointed end on which it spins ✿ ADJECTIVE ❺ The top thing of a series of things is the highest one ✿ VERB ❻ If someone tops a poll or popularity chart, they do better than anyone else in it ❼ If something tops a particular amount, it is greater than that amount

**top up** ✿ VERB To top something up is to add something to it in order to keep it at an acceptable or usable level

**topic** NOUN a particular subject that you write about or discuss

**torch**, torches NOUN ❶ a small electric light carried in the hand and powered by batteries ❷ a long stick with burning material wrapped around one end

**torn** ❶ Torn is the past participle of **tear** ✿ ADJECTIVE ❷ If you are torn between two or more things, you cannot decide which one to choose and this makes you unhappy

**tornado**, tornadoes or tornados [tor-**nay**-doh] NOUN a violent storm with strong circular winds around a funnel-shaped cloud

**tortoise** NOUN a slow-moving reptile with a large hard shell over its body into which it can pull its head and legs for protection

**torture**, tortures, torturing, tortured NOUN ❶ Torture is great pain that is deliberately caused to someone to punish them or get information from them ✿ VERB ❷ If someone tortures another person, they deliberately cause that person great pain to punish them or get information ❸ To torture someone is also to cause them to suffer mentally

**toss**, tosses, tossing, tossed VERB ❶ If you toss something somewhere, you throw it there lightly and carelessly ❷ If you toss a coin, you decide something by throwing a coin into the air and guessing which side will face upwards when it lands ❸ If you toss your head, you move it suddenly backwards, especially when you are angry, annoyed, or want your own way ❹ To toss is to move repeatedly from side to side

**total**, totals, totalling, totalled NOUN ❶ the number you get when you add several numbers together ✿ ADJECTIVE ❷ Total means complete ✿ VERB ❸ When you total a set of numbers or objects, you add them all together ❹ If several numbers total a certain figure, that is the figure you get when all the numbers are added together **totally** ADVERB

**totalitarian** [toe-tal-it-**tair**-ee-an] ADJECTIVE A totalitarian political system is one in which one political party controls everything and does not allow any other parties to exist

**touch**, touches, touching, touched VERB ❶ If you touch something, you put your fingers or hand on it ❷ When two things touch, their surfaces come into contact ❸ If you are touched by something, you are emotionally affected by it ✿ NOUN ❹ Your sense of touch is your ability to tell what something is like by touching it ❺ a detail which is added to improve something ❻ a small amount of something

**tough** [tuff] ADJECTIVE ❶ A tough person is strong and independent and able to put up with hardship ❷ A tough substance is difficult to break ❸ A tough task, problem, or way of life is difficult or full of hardship ❹ Tough policies or actions are strict and firm

**tour** NOUN ❶ a long journey during which you visit several places ❷ a short trip round a place such as a city or famous building ✿ VERB ❸ If you tour a place, you go on a journey or a trip round it

**tourism** NOUN Tourism is the business of providing services for people on holiday, for example hotels and sightseeing trips

**tourist** NOUN a person who visits places for pleasure or interest

**tournament** NOUN a sports competition in which players who win a match play further matches, until just one person or team is left

**tow** VERB ❶ If a vehicle tows another vehicle, it pulls it along behind it ✿ NOUN ❷ To give a

288

## towards - tragedy

vehicle a tow is to tow it ✿ PHRASE ❸ If you have someone **in tow**, they are with you because you are looking after them

**towards** PREPOSITION ❶ in the direction of ❷ about or involving ❸ as a contribution for ❹ near to

**towel** NOUN a piece of thick, soft cloth that you use to dry yourself with

**tower** NOUN ❶ a tall, narrow building, sometimes attached to a larger building such as a castle or church ✿ VERB ❷ Someone or something that towers over other people or things is much taller than them

**town** NOUN ❶ a place with many streets and buildings where people live and work ❷ Town is the central shopping and business part of a town rather than the suburbs

**toxic** ADJECTIVE poisonous

**toy** NOUN ❶ any object made to play with ✿ VERB ❷ If you toy with an idea, you consider it without being very serious about it ❸ If you toy with an object, you fiddle with it

**trace**, traces, tracing, traced VERB ❶ If you trace something, you find it after looking for it ❷ To trace the development of something is to find out or describe how it developed ❸ If you trace a drawing or a map, you copy it by covering it with a piece of transparent paper and drawing over the lines underneath ✿ NOUN ❹ a sign which shows you that someone or something has been in a place ❺ a very small amount of something

**track** NOUN ❶ a narrow road or path ❷ a strip of ground with rails on it that a train travels along ❸ a piece of ground, shaped like a ring, which horses, cars, or athletes race around ❹ IN PLURAL Tracks are marks left on the ground by a person or animal ✿ ADJECTIVE ❺ In an athletics competition, the track events are the races on a running track ✿ VERB ❻ If you track animals or people, you find them by following their footprints or other signs that they have left behind

**track down** ✿ VERB If you track down someone or something, you find them by searching for them

**tractor** NOUN a vehicle with large rear wheels that is used on a farm for pulling machinery and other heavy loads

**trade**, trades, trading, traded NOUN ❶ Trade is the activity of buying, selling, or exchanging goods or services between people, firms, or countries ❷ Someone's trade is the kind of work they do, especially when it requires special training in practical skills ✿ VERB ❸ When people, firms, or countries trade, they buy, sell, or exchange goods or services ❹ If you trade things, you exchange them

**trademark** NOUN a name or symbol that a manufacturer always uses on its products. Trademarks are usually protected by law so that no-one else can use them

**tradition** NOUN a custom or belief that has existed for a long time without changing

**traditional** ADJECTIVE ❶ Traditional customs or beliefs have existed for a long time without changing ❷ A traditional organization or institution is one in which older methods are used rather than modern ones **traditionally** ADVERB

**traffic**, traffics, trafficking, trafficked NOUN ❶ Traffic is the movement of vehicles or people along a route at a particular time ❷ Traffic in something such as drugs is an illegal trade in them ✿ VERB ❸ Someone who traffics in drugs or other goods buys and sells them illegally

**tragedy**, tragedies [*traj-id-ee*] NOUN ❶ an event or situation that is disastrous or very sad ❷ a serious story or play, that usually ends with the death of the main character

### how to remember

Hello Kitty...

remembers that the hero **raged** at the **trage**dy.

# tragic – tread

**tragic** ADJECTIVE ❶ Something tragic is very sad because it involves death, suffering, or disaster ❷ Tragic films, plays, and books are sad and serious **tragically** ADVERB

**trail** NOUN ❶ a rough path across open country or through forests ❷ a series of marks or other signs left by someone or something as they move along ✿ VERB ❸ If you trail something or it trails, it drags along behind you as you move, or it hangs down loosely ❹ If someone trails along, they move slowly, without any energy or enthusiasm ❺ If a voice trails away or trails off, it gradually becomes more hesitant until it stops completely

**trailer** NOUN a small vehicle which can be loaded with things and pulled behind a car

**train** NOUN ❶ a number of carriages or trucks which are pulled by a railway engine ❷ A train of thought is a connected series of thoughts ❸ A train of vehicles or people is a line or group following behind something or someone ✿ VERB ❹ If you train someone, your teach them how to do something ❺ If you train, you learn how to do a particular job ❻ If you train for a sports match or a race, you prepare for it by doing exercises **training** NOUN

**traitor** NOUN someone who betrays their country or the group which they belong to

**tram** NOUN a vehicle which runs on rails along the street and is powered by electricity from an overhead wire

**transfer**, transfers, transferring, transferred VERB ❶ If you transfer something from one place to another, you move it ❷ If you transfer to a different place or job, or are transferred to it, you move to a different place or job within the same organization ✿ NOUN ❸ the movement of something from one place to another ❹ a piece of paper with a design on one side which can be ironed or pressed onto cloth, paper, or china

**transform** VERB ❶ If something is transformed, it is changed completely ❷ To transform a shape is to change how it looks, for example by translation, reflection, rotation, or enlargement **transformation** NOUN

**transitive** ADJECTIVE In grammar, a transitive verb is a verb which has an object

**translate**, translates, translating, translated VERB ❶ To translate something that someone has said or written is to say it or write it in a different language ❷ To translate a shape is to move it up or down, or from side to side, but not change it in any other way **translation** NOUN **translator** NOUN

**transparent** ADJECTIVE If an object or substance is transparent, you can see through it

**transplant** NOUN ❶ a process of removing something from one place and putting it in another ✿ VERB ❷ When something is transplanted, it is moved to a different place

**transport** NOUN ❶ Vehicles that you travel in are referred to as transport ❷ Transport is the moving of goods or people from one place to another ✿ VERB ❸ When goods or people are transported from one place to another, they are moved there

**trap**, traps, trapping, trapped NOUN ❶ a piece of equipment or a hole that is carefully positioned in order to catch animals or birds ❷ a trick that is intended to catch or deceive someone ✿ VERB ❸ Someone who traps animals catches them using traps ❹ If you trap someone, you trick them so that they do or say something which they did not want to ❺ If you are trapped somewhere, you cannot move or escape because something is blocking your way or holding you down ❻ If you are trapped, you are in an unpleasant situation that you cannot easily change

**trash** NOUN ❶ Trash is rubbish ❷ If you say that something such as a book, painting, or film is trash, you mean that it is not very good

**travel**, travels, travelling, travelled VERB ❶ To travel is to go from one place to another ❷ When something reaches one place from another, you say that it travels there ✿ NOUN ❸ Travel is the act of travelling ❹ IN PLURAL Someone's travels are the journeys that they make to places a long way from their home **traveller** NOUN

**tray** NOUN a flat object with raised edges which is used for carrying food or drinks

**tread**, treads, treading, trod, trodden VERB ❶ If you tread on something, you walk on it or step on it ❷ If you tread something into the ground or into a carpet, you crush it in by stepping on it ✿ NOUN ❸ A person's tread is the sound they make with their feet as they walk ❹ The tread of a tyre or shoe is the pattern of ridges on it that stops it slipping

**treasure**, treasures, treasuring, treasured NOUN ❶ Treasure is a collection of gold, silver, jewels, or other precious objects, especially one that has been hidden ❷ Treasures are valuable works of art ✿ VERB ❸ If you treasure something, you are very pleased that you have it and regard it as very precious

**treat** VERB ❶ If you treat someone in a particular way, you behave that way towards them ❷ If you treat something in a particular way, you deal with it that way or see it that way ❸ When a doctor treats a patient or an illness, he or she gives them medical care and attention ❹ If something such as wood or cloth is treated, a special substance is put on it in order to protect it or give it special properties ❺ If you treat someone, you buy or arrange something special for them which they will enjoy ✿ NOUN ❻ If you give someone a treat, you buy or arrange something special for them which they will enjoy **treatment** NOUN

**treaty**, treaties NOUN a written agreement between countries in which they agree to do something or to help each other

**tree** NOUN a large plant with a hard woody trunk, branches, and leaves

**trek**, treks, trekking, trekked VERB ❶ If you trek somewhere, you go on a long and difficult journey ✿ NOUN ❷ a long and difficult journey, especially one made by walking

**tremble**, trembles, trembling, trembled VERB ❶ If you tremble, you shake slightly, usually because you are frightened or cold ❷ If something trembles, it shakes slightly ❸ If your voice trembles, it sounds unsteady, usually because you are frightened or upset

**tremendous** ADJECTIVE ❶ large or impressive ❷ INFORMAL very good or pleasing **tremendously** ADVERB

**trend** NOUN a change towards doing or being something different

**trendy**, trendier, trendiest ADJECTIVE INFORMAL Trendy things or people are fashionable

**trial** NOUN ❶ the legal process in which a judge and jury decide whether a person is guilty of a particular crime after listening to all the evidence about it ❷ an experiment in which something is tested

**triangle** NOUN ❶ a shape with three straight sides ❷ a percussion instrument consisting of a thin steel bar bent in the shape of a triangle **triangular** ADJECTIVE

**tribe** NOUN a group of people of the same race, who have the same customs, religion, language, or land, especially when they are thought to be primitive **tribal** ADJECTIVE

**tribute** NOUN ❶ A tribute is something said or done to show admiration and respect for someone ❷ If one thing is a tribute to another, it is the result of the other thing and shows how good it is

**trick** NOUN ❶ an action done to deceive someone ❷ Tricks are clever or skilful actions done in order to entertain people ✿ VERB ❸ If someone tricks you, they deceive you

**trickle**, trickles, trickling, trickled VERB ❶ When a liquid trickles somewhere, it flows slowly in a thin stream ❷ When people or things trickle somewhere, they move there slowly in small groups or amounts ✿ NOUN ❸ a thin stream of liquid ❹ A trickle of people or things is a small number or quantity of them

**tricky**, trickier, trickiest ADJECTIVE difficult to do or deal with

**tricycle** NOUN a vehicle similar to a bicycle but with two wheels at the back and one at the front

**trigger** NOUN ❶ the small lever on a gun which is pulled in order to fire it ✿ VERB ❷ If something triggers an event or triggers it off, it causes it to happen

**trim**, trimmer, trimmest; trims, trimming, trimmed ADJECTIVE ❶ neat, tidy, and attractive ✿ VERB ❷ To trim something is to clip small amounts off it ❸ If you trim off parts of something, you cut them off because they are not needed ✿ NOUN ❹ If something is given a trim, it is cut a little ❺ a decoration on something, especially along its edges

**trio**, trios NOUN ❶ a group of three musicians who sing or play together; also a piece of music written for three instruments or singers ❷ any group of three things or people together

**trip**, trips, tripping, tripped NOUN ❶ a journey made to a place ✿ VERB ❷ If you trip, you catch your foot on something and fall over ❸ If you trip someone or trip them up, you make them fall over by making them catch their foot on something

**triple**, triples, tripling, tripled ADJECTIVE ❶ consisting of three things or three parts ✿ VERB ❷ If you triple something or if it triples, it becomes three times greater in number or size

**triplet** NOUN Triplets are three children born at the same time to the same mother

**triumph** NOUN ❶ a great success or achievement ❷ Triumph is a feeling of great satisfaction when you win or achieve something ✿ VERB ❸ If you triumph, you win a victory or succeed in overcoming something

**trivial** ADJECTIVE Something trivial is unimportant

**trolley**, trolleys NOUN ❶ a small table on wheels ❷ a small cart on wheels used for carrying heavy objects

**trombone** NOUN a brass wind instrument with a U-shaped slide which you move to produce different notes

**trophy**, trophies NOUN ❶ a cup or shield given as a prize to the winner of a competition ❷ something you keep to remember a success or victory

**tropical** ADJECTIVE belonging to or typical of the tropics

**tropics** PLURAL NOUN The tropics are the hottest parts of the world between two lines of latitude, the Tropic of Cancer, $23\frac{1}{2}°$ north of the equator, and the Tropic of Capricorn, $23\frac{1}{2}°$ south of the equator

**trot**, trots, trotting, trotted VERB ❶ When a horse trots, it moves at a speed between a walk and a canter, lifting its feet quite high off the ground ❷ If you trot, you run or jog using small quick steps ✿ NOUN ❸ When a horse breaks into a trot, it starts trotting

**trouble**, troubles, troubling, troubled NOUN ❶ Troubles are difficulties or problems ❷ If there is trouble, people are quarrelling or fighting ✿ PHRASE ❸ If you are **in trouble**, you are in a situation where you may be punished because you have done something wrong ✿ VERB ❹ If something troubles you, it makes you feel worried or anxious ❺ If you trouble someone for something, you disturb them in order to ask them for it

**trousers** PLURAL NOUN Trousers are a piece of clothing covering the body from the waist down, enclosing each leg separately

**truck** NOUN ❶ a large motor vehicle used for carrying heavy loads ❷ an open vehicle used for carrying goods on a railway

**true**, truer, truest ADJECTIVE ❶ A true story or statement is based on facts and is not made up ❷ 'True' is used to describe things or people that are genuine ❸ True feelings are sincere and genuine **truly** ADVERB

**trumpet** NOUN ❶ a brass wind instrument with a narrow tube ending in a bell-like shape ✿ VERB ❷ When an elephant trumpets, it makes a sound like a very loud trumpet

**trunk** NOUN ❶ the main stem of a tree from which the branches and roots grow ❷ the main part of your body, excluding your head, neck, arms, and legs ❸ the long flexible nose of an elephant ❹ a large, strong case or box with a hinged lid used for storing things ❺ IN PLURAL A man's trunks are his bathing pants or shorts

**where does the word come from?**

*Did you know...*

that the word **trophy** comes from the Greek word *tropē* which means 'defeat of the enemy'?

292

**trust** VERB ❶ If you trust someone, you believe that they are honest and will not harm you ❷ If you trust someone to do something, you believe they will do it successfully or properly ❸ If you trust someone with something, you give it to them or tell it to them ❹ If you do not trust something, you feel that it is not safe or reliable ✿ NOUN ❺ Trust is the responsibility you are given to deal with or look after important or secret things ❻ a financial arrangement in which an organization looks after and invests money for someone

**trustworthy** ADJECTIVE A trustworthy person is reliable and responsible and can be trusted

**truth** NOUN ❶ The truth is the facts about something, rather than things that are imagined or made up ❷ an idea or principle that is generally accepted to be true

**truthful** ADJECTIVE A truthful person is honest and tells the truth **truthfully** ADVERB

**try**, tries, trying, tried VERB ❶ To try to do something is to make an effort to do it ❷ If you try something, you use it or do it to test how useful or enjoyable it is ❸ When a person is tried, they appear in court and a judge and jury decide if they are guilty after hearing the evidence ✿ NOUN ❹ an attempt to do something ❺ a test of something

**T-shirt** or **tee shirt** NOUN a simple short-sleeved cotton shirt with no collar

**tsunami** NOUN a large, often destructive sea wave, caused by an earthquake or volcanic eruption under the sea

**tub** NOUN a wide circular container

**tuba** NOUN a large brass musical instrument that can produce very low notes

**tube** NOUN ❶ a round, hollow pipe ❷ a soft metal or plastic cylindrical container with a screw cap at one end

**tuck** VERB ❶ If you tuck something somewhere, you put it there so that it is safe or comfortable ❷ If something is tucked away, it is in a quiet place where few people go

**Tuesday**, Tuesdays NOUN Tuesday is the day between Monday and Wednesday

**tug**, tugs, tugging, tugged VERB ❶ To tug something is to give it a quick, hard pull ✿ NOUN ❷ a quick, hard pull ❸ a small, powerful boat which tows large ships

*where does the word come from?*

*Did you know...* that the word **tulip** comes from Turkish *tulbend* which means 'turban'? That's because some people thought a tulip flower and a turban have a similar shape.

**tulip** NOUN a brightly coloured spring flower

**tumble**, tumbles, tumbling, tumbled VERB ❶ To tumble is to fall with a rolling or bouncing movement ✿ NOUN ❷ a fall

**tummy**, tummies NOUN INFORMAL Your tummy is your stomach

**tumour** [tyoo-mur] NOUN a mass of diseased or abnormal cells that has grown in a person's or animal's body

**tuna** [tyoo-na] NOUN Tuna are large fish that live in warm seas and are caught for food

**tune**, tunes, tuning, tuned NOUN ❶ a series of musical notes arranged in a particular way ✿ VERB ❷ To tune a musical instrument is to adjust it so that it produces the right notes ✿ PHRASE ❸ If your voice or an instrument is **in tune**, it produces the right notes

**tunnel**, tunnels, tunnelling, tunnelled NOUN ❶ a long underground passage ✿ VERB ❷ To tunnel is to make a tunnel

**turkey**, turkeys NOUN a large bird kept for food; also the meat of this bird

**turn** VERB ❶ When you turn, you move so that you are facing or going in a different direction ❷ When you turn something or when it turns, it moves or rotates so that it faces in a different direction or is in a different position ❸ If you turn your attention or thoughts to

# turn down - tyre

someone or something, you start thinking about them or discussing them ❹ When something turns or is turned into something else, it becomes something different ✿ NOUN ❺ an act of turning something so that it faces in a different direction or is in a different position ❻ If it is your turn to do something, you have the right, chance, or duty to do it ✿ PHRASE ❼ **In turn** is used to refer to people, things, or actions that are in sequence one after the other

**turn down** ✿ VERB If you turn down someone's request or offer, you refuse or reject it

**turn up** ✿ VERB ❶ If someone or something turns up, they arrive or appear somewhere ❷ If something turns up, it is found or discovered

**turning** NOUN a road which leads away from the side of another road

**turnip** NOUN a round root vegetable with a white or yellow skin

**turquoise** [*tur-kwoyz*] NOUN OR ADJECTIVE ❶ light bluish-green ✿ NOUN ❷ Turquoise is a bluish-green stone used in jewellery

**turtle** NOUN a large reptile with a thick shell covering its body and flippers for swimming. It lays its eggs on land but lives the rest of its life in the sea

**tusk** NOUN The tusks of an elephant, wild boar, or walrus are the pair of long curving pointed teeth it has

**tutor** NOUN ❶ a teacher at a college or university ❷ a private teacher ✿ VERB ❸ If someone tutors a person or subject, they teach that person or subject

**TV** NOUN ❶ TV is television ❷ a television set

**tweezers** PLURAL NOUN Tweezers are a small tool with two arms which can be closed together and are used for pulling out hairs or picking up small objects

**twelve** the number 12 **twelfth** ADJECTIVE

**twenty**, twenties the number 20 **twentieth** ADJECTIVE

**twice** ADVERB Twice means two times

**twig**, twigs NOUN a very small thin branch growing from a main branch of a tree or bush

**twilight** [*twy-lite*] NOUN Twilight is the time after sunset when it is just getting dark

**twin** NOUN ❶ If two people are twins, they have the same mother and were born on the same day ❷ 'Twin' is used to describe two similar things that are close together or happen together

**twinkle**, twinkles, twinkling, twinkled VERB ❶ If something twinkles, it sparkles or seems to sparkle with an unsteady light ✿ NOUN ❷ a sparkle or brightness that something has

**twirl** VERB If something twirls, or if you twirl it, it spins or twists round and round

**twist** VERB ❶ When you twist something you turn one end of it in one direction while holding the other end or turning it in the opposite direction ❷ When something twists or is twisted, it moves or bends into a strange shape ❸ If you twist a part of your body, you injure it by turning it too sharply or in an unusual direction ✿ NOUN ❹ a twisting action or motion ❺ an unexpected development or event in a story or film, especially at the end

**twitch**, twitches, twitching, twitched VERB ❶ If you twitch, you make little jerky movements which you cannot control ❷ If you twitch something, you give it a little jerk in order to move it ✿ NOUN ❸ a little jerky movement

**two** the number 2

**two-dimensional** ADJECTIVE A two-dimensional shape has height and width but not depth

**type**, types, typing, typed NOUN ❶ A type of something is a class of it that has common features and belongs to a larger group of related things ❷ A particular type of person has a particular appearance or quality ✿ VERB ❸ If you type something, you use a keyboard to write it

**typewriter** NOUN a machine with a keyboard with individual keys which are pressed to produce letters and numbers on a page

**typical** ADJECTIVE showing the most usual characteristics or behaviour **typically** ADVERB

**typist** NOUN a person whose job is typing

**tyrant** NOUN a person who treats the people he or she has authority over cruelly and unjustly

**tyre** NOUN a thick ring of rubber fitted round each wheel of a vehicle and filled with air

**ugly – uncommon**

**ugly**, uglier, ugliest ADJECTIVE very unattractive in appearance

**ultimate** ADJECTIVE ❶ final or eventual ❷ most important or powerful ✿ NOUN ❸ You can refer to the best or most advanced example of something as the ultimate **ultimately** ADVERB

**umbrella** NOUN a device that you use to protect yourself from the rain. It consists of a folding frame covered in cloth attached to a long stick

**umpire**, umpires, umpiring, umpired NOUN ❶ The umpire in cricket or tennis is the person who makes sure that the game is played according to the rules and who makes a decision if there is a dispute ✿ VERB ❷ If you umpire a game, you are the umpire

**unable** ADJECTIVE If you are unable to do something, you cannot do it

**unacceptable** ADJECTIVE very bad or of a very low standard

**unanimous** [yoon-**nan**-nim-mus] ADJECTIVE When people are unanimous, they all agree about something **unanimously** ADVERB

**unavoidable** ADJECTIVE unable to be prevented or avoided

**unaware** ADJECTIVE If you are unaware of something, you do not know about it

**unbearable** ADJECTIVE Something unbearable is so unpleasant or upsetting that you feel you cannot stand it **unbearably** ADVERB

**unbelievable** ADJECTIVE ❶ extremely great or surprising ❷ so unlikely that you cannot believe it **unbelievably** ADVERB

**unborn** ADJECTIVE not yet born

**uncertain** ADJECTIVE ❶ not knowing what to do ❷ doubtful or not known **uncertainty** NOUN

**uncle** NOUN the brother of your mother or father or the husband of your aunt

**unclear** ADJECTIVE confusing and not obvious

**uncomfortable** ADJECTIVE ❶ If you are uncomfortable, you are not physically relaxed and feel slight pain or discomfort ❷ Uncomfortable also means slightly worried or embarrassed **uncomfortably** ADVERB

**uncommon** ADJECTIVE ❶ not happening often or not seen often ❷ unusually great

**help with spelling**

Hello Kitty…

The letter **q** is always followed by **u** except in *Iraq*, *Iraqi* and *burqa*.

295

# unconscious – unfamiliar

**unconscious** ADJECTIVE ❶ Someone who is unconscious is asleep or in a state similar to sleep as a result of a shock, accident, or injury ❷ If you are unconscious of something, you are not aware of it **unconsciousness** NOUN

**uncontrollable** ADJECTIVE If someone or something is uncontrollable, they or it cannot be controlled or stopped **uncontrollably** ADVERB

**uncover** VERB ❶ If you uncover a secret, you find it out ❷ To uncover something is to remove the cover or lid from it

**undecided** ADJECTIVE If you are undecided, you have not yet made a decision about something

**under** PREPOSITION ❶ below or beneath ❷ You can use 'under' to say that a person or thing is affected by a particular situation or condition ❸ If someone studies or works under a particular person, that person is their teacher or their boss ❹ less than ✿ PHRASE ❺ **Under way** means already started

**undergo**, undergoes, undergoing, underwent, undergone VERB If you undergo something unpleasant, it happens to you

**underground** ADJECTIVE OR ADVERB ❶ below the surface of the ground ❷ secret, unofficial, and usually illegal ✿ NOUN ❸ The underground is a railway system in which trains travel in tunnels below ground

**underline**, underlines, underlining, underlined VERB ❶ If something underlines a feeling or a problem, it emphasizes it ❷ If you underline a word or sentence, you draw a line under it

**underneath** PREPOSITION ❶ below or beneath ✿ ADVERB OR PREPOSITION ❷ Underneath describes feelings and qualities that do not show in your behaviour ✿ ADJECTIVE ❸ The underneath part of something is the part that touches or faces the ground

**underpants** PLURAL NOUN Underpants are a piece of clothing worn by men and boys under their trousers

**understand**, understands, understanding, understood VERB ❶ If you understand what someone says, you know what they mean ❷ If you understand a situation, you know what is happening and why ❸ If you say that you understand that something is the case, you mean that you have heard that it is the case

**understanding** NOUN ❶ If you have an understanding of something, you have some knowledge about it ❷ an informal agreement between people ✿ ADJECTIVE ❸ kind and sympathetic

**undertake**, undertakes, undertaking, undertook, undertaken VERB When you undertake a task or job, you agree to do it

**underwater** ADVERB OR ADJECTIVE ❶ beneath the surface of the sea, a river, or a lake ✿ ADJECTIVE ❷ designed to work in water

**underwear** NOUN Your underwear is the clothing that you wear under your other clothes, next to your skin

**underwent** the past tense of **undergo**

**undid** the past tense of **undo**

**undo**, undoes, undoing, undid, undone VERB ❶ If you undo something that is tied up, you untie it ❷ If you undo something that has been done, you reverse the effect of it

**undress**, undresses, undressing, undressed VERB When you undress, you take off your clothes

**uneasy**, uneasier, uneasiest ADJECTIVE If you are uneasy, you feel worried that something may be wrong **uneasily** ADVERB

**unemployed** ADJECTIVE ❶ without a job ✿ NOUN ❷ The unemployed are all the people who are without a job

**unemployment** NOUN Unemployment is the state of being without a job

**unequal** ADJECTIVE ❶ An unequal society does not offer the same opportunities and privileges to all people ❷ Unequal things are different in size, strength, or ability

**uneven** ADJECTIVE ❶ An uneven surface is not level or smooth ❷ not the same or consistent

**unexpected** ADJECTIVE Something unexpected is surprising because it was not thought likely to happen **unexpectedly** ADVERB

**unfair** ADJECTIVE not right or just **unfairly** ADVERB

**unfamiliar** ADJECTIVE If something is unfamiliar to you, or if you are unfamiliar with it, you have not seen or heard it before

**unfit** ADJECTIVE ❶ If you are unfit, your body is not in good condition because you have not been taking enough exercise ❷ Something that is unfit for a particular purpose is not suitable for that purpose

**unfold** VERB ❶ When a situation unfolds, it develops and becomes known ❷ If you unfold something that has been folded, you open it out so that it is flat

**unfortunate** ADJECTIVE ❶ Someone who is unfortunate is unlucky ❷ If you describe an event as unfortunate, you mean that it is a pity that it happened **unfortunately** ADVERB

**unfriendly**, unfriendlier, unfriendliest ADJECTIVE ❶ A person who is unfriendly is not pleasant to you ❷ A place that is unfriendly makes you feel uncomfortable or is not welcoming

**ungrateful** ADJECTIVE not appreciating the things you have

**unhappy**, unhappier, unhappiest ADJECTIVE ❶ sad and depressed ❷ not pleased or satisfied ❸ If you describe a situation as an unhappy one, you are sorry that it exists **unhappily** ADVERB **unhappiness** NOUN

**unhealthy**, unhealthier, unhealthiest ADJECTIVE ❶ likely to cause illness ❷ An unhealthy person is often ill

**uniform** NOUN ❶ a special set of clothes worn by people at work or school ✿ ADJECTIVE ❷ Something that is uniform does not vary but is even and regular throughout

**unimportant** ADJECTIVE having very little significance or importance

**union** NOUN ❶ an organization of people or groups with mutual interests, especially workers aiming to improve their pay and conditions ❷ When the union of two things takes place, they are joined together to become one thing

**unique** [yoo-neek] ADJECTIVE ❶ being the only one of its kind ❷ If something is unique to one person or thing, it concerns or belongs to that person or thing only

**unit** NOUN ❶ If you consider something as a unit, you consider it as a single complete thing ❷ a group of people who work together at a particular job ❸ a machine or piece of equipment which has a particular function ❹ A unit of measurement is a fixed standard that is used for measuring things

**unite**, unites, uniting, united VERB If a number of people unite, they join together and act as a group

**universal** ADJECTIVE concerning or relating to everyone in the world or every part of the universe **universally** ADVERB

**universe** NOUN The universe is the whole of space, including all the stars and planets

**university**, universities NOUN a place where students study for degrees

**unjust** ADJECTIVE not fair or reasonable **unjustly** ADVERB

**unkind** ADJECTIVE unpleasant and rather cruel

**unknown** ADJECTIVE ❶ If someone or something is unknown, people do not know about them or have not heard of them ✿ NOUN ❷ You can refer to the things that people in general do not know about as the unknown

**unless** CONJUNCTION You use unless to introduce the only circumstances in which something will not take place or is not true

**unlike** PREPOSITION You can use unlike to show how two people, things, or situations are different from each other ✿ ADJECTIVE If one thing is unlike another, the two things are different

**unlikely**, unlikelier, unlikeliest ADJECTIVE ❶ If something is unlikely, it is probably not true or probably will not happen ❷ strange and unexpected

**unload** VERB If you unload things from a container or vehicle, you remove them

**unlock** VERB If you unlock a door or container, you open it by turning a key in the lock

**unlucky**, unluckier, unluckiest ADJECTIVE Someone who is unlucky has bad luck

**unmistakable** or **unmistakeable** ADJECTIVE Something unmistakable is so obvious that it cannot be mistaken for something else

**unnatural** ADJECTIVE ❶ strange and rather frightening because it is not usual ❷ artificial and not typical

**unnecessary** ADJECTIVE If something is unnecessary, there is no need for it to happen or be done

**unofficial** ADJECTIVE without the approval or permission of a person in authority

**unpack** VERB When you unpack, you take everything out of a suitcase or bag

# unpaid – upper

**unpaid** ADJECTIVE ❶ If you do unpaid work, you do not receive any money for doing it ❷ An unpaid bill has not yet been paid

**unpleasant** ADJECTIVE ❶ Something unpleasant causes you to have bad feelings, for example by making you uncomfortable or upset ❷ An unpleasant person is unfriendly or rude  **unpleasantly** ADVERB

**unpopular** ADJECTIVE disliked by most people

**unpredictable** ADJECTIVE If someone or something is unpredictable, you never know how they will behave or react

**unprepared** ADJECTIVE If you are unprepared for something, you are not ready for it and are therefore surprised or at a disadvantage when it happens

**unreasonable** ADJECTIVE unfair and difficult to deal with or justify

**unreliable** ADJECTIVE If people, machines, or methods are unreliable, you cannot rely on them

**unruly**, unrulier, unruliest ADJECTIVE difficult to control or organize

**unsatisfactory** ADJECTIVE not good enough

**unsteady**, unsteadier, unsteadiest ADJECTIVE ❶ having difficulty in controlling the movement of your legs or hands ❷ not held or fixed securely and likely to fall over

**unsuccessful** ADJECTIVE If you are unsuccessful, you do not succeed in what you are trying to do

**unsuitable** ADJECTIVE not right or appropriate for a particular purpose

**unsure** ADJECTIVE uncertain or doubtful

**untidy**, untidier, untidiest ADJECTIVE not neat or well arranged

**untie**, unties, untying, untied VERB If you untie something, you undo the knots in the string or rope around it

**until** PREPOSITION OR CONJUNCTION ❶ If something happens until a particular time, it happens before that time and stops at that time ❷ If something does not happen until a particular time, it does not happen before that time and only starts happening at that time

**untrue** ADJECTIVE not true

**unusual** ADJECTIVE Something that is unusual does not occur very often  **unusually** ADVERB

**unwanted** ADJECTIVE Unwanted things are not desired or wanted, either by a particular person or by people in general

**unwelcome** ADJECTIVE not wanted

**unwell** ADJECTIVE If you are unwell, you are ill

**unwilling** ADJECTIVE If you are unwilling to do something, you do not want to do it

**unwind**, unwinds, unwinding, unwound VERB ❶ When you unwind after working hard, you relax ❷ If you unwind something that is wrapped round something else, you undo it

**unwise** ADJECTIVE foolish or not sensible

**unwrap**, unwraps, unwrapping, unwrapped VERB When you unwrap something, you take off the paper or covering around it

**up** ADVERB OR PREPOSITION ❶ towards or in a higher place ❷ towards or in the north ❀ PREPOSITION ❸ If you go up a road or river, you go along it ❹ You use up to to say how large something can be or what level it has reached ❺ INFORMAL If someone is up to something, they are secretly doing something they should not be doing ❻ If it is up to someone to do something, it is their responsibility ❀ ADJECTIVE ❼ If you are up, you are not in bed ❽ If a period of time is up, it has come to an end ❀ ADVERB ❾ If an amount of something goes up, it increases

**upbringing** NOUN Your upbringing is the way that your parents have taught you to behave

**update**, updates, updating, updated VERB If you update something, you make it more modern or add new information to it

**upgrade**, upgrades, upgrading, upgraded VERB If a person or their job is upgraded, they are given more responsibility or status and usually more money

**uphill** ADVERB ❶ If you go uphill, you go up a slope ❀ ADJECTIVE ❷ An uphill task requires a lot of effort and determination

**upload** VERB If you upload a computer file or program, you transfer it from your computer into the memory of another computer

**upon** PREPOSITION ❶ FORMAL Upon means on ❷ You use upon when mentioning an event that is immediately followed by another ❸ If an event is upon you, it is about to happen

**upper** ADJECTIVE ❶ referring to something that is above something else, or the higher part of something ❀ NOUN ❷ the top part of a shoe

**upper case** ADJECTIVE Upper case letters are the capital letters used in printing or on a typewriter or computer

**upright** ADJECTIVE OR ADVERB ❶ standing or sitting up straight, rather than bending or lying down ❷ behaving in a very respectable and moral way

**upset**, upsets, upsetting, upset ADJECTIVE ❶ unhappy and disappointed ✿ VERB ❷ If something upsets you, it makes you feel worried or unhappy ❸ If you upset something, you turn it over or spill it accidentally ✿ NOUN ❹ A stomach upset is a slight stomach illness caused by an infection or by something you have eaten

**upside down** ADJECTIVE OR ADVERB the wrong way up

**upstairs** ADVERB ❶ If you go upstairs in a building, you go up to a higher floor ✿ NOUN ❷ The upstairs of a building is its upper floor or floors

**up-to-date** ADJECTIVE ❶ being the newest thing of its kind ❷ having the latest information

**upwards** ADVERB ❶ towards a higher place ❷ to a higher level or point on a scale
**upward** ADJECTIVE

**urban** ADJECTIVE relating to a town or city

**urge**, urges, urging, urged NOUN ❶ If you have an urge to do something, you have a strong wish to do it ✿ VERB ❷ If you urge someone to do something, you try hard to persuade them to do it

**urgent** ADJECTIVE needing to be dealt with as soon as possible **urgently** ADVERB

**URL** NOUN an abbreviation for 'uniform resource locator': a technical name for an internet address

**us** PRONOUN A speaker or writer uses us to refer to himself or herself and one or more other people

**use**, uses, using, used VERB [yooz] ❶ If you use something, you do something with it in order to do a job or achieve something ❷ If you use someone, you take advantage of them by making them do things for you ✿ NOUN [yoos] ❸ The use of something is the act of using it ❹ If you have the use of something, you have the ability or permission to use it ❺ If you find a use for something, you find a purpose for it **user** NOUN

**used** [yoost] VERB ❶ Something that used to be done or used to be true was done or was true in the past ✿ PHRASE ❷ If you are **used to** something, you are familiar with it and have often experienced it ✿ ADJECTIVE [yoozd] A used object has had a previous owner

**useful** ADJECTIVE If something is useful, you can use it in order to do something or to help you in some way **usefully** ADVERB

**useless** ADJECTIVE ❶ If something is useless, you cannot use it because it is not suitable or helpful ❷ If a course of action is useless, it will not achieve what is wanted

**username** NOUN a name that someone uses when logging into a computer or website

**usual** ADJECTIVE ❶ happening, done, or used most often ✿ PHRASE ❷ If you do something **as usual**, you do it in the way that you normally do it **usually** ADVERB

### how to remember

Hello Kitty...

knows how to spell **usual** by remembering that the **u**gly **s**isters **u**pset **a l**ady.

**utensil** [yoo-ten-sil] NOUN Utensils are tools
**uterus** [yoo-ter-russ] NOUN FORMAL A woman's uterus is her womb
**utter** VERB ❶ When you utter sounds or words, you make or say them ✿ ADJECTIVE ❷ complete or total **utterly** ADVERB

## vacant – valuable

**vacant** ADJECTIVE ❶ If something is vacant, it is not occupied or being used ❷ If a job or position is vacant, no-one holds it at present ❸ A vacant look suggests that someone does not understand something or is not very intelligent **vacancy** NOUN

**vacation** NOUN ❶ the period between academic terms at a university or college ❷ a holiday

**vaccinate**, vaccinates, vaccinating, vaccinated [*vak-sin-ate*] VERB To vaccinate someone means to give them a vaccine, usually by injection, to protect them against a disease **vaccination** NOUN

**vaccine** [*vak-seen*] NOUN a substance made from the germs that cause a disease, given to people to make them immune to that disease

**vacuum** [*vak-yoom*] NOUN ❶ a space containing no air, gases, or other matter ✿ VERB ❷ If you vacuum something, you clean it using a vacuum cleaner

**vacuum cleaner** NOUN an electric machine which cleans by sucking up dirt

**vagina** [*vaj-jie-na*] NOUN A woman's vagina is the passage that connects her outer sex organs to her womb

**vague**, vaguer, vaguest [*vayg*] ADJECTIVE ❶ If something is vague, it is not expressed or explained clearly, or you cannot see or remember it clearly ❷ Someone looks or sounds vague if they are not concentrating or thinking clearly **vaguely** ADVERB

**vain** ADJECTIVE ❶ A vain action or attempt is one which is not successful ❷ A vain person is very proud of their looks, intelligence, or other qualities ✿ PHRASE ❸ If you do something **in vain**, you do not succeed in achieving what you intend

**valentine** NOUN ❶ Your valentine is someone you love and send a card to on Saint Valentine's Day, February 14th ❷ A valentine or a valentine card is the card you send to the person you love on Saint Valentine's Day

**valid** ADJECTIVE ❶ Something that is valid is based on sound reasoning ❷ A valid ticket or document is one which is officially accepted

**valley** NOUN a long stretch of land between hills, often with a river flowing through it

**valuable** ADJECTIVE ❶ having great importance or usefulness ❷ worth a lot of money

### don't mix up
### Hello Kitty...
never mixes up **vain** (not successful) and **vein** (a tube that carries blood in your body).

**value – venue**

**value**, values, valuing, valued NOUN ❶ The value of something is its importance or usefulness ❷ The value of something you own is the amount of money that it is worth ❸ The values of a group or a person are the moral principles and beliefs that they think are important ✿ VERB ❹ If you value something, you think it is important and you appreciate it ❺ When experts value something, they decide how much money it is worth

**valve** NOUN ❶ a part attached to a pipe or tube which controls the flow of gas or liquid ❷ a small flap in your heart or in a vein which controls the flow and direction of blood

**vampire** NOUN In horror stories, vampires are corpses that come out of their graves at night and suck the blood of living people

**van** NOUN a covered vehicle larger than a car but smaller than a lorry, used for carrying goods

**vandal** NOUN someone who deliberately damages or destroys things, particularly public property **vandalize** or **vandalise** VERB **vandalism** NOUN

**vanilla** NOUN Vanilla is a flavouring for food such as ice cream, which comes from the pods of a tropical plant

**vanish**, vanishes, vanishing, vanished VERB ❶ If something vanishes, it disappears ❷ If something vanishes, it ceases to exist

**vapour** NOUN Vapour is a mass of tiny drops of water or other liquids in the air which looks like mist

**variable** ADJECTIVE ❶ Something that is variable is likely to change at any time ✿ NOUN ❷ In any situation, a variable is something in it that can change

**variation** NOUN ❶ a change from the normal or usual pattern ❷ a change in level, amount, or quantity

**varied** ADJECTIVE of different types, quantities, or sizes

**variety**, varieties NOUN ❶ If something has variety, it consists of things which are not all the same ❷ A variety of things is a number of different kinds of them ❸ A variety of something is a particular type of it

**various** ADJECTIVE Various means of several different types

**varnish**, varnishes, varnishing, varnished NOUN ❶ a liquid which when painted onto a surface gives it a hard clear shiny finish ✿ VERB ❷ If you varnish something, you paint it with varnish

**vary**, varies, varying, varied VERB ❶ If things vary, they change ❷ If you vary something, you introduce changes in it **varied** ADJECTIVE

**vase** NOUN a glass or china jar for flowers

**vast** ADJECTIVE extremely large

**vegetable** NOUN Vegetables are edible roots or leaves such as carrots or cabbage

**vegetarian** NOUN a person who does not eat meat, poultry, or fish

**vegetation** NOUN Vegetation is the plants in a particular area

**vehicle** [vee-ik-kl] NOUN ❶ a machine, often with an engine, used for transporting people or goods ❷ something used to achieve a particular purpose or as a means of expression

**veil** [rhymes with **male**] NOUN a piece of thin, soft cloth that women sometimes wear over their heads

**vein** [rhymes with **rain**] NOUN ❶ Your veins are the tubes in your body through which your blood flows to your heart ❷ Veins are the thin lines on leaves or on insects' wings ❸ A vein of a metal or a mineral is a layer of it in rock ❹ Something that is in a particular vein is in that style or mood

**velvet** NOUN Velvet is a very soft material which has a thick layer of fine short threads on one side

**vent** NOUN ❶ a hole in something through which gases and smoke can escape and fresh air can enter ✿ VERB ❷ If you vent strong feelings, you express them ✿ PHRASE ❸ If you **give vent** to strong feelings, you express them

**ventilate**, ventilates, ventilating, ventilated VERB To ventilate a room means to allow fresh air into it

**ventilation** NOUN ❶ Ventilation is the process of breathing air in and out of the lungs ✿ ADJECTIVE ❷ A ventilation system supplies fresh air into a building

**venue** [ven-yoo] NOUN The venue for an event is the place where it will happen

A B C D E F G H I J K L M N O P Q R S T U **V** W X Y Z

# verb - video

**verb** NOUN In grammar, a verb is a word that expresses actions and states, for example 'be', 'become', 'take', and 'run'

## how English works

### Hello Kitty...

knows that a **verb** is a word that describes an action or state, like *run* and *cry*. Verbs are sometimes called 'doing words'.

**verbal** ADJECTIVE ❶ You use 'verbal' to describe things connected with words and their use ❷ 'Verbal' describes things which are spoken rather than written **verbally** ADVERB

**verdict** NOUN ❶ In a law court, a verdict is the decision which states whether a prisoner is guilty or not guilty ❷ If you give a verdict on something, you give your opinion after thinking about it

**verge**, verges, verging, verged NOUN ❶ The verge of a road is the narrow strip of grassy ground at the side ✿ PHRASE ❷ If you are **on the verge** of something, you are going to do it soon or it is likely to happen soon ✿ VERB ❸ Something that verges on something else is almost the same as it

**verify**, verifies, verifying, verified VERB If you verify something, you check that it is true

**versatile** ADJECTIVE If someone is versatile, they have many different skills

**verse** NOUN ❶ Verse is another word for poetry ❷ one part of a poem, song, or chapter of the Bible

**version** NOUN ❶ A version of something is a form of it in which some details are different from earlier or later forms ❷ Someone's version of an event is their personal description of what happened

**versus** PREPOSITION Versus is used to indicate that two people or teams are competing against each other

**vertebrate** NOUN Vertebrates are any creatures which have a backbone

**vertical** ADJECTIVE Something that is vertical points straight up and forms a ninety-degree angle with the surface on which it stands

**very** ADVERB ❶ to a great degree ✿ ADJECTIVE ❷ Very is used before words to emphasize them

**vest** NOUN a piece of underwear worn for warmth on the top half of the body

**vet**, vets, vetting, vetted NOUN ❶ a doctor for animals ✿ VERB ❷ If you vet someone or something, you check them carefully to see if they are acceptable

**veto**, vetoes, vetoing, vetoed [vee-toh] VERB ❶ If someone in authority vetoes something, they say no to it ✿ NOUN ❷ Veto is the right that someone in authority has to say no to something

**via** PREPOSITION ❶ If you go to one place via another, you travel through that place to get to your destination ❷ Via also means done or achieved by making use of a particular thing or person

**vibrate**, vibrates, vibrating, vibrated VERB If something vibrates, it moves a tiny amount backwards and forwards very quickly **vibration** NOUN

**vice** NOUN ❶ a serious moral fault in someone's character, such as greed, or a weakness, such as smoking ❷ Vice is criminal activities connected with prostitution and pornography ❸ a tool with a pair of jaws that hold an object tightly while it is being worked on

**vice versa** ADVERB 'Vice versa' is used to indicate that the reverse of what you have said is also true

**vicious** ADJECTIVE cruel and violent

**victim** NOUN someone who has been harmed or injured by someone or something

**victory**, victories NOUN a success in a battle or competition **victorious** ADJECTIVE

**video**, videos, videoing, videoed NOUN ❶ Video is the recording and showing of

302

films and events using a video recorder, video tape, and a television set ❷ a sound and picture recording which can be played back on a television set ✿ VERB ❸ If you video something, you record it on magnetic tape for later viewing

**view** NOUN ❶ Your views are your personal opinions ❷ everything you can see from a particular place ✿ VERB ❸ If you view something in a particular way, you think of it in that way ✿ PHRASE ❹ You use **in view of** to specify the main fact or event influencing your actions or opinions

**viewer** NOUN Viewers are the people who watch television

**vigorous** ADJECTIVE energetic or enthusiastic **vigorously** ADVERB

**village** NOUN a collection of houses and other buildings in the countryside

**villain** NOUN ❶ someone who harms others or breaks the law ❷ the main evil character in a story

**vine** NOUN a trailing or climbing plant which winds itself around and over a support, especially one which produces grapes

**vinegar** NOUN Vinegar is a sharp-tasting liquid made from sour wine, beer, or cider, which is used for salad dressing

### how to say it

**Vinegar** should be said **vin**-ni-gar, with most force on *vin*.

**vinyl** NOUN Vinyl is a strong plastic used to make things such as furniture and floor coverings

**viola** [vee-**oh**-la] NOUN a musical instrument like a violin, but larger and with a lower pitch

**violate**, violates, violating, violated VERB ❶ If you violate an agreement, law, or promise, you break it ❷ If you violate someone's peace or privacy, you disturb it ❸ If you violate a place, especially a holy place, you treat it with disrespect or violence **violation** NOUN

**violence** NOUN ❶ Violence is behaviour which is intended to hurt or kill people ❷ If you do or say something with violence, you use a lot of energy in doing or saying it, often because you are angry

**violent** ADJECTIVE ❶ If someone is violent, they try to hurt or kill people ❷ A violent event happens unexpectedly and with great force ❸ Something that is violent is said, felt, or done with great force **violently** ADVERB

**violet** NOUN ❶ a plant with dark purple flowers ✿ NOUN OR ADJECTIVE ❷ bluish purple

**violin** NOUN a musical instrument with four strings that is held under the chin and played with a bow

**VIP** NOUN VIPs are famous or important people. VIP is an abbreviation for 'very important person'

**virtual** [*vur-tyool*] ADJECTIVE Virtual means that something has all the characteristics of a particular thing, but it is not formally recognized as being that thing **virtually** ADVERB

**virtual reality** NOUN Virtual reality is a situation or setting that has been created by a computer and that looks real to the person using it

**virtue** NOUN ❶ Virtue is thinking and doing what is morally right and avoiding what is wrong ❷ a good quality in someone's character ❸ A virtue of something is an advantage ✿ PHRASE ❹ FORMAL **By virtue of** means because of

**virus**, viruses [*vie-russ*] NOUN ❶ a kind of germ that can cause disease ❷ a program that alters or damages the information stored in a computer system

**visa** NOUN an official stamp, usually put in your passport, that allows you to visit a particular country

**visibility** NOUN You use 'visibility' to say how far or how clearly you can see in particular weather conditions

**visible** ADJECTIVE ❶ able to be seen ❷ noticeable or evident

**vision** NOUN ❶ Vision is the ability to see clearly ❷ a mental picture, in which you imagine how things might be different

**visit** VERB ❶ If you visit someone, you go to see them and spend time with them ❷ If you visit a place, you go to see it ✿ NOUN ❸ a trip to see a person or place **visitor** NOUN

**visual** ADJECTIVE relating to sight

# vital - vulnerable

**vital** ADJECTIVE ❶ necessary or very important ❷ energetic, exciting, and full of life

**vitamin** NOUN Vitamins are organic compounds which you need in order to remain healthy. They occur naturally in food

**vivid** ADJECTIVE very bright in colour or clear in detail **vividly** ADVERB

**vocabulary**, vocabularies NOUN ❶ Someone's vocabulary is the total number of words they know in a particular language ❷ The vocabulary of a language is all the words in it

**vocal** ADJECTIVE ❶ You say that someone is vocal if they express their opinions strongly and openly ❷ Vocal means involving the use of the human voice, especially in singing

**voice**, voices, voicing, voiced NOUN ❶ Your voice is the sounds produced by your vocal cords, or the ability to make such sounds ✿ VERB ❷ If you voice an opinion or an emotion, you say what you think or feel

**volcano**, volcanoes NOUN a hill with an opening through which lava, gas, and ash burst out from inside the earth onto the surface

**volleyball** NOUN Volleyball is a game in which two teams hit a large ball back and forth over a high net with their hands. The ball is not allowed to bounce on the ground

**volt** NOUN A volt is a unit of electrical force

**volume** NOUN ❶ The volume of something is the amount of space it contains or occupies ❷ The volume of something is also the amount of it that there is ❸ The volume of a device is the strength of the sound that it produces

**voluntary** ADJECTIVE ❶ Voluntary actions are ones that you do because you choose to do them and not because you have been forced to do them ❷ Voluntary work is done by people who are not paid for what they do **voluntarily** ADVERB

**volunteer** NOUN ❶ someone who does work for which they are not paid ❷ someone who chooses to join the armed forces, especially during wartime ✿ VERB ❸ If you volunteer to do something, you offer to do it rather than being forced into it ❹ If you volunteer information, you give it without being asked

**vomit** VERB ❶ If you vomit, food and drink comes back up from your stomach and out through your mouth ✿ NOUN ❷ Vomit is partly digested food and drink that has come back up from someone's stomach and out through their mouth

**vote**, votes, voting, voted NOUN ❶ Someone's vote is their choice in an election, or at a meeting where decisions are taken ❷ When a group of people have a vote, they make a decision by allowing each person in the group to say what they would prefer ❸ In an election, the vote is the total number of people who have made their choice ❹ If people have the vote, they have the legal right to vote in an election ✿ VERB ❺ When people vote, they indicate their choice or opinion, usually by writing on a piece of paper or by raising their hand **voter** NOUN

**vow** VERB ❶ If you vow to do something, you make a solemn promise to do it ✿ NOUN ❷ a solemn promise

**vowel** NOUN a sound made without your tongue touching the roof of your mouth or your teeth, or one of the letters a, e, i, o, u, which represent such sounds

## how English works

### Hello Kitty...

knows that these letters are all **vowels**: **a, e, i, o** and **u**.

**voyage** NOUN a long journey on a ship or in a spacecraft

**vulnerable** ADJECTIVE weak and without protection

**wade**, wades, wading, waded VERB ❶ If you wade through water or mud, you walk slowly through it ❷ If you wade through a book or document, you spend a lot of time and effort reading it because you find it dull or difficult

**waffle**, waffles, waffling, waffled [*wof*-fl] VERB ❶ When someone waffles, they talk or write a lot without being clear or without saying anything of importance ✿ NOUN ❷ Waffle is vague and lengthy speech or writing ❸ a thick, crisp pancake with squares marked on it often eaten with syrup poured over it

**wag**, wags, wagging, wagged VERB ❶ When a dog wags its tail, it shakes it repeatedly from side to side ❷ If you wag your finger, you move it repeatedly up and down

**wage**, wages, waging, waged NOUN ❶ A wage or wages is the regular payment made to someone each week for the work they do, especially for manual or unskilled work ✿ VERB ❷ If a person or country wages a campaign or war, they start it and carry it on over a period of time

**wagon waggon** NOUN ❶ a strong four-wheeled vehicle for carrying heavy loads, usually pulled by a horse or tractor ❷ Wagons are also the containers for freight pulled by a railway engine

**waist** NOUN the middle part of your body where it narrows slightly above your hips

**waistcoat** NOUN a sleeveless piece of clothing, often worn under a suit or jacket, which buttons up the front

**wait** VERB ❶ If you wait, you spend time, usually doing little or nothing, before something happens ❷ If something can wait, it is not urgent and can be dealt with later ❸ If you wait on people in a restaurant, it is your job to serve them food ✿ NOUN ❹ a period of time before something happens

**waiter** NOUN a man who works in a restaurant, serving people with food and drink

**waitress**, waitresses NOUN a woman who works in a restaurant, serving people with food and drink

**wake**, wakes, waking, woke, woken VERB ❶ When you wake or when something wakes you, you become conscious again after being asleep ✿ NOUN ❷ The wake of a boat or other object moving in water is the track of waves it leaves behind it ❸ a gathering of

### don't mix up

Hello Kitty...

never mixes up **wait** (to pass time until something happens) and **weight** (the heaviness of a person or thing).

# wake up – warmth

people who have got together to mourn someone's death ✿ **PHRASE** ❹ If one thing follows **in the wake of** another, it follows it as a result of it, or in imitation of it

**wake up** ✿ **VERB** ❶ When you wake up or something wakes you up, you become conscious again after being asleep ❷ If you wake up to a dangerous situation, you become aware of it

**walk VERB** ❶ When you walk, you move along by putting one foot in front of the other on the ground ❷ If you walk away with or walk off with something such as a prize, you win it or achieve it easily ✿ **NOUN** ❸ a journey made by walking ❹ Your walk is the way you walk

> **some other words to use**
> Instead of using **walk** too much when you are writing, try *stroll*, *march*, *ramble* or *stride*.

**walk out** ✿ **VERB** If you walk out on someone, you leave them suddenly

**wall NOUN** ❶ one of the vertical sides of a building or a room ❷ a long, narrow vertical structure made of stone or brick that surrounds or divides an area of land ❸ a lining or membrane enclosing a bodily cavity or structure

**wallet NOUN** a small, flat case made of leather or plastic, used for keeping paper money and sometimes credit cards

**wallpaper NOUN** Wallpaper is thick coloured or patterned paper for pasting onto the walls of rooms in order to decorate them

**walnut NOUN** ❶ an edible nut with a wrinkled shape and a hard, round, light-brown shell ❷ Walnut is wood from the walnut tree which is often used for making expensive furniture

**wander VERB** ❶ If you wander in a place, you walk around in a casual way ❷ If your mind wanders or your thoughts wander, you lose concentration and start thinking about other things

**want VERB** ❶ If you want something, you feel a desire to have it ❷ If something is wanted, it is needed or needs to be done ❸ If someone is wanted, the police are searching for them ✿ **NOUN** ❹ FORMAL A want of something is a lack of it

**war**, wars, warring, warred **NOUN** ❶ a period of fighting between countries or states when weapons are used and many people may be killed ❷ a competition between groups of people, or a campaign against something ✿ **VERB** ❸ When two countries war with each other, they are fighting a war against each other

**ward NOUN** ❶ a room in a hospital which has beds for several people who need similar treatment ❷ an area or district which forms a separate part of a political constituency or local council ❸ A ward or a ward of court is a child who is officially put in the care of an adult or a court of law, because their parents are dead or because they need protection ✿ **VERB** ❹ If you ward off a danger or an illness, you do something to prevent it from affecting or harming you

**wardrobe NOUN** ❶ a tall cupboard in which you can hang your clothes ❷ Someone's wardrobe is their collection of clothes

**warehouse NOUN** a large building where raw materials or manufactured goods are stored

**warfare NOUN** Warfare is the activity of fighting a war

**warm ADJECTIVE** ❶ Something that is warm has some heat, but not enough to be hot ❷ Warm clothes or blankets are made of a material which protects you from the cold ❸ Warm colours or sounds are pleasant and make you feel comfortable and relaxed ❹ A warm person is friendly and affectionate ✿ **VERB** ❺ If you warm something, you heat it up gently so that it stops being cold **warmly ADVERB**

**warm up** ✿ **VERB** If you warm up for an event or an activity, you practise or exercise gently to prepare for it

**warmth NOUN** ❶ Warmth is a moderate amount of heat ❷ Someone who has warmth is friendly and affectionate

306

**warn** VERB ❶ If you warn someone about a possible problem or danger, you tell them about it in advance so that they are aware of it ❷ If you warn someone not to do something, you advise them not to do it, in order to avoid possible danger or punishment

**warning** NOUN something said or written to tell people of a possible problem or danger

**warrant** VERB ❶ FORMAL If something warrants a particular action, it makes the action seem necessary ✿ NOUN ❷ an official document which gives permission to the police to do something

**warranty**, warranties NOUN a guarantee

**wary**, warier, wariest ADJECTIVE cautious and on one's guard

**was** a past tense of **be**

**wash**, washes, washing, washed VERB ❶ If you wash something, you clean it with water and soap ❷ If you wash, you clean yourself using soap and water ❸ If something is washed somewhere, it is carried there gently by water ✿ NOUN ❹ The wash is all the clothes and bedding that are washed together at one time ❺ The wash in water is the disturbance and waves produced at the back of a moving boat ✿ PHRASE ❻ If you **wash your hands of** something, you refuse to have anything more to do with it

**wash up** ✿ VERB ❶ If you wash up, you wash the dishes, pans, and cutlery used in preparing and eating a meal ❷ If something is washed up on land, it is carried by a river or sea and left there

**washbasin** NOUN a deep bowl, usually fixed to a wall, with taps for hot and cold water

**washing** NOUN Washing consists of clothes and bedding which need to be washed or are in the process of being washed and dried

**washing machine** NOUN a machine for washing clothes in

**washing-up** NOUN If you do the washing-up, you wash the dishes, pans, and cutlery which have been used in the cooking and eating of a meal

**wasp** NOUN an insect with yellow and black stripes across its body, which can sting like a bee

**waste**, wastes, wasting, wasted VERB ❶ If you waste time, money, or energy, you use too much of it on something that is not important or necessary ❷ If you waste an opportunity, you do not take advantage of it when it is available ❸ If you say that something is wasted on someone, you mean that it is too good, too clever, or too sophisticated for them ✿ NOUN ❹ If an activity is a waste of time, money, or energy, it is not important or necessary ❺ Waste is the use of more money or some other resource than is necessary ❻ Waste is also material that is no longer wanted, or material left over from a useful process ✿ ADJECTIVE ❼ unwanted in its present form ❽ Waste land is land which is not used or looked after by anyone

**waste away** ✿ VERB If someone is wasting away, they are becoming very thin and weak because they are ill or not eating properly

**watch**, watches, watching, watched NOUN ❶ a small clock usually worn on a strap on the wrist ❷ a period of time during which a guard is kept over something ✿ VERB ❸ If you watch something, you look at it for some time and pay close attention to what is happening ❹ If you watch someone or something, you take care of them ❺ If you watch a situation, you pay attention to it or are aware of it

**watch out** ✿ VERB If you watch out for something, you keep alert to see if it is near you

**water** NOUN ❶ Water is a clear, colourless, tasteless, and odourless liquid that is necessary for all plant and animal life ❷ You use water or waters to refer to a large area of water, such as a lake or sea ✿ VERB ❸ If you water a plant or an animal, you give it water to drink ❹ If your eyes water, you have tears in them because they are hurting ❺ If your mouth waters, it produces extra saliva, usually because you think of or can smell something appetizing

**water down** ✿ VERB If you water something down, you make it weaker

**watercolour** NOUN ❶ Watercolours are paints for painting pictures, which are diluted with water or put on the paper using a wet brush ❷ a picture which has been painted using watercolours

# waterfall – wear

**waterfall** NOUN A waterfall is water from a river or stream as it flows over the edge of a steep cliff in hills or mountains and falls to the ground below

**watermelon** NOUN a large, round fruit which has a hard green skin and red juicy flesh

**waterproof** ADJECTIVE ❶ not letting water pass through ❀ NOUN ❷ a coat which keeps water out

**watt** [wot] NOUN a unit of measurement of electrical power

**wave**, waves, waving, waved VERB ❶ If you wave your hand, you move it from side to side, usually to say hello or goodbye ❷ If you wave someone somewhere or wave them on, you make a movement with your hand to tell them which way to go ❸ If you wave something, you hold it up and move it from side to side ❀ NOUN ❹ a ridge of water on the surface of the sea caused by wind or by tides ❺ A wave is the form in which some types of energy such as heat, light, or sound travel through a substance ❻ A wave of sympathy, alarm, or panic is a steady increase in it which spreads through you or through a group of people ❼ an increase in a type of activity or behaviour

**wavelength** NOUN ❶ the distance between the same point on two adjacent waves of energy ❷ the size of radio wave which a particular radio station uses to broadcast its programmes

**wavy**, wavier, waviest ADJECTIVE having waves or regular curves

**wax**, waxes, waxing, waxed NOUN ❶ Wax is a solid, slightly shiny substance made of fat or oil and used to make candles and polish ❷ Wax is also the sticky yellow substance in your ears ❀ VERB ❸ If you wax a surface, you treat it or cover it with a thin layer of wax, especially to polish it ❹ FORMAL If you wax eloquent, you talk in an eloquent way

**way** NOUN ❶ A way of doing something is the manner of doing it ❷ The ways of a person or group are their customs or their normal behaviour ❸ The way you feel about something is your attitude to it or your opinion about it ❹ If you have a way with people or things, you are very skilful at dealing with them ❺ The way to a particular place is the route that you take to get there ❻ If you go or look a particular way, you go or look in that direction ❼ If you divide something a number of ways, you divide it into that number of parts ❽ Way is used with words such as 'little' or 'long' to say how far off in distance or time something is ❀ PHRASE ❾ You say **by the way** when adding something to what you are saying ❿ If you **go out of your way** to do something, you make a special effort to do it

**we** PRONOUN A speaker or writer uses 'we' to refer to himself or herself and one or more other people

**weak** ADJECTIVE ❶ not having much strength ❷ If something is weak, it is likely to break or fail ❸ If you describe someone as weak, you mean they are easily influenced by other people **weakly** ADVERB

### don't mix up

Don't mix up **weak** (not strong) and **week** (seven days).

**weaken** VERB ❶ If someone weakens something, they make it less strong or certain ❷ If someone weakens, they become less certain about something

**weakness**, weaknesses NOUN ❶ Weakness is lack of moral or physical strength ❷ If you have a weakness for something, you have a great liking for it

**wealth** NOUN ❶ Wealth is the large amount of money or property which someone owns ❷ A wealth of something is a lot of it

**wealthy**, wealthier, wealthiest ADJECTIVE having a large amount of money, property, or other valuable things

**weapon** NOUN ❶ an object used to kill or hurt people in a fight or war ❷ anything which can be used to get the better of an opponent

**wear**, wears, wearing, wore, worn VERB ❶ When you wear something such as clothes, make-up, or jewellery, you have them on your body or face ❷ If you wear a particular expression, it shows on your face ❸ If something wears, it becomes thinner or worse in condition ❀ NOUN ❹ You can refer

**wear down – weird**

to clothes that are suitable for a particular time or occasion as a kind of wear ❺ Wear is the amount or type of use that something has and which causes damage or change to it

**wear down** ✿ **VERB** If you wear people down, you weaken them by repeatedly doing something or asking them to do something

**wear off** ✿ **VERB** If a feeling such as pain wears off, it gradually disappears

**wear out** ✿ **VERB** ❶ When something wears out or when you wear it out, it is used so much that it becomes thin, weak, and no longer usable ❷ **INFORMAL** If you wear someone out, you make them feel extremely tired

**weary**, wearier, weariest; wearies, wearying, wearied **ADJECTIVE** ❶ very tired ✿ **VERB** ❷ If you weary of something, you become tired of it

**weather NOUN** ❶ The weather is the condition of the atmosphere at any particular time and the amount of rain, wind, or sunshine occurring ✿ **VERB** ❷ If something such as rock or wood weathers, it changes colour or shape as a result of being exposed to the wind, rain, or sun ❸ If you weather a problem or difficulty, you come through it safely ✿ **PHRASE** ❹ If you are **under the weather**, you feel slightly ill

**weave**, weaves, weaving, wove, woven **VERB** ❶ To weave cloth is to make it by crossing threads over and under each other, especially by using a machine called a loom ❷ If you weave your way somewhere, you go there by moving from side to side through and round the obstacles ✿ **NOUN** ❸ The weave of cloth is the way in which the threads are arranged and the pattern that they form

**web NOUN** ❶ a fine net of threads that a spider makes from a sticky substance which it produces in its body ❷ something that has a complicated structure or pattern ❸ The Web is the same as the **World Wide Web**

**website NOUN** a publication on the World Wide Web which contains information about a particular subject

**wedding NOUN** a marriage ceremony

**Wednesday**, Wednesdays **NOUN** Wednesday is the day between Tuesday and Thursday

**weed NOUN** ❶ a wild plant that prevents cultivated plants from growing properly ✿ **VERB** ❷ If you weed a place, you remove the weeds from it

**week NOUN** ❶ a period of seven days, especially one beginning on a Sunday and ending on a Saturday ❷ A week is also the number of hours you spend at work during a week ❸ The week can refer to the part of a week that does not include Saturday and Sunday

**weekday NOUN** any day except Saturday and Sunday

**weekend NOUN** Saturday and Sunday

**weekly**, weeklies **ADJECTIVE OR ADVERB** ❶ happening or appearing once a week ✿ **NOUN** ❷ a newspaper or magazine that is published once a week

**weep**, weeps, weeping, wept **VERB** ❶ If someone weeps, they cry ❷ If something such as a wound weeps, it oozes blood or other liquid

**weigh VERB** ❶ If something weighs a particular amount, that is how heavy it is ❷ If you weigh something, you measure how heavy it is using scales ❸ If you weigh facts or words, you think about them carefully before coming to a decision or before speaking ❹ If a problem weighs on you or weighs upon you, it makes you very worried

**weigh down** ✿ **VERB** ❶ If a load weighs you down, it stops you moving easily ❷ If you are weighed down by a difficulty, it is making you very worried

**weigh up** ✿ **VERB** If you weigh up a person or a situation, you make an assessment of them

**weight NOUN** ❶ The weight of something is its heaviness ❷ a metal object which has a certain known heaviness. Weights are used with sets of scales in order to weigh things ❸ any heavy object ❹ The weight of something is its large amount or importance which makes it hard to fight against or contradict ✿ **VERB** ❺ If you weight something or weight it down, you make it heavier, often so that it cannot move ✿ **PHRASE** ❻ If you **pull your weight**, you work just as hard as other people involved in the same activity

**weird** [weerd] **ADJECTIVE** strange or odd

# welcome - wheelchair

**welcome**, welcomes, welcoming, welcomed
**VERB** ❶ If you welcome a visitor, you greet them in a friendly way when they arrive ❷ If you welcome something, you approve of it and support it ❀ **NOUN** ❸ a greeting to a visitor ❀ **ADJECTIVE** ❹ If someone is welcome at a place, they will be warmly received there ❺ If something is welcome, it brings pleasure or is accepted gratefully ❻ If you tell someone they are welcome to something or welcome to do something, you mean you are willing for them to have or to do it ❀ **INTERJECTION** ❼ 'Welcome' can be said as a greeting to a visitor who has just arrived

**welfare NOUN** ❶ The welfare of a person or group is their general state of health and comfort ❷ Welfare services are provided to help with people's living conditions and financial problems

**well**, better, best; wells, welling, welled
**ADVERB** ❶ If something goes well, it happens in a satisfactory way ❷ in a good, skilful, or pleasing way ❸ thoroughly and completely ❹ kindly ❺ If something may well or could well happen, it is likely to happen ❻ You use well to emphasize an adjective, adverb, or phrase ❀ **ADJECTIVE** ❼ If you are well, you are healthy ❀ **NOUN** ❽ a hole drilled in the ground from which water, oil, or gas is obtained ❀ **VERB** ❾ If tears well or well up, they appear in someone's eyes

**well-off ADJECTIVE** INFORMAL quite wealthy

**wept** the past tense and past participle of **weep**

**were** a past tense of **be**

**west NOUN** ❶ The west is the direction in which you look to see the sun set ❷ The west of a place or country is the part which is towards the west when you are in the centre ❸ The West refers to the countries of North America and western and southern Europe ❀ **ADVERB OR ADJECTIVE** ❹ West means towards the west ❀ **ADJECTIVE** ❺ A west wind blows from the west

**westerly ADJECTIVE** ❶ When talking about a place, westerly means situated in the west ❷ coming from the west

**western ADJECTIVE** ❶ in or from the west ❷ coming from or associated with the countries of North America and western and southern Europe ❀ **NOUN** ❸ a book or film about life in the west of America in the nineteenth century

**wet**, wetter, wettest; wets, wetting, wet or wetted **ADJECTIVE** ❶ If something is wet, it is covered in water or another liquid ❷ If the weather is wet, it is raining ❸ If something such as paint, ink, or cement is wet, it is not yet dry or solid ❹ INFORMAL If you say someone is wet, you mean they are weak and lacking confidence ❀ **NOUN** ❺ In Australia, the wet is the rainy season ❀ **VERB** ❻ To wet something is to put water or some other liquid over it ❼ If people wet themselves or wet their beds, they urinate in their clothes or bed because they cannot control their bladder

**whale NOUN** a very large sea mammal which breathes through a hole on the top of its head

**what PRONOUN** ❶ What is used in questions ❷ What is used in indirect questions and statements ❸ What can be used at the beginning of a clause to refer to something with a particular quality ❀ **ADJECTIVE** ❹ What can be used at the beginning of a clause to show that you are talking about the whole amount that is available to you ❺ You say what to emphasize an opinion or reaction

**whatever PRONOUN** ❶ You use whatever to refer to anything or everything of a particular type ❷ You use whatever when you do not know the precise nature of something ❀ **CONJUNCTION** ❸ You use whatever to mean no matter what ❀ **ADVERB** ❹ You use whatever to emphasize a negative statement or a question

**wheat NOUN** Wheat is a cereal plant grown for its grain which is used to make flour

**wheel NOUN** ❶ a circular object which turns on a rod attached to its centre. Wheels are fixed underneath vehicles so that they can move along ❷ The wheel of a car is its steering wheel ❀ **VERB** ❸ If you wheel something such as a bicycle, you push it ❹ If someone or something wheels, they move round in the shape of a circle

**wheelbarrow NOUN** a small cart with a single wheel at the front, used for carrying things in the garden

**wheelchair NOUN** a chair with wheels in which sick, injured, or disabled people can move around

310

**when** ADVERB ❶ You use when to ask what time something happened or will happen ❀ CONJUNCTION ❷ You use when to refer to a time in the past ❸ You use when to introduce the reason for an opinion, comment, or question ❹ When is used to mean although

**whenever** CONJUNCTION Whenever means at any time, or every time that something happens

**where** ADVERB ❶ You use where to ask which place something is in, is coming from, or is going to ❀ CONJUNCTION, PRONOUN, OR ADVERB ❷ You use where when asking about or referring to something ❀ CONJUNCTION ❸ You use where to refer to the place in which something is situated or happening ❹ Where can introduce a clause that contrasts with the other part of the sentence

**wherever** CONJUNCTION ❶ Wherever means in every place or situation ❷ You use wherever to show that you do not know where a place or person is

**whether** CONJUNCTION You use whether when you are talking about two or more alternatives

**which** ADJECTIVE OR PRONOUN ❶ You use which to ask about alternatives or to refer to a choice between alternatives ❀ PRONOUN ❷ Which at the beginning of a clause identifies the thing you are talking about or gives more information about it

**whichever** ADJECTIVE OR PRONOUN You use whichever when you are talking about different alternatives or possibilities

**while**, whiles, whiling, whiled CONJUNCTION ❶ If something happens while something else is happening, the two things happen at the same time ❷ While also means but ❀ NOUN ❸ a period of time

**while away** ❀ VERB If you while away the time in a particular way, you pass the time that way because you have nothing else to do

**whine**, whines, whining, whined VERB ❶ To whine is to make a long, high-pitched noise, especially one which sounds sad or unpleasant ❷ If someone whines about something, they complain about it in an annoying way ❀ NOUN ❸ A whine is the noise made by something or someone whining

**whip**, whips, whipping, whipped NOUN ❶ a thin piece of leather or rope attached to a handle, which is used for hitting people or animals ❀ VERB ❷ If you whip a person or animal, you hit them with a whip ❸ When the wind whips something, it strikes it ❹ If you whip something out or off, you take it out or off very quickly ❺ If you whip cream or eggs, you beat them until they are thick and frothy or stiff

**whip up** ❀ VERB If you whip up a strong emotion, you make people feel it

**whirl** VERB ❶ When something whirls, or when you whirl it round, it turns round very fast ❀ NOUN ❷ You can refer to a lot of intense activity as a whirl of activity

**whisk** VERB ❶ If you whisk someone or something somewhere, you take them there quickly ❷ If you whisk eggs or cream, you stir air into them quickly ❀ NOUN ❸ a kitchen tool used for quickly stirring air into eggs or cream

**whisker** NOUN The whiskers of an animal such as a cat or mouse are the long, stiff hairs near its mouth

**whisky**, whiskies NOUN Whisky is a strong alcoholic drink made from grain such as barley

**whisper** VERB ❶ When you whisper, you talk to someone very quietly, using your breath and not your throat ❀ NOUN ❷ If you talk in a whisper, you whisper

**whistle**, whistles, whistling, whistled VERB ❶ When you whistle a tune or whistle, you produce a clear musical sound by forcing your breath out between your lips ❷ If something whistles, it makes a loud, high sound ❀ NOUN ❸ A whistle is the sound something or someone makes when they whistle ❹ a small metal tube that you blow into to produce a whistling sound

**white**, whiter, whitest NOUN OR ADJECTIVE ❶ White is the lightest possible colour ❷ Someone who is white has a pale skin and is of European origin ❀ ADJECTIVE ❸ If someone goes white, their face becomes very pale because they are afraid, shocked, or ill ❀ NOUN ❹ The white of an egg is the transparent liquid surrounding the yolk which turns white when it is cooked

**whizz**, whizzes, whizzing, whizzed (also **whiz**) VERB INFORMAL If you whizz somewhere, you move there quickly

**who** PRONOUN ❶ You use who when you are asking about someone's identity ❷ Who at the beginning of a clause refers to the person or people you are talking about

**whoever** PRONOUN ❶ Whoever means the person who ❷ Whoever also means no matter who ❸ Whoever is used in questions give emphasis to who

**whole** ADJECTIVE ❶ indicating all of something ✿ NOUN ❷ the full amount of something ✿ ADVERB ❸ in one piece

**whom** PRONOUN Whom is the object form of who

**whose** PRONOUN ❶ You use whose to ask who something belongs to ❷ You use whose at the beginning of a clause which gives information about something relating or belonging to the thing or person you have just mentioned

**why** ADVERB OR PRONOUN You use why when you are asking about the reason for something, or talking about it

**wicked** ADJECTIVE ❶ very bad ❷ mischievous in an amusing or attractive way

### Did you know...

that the word **wicked** comes from the Old English word *wicce* which means 'witch'? That's because people thought that witches did wicked things.

**where does the word come from?**

**wide**, wider, widest ADJECTIVE ❶ measuring a large distance from one side to the other ❷ If there is a wide variety, range, or selection of something, there are many different kinds of it ✿ ADVERB ❸ If you open or spread something wide, you open it to its fullest extent

**widen** VERB ❶ If something widens or if you widen it, it becomes bigger from one side to the other ❷ You can say that something widens when it becomes greater in size or scope

**widespread** ADJECTIVE existing or happening over a large area or to a great extent

**widow** NOUN a woman whose husband has died

**widower** NOUN a man whose wife has died

**width** NOUN The width of something is the distance from one side or edge to the other

**wife**, wives NOUN A man's wife is the woman he is married to

**wig** NOUN a false head of hair worn to cover someone's own hair or to hide their baldness

**wiggle**, wiggles, wiggling, wiggled VERB ❶ If you wiggle something, you move it up and down or from side to side with small jerky movements ✿ NOUN ❷ a small jerky movement

**wild** ADJECTIVE ❶ Wild animals, birds, and plants live and grow in natural surroundings and are not looked after by people ❷ Wild land is natural and has not been cultivated ❸ Wild weather or sea is stormy and rough ❹ Wild behaviour is excited and uncontrolled ❺ A wild idea or scheme is original and crazy ✿ NOUN ❻ The wild is a free and natural state of living ❼ The wilds are remote areas where few people live, far away from towns **wildly** ADVERB

**wilderness**, wildernesses NOUN an area of natural land which is not cultivated

**wildlife** NOUN Wildlife means wild animals and plants

**will** VERB ❶ You use will to form the future tense ❷ You use will to say that you intend to do something ❸ You use will when inviting someone to do or have something ❹ You use will when asking or telling someone to do something ❺ You use will to say that you are assuming something to be the case

**will** VERB ❶ If you will something to happen, you try to make it happen by mental effort ❷ If you will something to someone, you leave it to them when you die ✿ NOUN ❸ Will

**willing - wipe**

is the determination to do something ❹ If something is the will of a person or group, they want it to happen ❺ a legal document in which you say what you want to happen to your money and property when you die ✿ PHRASE ❻ If you can do something **at will**, you can do it whenever you want

**willing** ADJECTIVE ready and eager to do something **willingly** ADVERB **willingness** NOUN

**win**, wins, winning, won VERB ❶ If you win a fight, game, or argument, you defeat your opponent ❷ If you win something, you succeed in obtaining it ✿ NOUN ❸ a victory in a game or contest

**win over** ✿ VERB If you win someone over, you persuade them to support you

**wind**, winds [rhymes with **tinned**] NOUN ❶ a current of air moving across the earth's surface ❷ Your wind is the ability to breathe easily ❸ Wind is air swallowed with food or drink, or gas produced in your stomach, which causes discomfort ❹ The wind section of an orchestra is the group of musicians who play wind instruments

**how to say it**

**Helpful hints...**

**Wind** rhymes with *tinned* when it's to do with air, and with *kind* when it means 'to turn'.

**wind**, winds, winding, wound [rhymes with *mind*] VERB ❶ If a road or river winds in a particular direction, it twists and turns in that direction ❷ When you wind something round something else, you wrap it round it several times ❸ When you wind a clock or machine or wind it up, you turn a key or handle several times to make it work

**wind up** ✿ VERB ❶ When you wind up something such as an activity or a business, you finish it or close it ❷ If you wind up in a particular place, you end up there

**wind instrument** NOUN an instrument you play by using your breath, for example a flute, an oboe, or a trumpet

**windmill** NOUN a machine for grinding grain or pumping water. It is driven by sails turned by the wind

**window** NOUN a space in a wall or roof or in the side of a vehicle, usually with glass in it so that light can pass through and people can see in or out

**windscreen** NOUN the glass at the front of a vehicle through which the driver looks

**windsurfing** NOUN Windsurfing is the sport of moving along the surface of the sea or a lake standing on a board with a sail on it

**windy**, windier, windiest ADJECTIVE If it is windy, there is a lot of wind

**wine** NOUN the red, white, or pink alcoholic drink which is normally made from grapes

**wing** NOUN ❶ A bird's or insect's wings are the parts of its body that it uses for flying ❷ An aeroplane's wings are the long, flat parts on each side that support it while it is in the air ❸ A wing of a building is a part which sticks out from the main part or which has been added later ❹ A wing of an organization, especially a political party, is a group within it with a particular role or particular beliefs ❺ IN PLURAL The wings in a theatre are the sides of the stage which are hidden from the audience

**wink** VERB ❶ When you wink, you close one eye briefly, often as a signal that something is a joke or a secret ✿ NOUN ❷ the closing of your eye when you wink

**winner** NOUN The winner of a prize, race, or competition is the person or thing that wins it

**winter** NOUN Winter is the season between autumn and spring

**wipe**, wipes, wiping, wiped VERB ❶ If you wipe something, you rub its surface lightly to remove dirt or liquid ❷ If you wipe dirt or

A B C D E F G H I J K L M N O P Q R S T U V **W** X Y Z

313

**wipe out – wolf**

liquid off something, you remove it using a cloth or your hands

**wipe out** ✿ VERB To wipe out people or places is to destroy them completely

**wire**, wires, wiring, wired NOUN ❶ Wire is metal in the form of a long, thin, flexible thread which can be used to make or fasten things or to conduct an electric current ✿ VERB ❷ If you wire one thing to another, you fasten them together using wire ❸ If you wire something or wire it up, you connect it so that electricity can pass through it

**wireless**, wirelesses NOUN OLD-FASHIONED a radio

**wisdom** NOUN ❶ Wisdom is the ability to use experience and knowledge in order to make sensible decisions or judgments ❷ If you talk about the wisdom of an action or a decision, you are talking about how sensible it is

**wise**, wiser, wisest ADJECTIVE ❶ Someone who is wise can use their experience and knowledge to make sensible decisions and judgments ✿ PHRASES ❷ If you say that someone is **none the wiser** or **no wiser**, you mean that they know no more about something than they did before

**wish**, wishes, wishing, wished NOUN ❶ a longing or desire for something, often something difficult to achieve or obtain ❷ something desired or wanted ❸ IN PLURAL Good wishes are expressions of hope that someone will be happy or successful ✿ VERB ❹ If you wish to do something, you want to do it ❺ If you wish something were the case, you would like it to be the case, but know it is not very likely

**wit** NOUN ❶ Wit is the ability to use words or ideas in an amusing and clever way ❷ Wit means sense ❸ IN PLURAL Your wits are the ability to think and act quickly in a difficult situation ✿ PHRASE ❹ If someone is **at their wits' end**, they are so worried and exhausted by problems or difficulties that they do not know what to do

**witch**, witches NOUN a woman claimed to have magic powers and to be able to use them for good or evil

**with** PREPOSITION ❶ With someone means in their company ❷ With is used to show who your opponent is in a fight or competition ❸ With can mean using or having ❹ With is used to show how someone does something or how they feel ❺ With can mean concerning ❻ With is used to show support

**withdraw**, withdraws, withdrawing, withdrew, withdrawn VERB ❶ If you withdraw something, you remove it or take it out ❷ If you withdraw to another place, you leave where you are and go there ❸ If you withdraw from an activity, you back out of it

**withdrawn** ❶ Withdrawn is the past participle of **withdraw** ✿ ADJECTIVE ❷ unusually shy or quiet

**within** PREPOSITION OR ADVERB ❶ Within means in or inside ✿ PREPOSITION ❷ Within can mean not going beyond certain limits ❸ Within can mean before a period of time has passed

**without** PREPOSITION ❶ Without means not having, feeling, or showing ❷ Without can mean not using ❸ Without can mean not in someone's company ❹ Without can indicate that something does not happen when something else happens

**witness**, witnesses, witnessing, witnessed NOUN ❶ someone who has seen an event such as an accident and can describe what happened ❷ someone who appears in a court of law to say what they know about a crime or other event ❸ someone who writes their name on a document that someone else has signed, to confirm that it is really that person's signature ✿ VERB ❹ FORMAL If you witness an event, you see it

**witty**, wittier, wittiest ADJECTIVE amusing in a clever way

**wives** the plural of **wife**

**wizard** NOUN a man in a fairy story who has magic powers

**wobble**, wobbles, wobbling, wobbled VERB If something wobbles, it shakes or moves from side to side because it is loose or unsteady

**wobbly**, wobblier, wobbliest ADJECTIVE unsteady

**woke** the past tense of **wake**

**woken** the past participle of **wake**

**wolf**, wolves; wolfs, wolfing, wolfed NOUN ❶ a wild animal related to the dog. Wolves hunt in packs and kill other animals for food ✿ VERB ❷ INFORMAL If you wolf food or wolf it down, you eat it up quickly and greedily

**woman - workshop**

**woman**, women NOUN ❶ an adult female human being ❷ Woman can refer to women in general

**wonder** VERB ❶ If you wonder about something, you think about it with curiosity or doubt ❷ If you wonder at something, you are surprised and amazed at it ✿ NOUN ❸ Wonder is a feeling of surprise and amazement ❹ something or someone that surprises and amazes people

**wonderful** ADJECTIVE ❶ making you feel very happy and pleased ❷ very impressive

**wood** NOUN ❶ Wood is the substance which forms the trunks and branches of trees ❷ a large area of trees growing near each other

**don't mix up**

**Hello Kitty...** never mixes up **wood** (what trees are made of) and **would** (the verb).

**wooden** ADJECTIVE made of wood

**woodwind** ADJECTIVE Woodwind instruments are musical instruments such as flutes, oboes, clarinets, and bassoons, that are played by being blown into

**wool** NOUN ❶ Wool is the hair that grows on sheep and some other animals ❷ Wool is also yarn spun from the wool of animals which is used to knit, weave, and make such things as clothes, blankets, and carpets

**woollen** ADJECTIVE ❶ made from wool ✿ NOUN ❷ Woollens are clothes made of wool

**woolly**, woollier, woolliest ADJECTIVE ❶ made of wool or looking like wool ❷ If you describe people or their thoughts as woolly, you mean that they seem confused and unclear

**word** NOUN ❶ a single unit of language in speech or writing which has a meaning ❷ a remark ❸ a brief conversation ❹ A word can also be a message ❺ Your word is a promise ❻ The word can be a command ❼ IN PLURAL The words of a play or song are the spoken or sung text ✿ VERB ❽ When you word something, you choose your words in order to express your ideas accurately

**work** VERB ❶ People who work have a job which they are paid to do ❷ When you work, you do the tasks that your job involves ❸ To work the land is to cultivate it ❹ If someone works a machine, they control or operate it ❺ If a machine works, it operates properly and effectively ❻ If something such as an idea or a system works, it is successful ❼ If something works its way into a particular position, it gradually moves there ✿ NOUN ❽ People who have work or who are in work have a job which they are paid to do ❾ Work is the tasks that have to be done ❿ something done or made ⓫ IN PLURAL A works is a place where something is made by an industrial process ⓬ IN PLURAL Works are large scale building, digging, or general construction activities

**work out** ✿ VERB ❶ If you work out a solution to a problem, you find the solution ❷ If a situation works out in a particular way, it happens in that way

**work up** ✿ VERB ❶ If you work up to something, you gradually progress towards it ❷ If you work yourself up or work someone else up, you make yourself or the other person very upset or angry about something

**worker** NOUN a person employed in a particular industry or business

**workforce** NOUN The workforce is all the people who work in a particular place

**workout** NOUN a session of physical exercise or training

**workplace** NOUN Your workplace is the building or company where you work

**workshop** NOUN ❶ a room or building that

A B C D E F G H I J K L M N O P Q R S T U V W X Y Z

315

# world – wrap up

A B C D E F G H I J K L M N O P Q R S T U V W X Y Z

contains tools or machinery used for making or repairing things ❷ a period of discussion or practical work in which a group of people learn about a particular subject

**world** NOUN ❶ The world is the earth, the planet we live on ❷ You can use 'world' to refer to people generally ❸ Someone's world is the life they lead and the things they experience ❹ A world is a division or section of the earth, its history, or its people, such as the Arab World, or the Ancient World

**worldwide** ADJECTIVE throughout the world

**World Wide Web** NOUN The World Wide Web is another name for the internet, the worldwide communication system which people use through computers

**worm** NOUN ❶ a small thin animal without bones or legs, which lives in the soil or off other creatures ❷ an insect such as a beetle or moth at a very early stage in its life ✿ VERB ❸ If you worm an animal, you give it medicine in order to kill the worms that are living as parasites in its intestines

**worm out** ✿ VERB If you worm information out of someone, you gradually persuade them to give you it

**worn** ❶ Worn is the past participle of **wear** ✿ ADJECTIVE ❷ damaged or thin because of long use ❸ looking old or exhausted

**worn-out** ADJECTIVE ❶ used until it is too thin or too damaged to be of further use ❷ extremely tired

**worried** ADJECTIVE unhappy and anxious about a problem or about something unpleasant that might happen

**worry**, worries, worrying, worried VERB ❶ If you worry, you feel anxious and fearful about a problem or about something unpleasant that might happen ❷ If something worries you, it causes you to feel uneasy or fearful ❸ If you worry someone with a problem, you disturb or bother them by telling them about it ❹ If a dog worries sheep or other animals, it frightens or harms them by chasing them or biting them ✿ NOUN ❺ Worry is a feeling of unhappiness and unease caused by a problem or by thinking of something unpleasant that might happen

**worse** ADJECTIVE OR ADVERB ❶ Worse is the comparative form of **bad** and **badly** ❷ If someone who is ill gets worse, they become more ill than before ✿ PHRASE ❸ If someone or something is **none the worse** for something, they have not been harmed by it

**worship**, worships, worshipping, worshipped VERB ❶ If you worship a god, you show your love and respect by praying or singing hymns ❷ If you worship someone or something, you love them or admire them very much ✿ NOUN ❸ Worship is the feeling of respect, love, or admiration you feel for something or someone

**worst** ADJECTIVE OR ADVERB Worst is the superlative form of **bad** and **badly**

**worth** PREPOSITION ❶ If something is worth a sum of money, it has that value ❷ If something is worth doing, it deserves to be done ✿ NOUN ❸ A particular amount of money's worth of something is the quantity of it that you can buy for that money ❹ Someone's worth is the value or usefulness they are considered to have

**worthless** ADJECTIVE having no real value or use

**worthwhile** ADJECTIVE important enough to justify the time, money, or effort spent on it

**would** VERB ❶ You use would to say what someone thought was going to happen ❷ You use would when you are referring to the result or effect of a possible situation ❸ You use would when referring to someone's willingness to do something ❹ You use would in polite questions

**wound** NOUN ❶ an injury to part of your body, especially a cut in your skin and flesh ✿ VERB ❷ If someone wounds you, they damage your body using a gun, knife, or other weapon ❸ If you are wounded by what someone says or does, your feelings are hurt

**wow** INTERJECTION Wow is an expression of admiration or surprise

**wrap**, wraps, wrapping, wrapped VERB ❶ If you wrap something or wrap something up, you fold a piece of paper or cloth tightly around it to cover or enclose it ❷ If you wrap paper or cloth round something, you put or fold the paper round it ❸ If you wrap your arms, fingers, or legs round something, you coil them round it

**wrap up** ✿ VERB If you wrap up, you put warm clothes on because it is cold

**wrapper** NOUN a piece of paper, plastic, or foil which covers and protects something that you buy

**wreck** VERB ❶ If someone wrecks something, they break it, destroy it, or spoil it completely ❷ If a ship is wrecked, it has been so badly damaged that it can no longer sail ❀ NOUN ❸ a vehicle which has been badly damaged in an accident

**wrestle**, wrestles, wrestling, wrestled VERB ❶ If you wrestle someone or wrestle with them, you fight them by holding or throwing them, but not hitting them ❷ When you wrestle with a problem, you try to deal with it

**wriggle**, wriggles, wriggling, wriggled VERB ❶ If someone wriggles, they twist and turn their body or a part of their body using quick movements ❷ If you wriggle somewhere, you move there by twisting and turning

**wrinkle**, wrinkles, wrinkling, wrinkled NOUN ❶ Wrinkles are lines in someone's skin, especially on the face, which form as they grow old ❀ VERB ❷ If something wrinkles, folds or lines develop on it ❸ When you wrinkle your nose, forehead, or eyes, you tighten the muscles in your face so that the skin folds into lines **wrinkled** ADJECTIVE

**wrist** NOUN the part of your body between your hand and your arm which bends when you move your hand

**write**, writes, writing, wrote, written VERB ❶ When you write something, you use a pen or pencil to form letters, words, or numbers on a surface ❷ If you write something such as a poem, a book, or a piece of music, you create it

### don't mix up

### Hello Kitty...

never mixes up **write** (to put words onto something) and **right** (correct).

**write down** ❀ VERB If you write something down, you record it on a piece of paper

**write up** ❀ VERB If you write up something, you write a full account of it, often using notes that you have made

**writer** NOUN ❶ a person who writes books, stories, or articles as a job ❷ The writer of something is the person who wrote it

**writing** NOUN ❶ Writing is something that has been written or printed ❷ Your writing is the way you write with a pen or pencil ❸ Writing is also a piece of written work, especially the style of language used

**written** ❶ Written is the past participle of **write** ❀ ADJECTIVE ❷ taken down in writing

**wrong** ADJECTIVE ❶ not working properly or unsatisfactory ❷ not correct or truthful ❸ bad or immoral ❀ NOUN ❹ an unjust action or situation ❀ VERB ❺ If someone wrongs you, they treat you in an unfair or unjust way **wrongly** ADVERB

**wrote** the past tense of **write**

### how to say it

### Helpful hints...

**Wound** rhymes with *swooned* when it means 'hurt', and with *found* when it's the past form of wind.

wrapper – wrote

A B C D E F G H I J K L M N O P Q R S T U V W X Y Z

**Xmas** NOUN INFORMAL Xmas means the same as Christmas

**X-ray** NOUN ❶ a stream of radiation of very short wavelength that can pass through some solid materials. X-rays are used by doctors to examine the bones or organs inside a person's body ❷ a picture made by sending X-rays through someone's body in order to examine the inside of it ✿ VERB ❸ If you are X-rayed, a picture is made of the inside of your body by passing X-rays through it

**xylophone** [zy-lo-fone] NOUN a musical instrument made of a row of wooden bars of different lengths. It is played by hitting the bars with special hammers

**yacht** [yot] NOUN a boat with sails or an engine, used for racing or for pleasure trips

**yam** NOUN a root vegetable which grows in tropical regions

**yank** VERB ❶ If you yank something, you pull or jerk it suddenly with a lot of force ✿ NOUN ❷ INFORMAL A Yank is an American

**yard** NOUN ❶ a unit of length equal to 36 inches or about 91.4 centimetres ❷ an enclosed area that is usually next to a building and is often used for a particular purpose

**yarn** NOUN ❶ Yarn is thread used for knitting or making cloth ❷ INFORMAL a story that someone tells, often with invented details to make it more interesting or exciting

**yawn** VERB When you yawn, you open your mouth wide and take in more air than usual. You often yawn when you are tired or bored

**year** NOUN ❶ a period of twelve months or 365 days (366 days in a leap year), which is the time taken for the earth to travel once around the sun ❷ a period of twelve consecutive months, not always January to December, on which administration or organization is based ✿ PHRASE ❸ If something happens **year in, year out**, it happens every year **yearly** ADJECTIVE OR ADVERB

**yeast** NOUN Yeast is a kind of fungus which is used to make bread rise, and to make liquids ferment in order to produce alcohol

**yell** VERB ❶ If you yell, you shout loudly, usually because you are angry, excited, or in pain ✿ NOUN ❷ a loud shout

**yellow** NOUN OR ADJECTIVE ❶ Yellow is the colour of buttercups, egg yolks, or lemons

### help with spelling

*Hello Kitty...*

knows that the letter **y** is unusual because sometimes it acts like a vowel, as in *tyre*, and sometimes it acts like a consonant, as in *yes*.

## yes – your

❀ VERB ❷ When something yellows or is yellowed, it becomes yellow, often because it is old ❀ ADJECTIVE ❸ INFORMAL If you say someone is yellow, you mean they are cowardly

### where does the word come from?

### Did you know…

that the word **yolk** comes from an Old English word *geoloca*? And *geoloca* comes from *geolu* which is the Old English for 'yellow'.

**yes** INTERJECTION You use 'yes' to agree with someone, to say that something is true, or to accept something

**yesterday** NOUN OR ADVERB ❶ Yesterday is the day before today ❷ You also use 'yesterday' to refer to the past

**yet** ADVERB ❶ If something has not happened yet, it has not happened up to the present time ❷ If something should not be done yet, it should not be done now, but later ❸ 'Yet' can mean there is still a possibility that something can happen ❹ You can use 'yet' when you want to say how much longer a situation will continue ❺ 'Yet' can be used for emphasis ❀ CONJUNCTION ❻ You can use 'yet' to introduce a fact which is rather surprising

**yield** VERB ❶ If you yield to someone or something, you stop resisting and give in to them ❷ If you yield something that you have control of or responsibility for, you surrender it ❸ If something yields, it breaks or gives way ❹ To yield something is to produce it ❀ NOUN ❺ A yield is an amount of food, money, or profit produced from a given area of land or from an investment

**yoga** [*yoe*-ga] NOUN Yoga is a Hindu method of mental and physical exercise or discipline

**yogurt** or **yoghurt** [*yog*-gurt or *yoe*-gurt] NOUN Yogurt is a slightly sour thick liquid made from milk that has had bacteria added to it

**yolk** [rhymes with *joke*] NOUN the yellow part in the middle of an egg

**you** PRONOUN ❶ You refers to the person or group of people that a person is speaking or writing to ❷ You also refers to people in general

**young** ADJECTIVE ❶ A young person, animal, or plant has not lived very long and is not yet mature ❀ NOUN ❷ The young are young people in general ❸ The young of an animal are its babies

**youngster** NOUN a child or young person

**your** ADJECTIVE ❶ Your means belonging or relating to the person or group of people that someone is speaking to ❷ Your is used to show that something belongs or relates to people in general

### don't mix up

### Hello Kitty…

never mixes up **your** (belonging to you) and **you're** (you are).

**yours - zucchini**

**yours** PRONOUN Yours refers to something belonging or relating to the person or group of people that someone is speaking to

**yourself**, yourselves PRONOUN ❶ Yourself is used when the person being spoken to does the action and is affected by it ❷ Yourself is used to emphasize 'you'

**youth** NOUN ❶ Someone's youth is the period of their life before they are a fully mature adult ❷ Youth is the quality or condition of being young and often inexperienced ❸ a boy or young man ❹ The youth are young people thought of as a group

**yo-yo**, yo-yos NOUN a round wooden or plastic toy attached to a piece of string. You play by making the yo-yo rise and fall on the string

**zebra** NOUN a type of African wild horse with black and white stripes over its body

**zebra crossing** NOUN a place where people can cross the road safely. The road is marked with black and white stripes

**zero**, zeros or zeroes, zeroing, zeroed ❶ nothing or the number 0 ❋ NOUN ❷ Zero is freezing point, 0° Centigrade ❋ ADJECTIVE ❸ Zero means there is none at all of a particular thing ❋ VERB ❹ To zero in on a target is to aim at

### where does the word come from?

### Did you know...

that the word **zero** comes from an Arabic word *sifr* which means 'empty'?

### Hello Kitty...

knows that some words that sound as if they begin with z actually begin with *x*, like *xylophone*.

**zigzag**, zigzags, zigzagging, zigzagged NOUN ❶ a line which has a series of sharp, angular turns to the right and left in it, like a continuous series of 'W's ❋ VERB ❷ To zigzag is to move forward by going at an angle first right and then left

**zinc** NOUN Zinc is a bluish-white metal used in alloys and to coat other metals to stop them rusting

**zip**, zips, zipping, zipped NOUN ❶ a long narrow fastener with two rows of teeth that are closed or opened by a small clip pulled between them ❋ VERB ❷ When you zip something or zip it up, you fasten it using a zip

**zone** NOUN an area that has particular features or properties

**zoo**, zoos NOUN a place where live animals are kept so that people can look at them

**zoom** VERB ❶ To zoom is to move very quickly ❷ If a camera zooms in on something, it gives a close-up picture of it

**zucchini** [zoo-**keen**-nee] PLURAL NOUN Zucchini are small vegetable marrows with dark green skin. They are also called **courgettes**